The Awakening

1963 Lectures

NEVILLE

Order this book online at www.trafford.com
or email orders@trafford.com

Most Trafford titles are also available at major online book retailers.

(1963 lectures unabridged, verbatim, and all transcribed from tapes
recorded in live audiences in Los Angeles, CA)

Reel-to-reel tapes transcribed and books compiled by Natalie.

Printed in the United States of America.

ISBN: 978-1-4669-8164-5 (sc)
ISBN: 978-1-4669-8165-2 (hc)
ISBN: 978-1-4669-8166-9 (e)

Library of Congress Control Number: 2013903110

Trafford rev. 05/01/2013

 www.trafford.com

North America & international
toll-free: 1 888 232 4444 (USA & Canada)
phone: 250 383 6864 ✦ fax: 812 355 4082

OTHER WORKS BY NEVILLE

Your Faith Is Your Fortune
The Search
Awakened Imagination
He Breaks the Shell

The Neville Reader (reissue of *Neville*) containing:

      Out of This World
      Freedom for All
      Feeling Is the Secret
      Prayer—The Art of Believing
      Seedtime and Harvest
      The Law and the Promise
      Resurrection

CONTENTS

NOTE FROM AUTHOR

(This is Neville's last piece of writing, given to me by Mrs. Goddard after his death in 1972. Neville felt "that the chapter *Resurrection* needed something to lead into it.") Natalie

Introduction to *Resurrection*

If I tell you what I know and how I came to know about it, I may give hope to those who would gladly believe the Bible but who do not understand it or who may have thought that the ancient scriptures is but a record of extravagant claims. Therefore, the reason for this report from me, rather than from another whose scholarly knowledge of the scriptures is more erudite, is that I am speaking from experience. I am not speculating about the Bible, trusting that my guesses about its meaning are not too wide of the mark. I will tell you what I have experienced, that I should convey more of God's plan than the opinions of those who may know the Bible so intimately that they could recite it from end to end, although they have not experienced it.

He who knows something out of his own experience knows something that makes the finest and wisest opinion look shadowy. True knowledge is experience. I bear witness to what I have experienced. Looking back, I do not know of anything that I had heard or read to call forth this knowledge. I did not receive it from man, nor was I taught it, but it came through a series of supernatural experiences in which God revealed himself in action for my salvation.

He unveiled me. And I am he. We mature only as we become our own Father.

I do not honestly expect the world to believe it, and I know all the varieties of explanation I myself should give for such a belief had I not experienced it. But I cannot unknow that which I have experienced. When it occurred, it was the most amazing thing that ever happened to me. I could not explain it with my intelligence. But God's plan of redemption unfolded within me with such undeniable insistence that finally it became both a mystery and a burden laid upon me. I literally did not know what to do with what I knew. I tried to explain it to friends, and I know that with all good will, they could only think, Poor Neville, he has evidently had a very bad time.

From the first experience, I felt commissioned. I could not unknow it, and I am burdened with that knowledge. The warnings of my friends could make no difference to the truth I had experienced. That truth remained. Whether I could be a living instrument of it or not, I could not say at all. But until I put it into words so that others could read it, I did not feel that I had accomplished the work I was sent to do.

Now that I have written it, I feel that I have finished what I came to do. And that is to reveal the true identity of Jesus Christ. Jesus is the I AM of everyone. He is the Lord, the one God and Father of us all, who is above all and through all and in all. Therefore, if the words *Lord, God, Jesus* convey the sense of an existent someone outside man, he has a false god. Christ is the Son of God. The Son of God is David, the sweet psalmist of Israel.

It's the Father's purpose to give himself to all of us, to each of us. And it is his son, David, calling us Father, who reveals the Father's gift to us. The Father's gift of himself to us is not discovered until the very end. And all discovery implies suffering to be endured in the process of discovery.

The Father became as we are that we may be as He is. He is never so far off as even to be near, for nearness implies separation. He suffers as us, but we know it not. God as Father is made known only through his son, David. The core and essence of David's work is his revelation of the Father. Can one come to an identity of oneself with the Father without the Son's revelation of him? Personally, I feel quite sure the answer is no—one cannot. "No one knows the Son except the Father, and no one knows the Father except the Son and anyone to whom the Son chooses to reveal him."

If two different witnesses agree in testimony, it is conclusive. I now present my two witnesses: the internal witness of the Spirit, my experience, and the external witness of scripture, the written Word of God.

Neville
September 1972

FOREWORD

(to the 1963 book)

Welcome to the world of the visionary, of mystical experiences, of a deeper appreciation of the meaning of life, and of practical imagining.

We are led to the truth when we are ready for it. I was led to Neville when a point in life was reached where answers had to be found, where changes in thinking had to take place, and where there was a need to expand spiritual awareness. The first most compelling concept I encountered was that a change in attitude begets a change in the outer world, stated by Neville as "imagining creates reality." It followed that one's world is a reflection of one's inner thinking plus the attendant emotions; and that to dwell on anything you desire, feeling the possession of it in the present, not the future, remaining faithful to that feeling of having, believing it wholeheartedly, produces that result. I tried it and it worked.

To my joy, a three-and-a-half-month trip through Europe, all expenses paid, came in within about a month after doing an imaginal act of flying in a jet over the ocean to Europe. I did not lift a finger to make it so. This is the pragmatic and provable law that everyone can test to their satisfaction. It's the way to everything in the world, and it's being done by every person every moment in time, either wittingly or unwittingly. It's a magical overcoming of limitation when done deliberately. And it is God in action.

Neville taught from his own visions, mystical experiences, and discernment (not speculation) not only that imagining creates reality but that every soul is destined to spiritually awaken eventually as God, yet retaining one's identity. This book of 1963 talks (and those to follow) chronicles a steady growth in understanding of his six major visions that occurred starting in 1959 and continued over a period of three and a half years. Through extensive study and insight, these visions paralleled those found in the Bible and proved to be the keys to explaining the hidden mysteries of the prophetic Old Testament and their fulfillment in the New. Perhaps an analogy would be what the Rosetta stone did for Egyptian hieroglyphics. Once understood and accepted, the larger picture emerges. The questions "Who am I? What am I doing here? Where did I come from? What is the purpose?" are all answered. A sense of power is returned to the individual, plus a great sense of peace ensues, knowing life really does have a glorious meaning in spite of the seeming chaos and horrors of the world.

As Browning said in his *Paracelsus*, "Truth is within ourselves; it takes no rise in outward things . . . There is an inmost center in us all, where truth abides in fullness . . . and to know rather consists in opening out a way whence the imprisoned splendor may escape, than in effecting entry for a light supposed to be without." Neville's teaching gives us the way to that center and how to help open out the way that the imprisoned splendor may escape. But the story needs time to be understood, to be heard repeatedly, and to be internalized by the seeker. And that is why the eleven years of lectures are so precious, gradually leading one into and through the process. Study helps stir the sleeping giant in all who have been made into the good soil, that is, ready to awaken. To awaken is to experience those same six visions—resurrection, birth from above; finding David and the fatherhood of God; the splitting of the temple and ascension into Zion; and the descent of the Holy Spirit as a dove. These are the signs that the transformation has been completed and that our divine identity and heritage have returned.

May the reader enjoy the journey from the senses back to the soul. And may all of your loving imaginal acts be quickly fulfilled.

Natalie
2013

ACKNOWLEDGMENTS

First and foremost, thanks to Neville for being the inspiration of our lifetimes —and therefore the incentive to help preserve his work for posterity.

Thanks and deepest appreciation from the one who produced these typed lectures and then conceived of publishing them to those whose efforts go to make publication of this first book of a series possible.

(In memory), thanks to Gary Nordgren, for his technical skills and his dedication to disseminating Neville's teaching.

To William Machgan, for his love of Neville's teachings, which led him to lend support to this project.

To Faye Shelton and Dr. Neeta Blair for their voluntary efforts.

N.

ESAU, JACOB, AND ISRAEL

February 12, 1963

We are told by Paul in 2nd Timothy 3:16 that all scripture is inspired by God and profitable for teaching, for reproof, for correction, and for training in righteousness. Well, the word righteousness is defined for us in the *Encyclopedia Britannica* as "right thinking," and we're told *all* scripture, any section of it, any part of it. We're also told that it's a threefold cord that is not quickly broken. It's built like the ark on three levels: the physical (the literal level here), psychological, and spiritual levels.

So tonight, we have taken three characters of scripture: Esau, Jacob, and Israel. I think I have broken this cord; in fact, I am convinced of it. And so I have to share with you tonight what I know of these three levels. They're not persons as we are; they are states of consciousness through which the immortal soul passes on its way to God.

We read this story in the 25ᵗʰ chapter of the Book of Genesis. We are told that Rebecca was childless and that she and Isaac prayed to God that they may be blessed with a child, and God responded, as we are told all through the Bible, this response to a prayer for a child. In this case, there are twins. The Lord said unto her, "Two nations are in your womb, and two peoples, born of you, shall be divided; one shall be stronger than the other, and the elder shall serve the younger" (verse 23).

Now, here is a prophecy. Before they were brought into the world, it was prophesied which one would excel. Here is predestination, and you cannot in any way interpret it in any other way—one is *predestined* to excel. And yet they are brought into the world; they haven't committed anything good or evil, and yet one was predestined to excel. He is the younger, Jacob, the supplanter, and the first one, Esau, must serve him. But I tell you that these are states of consciousness, for we can take them on different levels.

So we are told in the same 25th chapter of Genesis that the first one came in and he was red all over, like a hairy mantle, and so they called his name Esau. His other names were Edom—like Adam, spelled in the same way—Aleph, Daleth, Mem, the red earth, the red being. But he was covered with hair all over. That's the first one who must now serve the younger. The second came out holding, taking his hands, the heel of the first, and he was called Jacob, the supplanter. Then we are told that the first one was a hunter, a man of the field, and the second one was the smooth-skinned lad who lived in a tent. So on this level, it's the outer and inner man.

No matter how hairless you seem to be, just put a magnifying glass on the body and you will see the body is completely covered in hair. You may call it fuzz, but it's hair. The most external thing in this world of man is hair; next would be skin. The second one had no hair; he was hairless—that's the inner man. Putting it out in our language that you and I can understand and apply it, the outer man is the man of sense. I am in this room right now, and everything seems so real, more real than anything else in this world. I know this room by reason of my bodily organs. My senses allow it, and my reason dictates it, so this is fact, this is real, and all this is real.

There is an inner man, and he is skilled in arranging, arranging things so that they lead to desired ends, not based upon the evidence of the senses at all. There is an inner man. So I stand here. I could desire to be elsewhere and, denying the evidence of my senses, denying reason, dare to assume that I am where I would like to be and rearrange the furniture of my mind. Instead of using this to tell me that I am here, I use other furniture, other objects of the mind. And here, I rearrange it and remain faithful to that state until it takes on tones of reality, until it seems to be sensorially vivid. So when I open my eyes upon it, I am shocked to find I am still here. That is the inner man, called Jacob, the supplanter—he takes the place of the outer man. He supplanted his brother twice. First, he took his birthright and then he took his blessing. So these are the two in conflict, and the whole story is one of conflict.

But eventually, after unnumbered ages, Jacob will be given the name of Israel, a man after God's own heart. It seems to come soon, but it doesn't really. No one knows the length of time between the awakening to these two states of consciousness and the fulfillment in the form of Israel. But we must read the Bible from all angles to see it. First, Esau is Edom. In the story of Job, the hero is an Edomite, all of the characters are Edomites, and the whole place is laid in Edom. *Edom* means red earth.

We are told that the first one to make a name for himself by subduing all the Edomites was named David. You read it in the 8th chapter of the 2nd Book of Samuel: And David subdued the Edomites and made for himself a name. He is the first king of Israel chosen by Jehovah. Saul was chosen by the *people* but rejected by Jehovah. So here is one, David, *chosen* by Jehovah, the first king of Israel. *Israel* means "a man after my own heart." "Behold, an Israelite indeed in whom there is no guile"; that's what he said when he saw Nathanael, and "only the pure in heart can see God." So "I have found David, a man after my own heart," one who could subdue the Edomites. Well, that comes a way beyond this initial story of the appearance of two boys. It's all in us.

I am told, and you are told tonight, that it's possible that I could assume that I am the man that I would like to be. And if I dare to remain faithful to that assumption and not waver in it, just as though it were true, and to the degree that I am loyal to that assumption, it will crystallize and become a fact. I need not appeal to any person in the world to help it. I can do it all by myself if I know of the existence of the being in me who is skilled in arranging things so that it leads toward a desired end. How would I arrange the furniture of the mind to lead toward the desired end? Well, name the end first, for the end is where I begin. In my end is my beginning. So I name the end "I would like to be," and I name it.

Take a very simple story, a true story, a man who had never earned twenty thousand dollars a year, he'd never earned beyond ten. He was an engineer. I said to him, "Where would you work if you made your twenty thousand?" He said, "I've picked out the job. They don't know it, but the building is on Madison Avenue. I know exactly the floor. I've ridden up in the elevator, I've gotten off on the floor, I've walked into the office, and I know where I would sit were it true that I worked there, where I would hang my hat, and were I to take off my coat, where I'd put it. I know exactly what I would do." I said, "All right, now just stand on that elevator and go up and get off at that floor. See it stop at that floor and get off, walk right into the place, take off your hat, take off your jacket if you want to, and just simply be natural in the job." Within two weeks he was on that job at twenty thousand dollars a year. And for five years, he traveled all over the Near East, aiding in the building of dams and all kinds of things, after this last Second World War. One day, he didn't feel well, closed his eyes, and made his exit from this world. But he had five years of exercising Jacob.

What does it matter when we go from this sphere? It doesn't really matter. Before he made his exit from this sphere, he discovered Jacob; and if there's evidence for a thing, what does it matter what you or I or anyone else thinks about it, or even wish about it? Many of you don't wish this thing to work, but it doesn't matter. If it works and there is evidence for it, that's all that matters. But he *proved* it and lived by it for five years. I can see him now sitting in my living room in New York City when we agreed on a certain technique of the rearrangement of the furniture of his mind—that he was not in some former job; he's now in the new job, and the job is on Madison Avenue. He gets off on a certain floor, and his income is twenty thousand a year. And so, that was just his salary. He had expenses; all these things were paid, traveling expenses, and all other kinds of expenses. Maybe his job was worth thirty-five thousand a year—I do not know. But I know his salary was twenty and he traveled all over the Near East, building these fantastic things that he loved.

I can multiply that by hundreds and hundreds and hundreds of the exercising of Jacob. Jacob comes second—bear this in mind. The whole vast world, 3 billion of us, we only know of the existence of Esau. We know the man; he was born in a certain social structure, and that's it. He has no financial, social, intellectual, or other support behind him, and life is rugged. That's Esau; that's Edom. And then comes this story. He's made aware of another one that's going to be brought forth, another one, and his name is Jacob, the supplanter. And you tell him what you would do, were you he, to achieve a certain goal, and he tries it and he does it. He doesn't always succeed; and quite often having succeeded once, he forgets it, and he goes back and serves Esau.

Then comes that moment in time when he hits the third level, the spiritual level, and knows a thing to be literally true on the third level. All of these stories are literally true on the spiritual level. It's only on the psychological level that it's something different. Like, I stand here and I assume that I am elsewhere and then I see the world as I would see it were I standing there physically. Then I open my eyes upon it, and there isn't any difference. I'm shocked to find I'm not actually there. I've done it. I have gone and prepared a place. Having gone and prepared the place, I return here; but I will now move across a bridge of incidents, a little series of events, leading from where I am physically to where I am in consciousness. And it worked. I may forget it tomorrow when I get there because on reflection, it will seem so natural I may say to myself, "Why, it would have worked anyway. This thing would have happened anyway. Look at all the things that happened in the interval, and therefore, they would have happened in spite of what I did." So I may be inclined to forget that I actually determined the event by an imaginal act. I ___(??). So I try it again and it works. Then I try it again. Then, as I try it and it works, I'm becoming aware of Jacob.

But what about Esau? Jacob wrestled all through the night of human darkness, human ignorance, with the Lord himself. But he couldn't grant him what he asked for. He had to change his name before he could give him what he asked for, and he changed it from Jacob, the deceiving one. For he deceived his father-in-law, he deceived his brother, he deceived his father—he deceived everyone; but even though he deceived them, he was God's chosen vessel. I deceive myself when I stand here and persuade myself that I am elsewhere. I deceive myself when you tell me a story and I persuade myself that you *are* what you would like to be. So I forget what you told me that you are, and only think of what you would like to be. When I am self-persuaded that you are such a person, I'm self-deceived.

So Jacob is the deceiving one. He comes into the presence of his father, and he has no hair, while his brother is all over with red hair. So with the aid of Rebecca, the mother, he takes two goats, slaughters the goats, takes the hair and the skin, and covers his hands and covers the nape of his neck, and then puts on the robe of his brother that he may deceive his father when he comes into the father's presence. The father said, "Who are you?" He said, "I am your son, Esau." He said, "Come closer. I can't see you. Come closer that I may feel you." He comes closer, and as he comes closer, the father feels him. He said, "You know, you feel like Esau, but your voice sounds like Jacob." He said, "No, I am your son, Esau." And he persuaded the father to believe he *was* Esau, and the father gave him the blessing that belonged to Esau. Then, when the father had completed the act and could not now take it back, because God swears by himself and can't take back his oath or change it, then Esau comes in from the hunt to discover the treachery and that "he is well named, for twice he has taken from me and supplanted me." So the father gave him the blessing.

I clothe myself in the ___(??) by rearranging the structure of my mind, rearranging the furniture of the mind. I see myself and have you see me as I would like to be seen by you. And when I see you in my mind's eye, seeing me as you would see me were it true that I am what I am, assuming that I am, then I am re-clothed. Now, to what degree can I fool myself? To what degree can I actually become all the characters—I'm playing other parts, of Isaac—and let myself be Isaac, believing that what I'm doing is real and true? Can I believe in the reality of that imaginal act? Yes, I've done it, unnumbered times, and it worked. Whenever I do it with self-persuasion to the point of acceptance, it worked. So I found my Jacob.

But now there's another one. I've got to find Israel. Israel is on the highest level: one after God's own heart, a man without guile. How do you find him? There's not a thing in this world you can do to find him; it's revealed. This is completely revealed. You can't go about bringing it to pass; it just happens. And this is how it happened to me. One night, I saw these two fantastic creatures. I saw Esau and Esau is just as he's described, covered from the crown of his head to the sole of his feet in red hair, just like a huge, big ape. And here, Jacob, instead of being a man, Jacob is the most glorious female you could ever imagine. Here is an angel beyond angels in this ___(??), and here is Esau, this *monstrous* thing, thriving on violence, thriving on everything that is evil in this world, living on it.

And I thought when I saw the two of them that they existed independent of my perception of them. I didn't know they did not. I did not know that I had never severed the umbilical cord, that they are *my* children. *I am* the being spoken of as Rebecca. I am Rebecca who gave birth to those ___(??). And one the embodiment of every lovely thought that I have ever entertained. Every time I ever exercised my Imagination lovingly on behalf of another, it simply energized this lovely creature; and every time that I acted or reacted violently, I fed and energized Esau. Looking at Esau, no one spoke to me; I had a desire, without turning to anyone to ask their help or to pledge myself in their presence, and I pledged myself that I would redeem this monster if it took me eternity. Such a thing should not live in this world, and I gave him birth. In my ignorance, I gave him birth, this monstrous thing that fed and lived on violence and only violence. That in my blindness, he would whisper in my ear throughout the twenty-four-hour day—yes, even in my dreams—and urge me to violence and urge me to react in the unlovely way.

Then I saw what he was. I still did not know at that moment that he was not independent of my perception of him, but I pledged I would redeem him. At that very moment that I pledged, I would redeem him if it took me eternity. I discovered that he was not an entity, as you are; he was nothing more than an embodied force. It was all my misused and misspent energy throughout eternity. For here, this monstrous thing before my eyes melted and left no trace of ever having been present. But as it melted, all the energy that it embodied came to me. It returned to me, who gave it. I have never felt such power in my life. Everything came back to me. And this glorious creature was the personification of all of my noble acts, my lovely acts, and every loving thought I ever entertained fed her, and she glowed. And this one melted before my eyes.

So I tell you, you will meet both of them. They're present now. You can't see them at the moment, but they're present. Wherever you go, they're present. But I tell you of them and ask you to exercise Jacob. Every time that you persuade yourself of something loving, something lovely, even though reason at the moment denies it and your senses deny it and everything denies it, to that degree that you are self-persuaded you are feeding this glorious creature, and you are denying food to this monster. It isn't his fault; we gave him birth. As the poet said, "Alas, two souls are housed within thy breast, one to heaven does aspire, and the other to earth does cling." So two are housed in the breast of every being, and that's part of the structure of this world.

Everyone is bringing to birth these two, and they are invisible until that moment in time when you wrestle successfully with God, and your name is changed from Jacob to Israel. Then you will know why David, the true king of Israel, was the *first* to make himself a name. He won a name for himself by being the first to subdue the Edomites. And you will see the Edomites embodied in a single man, and that being is a monster. His name is Esau. And you will redeem him, not by blows as historians tell you, for they will tell you that he slaughtered in one night 18,000 Edomites. No, he doesn't slaughter any 18,000 Edomites as individual units. He conquered the *whole* of Edom by melting the embodiment of all of Esau. And when he melted the whole of Esau, he was a man after God's own heart.

So we are told, "I have found in David a man after my own heart. And he is mine forever, he's now my son, and I will do good for him" (Acts 13:22). "I will raise up now from this man after my own heart, a son, who will come forth from his body. I will be his father and he shall be my son" (2 Samuel 7:12). And that one that is being brought forth from the body that is God's only begotten, who becomes in time the father of that son that has emerged, Christ Jesus. You're giving birth to Christ Jesus. Every being in the world has to give birth to him. When he gives birth to that Christ Jesus, *that* is the father of David. And David will call him "my Father, my Lord, and the Rock of my salvation" (Psalms 89:26). So every being in the world because of this conflict within himself is actually molding and shaping within himself Christ Jesus. So Paul tells us, "I have travailed with you and will continue in travail, in labor until Christ be formed in you" (Galatians 4:19). When Christ is formed in you, it's because he comes from a heart which is the heart of God. And so, "I have found in David a man after my own heart."

So I ask you to try it. Try it tonight for a friend. If some friend needs a job, if some friend needs more money, and if some friend want something that reason can't imagine, assume that they are telling you that they have what they want. Don't raise a finger to make it so. Believe that what you've imagined is so. And go about your merry way, believing in the reality of your imaginal act. And to the degree that you are self-persuaded of the reality of this imaginal act; to that degree, they will conform to it.

This whole vast world on the outside is Edom, that is, Esau. And the victory belongs to Jacob. It's prophesied that "there are two nations within your womb and two people born of you shall be divided; one shall be stronger than the other, and the elder shall serve the younger." This [body] is the elder; it comes first. So reason tells you it can't be, and your senses confirm that what reason dictates, it can't be—that's confirmed. But the prophecy is that the victory belongs to the younger; it belongs to Jacob, and Jacob is your ability, your skill, in rearranging things so as to determine or predetermine an outcome. How would I feel tonight were I . . . and I name it? What would I see were it true? Well then, see it. How would I feel were it true? Well then, feel it. What would I say to my friends were it true? Well then, say it. Not audibly, for this being is a psychological being; you say it inwardly. So you talk to yourself inwardly as though you spoke outwardly. You carry on these inner mental conversations from premises of fulfilled desires. And you talk to all your friends from these premises. That is Jacob.

But do it lovingly. The more that you do it lovingly, the nearer you are to meeting God in that successful wrestling match. And so, one day, it's going to happen. When it happens, you'll say exactly what he said in the Book of Genesis: "I have seen God face to face, and yet my life is preserved." Here, I stood in the presence of God, and I didn't know it. This is the *house* of the Lord, and I didn't know it. And so, he takes the stone on which he slept that night and puts the stone down to mark the place of the house of God, and he calls it Bethel, the house of the Lord, the house of God. And in this dream, what did he see? He saw the contact between infinity and finite man. For here a ladder rested on earth and stretched to the heavens, and above it all stood God. He saw on that ladder, ascending and descending gods. The Bible translates the word *Elohim* "angel"; it's not angel, it's Elohim. He saw the gods rising and descending, and above it all stood the Lord. The Lord said to him, "I am the Lord, the God of Abraham your father and the God of Isaac" (Genesis 28:12, 18; 32:30).

Now, if you read it as a historical document, Abraham was not his father; Isaac was his father. If you read it through the eyes of the Spirit, the voice is telling the truth: Abraham is the father of all. All through the ___(??), we all come out of Abraham. And so here, "I am the Lord, the God of Abraham, your father." Now we go to the first verse of the Book of Matthew, and this is "the book of the genealogy of Jesus Christ, the son of David, the son of Abraham" (Matthew 1:1). Here we find the nations, all coming out of Abraham. All the promises are made to him. And then comes this most complex statement of the fight, the battle within man.

Now a question is asked because he is the Edomite of Edomites; his name is Job. He doesn't understand the conflict within him. Jehovah spoke to him and said, "Why should a man—a mere man couldn't see him—___(??)? Then he asks three very important questions. He said, "Did you know the period of gestation of the wild goat? Did you know the habits of the wild ass? Can you domesticate the wild ox?" (Job 39:1) You read that and you wonder what it is all about . . . and what beautiful imagery. For in my vision, I saw Christ as the ox, as the wild ass, and as the wild goat. Was not the wild goat the substitute for Isaac to sacrifice for the sin of the world? And he found the wild goat. Well, can you tell me the period of gestation of the wild goat? How long would it take Christ in man to really come to birth? Can you domesticate the wild ox? How long would it take you to take that wonderful Imagination of yours and actually tame it? Everything denies him, and so you go wild in your reactions, and so he still remains a wild ox. So can you *domesticate* the wild ox? And do you know the habits of the wild ass? Are we not told that "a *stupid* man will get understanding when the wild ass's colt is born a man" (Job 11:12). Everything in the world—a stupid man will get understanding when the wild ass's colt is born a man. And did he not ride on the ass into the most triumphant ride in the world into Jerusalem? He came riding on an ass. He couldn't if he was still wild. He had to be controlled; he had to be domesticated and broken in. So he comes riding on that which *he* has broken in, his own wonderful human Imagination.

So take that Imagination of yours, which is God, God in man. So no matter what the appearance seems to be, what would you like it to be? Well, then, see it as though it were as you want it to be. Believe me, imagining creates reality, for all things are created by him. I tell you, I have proven to my own satisfaction that imagining creates reality. Therefore, if I know it and live by it, then I have found him. Then I too can ride triumphantly on this domesticated wild, wild beast. He was a wild beast but no more. For the wild ass was given to us through man. And so Christ in man was wild, but man didn't know it. Then he starts the training process with the state of consciousness called Jacob. That's when he's given. So I have told you the story. I hope you believe it. You try it. Every time you try it, even if you fail, Jacob is being exercised. But may I tell you, ultimately you cannot fail because it is predestined: Jacob cannot fail.

A clue was given to us as to who he is when we see the one of the twelve sons he loved most. He loved Joseph most of all, for Joseph was the comfort of his old age. For Joseph was born to the woman he wanted most, but in his conflict, he had to marry Leah. Then, after he served seven years, seven for Leah, he was tricked. As he had tricked the father-in-law, the father-in-law tricked him. And then he had to serve another seven years, this time to get Rachel. Out of Rachel comes Joseph and his last, Benjamin. But Joseph was his love, the joy of his old age, and Joseph was a dreamer. Listen to the words, "Behold this dreamer cometh. Let us shun him. Let us kill him" (Genesis 37:19).

So the purpose of the killing was ___(??). He was a dreamer and the interpreter of dreams. He could not only dream but also interpret dreams. Well, this faculty in man that dreams is man's Imagination, and any interpreter of a dream is man's Imagination. And so, "Behold this dreamer cometh. Let us kill him." And then Judah . . . Judah said, "No, let us sell him to the Ishmaelite, let us sell him to the Ishmaelite, as the caravan moves on toward Egypt." And so they sold him, the dreamer. That's what everyone does in this world. But the dreamer rose to the heights of Pharaoh and saved them in their famine. When they sought food, it was Joseph who would save his father and save his own brothers. And so the dreamer in man will *save* you—that's Joseph. But what a long period between that moment in time when they sold the dreamer into slavery and the one called David, who could bring down the giant and bring down the Edomite and make for himself the name of names in all of Israel so that God could say of him, "I have found a man after my own heart."

But the day will come that you will prove every word I have told you this night. You'll meet Esau, and he's just as I have described him, just as I experienced him. And you'll meet the most radiant being, and you know who she is. It doesn't make sense, but these two are not detached from you. They are formed in you; and at that moment in time, they seem to be external to you, but the umbilical cord has not been severed. And you will see they are holding embodied energy, one well used and the other misused. Instead of spending any time to correct that mistake, right before your very eyes it melted. But it doesn't vanish; all the energy held there returns to you. Then you know the words, "Nothing is lost in all my holy mountain." In all my wanderings, I have misspent so much that I thought it was lost, and yet nothing is lost. It was embodied in a monstrous thing, but then it came back, and all that energy that I had misused wasn't really wasted or lost; it returned.

It only caused me frightful suffering in the interval when it first began to form within me and I gave my whole body over and my life over to my senses, to my passions, based upon this garment that was hairy from head to foot. And then I began to work on something entirely different, a Jacob that was smooth-skinned and that no one could see. And he was the supplanter. I heard about him and I began to trust him and it worked. And then things worked, and then one day, I saw that he was not forever an invisible state. He became a concrete reality. I saw him, and what beauty! And I saw Esau, but I redeemed Esau. Jacob does not need redeeming.

And so I tell you, try it. It will not fail you. But these are the three states through which the immortal soul will pass. You are doing it now anyway—everything that you have said within yourself this night as you go. If you said, "Well, I don't believe it," it's perfectly all right. That's your privilege. But that is part of the feeling you give to these two that are now struggling within your womb. For long before they come out and you see them, the struggle is on. Because she asked the question, "Why is this so? Why am I alive if this fight is so within me?" And then he answered and told her that there are two nations within her, and the war is on; one will serve the other. He tells her exactly which will do which: the elder will serve the younger.

The one who comes first—Esau, he comes out first—that's the elder. Here's the younger, and who is he? Jacob. What's Jacob's name? The supplanter. He supplants: he looks at the world; he doesn't like it. Like that vision I had on Fifth Avenue, looking at an empty lot, I would say, "I remember when it *was* an empty lot." It still is an empty lot to my outer senses, but I'm not using my outer senses. Then I would build a word picture for this lot as I desired the lot to be, and I would say, "I remember when it *was* an empty lot." And yet it still, to my outer senses, is an empty lot, but it's not to me and not to those to whom I describe my dream for that so-called empty lot. That's exercising the inner man, exercising Jacob.

And the day will come—when? God and only God will know, as your own wonderful being, for that's God. He sees the heart just as he wants it, and you're wrestling all along with yourself. And one day, when he sees the *heart* and the heart is owned by one called David, "a man after my own heart," suddenly he sees Israel, and David is his son, his only begotten son. And David reveals to him who he is: God the Father. Everyone will one day find David, a man after God's own heart, and David will reveal to you when you find him that *you* are the one he's been seeking all through eternity: you are God the Father.

Now let us go into the Silence.

*   *   *

Q: (inaudible)
A: ___(??) three other great states called Moses, Elijah, and Jesus. I think you will be surprised when you hear what these states are, which are the same three levels—the physical, psychological, and spiritual. These are the threefold cord that we're told in the 4th chapter, the 12th verse of Ecclesiastes, it is not quickly broken. I can tell you from experience again that I have broken this cord.

Are there any other questions, please?
Q: (inaudible)
A: What does it mean "I beheld Satan like lightning fall from heaven"? That's when the disciples return, glorifying God and telling what marvelous things they did with the teaching, ___(??) all kinds of people, casting out the unlovely things in people. And then he rejoiced himself

when he heard of the great work that was being done by those that he had taught, and then he said, "I beheld Satan falling like lightning from heaven" (Luke 10:18). Well, Satan is a state. Satan is only the embodiment of unbelief. He saw the entire thing fall because here, it would have done nothing unless it was believed. "According to your belief be it unto you. Your faith has made you whole." And so when the seventy returned, filled with good news about what they had done with the teaching, then he saw unbelief tumble from heaven. For heaven is within you, and therefore that exalted state within you that dictates audibly what you'll believe and what you'll not believe, then from that heavenly state unbelief is cast out.

Q: (inaudible)

A: Did you hear that question? The lady is equating this Jacob to "Seek ye first the kingdom of heaven." Well, Jacob, as we told you earlier, ___(??) and practice this art of rearranging the structure of my mind. So I would equate it. Because we're all being raised into a world completely subject to our imaginative power, and in that world where you are going, you need ask no one to aid you in what you're going to do. But you start the practice here before you can see the forces. You can't see them, but the forces are all around us. But we reach these two states; they are embodied. And may I tell you, you'll see them. The night I saw him, I beat him. I was violent in my attempt to destroy him through violence. And then I not loved him, but I had compassion for him. An inward mercy flowed out of me because I realized I gave him birth, and nothing so monstrous should have been brought into this world. And I, lost in my compassion for *it*, dissolved it.

So I know beyond all doubt the greatest power in the world is love. Because I could have beaten him forever and he would only have grown on it. So today, the world, not knowing this power of love, may think they will destroy a seeming enemy through effort and through force, and build bigger and bigger missiles to destroy it. People do it in ___(??); they do it murdering. They do all these things; and you will never destroy the enemy, not with force, not in eternity. You can disarm him through mercy. Mercy is the greatest power in the world. Mercy is love in action. And so when I had mercy on this thing, that infinite might that he seemed to embody dissolved before my face. So when people think they're going to really change the world through force, well, they are simply keeping alive Esau.

Q: (inaudible)

A: ___(??) a little female sheep? Really, if you break the word *Resh*, it means spirit, or wind and air, is power. But by definition, it is a ewe, a little ewe lamb that's going to be sacrificed. Because she's giving birth to these, and the whole battle is in her. She wonders, "Why is this battle in my womb? What have I done?" and she's told, "There are two nations in you." And that *Judah* means praise, it's the hand, Yod, but the word itself, *Judah*, means praise. (Tape ends.)

MOSES, ELIJAH, AND JESUS

February 15, 1963

___(??) Moses, Elijah and Jesus. In biblical language, a man's name reveals his character. The name is an expression of the essential nature of its bearer. As I've said in the past, these characters are not persons—they are eternal states through which the immortal soul passes to awaken as God. These are eternal spiritual states.

To understand tonight's subject, let us go back just for a moment. As you know, as I told you, the Bible is God's plan, something to be understood only through revelation. It's revealed; it's true. What seems the most impossible thing in the world will prove itself true in time. The Book of Genesis is the seed plot of the Bible. As we remember, it began with God: "In the beginning God," and the book ended on the note "in a coffin in Egypt." The one in the coffin was called Joseph. Joseph is human Imagination. It is of one tissue with divine Imagination, but here it is human Imagination placed into a body. He exacted from his brothers a promise that they will not leave his body in Egypt; they will take it up to the land that was promised by God to his forefathers, Abraham, Isaac, and Jacob. That was a pledge by the brothers, exacted by the brother Joseph. That ends the book, the seed plot of the Bible. Then we start toward the unfoldment of the seed planted in the Book of Genesis.

The next Book is Exodus, and that's where Moses comes in for the first time in the Bible. As I told you earlier, a name is the expression of a character. It's not something that you call a name and someone replies. It simply is a true expression of the character of the one who bears it. Now we are told that Pharaoh's daughter found Moses floating on the river, and she named him Moses because she drew him out of the water. Well, I will not deny that; that's one part of the name Moses, "to draw out, to rescue, to fetch." But, it has another name, another meaning. She was Egyptian, and the boy was raised in the courts of Pharaoh. The word Moses is, as a root, the Egyptian word for the verb "to be born." That's what it means, to be born. Something is now to be born, and it is buried in man, in the Book of Genesis. It's completely contained in this part, in this coffin called man. But now it must be awakened; it must be born. And we are told that *he* did not volunteer for the task; he was drafted.

Now let me stop here and tell you this is not a man as you are, as I am; this is a state of consciousness. All these characters are states of consciousness. And so Moses is playing the part now leading you, leading me, and leading everyone in the world, out of the state known as Egypt, taking us out of Egypt into the Promised Land. Moses is true. In this case, in him in germinal form is the entire future life of Israel. All the figures that you read concerning him are contained in us. He was a prophet, a priest, a lawgiver, a shadow of the king or a foreshadowing of the king, a victor, an exile, a fugitive, and a man of God. All these are figures in the state called Moses. Now he's leading us out.

Let us see what he has in common with the other characters named in tonight's subject, Elijah and Jesus. No one knows the burial place of Moses. As we're told in the very last book of the prophets, called Deuteronomy, Moses died and he was buried. Who buried him? The Lord buried him, and to this day, no one in Israel knows the burial place of Moses. You'll find it in your Bible, the 34th chapter of Deuteronomy,. No one knows. You're told that Elijah—now the word *Elijah* means "my God is Jehovah"—while talking to his disciple, Elisha, parted by this fiery chariot and fiery horses as he was lifted up into heaven by a whirlwind. Therefore, no one knows his burial place because he wasn't buried; he was transported. We're told of Jesus, when they came early in the morning and they found the stone rolled away, that his body had been removed. And you could say that no one knows where they laid the body. "Where have they laid the body of my Lord?"

So here we find that at the end there were three, each having the same exit from this world and no place where they could find the body. Now here's a progression leading up toward God. *Moses* means "to be born," or Hebraically, "to draw out." Yes, something is being drawn out, that which must be born. Elijah, "my God is Jehovah." And Jesus, "Jehovah is Savior." In keeping with the statement in the 43rd chapter of Isaiah, and if you read ththose three verses, the 3rd, the 7th and 11th, "I am the Lord your God, the Holy One of Israel, your Savior"—if you read it on the surface, it will mean nothing to you, but we go back to find what was the great revelation as Israel is being moved out in this exodus from Egypt. It took forty years, and forty is the numerical value of the thirteenth letter of the Hebrew alphabet, whose symbol is a womb. So something is going to be born; something is coming out of the womb in a so-called forty years. It doesn't mean forty years as you and I measure time. But something is coming out of man, and everything that is coming out is God, moving through the second stage, called Elijah, and flowering in its fullness in Christ Jesus.

Moses is the first to have the name of God revealed to him. There are many names for God, but never before was it revealed as it was to him, that state—and you are in it now, as I am in it—and the name revealed of God the Creator is I AM. The 3rd chapter . . . read the 13th through the 15th verses of the 3rd chapter of Exodus: "When I go to the people of Israel and tell them that the God of their fathers sent me, the God of Abraham, Isaac, and Jacob, and they ask me, 'What is his name?' What shall I say?" The voice answered, "I AM THAT I AM. Say unto them, 'I AM has sent you.'" It was never revealed before that that was the name of God.

Now we are told in the 9th Psalm, the 10th verse, "Those who know thy name put their trust in thee"—if you know the name. And you and I have heard the name, but if you really know it, you'll put your trust in the name. Well, I tell you, the name is I AM. It's not John, it's not Jesus, it's not God, it's not Lord, it's nothing outside of I AM. The word translated "Lord," which is *Jehovah*, means I AM. When I say "I AM the Lord thy God," I really should say, if one would understand it, "I AM the I AM, your Creator." For the word translated "God" is the word *Elohim*, the word used in the first chapter of Genesis—"And *God* said"—that is *Elohim*; it's a plural word. "Let *us* make man in our image." When you read the words in the sentence, "I am the Lord thy God," the word *I AM* is the same word translated Lord. So I AM the *I AM*, the God who created you in his image; and besides me, there is no other God, no Creator, and no other Savior. That is what was revealed in the state known as Moses. If you take the word Moses—Mem, Shin, and He—and you turn it backward, it spells the name "name"—He, Shem. The common word in Hebrew for name is *Shem*. It's Heshem, "the name." If I take the middle letter out, which is *Shin*, and put it first of the three little letters, *Shema*, it spells "heaven."

So here, the name means so much. I call everything out. I'm going to be born and, being born, bringing all things hidden within me to the surface to be born; I do it in his name. So I'm drawing it out. The word in Egyptian means "to be born." I am drawing it out of myself; that's Moses, Mosheh. I turn the name around. I do it in his name, Heshem. And where do I draw it from? Shameh: "Out of the heavens." And where is heaven? "Heaven is within you" (Luke 17:21). From my own being, I am drawing everything, but I draw it in his name. There is no other name under the sun by which this thing is done. And so, how do I draw anything? I draw it only in his name.

We are told he draws it all out, but he cannot enter the kingdom of heaven, the Promised Land, called Canaan. The one that will take the Israelites in—his name is Joshua. Well, the word *Joshua* is the same word as *Jesus*, the identical word, spelled the same way. He cannot go in; he's only the power that draws out. But he cannot take us into the Promised Land; Jesus does, whose name is Joshua. Before we reach that state called Joshua, which is Jesus, we pass through the state of Elijah. The word Elijah means "my God is Jehovah." But if I say, "My God is Jehovah," I think in terms of some external force. If I say, "My God is I AM," then you might think me arrogant, think me blasphemous, and yet that is exactly what the word means.

His story is told us in the Book of Kings. In the Book of Kings, there is nothing but sheer, unadulterated power. When a man feels it and knows what it can do, *untempered* by love, he does everything. That's what Elijah did. He called down the fire and destroyed the sacrificial bull, turning it to ash; he destroyed the children who criticized him and then the 450 prophets of Baal who could not bring down any fire. Then he did in a twinkle of an eye, he ordered the destruction of all of the prophets of Baal. Violence in the extreme! Then we move from this state to the Joshua, which is Jesus. They're the same power, infinite power, *tempered* with love.

Now let me give you my own personal experience concerning these states. They are states, for when you meet these states, they are personified as men. Thirty-odd years ago, I was taken in spirit into a divine council, a divine society, and the first one to meet me was the embodiment of Infinite Might. He was seated—and the symbolism is perfect—in a chariot, and hitched to that chariot was this perfectly marvelous pair of horses, beautifully harnessed and hitched to the chariot. Seated in it was Infinite Might, eyes of steel; not an nth part of love came from that face to mine. As he thought, I heard what he thought. Whatever he thought, I heard it. He looked at me, eye to eye, but no emotion or feeling concerning love or mercy or tenderness came from his eye to mine, just sheer might, sheer power. No power on earth can compare to the embodiment of that power. And just as we are told, he then ascended in his fiery chariot, leaving not a trace behind. It seems such a stupid statement to make that not a thing on earth would lead one to believe that it could be literally true, and yet my mystical experience confirms the truth of that statement. For there is the perfect embodiment of the chariot and the horses, beautifully harnessed, and the charioteer is Elijah himself—Infinite Power. The horse has always been the symbol of the mind. In this case, the mind is harnessed; it's disciplined and directed by the charioteer, the one who is in control of that disciplined mind, but without feelings, no emotion of love.

Then I was taken into the presence of Infinite Love, Infinite Mercy, and here I stood in the presence of Christ Jesus—a state, yes, a living state—and talked and communed with him. He asked me, "What is the greatest thing in the world?" and I answered in the words of Paul, "Faith, hope and love, these three abide, but the greatest of these is love." At that moment, he embraced me; I became one with Infinite Love. I have never known such joy in my life, such peace, such mercy, and such anything concerning these attributes. While in this embrace came this voice from out of space, and I found myself once more in the presence of Infinite Might—he's called Elijah. Another word for him in the Bible is *El Shaddai*, "God Almighty." But no mercy there as yet, and no love there as yet, just sheer power. And it was he who sent me back to where I am today with the command, "Time to act!"

All of this was done in the state of Moses. It is Moses, that state that I entered. Not voluntarily, I was drafted—as I was drafted into God's army, without my permission, without my consent—for a purpose: to lead me out of Egypt into the Promised Land. But I had to pass through these states, and everyone passes through these states. And so Moses is the mediator, the state that is the mediator of all the things that happen to him so that he, in turn, may share with those *for whom* it happened. And so it happened to me, and in that state, the state of Moses, and then I in turn must; I'm compelled to share with you the things that happened to me, for they happened *because* of you, to tell you it is all true. And you say, "A little handful like this and three billion of us in the world?" It doesn't matter if only one came. If one came and one heard of God's Word and the truth of that Word, it would be infinitely greater than the three billion who didn't hear of it, for we enter the kingdom of God one by one; we do not enter in pairs.

I can't take with me into that state the dearest soul to me in this world. We have to go alone, singly. We're known singly and loved singly, and no two can go together. So it doesn't matter if I speak to hundreds or to one or speak across the nation on radio to a million; it makes no difference. Do they believe it? So the story is tell the story as you experienced it, in the hope, yes, that they will believe it. But no one has any assurance that they will believe it. But only as it is believed and accepted by the individual does he start the journey out of Egypt.

Now, Egypt is not in the Near East—you're Egypt. Joseph, which is your own wonderful human Imagination, is buried in Egypt. This is Egypt. He contains within himself the whole vast world, and now it has to be led out. It's led out by the true revelation of the true name of God. It was never revealed before. In the fifty chapters of Genesis, the word is not revealed, not used. And now comes the revelation of the 3rd chapter and the 6th chapter of the Book of Exodus: "Go and tell them I AM sent you." All through the entire book, when you read this strange translation, "I AM the Lord," it is simply "I AM the I AM." Why take the second I AM and then call it Lord? The average person reading it can't quite understand it, but the identical word that begins the sentence "I AM"—which is *Yod He Vau He*—is the word that comes when just two words are removed, "the Lord." So I AM the I AM, your God; and besides I AM, there is no God. "I AM your Maker." Therefore, you are really self-begotten in the true sense of the word.

So these three are three fantastic states through which man moves. And the day will come that you too will be taken by a whirlwind into heaven, and you will be brought into the presence of a state; but to you, it's something completely independent of your perception of it. When you look at him, he's a power—I mean a power beyond the wildest dream of man—and it's man. I could paint a picture for you could I draw. If I could only paint, I would paint him; I can see him so clearly, and it's thirty-odd years ago. More vivid than anything that happened to me today, it's so indelibly impressed upon my mind. And yet it's the state called Elijah, and one passes through that state where it is nothing but sheer might. You see it in the world today—it could be economic power, where there's no feeling whatsoever but simply to get a new power. It could be economic power, military power, social power, intellectual power, or any other kind of power, without feeling or compassion, just sheer might. We see it described in the world. There isn't a morning paper or a program on the radio or TV that doesn't describe this might, sheer might. Whether I can get the better of that nation or nations without feeling doesn't matter; it's power—that's Elijah. Read his story in the Book of Kings.

But it passes from that to God himself, and that is Christ Jesus. When you stand in his presence, again, he is *other* than you. He communes with you, he asks you questions, and you answer the question, and he embraces you, and it all seems so much the *two* of you. And yet you are told in the 14th chapter of Zechariah, "His name is one. God is one and his name is one" (verse 9). They aren't two. He seems to be another. He embraces you; but at that moment of the embrace you become one. The Lord, the I AM, is one, and his *name* is one. And then, you find yourself fused with God himself, and there aren't two of you, not you *and* God; you *are* the very being that you've been seeking. You *are* he.

Then comes the savior. "To be called" also means "to be sent." You are called and then sent to reveal all that has happened to you in the hope that those who hear it will accept it. For we are told, many rejected it and many accepted it; that's how it's all sealed up. Eventually all will accept it.

It's a form of preparation leading up toward the fulfillment of his purpose, which is to give himself to us. For it is God's purpose to give himself to you individually, as though there were no others in the world, just God and you. And because God is one and his name is one, there can't be God *and* you. For you stand in his presence; and as you answer the question, which you will, you'll answer it without knowing and without thinking. You won't speculate—you'll answer it automatically—at that moment of answering that "God is love." "What is the greatest thing in the world?" You'll say God. But you don't say that; you say love. Then you are embraced by Love himself, and you aren't you *and* Love; you *are* Love. You are the embodiment of Love, and you never felt such mercy, such compassion, and such love. And you are one with. But there aren't two of you; you are God.

While in the very embodied state of infinite love, you are sent, sent to do what you'll be doing right in this world because everyone must be led out of Egypt: "Bring my people out of Egypt. Even though I will harden the heart of Pharaoh and keep them back in Egypt, I will still tell you 'Bring them out of Egypt.'" And so, harden, harden them against what you have to say. Because tonight, in this audience, we are Christians and Jews—undoubtedly all of us. There may be one who does not call himself a Christian or a Jew, who would think, But I'm not either. I'm an agnostic or I'm an atheist or maybe I'm of some other creed. But I'd say on a whole that as I go across the country, I speak to essentially a hundred percent Christians and Jews. Therefore, the word *Moses* to the Jew is a sacred name, the one that was the leader chosen by God to lead his people, his chosen people, out of Egypt into the Promised Land; and Elijah, the great prophet; then to the Christian what's more sacred than the name of Christ Jesus. And I tell you, these are states, infinite states and eternal states, through which the *immortal* soul passes, and he awakens in the very end, being confronted by God himself, the Ancient of Days.

And then he goes back into the place. And then you will know on the Mount of Transfiguration that these were the three who appeared: There were Moses, Elijah, and Jesus. Then they all shone until their faces were like the sun. That's true. We are told that when Moses came down from the mount, they all were afraid because he shone so. And then he covered himself with a veil. Then he could talk to the people while he was veiled. Well, the veil is the human body. This garment is the veil to talk to man, for if you would see him unveiled, you couldn't stand the light. So when he went into the presence of God, he took off the veil. He was carried in spirit into the presence of God, and he's one with him. You can't stand the light. He comes down. Before he can put on the veil, there's a light that dazzles the eye of mortal man.

But may I tell you that whether you believe it or not, the morning it first happened to me, I was alone in my own room in a hotel on Forty-ninth Street in New York City, at four in the morning. There was no moonlight, and there was no reason for light in my room, so the light wasn't on. But here was this unearthly light that filled the room, and it did not subside until the sun came out. The entire room was completely radiant with light, but no one could see it but myself. But it was light; the room was completely diffused with light, and it wasn't any moonlight, as it was four in the morning. The light, the artificial light, was not on.

So I tell you that the symbolism is true, and it's all about you. Everything in the book is about you. As we are told in the fortieth Psalm, "In the volume of the book"—some translate it—"In the volume, it's all about me." It is. The whole book is about you. And these fantastic characters are the eternal spiritual states through which *you* move. So everything is planted in you and recorded in that first book, the Book of Genesis. Then comes the beginning of Exodus, where man is making his exit from the world of slavery, the world of Egypt. And it's not in the Near East. This, wherever I go, this is Egypt. I am pulling myself out.

And there are a series of signs that will accompany my exit from Egypt. One of the signs, as you're told, only occurs in connection with Israel's departure from Egypt, and that is the serpent (Numbers 21:9). Moses chose the serpent and showed them, but no one understood it, no one. Today, how many people understand that that symbolism is true? It's recorded for us in the 3rd chapter of John that it must take place in the same manner—just "as Moses lifted up the serpent in the wilderness, so must the Son of man be lifted up" (verse 14). You will find yourself one day actually experiencing the state of being lifted up in serpentine form, lifted up into heaven. And so signs follow, as told us in the Book of Deuteronomy: "And Jehovah delivered his people from Egypt by signs and wonders." Always signs and wonders—everything was a sign. But how are we to interpret a sign? Wait for it; all these signs will happen. At the nativity, the angel gave a *sign* to the shepherds, and people have completely misunderstood the sign and thought it was the event. He told you the sign, which is a deliverance of an individual into heaven from the land of Egypt.

Simeon comes into the temple, and he looks at the child. He tells them, "This is a *sign* that is spoken against." Now in this audience, for the last three years, I would not say there were many, but I have heard, personally and through the grapevine, those who spoke against the sign, some never to return in the interval of three years. So this is a sign that will be spoken against. How true is the prophecy? To those who would come home today socially, and they still come socially, we dine together, but they will not be seen here. When we are together socially, we never discuss signs. And so Simeon comes into the temple and sees the child and makes the prophecy, "This is a sign that will be spoken against." And those who come, you come, you haven't spoken so far against it, but I know dozens who have spoken against it to the point of never having returned to this auditorium. How true is the prophecy?

And so he gives us signs and wonders as he brings us out of Egypt. The story of Christ Jesus, every event of it, is only a sign. Not a thing takes place here on this level. Everything recorded about him—from his birth to the very end, the ascension—is a sign. Everything is going to take place in you: the birth, all the miracles, the fantastic things, and yes, the transfiguration too. May I tell you, when it does take place, you too will swear those who are present to secrecy. And yet, *after* the thing, it is so fantastic that you need not even swear them to secrecy, but you do it automatically because like Peter, James, and John, they were not asleep, but they were drowsy. They look at you; they can't believe the wonder of it all, and you swear them to secrecy. But you need not because when they return here to this level, they don't remember; or if they do, they only vaguely remember.

Peter was filled with sleep, yet he kept awake, but he was drowsy. And so he couldn't quite see the glory that was given at that moment to the one whosever name he was. He is called Jesus because in the end, when the whole thing vanishes, "there was Jesus only." These states remain behind for all to pass through, and one who's ___(??); and at the very end, *he* is Christ Jesus. *Everyone* becomes Christ Jesus. There's nothing in the end but Jesus. And Jesus means "Jehovah saves." He is a savior. And he saves who? He saves you because you are he. You are self-begotten. In the end, you come right out, and you are one with the Being who begot himself as you. So these are the states through which you, the *immortal* you, *must* pass to awaken as God. And there's none but God, only God.

So *Moses* means "to draw out," no denying that it does. My old friend, Abdullah, could spend two hours on the platform, taking three little letters and analyzing them for us. Mem Shin He, took one letter at a time and put them together in many combinations. And the word *Moses* as it is spelled is "to draw out." ___(??), "To lead one out" of the great land of Egypt. You turn it around. How does he do it? He does it by the name that was revealed to him, Heshem, which means "name." Well, what was the name? I AM. "Go and tell them I AM sent you." Well, that's Heshem. Now take the middle one out, Shin, put it first, and that's Shema, the heavens. And he draws it out of heaven. Where is heaven? "Heaven is within you." So he draws the whole thing out of himself.

So Moses is sent. He didn't want to return. He is drafted. So man is put into the state of Moses and becomes one with the state. Then he is leading *himself* out of the confusion of Egypt into the calmness, the peace, and the joy that is God. But he had to pass through the state of Elijah, and Elijah is sheer might, nothing but power. So he's called the personification of all the prophets. No mercy in it, just cold-blooded prophecy and destruction. But he has to move through that, and he moves up to Jesus. And so, at the end, everyone is Jesus. And yet may I tell you that you will not lose your individuality. Everyone will be Christ-like without losing his wonderful, definite individuality. I will know you, you will know me, and yet you'll be transformed and I'll be transformed. I can't describe what I saw. I can't find the words to describe what I revealed to the one who is not here tonight and swore her to secrecy. But I'm quite sure she was in the state of semi-sleep and would not or could not remember. But it's more vivid than this room is now, what happened.

So I tell you, everyone is destined for it. You may take it lightly and think, Well, that's silly! because that's the whole vast world. They've been teaching this story for 2,000 years or beyond that, but they don't see the mystery. It's all a mystery. As I told you earlier, a mystery is not a matter to be kept secret but a truth that is mysterious in character. ___(??) a secret. I've been asked in this auditorium, "Is it right to tell it?" Certainly it's right to tell it. You can't restrain yourself. But it's something difficult to describe because it's mysterious in character, not a thing to be hidden from the world, for you are *destined* to be Christ Jesus. But you will not become aware of your heavenly inheritance so long as you still wear the garment, which is a veil. For this is the veil. But you will continue to do your work and tell your story to all who will listen, but you will not become fully aware of the inheritance while you're still clothed in a garment of flesh and blood.

So Moses begins the great exodus. It really is the beginning of the birth of Israel. He not only attends the birth but also in *him* Israel is born. So in the state called Moses, Israel is born. Everyone without their permission is put into the state of Moses, and then he is pulled out and pulled out to the flower that is Christ Jesus. But he passes through that mighty state, Elijah, one who could bring down the very fires of heaven and destroy the world. There are moments that they do it: watch the world and see it. They do it unmoved by mercy, unmoved by any compassion whatsoever. But it's a state. One day you'll be taken in Spirit into the presence, and you're awed by the presence of this might. And it's man, and it is Elijah. He is actually seated in his chariot, and there are horses, the symbol of the mind, beautifully harnessed—meaning a disciplined mind—and hitched up to the chariot, and he the charioteer.

Then you go past him; taken by the wind, he doesn't take you past but you go past him into the presence of the Ancient of Days. Then comes the most glorious thing in the world, Love. Here, Love stands in your presence, and it's still a state. You answer the state and then you become one *with* the state and that state is God. It is Christ Jesus. All states are granted, but you'll meet them and meet them in this holy assemblage. Each will be identified, and they are all part of the stories of the scriptures. So I tell you, these are not characters. The name signifies the eternal state through which you and I pass. Everyone is destined to meet the same end, and the end is God. We all awaken as God. So "Let us make man in our image" is true. That is Elohim. But the name isn't really revealed until the journey starts.

Now tonight, I hope you believe the name. If you *believe* the name, read the 9th chapter, the 10th verse of the Book of Psalms: "Those who know thy name will put their trust in thee, for, O Lord, thou would not forsake those who seek thee." It should not be "But, O Lord," for again you get off the beat. For God—the word now "O Lord" is Yod He Vau He, I AM—is addressing himself. Having found the name, I put my trust in thee. I believe *I am* the man that I want to be. I put my trust in thee. Can I dare to assume that I am *now* the man that I want to be even though everything in the world denies it? If I dare to, I'm putting my trust in thee, and your name is I AM. For I AM would not forsake myself who seeks thee. That's what it means. Read it carefully in Psalms 9:10. So if I find the name, I must put my trust in him.

Now, we go to church, get on our knees, and pray to something other than I AM. We make our appeal to everything but I AM. So the journey has not started. No man starts out of Egypt toward the Promised Land—made by God himself (the I AM) to the fathers, as told us in Genesis—until he finds the name that leads him out. No other name can lead him out. He sends his leader, which is Moses, "something to be born," that's what it means, that's what the word means. But it draws you out—also means "to draw out, to rescue"—but it is something to be born, heading toward the perfect, itself being not the perfect but tending toward the perfect.

So do *you* believe the name I told you this night, that is, the name of God? If you really do, you'll put your trust in him. If you go out of here tonight, hoping that something other than this name will draw you out of sickness or poverty or being unknown or anything else in the world, you have not put your trust in him. If you really believe it, you'll put your trust in his name. Now, it's entirely up to you. I can do no more than tell you the name and hope that you will trust in his name. Trusting in his name, you are moving out of Egypt into the land that was promised. He himself who pulls you out does not enter the land. He cannot go in, but Joshua will take you in, "my servant" Joshua, who is Jesus. So you go into the land by becoming one with Jesus. That's the land. For he himself is the kingdom; he is the king and the kingdom. For you rise into a land completely subject to your imaginative power. And so Christ Jesus is both king and kingdom, and you rise into it. But he who pulls you out by revealing his name can't take you in. He brings you to the border. Then, you are told, as he said to Moses, Look to the north, the south, the east and the west, as far as the eye can go, that is the land. But you can't go in, Joshua takes them in. All Israel will go in, but led only by Joshua. So you're led right up to Joshua to answer the question correctly, you become one with him, and you're one with the king. You *are* the king and you are the kingdom (Deuteronomy 34:4; Joshua 1:1).

So believe me, the story is true; the symbolism is true, everything about it. But if you do not believe in the name, why then, you may still be playing the part of Jacob. Before he can start, he's not leading Jacob out of Egypt; he's leading Israel. Jacob has to be transformed into Israel before the journey from Egypt can start. But Jacob is a very smart wonderful fellow (the psychological you) that can play all kinds of games by self-deception and get results. Persuade myself that things are as I would like them to be, and to that degree that I am self-persuaded, I'll become them. That's Jacob. But he cannot start the journey out of Egypt until his name is transformed into Israel. As he's transformed into Israel, Israel is led by the state known as Moses, one who is about to be born. All the things buried in him—and it's God buried in him—brings them all to the surface in full bloom.

So I ask you tonight to, above all things, believe in the name, above all things. If tonight you are unemployed, use the name. Trust in his name: "I am gainfully employed." If you're not in the chips as it were, well then, "I've never had more in my life, never enjoyed such comfort, such freedom from the pressure from the wants of this life!" Use the name. And so I must repeat it again, the 9th chapter, the 10th verse of Psalms: "Those who know thy name put their trust in thee," if you know the name. If you don't believe the name, you will not put your trust in that name. And tonight, millions of people are going to the churches across the Christian world, lighting candles and putting their trust in a candle or something on the wall or some little thing on the outside. I have seen them. All of the Christian churches—I'm not singling out one denomination—I've seen them. I've seen people on Fifth Avenue in New York City get right down on the street, on the sidewalk, and prostrate themselves before a man-made edifice called a cathedral—whether it was St. Thomas' cathedral or St. Patrick's cathedral or some other cathedral—and worship a man-made structure. And that's where they put their trust.

But if you know his *name*, you'll put your trust in his name, and his name is I AM. Tell no one what you're doing; just simply quietly appropriate the state in his name. But we told you earlier that when we're told to ask in his name and call upon his name, it really means—that phrase means—to ask *with* and to call *with* his name. Not call *upon* his name as millions do, saying, "In the name of Jesus Christ, so and so." No, his name is not Jesus Christ; his name is I AM. So call *with* his name. Don't call *upon* any name; call *with* his name. And the name is I AM.

Now let us go into the Silence, and call with his name.

*   *   *

Now, are there any questions, please?

Q: (inaudible)

A: My dear, Armageddon, bring it in. This is it. This whole vast world is really Egypt, and we, individually, we are Egypt. ___(??). And then you begin to believe in his name. ___(??) When no doctor could help and no one could help and then you go up in your Imagination—that's Joseph. You dare to enact a scene implying the fulfillment of your dream. Then came this most excruciating pain that lasted, oh, several minutes. Then came the breaking of all the wires that bound you, and you were free. That was Armageddon. But the whole vast world is Armageddon.

Q: Are the characters all myself? Are they all states and stages of my consciousness?

A: Yes, my dear. For instance, seated as you are now you could be in as many states as it would be molded in this section of time. But the state to which you most often return and occupy most of the time, that state constitutes your real self for the moment. When someone feels more depressed in the course of a day than they feel elated, well, depression is the state that is their home. Others would feel secure, would feel powerful. These are only states. But you see, every state needs a man as an agent to express it. So a man has to express the state of Moses. Moses is a state. Elijah is a state. But it can't express itself; it needs an agent, and the agent is always man. So a man, the pilgrim, moves into a state and then the state becomes animated. If you saw it, it's personified as man only because you occupy it. And so these are states. All states need agents, and the agent is always a man. The state of love needs a man to express it; the state of hate needs a man to express it. It can't express itself; man is the operant power. "Where man is not, Nature is barren." The states are barren; they don't bear, but where man is, the state begins to bear. But these are the important states through which we pass, and we go right up to that final state. There is no state beyond that in this drama, which is Christ Jesus. That's the final state. "In many and various ways, God spoke of old to our fathers by the prophets; but in these last days, he has spoken to us by his Son" (Hebrews 1:2). That's the final state.

Q: (inaudible)

A: My dear, I AM is the operating power. It's God himself. So you say, "I am nothing"—that's a state. "I am ill"—illness is a state. The same I AM is playing and clothing himself differently. "I am wealthy." "I am poor." Poverty, wealth, health, and sickness are states. But I AM clothing himself in any state takes upon himself the consequences of that state. Why not become selective in choosing states? But all these parts we live are still moving him toward—after he finds the name I AM—he then moves toward the final goal in spite of himself. In spite of himself he moves toward that wonderful state where he is brought into the presence of the Ancient of Days. And the story told us in that 7th chapter of Daniel is true. Who did he see in the presence of the Ancient of Days? One that resembled the Son of man. ___(??) Right in the presence of the Ancient of Days . . . and then you'll answer correctly, and you're one with him. There aren't two of you. In that day, his name is one; God is one and his name's one. He said, "What is the greatest commandment in the world?" and he answered—and he's quoting now from Deuteronomy—"Hear, O Israel, the LORD,"—which means I AM—"thy God"—Elohim—"is one I AM." The word is—you hear it if you go to the synagogue, and you hear that wonderful statement every service in synagogue—"Shema, Israel,"—"Hear, Israel: The Lord our God is one Lord"—Achad. It's a compound unity, one made of many. But the word translated, we sound it *Jehovah*—"Hear, O Israel, the Lord"—that's Jehovah—"our God"—Elohim—"is one Jehovah." But the word translated Jehovah in the first revelation to man, in the 3rd chapter of Exodus, is I AM—Yod, He, Vau, He. So "Hear, O Israel: I AM"—Elohim, our Creator—"is one I AM."

I'm trying to bring out . . . in the end when you see God's only begotten Son and know him to be your son, and I know he is my son, are you and I not one being? I'm not sharing him. I'm his only begotten father; he's my only begotten son. Well, when you have the same conviction through experience, then are you and I not one? And his name is one. But "Hear, O Israel, the Lord our God is one Lord"—one I AM.

Q: My father's name, Moses, was given to him, Moses. Would that have
   any significance in this life? ___(??) He walked across the prairie?

A: My dear, I feel that every name has a significant value. If he gave to that
   great name Moses the value that it really contained, no wonder he did
   what he did—walked through the country, across the prairie and braved
   it before there were any compasses in the world—if you want to give the
   name significance because the word Moses is a powerful name. In fact,
   we have no names comparable to the names in the Bible. The name
   David—now my family, because of my experience with some other
   David, I think they have a bunch of Davids now. A little nephew was
   born two weeks ago, David. And so others ___(??) another; it's my great
   nephew, so I believe that in the next fifteen years, we're going to have a
   bunch of Davids and Moses and all kinds of these names because ___(??).
   They're the most glorious names. The word *Mark*—for instance, my
   little godson, I saw him in my vision, and I called him Mark. So I told
   the mother when the child was born that I called him Mark in my
   vision. Well, Mark was the name, so there's another little Mark. And I
   can't find any name comparable to these biblical names. They have great
   significance. So I would say, your father and your mother named him
   Moses—marvelous!
   Goodnight.

THE SIN AGAINST THE HOLY SPIRIT

February 19, 1963

Tonight's subject is "The Sin Against the Holy Spirit." Undoubtedly you have heard numberless concepts of this statement in scripture. The most common interpretation is a violation of the sex act. There are unnumbered concepts of it. But that is not my picture, not as has been revealed to me. As I have told you, the Bible is not something that you open up and just read as you would a novel. It's a building of three levels. As we are told, a three-fold cord is not quickly broken. And so they are on levels.

I, personally, cannot conceive of a violation against the Holy Spirit, I really can't. I'll give you my reasons for it afterward, but I can't. And so if I can comfort you, may I tell you don't be anxious. I can't conceive that you can violate and blaspheme the Holy Spirit, I can't. That you will simply sin, yes, certainly, we all sin. Every moment of time we sin, and all sins are forgiven, all blasphemies are forgiven. But the only blasphemy that cannot be forgiven is that against the Holy Spirit, as we're told in Matthew, Mark, and Luke. If you want the quote, the 3rd chapter of Mark, and the 12th chapter of Mathew, and the 12th of Luke. I find in the Book of Luke a more advanced development of the theme than I do in Matthew and Mark. Mark is the earliest revelation of this theme, but I find that Paul later advanced in this development of the theme in the Book of Luke. But each statement is followed by the strangest, most irrelevant thought in the three books. But that which follows in the Book of Luke is tonight's theme.

And in the Book of Luke, after he made the statement "that blasphemy against the Holy Spirit is not forgiven," then you will think you are reading an entirely different chapter on a different theme. For then it goes right

29

into this statement: "And when you are taken before the synagogue and the rulers and the authorities, do not be anxious how or what you are to answer or what you are to say; for the Holy Spirit will teach you in that very hour what you *ought* to say." That little word *ought* reveals so much. That implies you need not say what you should say; the Holy Spirit will teach you in that very hour what you ought to say, and that is the crux of the whole thing. Man is free, and because he's free, he need not say what he should say. So he will teach you in that very hour what you ought to say.

Now first of all, you must understand what a synagogue is. A synagogue is a gathering; it's a community called by Jehovah. We think a synagogue is built with human hands; but a synagogue, in the true sense of the word, is a place of worship, a place of instruction. The only worship in the synagogue is the reading of scripture. No getting up and saying prayers, it's the reading of the Word of God, as told us in Nehemiah 8:8, "And they read from the book, the law of God, clearly; and they gave the sense, so that the people understood the reading." And here, for almost two thousand years, in the most populous of our Christian denominations, they read it in Latin, in a tongue not understood by anyone in the congregation. And here we are warned, "They read from the book, the law of God, clearly; and they gave the sense, so that the people understood the reading."

Were I in France and speak only English, I couldn't go to any church and hear someone read to me in French. You have to read to me in the English tongue and read it with understanding that I may understand it. For here is the Word of God. Were I in any part of the world, I would only understand were it read in English. But if I could not understand English and understood some other tongue, then read it to me in that tongue, and read it with the sense so that I may understand it. And this is the story all over the world. You take one little passage, and we, ourselves, don't understand it. And then we go off and criticize the president or some other person. Hasn't a thing to do with anything taking place in the outer world. It's all about you; it's all about me.

Before we go into this statement, tonight's theme, let me show you the difference between Jesus and the Christ. For the whole thing is about the Christ. And so the connection between Jesus and the Christ is not that of an historical figure and some metaphysical entity but that of a visible history condensed into a few years and a history that is continuously unfolding throughout the ages—a history that is known as the history of salvation. Christ is divine history inwoven in every child born of woman. The whole vast history of God is inwoven in you, inwoven in me, and inwoven in *every* being. And when it reaches maturity in you, in one short little interval of time, that condensed moment of time, just a few years, the whole thing unfolds. And no one, may I tell you—well, I'll modify that, as I wouldn't say no one—but so very few will believe it. The entire divine history inwoven in man like a seed matures through the ages—all the pains, all the violence, everything in the world—and suddenly, what you heard about another begins to awaken in you. The whole thing flowers in you, and you are him. That's the story.

Now, why do I not believe that you could ever sin against the Holy Spirit? I'll tell you. "When they bring you before the synagogue and before the rulers and before the authorities, do not be anxious how or what you *are* to answer." If I must answer, someone asked me a question. "Do not be anxious how or what I am to answer"—but then who asked me a question? Some question must be asked for me to answer. Or what I am to say? "For the Holy Spirit will teach you in that very hour what I *ought* to say." So when I am brought into the wonderful gathering and presented to the Holy of Holies, God himself, I am told supernaturally—yes, I am prompted as though I were on a stage and the prompter is telling me what I ought to say. So I am supernaturally *prompted* what to say. And I can't, from my own experience, believe that anyone in this world could falter. It's automatic.

When you stand in his presence and he's infinite love, he will ask you, "What is the greatest thing in the world?" and you, without taking thought, without batting an eye, and without trying to rationalize, will automatically, like a response and like an echo, will say, "Faith, hope and love, these three abide; but the greatest of these is love" (1 Corinthians 13:13). You will do it automatically. He who asked the question and prompted you supernaturally what to say will then embrace you, and you are one with God forever and forever. Then you'll be sent to tell that story to the whole vast world, who will listen. Some will listen and accept it, others will reject it, and the majority will not even listen. It doesn't really matter.

It doesn't matter. This tree is growing in us; and when it matures in us in a short, very short interval of time, in a matter of years, a few years, the whole thing will unfold. It doesn't take fifty years (I am fifty-eight), not fifty-eight years, but just a few years to begin to happen; and then one after the other, everything said of him unfolds in you, and you are him. So Christ is divine history; and Jesus, the first to be raised from the dead, is the one in whom that divine history unfolded in this little short interval of time, and you are him. Everyone then becomes Jesus because everyone in one little moment of time is going to have it, in a matter of years. Then when the curtain comes off—the curtain being this little garment of flesh—you will know exactly who you are.

So I say that I personally cannot believe, although the word *ought* is used, and I am told in scripture, in Deuteronomy, in the Book of Proverbs, and the Book of Revelation, "Do not change one word of scripture. Do not add to it and do not take from it. Leave it just as it is." Therefore, I cannot alter the word *ought*, and it's used advisedly in both the King James Version and the Revised Standard Version. And so he will tell you what you *ought* to say, giving man freedom to deny it and *not* say, "The greatest thing in the world is love." That's man's choice. He's free. He could *not* say it, but I don't believe man would ever not say it. Because in my own case, it was like a response, like an echo, and how can you change an echo? If I screamed in some canyon and the voice came back, it's going to come back exactly what I said. But he was supernaturally prompted what to say, and so I can't see how you who are prompted in the depth of your soul what to say after the question is asked, that you're going to fail. So I would say, don't despair. You will not sin against the Holy Spirit.

But all other sins are forgiven, all of them. And what are the other sins? It is stated so clearly for us if we understood the Bible that every sin in the world is forgiven, all blasphemies are forgiven, and we hold the key. So in the end of the Book of John—that is, the first ending, the twentieth chapter—there are two endings, but the first and real ending is the twentieth chapter, in that he appears but in a room that was completely sealed. The doors were closed, and he's completely shut out, as it were; and they wondered if he really rose. Then he appears in the midst of those he told that he would return to them, appearing in their midst and showing them the marks upon his body to testify to the reality of his presence. Then he said to them, "Peace be unto you." And then he breathed upon them (John 20:19).

Listen to it carefully. "He breathed upon them and they received the Holy Spirit." Following this, he said, "If you forgive the sins of anyone, they are forgiven; and if you retain the sins of anyone, they are retained." He breathes upon them and gives them the Holy Spirit. The word *breath*, the word *wind*, and the word *spirit* are one, the same word, in both Greek and in Hebrew. So he breathes upon them. I'll tell you what that breath is. It's a vibration, the most intense vibration that you've ever felt, nothing comparable to it. That breath that transfers to you the gift promised, the gift of the Holy Spirit, is the most intense vibration. It awakens you, for this took place in the upper room. If you read the story correctly, they are all gathered together in the upper room and the doors were closed. And suddenly he appears, gives them peace, breathes upon them, and then gives them the power to hold or to release.

Well, I tell you, you can exercise this faculty right now. You can take someone in your world and represent that one to yourself, as you would like to see him in this world. And to the degree that you are self-persuaded that he *is* such a being, he becomes that being. You can actually free him. And you can hold him enslaved forever by fixing in your mind's eye the being who is now limited as though he could never come out. That's your privilege. Yet these are only states of consciousness, and in every state a man lives, he grows. As Matthew brings out right after his statement, "If the tree be good, it bears good fruit; if the tree be bad, it bears bad fruit," he invites us to make it a good fruit.

That's why I say that Luke went beyond Matthew and Mark in that statement of sinning against the Holy Spirit. They confine themselves after the statement that if you sin against the Holy Spirit, there is no forgiveness; but to sin against everything else, there is forgiveness. Then Matthew shows you how they're all trees bearing fruit. So everyone in this world is bearing fruit. You can bear the fruit of poverty, the fruit of wealth, the fruit of being known, the fruit of being completely unknown, the fruit of health, the fruit of wealth—anything in this world. And you who know this law can take anyone from the state where you find him and put him in the state that you desire to see him. You don't need his consent. You don't need his knowledge of what you're doing. Don't tell him what you are doing. Trust this power in your own being. Bring that individual before your mind's eye, represent him to yourself as you would like to see him, as you feel he would like to be seen by the world, and persuade yourself that this imaginal act on *your* part is true and real. And to the degree that you are self-persuaded that it is real, it becomes real.

And so I tell you, if you forgive anyone, he is forgiven; if you retain his sin, it is retained. So don't blame him. If he does not find the good job you think he should find, don't give an argument. It's entirely up to you. Do you know he needs a good job, a better job than he has, and that he must be more gainfully employed than he is? And you are telling him go and find the right people and go and make a greater special effort? You aren't applying this principle. Only as *you* become self-persuaded that he *is* gainfully employed have you applied this principle of forgiving his sins. For sin means "missing the target, missing the mark, missing the goal." For he has a target; his target is that he would like to be gainfully employed—that's his goal. And if he misses it and you know he's missed it and you would like to help him, you can help him.

Now listen to these words, "If I had not come and spoken unto them, they would not know sin; but now they have no excuse for their sin" (John 15:22). He comes and he shows man that causation is mental and that it isn't physical, and now man has no excuse for his sin, for missing his mark. For every man has a mind; every man has Imagination. He can exercise it. And "I tell you, 'You have heard of old that you should not commit adultery.' But I say, to look on a woman lustfully is to have already committed the act in your heart" (Matthew 5:27). He raises the act from the physical state to the mental state, so then he makes every man now responsible for missing the goal. And yet every goal on this level is forgiven. If I don't get the job, he doesn't condemn me. He only asks me to apply the law as he revealed it to me.

And so, "He read from the book." You're told, "Then he read from the book, the law of God, clearly; and they gave the sense so that the people understood the reading." And so you read from the book, God's revealed word, and he tells you that causation is mental, that imaginal acts create facts. So what are you imagining? I can say morning, noon, and night that I am thinking and holding a thought for you; and yet every time I think of you, I think in my heart, *I* hope *he gets it.* I am not doing a thing about it. I must so persuade myself that I can't see any other *you* than the *you* that I would like to see and you would like to see in the world. Any other *you* is not doing it. That's what he taught us to do.

And I tell you, the day will come—maybe tonight, and I hope it's tonight, because it begins in one moment that you least expect—when suddenly the whole thing begins to awaken and the flower begins to bloom within you. Everything is condensed within a few years that took eternity as you saw it. For in the beginning of time, you were shown it, shown it on Mt. Sinai. They can't find Mt. Sinai. No matter how the archaeologists look, they can't find it. They never will find it. God's sacred mountain, where all of us—but all of us, not one was left out—gathered together around and heard Jehovah pledge us. He called us his bride; we were then Israel. Then he took us, and he pledged Israel to himself in this wonderful holy covenant and showed us exactly what we would go through. And then we'll forget it in the passage through, and we couldn't remember it until the very end. In the very *end,* memory returns.

These wonderful words come to me from Edward Thomas's great poem: "All was foreshown me, naught could I foresee; but I learned how the wind would sound, after these things should be." You do. Suddenly, when the thing begins to unfold and you hear the wind, the ___(??) wind—this terrific hurricane of a power—and then all things begin to unfold, and everything said of Jesus Christ in the scripture you will experience, from the birth to the very end, everything. So do not see him as something on the outside. See Jesus, as I told you earlier, as a history condensed in a few years, just a few, few years, and see Christ as history continuously unfolding throughout the ages and you, the individual, matching this already unfolded divine history. You went through all the fires of the world, and suddenly you reached the point of blooming. Then suddenly, in this quick moment of a few years, you bloom. All that was foreseen and foretold, you suddenly awake, and you are it.

So everything in the world is forgiven. I don't care what you've done. I don't care what you are planning to do. It's all forgiven because these are only states. The only thing that is *not* forgiven is the sin against the Holy Spirit; and that is, as I see it from my own experience, when the individual refuses to confess his faith when supernaturally prompted to do so. When you're brought into the presence of the God of gods, the only God, and here in his presence, you are prompted to confess your faith. You don't initiate the words; they're told you. But you heard them before—we all heard these words before—but in that very moment, they are still uttered in the depth of your soul that you may not make any mistake: "What is the greatest thing in the world?" Then without batting an eye, without thinking, without any thought, you say, "Faith, hope and love, these three; but the greatest of these is love."

And here is the infinity embodied before you, the Holy Spirit, Jehovah himself; he embraces you, and you are merged with him. You are one with God, never in eternity to be divorced from him—one with God because you answered correctly. And yet you did not write the words; you didn't initiate them. So I cannot see how anyone could sin against the Holy Ghost. But again, I would like to say, as earlier, I cannot change the scripture; and the word *ought* is there, as far back as we can go to the earliest manuscripts. And so there is a possibility that one having been supernaturally prompted what to say could change the script, and then that's the sin against the Holy Spirit. But I don't think you will. But then again I can't conceive of anyone ___(??). So I can't conceive of God failing. He can't fail.

But in the interval, in all these things that we sin against, we fall into states. A man falls into a state of feeling sorry for himself; all right, then things begin to grow. He has so much to feel sorry about after he falls into the state. You, knowing the law, instead of lecturing the man or arguing with the man, just take him out of it. He may fall in twenty-four hours later. A friend called me today, all excited; it would not be the first time. ___(??). But my wife said that when she spoke to him earlier, he asked a very simple question. I didn't really want to discuss my daughter at all. Well, he said, "What news have you of Vicki?" because he knows she's back in New York City, and she said, "Well, we are very pleased with her report." And he said, "Pleased? Oh, I wish I could use that word pleased about anything about myself."

He's been coming to my meetings for years. I mean years. A way back in New York City, he came two, three times a week. He's in pictures, so he's out here now; he'll return back East. I said, "Do come, as often as you can. Be my guest. You don't have to put two dollars out at all, be my guest. Just come and saturate yourself." But after years of this saturation, he can't conceive of being happy, just can't conceive of it. And you tell him morning, noon, and night that these are states. So if you put yourself into a state of being wanted, you'll become wanted. If you put yourself in the state of being *not* wanted, well then, you'll find all the evidence in the world where you're not wanted. No agent will call you; and if they do call you, they'll say, I'm sorry but the other one got the job. So it will go on forever.

But he can't quite believe in this reality ___(??). And so I brought him out unnumbered times, and yet I must never falter. "How often must I forgive? Seventy times seven." And so if he calls me a thousand times, I still must pull him out. So he'll get a job for a couple of days. Makes himself, maybe a couple of hundred dollars; and then on the fourth day, he calls, "Nobody called me on the fourth day." And there you go, all over again. And you could take him down and just put it into his head, but he can't quite see it. Yet you and I who know this principle must forgive seventy times seven and not ignore him because he will not himself do this. If he wants to lean forever, let him lean forever until that tree begins to take root. And one day, when he least expects it, suddenly the whole story of Jesus Christ will unfold within him, and *he* is Jesus Christ.

Christ is divine history, the history of salvation—that's Christ. And Jesus is history condensed into a few years that matches. Suddenly, the whole vast thing that has been stretched out and continuously unfolding throughout all the ages is now telescoped in one short little interval of time in the life of one man. And so Christ is born in everyone and telescoped in just one ___(??). May it happen to you now. When it will happen only God knows. I do not know, but he knows. And the day it starts to happen, you can't stop it. Just one petal after the other will come out, and the whole thing will form the flower that is Christ. And then when you make your exit from this world you've made it for the last time, and then you are in eternity. But not better than those who have not yet arrived because *all* are destined to be one with God, all. No one is better because they preceded you. "Christ is the first fruit of those who slept; the first that has been raised from the dead" (1 Corinthians 15:23). But he is the beginning of the process, not better than any being in this world, because *all* are awakening and all will be one, and that one is God.

So the sin against the Holy Spirit . . . may I ask you, do not be too concerned. If you will trust me, I can't conceive that you will in any way not respond when you are prompted supernaturally what you should say. Listen to the words, "And when they bring you before the synagogue"—yes, it will be a divine gathering, may I tell you, a heavenly gathering of the gods, those who preceded you; that's the synagogue, it's the assembly called by Jehovah himself in fulfillment of the eighty-second Psalm: "God has taken his place in the divine council; in the midst of the gods he holds judgment" (verse l). And you are brought into his presence and presented to the Ancient of Days, the Holy Spirit, and he's man, the embodiment of love. He will ask you a very simple question. He is the ruler. He is the authority.

But don't you be anxious how or what you are to answer or what you are to say, for the Holy Spirit will teach you in that very hour what you *ought* to say. And I tell you, what you ought to say you're going to say. You are going to say it automatically. Then he embraces you with his infinite love and infinite delight, a joy beyond the wildest dreams. No one could conceive of the joy when Jehovah embraces you. And then you are sent, sent to do what you'll be doing, telling the word of God, just speaking it. You can't add to it, and please don't take from it, but just tell the Word of God just as you are told in Nehemiah 8: 8. In fact, there are four chapters, from the eighth through the eleventh, that tells you all about simply talking about the word of God, nothing else.

And so let no one tell you that it means any sexual departure or misuse or abuse or all the things; and there are unnumbered, hundreds of books written on that theme, and it isn't so at all. They are rationalizing God's word. You can't rationalize it; it has to be revealed. And so this is a mystery known only by revelation. I read those books. I bought them; I have them at home, so I know what people have read about it. And then having had the experience, I know everything is forgiven but in the true sense of the word. No matter what a man has ever done, it's completely forgiven. Take him out of one state; put him in the other. If he falls into the state a thousand times, pull him out of that state a thousand times.

And do the same thing for yourself. You do it by representing yourself to yourself as though you were the man that you would like to be, and walk the earth just as though it were true. And although reason, for the moment, may deny it and your senses deny it and everything denies it, it doesn't matter. You remain faithful to it; and you, the only living reality in the world, will take that state and animate it, and that state will bear its fruit. So you are told in the twelfth of Matthew—after the statement of the Holy Spirit and the great blasphemy against him—that he jumps completely with a new thought and just build you a good tree that bears good fruit and not the bad tree that bears bad fruit. And so someone doesn't like what he's doing in this world—that's a bad tree. It's a tree bearing the fruit. Take him out of that and build a good tree, and leave him there. Let him bear the good fruit of the good tree.

But he is neither a good tree nor a bad tree. He is the immortal soul falling into these states, one after the other. That's what Blake meant when he said, "I do not consider either the just or the wicked to be in a supreme state, but to be every one of them states of the sleep which the soul may fall into in its deadly dreams of good and evil." But he's neither good nor evil; he falls into these states unwittingly. And so you can take someone and, without their knowledge, without their consent, put them into a state, a lovely state, and persuade yourself that it's true, although you have no evidence to confirm it as yet. You haven't seen him, and you haven't heard from him, but you persuade yourself that it is so. And if you do, suddenly you'll meet him or hear of him or hear from him, and he will confirm the fruit that you bear him. But if you don't do it and you believe all the things you hear and see in the course of a day, well then, you are moving unknowingly into all kinds of confusing states.

But may I tell you that you will not—even though the Bible tells us, using the word *ought*—I say from my own experience, sin against the Holy Spirit. So don't be concerned; don't be anxious about what must I do to avoid it. You will not sin against the Holy Spirit. I can't conceive of someone in the presence of God being supernaturally prompted what to say other than what you're told to say. I can't conceive of it. As I told you that, automatically, how easy it was to do. You will believe it, and you'll become it. Because I didn't take a thought, I was taken in Spirit right into his presence. And then I could not ___(??), just like an echo. I simply echoed what was ___(??) in the depth of my soul. I can tell you, and that was enough. That brought me the embrace of God.

Here, from then on to this moment, I can't forget it. It's more vividly impressed upon me than this morning's, or tonight's dinner for that matter. I've had many lovely letters today, cards today, and experiences today; but yes, sweet as they are to me, nothing is as indelibly impressed upon my mind as this that happened to me thirty-odd years ago. It is this part of my vision as though I saw it only five minutes ago or minutes ago. I can still see him. If I could paint as Blake painted or the great artists of the world, I'd paint him, and show you this—just as Daniel describes him, just like that—this Ancient of Days.

So I say, don't be concerned, but do practice freeing individuals from the sin that is forgivable. You can forgive every being in this world before he breathes upon you and gives you the gift of the Holy Spirit. You still can forgive. Everyone can do it. My friends in San Francisco and my friends here, dozens of you, whose stories I have told in my latest book, you forgave—that's forgiving. You took certain things that you want in this world and denied that you didn't have them by assuming that you had them, and you got them. Whether it was a lovely painting of a ship that you now have on the wall, whether it was the getting of a home that maybe you don't want anymore—perfectly all right. These are all states. But you *got* them. And you took others, and you changed others and made them conform to your dream of them and they all conformed to it.

Now let us not go back to sleep. Let us remember what you did and continue to do it. Knowing that at any moment in time, when you least expect it, just like a thief in the night, he comes upon you. Then he breathes upon us and our head becomes a vibrant center, an intense vibration, and then we will awaken from the dream. It is Christ breathing upon himself in us, for Christ, being divine history, is simply awakened and unveiled in us, and we suddenly become aware as we awaken in ourselves, and we are him. Then we rush to our scripture and reread the story as told us in Matthew and Luke, and everything said of his birth we just experienced. Even to the three who are present and everything about him, even to the swaddling clothes—but everything. And then you stand in ___(??), bewildered.

And then five months later, something equally fantastic happens. Then we are told, "If the Son makes you free, you are free indeed," if the *Son* makes you free. For the promise is made that the Son will make the Father free in the Book of 1st Samuel, the 17th chapter, the 25th verse. He will set the Father free. If he sets the *Father* free, there must be a child. And he tells you that he's trying to find that child. Finding the child, he must know who the Father is; and when he finds who the Father is, he sets the Father free. So it takes the *Son* to set the Father free. So in the 8th chapter of John he said, "The Son abides forever. When the Son sets you free, you are free indeed" (verse 36). And then you see the Son after another breathing of the wind upon you, for your head becomes a vibrant space, more intense than anything you've ___(??). All of a sudden, here he comes, and he sets you free, for he calls you "Father." You know who he is, God's only begotten Son, and he calls you "Father." Then you know exactly who you are. And then comes one after the other, but everything. The whole thing is telescoped.

So let me again repeat the connection between Jesus and the Christ is not that of an historical figure and a metaphysical entity but that of an history condensed within a few years, a history that is unfolding forever, continuously unfolding throughout all the ages. Suddenly, this matches that and it telescopes, and all that is unfolding forever is telescoped in you in a few short years; and you are he.

Now let us go into the Silence.

*   *   *

Q: (inaudible)

A: No, I saw it in this morning's *Times* ___(??), the Torah, the new Torah. This would be the first five books; this would be Genesis through Deuteronomy. No, I ___(??) the Book of Mark, "If anyone should say to you, 'Look, there he is!' or 'Look, here he is!' believe him not." Don't believe him if anyone tells you that I've found him. Come and go hear him. That's not him. You'll never see him because you can only see a veil. Wherever you go, you're going to see a veil because the body that man wears is a veil. So don't let anyone mislead you in telling you they've found Christ and come with me, I'll show you who he is. Don't believe it. He unfolds *in* you; and the whole story of him, as recorded in the gospels, totally telescopes, and the whole thing unfolds within you and every experience you have. (Tape ends).

PAUL'S AUTOBIOGRAPHY

February 22, 1963

Tonight we have Paul's autobiography. It is the story of Paul, and Paul is the greatest and most influential figure in the history of Christianity. After you hear his story, you may judge just who he is. Paul begins where everyone who aspires after public confidence must begin: with his own credentials. Paul wrote thirteen letters; that is, we have thirteen if you will take the double letters as two, like 1st and 2nd Corinthians, 1st and 2nd Timothy, and 1st and 2nd Thessalonians. If you take these as two letters, then he gave us thirteen.

He first appears in scripture in the Book of Acts, and bear in mind that the Book of Acts was once part of the Book of Luke. The same author who wrote the Book of Luke wrote the Book of Acts. They were once one volume, or one Book in two volumes. Our early fathers divided the two and placed the Gospel of John between them. But he first appears you may say in the book you would call the gospel of Luke, but we now call it the Book of Acts. He was present when the first Christian martyr was stoned to death, Stephen, and Paul consented unto Stephen's death. He was present when those who stoned Stephen placed their coats at the feet of Saul—his name was then Saul—and that is the 7th chapter of the Book of Acts.

In the ninth chapter, he starts this great journey to Damascus, and he bears with him letters to the high priest in Damascus. He pledges himself that if he finds anyone belonging to the Way—capital W-a-y—be he man or woman, he will bring them bound to Jerusalem. The earliest name given to the Christian was "the Way." Everyone who believed it, they were called followers of the Way, not Christians. So if he found anyone who belonged to the Way, he would bring them bound to Jerusalem. And on the way to bind those who belonged to the Way, he was blinded by the light; and then the whole thing was revealed to him, and his name was transformed from Saul to Paul. And then we have the remaining portion of the Book of Acts devoted almost exclusively to Paul—at least the last sixteen chapters, which would begin with the very first verse of Acts 13, right through to the twenty-eighth, where he ends his days still propounding this mystery and trying to persuade everyone of the truth of Jesus. Beginning with the law of Moses and all through the prophets, he explained to them in all the scriptures the truth concerning Jesus. And some were convinced by what he said, while others disbelieved (Luke 24:27). That's the story.

But if I will read Paul and take one of his letters that would really explain Paul to me, I would go to the letter of Galatians. For in Galatians—which scholars claim to be the very first book of the New Testament, as it came before the gospels, before any book, so they claim—and in this letter he makes the claim, I, "Paul an apostle—not from men nor through man, but through Jesus Christ and God the Father, who raised him from the dead" (Galatians 1:1). Here is a declaration of complete religious independence from all men and dependence on God, repudiating in this letter all authorities, institutions, customs, and laws that interfered with the direct access of the *individual* to his God. No intermediary between the individual and his God; none called by any name. Then he said, "The gospel which I have preached is not the gospel of man. For I did not receive it from a man, neither was I taught it, but it was given to me by revelation of Jesus Christ" (verse 11). "And when it pleased God to reveal his Son *in* me, then I conferred not with flesh and blood" (verse 16).

And you ask the question of Paul, "Was your Christ once really a man?" If you asked that of Paul, he would say, "Was? He *is* the *heavenly* man." And then they'll answer—to answer the question—"Was he really ever a man?" and he replied, "Not was. He is the heavenly man," and "As we have borne the image of the man of dust, so shall we also bear the image of the heavenly man" (1 Corinthians 15:49). That still doesn't satisfy. "Was he *really* a man as we understand a man?" He doesn't respond in kind. Then you read his words, "From now on, we will regard no one from a *human* point of view; even though we formerly regarded Christ from a human point of view, we regard him thus no longer." For you who take notes: the 2nd Corinthians, the 5th chapter (verse 16). Then he makes the following statement in the same 5th chapter:: "God was in Christ, reconciling the world to himself, not counting any trespasses against them, and entrusting *us* with the message of reconciliation" (verse 19). You will see later on what Paul is trying to tell us. If I would substitute the word *Imagination* for God and *imagining* for Christ—imagining being the activity of Imagination—that Imagination was imagining, reconciling the world to himself and not counting any trespasses against them and then entrusting to us this message of imagining.

Now we'll go to this great Galatians. He said, "I have been crucified with Christ: It is not *I* who live, but Christ who lives in me; and the life I now live in the flesh I live by the faith of the Son of God, who loved me and gave himself for me" (Galatians 2:20). You bear in mind imagining being that Son and Imagination being God the Father. And now let us go to the first two verses of the 3rd chapter of Galatians, "O foolish Galatians! Who has bewitched you, before whose eyes Jesus Christ was publicly portrayed as crucified?" Listen to the words carefully: "Before whose eyes Jesus Christ was *publicly portrayed* as crucified." Know what portrayed means? I think we all know, but let me refresh your memory: "to depict in a drawing, or a painting, or in some verbal description, or as an action on a stage, a play on a stage." "O foolish Galatians! Who has bewitched you, before whose eyes Jesus Christ was publicly *portrayed* as crucified? Now answer me only this"—he asks a very simple question—"Did you receive the Spirit by the law, by the works of the law, or by *hearing* with faith? Are you so foolish? Having begun with the Spirit, are you ending with the flesh?" (Galatians 3:1-3) Do you get it? The whole vast world has fallen victim to the flesh being of Jesus. Have you, having *begun* with the *Spirit*, are you falling now actually blind and a victim of the flesh?

You were shown the whole thing like a play. Go into a stage tonight and someone moves across the stage and they play the perfect play of God's *only* salvation, the *only* way that man could be saved; he walks across a stage and he plays it. Every scene that he enacts is a mystical scene to be experienced by the individual. That was all done. Well, now are you going to confuse it? Can't you now have that little spiritual observance and separate the actor walking across the stage from what he's trying to portray? For he's *portraying* it! Listen to the words, the first three verses of the 3rd chapter of the epistle to the Galatians: "Before whose eyes Jesus Christ was publicly portrayed as crucified." He was *portrayed* as crucified. You go to a play tonight and somebody is shot. You know he goes home tonight after being shot and has the most wonderful time. Their day begins at night, for they work at night. So they go home and the actor goes home and that's night; his day begins. But you will weep sitting in the audience as you see him being shot and being abused. But *he* wasn't shot, and *he* wasn't abused save as an actor, but not the being who put on the mask who played the part. So let me repeat it: "Whose eyes beheld Jesus Christ publicly portrayed as crucified." And then the words: "Are you foolish? Having begun in the Spirit"—it was revealed to you, the spirit of the play—"are you ending now with the flesh?"

So the world thinks he was flesh and blood. No, he wasn't flesh and blood. This is the fulfillment of all that was told in the Old Testament, but no one understood it, except to one to whom it was revealed—you can call him Paul now. "And when it pleased God to reveal his Son in me, I conferred not with flesh and blood" (Galatians 1:16). "The gospel I preach to you is not man's gospel. I did not receive it from a man, nor was I taught it, but it was revealed by Jesus Christ." The whole thing was revealed, and I saw the mystery of it all, the mystery of salvation—that Christianity is based upon the affirmation that a series of events happen in which God revealed himself in action for the salvation of man.

Did they happen? Well, the play said they did. I went to the play, and I saw it. I was part of the gathering, and they hoped that I would have the spirit of discernment to separate the action of the actor from what he was acting and see the Spirit, not the flesh. Did I see the Spirit? Well, then after a while come the teachers who did not participate, and they tell you he is flesh and blood and that he was born of a certain woman on a certain day, in a manner that you were born, only he didn't have a physical father; and that isn't true at all. This birth is something entirely different, as told us in the Book of John: "He is born not of blood nor of the will of the flesh nor of the will of man, but of God" (John 1:13). An entirely different birth takes place, which is all explained as the play unfolds. You saw the Spirit, but don't go back now to the flesh.

And now the story begins. We were called the followers of the Way. That's what we were called—all of us who believed it as we saw the play unfold. Is that the Way of salvation? I'll believe it. I will wait patiently until it unfolds in me, for that's the Way of salvation. Then in the fourteenth of John, we are told, "And now you know the way," and "Thomas said, 'We do not know the way. We do not know where you are going, so how do we know the way?'" "He said, 'I am the way. I am the way, and the truth, and the life.'" It's not a man. Follow me closely. All that you have seen me do upon the stage, that is the way, for I am the way. He didn't say I am this, that, or the other. I am the way. You follow the whole thing as Spirit that moved before you, and you have seen the *way* of salvation. They still didn't understand it. The way to what? Well, the way to everything, but primarily the way to the Father. "For no one comes to the Father but by me" (John 14:6). You can't come to the Father save by me, and I am the way. So don't look upon me as flesh and blood; I am the way. Follow my story: through this series of events, you'll come to the Father.

So the state unfolds on the stage, and they all see the Spirit, but many could not discern and discriminate between the action of the actor and what the actor was portraying. So we come back to Galatians: "Before whose eyes Jesus Christ was publicly portrayed as crucified." There you see it. The whole thing is unfolding on a stage. But man cannot lose himself to the point where he gets beyond the action of an actor and cries and weeps with the actor. As to the actor, he can't see what he is portraying. He's *portraying* something, and they can't get what he is portraying. So I tell you, read the story of Jesus and don't think of Jesus as flesh and blood. He is God himself, unfolding it before you in the form of a man that can see a man walking across the stage.

So is Paul the initial awakened being? You can judge it; I don't know. I am led to believe that he is. That Paul, the most influential, the most important figure in the history of Christianity, is the one to whom it was revealed. He was violent in his destruction of everything other than the outer observation of law, and to him it was revealed. So take courage. If you are violent today in supporting something that is external that you must observe, it doesn't matter. Paul did the same thing. And suddenly he was blinded by the revelation, and he saw the mystery of Christ. He saw that Christ was within him: "And when it pleased God to reveal his son *in* me, then I conferred not with flesh and blood" (Galatians 1:16). To whom would I turn? To whom would I turn and ask them to throw light upon an experience that is not understood by mortal mind? But having known the Bible as he did, he was well grounded in it, he could return to his Bible and see where it was all foretold. But he could not, on that level, understand it. It had to be unveiled. As it was unveiled, he saw the interpretation of the ancient scripture. And then in the end of Acts, when he stands before King Agrippa and he says, "Here I stand before you chained, condemned, for my hope in the promise made by God to our fathers. Here, I have hope in that promise that I stand in chains before you, because I know it's true." And then he spent the rest of his days expounding this story concerning what he called then, Jesus.

And the whole vast world of Christendom thinks it is a man of flesh and blood. And *Jesus* means "Jehovah saves; Jehovah is salvation." There's nothing in the teaching of Paul but God and man—no intermediary, nothing in between. So God himself is being woven in man and unfolds himself in man in a series of events. As these events unfold—and they unfolded in Paul—then he knew the mystery of the scripture. Then he tried to tell it to those that followed him in the path because he condemned and allowed the death of others for believing in it. Then he himself fell victim to his belief.

So who will believe it? I know that across this country as I go, the one question that is always asked me no matter where I go, whether it's a little social gathering, is "Well, don't you believe in a physical Jesus?" No matter where I go, I get it. When I go to a small little dinner party of four, five, or six, I'm asked, "I know what you say, Neville, but don't you *really* believe he did live, that he walked 2,000 years ago on this earth and he was called Jesus, and he walked and his mother was Mary and his father was Joseph, or maybe his father wasn't Joseph?" And then they ask all these questions, and all these are asked. The unprepared mind—how can you explain to a mind unprepared what Paul said in the first three verses of the 3rd chapter of Galatians: "O foolish Galatians! Who has bewitched you,"—for they went astray to some physical state—"before whose eyes Jesus Christ was publicly portrayed as crucified"? You sat with me and you saw the play—before our eyes he was publicly portrayed as crucified. "Now I ask you one thing: Did you receive the Spirit from the works of the law, or by hearing with faith?" You saw it, you heard the words, and you accepted what you heard on *faith* that this thing is true. Now, said he to them, "Are you so foolish? Having *begun* with the Spirit, are you now ending with the flesh?" You began with the Spirit when you heard it and saw it, are you now going to end with the flesh? For the whole vast world today is ending with the flesh and they can't see the *Spirit* that is Christ Jesus.

Christ Jesus is in man. It's a way. "Christ in you is the hope of glory." And the same author, Paul, in his 13th chapter of his 2nd Corinthians, "Do you not realize that Jesus Christ is in you?—unless of course you fail to meet the test!" (verse 5). I hope you realize we have not failed. If Jesus Christ is in you, then I should start looking to find out where he is. I have found him by a search and an experiment. When he said, "God is in Christ, reconciling the world to himself, not holding any trespasses against them and entrusting to us the spirit of reconciliation." So then God is in Christ, and Christ is in me, then who are we? God is in Christ and Christ is in me and I discover that God is my own wonderful human Imagination. God in action is Christ, and Imagination in action is imagining, so Imagination imagining is reconciling the world to himself.

Now, to those who discover it, he entrusts this great secret of reconciliation. So you take every being in the world. All right, let them go astray; it doesn't matter. If with God all things are possible and he works and creates only through Christ and Christ is now imagining, I could imagine that you are what I want you to be, if I really believe in Christ—for Christ in you is the hope of glory—and he's my own wonderful imagining. So I could imagine that you are the lovely one that I would like you to be, and although at the moment you don't respond and tomorrow you still don't respond, I will persist, for one of his attributes is patience. Read the fruits of the Spirit. It's not only love and joy and peace but also patience—it's persistence. In the end of the Book of Galatians, he gives us the fruit of the

Spirit (Galatians 5:22). And so I can persist. I can be patient. I will imagine things are as they ought to be, although at the moment, reason denies it and my senses deny it and everything denies it. But this is the fruit of the Spirit. I'll be patient. I will imagine things are as I would like them to be. And that's God in action, and God in action is Christ. And so I will persist, and I'll be patient. I like what I'm doing; therefore, the Spirit bears the fruit of love and joy and peace. These are the first petals that come out: love, joy, and peace, and then come the other attributes, among which you will find there is patience—there is persistence.

So Paul, to me, is the first in whom the visions took place. It came to one of the smallest tribes, Benjamin. He was born in the tribe of Benjamin, a child of Abraham. So Abraham is faith, for it was all shown to Abraham, and he believed it and waited patiently for the fulfillment of what was shown him. He saw the play too. It was all *portrayed* to Abraham. And "Abraham rejoiced that he was to see my day; he saw it, and he was glad" (John 8:56). Then he went into the foreign land, as he was led by the Spirit. But he still remained faithful to what he had seen in the play. The play unfolded before him. God played the part, and God was Christ Jesus.

So you say, "Well, how could this Lord, this exalted Lord, become human?" Again Paul answers in his letters to the Philippians, "He emptied himself . . . and became obedient unto death, even death upon a cross" (2:5-9). Again, he's speaking in a mystery. For Paul is very fond of using the word *mystery*; in fact, he uses it no less than eighteen times. And so he said he emptied himself and became obedient unto death, even death upon a cross. Well, this [body] is the cross I can tell you, and to him the cross was not the grievance of God but the love of God, may I tell you. And that crucifixion is the most delightful state; it's not a painful state at all as the churches portray. They don't portray the true thing at all. It's the most delightful state, for it happened to me right in this present embodiment, where it was shown me so vividly how it was done. And the thrill that was mine the night that my hands became vortices; my head, a vortex; my side, a vortex; and the soles of my feet, vortices!

Here I was on a pilgrimage toward some invisible Mecca. As I walked toward this invisible Mecca with unnumbered thousands, a voice out of the blue announced, "And God walks with them." Then a lady to my right, dressed in Arabic costume, asked the voice, for she heard it—they all heard it—"If God walks with us, where is he?" The voice answered, "At your side." She, like the whole world, takes it literally, so she turned to her side, to her left, where I walked with her. Then she became hysterical. She laughed beyond the wildest dream of laughter; she was hysterical. She said, "What? Neville is God?" The voice replied, "Yes, in the act of waking." And then a voice in the depth of my soul—and no one heard the voice now, but they all heard the conversation I've just given you, but no one heard this, except I and I alone—and from the depth of my being, the same voice now spoke. The voice said, "God laid himself down within you to sleep, and as he slept, he dreamed a dream. He dreamed . . ." and I knew the end of it: he was dreaming that he's Neville. He's dreaming that he's you. He's dreaming that he's every being in this world. He laid himself down within us to sleep. This is a sleeping God, and as he slept, he dreamed a dream; he's actually dreaming that he's you. Whatever your name is, he's dreaming that he's you. So the voice said to her who questioned the voice, "Yes, he is God in the act of waking from this sleep." When he awakes from the sleep, he is one with the dreamer who dreamed him into being, and he is God." So that's the story.

He said, "I have been *crucified* with Christ; it is not I who live but Christ who lives *in* me; and the life I now live in the flesh I live by the faith of the Son of God, who loved me and gave himself for me" (Galatians 2:20). Now listen to these words, "If we have been united with Christ in a *death* like his, we shall certainly be united with him in a resurrection like his" (Romans 6:5). The resurrection has taken place, but it is taking place. It took place; and that first one, whether you believe it or not, is Paul. It took place, and from that moment on, it is *taking* place in every being in the world as we march toward this invisible Mecca. Along the way, we are pulled out of the crowd—unnumbered are moving—and one by one we are pulled out; he awakens in the individual. That one without losing his distinctive individuality is God. So Jesus Christ is God himself.

The play is on. God became man and played the parts and showed us all before we started the journey. But we can't quite discriminate between the action of the actor and what the actor is trying to portray. So go back and read the words carefully, "Before whose eyes Jesus Christ was publicly *portrayed* as crucified." You go to any dictionary and look up the word *portray* and see its definition: you can depict it in a drawing, depict it in a painting, in a verbal description of it, or as an actor. An actor depicts the thought, but man can't quite discriminate between the thought depicted and the actor depicting the thought, and he thinks now the thing is flesh and blood, but it isn't.

Well, you dwell upon it. And one day you too will find yourself in that journey, the most colorful crowd in the world, I mean really colorful. Nothing on the screen compares to it in the color and the joy as you move toward this invisible Mecca. You'll hear a voice, and the voice will scream out, "And God walks with them." Someone in the crowd—and chances are if it always repeats itself in the same way, that someone will be standing at your side—and you will ask . . . but they will ask, "Well, if God walks with us, where is he?" And the voice will come back, "At your side." They will look into your face and become hysterical; it will strike them so funnily that you, a normal man with all the weaknesses of a man, would be God. The voice will come back that all will hear, "Yes, in the act of waking." Then from the depths of your soul will come the same voice, and no one but you will hear it. I put it in words that the world would understand, but the words differ: "And God laid himself down within you to sleep." It isn't that "*I* laid myself down within you to sleep, and as I slept I dreamed a dream. I dreamed"—he's going to complete it—"I dreamed I am you." That's what you're going to hear in the depth of your soul.

And then, at that moment, you are going to find yourself being crucified in the most thrilling manner in the world. You'll be sucked back into the body that was on the bed, and your hands are real vortices and your feet vortices, your head a vortex, and the right side a vortex. It's a thrilling joy as you are nailed once more to this body. Then you will know Paul's words: "I have been crucified with Christ; it's not I who live, but Christ who lives in me; and the life I now live in the flesh I live by the faith of the Son of God, who loved me and gave himself for me." And the Son of God in whom there is life is your own wonderful human imagining. Imagining is life itself. What you imagine becomes animated; it takes on life, takes on motion, vibration.

So here, when you go home, you read it and take that wonderful third chapter—take the whole book; there are only six chapters in the Book of Galatians—and see Paul's confession. No one taught it to him; he didn't receive it from a man. It came through a revelation of Jesus Christ. "And when it pleased God to reveal his Son in me, I conferred not with flesh and blood." And God will reveal his Son in you, he explodes you, and you will see his Son standing before you. You will see that Son as your Son. Then you know the meaning of the words, "No one comes unto the Father but by me . . . for I am the way, I am the truth, I am the life." Not a man called Jesus or Neville or Peter or any other name—no, the Way. "I am the way." The way is a series of mystical experiences, that's the Way. "I am the way," and "you come to the Father in no other way, save by me." So watch this picture as it unfolds. For before you unfolded the story, before your eyes, Jesus Christ was *publicly revealed* in this drama. So that is the play.

So when you see me, you see the Way. If you heard my story, you heard the Way. There is no other Way. So "I am the way, the truth and the life." Not a man called Neville; what he has experienced is the Way. And there is no other way to come to the Father. You will be brought by these series of experiences, for Christianity is based upon the affirmation that a series of events happened in which God revealed himself in action for the salvation of man. This series of events he unfolds in you, and you are the participant; you go through it, and you're brought right up to fatherhood. But "no one comes to the Father but by me . . . and I am the way." You go back, and you see the first appearance of the Way in the story of Paul, the 9th chapter of the Book of Acts. He went out to destroy everyone who believed in the Way, and he's going to bring them captive, bound, into Jerusalem. As he walked toward Damascus to bind male and female who were followers of the Way, he was blinded by the experience.

And *he* went through the experience of the Way. Then he comes back and goes through hell, but not for one moment could he relinquish the experience. And so he closed his days, explaining to everyone who would listen to him the story of the Way, and some believed him, while others disbelieved him.

Now let us go into the Silence.

*   *   *

Q: (inaudible)
A: The question is, will I say something about "My yoke is easy and my burden is light." Well, that's a talk in itself. He declares himself to be the light of the world. Yoke is union. Union with Christ is really very easy. If you saw that unfolding picture, just like a screen, could you believe it? Belief is union; that's yoke. It's very easy to believe it, but man has to be free from his prefabricated misconceptions of Jesus. If you come with your prefabricated misconceptions and you see it, you will not find the yoke easy. Many in this audience tonight, that is, a few, who are unwilling to believe what I said this night, still believe in a Jesus of flesh and blood, and flesh and blood cannot inherit the kingdom of heaven (1Corinthians 15:50). For God is Spirit, and those who worship him worship in Spirit and truth. Therefore, if you insist that he is flesh and blood, well then, you'd be unwilling to believe that he is simply portraying the state of God becoming man that man may become God. It may not be difficult; it is very easy to accept it if you saw it and could extract from the actual actor what the actor is trying to portray. So he's portraying it.

But I know; I was raised a Christian, and I was raised to believe that he was a little boy of flesh and blood. And all these things were told me and my family, and I'm quite sure the 900 million Christians of the world have been told the same story. Because I know from experience that no matter where I go, "Well, don't you believe"—they want to pin you right down—"that he did live and walk this earth as flesh and blood?" And then you say, "No. Do you believe?" and then you ask some more questions: "You know the man called Barrymore, a very good actor, who played the part of Hamlet? But he wasn't Hamlet. He explained and he portrayed this melancholy Dane, this prince, but he wasn't a Dane and he wasn't a prince; he's an actor. Can you believe it for one moment?" No, they don't want to believe that. And may I tell you that this comes from every walk of life. Not just those who are out of high school or grammar school, but out of colleges and great universities, with their highest honors and highest degrees, and they don't want to believe it. If you don't want to believe it, you don't believe it. And so how can you share your vision with another who is unwilling to share it with you?

But you tell it anyway. You tell it until the end of your earthly days because you are making your departure, as he said, "The time for my departure is come. I have fought the good fight, I have finished the race, I have kept the faith" (2 Timothy 4:6). That's Paul's last word. And so he kept the faith. The faith of what? The faith of Abraham. He said, "My kingdom is not new; it is as old as the faith of Abraham." It's the fulfillment of that faith, but no one knew it. And suddenly all that Abraham was shown in the beginning is now fulfilled in him. And so "I do not bring a new religion; it's not man-made; it is one that is as old as the faith of Abraham."

But who will believe it? People think of Paul being a convert, and you think of a convert as one who was once a Jew who became a Christian or vice versa. That's not a convert, not in the true mystical sense of the word. It's the *fulfillment* of the vision. He never once—not for one moment did Paul ever give up Judaism. His last plea before King Agrippa is "I stand here in chains for the hope of the promise made to our fathers by God through his prophets." He isn't denying that faith and that hope. That's why I am here, but I tell you that my experience is only the fulfillment of what God said to my father, Abraham. He promised him a son even though he couldn't beget him, and that son has been revealed in me. And now that I see the son, I tell you about the Way, and you don't believe me and you enchain me and you beat me because I tell you of these stories. He was only fulfilling scripture, the 53rd chapter of Isaiah: the servant of the Lord must suffer, and he comes to bring a message. He doesn't have to suffer physically, although he may, but he can suffer by abuse and be ostracized, put apart. He doesn't know—poor fellow, he's stuck. And there it goes.

He knows that one day, he takes off the garment and he'll be taken into an entirely different world because then he's equipped to function consciously there. And those who beat him and then ostracized him are the beaten people, and over and over they go playing and replaying the same part until, in that wonderful journey, the voice comes out: "God walks with them." Now you see the light, or you don't. What a glorious play!

Q: (inaudible)

A: Certainly, my dear. ___(??) "made into the image of the man of dust, he shall also be made into the image of the heavenly man," for we are destined to be conformed to the image of his Son (1 Corinthians 15:49). And then you say, how can the Imagination be a son? It is, believe it or not. When Blake made the statement "Man is all Imagination, and God is man and exists in us and we in him . . . the eternal body of man is the Imagination and that is God himself," he was right. Because Imagination always *personifies* itself, and it is man.

Q: Nehemiah 8, where you said about the reading of the book, would that be equated with the portrayal, the reading of the book?

A: Certainly. Nehemiah 8:8, "And they read from the book, the law of God." But see, they gave it the sense. Not only they gave it the sense but those who heard it—all who heard it understood the reading. And so the purpose of the teacher is to instruct. He not only has to read the script but also must read it with meaning. They must understand the meaning.

Q: Was Paul a person like we are?

A: Yes, my dear, Paul is just as you are. Paul is just as I am. And in Paul, the vision began to unfold. And so he's the most important figure, the greatest figure, the most influential figure in the history of Christianity. More is said of him in the New Testament than of anyone else. The Book of Acts, which was part of the Book of Luke, devotes more than half the book to Paul; then Paul gave us what we have preserved today, thirteen letters. He's been most controversial; and today in certain denominations, they speak of the Paulist, meaning the convert. Everyone who was not of that faith, in an orthodox sense, when they adopted is the Paulist. So the Paulists simply are the converting ones, as it were. But it's a complete misunderstanding of what Paul meant. Paul was a convert to the Way, but never did he ever give up the root of Israel.

Good night.

HIS NAME

February 26, 1963

Tonight's subject is "His Name." I think you know how I feel about the Bible—that the Bible is not the product of human___(??); it is not constructed by man. It's the history of man's discovery by God's revelation of the changing name of God, and it increases in its value to man.

In the 4th chapter of Genesis, the very last verse, we are told that a child was born whose name was Enosh, born of Seth, and many began to call upon the name of the Lord. That's the first time that man began to call upon the name of the Lord. The word *Enosh* means "mortal man, something that is fragile, something that simply wears out and is buried." Mortal man began to ask concerning origins: Why am I here? What is the cause of the phenomena of life? So man began to ask concerning origins.

The next time we see it, it's in the 32nd chapter of the Book of Genesis. And this is the night, so we are told, a man called Jacob, the supplanter, wrestled with God. When it came to the breaking of the day, God said to him, "Let me depart"; and he said, "I will not let you depart until you bless me," and God blessed him. Then he said to God, "What is your name?" and God answered, "Why do you ask my name?" He would not tell him. But he called the spot where God touched him Peniel, which means "the face of God." "For, said he, I have seen God face to face and yet my life is preserved." Then as the sun rose, Jacob halted because where God had touched, it shrank; it shrank upon his thigh. It was a sinew upon his thigh (Genesis 32:24). But we're all adults; *that's* what man at that level of consciousness believed to be the creative power of the universe.

For today, 1963, you and I are witnesses to the most fantastic things that man has conceived—missiles in space that can reach the sun, these IBM machines, electronic brains—but nothing that man has ever devised or brought to birth can compare to a child. Nothing in this world that man could ever conceive is comparable to the brain of a child. For the child conceived the instrument that now frightens him. We have a bomb, a nuclear bomb, but that can't compare to the brain that conceived it, no matter what we do with it. So a little child, this living organism, was what man thought; and he goes back to the origin, and you realize the sex act and he thought that could be God. Well, you read the 32nd chapter of the Book of Genesis, where man once thought that that was God: the very act of producing the most sensitive, creative thing in the world in the form of a child. And all over the world, we find these phallic images; all over the world you can see them. There isn't a part of the world that someone hasn't erected some phallic image in his worship of God.

Now we turn to the second book of the Bible, the Book of Exodus, where the name changes because it wasn't yet revealed. Men began to call upon the name of the Lord. They didn't know what to call upon, and many thought it was sex. And then comes the 3rd chapter of the Book of Exodus, and you read through, say, the fifteenth, and now God reveals himself to his chosen vessel, Moses. "And Moses said to the Lord, 'When I come to the people of Israel and I say to them that the Lord your God has sent me unto you' and they ask me, 'What is his name?' what shall I say?" And the Lord answered, "I AM who I AM." In other words, every form of the verb "to be." I am that I am. I will be what I will be. "Say unto them, I AM has sent me unto you. And so when you come to the people of Israel and you say to them, 'The God of your fathers, the God of Abraham, the God of Isaac, and the God of Jacob has sent me unto you, and this is my name forever . . . I AM.'" No other name, my name forever, and this will lead you out of the wilderness into the Promised Land. So that was the second grand revelation of the name of God. Man thought it was simply the creative act. Who can deny that nothing in this world man has ever created compares to that of a child? Nothing. And he has to trace it back to its origin of the act. All of a sudden comes out of this fantastic part of him. And then comes a revelation of another kind: that the name is I AM.

Then comes the *final* revelation, which we find in the New Testament. He brings something entirely different that man has not quite seen before, and he reveals the name now as Father. "Holy Father, keep them in thy name, which thou has given unto me, that they may be one, as you and I are one" (John 17:11). So he gave him the name that was his name, and the name was Father. The final revelation of God to man concerning who he really is: he's Father. So "In many and various ways God spoke of old to our fathers by the prophets, but in these last days he has spoken to us by a Son" (Hebrews 1:1). If he's spoken by a Son, then he's Father. And so God speaks in his final day to man through a Son, his Son, and the Son reveals to that man that he is the father of that Son. And then and only then, does man know who he really is.

But until that day comes, take the second revelation of the name of God, which is I AM, and use it and use it wisely. You can use it for anything in the world. You are told, "If you blaspheme against this name, you must be stoned to death" as told us in the 24th chapter of the Book of Leviticus. Stone him to death—if you want to hear it, the twenty-fourth of Leviticus, the sixteenth verse—anyone who blasphemes against the *name*. The name has already been revealed because Leviticus is the third book; the second book, Exodus, has revealed the name. Now if you blaspheme against this name, stone him to death. But everyone must do it. One who was born of a Hebrew woman who knew an Egyptian man, and he cursed the name of God, and they listened to see what God should say to do to such a man: to stone him to death. Well, a stone does not mean you take stones and throw at him, as people will do, but the stones are the literal facts of life. How would I blaspheme against the name of God? With God, all things are possible; there's nothing impossible to God, and his name is I AM. And I dare to say I am unwanted, I am poor, I am ill, and I am completely ignored in this world? All of this is blasphemy against *God* to whom all things are possible, for it's not seeing what I want for myself or for anyone in this world that I love. So here, I am blaspheming against God.

Now I am told in the 8th chapter of the Book of John, "Except you believe that I am he, you die in your sins" (verse 24). Sin is "missing the mark." So if I don't believe that *I am* the man that I want to be, I remain where I am at that moment of not daring to assume that I am the man that I want to be and remain in that limitation. So I die missing the mark. I die in my sins. And so the being that you really are if the second revelation is true—and I can tell you it is true—that his name is I AM. It doesn't mean you worship something on the outside when you say "I am." And the day that you actually contact it as though the I-Thou concept within yourself, and feel who you *really* are, but really feel it . . .

Now, here is a true story that I heard this past Saturday. I go occasionally when I'm invited, but I'm not a member of the Turf Club; I go only when someone takes me. So last Saturday, my wife and I were taken to the Turf Club. I was introduced to this man who sat just one little row below. Awfully nice chap—he could play the part of Lon Chaney—strange, strange, weird little fellow. And then they told me his story. He came here penniless from Kentucky, not a nickel. How he got the money necessary to buy a small plot of land I do not know; that was not told me. But he bought a small plot of land in Ventura County. He wanted to have oil, so he would sleep on the land itself. He didn't build some little shack; he slept right on the ground; and with his head to the actual ground, he would hear oil coming in. He would smell oil.

He would come home sometimes in the morning at 6:00 a.m., and his wife was distraught. "What has happened to you?" He was sleeping on the land, bringing it in. Today, the man—I would say he's ten years my senior, about sixty-eight, pushing seventy—has no financial problems. He has given away fortunes. He's worth over six million so he told me himself. But now he has another problem, and he's forgotten the name of God. His present problem is boredom. He goes to the track five days a week, Tuesday through Saturday. If he drops ten thousand, it's no problem. If he drops twenty thousand, that's no problem. He can drop what he wants. But he's bored and he's not physically well and he doesn't remember how he brought all this into being by the name of God.

When he put his head on that earth and began to listen, who was listening? If you said, "Hey, what are you doing?" "*I am* smelling oil"—that's what he would say. You would have called the name of God. "*I am* smelling oil. *I am* hearing oil"—that's what he would say. He brought it all in, brought his six million. He's given away a fortune; because it comes in so rapidly, he gives it away, still leaving himself millions. But he doesn't remember the name of God. Now he's saying, "*I am* unwell." He's blaspheming the name of God. So you are told, "The man who blasphemes the name of God, stone him to death." To stone is to show him the facts of life. And so show him the facts of life. "You aren't feeling well, are you?" "No." And you see the world with all the things with it and these are the stones and you tell him. But he has forgotten, and those around him don't know; he once used the name of God wisely and brought wealth into this world. He can bring anything into this world if he would use the name of God. "It is my name forever," said God in the 3rd chapter of the Book of Exodus, "my name forever."

But I will reveal a still greater name as man begins to awake, and the final name is Father. And so, "Show us the Father, and we'll be satisfied." "I have been so long with you, and yet you do not know me, Philip? He who has seen me has seen the Father; how then can you say, 'Show us the Father'?" (John 14:8) And so here, "I tell you I am the Father," and no one knows he is the Father. So, "Holy Father, keep them in thy name, which thou has given me, that they may be one, even as we are one." There's no way in this world that you and I will know we are one save through this last act of God's revealing himself when he gives you his last name, which is Father. He'll give it to you and you'll be Father. I am the father—that I do know—and you'll be the father of the same and only begotten Son of

God. When you see him as I have seen him and you will see him *as* I saw him and you are his father, then you and I are one. For I can't be the father of your son and not be you. That's God's final revelation to man on this level. So, "In many and various ways, God spoke of old to our fathers by the prophets; but in these last days, he's spoken to us by a Son." And the Son reveals the nature of the Father, for "No one knows the Father except the Son and anyone to whom the Son chooses to reveal him" (Matthew 11:27).

Until that day comes, use that second revelation, which is forever his name, and use it wisely. As we are told in the ninth Psalm, the tenth verse, "Those who know thy name . . . trust in thee," if they know the name. If they know that name they'll trust in thee, for that's your very being; a name is the individual himself. So God's name is I AM, and that *is* God. If you know the name, well, trust in him. So tonight, if you know the name, believe it; *trust* in his name. You listen as though you heard what you would hear were you now the man or woman that you want to be, and trust in his name. His name is I AM. Well, who is hearing what you are hearing? Well, you are; and if I asked, you would say, "I am hearing it." Well, that's God. What is God in you hearing? "I am" and you name it. Whatever you name, that's it. Now trust in his name, for "Those who *know* thy name trust in thee," for you will never forsake them.

So here, the name changes as man begins to awaken as God. And for the final revelation, I know of no greater chapter than John 17, where he reveals himself and gives himself to man: "Holy Father, glorify thou me with thy own self" (verse 5). He doesn't want any other glory. It's God himself giving himself to man, for that's his purpose. When he succeeds in his purpose, the man to whom he's given himself *is* God. And God is father—that's the final revelation; therefore, there must be a child. Where is the child if I am a father? Here comes the child in view, and he's David. God's only begotten son is David: "Thou art my Son, this day I have begotten thee" (Psalm 2:7). That is concealed in man until that last moment when the veil is lifted and the fatherhood is revealed to man through the nature of the Son. And there you see David, and David tells you who you are. You are his father, and he calls you Father. Calling me Father, the eighty-ninth Psalm is then fulfilled: "I have found David. He has cried unto me, 'Thou art my Father, my God and the Rock of my salvation'" (Psalm 89:26).

So David calls you Father. And there is no doubt, no uncertainty, in your mind when you see him; there he is. Yet there is no change in your sense of I-ness. The self that becomes his father is the same self that was self before, only now a far greater self. It includes fatherhood, but the same sense of I-ness. You haven't changed your distinctive individuality—the same sense of I. But now it is enlarged to include fatherhood, and that Father is God.

You tell it to the world in the hope that you can make it as clear as it is to you—in the *hope* that you can. So you know, whether they reject it or accept it, it is true; and the day must come in time when each individual will have the same experience. He'll pass through it all.

Until that happens, use his name wisely, as revealed to us through his prophet Moses in the 3rd chapter of Exodus. Use it for wealth, for health, and for recognition. But don't blaspheme against the name of God: "Unless you believe that I am he, you die in your sins." So we are told, they took up stones to throw at him because he had offended. To them he had blasphemed the name of God, for he claimed, I am God. And so that was blasphemy on their level, and they took up stones to throw at him. What stones? They told him that they knew his father, they knew his earthly mother, they knew his brothers and his sisters, and they named them; and so if I know your brothers and your sisters and I know your father and mother, Joseph and Mary, and they named the four brothers and they implied multiple sisters and then they began to show him the facts of life and the facts contradicted his claim, therefore they were stoning him with the facts of life. These were the stones. He simply disappeared out of their midst. You could not argue with that mind because they knew exactly your physical background.

He is telling them, "If you will receive what I tell you, I will give you power to become children of God; who were born not of blood nor of the will of the flesh nor of the will of man, but of God" (John 1:13). This verse is something entirely different. In Greek physiology, to be born of blood, they meant that the seed of the man mingled with that blood of the woman; and from this union came a child. But it wasn't born in that way. To be born of the will of the flesh is by sexual impulse. It wasn't born *that* way. To be born of man is to have human parentage. It wasn't born *that* way; it was born of God. Something entirely different, where a man suddenly awakes within himself and he steps out of his own skull to find that all along, he has been sleeping.

And then we read these words in the Book of Revelation, "And he thought himself alive and he was dead" (Revelation 1:18). Here a man was dead, and all along he believed that he was alive. You read it. In the whole vast world, the sleep is so profound and so deep that he doesn't know that he is sleeping, and the sleep is so deep that he is likened spiritually to a dead man. Then one day, in God's own wonderful time, he awakens himself in man and he brings him forth. Then he awakes for the first time to realize all through the ages that he *had* been dead, but he didn't know it. But now he's resurrected by the mercy of God. So he thought he was asleep while he thought he was awake, and yet he was dead. You read it; I think it's the third chapter, the first verse of Revelation: those who were dead and yet thought themselves alive.

But in the meanwhile, you think yourself alive; well, try this principle by the use of God's name. He will not fail you. I promise you he will not. But one thing to bear in mind is this: you may have wealth tonight and have it heavily insured—furniture, jewelry, and furs—but you left it when you came here tonight. Wherever you have this wealth, this outside wealth—you may have stocks and bonds and they may be insured, but you left them wherever they are, maybe in a vault or your home. You know, standing here just about two years ago when I left this platform and looked over here, I saw this enormous flame and all these beautiful homes burning. They were all left behind where other people were, all consumed in a matter of moments. But there is one thing you can't leave behind and you always take with you; after you find the name, you can't leave it behind you. Can you go any place where you leave behind you I AM? Where can you go in this world where you leave behind you the only power in the world, which is I AM? For "those who know thy name put their trust in *thee.*" Not in the bank, not in their social position, their financial position, their intellectual position, or any other position: put your trust in thee.

Now, who are you? I AM. So anyone who came in here tonight brought that name with them; when you leave here tonight, you're going to take it with you. And you can't go any place in this world where you can leave it behind you. But maybe you don't know that you are carrying it with you. You can have a treasure and not know you have it. If I had a billion dollars deposited in the bank but I didn't know it, I could die of starvation for want of a dollar. Yet I could sign a check if I *knew* I had it and withdraw for my earthly needs. For here, you can't leave behind you God's name. He's put himself *in* you, your very being; your own I-am-ness—that's God. And because it is God, don't blaspheme against the name; use it wisely, and use it lovingly. I say to you, "What are you hearing?" and then you tell me, "I am"—before you even answer. "I am hearing so and so," or "I am thinking so and so." Well, see to it that what you are hearing, what you are feeling, and what you are thinking is in harmony with your highest ideal. For you can draw it out, just like this man drew out his oil from this little bit of dirt, and today he's worth millions but bored. But if you know the name and don't forget the name, you won't be bored. You'll be able to use it wisely through your entire earthly days.

And then in this embodiment, the final one will be revealed to you. But only God knows when he reveals the final one. I can talk about it and tell you about it, but I cannot lift the curtain for you. Only the Son himself can reveal you as the Father. I can *tell* you that you're going to be the Father, that

I do know, but I have no power to tear that curtain and show you David. He and he alone will reveal you as the Father. And so, "No one knows who the Son is save the Father; and no one knows who the Father is save the Son, and anyone to whom the Son chooses to reveal him." But I will tell you, he will be David. One day he's going to tear that curtain from the vine and stand before you and call you Father. You know exactly who he is. And there'll be no doubt in your mind, but none whatsoever: you're looking at your own begotten Son. Begotten, not by any woman in this world, but begotten out of your own wonderful being, your mind, and it's David, the eternal David. He will be just as he's described in the Book of Samuel, just as he's described, no doubt about it.

I can't tell the thrill that is in store for you after it happens. You are so excited that you can't think of anything, but you may bore your friends; you may bore anyone that you meet because you can't think of anything *but* this enormous event that has happened to you. You can't really think that it's taken place. You may be a single man, a man who has never known a woman in this world, but it makes no difference; all of a sudden you are a father. And you are father in the true sense of the word. Then you will know he was born not of blood nor of the will of the flesh nor of the will of man but of God. He calls you, Father, and you know God is his father. He tells you exactly who you are. Then you've got to walk the earth for the remaining years shut out because you are still wearing the garment of flesh. And although you are now heir to a presence and to a promise that's already been fulfilled, you still cannot share it with others. So that it cannot become to you actual or fully realized in you until you take off the garment for the last time. Then you are one with the heavenly host.

But *everyone* is destined. You can't brag about it; you can't crow about it because you didn't earn it. No one can brag about it for the simple reason that you didn't earn it. It was all God's plan from the beginning. He who began a good work in you (at that moment) brought it to completion at the day of Jesus Christ . . . And Jesus Christ is God the Father. Therefore, if Jesus Christ is God the Father and David calls him Lord and then David calls you Lord, who are you? Are you not then Jesus Christ? Then you realize the words, "Do you not realize that Jesus Christ is in you?—unless, of course, you fail to meet the test!" (2 Corinthians 13:5) I hope you realize that we have not failed in our test.

And so eventually you read the words, "And the whole thing disappears and there was Jesus only." Moses was present. Elijah was present. They all saw the *glory* of God. And when it all subsided, there was Jesus only (Matthew 17:2-8). "For at the name of Jesus Christ every knee will bend and every tongue will confess that he is Lord, to the glory of God the Father"

(Philippians 2:11). There is only Jesus, and he has one Son; he's sharing his Son with you, not walking the street with you as a friend but as your Son. So he gives himself to every being in the world. And there's no way in the world that he can actually prove that he gave that gift of himself save that he gave his only begotten Son to you *as your* Son.

So the Bible in miniature is in the 16th verse of the 3rd chapter of John: "And God so loved the world he gave his only begotten Son." It's in miniature in that one verse. And people think he gave his only begotten Son and his name is called Jesus Christ. No. Jesus Christ, by his own confession, is God the Father. "You see me, Philip, and yet you do not know me? He who has seen me has seen the Father; how then can you say, 'Show me the Father'?" (John 14:9) And so the Son given could not be that being who calls himself Father. And the Father is Jesus Christ. Who calls him Father? David. Then he asks the question nobody asked him when he said, I am a father, then where is the child? So he brings up the question, "What do you think of Christ?" and they said, "Well, the son of David." He said, "Why then did David, in the spirit, call him Lord? If David calls him Lord, how can he be David's son?" And no one asked any further questions (Matthew 22:41-45).

David in the spirit calls him Adonay, a word used by every child when it refers to his father. Every child spoke of his father as Adonay, translated in the English "my lord." And so David called him "my Father." So he tells you who he is and who David is relative to himself. So David's going to call every being in this world "my Father." And because God is one and his name is one and that name—every knee must bow at that name—not only you are destined to know yourself to be Christ Jesus or God the Father but everyone.

But until it is revealed to you, use his name as revealed through his prophet, Moses. When you go to them, just tell them, "I AM sent me unto you." Lead them out of that wilderness into light by my name. Well, you can lead yourself today no matter where you are. Whether you are now bewildered because you are unwanted as you think you are, or unemployed as you may be, lead yourself from these states of violence into states of fruition, a fruitful state, by the name. And the name is I AM. Just simply assume "I am," and name it and hear it, smell it, and see it to the best of your ability. To the degree that you remain loyal to this what you are imagining and hearing, you will actually externalize it within your world. Now don't judge it before you try it. Try it.

Now if what I've said this night offends, I'm not ___(??) to offend anybody should it be in conflict with what you believed when you came here. Yet I will go back to scripture, he offended them, and then they sold him for thirty pieces of silver. Then we go back to the Book of Leviticus; and here we are told, "If an ox gores a slave, male or female, then the owner of the ox must pay to the owner of the slave thirty pieces of silver, and then the ox must be stoned" (Exodus 21:32). The symbol of Christ is that of an ox. And so if the Christian gospel offends, well then, he is goring you by whatever he has to say. And now, having gored him, the slave will resent it; then he must be sold for thirty pieces of silver.

And so you always fulfill scripture. The Word will always be fulfilled. The prototype of Jesus Christ was Joseph, and he was sold for twenty pieces of silver. Twenty means "disappointed expectancy." Thirty is "divine perfection." You reduce it to a three, and three is also associated with resurrection, for on the third day, the earth rose up out of the deep. And so here, if I should offend you by what I say, then mentally sell me for my thirty pieces of silver. That's what you're called upon to do. For if the ox gores and in any way hurts the slave, male or female, then the owner must pay to the owner of the slave thirty pieces of silver and then the ox must be stoned with the *facts* of life.

People will always throw the bricks at and remind you of when they knew you, or even as they know you, for we are all limited as we wear these garments. No man in this world can tell me while he wears the garment that he isn't limited. Tonight, President Kennedy is frightfully limited in his office as president. Bricks are coming all over the place—what he promised in his campaign to get the office and what he's delivered. And because of this conflict between what he promised and what he's delivered so far, well, they'll throw all the bricks in the world at him. He's fully aware of it. You can throw it at the pope, throw it at the queen of England, and throw it at any person in this world—the facts against any ambition of theirs. If I took you into my secret and told you my ambition and you as a friend know I did not realize it, you could throw me all the rocks in the world and remind me of what I told you as against what I have accomplished. That is true of every being in the world.

But nevertheless, whether you've accomplished them or not, go back and apply this principle toward the fulfillment of your dreams. I can tell you in my own case, for it has been, it has all been when I was faithful to the use of God's name. When I dared to assume that I am what at the moment reason denies and my senses deny and I remained faithful to it, then I invariably realized that; the unnumbered times when I had not been faithful to it, I coasted. We all coast after a while, and then we're jacked up suddenly. We have to go back to the use of the name. And so "Those who *know* thy name put their trust in thee"—not in anything outside of thee. And your name is I AM, and it's your name forever and forever. So put your trust in the name of God by walking out of here tonight in the belief that you are already the man or woman that you would like to be. See the world as you would see it, as though it were true, just as though it were true. And to the degree that you remain loyal to that assumption, to that degree you will externalize it and reap it as a fruit within this world.

Now let us go into the Silence.

*   *   *

Q: Is Paul a man just as we are?

A: Did you hear the question, "Is Paul a man as we are?" If there's any man in the entire Bible that is a man as I am, it's Paul. If there's any man in the entire Bible who walked this earth as you walk it and as I walk it, it is Paul. It's the story. The others are states of consciousness. Here is one person in whom it began to awaken. He was grounded in orthodoxy; as he said in his own confession, "I am of the tribe of Benjamin, a child of Abraham, grounded in the law." And then he didn't understand it, the fulfillment of that law, until it happened in him. Then he denied he ever heard it from a man, for no man could have taught it to him. So "the gospel that I preach, said he, is not the gospel of a man, for I was not taught it, nor did I hear it, but it came through a revelation of Jesus Christ. And when it pleased God to reveal his Son in me, then I conferred not with flesh and blood" (Galatians 1:11, 16). And here is a perfect revelation of how this thing takes place.

I can tell you I hadn't the slightest concept. I was raised in an orthodox Christian environment, a strict Christian environment, and I had no idea that this thing actually was alive in man. He wove it into us. Then it happened just as you're told in the scripture, only it happened in the depth of the soul and you go through all the experiences. I had no idea. When I started to teach this, I was teaching only the law of God. I started in 1938, on the second day of February, and I only spoke of God's law because I've proven it and it works, which is I AM. So I went across the country, telling anyone who would listen to me that you can assume that you are what you want to be and you'll become it. And they did. It worked. But I had no idea of the profundity of this teaching until it began to happen in me that all of a sudden the birth from above took place and everything as described in the gospels, even to the story of the dove. *That* I never conceived to be an actual fact until it happened in the depths of myself. So I say it happened to Paul. He is the one character that I would swear actually walked the face of the earth. (Tape ends.)

THE PURE IN HEART

March 1, 1963

Tonight's subject is "The Pure in Heart." I think you are all familiar with it, the sixth beatitude: "Blessed are the pure in heart, for they shall see God" (Matthew 5:8). I dare say that it would be unwise to pick and choose among the beatitudes, and yet I hear that most people look upon this beatitude as the brightest particular star in the heavens. It really seems the most inaccessible, not only the promise but the condition that must be met in order for the promise to be fulfilled: for we must be pure in heart to see God. And what wouldn't man give to see God? And yet all he needs to do in this world is to fulfill the condition: to be pure in heart.

And so what do we mean by pure in heart, just what is it? First of all, may I tell you that you need not think of moral perfection; and certainly, it does not refer in any way to sexual purity. For we are told by the same one who uttered the beatitude that the harlot given to love will go into heaven before the Pharisee. The Pharisee was *perfect* in keeping these outward laws—the washing of the outside of the cup and the washing of the hands and feet. He abided by the law, outwardly, and yet he was told that the harlot given to love would go into heaven before he would. So it isn't that. So what is this purity spoken of: "Blessed are the pure in heart, for they shall see God"?

You see, the Bible is a mystery; and although on the surface it seems so simple, anyone should be able to understand that simple statement, but anyone: "Blessed are the pure in heart, for they shall see God." But the Bible isn't that simple. So what is this purity, and what is the heart? For the word pure is Tahor, which means clear, which means "unalloyed, pure, pure gold." It was used as a tract of land completely cleared of trees, without structures, none whatsoever; but here, it is pure gold. But to understand it, we've got to go all over the Bible to get it. And here in the seventy-third Psalm, the very first verse, "Truly God is good to Israel, to those who are pure in heart." So right away he set up Israel as the pure in heart. And then in John 1, he sees Nathanael—Nathanael means "the gift of God"—and Nathanael looks at him. At the moment, he is not quite sure that anything good could come out of Galilee. And Jesus looking at him said, "An Israelite indeed, in whom there is no guile" (John 1:47). So that's an Israelite, one in whom there is no guile, no deceit, and incapable of duplicity—that's the true Israelite, and that's the heart.

Now, in the 24th Psalm, the 3rd and 4th verses, the question is asked, "And who will ascend the hill of the Lord? And who shall stand in his holy place?" Then comes the response, "He who is of clean hands and the pure heart, who does not lift up his soul to what is false, and does not swear deceitfully." So "Who can ascend the hill of the Lord? Who could stand in his holy place? He who has clean hands and the pure heart." Then you are told in the next line exactly what he means by it: he doesn't lift up his soul to what is false and does not swear deceitfully. So we bring the whole thing down just to one simple, simple voice: a man that is incapable of deceit for personal gain. If I tell you a story for amusement where you and I can laugh together, that's not deceit. But if I do it for personal gain, say, in politics—whether politics being government or in religion or in business—anytime that I plot and plan a little scheme to get the better of another for my own personal gain, then I am not pure in heart.

So he's looking for one who is pure in heart because no one but such a one can see God. No one can be brought into the presence of the Ancient of Days and be presented to him but the pure in heart. He may have no intellectual, social, or financial background, but nothing in the world of ___(??), but he is incapable of deceiving another for his own personal gain. That one has the heart of the Israelite. At the very moment that it's observed by God, who sees all and knows all, he brings him right into his presence and you see God. When you see God, you see that only reality and you become what you see. At that very moment, like a seal upon wax, the impress is made and you bear the image of God. Not on this physical garment, but you bear it on your eternal garment, which was waiting for that moment in time when the heart was pure gold. It's the unalloyed gold.

When you start with this homogenous substance called the body—for this is simply containing all, all minerals, all things—and then we are put through furnaces, furnaces of affliction as the Bible speaks of them. I'd rather speak of them as furnaces of experience. But every test in the world is given to the individual by himself (but he doesn't know it) to do what is called, not the right thing but the loving thing, where you could never deceive. And when you've been put through all these tests and you'd still, in front of your own being and your own poverty, rather die than take advantage of another and that heart becomes pure gold, only *it* can receive the imprint of the King of kings.

Now he finds such a person. Now this is the mystery. He's been looking and looking, and he finds him, and his name, he calls him David. After putting himself through all the furnaces, he extracts the pure gold that can take his imprint, and that he calls David. "I have found in David"—the 13th chapter, the 22nd through the 24th verses of the Book of Acts—"I have found in David the son of Jesse a man after my heart." Here, for the *first* time, I brought forth exactly what I wanted: "I found in David, the son of Jesse, a man after my heart. Of whose posterity God has brought forth a Savior, Jesus, as he promised."

Now the word *Jesse* actually means I AM. He is the father of David. So who is begetting *that* heart? "I am." You put yourself unknowingly from your present level into every situation in the world to test that goal. So here you are embedded in this homogenous substance containing all things, but you've got to extract only pure gold. And that pure gold is David. So I have found in David—I brought him forward—the son of Jesse, the son of I AM. So I bring it out, and out of *it* now I make myself a pledge. This is the pledge that's told us in the 7th chapter of the Book of 2nd Samuel, and I will now bring forth from your body your son. The words are "And when you lie down with your fathers, I will raise up after you your son, who shall come forth from your body. *I* will be his father, and he shall be my son" (verse 12).

And now the process begins. He's found him; and from him, he's going to bring forth now his own likeness. He's found David, his only begotten son—that's pure gold. Now God *now* begins the process of making what he has brought forth into his own image. Now, "Let us make man in our image, after our likeness" (Genesis 1:26). You can't make man until first you produce this pure metal, this pure gold. And so God became embedded in what is called a garment of flesh; and in it he moves through all the furnaces of experience until he can produce out of it the pure gold. Then from it he now brings forth himself. He's going to make himself; and making himself, he's making us, individuals.

Now it doesn't make sense, but you listen to it carefully. In the 44th chapter of Isaiah, the very last verse, what is said of Cyrus is said of David, and the name only appears twice in the book, just a couple of times in the book, in the forty-fourth and beginning the forty-fifth of Isaiah. Cyrus is called "my shepherd." That's what David was called: I have found my shepherd and he will do all of my will. David will do all of my will, so you can see the two are as one. Now in a wonderful manuscript, which is used in the *Apocrypha*, also in the traditional books of our Bible; and Cyrus is made to say—it's supposed to have this manuscript, this parchment—"I am Cyrus the king, the great king, the mighty king. I am the son of Cambyses the great king. I am the grandson of Cyrus the great king, exalted according to the beneficence of their hearts." Now here we find Cyrus, Cambyses, and Cyrus. I make the claim that man awake matures completely when man becomes the father of his own father. He's Cyrus; his father is Cambyses, and his grandfather is Cyrus. So Cyrus awakes, and he says, "I am Cyrus the king, the great king, the mighty king. I am the son of Cambyses the great king, the grandson of Cyrus the great king, exalted according to this love of their hearts."

Now here we come back. David seems to be something that I begot. I promised myself I'm going to extract something that is gold, my very being. "I will raise up after you, raise up out of your very body, your son, who will come forth from your body." Well, that's gold. "I will be his father, and he will be my son." Now we are told that he buried this in the mind of man. The word *mind* and the word *heart* are the same in Hebrew.

When we are told in the 3rd chapter, the 11th verse of Ecclesiastes that "God has put the world into the heart of man, yet so that he cannot find out what God has done from the beginning to the end," that word translated heart and the word translated world are now changed in the modern version of the Bible, and the word *heart* now becomes mind and the word world becomes eternity. So, "And God has put now eternity into the mind of man, so that he cannot find out what God has done from the beginning to the end." That same word translated world is now translated eternity, and the word translated heart, in the King James Version, is now translated mind. It's the identical thing.

What did he put into the mind and the heart? The whole personality of a man is that gold. He had to first make him. When man becomes incapable of duplicity but incapable of deceit, he has the gold, and the gold is in that man. And now that's placed in man by whom? By the one who brought it into being. Who is that being? Jesse. Jesse is producing David and David is pure gold, and "I have found in David, the son of Jesse, a man after my heart." Now out of him I am going to actually extract my own being. I can't extract it from anything but pure gold. And now he begins to make man in his image after his own likeness. And it takes *that* gold to take the imprint of God Almighty, of Jehovah himself. So everyone in the world will do it because Jesse is buried in you as your own wonderful I-am-ness.

If you should drop dead this very second, it doesn't make any difference; the play goes on. And he'll put you into situation after situation after situation until finally you become incapable of deceit. What you do sexually is not his concern, unless it is to deceive for personal gain. To marry someone with all the outer appearance of love, when basically you really want to get rid of them within twenty-four hours for what they have, that's marrying for personal gain. That's deceit. But if you married a thousand people, if you lived without marrying to a thousand people, that's not a thing to do with it. No matter how you are given to such love, you are told that you will get into heaven before the Pharisee, in the 9th chapter of the Book of Luke.

But the question is asked to lead up to it. So I ask you a question, said he, "A man said to his first son, 'Go into the vineyard and work.' And he said, 'I will not,' but afterward repented and went into the vineyards. He said to a second son, 'Go into the vineyard and work.' And he said, 'I'll do it,' but he did not. I ask you, who obeyed the will of his father?" They said, "The first one." He said, "I tell you, the tax collectors and the harlots will get into the kingdom of heaven before you" (Matthew 21:28). For you are just then like the second son; he says, "I'll do it," but you don't do it. The first son repented. He said, "I won't do it," but he repented and changed his mind and he did it.

And so everyone in the world is brought into these unnumbered situations where they are faced with it, and though you starve, you still can't take advantage of another. You'd rather be dispossessed; go through all the things of the world that would seemingly dishonor everyone. You'd rather do it than take advantage of another for personal gain. Can't do it. When man comes to *that* point, he's the pure in heart. And it hasn't a thing to do with the moral code of the world. So don't think of this in any way as *moral* perfection that is attained by an individual; and don't think of it, as the world would naturally think of it, as sexual purity. Nothing has to do with sexual purity, as the world sees it; it is all to do with duplicity. Can you really be double-minded and say one thing as a promise when you intend another, which is to get personal gain at the expense of the other, whether it be a party, an individual, a family, or a government? And so, "Blessed are the pure in heart, for they shall see God." And that pure in heart is that when the gold is actually there, having been put through all the furnaces of experience, and finally, when I arrive at the point, "Just let me die. I haven't eaten this day; I haven't eaten this week, but let me die. But I can't take advantage of another for personal gain." At that moment, may I tell you, and I'm speaking from experience, that you are taken into the presence of the Most High.

For my experience, I go back to the days of the deep Depression. I mean that when I didn't know where to find a nickel. There's a lady in the audience tonight who, along with my wife, came to my very first meeting, and she knows the truth of which I speak. I would walk from my little place in the village in the hope of finding a friend, fifty blocks away—I couldn't ride the subway; that was a nickel. In the hope I could find some friend who would give me—I couldn't borrow it with collateral—in the hope that eventually someone would give me a quarter and I would make something and pay it back. For I had four mouths to feed—my dancing partner and her parents. If I could I find a quarter, I would buy vegetables and a little olive oil and walk back the fifty blocks. Many a day I couldn't find a friend who had a quarter. But I would pass the places, and I couldn't take one piece of lettuce. I could not take anything from these trays all exposed, I couldn't. I'd go back hungry, just tell them of my experiences. I couldn't lift a thing from anyone who I hadn't paid. It wasn't mine.

So I know exactly how this thing works. While I was in that state where I was incapable of stealing, but incapable of stealing, and I could not deceive for personal gain, one night, taken in Spirit right into the presence of the Ancient of Days, he asked me the eternal question, "What is the greatest thing in the world?" I was by him prompted what to say what I ought to say, and I simply repeated the 12th chapter, 12th verse of the Book of Luke. So when you're brought into his presence, don't be anxious how or what you are to answer or what you are to say, for the Holy Spirit will teach you in that very hour what you ought to say. So in that moment, what I ought to say I said it, that the greatest thing in the world is love.

Well, you couldn't steal from one you love. You couldn't steal from anything in this world if you loved them—you couldn't. If you asked them for it and they had reasons, without explaining the reasons for not giving it, you couldn't condemn them for their reasons they didn't give it. You couldn't condemn them for their actions and their reactions. So you accepted it; that was all right, perfectly all right. So when you are brought into that state, it's because the heart is guileless. And so he finds some Israelite. "Behold, an Israelite indeed in whom there is no guile." No guile whatsoever; he is guileless. And then he can see the face of God, for he looked into the face of God. But you're told in the same book, the fourteenth chapter, "When you see me, you see the Father." So he saw the Father because he was without guile. And his face was unveiled.

Now we are told in Paul's letter to the Corinthians, the 2nd Corinthians, the 3rd chapter, "So take heart. Not one will despair. And we all, with unveiled face, beholding the Lord, will be changed," but rather, it is said in the present active sense: "we are *being* changed from one glory to another glory" by the Spirit (verse 18). We are actually being changed by beholding the face from one glory to another glory. He uses the word advisedly, "We *all*, unveiled, beholding the Lord, are being changed into his very image from one glory to another glory."

So I tell you, don't despair. If today you think, well, it's *easier* to get away with it than to face society and you get away with it, perfectly all right, do it. Tomorrow you'll be faced with a similar situation, whether it be in this little world of ours or another world—there are worlds within worlds within worlds—but you will not come out of the furnaces until it's pure gold. No one in the world gets away with anything, but no one. And so when we are told in that sixth beatitude, "Blessed are the poor . . . blessed are the pure in heart, for they shall see God," believe it. Nothing but the unalloyed gold can come out.

Now, I just love *all* the beatitudes, but I must confess that this excites me. There are eight if you read it in one way; you could make them nine in another way; and at maximum, you could get ten of them if you read it in another way. Some are inclined to read them as ten because it gives the feeling of a new Torah, a new Ten Commandments. But that's stretching it a bit; but we can—you can read it in ten. But there are definitely eight. You can't miss the eight, and you can push them into nine, or even ten. But it *is* a new code, a new law, where causation becomes mental and not physical. As you're told, "You've heard it said"—as the eight are given and then we go into an explanation of the eight—"you shall not kill" but I say unto you, to even entertain it in your heart is to have committed the act. "You've heard it said you should not commit adultery, but I say to look upon a woman lustfully is to have already committed the act in your heart with her" (Matthew 5:27). Therefore, the whole thing is raised from the physical level, the Pharisee, where he doesn't do it physically, but he does it mentally. And it's now raised to the level of the mind where if you do it mentally you've done it.

To plot and plan to take advantage of another but to restrain the impulse because you contemplated the act along with its consequences to yourself and to your friends and your family and because you couldn't stand the, well, embarrassment if you were caught, and then you restrained the impulse to do it, but that wasn't good enough. Shouldn't even entertain the thought! And so to entertain the *thought* is to perform the act with the new code. And so you can't even entertain the thought. And when you can't ___(??), do not restrain the impulse. So if I contemplate an act and it seems pleasant, I might be inclined to do it if I could get away with it; but if I contemplate it along with its consequences to myself and to others, well then, I may restrain the impulse. But I'm told that's not good enough. You don't even contemplate the act if the act is to take advantage of another for personal gain.

And may I tell you, maybe you've all had the experience and you'd rather die than steal. Maybe you've had that experience. If you haven't had it, may I tell you that you're not going to avoid it. So don't think that man is judged today because of his fabulous wealth. Sometimes I think that God starts us on the play at the top of the ladder. If all the honors are given to the world and they receive all the mortal honors—things that vanish—and how they love them, and then the play unfolds because they aren't strong enough as yet to withstand the temptation if they're up against the pressures of things when they have more than their own mouth to feed. If you have your own mouth to feed and that's the only mouth to feed, oh well, so what? You won't die. You can just go to bed hungry—sleep it off. But when there are others that you love and they depend upon you to find that quarter and you won't steal it, and so you come back without the quarter. And you all have to amuse yourselves with fun—just turn on the radio or something—and you haven't even paid the rent. And just simply play the game until that moment in time when pure gold comes out and he found David. Having found David, of pure gold, he leaves David in you and then out of you he brings himself.

Well, who is the very being he's bringing out? He's bringing out Jesse. Well, who is Jesse? Jesse is the father of David. So he's pulling Jesse out of his own being, and Jesse is I AM. So he leaves David. So who is the one that he placed in the mind in the beginning? In the beginning was when the gold became pure unalloyed gold; that was the beginning. So he leaves it in the mind of man. And then he pulls out now his *own* image and the image is Jesse, for his name is I AM and Jesse's name is I AM. But Jesse is the father of David, so he's pulling himself out of himself, and he sets up in himself a son called David, pure gold, a man after my own heart. You get it?

This is a mystery. It's not the easiest thing in the world to reveal, but may I tell you that it's the most glorious thing when you contemplate it. Here, God himself, his name is I AM, decides to make his own being and bring forth himself, the image of himself. He sinks himself in this we call the tent—in the Bible it's called the tent—flesh and blood, with all of the passions; this complete state that contained everything, all the memory, all the fires of the world. But he can't use them. He has to extract from *it* pure gold, and that pure gold is David. He can't start his work until he brings David out. And finally, he brings David out and only David is pure gold. "I have found in David the son of Jesse a man after my heart, who will do all my will." And I will bring forth from him a Savior, Jesus, as I promised. And so he starts the work of bringing him forward; and bringing him forward, he brings forward himself, the father of David.

So he first creates David, as told you in the 2nd chapter, the 7th verse of the Psalms, "Thou art my Son, today I have begotten thee." And now out of this I'm going to bring that which is my *real* being, and he brings his own being out who is the father of the son, and the father is Jesse. Well, Jesse is the father of David, and Jesse is I AM. And so, all of a sudden, this begins to unfold within you. But it will not start until you reach that point where the pure gold is produced within you through all the experiences, all the fires of experience, where you are guileless.

So let no one tell you that your excessive energy expressed in anything in this world is *wrong*. It isn't wrong, unless it was expressed falsely. Let me quote you the words "Who will ascend the hill of the Lord? And who will stand in his holy place? He who has clean hands and a pure heart, who does not lift up his soul to what is false, and does not swear deceitfully." In any deceitful act on your part, there is still more fire that you must pass through, still more experiences, until finally, when you're faced with everything and the world is against you and it means life or death, you still will choose death. You cannot violate your code of the guilelessness—you can't. So when you could not raise a finger to take anything, then there's harmony. It's the harmony he's looking for. Now he starts to mold it into his own image, as told us in the 1st chapter of Hebrews. Then he starts, and it takes on the imprint of God himself. So don't be concerned. It's going to work because the one who does it is doing it in you. Your own wonderful I-am-ness that's doing it. That's the great Elohim, who sunk himself in you and began the process of extracting pure gold that he may work on it to mold his image upon it. And that's you.

So you believe it. And when you go home—that 24th Psalm, it's a short one and what a beauty! It begins with the words, "The earth is the Lord's and fullness thereof, the earth and those who dwell therein; he's established it upon the seas, and founded it upon the rivers." He tells you who you are. For right now, you're going to come into his presence if you are one who cannot lift up your soul to that which is false. And so he tells you who he is. The earth is the Lord's and the fullness thereof and all those who dwell therein. ___(??). And you'll find it one day, the whole vast world, all yours. You appear to it. And then if you can fit that bill where you can actually rise into the presence of the Lord, it's because you do not swear deceitfully. Regardless of the temptation, you couldn't swear deceitfully. And then you're brought in. And when you take off this little garment after that moment in time, you'll take it off for the last time. And then you will read in that wonderful chapter, the 5th chapter of 2nd Corinthians, what is waiting for you and what body of glory is waiting for you (verse 1). And so you'll fit it. It's all perfect.

But don't despair and don't be concerned. You won't fail; may I tell you that no one in the world is going to fail. So if today we seem to be on different levels, forget it. We'll all pass through similar levels, moving toward that one point in time when we are fitted to come into the presence of the

Holiest of Holies. So who will stand in his holy place? You will. And when you stand, you'll see him and you'll be just like him. You'll take the imprint of the being that you behold, and in that moment, you become one with the being you behold. And although when you put on the veil once more and return to this world, no one sees it; they see the being that they have always known, but you're veiled. You're veiled, and all are veiled. And when it's taken off, it's taken off *after* that experience for the last time.

So when he is asked the question after the statement is made, "The foxes have holes, and the birds of the air have their nests; but the Son of man has no place to lay his head" (Matthew 8:20). The Son of man is waiting for just such: it's unalloyed gold in the hearts of man. Because, literally, a nest means this moving tabernacle, this thing called the flesh. He's waiting for it to be just right. And at the moment when it's just right, when you least expect it, he's taken into the presence where he receives the imprint, just like a seal upon wax. He returns once more veiled, and no one knows because he's the being that he was prior to that. But he's not so to himself. He knows what he saw, and he knows what he became at that moment. He was like the molten gold that took it and returned to tell it.

So I tell you, don't seek the opportunity because he in you, your own I-am-ness; he's working it out for you. He'll take you through all the experiences necessary to reduce you to pure gold. And chances are the majority of you here—maybe all of you, I hope—have reached that point. But don't test yourself, don't. Life does that; all the thing is moving. And the day will come that you'll have the experience. When you can meet them, it doesn't matter if you die or not, but you cannot be double-minded about it. Knowing you couldn't be, well then, it's done; and he sees in you the David he's been looking for. He's always looking for David. So in the 89th Psalm, he said, "I have found David . . . he has cried unto me, 'Thou art my Father, my God and the Rock of my salvation'" (verse 26).

And all these things are but true; they're unbelievably true. Suddenly you actually have an experience that was written 4,000 years ago. These words were written and put on parchment thousands of years ago, and you thought they were relating some little incident of 4,000 years ago when they were not. They were telling God's eternal mystery, how in everyone it happens, and suddenly you find him. Well, where was he all along? He was in you. After he has made you David: "Thou art my son, today I have begotten thee," now he hides him in the one in whom he made him. He hides him, as told you in the 3rd chapter, the 11th verse of Ecclesiastes, he hides him right into the mind of that man. But he so does it that that man cannot find out what he did from beginning to end—until that moment in time when he finds him—and there is David. And who is he?—*your* son. If he is your son, who are you? Jesse. And who is Jesse? I AM. That's what the word means, just I AM. And that's the name of God.

Now let us go into the Silence.

*   *   *

Q: (inaudible)

A: Do we have responsibility to ___(??)? My dear, it's an excellent question. The name of the being who is doing it is I AM. If I ask you a question now, "Tell me your name," you would reply, "I am" before you gave the name, wouldn't you? Well, that's the being who's doing it. He's buried in you. And he's gone through unnumbered ages, purifying that homogenous substance, separating it so he can only bring out the unalloyed gold. And so all the mixtures cause one to act in the unnumbered ways that they do. So your answer is that in the sense that the being who is doing it you named before you gave me your earthly name that you now, at the moment, bear. Is that clear?

Q: [inaudible]

A: He'll never in eternity depart from that homogenous substance into which he sunk himself when he decided to make man in his own image. But he has to make it, first of all, out of pure gold. May I tell you that it is really pure gold—I'm not kidding—when you see it one day after the temple has been torn from top to bottom. As you're told in the Book of Hebrews, it identifies the spiritual body with the curtain of the temple: "And the curtain was torn, from top to bottom . . . and then he entered into the Holy of Holies forever" (Hebrew 9:3). No intermediary thereafter. But when it's torn, you look and you see molten gold, glowing, liquid gold, and you *know* it is yourself. You will say with Blake, "I behold the vision of my deadly sleep of 6,000 years, circling around thy skirts like a serpent of precious stones and gold." Then suddenly you'll say, "I *know* it is myself, O my Divine Creator and Redeemer." At that very moment, the being who created you, you are he; he made you into his own being and succeeded in giving you himself. So you are looking at pure gold, and then you, as that molten gold, up you go, like a serpent, to fulfill the statement in the 3rd chapter of the gospel of John: "As Moses lifted up the serpent in the wilderness, so must that Son of man be lifted up." And suddenly, as *gold*, up you go; and you are really molten gold then, and up you go (verse 14).

It's an incorruptible element. Gold could not corrode, not in eternity. Gold, the pure gold, is incorruptible. And this is only the symbol of the true spiritual gold that you are; therefore, Paul is right when he said that the body you will wear is imperishable, incorruptible, immortal, and imperishable. But you first have to get that metal out of this very *alloyed* state into the unalloyed state. And when you see it, may I tell you that you will know at that moment you've always known it.

So to come back to your question, yes, the being *in* you as your own I-am-ness is doing it. But having heard it, believe it. The question is asked, "What must I do to do the will of him who sent me?" What must I do to do the work of him that is called God? He said, "Believe in him whom he has sent." Believe it. It's true.

____(??) forget the sex angle. What you do in your life sexually, I don't know and I don't care and God doesn't. Maybe some moral ____(??) will care, but that's not God and that's not your judge. And so it is not that. It's not any moral purity; it's not any sexual purity as the world understands *that* word; it is duplicity. Don't you promise one, intending while you promise it not to keep it but to fulfill another state for personal gain. That's what I'm getting at, the sixth beatitude, the 5th chapter, the 8th verse of the Book of Matthew: "Blessed is the pure in heart" or "are the pure in heart," either one. "Blessed are the pure in heart, for they, and only they, shall see God." And that purity has not a thing to do what the world will tell you. It's all based upon guilelessness, for he is the true Israelite. "Behold an Israelite indeed in whom there is no guile." And that's called Nathanael. Nathanael means gift of God. Pure gold now. "Now who will ascend the hill of the Lord? Who will stand in his holy place? He who has clean hands and a pure heart."

And you know what clean hands and pure heart represents now. To murder is better than the other; to murder for personal gain is full of guile. Moses murdered the Egyptian who killed a Hebrew boy, and yet he saw God. So even murder in the heat of passion, when someone that you love was injured; and you in a moment of violence, may I tell you, that is not in the eyes of God comparable to deceiving your neighbor. If you murdered for personal gain, as some do, many do, and you go into that world, those who plotted and planned it; they have plotted and planned the destruction of millions for personal gain for their individual governments, *that* is deceit. But in the heat of battle, as we're told, that Moses murdered the Egyptian when he had killed the Hebrew boy, and yet Moses saw the face of God. David was chosen, and he killed Goliath.

So deceit is that one little bit of alloy left among the gold that *must* be burned away before it becomes unalloyed gold. It seems to be the most difficult thing when man is under pressure to eat, to pay rent, and to do these things that he would take advantage of another for personal gain. And that's what he calls guile in the Bible. The sixth beatitude tells you that such a person cannot see God. If you can't see God, then you can't receive the impress of God. He can't make you into his image. But when you're brought into his presence, at that very moment, it's like a seal upon wax; and you are one with him, and you take on the whole impress of God forever. It's your immortal body, your indestructible body. But you can't be brought into his presence until you are pure gold in his eyes, the one he calls David. (Tape ends.)

THE FOURFOLD GOSPEL

March 5, 1963

Tonight's subject is "The Fourfold Gospel." As you know, for I think you do, the Bible is a mystery, a mystery to be known only by revelation. As I told you in the past, a mystery is not a matter to be kept secret but a truth that is mysterious in character. The four gospels are the plot of the entire Bible. Everything that was promised Israel as we have it recorded in the thirty-nine books of the Old Testament came into flower, into fulfillment, in the four gospels. But even to this day, two thousand years later, many are still seeking in the Bible for the Christ of whom the fathers spoke and whose coming they foretold. As we are told, "The prophets who prophesied of the grace that was to be yours inquired and searched about that salvation; they inquired what person or time was indicated by the Spirit of Christ within them when predicting the sufferings of Christ and the subsequent glory" (1 Peter 1:10).

Well, they could not find him. They were all looking for a *man*, and today the whole vast Christian world still turns to a man. And those who deny it think in terms of a man that they deny. They do not know the Christian mystery. So Paul made the statement, "From now on we'll regard no one from the human point of view; even though we once regarded *Christ* from the human point of view, we regard him thus no longer" (2 Corinthians 5:16). Yes, even though I once thought of Christ from the human point of view, I think upon him so no longer; he is something entirely different.

To understand this mystery, we have to find the root, and that is in the Old Testament. What did they promise? The promise is in the eleventh chapter, the first three verses, called the Messianic book, one of the many chapters, but this one is prominent. "There shall come forth a stem from the stump of Jesse, and a branch shall grow out of that root. And the Spirit of the Lord shall be upon *him*." The imagery turns from a root, from a branch, and from a stem into a man. And the Spirit of the Lord shall be upon him, the spirit of understanding, the spirit of knowledge, the spirit of counsel, the spirit of the fear of the Lord—all these will be upon him. He shall not judge by what his eyes see or decide by what his ears hear" (Isaiah 11:1-3).

So here, something is said about a branch. Something is said about a stump out of which this branch will come. So we search the scripture, and we find in the Book of Daniel: "And the king said: 'I beheld the visions of my head as I lay in bed, and a watcher, a holy one, came down from heaven.' And he cried aloud, 'Hew the tree down, cut off its branches, strip its leaves, scatter its fruit. But leave the stump'" (Daniel 4:13). Do not disturb the stump. And now he turns from the imagery of the tree, with its branches, its leaves, and its stump, to that of a man. "Let *him* be watered with the dew of heaven"—speaking now of a stump, and it becomes now a man—"let him dwell with the beasts of the field; take from him the mind of a man and give to him the mind of a beast; and let seven times pass over him . . . until he knows the Most High rules the kingdom of men, and gives it to whom he will" (Daniel 4:15-17).

You ask, "What is it all about?" For this is a prophecy that is fulfilled in our gospels. The word *Jesse* means I AM. It's called the stump of Jesse. The word I AM is simply called Jehovah, the name of God. In its root meaning, it means "to fall" or causatively "to cause to fall." The only being that fell, this tree of life, is God himself. And for us, God fell; he sacrificed himself to redeem us, to give us life in ourselves, and the mystery of life through death, the death of God. So this Branch, now, ____(??) and we begin to study the word branch in the Bible, for branch comes out of the stump of Jesse. The stump is I AM. The first presentation is Matthew, and Matthew presents the Lord as a king. So where is the Branch identified in the Bible as a king? We find it in the 23rd chapter, the 5th verse of Jeremiah: "And the days shall come where I will raise up for David a righteous Branch, and he shall reign as king."

So here we find a presentation of this Branch, which is not a tree, for we see now it is a man. But he is presented as a king, so Matthew gives us the genealogy of a king. He comes down through the royal blood. But Matthew begins the book with "This is the book of the genealogy of Jesus Christ, son of David." David is the source of the dynasty. The first king of Israel was Saul, chosen by the people, but Jehovah rejected Saul and chose David. David is the first king of Israel as chosen by God. So this is the book of the genealogy of Jesus Christ, son of David. When I trace the genealogy of a king, I always must begin at the source of the dynasty and come down and finish with the king. When I trace the genealogy of a man, I begin with his father and go back as far as I may. But not with a king; you do not say this is king ___(??) so and so, the son of so and so. You go right back to the source of the dynasty and then you bring him forward and it culminates in the king himself. That's how you get the genealogy of a king. That's what Matthew does in presenting the Lord as king to fulfill the 23rd chapter, the 5th verse of Jeremiah.

Mark presents him as a servant; therefore, there is no need for a genealogy—the perfect servant, the ideal servant. So God is now presented as a servant. And here, where is the Branch of the servant? The 3rd chapter, the 8th verse of Zechariah: "Behold, I will bring forth my *servant* the Branch." All this is prophecy. He hasn't brought him forth; he's bringing him forth, going to do it, by "bringing forth my servant the Branch." So Mark does not have a genealogy. Who are you? Well, "I am the servant of the Lord." That's good enough. If you are the servant of the Lord, there's no need for any further credentials. So his credentials are simply his position in life: he is the ideal servant. That's Mark.

Now in the 10th chapter of Mark, he makes this statement, "I came not to be served but to serve." He is the servant in Mark. Luke presents him as the ideal man, Jehovah's man. Where is the Branch concerning him? Again in Zechariah, the 6th chapter, the 12th verse. First of all, Isaiah claims it in the fortieth chapter, "Behold, the man," but he doesn't use the word *Branch*. But Zechariah, to fulfill the prophecy, brings in the Branch: "Behold the man whose name is the Branch." So Luke presents him—the ideal man *should* have a genealogy—so Luke presents him as man. When you read the two genealogies of Matthew and Luke, they differ. At the beginning of David the king, they part and David's older son, Nathan, becomes the line through which Luke takes Jesus Christ. His younger son, Solomon, becomes the one through whom he takes the one bringing him into a king.

So here, you find a complete different genealogy for fourteen generations, then another fourteen following that. Here you have these many, many generations where there are entirely different backgrounds; and people think you can't be telling the story of the same person, but people don't know the mystery. You're presenting not a person; you're presenting not a man, but you're presenting something that is altogether different. Christ is not *a* man, *a* king, *a* servant; Christ that saves is a series of mystical experiences through which God reveals himself for the salvation of man. That's Christ.

The whole vast New Testament is based upon the assumption that a certain series of events happened in which God revealed himself in action for the salvation of man. Did they happen? Now we are told in scripture

that they happened. I claim that the evangelists were telling their own
story, as told us in the end of Luke: "And they told what had happened"
(Luke 24:35). As Moffatt takes that phrase and describes it and translates it,
"They related their own experiences." They are relating a series of mystical
happenings in the soul of the individual where God revealed himself in
these actions for the salvation of that individual. So Luke presents God as
the ideal man: "Behold, the man whose name is the Branch"—6th chapter,
12th verse of Zechariah. He must have a genealogy, and this goes all the way
back, unbroken, back to Adam, the son of God.

John, on the other hand, presents him as God himself—no need of a
genealogy, none. And this you find in the 4th chapter, the 2nd verse of Isaiah,
"And the day is coming"—and the day is always in the future, for this is all
prophecy—"when the branch of Jehovah will be beautiful and glorious." All
this is in the future, and men are still looking for this branch to flower in
some mighty conqueror who will come and save humanity from the tyrants
loose in the world. And he doesn't come that way. So they denied he was a
king because they did not read carefully: "My kingdom is *not* of this world."
They are still expecting him to, in some way, entrench himself in the world
and establish a kingdom and rebuild what they believed to be David's
kingdom. And all these must be spiritualized. All the characters mentioned
as his background, his genealogy, are *states of consciousness*, all of them.

Here, it begins: "This is the book of the genealogy of Jesus Christ, the
son of David"; the very end of the genealogy, Joseph's father is called Jacob,
that seventeenth verse (Matthew 1:1-16). A few verses on, on the 20th verse,
the angel of the Lord appears unto Joseph in a dream and says, "Joseph, son
of David, do not be afraid to take unto thyself Mary thy wife." Three verses
before, it is stated in the genealogy that his father was Jacob. And along the
way, just a few verses down, the angel of the Lord addresses him as Joseph,
son of David. Here, in the genealogy, Joseph is called "the father," and the
genealogy begins with Jesus Christ, son of David. Don't you see it? You've
got to spiritualize all of these characters. They are states of consciousness;
they are not persons any more than Jesus Christ is a person. Jesus Christ is
that series of events unfolding, like a tree, in man for the salvation of that
man in whom this series unfolds. That is Jesus Christ. And man cannot
think that way if he wants to personify it and put it on a wall, put it in some
little hole, and do something with it. And it isn't that.

So here we find the presentation of God as a king in Matthew, the
presentation of God as a servant in Mark, and the presentation of God as the
perfect ideal man in Luke and God himself in John. So in John, he speaks
and calls himself constantly I AM. "I am the vine. I am the way. I am the
truth. I am the resurrection. I am the door." All through he is emphasizing

who he *really* is—the being that *you are*. But the series of events, I promise you, will unfold within you. When they unfold within you, you know who you are. And you could no more keep it to yourself than the evangelists who experienced Christ could have kept it to themselves. They couldn't if they experienced it. Having experienced Christ, they could not keep their experience of Christ to themselves, so they tell it.

Now, let me show you what Luke tells us in his own way. Why they translated it this way, I don't know. Luke begins his book: "In as much as many have undertaken to assemble a narrative of the things which have been accomplished among us, as it was revealed to us by those who were eyewitnesses from the beginning, it seemed good to me also, having observed closely for some time past." Now that phrase "for sometime past" is a translation of the Greek word *Anothin*, which means "from above." When it is used in the third chapter of John, it is used "from above." It is said to Nicodemus, "You must be born from above. Except you be born from above, you cannot enter the kingdom of heaven" (John 3:3). Yet here, in the Book of Luke, the same word, no alteration, the identical word is translated into this phrase "for sometime past." So he's telling you, if you go back to the original tongue where he got it. "Having observed all things closely from above, it seemed good to me also to write an orderly account for you, Theophilus—one who loves God—that you may know the truth concerning these things of which you have been informed."

He's writing it down for all of us who claim we love God, for we are Theophilus, a lover of God, one who seeks God. He's telling you where he got it. He is not making any claim that his arrangement is a greater chronological arrangement of the source material. What he's telling us is God is from above, and he's going to write it in an orderly arrangement, which he claims this arrangement is better, better understood by man; for he begins with a birth and he ends, for man's sake, with a crucifixion. That's not the way in which Luke got it. For Luke is not his name—all this is anonymous—but whoever calls himself Luke did not receive it in that order. But he thinks it's a better arrangement to be understood by mortal minds until they, themselves, have the experience.

So what the gospels are telling us, believe this, believe it for the works' sake. Then he tells us how to prove the law of God, and in proving the law of God, you may believe his promise. Then he tells us what to do about the law of God. "Ask anything in my name"—but don't forget my name; my name is I AM—"and it will be done unto you." Ask anything in my name and it will be done unto you, but my name is I AM. But don't call it by any other name. And when you call *upon* my name, call *with* my name. Don't call upon it, for I have no other name. So don't say, "In the name of I AM";

just prepare yourself to be "I am." Now, I am what? You name it. Whatever you want to be, just name it. But call with my name; don't call upon my name. So call, I am healthy, I am wealthy, I am known, and I am anything that you think lovely in your world. Call upon it by calling *with* the name.

Then he tells them, "I have come to testify of things that I know and that I have seen. If you will not receive the testimony that I bring you of things of earth, how may you receive the testimony of mine if I tell you of things of heaven?" Now, let me give you a vision of mine that happened many, many years ago to show you it was revealed to me long before it began to awaken in me. Just like the vision of the fourth of Daniel, only in my case it wasn't a tree. But just as he starts off the vision, "the visions of my head as I lay in bed," suddenly I saw this fabulous field, and consciousness followed vision. I entered the field. It had no limit; it was infinite. At first I thought them to be flowers, long, tall flowers, like sunflowers, huge, big flowers. As I approached them, they were not flowers. They were all rooted like a flower into the earth, but the faces, beautiful faces, human faces—everyone was a face. As I came upon them, they moved in concert as though someone led them in some orchestra. And they all moved; if one bent over, the whole vast field of them bent over; if one smiled, they all smiled. They all did everything in concert.

When I walked among them, admiring the beautiful human faces that were anchored and stationary like a flower, I realized right at that moment that I am not comparable to them in beauty, nothing in that rhythm, and yet I enjoyed greater freedom, limited as I was, than all of them put together. They moved in concert, and I had freedom of movement even though my motion was not in harmony. I had freedom of choice even if I made the wrong choice. I could choose evil, and they could do nothing. They could do nothing but move as some invisible power moved them. They could do nothing of themselves. And I realized that with all of my limitations, I was greater. I could make mistakes, and they couldn't make a mistake. I could actually move without the consent of another, and they couldn't do it. And beautiful as they were, I realized how much infinitely greater I was, limited as I was, because I was detached from that field.

And I thought, in the depths of me, that at one time, I must have been one of that orchestra. And God in his infinite mercy fell with me and then took up residence in me. Then seven times had to pass over me, the fiery ordeal. I had to be given . . . this is a human face . . . "take the mind of man from him and give him the mind of a beast. Let him now live with the beasts of the field, sever everything from him, cut off the branches, strip the leaves, scatter the fruit, but don't disturb the root." And the root is God himself; that's Jesse. But "seven times will pass over him until he knows that the Most High rules the kingdom of men and gives it to whom he will." He gives it in that moment that he gives us Christ, and Christ is that series of mystical experiences taking place in the individual's soul for that soul's salvation.

I can see that field of flowers now. Perfectly beautiful human faces, not a blemish, everything perfect and everything moving in this perfect rhythm as some invisible director directed them, and they all moved in concert. So you and I were once part of that harmony, and then the harmony became broken for our salvation. We descended because *God* descended with us; he doesn't push us out. The word *He Vau He* means "to fall," and that is the root of the verb that we have as Yod He Vau He, which we call Jehovah, the great sacred name, the name by which all things are made.

So here, Matthew, Mark, Luke, and John present this mystery of the branch; and I tell you, it grows in us. As Blake said, "The gods of the earth and the sea sought through nature to find this tree, but their search was all in vain; there grows [one] in the human brain." And that tree is turned down. If you saw the human being and take off the skin and see just the nervous system, it's just like an inverted tree, where the brain is the root and the whole tree grows down. But that tree is going to be turned up. One day, you'll see it turned up. There will be a complete severance of your being, called "the curtain of the temple," and then *you* that were living down, not even knowing it, that it turns right up. And all the currents of eternity are now reversed in you, and you've turned up, and from then you grow up.

And the vision I had of this many years ago startled people. I first told it in San Francisco. Why, the reaction was horrible. Yet, the Book of Mark, speaking of the servant of the Lord, who is the Branch, speaks of it. When the blind man's eye was opened, the Lord opened the eye of the blind man; he said, "What do you see?" He said, "I see men like trees walking." There it is, "I see men like trees, walking" (Mark 8:24). This night when I had this vision of the majesty of man when he is turned up, you will think, "How could I be a tree?" but I am telling you, such beauty, and such joy when you see it! Something altogether different, but how could you describe it? You can't describe it to the satisfaction of anyone because who wants to be a tree? And yet here inverted and we're called the branch; don't forget it: "And there shall come forth a stem from the *stump* of Jesse"—from the stump of I AM—"and a branch shall grow out of its root, and the Spirit of the Lord shall rest upon him, the spirit of wisdom and understanding, the spirit of counsel and might, and the spirit of knowledge and the fear of the Lord" (Isaiah 11:1). Fear, by the way, means reverence of the Lord, the awe of God, not fear as we understand it.

Again, these same four, Matthew, Mark, Luke, and John, it is revealed to us in a strange way when the child is given a name. This is now the 9th chapter of the Book of Isaiah: "To us a child is born, to us a son is given"—two entirely different experiences, a child is born, a son is given—"and the government shall be upon his shoulder, and his name shall be called 'Wonderful Counselor.'" Don't put a comma between Wonderful and Counselor as so many Bibles have. Bear in mind that there were no punctuation marks in the ancient Hebrew, none whatsoever, not even breaks as paragraphs, just all continuous. And they put a comma in between Wonderful and Counselor. It is not. There are four names given, in keeping with the fourfold gospel: "His name shall be called Wonderful Counselor, Mighty God, Everlasting Father, Prince of Peace," the four titles.

Wonderful Counselor, that's omniscience itself. You could ask nothing of a being who is completely awake that would not have the automatic answer, for there is omniscience. Mighty God, divine omnipotence. And here, Everlasting Father, Father forever. That's when the Son is given; that's when the third title comes. And then, Prince of Peace; that's at the very end, when you are about to take off the garment for the last time, as told us in the Book of John: "And my peace I leave with you; not as the world giveth give I unto you" (John 14:27). He gives a peace that is beyond understanding. You can't disturb that peace, for he's the Prince of Peace. He is an Everlasting Father; he is Father forever. When you see me, said he, you see the Father, Father forever. Almighty God, a might beyond the wildest dreams of anything you've ever seen. And when you see that might, you see it personified as a man. Look into his eyes, and you see might like you've never known might before, and it is man. And then Wonderful Counselor, so he promises to send us the Counselor. When he withdraws, he will send to those who have the understanding to follow him as he revealed what happened in him.

So when you read the gospels, whether it be Matthew, Mark, Luke, or John, do not see a man walking through the pages. See the great mystery of Christ the Branch unfolding in you. And it takes root. There must come out a root from that stump. It takes root. How does it take root? Well, you first hear the story and you believe it, then the Word is planted. As one believes it, he's accepted the Word. The Word he translates in the Book of John, called logos, that's, "In the beginning was the Word"—that's the Greek logos—"and the Word was with God, and the Word was God." That's really the translation of the Hebrew Dabar, which means "the Word of God which contains within itself the power of its own expression." That Word in the Book of John, the first verse, is Christ: "In the beginning was the Word, and the Word was with God, and the Word was God."

Now turn to the 55th chapter of the Book of Isaiah: "So shall my word be that goes forth from my mouth; it shall not return unto me empty, but it shall accomplish that which I purpose, and fulfill *that* where I sent it" (verse 11). So the word when it comes, it's the word called Christ. I tell you the story. Believe it. The minute you believe it, you've accepted it; it has fallen on fertile ground. It will then take root, and the Word contains within itself the power of its own expression. And the whole vast program of God for man's salvation is contained in that Word, the seed. It falls upon man; man hears it. He either believes it, or he rejects it. And so here, we move across the world, and seven times pass over us until one day, we hear it with acceptance; and then the little root takes place in that stump of Jesse, the stump of I AM. Then out of it comes the Branch, and then the Spirit of the Lord descends upon him. From then on, it moves and you can't stop it.

So you can't earn it. Accept it. Believe the story as it was intended when it was first written, completely misunderstood through the centuries. It told us of a certain individual who was born in a strange way and raised in a strange way and died a horrible death. But that's not the story at all. If I would comfort you with a death, the 6th chapter of the Book of Romans should comfort you. For here in this sixth chapter we are told that "if we have been united with Christ in a death like his, we shall certainly be united with him in a resurrection like his" (verse 5). He uses the past tense when it comes to death and the future when it comes to resurrection. If we *have been* united with Christ in death like his, then we *shall be* united with him in a resurrection like his. So the unity took place in his death, for he fell and all of us are in it. Now he's asking us for acceptance through the Word. We have union with him in a death like his; we shall have union with him in a resurrection like his. He resurrects us one after the other by this series of fantastically wonderful mystical experiences, one after the other. And you can't contrive them; they come like a thief in the night when you least expect them, one after the other. So everything said in the gospels concerning the central figure is all about you, everything, from the beginning to the end.

But I tell you, the death has already taken place. But even though the death *took* place, for the tree has fallen, it's been felled: "Hew down the tree, cut off the branches"—that's all over—"strip the leaves, scatter the fruit, give him the mind of a beast." Well, haven't we the mind of a beast? Go back twenty years, what beast in the world would have conceived of ovens to burn innocent people by the millions? Isn't that the mind of a beast? Have you read here recently the current stories of Stalin? The things the man did to those, even the most intimate circles, that no one felt at ease in his presence. Molotov down to all like little children, shaking, every one of them. This came up last Sunday in the Sunday *Times*, in yesterday's *Observer*, in today's

New York Times, for I get that every day, and all these stories because today is the tenth anniversary of his death. Here was the strangest—call it a beast; there is no beast that would have done the things the man did to his own people. He hated everything in the world. And so did Hitler, who hated everything. And so take the man's mind from him and give him the mind of a beast. Who gave the order? God. And this is the order from on high.

Now in the eyes of the world, they seemed to be so far advanced because they were so powerful in the exercise and misuse of power. They are on the down; they're descending. They have . . . seven times must pass over this mind of a beast before it could accept the story of Christianity. Both rejected it. Both called it foolish, that the whole thing was stupid. The opiate of humanity, said one, quoting his master Karl Marx, and the other looked upon Christianity as the weakest thing in the world. Christ to him was simply nothing but a weakness because he couldn't kill. He said, "Put up the sword . . . and turn the other cheek . . . and Father forgive them, they know not what they do."

And so here you see the beast of beasts, and it was all at God's command. "Take from him the mind of a man and give him the mind of a beast, and let his lot be among the beasts. But do not disturb the root. Leave that stump and let it be watered with the dew of heaven." And then there's a reversal; it just suddenly appears, and all of a sudden, the stump puts out a shoot. It can't put out the shoot until it first heard the Word of God. So we're told, "Go and tell the Word, and it must start in Jerusalem and spread to Judea, Samaria, to the ends of the earth. Go and tell it. And some will accept it and some will reject it. But those who reject it, all right, because seven times has not passed over.

And what are the seven times? Read the 3rd chapter of the Book of Daniel, and "heat the furnaces seven times more than they were wont to be." And then comes the three Hebrew boys, and they are put into the furnaces, clothed. And then the king said, "Were there not three?" They answered yes. "But I see four . . . and the fourth has the form of a Son of God" (verse 24). So here there were four, not three. Three were put in, the threefold man, the three-dimensional man, but goes with them the fourth, God himself. For the fourth ___(??) is God himself altogether. When they came out, not even with the smell of fire, their hair was not singed, and not even the smell of fire upon their garments. Then he, Nebuchadnezzar, worshipped the God of Israel, worshipped the God of Shadrach, Meshach, and Abednego.

Here, this whole thing is a mystery to be unfolded in the simple way it began: by telling you that Christ of the scripture is unfolding in *you* in a series of events, revealing to you your salvation. So not only before, ___(??), for Peter in his epistle said that the prophets saw how they searched and inquired about this grace that was to be yours, and how they inquired about this salvation; and asked him what persons, what time was indicated by the Spirit of Christ within him when prophesying and predicting of the sufferings of Christ and the subsequent glory (1 Peter 1:10). But they didn't find him. They couldn't find the Christ of whom they wrote and whose coming they foretold. They couldn't find him because they were looking for *a man*. And today they are still looking for a man and looking for a time. They think maybe 1963 will bring him, 1964, and all through the ages, people have thought of just a moment in time was the coming of Christ, or the coming of a person. And he doesn't come that way.

He comes in you. And when you have him, you share him with everyone who will listen. But many will say because they know you so well, "But don't I know him? Isn't he Mary's child and his father named George? Doesn't he work in a factory with me? I know him. What's he talking about?" And so they expect an entirely different kind of person to come. They don't expect this garment to have within it an experience that no mortal man possibly could ever have. And it all happens *in* the man, in the depths of the soul of the man. Then he goes back, and he sees where it was all foretold, but naught could he himself foresee. It was all there, but he couldn't really dig it out any more than the scholars can, until it happens.

After it comes to the surface in him and he's bewildered, when the dust settles so that he can really talk about it without excitement, a few will listen and a majority will turn their backs. And they'll say, that poor fellow. He used to be so normal, used to be a very normal person. Used to tell me how to get a better job, and I used to get the job. He used to talk about how to get enough money, and I got the money. I went to the track and made $84,000. I went to the track and made $54,000. Went out ___(??), and I met all kinds of things. But now he's talking of stranger things. He's talking about a Christ I never heard of before. I'd rather have my old Christ because to him I can kneel and to him I can say a prayer in the *hope* that he will have compassion on me and respond. But *this* Christ, a series of mystical experiences in the soul of man, where the whole tree unfolds? And suddenly the tree fell down and turns around, and then the whole thing goes up right back into the great stump itself, the skull of man; and from then on, it begins to really grow?

And then he knows what the glory is that Paul spoke of, for there is laid up for me in heaven a crown of glory. But he himself grows it; no one puts it upon him. It's a living crown, but not a crown as the human eye sees when they see the queen's crown. This is entirely different, a *real* crown. Do you know of any crown comparable to the antlers of a stag? Have you ever seen such majesty in your life when you see this beautiful thing? Did you ever see such majesty as a tree in full bloom? No. Don't even try to visualize it when I tell you. The writer of the Book of Mark could see it correctly: "What do you see now with the eye open?" "I see men like trees walking." Don't even try to visualize it because it frightens people.

But believe the story as I told you this night concerning Matthew, Mark, Luke, and John: the fourfold man you are. One presents you as a king to fulfill the 23rd chapter of Jeremiah. For he said, "I have come to fulfill the scripture. Scripture must be fulfilled in me. And beginning with Moses and all the prophets, he interpreted to them in all the scriptures the things concerning himself" (Luke 24:27). It's all about this being that you are. And then comes the presentation of the ideal servant: "Behold, my servant the Branch"—the 3rd chapter of Zechariah. "Behold, the man, the Branch, whose name is the Branch"—the 6th chapter of Zechariah (verse 12). Then comes the fulfillment of the 4th of Isaiah. For all must be fulfilled, and so these four branches *must* take root and all grow and mature in man. So here you have the king, the servant, the ideal man, and God himself.

Now don't neglect the use of the law, even though it will never justify you before God. You have the law. Now let us go into the Silence and use the law wisely by assuming that we are the man, or the woman, that we really want to be. Try to persuade ourselves in this short interval of a minute that we really *are* this being. And if you believe it, that's another form of the word that now cannot return unto you empty but must accomplish that wherein you sent it. By assuming that you are, you have sent it on its way, and you'll be transformed into the likeness of your assumption. Now let us go.

*   *   *

Q: (inaudible)

A: To me it's ___(??), but I do not go for that. So Adam is supposed to be the beginning of just the most primitive concept of what man could be. But it goes back to Adam and you can't break the line because God creates it. And so it has to go through the flower ___(??) by Jesus, right straight back to Adam, the most primitive concept, the dust itself. For he's of dust, and to dust he will return. So Luke gives it through the physical line. Yet Nathan, the word *Nathan*, who is to come, is "gift." But Nathan, you see is the third son; and in the Bible, it is always given to the second. It's all this reversal of order. So Esau was denied, and Jacob was given; Manasseh denied, and Ephraim was given; and all through we have this first denial and the second accepted.

So Solomon was the second. But in Solomon we have, by tradition, a king; Nathan, by tradition, was simply a good man. He was a gift. Not

Nathaniel. Nathaniel was a "gift of God." But this is simply Nathan, just "gift." And so through this gift, for this [body] is a gift. And he clothed me in the Spirit in a garment of flesh, called in the Bible skin. He made skin for me. So he made a skin for the first Spirit, called Adam. And that's the line that Luke gives it, and then there were seventy-five before it flowered in Christ Jesus.

Q: (inaudible)

A: "I am Mary and birth to Christ must give if I in blessedness for now and evermore would live." She gave birth to Christ Jesus, and Christ Jesus is a *series* of wonderful mystical experiences by which God revealed himself in action for the *salvation* of man. So then the one in whom these experiences take place must be Mary, for in him the experiences called Christ Jesus are taking place. So she is blessed and the womb is blessed because she gave birth to the savior of the world. But everyone in whom it takes place is Mary because Christ is eternal and the same being is unfolding in everyone. Everyone will be Mary when it happens.

Q: (inaudible)

A: My dear, it is called election. But I must confess I do not know the mystery of God's election. I am convinced that not one can fail, as told us in that same 11th chapter of Isaiah that I quoted tonight, "None is lost in all my holy mountain," no, not one. Therefore, not one can really be lost because *God* would be lost. He himself fell for our salvation. He actually is the tree of life commanding himself to fall, and then we are redeemed by his fall—the mystery of life through death. So we are called one by one. But I could not tell anyone . . . in fact, that question was asked and answered in the 1st chapter of the Book of Acts: "It's not for you to know the times or the place, but only the Father." So men are asking, "Well, when will it happen to me?" No one has this power to see the root or the branch. The root must take place from this stump—acceptance must be there—and then the branch will come out. And the branch will bear the fruit of these experiences.

But who can see it? And so when they tell you they can see it and they see auras and see all these things, well, let them believe it. I can look at you and see auras, but that hasn't a thing to do with it. But the ancient prophets of this world instead of looking at it, look through it, and you'll see it's man, and you'll see it a circle of light. Don't look at it, just look in it and beyond it. It's no great problem but simply a change the focus, that's all. Try it. It's very easy. __(??) on the bathroom floor and all these little tiles. Don't look at them, just look in them and beyond them, and they will all enlarge. You'll find clarity you've never known before between your vision and what you're seeing ___(??). But that doesn't mean what I'm talking about tonight. It has not a thing to do with the Spirit. But there are those who teach it, and these others taught it; that's not my cup of tea. This is truth. The Bible is truth, but it's a mystery. The Old Testament contains the entire promise of God: the four chapters, the four books—Matthew, Mark, Luke, and John—that's the fulfillment, complete fulfillment. The rest are commentaries on the fulfillment.

Any other questions, please?

Q: God is my own consciousness and awareness of the being that I am, is that right?

A: Yes, my dear. He actually became you that you may become him. He actually became you. For God to become you, he would have to fall. He would *have* to fall. *Infinity* took on a finite mortal state. Here is immortality becoming mortal; that which is forever becoming something that's sentient so that which is finite may become as he is. So God became man that man may become God. That's the great mystery.

Until Friday.

THE ORIGINAL SIN

March 8, 1963

Tonight's subject is "The Original Sin." Undoubtedly you've heard time and again that it's some sex violation. It hasn't a thing to do with sex. It's ancient, yes, but not a thing to do with sex. The Bible is a mystery. You can only understand it as it is revealed to you or believe it when you are told it by one to whom it has been revealed. It's not a book that you just pick up and read as you would a novel. As we know, there are sixty-six books and you would start at taking Genesis and go through Revelation, and say that's the way that it's done. Because that's not the way the Bible really is presented.

All the attributes of mind are personified in the Bible, and you and I take them as persons, and they're not persons. All the characters are simply personifications of attributes of mind, eternal states of consciousness. So we must find out the first state that appeared in the Bible. What is that first state? For it is against *that* state which is the ideal that man has sinned. Sin means "to miss the mark," or I could disbelieve it or I am ignorant of it. And these are different levels of sinning: To know it and not to heed it is the most serious state; to hear of it and disbelieve it, that is a secondary state; never to have heard of it, that is not really a severe case. Yet all carry with it certain responsibilities. So we must search the Bible for this initial state that was presented to man. Man heard it but didn't believe it; man heard it and believed it but didn't quite find it; and man never heard of it.

So this initial state is personified as a little child. You will read it in the 8th chapter of the Book of Proverbs: "The Lord created me at the beginning of his way, the *first* of his acts of old. Ages ago I was set up, at the first, before the beginning of the earth. When he marked out the foundations of the earth, I was beside him like a little child, delighting, ever a delight before him, rejoicing in his inhabited world, delighting in the sons of men. He who finds me finds life and obtains favor from the Lord; he who misses me injures himself; all who hate me love death." Now that's Proverbs 8:22-36. That's the first state that is set up.

As we told you last Tuesday night, Jesus Christ is not a person. Jesus Christ is this eternal state, a state of salvation, and a series of mystical experiences in the depths of the soul. If man finds it, he passes through this series of experiences, which leads him to God. "For no man comes unto the Father save by me." This is the state called Christ Jesus. But no man comes—"I am the way"; there is no other way. The earliest Christians were called the people of the Way—as told us in the 9th chapter of the Book of Acts and all through the Book of Acts, the people of the Way. For here is the way: "*I am* the way and the truth and the life."

So here is a state personified as a little child, as told us in the 11th chapter of the Book of Isaiah: "And a little child shall lead them" (verse 6). Lead them where? Lead them to the Father. Everything is personified. Well, here is the personification of the initial state that was his eternal delight, delighting in his inhabited world, rejoicing ever before him, and delighting in the sons of men, hoping that the individual man would find him. If he found him, then would come the unfoldment within that man who found him of the series that would take him to the Father. There's no other way to go to the Father than through that *series* that he laid down.

So here, the first state is the state ___(??), the original state. Man hears it, and he doesn't believe it. Paul heard it and Paul didn't believe it. But Paul then confessed in his first letter to Timothy: "Formerly, I blasphemed and persecuted and insulted him; but I received mercy because I ignorantly acted in unbelief." I didn't believe it. I heard it, but I just did not believe it. And so I received mercy. And so mercy is in all of us. If you don't receive mercy, which completely sets you free from your horrible acts, as he confessed, well then, it is from the extreme state to the modified state because he never heard of it.

Now listen to this chapter, the 12th chapter of the Book of Luke, say from the 46th through the 48th verse. It's the story of a master, and the master has made known his will to his servants. One servant knows his will, but he doesn't do it. He doesn't act upon what he knows the master desires, so when the master comes, he is severely beaten. Another servant does not know, but he does what is deserving of beating, but he is lightly used. You are not set free from the responsibility of falling into a state, any state in this world. So I am in the state of being poor, all right, I will reap the fruit of poverty. But I will not experience the beating in the state of poverty comparable to you who know how to use God's law. If you dare to assume that you are unwanted, knowing that you are only in a state and knowing it, you deliberately allow yourself for unnumbered reasons to enter into a state where you feel unwanted, feel beaten, and feel poor, then you *really* will be beaten by the events and the circumstances of life. If you never heard it and you don't know it, you cannot avoid reaping the fruit of the state, but it will be a light beating. It will be modified, as told you in that 48th verse of the 12th chapter of the Book of Luke. The forty-seventh tells you that if you *know* what the will of the Father is, the will of God, and you don't do it, you will be *severely* beaten.

Now, what is the other aspect that Paul spoke of where he received mercy? You can exercise that. So someone doesn't know it. Paul didn't know it; he confessed he did not know it, and he received mercy. Like my friend in San Francisco, he meets a man who never heard this story; but he, my friend, heard it. The man is unemployed and wants a bill for a dinner. My friend made himself a pledge he would not give any panhandler a dollar at any time. He had an experience when he was a boy at fifteen, so true to form, he did not give the dollar. But now he knows this story; he can't get away with it anymore by simply ignoring the request. The man wants food. The man wants a job. The man is in need. Well, he cannot ignore it and walk by knowing *this*. He is confronted now with a request. He has to stop right on that street and see that man gainfully employed, knowing in his heart that that imaginal act of his has its own appointed hour. It ripens; it will flower. If to the man, who doesn't know this law, it seems late, it seems long, in getting the job, well then, he isn't concerned. He did what he was called upon to do; and although it seems long, he will wait, confident that it will not be late, and it will simply come into complete flower in that man's life. He knows it. So he was merciful and forgave the man. If he, knowing what he knows today, daring to teach this law to others, asking them to join with him in simply setting the world free, that he met a man because *he* had a good meal, the man didn't, and instead of doing this, simply ignored it and walked by, went home to his own home where he's sheltered, comforted, and has a full larder; *he* will be held responsible. He was not merciful.

So here is the story. The original sin is to hear this story. The story of salvation is set forth for us in the gospels. Follow the story of one called Christ Jesus. It's not a person. Christ Jesus is simply God's method of salvation. The first state he ever created was that state. He is ever before him as sheer delight, delighting in the sons of men, always rejoicing before God, for this is his only way of salvation. And so he created—he didn't improvise *after* he created the world; before he brought forth anything in the world, he created the means of redemption; and the means of redemption is personified as a little child—"and a little child shall lead them"—to us, Jesus

Christ. That is God's eternal method of salvation. So read the story, and exactly what happened to him as a *seeming* person, *that* is going to happen to you.

Now, how? Believe it. First thing, you hear it, and then you either accept it or you reject it. I plead with you to accept it, just accept it, for we are told in that same 8th chapter of Proverbs, "He who finds me finds life and obtains favor from the Lord; he who misses me injures himself; all who *hate* me love death" (verse 35). Love death? Yes, they love this world more than anything else in the world. And the world here that seems so alive to us, may I tell you, is the world of death. I'm speaking from experience; this is the world of death. So they'll give anything to extend what they consider life by twenty-four hours. Promise them a month, oh, they're thrilled. Promise them an extra year and that's marvelous. And this is death.

For in my vision, when I saw the world not yet descended here, and all must come through death. For the mystery of life is life through death; the mystery of the grain of wheat is that it must fall into the earth and die before it can be made alive. If it doesn't fall into the ground, then it remains alone; if it falls into the ground and dies, it brings forth much (John 12:24). So God falls into the ground. This is the ground, this flesh. The world of flesh is the element of death where God falls into death, into this ground, called a fleshly being. And so those who hate me, they love the flesh; they love death. And they will give anything to perpetuate if only for an hour, one more breath in the world of death. Those who hear it, they know the Spirit is the element of resurrection, and so they are not completely attached to the world of death. But those who hear it and do it have life. Those who hear it but would not do it are the ones condemned, severely beaten. Beaten only to get them back upon the track as it were and put through the furnaces of affliction, these fiery, fiery states. Those who have never heard of it are not completely free of the responsibility of falling into that state, but it is modified for them. It is lessened for them. They're not as hurt as those who know it who did not do it.

So the original sin begins with hearing this story and either rejecting it or seeing it in a way. So I ask you not to reject it, for if you find him, you find life. The minute you find him the entire series awakens in you, and it's the *only* way to the Father. So the only intermediary, really, is the Way, called in the Bible Christ Jesus, who is not a person. It's the Way, a series of mystical experiences inwoven into the soul of man, that man, individually, finding it then begins to go through. He goes through these states automatically at stated intervals known only to God the Father. At the very end, he awakens, and he is one with the Father. That's the purpose. God is bringing us not only into his world but bringing us into his world as himself. So in the end, there is no one but God. Because God's purpose is to give us himself, as though there were no others in the world, just God and you, God and us. But in the end, not even God and you, or God and I, just God. But you, in that moment, will be he.

As told us, he leaves everything and cleaves to his emanation, his bride (Genesis 2:24). For we are his bride, as told us in the 54th chapter of the Book of Isaiah, "Your Maker is your husband, the Lord of hosts is his name." And a husband must leave everything and cleave to his wife until they become one flesh, one being. So in the end, they will not even be two, just you, and you will be he. So God is giving himself to me; he's giving himself to you. And in the end, when he completely completes his purpose, there's only God, and you are he.

So the original sin is to have heard this wonderful first state. Listen to it carefully: "The Lord created us at the beginning of his way, the *first* of his acts of old. Ages ago, I was set up at the first, before the beginning of the earth. When he laid the foundation of the earth, then I was beside him, like a little child, I was daily his delight, rejoicing before him always, rejoicing in his inhabited world, delighting in the sons of men." Here was the Way personified, really personified, as a child. For everything in this world is God, and God is man; therefore, everything becomes man—everything's personified. So the first state that is personified ___(??) God is a delightful child, and it's the Way to bring man to himself as himself. It seems silly and it seems stupid, but not when you go into the depths of your soul and see this personification of all the attributes of mind.

Five years ago, when my daughter was in high school, it was my pleasure every morning to get up early and prepare breakfast for the two of us, then make a little lunch basket for her, and then bid her good-bye as she went off to school. Well, this morning, after she went off to school, I went back to my library where I'm reading my Bible because my wife slept late and we would meet at brunch. This morning, when she came out and we were having brunch, she said, "I had the strangest experience this morning. I woke, I was sitting up in bed, you were sitting on the bed, and then my hand was engaged with another hand. You turned—I couldn't see the face who had the hand—but you turned, and you evidently recognized him. You seemed to know him quite intimately and you said to me, 'Why, it is death.'" Then I said to you, 'I don't want to die.'" Then I said to her, "Are you afraid to die?" She said, "No, I'm not afraid to die, but I have unfinished business. I don't want to die." I said, "All right, if you are not afraid to die, all right." Then the two hands disengaged, and as they disengaged, she then began . . . she thought she was sitting on the bed, she thought I was sitting on the bed next to her, and then she came to.

This was an experience in the depths of her soul where death was personified as the cold hand of death. Haven't you heard it? Haven't you heard of the king of terrors, the jaws of death? All poets use it. And here she had the experience of an actual hand, the hand of death, that I, sitting on the bed, in the depth of her soul, recognized him, and I knew him quite intimately. Being not afraid of death, I asked her, "Are you afraid of him?" She said, "No, I'm not afraid to die. But I don't want to die. I have unfinished business." At that moment, when she didn't feel afraid of death, the two hands disengaged, and then she woke. ___(??). And I was not in the room; I was in my library reading my Bible.

So I tell you, all the states of the Bible that we call characters are simply personifications of these infinite attributes of the human mind, which is divine mind. So what we speak of as this little child that leads them—"a little child shall lead them . . . and I stood beside him as a little child . . . and I was daily his delight, rejoicing before him always, rejoicing in his inhabited world, delighting in the sons of men." Then comes that wonderful statement, "He who finds me finds life." Here I am delighting among all the people of the world, trying to encourage everyone to find me. If you can only find me you'll find life. He's asking everyone to please believe him. How would I find him? Believe it. Believe what I've told you. Believe that he is really a series of mystical experiences, inwoven in the soul of man. Believe it. And if you believe it, maybe tonight you'll find him. If you find him tonight, the first one, like a little petal on a flower, opens as an actual experience. Having opened up one, you know from actual personal experience it's true. You'll never then waver. Then, in the not distant future, a second petal will open, and all will open. As they open, they lead you to God, God the Father; and when you get there, you are he.

So the whole story is inwoven in man. Hasn't a thing to do with your violation of any sexual ___(??), which would be implied if you read the story in a certain way. But it isn't that at all. And may I tell you, that first so-called disobedience, which we find in the 3rd chapter of the Book of Genesis, that very first disobedience was God. As we are told in the 11th chapter, the 32nd verse of the Book of Romans, "And God consigned all men to *disobedience* that he may have *mercy* upon all." So don't think for one moment any Eve or any Adam disobeyed. It was *God* who disobeyed. God commanded himself, and the only way he could bring about this fabulous dream of his into its complete bloom was his play. God entered into every one of us. And God is the one who disobeyed. He knew in his heart he couldn't die, but he also knew he would have the illusion of death in the world of flesh. And so God disobeyed his command of God. God became man that man may become God. And so he's sunk in all of us as our own wonderful I-am-ness—that's God.

And in it now they're trying to find out the way back. There's only one way back and that was in the beginning. He wrote that story in the very beginning. "God created me at the very beginning of his way, the first of his acts of old. Ages ago, I was set up at the first, before the beginning of the earth." You mean the way of salvation? Yes. The way of salvation was the very first act of God. It wasn't improvised. It wasn't something thought of *after* the event; it was before anything was brought forth. And God is playing all the parts, and he's written out completely in detail the means of salvation.

And the means of salvation? You'll be born again—that's the very first act, in the true sense of the word—and be born from above. Then will come another act. He will give you what he promised you. To prove how much he loves you, he will give you his Son. That's the second act. Then you are a father. If you have a son, you are a father. Then will come a third act. In the third act, he will unveil himself in you, spiritual circumcision, and you will see the true head of creation; and you are it. You'll know exactly who you are, and you are he. You'll still be clothed in a garment of flesh; therefore, your ultimate inheritance is delayed, delayed until you take off this veil for the last time. But the veil has been split. You'll wear it, but it's split, so you aren't as shut out from the vision of eternity as you were prior to the splitting of the veil.

And then all the stories told in the gospels concerning Christ Jesus begin to unfold in you, every one. Then you will know that Christ Jesus is not a person. Christ Jesus is the way, just as told us in the 14th chapter of the Book of John, "I am the way, I am the life, I am the resurrection . . . I am the way; no one cometh unto the Father save by me." There is no possibility of coming to the Father. I have had unnumbered arguments across the country: "Well, after all, Neville, you were born and raised a Christian in the Hebrew-Christian faith." They are one: Hebrew and the Christian faith are both interwoven because one is the fulfillment of the other. "But, after all, don't tell me that the Buddhists haven't the same thing and the Hindu's haven't the same thing and the others haven't the same thing." And may I tell you, as I stand before you, there's only one way.

There's *only one* way, and this series of events is the only way to the Father. You will be born from above; you will see his only begotten Son as your son; you'll be torn in two from the top to the bottom; the dove will descend upon you and smother you with affection. All these things will happen to you just as it's recorded it happened to him. That was only the personification of the Way. That's not a person. He personifies the Way, from beginning to end. So everything claimed of him you will experience. When you experience it, you will tell it, tell it to the best of your ability, in the hope that they will believe it. Some will believe it, and some will not believe it.

But may I tell you, in our world where we live now, you have heard it and you have ___(??). Having heard it, you carry out full responsibility for all the states into which you fall. You'll be beaten severely because you've heard it. If you never heard it, then the trial would not be as severe. Read it carefully when you go home, and here is the story. I think it's the 18th of Matthew. A king calls his servants together. He wants all the accounts settled. One servant owes him ten thousand talents, and he didn't have it, so the king ordered that the man, his wife and children be sold, and whatever they had, to settle the account. He fell on his knees and pleaded with the king for patience and for mercy. Then he would, if the king were patient, he would pay in time. The king heard his plea and forgave him, completely forgave him. Then the man went out and saw a man who owed him a hundred denarii, and he grabbed him by the throat and demanded immediate payment. The man couldn't pay, and he had the man thrown into jail as a debtor. And when the king heard what the one he forgave did to another who only owed a hundred denarii, not ten thousand talents, then he treated him severely and threw him in until every last talent was paid (Matthew 18:23).

So they know to pray in this manner: Father, forgive us our debts as we forgive those . . . just ___(??) forgive the other. Father, forgive us in proportion to our ability to forgive the other who owes us. So when you meet anyone in this world, no matter who you ___(??) another, don't pass by. Doesn't cost you one nickel; it only costs you an imaginal act. It'll take you just a second. So think of anyone that now needs something in this world but anyone in your world, and imagine that they are as you would like them to be but *everyone* and don't you raise a finger to make it so. Believe in God. God is creative. That imaginal act of yours has a little interval of time between the imaginal act and its fulfillment. Like every vision in the world, "The vision has its own appointed hour; it ripens, it will flower. If it seems long, then wait; for it is sure and it will not be late" (Habakkuk 2:3).

So in your imaginal act concerning any person in this world, make it loving and make it altogether marvelous. And if you do it, then drop it. It's done! Without the man's knowledge or his consent, you did it for him. Forgive every being in the world, and as you forgive others, the Heavenly Father forgives you. And so you may not know it but at the moment that you did it, it is really done, although it hasn't yet appeared within the world of effects, on this very, very low intensity. This is very low. But you believe it and try it.

But you have been exposed to it, and no one who has been exposed to it from that moment on is free of a severe beating. If you're not exposed to it, the beating is light. If you are exposed to it and feel sorry for yourself, the beating is really severe. No man can afford to feel sorry for himself having heard that these are infinite states of consciousness into which the soul, moving to God, falls either knowingly or unknowingly. So if you feel sorry for yourself knowing that you are in a state, when you reach the fruit of that state, it really will be severe. So I ask you not to feel sorry for yourself, not to feel sorry, just simply move out of one state into another state and lose yourself in it just as though it were true. In the not distant future, you will reap the fruit of that state.

For listen to what he tells us. You know the tree by its fruit; the good tree bears good fruit, and the evil tree bears bad fruit. So if that is truly right, that this is the law of harvest, identical harvest, that I am in a state and I can't reap the fruit of any state other than that state into which I have gone knowingly or unknowingly, so we try it, try it tonight. Take someone in this world of yours who you would like to help and see him or see her as you would like to see him, as you would like to see anyone, and believe in the reality of your imaginal act and that act will come to pass just as surely as I am standing here. But you are held responsible for it. You must do it.

So the original sin is to have heard this story of God's plan of salvation: "I have prepared a way for my banished ones to return." The first thing I did, said he, was to prepare the way. I didn't banish them and then contrive a way, improvise a way; I prepared the way in the beginning. He planned everything that has come out and as it *will* be established. So he's prepared the way, and the way is told us in the story of Jesus Christ. So we read it, and the churches encourage us to read it as the history of a man. No, the story of Jesus Christ is just like an actor on a stage. When he walks across the stage, he plays a part, and the audience either understands it or they don't. If they don't understand it, they aren't held responsible. If they understand it and don't believe in it, then the beating is severe. If they understand it and make the effort but still don't find him, then read the second ___(??). First, "He who finds me has life and obtains the favor of the Lord; he who misses me injures himself (that's not fatal, he injures himself); all who hate me love death." They may hate the story having heard it, for they like the fleshpots. They'd like to be here more than any other place in the world.

May I tell you from experience that when I entered the world and saw people who had not yet descended this low—for this is the very limit of opacity, this is the limit of contraction—when I talked to them, they thought I was telling tall, tall stories. They couldn't believe that I had just come from this world and that I would go back to this world because I came there consciously. So when I looked at them and saw them, I was told by one who was here years ago—I never met him here; he was a German, Heine, you know the works of Heine—and Heine said to me, "You know, Neville, they don't speak of earth as earth, they call earth Woodland and they don't believe that anyone who ever goes to Woodland could ever come back to what they call life."

Because Woodland, this is the earth, is the limit of contraction, the limit of opacity, and so those who are here are in Woodland. It's a tremendous accomplishment to be here because you can't turn around and hear this story and find God until you come here. You must reach the limit of contraction before you can hear the story of salvation. While you are here, you hear it, hear it, and believe it. It's a series of mystical experiences in the soul of man that leads you from wherever you are when you find him, to God, and arriving there, you are one with God. There's nothing but God.

So all the characters of the Bible are personifications of the infinite states of mind, these states of consciousness. But the first state that he created was the "Way of salvation," and he personified it for his own delight as a little child. And may I tell you, it is sheer delight when you see the little child. It's infinitely beautiful, and it is the personification of this state. For it comes first and as you encounter it and have the experience of your own birth from above, here comes the child. It's a babe. "And a little child shall lead them." They speak of it as child, but the word translated child is really "a babe." And the little babe shall lead them through the series of experiences up to the fulfillment of it all where he awakens *as God.*

So the very first thing that he created was the way of salvation, personified for us as a child, but told to us in the Bible as a person called Christ Jesus. But Christ Jesus is not a person but the way of salvation. "I am the way," he's made to say. But I do not know the way. Well, I am the way. The way to what?—well, the way to everything, but specifically to the Father. I am the way to the Father. "No one comes unto the Father but by me," but no one. So you can't get to the Father save you come in this manner and this is the way. He marked it out for you. This is how you come. So you believe the story. Believe in the story and you may this night find him. And "he who finds me finds life," for "as the Father has life in himself so he has granted the Son also to have life in himself." And then you have life in yourself. So tomorrow, arriving at the Father who has life in himself, and you are one with the Father, you have been ___(??) life in yourself. And then you can animate anything in the world, make anything become alive.

In the meanwhile, believe it. Believe it and I promise you it's my sincere desire that before I leave this platform, whenever I will leave it in the future, that many of you, if not all of you, could tell me that you had the identical series of experiences because you've got to have them anyway. But I can't think of any greater thrill to me than to hear you tell me that "it happened to me last night," and tell me the story that I know you are going to tell me. Because everyone must have it and having it, then you're on the way toward the Father; and when you arrive there, you are one with the Father. Because I am one with the Father, when you get there, you and I are one, and yet we do not lose our distinctive individuality. ___(??) the one, because it's the same Father, so we have the same Son. And that's how he set the whole thing up in the beginning. Before he did anything he set up this state.

Now take it on this level and think of a friend that you would like to help. There must be some friend who today knows they'd like to be gainfully employed. Regardless of what he made in the past, regardless of the figures you see on the paper's headlines today, forget that! Everything is possible to God. I wouldn't care if you doubled that unemployment figure by ten, it still doesn't stop your imaginal act from working. But you take a friend, bring him into your mind's eye, bring her into your mind's eye, and see him and see her gainfully employed, making more than they've ever made before. Don't raise a finger to make it so, but just imagine that it is so. Leave it just like that and believe in God. God is your own wonderful Imagination. God is your own wonderful I-am-ness that's imagining. So believe it, believe in it. Know in your own being that it takes an interval called incubation between what you imagined and the fulfillment, the birth, of that state. So don't be anxious in the interval. You imagined it. You're still imagining it. You will continue to imagine it until what you have imagined is completely externalized in your world.

Try it now with someone. And don't tell them what you have done. Don't ask for any praise. Don't tell any being in this world what you have done. Without their knowledge, without their consent, you be merciful. You are encouraged to be merciful. Let me remind you of that first chapter of Paul's letter to Timothy: "I blasphemed, I persecuted, I insulted him; but I received mercy because I acted ignorantly in unbelief" (1 Timothy 1:13). All right, now you are not going to act ignorantly in unbelief. Maybe he did. Maybe he thinks the whole thing is stupid. But don't you argue with him. Maybe you tried to persuade him to come here. Maybe you tried to persuade him to read one of my books. Maybe he thought the whole thing stupid. But in spite of that, God is love. It doesn't matter what he did or what he said. You now bring him into your mind's eye and see him as gainfully employed. And don't tell him what you did. Let no one know what you're doing, and you remain faithful to what you have done. He will get the job, even if he doesn't know that you did it. Doesn't really matter. Try it.

Now let us go into the Silence. (Tape ends.)

GRACE VERSUS LAW

March 12, 1963

Tonight's subject is "Grace versus Law." We're told in the very first chapter of the Book of John, "The law was given through Moses; grace and truth came through Jesus Christ." Unnumbered volumes have been written about this grace versus law.

Tonight I'm speaking not through theory; I'm speaking from experience. And so we're called upon to pass on to other generations, succeeding generations, our testimony. As we're told in the 1st epistle of John, 1st chapter, the first three verses: "That which was from the beginning, that which we have heard and seen with our eyes . . . that which we have seen and heard we proclaim also unto you, so that you may have fellowship with us." For these are the two births that take place in every individual in the world. No one brings about his own physical birth; he is born by the action of powers not his own. And no one brings about his own spiritual birth; he is born by the action of powers beyond his own. The first, we admit we are here, clothed in this garment of flesh. We find ourselves here, but we know we never had a thing to do about it; it's simply we found ourselves here. So you will find yourself born spiritually in the same miraculous manner. You'll be born from above, just as you are born here from below. Here, we are born from below from the womb of a woman. Then will come another act, God's mightiest act, and you will be begotten and born from above by the action of powers not your own.

We turn first to the law. In the very beginning, God established the law of identical harvest: "And let the earth put forth vegetation, trees yielding seeds, and fruit trees bearing fruit in which is their seed, each according to its own kind" (Genesis 1:11). Here we find the harvest is nothing more than the multiplication of the identical seed. "Be not deceived; God is not mocked, whatever a man sows, so shall he reap" (Galatians 6:7). That's in this world, this law. Tonight I will show you what I have found about this sowing.

Causation in our world is really mental. It was not always known as a *mental* state. It was believed in the beginning to be physical, and so laws were instituted and men abided by these laws outwardly; they observed the law. Then came the great revelation of "grace" that interpreted the law, thus bringing grace. "For," said he, "do not think that I have come to abolish the law and the prophets. I have come not to abolish them but to fulfill them." And then he interprets law for us and puts it on a *mental* plane: "You have heard it said by men of old, 'Thou shalt not'" and he states it; "But I say unto you," and then he puts it on an entirely different level. And not one statement conveys it more graphically than, "You've heard it said of old, 'Thou shalt not commit adultery.' But I say unto you, to look upon a woman lustfully is to have already committed the act with her in your heart'" (Matthew 5:27). Not to restrain the impulse, that's not good enough; but not having the desire, then you haven't committed the act. But to have the desire and because of the consequences of your act, you restrain the impulse, that is still not good enough. The act was committed with the impulse.

Now here, we are on an entirely different level, a mental level, and this is what I discovered about this level. I could stand here physically and see any part of this world mentally by assuming that I am there, and then viewing the world *from* that assumption rather than thinking *of* that state. Standing here, if I desire to be elsewhere, although at the moment, my reason tells me I can't afford it, my senses tell me I haven't the time—you're committed, you'll be here next Friday; you couldn't get there and be back, so here you are—you're stuck. But I desire to be elsewhere. So reason and my senses deny that I could be because I just shouldn't be there. But standing here, let me now assume that I am where I would like to be, and then let me mentally view the world *from* that assumption as though it were true, just as though it were true.

Well, I know from my own experience that if I dare to do it, everything in this world that would tie me here, there will be a reshuffling of the events of life and compel the journey on my part. And it would; that assumption of mine would build a bridge of incidents across which I would move to the fulfillment of that state, and no power in the world could stop it. I would walk across a series of events. From the very moment that I do it, things would happen to compel me to go, and I physically as a man could not resist it. Things would happen to *compel* the journey if I dare to assume that I am elsewhere while physically I am really here.

Now the same thing is true not only of a physical journey but a journey into other states like wealth, like fame, and like anything in this world. What would it be like were I—then I name the experience. Suppose now, at this very moment, I desired, say, a certain security that I do not now enjoy. But I want it; I hunger for it. What would it be like were I now in possession of security? Let me now make the same psychological motion, all in my Imagination, and then view the world from that assumption just as though it were true. If I dare to assume that it's so, I may regret tomorrow that I did it, I may, but that's my choice. I can acquaint you with this law and then leave you to your choice and its risk. Many a person had nothing and hungered for wealth and they got it, but, oh, what things happened to them when they got it. They wanted it. And if you want it, take it. You can always give it up.

But here is the law by which man *moves* in this world. So I will acquaint you with the law and show you how I operate it and how it works. But may I tell you, no matter how good you are in this world and no matter how wisely you operate the law, it doesn't in any way qualify you for the second radical change in your life, which is called grace. That's the second birth. The twice-born man has received grace, and grace is God's gift of himself to man—that's grace. No matter how wise you are, you're on the wheel with the first birth, playing it as wisely as you can—and I hope you will play it wisely when you hear the law and how to operate it. But it cannot in any way qualify you for the second birth. That is grace—that's the gift. You cannot bring that about any more than you brought about the first.

Now the second birth, it's sheer fantasy. It's called not salvation; grace is salvation. "What must I do?" they ask the question. Well, he made the statement, "What if you owned the whole vast world and lose your life?" Then said he, "It's so much easier for a camel to go through the eye of a needle than a rich man to enter the kingdom of God" (Matthew 19:24). And they said to him, "Then *who* can be saved?" He said, "With men it is impossible; but nothing is impossible to God." With men, yes, it's impossible; he can't save himself. When a man tells you he is a self-made man, he's not speaking from any knowledge of this mystery, no self-made man. For this is a gift, the second is a complete gift.

And what is the secret of God's election? I do not know. I can't tell you. I can only share with you what I've experienced and tell you how it comes. It's a process, and it happens so suddenly. It comes without any warning. No one knows the moment it's going to come, and suddenly you're born. You are actually born, without . . . you are consciously born. I have no conscious memory of being born from my mother's womb, none whatsoever. I was born on a certain day of a certain month of a certain year in a certain little island in the West Indies. I was born; I had no knowledge of it, and then gradually consciousness possessed me. Then when I was maybe three or maybe not quite four, I began to function consciously with memory, but memory didn't go back to my mother's womb.

But the second birth is something as though you're actually doing it to yourself, and every moment of time is conscious and so vividly and vividly alive. The whole thing *you* are doing. From the very moment to the very end of the birth it is taking place in you, and out of your own wonderful being, you are coming. Until that moment, you didn't know that you were dead. You took it for granted that you were alive and that one day the body would die; and so whether you survived or not, you didn't know, but that would be death. Those who saw you put away, whether cremated or in the earth, they would say good-bye to you, and they would speak of you as someone who's dead . . . but not while you walked the earth with them. And yet here comes the moment in time when suddenly a power beyond your wildest dream is taking place *in* you. You aren't doing it; you have no control; it's being done to you. And as the power is intensified, you awake. You always thought prior to that moment that you were awake. You always thought prior to that moment that you were alive and walking about the earth. Here, for the first time in eternity, you are awakening in a tomb, and the tomb is your skull. You find yourself completely sealed and entombed in your own skull, and you're fully awake for the first time in eternity.

Then begins the birth, and you come out like one being self-born, truly begotten by yourself. Out you come, and the entire drama as described for us in the gospels you are enacting. You are being self-born. The witnesses become present, and they appear to witness this event in eternity. They can't see you because you are invisible. But you're more real than they are, more real than anything in the world at that moment and yet you are invisible. And then you know what it means: "God is spirit, and those who worship him worship in spirit and in truth" (John 4:24) and "As God has life in himself"—God the Father—"so now he grants the Son to have life in himself" (John 5:26). And so all of a sudden, you awake; and the force, this intense power that you feel coming from you, now seems to be in the corner of the room and centered all over. And all of a sudden, it comes to the end, and you return once more, enclosed in this simple little garment out of which you had just for a moment emerged with the most fantastic drama in the world.

That was grace, but it comes in stages: it has three fantastic parts. That first one is simply your birth from above to fulfill the 3rd of John: "You must be born from above, for unless you be born from above you cannot in any wise enter the kingdom of heaven," which fulfills that chapter (verse

3). Then comes the second, when God really gives you himself. And then suddenly a similar power possesses you and you're carried with it; you can't stop it, not a thing you can do about it. Suddenly, as you are carried with it, you explode; your whole being explodes, and here he presents you with his Son.

Now the eighteenth verse of the first chapter, we are told, "Grace and truth came through Jesus Christ," right after we're told how it comes: it comes through Jesus Christ, grace comes and the truth comes. Then we are told, "No man has ever seen the Father; the Son, who is in the bosom of the Father, he has made him known." You didn't know that you contained within you the Son of God. You had no idea you did. Suddenly there's an explosion, and he stands before you, and he calls you Father. You don't see yourself; *he* calls you Father, and you know he's your son. And here, the father-son relationship is established forever. He calls you Father to fulfill the eighty-ninth Psalm: "I have found him . . . I have found David, and he cried unto me, 'Thou art my Father, my God, and the Rock of my salvation,'" the fulfillment of the great 89th Psalm, the Messianic psalm (verse 26). You look at him, and there's no doubt in your mind who he is; there's no doubt in his mind who you are. It takes the Son to reveal the Father, and you didn't know for one moment you were he until the Son reveals you to yourself. And then the third in the great gift is when out of the blue, you are torn in two, from top to bottom; and then you ascend, a living being, something that is fiery and alive. You ascend right into Zion, which is your skull.

And these three parts mark the great gift, called in the Bible "grace," an unearned, unmerited gift. No one in this world is good enough to earn it; therefore, *all* will get it. God actually expresses to man a mercy with which man is incapable with his conscience of ever judging himself as worthy of redeeming. No man in this world with conscience and memory could ever judge himself as mercifully as God does. So what man has done, I've certainly done it, you've done it, and the whole vast world has done it; and we are so sinful while we are here in this world of law, of doing it. And in spite of our limitations, in spite of our weaknesses, God's infinite mercy brings about the second birth. And we're all lifted up in this eternal place where we're put into the everlasting temple that God is making out of us, making out of himself, for he gives himself to man before man can be fitted into the everlasting temple. And no one can fit your place. No one can fill my place. Not one can be displaced; not one in any way can be rubbed out. The temple would be unfinished. I know from my own experience that not one can be unsaved. I don't care who he is; no matter what he has done in this world, everyone will be saved. What must I do to be saved? *Believe* the gospel.

Now we are told that we could delay it That's why I find it difficult to believe that. But still it's scripture; the 4rh chapter of the Book of Hebrews, "And the good news preached unto us was also preached unto them; but it did not benefit them, because it was not mixed with faith in the hearer." Now tonight some of you could reject it, and that may appear on the surface to delay your call and it may—I do not know. I have no assurance that you could delay it. But it would appear that rejection on the part of one because he heard it but did not accept it because it didn't make sense to him, therefore, he rejected it. And I tell you, those who reject it—and maybe by your rejection, you delay your call—eventually you're going to be called. Because he'll put you through all the paces of the world until finally you have no power to reject the story when you hear it.

But while we're here in this world of law, let me now quote you the 1st Psalm—it's a marvelous benediction: "Blessed is the man . . . who delights in the law of the Lord . . . who meditates on it day and night. For, in *all* that he does, he prospers" (verses 1-3). But in *all* that he does, not a few things but in everything. And the law is so simple if you jump to the foundation that is *mental*, it's not physical. Go to church as the people who practice it outwardly thought it would in some way bring good for them, but that wasn't it. It's mental. Causation is mental, so the law is mental. So *I'm* the law. For "blessed is the man who delights in the law . . . meditating it day and night . . . for in all that he does, he prospers"—in *all*.

So you think now of the man you would like to be, and you seem so remote from such a man and can't conceive of being that man in the immediate present. All right, you think so. I tell you, try this law: What would it be like if now my closest friend saw in me what they wouldn't dream ever, prior to this moment, of ever seeing me? What would it be like? How would I see him? How would he see me were it true? What would the world think if they knew that I am and I name it? What would they see? Well, then sit perfectly still and let them see you. Walk now by faith not by sight. I'm going to call a thing that is not as though it were, knowing that the unseen will become seen. So I call myself just as though I were the man that I'd like to be. So you who are taking notes, that's the fourth chapter, seventeenth verse of Paul's letter to the Romans: "He calls a thing that is not seen as though it were seen, and the unseen becomes seen." So I will call something that is not seen just as though it were seen and let the unseen become seen.

You try it. May I tell you that it will not fail you. No power in the world can stop it from crystallizing into fact if you try it. For the things that are seen, we're told in the 11th chapter of Hebrews, were made from things that do not appear. All the things you see were made from things that do not appear ___(??)—you'll find it in the 3rd verse—all the things in the world. You see a man, well, what made him what he is? Well, he once assembled a certain mental state, and knowingly or unknowingly, he fell into it. Falling into it, he remained there long enough for it to take on that initial statement of God: "All things must bring forth after their kind," the law of identical harvest. The harvest is only the multiplication of the identical seed.

So I fall into a state. I do it wittingly or unwittingly, but I fall into a state. Remaining in the state, suddenly the ___(??) comes out. Someone begins to appear in my world; he seems to be instrumental in making me move forward in the direction that I should go. I may, on reflection, think *he*, the instrument that moved me forward by certain contacts, was the cause of my being forward. No, the cause was unseen. As you are told, things seen were made from things that do not appear. He appears, so he can't be the cause. And so I look back on my world and see all the people that seemed to be instrumental and helpful in moving me forward, but they're seen, and causation is mental. So things that are now seen that are made were made from things that do not appear. But if that is true, then he—I'll thank him for what he did, but I can't claim that he was the cause of my good fortune. So he introduced me to the right people and all things added up to the things that I am assuming. But the cause of it all was my assumption and my faithfulness to that assumption. So I dare to assume that I am or that you are what I would like you to be. Assuming that you are what I would like you to be and I feel that you would like to be, I am unmoved in that assumption and you become it, without your knowledge or your consent. I don't need your consent and I don't need your knowledge if causation is mental.

So I warn you of the law and leave you to your choice and its risks because you could use it unwisely. But my hands are now washed of that. I cannot stop it. I tell you the law and leave you to your choice. I can't be like a mother over you, saying that you should not do this. For you're told in the Book of Deuteronomy, "I place before you this day good and evil, life and death, blessings and cursing; choose life" (30:19). He suggests that you choose life, but he can't take from you the right, having set you free, to choose anything you want. So he puts before you life and death, good and evil, blessings and cursing, and suggests you choose life; but he cannot deny you the right to choose anything. It's all spread before you. When you imagine something unlovely of another, it will come to pass. It will boomerang too, but it will come to pass. So you are entirely free to imagine anything in this world, for imagining creates reality. A man imagines. If he imagines it and persists in that imaginal act, it will come to pass. And that's the law.

For if there were no other than the wise use of law, to own the whole vast world and yet not to be redeemed from that wheel of recurrence, this would become the most horrible hell in the world. Fortunately, God started in the beginning a plan of redemption, and it's grace where he saves us from the wheel of recurrence. What is his great secret where he picks you at one moment of time and picks another at one moment of time to put him into that eternal structure, the everlasting temple, not made with hands? I do not know. I must confess I do not know. I only know he promises to build a temple for us, anonymously, and we are the temple. We are the temple of the living God, a temple in which God will dwell. And yet we are free beyond the wildest dream of man, for we are God himself in the structure called the New Jerusalem.

So here, use the law wisely for yourself and for others. Every time you exercise your Imagination lovingly on behalf of another, you are literally mediating God to a man, literally. Do it. But may I tell you, if you are the most loving being in the world, the most generous being in the world, and the kindest being in the world, you still cannot by your own effort be born from above. It's a gift, an unearned gift. You can't be good enough. To me that's the most exciting thought in the world because no man could look me in the eye and tell me that he feels himself worthy of such a birth. With a memory and a conscience, he couldn't possibly do it. I know I'm twice born. The second, every second of it, is so vividly alert in my mind's eye. I can go through the whole thing now mentally and reenact the entire scene. And yet with the memory of my past, I would say, "Neville, you are unworthy of this." And therefore, because I know in my heart I am unworthy of it, I can say to every being in the world, "You're going to get it."

If I felt I was *worthy* of it, then I'd have to go out and try to make everyone good as I would conceive myself to be. But I don't conceive myself to be good, as the world calls good. I've done unnumbered things of which I would be ashamed, and I still feel I am capable under stress of doing things of which I would be ashamed. And yet I have had the grace of God, the second birth from above. And I can't conceive of anything more encouraging in the world than to share with others your own experiences and tell them that they cannot lift themselves by their own bootstraps. This is an act of mercy, and mercy is God in expression, for God is love and mercy is love in action.

The mightiest act of God is that act when you, the sound sleeper, he awakens. And you don't know you're asleep. I certainly did not know I was asleep. I hadn't the slightest idea that I was dead, and to find myself walking this earth for fifty-odd years and suddenly to find myself awakening in a tomb? And then discover the great mystery of it all: that he was buried in

Golgotha, and Golgotha is the skull? And that was literally true, and it was *he* who was buried? And then to go back and reread the scripture and to read: "I have been crucified *with* Christ; it is not I who live, but Christ who lives in me; and the life I now live in the flesh I live by the faith of the Son of God, who loved me and gave himself for me" (Galatians 2:20). He gave himself for me the second he became me, but I didn't know it.

I didn't actually know that the being that I think I am, that I am he. That he is every being in the world or that being couldn't live. That no child born of woman could cross the threshold that admits to conscious life without the death of God. That he died to make me alive. The mystery of life through death: that I became alive through his death. And then this mighty act of resurrecting himself, but he resurrects himself as you. And so all of a sudden, there's no change of identity; you awake, but you are he. Then you know the great mystery of the epistle of John: "It does not yet appear what we shall be, but we know when he appears we shall be like him" (1 John 3:2). We shall be like him. Well, if there's no change in your identity, therefore, who is he? No change whatsoever in your identity, therefore, who is he?—your very being.

All of a sudden you awaken. But may I tell you that the full glory of your inheritance—you inherit heaven—but the full glory of that inheritance is not fully realized in you or, for the moment, it's not fully grasped by you while you are still in this body. You must then play the part of the apostle and share it with those who will listen to you until that moment in time comes when he takes off the garment. And then that which ascended is completely displayed to you and to the heavenly host. But you have played and shared with the others all that you have experienced. It's called the apostolic testimony: "That which was from the beginning, that which we have heard and seen with our eyes . . . that which we have seen and heard we now proclaim unto you, that you may share with us this fellowship" (1 John 1:1-3).

And then that fabulous passage that always closes the Anglican service, which in our country is the Episcopal service. It's taken from the last verse of Paul's second letter to the Corinthians: "The grace of the Lord Jesus Christ and the love of God and the fellowship of the Holy Spirit be with you all" (13:14). What a benediction! To say to a gathering like this that, May the *grace* of the Lord Jesus Christ—that was the second birth that comes from the love of God, that through such a birth you may have and share the fellowship of the Holy Spirit, and may it be with you all. And so that's how in all Anglican services they told it in the hope that someone or maybe all would in the not distant future share in that fellowship. But it's the last verse of that 13th chapter of 2nd Corinthians, and to me, it's the most inspiring, just to read it and just try to feel it.

And so grace versus law is not really in conflict. For he said, "I have come not to abolish the law or the prophets but to fulfill them" (Matthew 5:17). Peter in his first letter, that tenth verse of the first chapter, identifies grace with salvation. He said, "The prophets who prophesied of the *grace* that was to be yours, they searched and inquired about this salvation." So he associated grace with salvation—that when it is given, he's saved, he's been redeemed. But because no one can play *your* part, *you* will be redeemed. Don't go back in memory and try to find other things you could undo toward salvation. Do that toward this world to make yourself happier and freer in this world, but not toward salvation. Because if it was not for God's infinite mercy to hide your past from you, you couldn't live with yourself. No man in this world could live with himself if he could now bring back into memory the past; he couldn't because you have played all the parts. You've been a long, long time in coming; and at the very end, you will have played *all* the parts. Therefore, in the end, you too can say, "Forgive them; for they know not what they do" (Luke 23:34).

There's a purpose to God's play, a fabulous purpose. As Blake said, "Do not let yourself be intimidated by the horror of the world. Everything is ordered and correct and must fulfill its destiny in order to achieve perfection." But you've played it. I have played it. Had I not played all the horrible parts of the world, I could not have be merciful when I read about them in the papers. I could not in my heart feel that some mercy should be expressed when you see these horrible stories told in the press. Had I not played it, I couldn't have been the impulse for mercy. But in the end, having played all, you'll forgive all. And so every being in the world will have played all and therefore fitted himself for God's use in the building of his temple.

I can't get away from a sense of predestination when I read scripture, the 8th chapter of the Book of Romans: "We are called according to his purpose. For those whom he *foreknew* he also predestined to be conformed to the image of his Son. And those whom he predestined he also called; and those whom he called he also justified; and those whom he justified he also glorified" (verse 29). You cannot take these five terms, foreknowledge, predestination, called, justification, and glorification, and interpret them in any way to avoid the conclusion of predestination. I don't see how you can. We were with him in the foundation of time, we're told. He called us in the beginning before that the world was, and now he calls us according to his purpose, when this section of his fabulous—you can't conceive of it—living structure is about to be completed. And only you can fit, but *only* you, that one portion of it. So he calls you. And the one called he had predestined to be called. And the one called he justifies—you can't be justified by your actions—*he* justifies you. And then he glorifies you. And glorification is his gift of himself to you, as told us in the 17th chapter of the gospel of John: "Father, glorify thou me with thine own self." So he glorifies the individual with himself. So the entire five terms lead to one conclusion of a predestined, foreknown state. He foreknew the entire thing and was building toward it.

Now the opposite of grace is disgrace. The Bible speaks of it as "the wrath of God, the anger of God." We know what it is to be in disgrace. Grace is the unearned gift, the greatest thing in the world, and the gift of God himself. And the opposite would be the almost *absence* of God. Now the 23rd chapter of the Book of Jeremiah makes this statement: "The anger of the Lord will not turn back until he has executed and accomplished the intents of his mind. In the latter days you will understand it clearly" (verse 20). It seems that God has forsaken us when we go through a war, when we go through some horrible disgrace, where the world has collapsed upon us. A child has gone astray, and society frowns upon us because we are the parents of that child. Or maybe my husband or my wife has done something that has disgraced the family and the community. And God has forsaken us. And so I'm passed through the fires of affliction, these horrible fiery ordeals; disgrace, the opposite of grace where God seemed to be with me and guided me. But he will not turn back until he's accomplished the intents of his mind. In the latter days, you will understand it clearly and forgive all and be happy that he in his infinite wisdom and mercy could put me through that fiery ordeal to bring me out qualified to fit into his eternal temple.

So no one will be condemned in the end. No one will be unsaved. So when they ask you, "What must I do to be saved?" Go to scripture and show them that "with man it is impossible"—that's the 10th chapter of the Book of Mark. With man, no, it isn't possible—Mark 10:26, 27—but "with *God all* things are possible." But they couldn't understand how any man could be saved after he told them what he had told them, about the camel and the rich man. Now the rich does not mean necessarily a man who has money. As the very first beatitude tells you, "Blessed are the poor in spirit, for they shall receive the kingdom" (Matthew 5:3). The *poor* in spirit is the one who is not complacent. In other words, not everyone who has money is complacent. You could be socially prominent and be very complacent—you're above it all. Or you could be intellectually a snob. You have your PhD, you have all these degrees behind you, and you're above it all. You know everything because conferred upon you is a degree given by man. You ask others, "Have you a degree?" No. "Not even a little one?" No. And so then all of a sudden you become the grand snob. And they are all over the world. In this world of ours, there is so much of real *learned* ignorance.

I'm not saying that all who have their degrees are. You should get it, but you cannot by these earn the kingdom no matter what you do, for the wisdom of this world is *foolishness* in the eyes of God. Not a thing that man knows here through his efforts will in any way function where he is destined to be. For he's rising into a world that will be completely subject to his imaginative power, but completely subject to it. Everything in the world will be under his control, but everything. Because God, having given himself to man and being all-wise, he'll be all-wise; God being all-powerful, he'll be all-powerful; God being all-loving, he'll be all-loving. For he gives himself to man. And in that world, there's nothing that is not under his control but nothing. And so you will not be replaced by anyone, and all will be equal in the eyes of God because it's himself. He can't be more than what he gave you. So one cannot be greater, because he can't get more than God gave him, for he gave him himself. It is his purpose to give you himself as though there were no other in the world, just God and you, and finally, only you because he actually gave himself to you.

Now let us go into the Silence.

*   *   *

Q: (inaudible)
A: (inaudible)
Q: (inaudible)
A: No, my dear. The wheels of Ezekiel are not incarnations. There are two births: this birth and the spiritual birth. But man does not die when he appears to die. I have gone into worlds as real as this world, just as real. And so if you do not have the second birth before the world calls you dead, don't think you're dead. You will have it. And in that world into which I have gone, people are just as solidly real as they are here. I don't put my hands around them and go through them; they're solid, just as solid as you are. And yet it's not this world. Seated in my chair or on my couch, I have seen a world that I should not see because reason drifted and I knew that my eye is closed. I am seeing something that is so vividly real, and with my eyes open, I should not be able to see that. I should see the familiar pictures on the wall and the familiar objects in my room, but I'm not seeing that. And then consciousness follows my vision, and I stepped into the world that I contemplate. Stepping into that world, it closes around me like closing the door, and I'm completely shut out of this world. I'm in that world, and that world is just as real as this. But that's not heaven; that's this world. These are worlds within worlds within worlds where man completes his wonderful—call

it evolution, if you will; I don't like the name or the word but call it that—completes his evolution within this peculiar time slot. Within that time slot, he completes it.

Q: (inaudible)

A: How would I explain my experience in the void? Well, when I step into these worlds, the world is just as real as this, just as real as this. That I have had an experience of the void? Yes. We've all had ___(??), but that's not the world of which I speak. When a man dies here, he doesn't really die. I've made the statement time and again: the little flower that blooms once blooms forever. It doesn't die. I'll take it from my lapel, pluck it out of my lapel, and throw it away. But it cannot die. He's the God of the living, not the dead.

It was revealed so vividly, but man doesn't quite see it. And all of a sudden, Moses of thousands of years and Elijah of thousands of years appear on the mount of transfiguration, proving I am the God of the living not the dead. Nothing dies. You can be shot and be perfectly riddled with holes, but you can't die. And you're not gossamer; you're solidly real. You can be hurt in that world as you can be hurt here. There's a difference between survival and resurrection. Survival is continuity; resurrection is discontinuity. Entirely different worlds. When one is resurrected, they enter heaven; they enter an entirely different world. But when one survives, it's a continuous state. But memory is short, and the presentation is not quite the presentation as it was here; therefore, he doesn't remember. He doesn't remember. He comes upon a scene that he *should* remember, but it came in a different sequence and so he doesn't remember.

Q: (inaudible)

A: I say, in my own case, I fused with God. That was not any fourth dimension or any other dimension; it was simply heaven. I was brought into his presence and presented to the Ancient of Days. And when I answered the question he asked of me and I answered it correctly, "the greatest thing in the world is love," he embraced me. In that vivid embrace, I fused with his body and became one with the body of God—a delight that you cannot describe in words. There's no way to describe it. And in that sheer delight in the body of God, I was then brought before the presence of infinite might and commanded to act. So I can't say it was any fourth dimension or sixth dimension or any other dimension. I only know that I became one with the body of the being who embraced me. And I have no knowledge that there was ever a divorce, one with that body, although I am individualized here.

And so the drama was completed as stated in the very beginning of the Book of Genesis. Read it in the end of the second chapter. For the commandment of God to man is really God to himself. And so a man must leave all and cleave to his wife until they become one flesh (verse 24). As you're told in the 54th chapter of the Book of Isaiah, "Your Maker is your husband, the Lord of hosts is his name" (verse 5). So my Maker is my husband, and the Maker is God. He has to leave all and cleave to me until we became one flesh. And in *that* day we became one flesh, and there's been no divorce or separation since. Yet I'm wearing this garment that is subject to all the ills and misfortunes of the journey.

But that drama took place in the soul. And he had to create me, and he was my Maker and he's my husband and I am his bride. I must bear his Son. And I bore his Son. And yet we are one. I, a man, a father of two in this world, and have no compunction whatsoever when I mention that I am the bride of God.

Goodnight.

CHRIST UNVEILED

March 15, 1963

Tonight's subject is "Christ Unveiled." That's quite a tall order, for we are told in the Book of Mark, the 13th chapter, the 21st verse, "If anyone says, 'Look, there is Christ!' or 'Look, here he is!' believe him not." And I endorse that 100 percent. "If anyone dares to tell you, 'Look, there is Christ!' or 'Look, here he is!' believe him not." But listen to it carefully and see the pronoun used in that sentence: "Here *he* is," believe him not.

So here, who is Christ? What is Christ? Where is Christ? Paul found him; and having found him he said, "From now on we regard no one from a human point of view; even though we once regarded Christ from a human point of view, we regard him thus no longer." If you're taking notes, that's Paul's second letter to the Corinthians, the 5th chapter, the 16th verse. He regards him not from now on as man. He thought he was man and went out to destroy those who believed in Christ as a man. Then we are told in Peter's letter, his 1st letter, the 1st chapter, read the 10th and 11th verses: "That the prophets who prophesied . . . they inquired what person or time was indicated by the Spirit of Christ within *them* when predicting the sufferings of Christ and the subsequent glory." They thought they were looking for a person, and they wondered when he would come. There was no reply to that save "it was revealed to them that they were not serving themselves, but serving you." So what is Christ? I tell you, Christ is the *way* of salvation; Christ is the *way* to the Father.

Now we'll turn back to the gospels, where we have all these events together. For scripture, as we understand it, says, the New Testament, Christianity is based on the affirmation that a certain series of events happened in which God revealed himself in action for the salvation of man. Did they happen? I tell you from *experience* that they happened. Not only did they happen but also they are *happening*—they are taking place at every moment of time in our world. If you have not experienced these events, may I tell you that you are going to. Not a thing in this world that you will ever do that would stop it. You are going to because God will not fail, no, not in one being in this world.

So here we are told the events were assembled. Luke, in his first four verses, makes the statement: "That many undertook to compile a narrative of the things which have happened or have been accomplished among us, just as they were delivered by those who from the beginning were eyewitnesses and ministers of the word." So here we have the oral tradition. They're all talking about it; these things happened, and they're telling it. But then came the moment in time that many undertook to put it into written form, And so he thought it wise to do the same thing. So he said, "Having observed all things closely for some time past." Then he thought that he too would put it into the written form for one called Theophilus. Theophilus means "one who loves God."

So he's speaking to you. You love God and I love God, for he's the source of everything. He's the source of our life; he is the end of all things. And so he is addressing his remarks to you, "O dear Theophilus, that you may know the truth concerning the things of which you have been informed." And so we heard it orally. I did as a child. And then when I began to read and write, I could read it for myself, but I didn't understand it. But before I could read it, Mother taught it to me. Then I was sent to school, and then they taught it to me in school. Then I go to Sunday school, and there I heard the story by the teacher. And so we heard it orally; then came the moment in time that we could read it for ourselves, and then came this closed book.

Let us see if we can find and unveil Christ tonight. In the 16th chapter of the gospel of Matthew, one called Christ Jesus turns to his disciples, and he asks the question, "Who do men say that the Son of man is?" They replied, "Some say John the Baptist, others say Elijah, and others say Jeremiah or one of the prophets." And he said to them, "But who do *you* say that I am?" Right away that second question identifies it with the Son of man. The first question is "Who do men say that the Son of man is?" and the second question is, "But who do *you* say that *I am*?" So he's asking the question about the Son of man, and then he's asking the question about himself. "But who do you say that I am?" Now he identifies himself with the Son of man. And Peter replies, "You are the Christ, the Son of the living God." To this, he answered, "Blessed are you, Simon Bar-Jona! For flesh and blood has not revealed this to you, but my Father who is in heaven" (verse 17). He confesses that no flesh and blood could have told him; it had to come by revelation. Now, where do we find this same flesh and blood revelation? We find it in Galatians, the 1ˢᵗ chapter, and Paul said, "When it pleased God to reveal his Son *in me*, I conferred not with flesh and blood (verse 16)." That mortal mind could not reveal no matter how it rationalized; no matter how it tried to unravel this mystery, it can't. It has to be revealed. It has to be completely unfolded in the individual. So he said, "I am the Son of man."

Well, now we go back into the Old Testament to find this cue. Where did God promise this? We turn to the 7ᵗʰ chapter of the 2ⁿᵈ Book of Samuel and this is a vision, for we are told between the 8th verse and 17th verse that Nathan received the vision, and according to all these words and according to all this vision, Nathan spoke unto David. This is what he told David: "And the Lord of hosts said unto me, 'Go to my servant David . . . and say to David that when your days are fulfilled and you lie down with your fathers, I will raise up your son after you, who shall come forth from your body. *I* will be his father, and he shall be *my* son." Here we have to now spiritualize the mission of David. Here is David, a man. If "I will raise up your son after you," then he's David's son. I can't deny that. "I will raise up *your* son after you, who will come forth from your body. I (now the Lord is speaking) will be his father and he shall be my son." So if he is the son of David, then he is the Son of man. If, on the other hand, the Lord adopts him—"He shall be my son"—then he is the Son of God.

So in this question, "Who do men say the Son of man is?" and they all thought of all kinds of things. He said, "But who do you say that I am?" "You are Christ the Son of God." And right away you think in terms of Christ the Son of God, and yet he's Son of man, then you think of *a* man. And it isn't so at all. Here is a man as you are, whether you be male or female, walking the earth. You've heard this story orally, and when you began to read you could read it for yourself. You didn't understand it but you read it. And you are playing your normal part in this world; and one day, when you least expected it—in fact, you never expected it, as you always thought it happened 2,000 years ago to one person and that was *it—you* are that person. It is happening to you, and you go through the entire series of events as recorded in scripture. And then you know who Christ is.

Christ is the *way* to the Father, and there is no other way. "I am the way." To what? ___(??) to everything in this world, but specifically to the Father. "I am the way. No one comes unto the Father but by me" as told us in the 14ᵗʰ of chapter of John. But no one comes unto the Father but by me, so here is the *way*. Well, what is the way? And then you search the scripture and you find the way. The way you just determined is ___(??) in the beginning. Now listen to these words, this statement, carefully—Paul's letter to the Ephesians—"He is the image of the invisible God, the firstborn of all creation.". "He is the image of the invisible God, the firstborn of all creation." I think that's the fifteenth verse, but you can easily check it (Colossians 1:15).

Now where is this statement in the Old Testament, because the New is only the fulfillment of the Old? The whole is in the Old, and the New is simply fulfillment. Well, where is it in the Old? You'll find it in the 8th chapter of the Book of Proverbs: "The Lord created me at the *beginning* of his way, the *first* of his acts of old" (verse 22). "Ages ago I was set up, before the beginning of the world. When he laid out the foundation of the world, I was with him, beside him, like a little child" (verse 30). Here is God's *way* of salvation. But God's way in scripture is always personified. Every attribute of man's mind, which is God's mind, is always personified. When it's wealth, you see wealth as a man. When it's power, you see power but it's a man. When you meet infinite might, it's a man. ___(??) it's a man. And so all the attributes of mind are always personified because God is man and man is God.

So he personifies this *way*, that *way* that was in the beginning. This is not improvised. Before God brought the whole vast world into being, he plotted and planned a *way*, a way of redemption for all of us. This is not an afterthought of God; it came first: "I am the first of his acts of old." Before he brought forth the world, the universe, anything, he planned a *way*; and the way was to God personified as a little child. "I was daily his delight, rejoicing before him always, rejoicing in the inhabited universe and delighting in the sons of men." Now listen carefully, "He who finds me finds life and obtains the favor from the Lord; he who misses me injures himself; all who hate me love death." That's the eighth of Proverbs (verse 35).

Now where do we find this in the New Testament, this second part we just quoted? The very first words uttered by Jesus recorded in scripture you find in the last few verses of the 2nd chapter of Luke. It takes place in the synagogue, in the temple, and his parents said, "Why did you do this unto us?" He replied, speaking about seeking him, "Why did you seek me? Do you not know that I must be in my Father's house?" And they did not understand the saying . . . but the mother kept these things in her heart. Then Jesus grew in years, in wisdom . . . and in the favor of the Lord." The first recorded utterance of Jesus in scripture, when he was only a lad, a child, in his father's presence: "Do you not know I must be in my Father's house?" Well, where's my Father's house? He said, "Heaven is the throne of God and heaven is within you" (Luke 17:21). Where do you find him? You will seek him. Where would you seek him? They sought him elsewhere. They couldn't find him until they found him *in* the Father's house. For you are the temple of the living God. It's called the synagogue, outwardly; that's only a symbol of what you really are. *You* are the synagogue; you are the temple of the living God. I will not find the *way* until I find it in myself.

And I find him without searching for him. One day, it's going to please God—for this comes at the fullness of time—when it pleases God, and he sees in me the ripeness that he's looking for, and then he unfolds me in his home by the series of events. First, the birth, then the discovery of his Son, and then the splitting of the temple. And there I am taken into his home, and his home is within me. And may I tell you, just as it's described in that 13th chapter of Mark, there is a most frightening earthquake when you are taken into the home. And you are the cause of it. When you move up and move into that heavenly state within you, there is a vibration that you've never experienced before. Speak of an earthquake! The whole vast world within you begins to shake because *you* have been redeemed. You are brought in, and there's a joy beyond the wildest dream you've ever conceived because one more has been brought into the temple, into the house of God. It's true, just as I've told you.

So Christ? Christ is a *way*, the way of redemption, and the *way* is in man. "The Lord created me at the beginning of his way, the *first* of his acts of old." So before he brought forth a star, anything in the world, he created a way of return to himself, and that way is called Christ in the Bible. And the people sought it: "The prophets who prophesied inquired as to what person," and to this day in 1963, they're still looking for a person. Every year, you see the papers; they're always looking for some person coming into the world that will be Christ. And they're always so eager to find a Christ on the outside that they will follow. They found one in Hitler, one in Stalin, and one in someone else; they were always the savior of the world. But read now that same one we quoted earlier, the 13th chapter of Mark, the 21st verse, "If anyone says to you, 'Look, there is Christ!' or 'Look, here he is!' do not believe it." You'll never find him in another.

But in no being in this world would you find Christ. You either find him in yourself as the way that leads you to God or you never find him. But you will find him. Everyone will find him. And when they find him, they'll find him as the *way*. So he said, "I am the way. I am the truth. I am the life. I am the resurrection. I am the door." There is no other door. You can't get through any other way. And this is the *way* to the Father. And so the way is inwoven in every child in this world, and that child will find the way when God is ready for him; for only God knows that moment in eternity when he will awaken that child.

Now why are we called, in the 7th chapter of 2nd Samuel, "those who sleep with the fathers"? Here we are three billion in the world today. And "When your days are fulfilled and you lie down with your fathers, I will raise up your son." "When you lie down with your fathers, I will raise up your son after you, who will come forth from your body." And you think therefore of the fathers. May I tell you, *you* are the fathers. You've already fulfilled your day in preparation and now you are sleeping with the fathers. You are sound asleep, but you don't know it. You came here tonight as a conscious being and you go home tonight very hungry, drive your cars, or walk or take the bus to get off at the right point and to go to bed; and you'll be fully conscious of the fact *that's* where you're going to sleep. But all prior to that, you were awake, for you did all these things consciously. And may I tell you, I have observed my brother, Bruce; from the time he was born, he was a sleepwalker. Bruce would come downstairs, go to the larder, unlock the larder, pour some milk, put some jam on a piece of bread, eat it and drink his milk, walk around objects that we put in his place, and we would do everything to make him fall on his neck. Boys will do that. But he never did. He never struck a chair, but walked around the chair. He would go upstairs, go back to bed, and go sound asleep; and he was totally unaware that he'd done anything in this world that was to him unnatural.

The only person in this world that convinced him that he did it, as we told him he did it, was my mother. Mother would say, "Yes, Bruce, you did it." "But, mother, I couldn't have done it." But he would not oppose mother. He would oppose us but not mother. Not that she would have done anything violent to him because mother wasn't that way. But he couldn't distrust my mother. Not one of us could distrust her. She was to us the ideal. After all, she wouldn't lie to us; that's what we believed. And so our brother Bruce trusted her. But he couldn't; he would rack his brain to find out how he did it. He would get out of bed, go down the stairs, open the larder, put some butter on the bread or put some jelly on the bread, eat it, drink some milk, walk around the objects that we put in his way, go back to bed, and be totally unaware that he'd done it.

That taught me a lesson in my mature years. Not when I did it to him as a child but in my mature years, when I was awakened to find that I had been asleep all through the ages, and I didn't know it. All through the ages I had been sleeping, and how long are these ages? Now Paul tells us in his letter to the Colossians, I will tell you a mystery, a mystery that has been hidden for ages and generations. The mystery is Christ in you, the hope of glory (1:26). He tells us a mystery. The mystery is Christ in *us*, the hope of glory. Well, here, I didn't understand it any more than the world understood it, and one day it happened. God in his infinite mercy looked upon me and found me ripe at that moment, and he awoke me. As he awoke me, I awoke for the first time in eternity, and I was sealed in a tomb, and the tomb was my skull. I was completely sealed in a tomb, and the tomb was my skull. And then

God rolled away the stone, and I came out. But until that moment, I never thought for one moment I was asleep. Not only asleep but the sleep was so deep, so profound I was dead. So profound was that sleep that I was dead, for when I awoke, I was in a tomb, and you don't put anyone in a tomb unless they are dead. And so when you enter that tomb, you're dead.

So you are one with Christ who *died* for you—he is the Way—and together you are completely sealed in a tomb. But you don't know it. I didn't know it. But may I tell you, I have never been more awake in eternity. And when I saw things round about me and saw them all objectively, and they couldn't see me, then I understood the words, "He is the image of the invisible God" (Colossians 1:15). The image, how can you be the image of something invisible? These are the words: "He is the image of the invisible God, the first of all that was created." How could I actually reflect something that's invisible? But it's true that you are the image of the invisible God. And nothing that is mortal that looks at you can see you. You are more real than any being in the world when you look at them.

And then the whole thing began to come back, and I began to see these experiences that I had gone through. And I wondered, for it puzzled me, looking at you and looking at myself, bathing, shaving, taking care of the body; and it seemed so alive. It seemed so independent of any man's perception of it. I could leave the room in spite of what my wife would suggest; I could do what I wanted to do within certain areas, and yet at this moment in time, I realized that this isn't so at all. When I awoke, *then* I realized an experience I had many years before of God bringing me to that point of awakening. When one moment in time he took me, took me into a world just like this, and showed me the power that was mine tomorrow, mine in complete control.

But he allowed me to exercise it just for a moment, and I saw people just like you. As I saw them, I ___(??) within myself arrested a rhythm, an action. As I did it, the people that I observed stood still. They couldn't move and nothing moved. Things that were in space stood still; everything stood still. And now how could this be? ___(??) and they couldn't move. But when I released within myself that activity that I had arrested, they all moved on and completed their intentions. And then it broke. Then on several occasions, he has taken me into the same, not the same scene but similar scenes. So I would come upon a scene, and I knew if I could stop within myself an activity which I felt it would stop. I did it and it stopped. Then I understood what he meant: "As the Father has life in himself, so he has granted unto the Son to have life in himself" (John 5:26).

So everyone is destined to have life in himself. And then you wonder, then what are all these garments? What are all these things round about us, this thing called Neville, and you that I know and love? What are all these? Are these really costumes? Is something being formed in us that is the image of the invisible God, and we have to play these parts and wear these costumes for a moment? I have concluded that that's so. That the whole vast world is truly, as Shakespeare said, a stage; and all the men in it are merely players, and one man plays many parts in his time. And so the being playing it all is God, individualizing himself, begetting himself. Just as we are told in that 7th chapter of 2nd Samuel: "I will raise up your son after you, who will come forth from your body. *I* will be his father and he shall be my son." So out of this human body, something is coming forward that is going to be called Son of man because it comes out of a man; but it is going to be the Son of God, and it's the image of the invisible God. Something is being formed in man, and he brings him forward.

And may I tell you, it's your own sense of I-ness. No loss in identity when you are awakened, but none whatsoever, none. So I will know you in eternity; you'll know me in eternity. But for all the sameness of identity and we know each other, there's going to be a *radical* discontinuity of form, a radical discontinuity of form. You have no idea how beautiful you really are. Human face yes. Human hands yes. Human feet yes. The human body no. Not this body, not for one moment! And I can't describe it to you. Not that I wouldn't if I could; I can't describe it. You are beautiful beyond measure, the being that you really are. If I made an attempt, it would only be just radiant light, like, well, a rainbow. How would I describe it, the being that you really are? But I will know you, and you'll know me, for there's a sameness of identity and human enough to recognize each other. But the form, a radical, radical discontinuity of form, and I can't describe it. You can display it; and you know who you are; and then you return to this that someday you'll put down and put down forever. And this is essential.

But before these came into being, God mapped out his Way, and the Way was called Christ. No one understood what Christ was. They thought it was a man who would come and save the world. Men were always looking for the coming of Christ as a man, and Christ is the *way* of salvation, not a man. But *in* man, in you, you are David; he brings forward your son, but that's his son. Then you will understand that great opening statement in Matthew: "This is the book of the genealogy of Jesus Christ, son of David." But then *he* brings up the question, "What think ye of the Christ? Whose *Son* is he?" (Matthew 22:42). The question isn't complete until you listen to the last part, "Whose Son is he?" "The son of David." Well, then, "Why did David call him Father?" You see the Son of man is also Son of God. But the Son of God and God are one: "I and my Father are one" (John 10:30). You get it? I and my Father are one, and yet I am Son of man. This is man and out of man comes a being that is God's son. Then, David, who played this fantastic part, which is now universal humanity, becomes the Son of man. You follow it? Son of man is one with the Son of God. And that out of which the Son of man comes who *is* the Son of God in turn becomes the Son of man. You follow me? If you don't, ask me when the questions are in order. Son of man—Son of God—God. The Son of God and God are one; yet the Son of God cannot deny he's a father, a man, and therefore, the Son of man.

There's a question asked in that sixteenth of Matthew, "Who do they say the Son of man is?" Naturally, because he's Son of man, you've got to think in terms of man; so they say, "Well, he is John the Baptist, he is Elijah, he is Jeremiah or one of the prophets," so they mention man. Now he doesn't follow with that, he doesn't ask any further question about that. He changes now: "But who do *you* say that *I am*?" He's asking now, "Who am I? I asked you of the Son of man. I'm telling you I am the Son of man, but who am I? And they mention, "You are the Christ, the Son of God." Now he tells them, "Simon, flesh and blood could not have told you this. It had to be revealed by my Father who is in heaven" (verse 13-17).

So here, he comes down to the foundation: Who is the Son of man, who is the Son of God, and who is God? It comes out of David. Well, that was the promise given to him. So David is collective humanity; out of David comes the Son of man, and that Son of man is the Son of God. Well, when the Son of God awakens, he has to have a son, and it is David. David never got beyond that age of twelve, where he appears (in that 2nd chapter of Luke) in the temple. They ask, "Where were you? We've been looking all over for you. Why did you do this unto us?" And "Why did you seek me?"—they were seeking him. "And you couldn't find me until you found me in my Father's house." Why would you seek me elsewhere? You were looking all over for me. "Do you not know I must be in my Father's house?" (verse 49). You can't find me, but if you find me, you find life: "He who finds me finds life and receives the favor of the Lord."

And when you find life, you'll do to every form in this world what has been my privilege to do at these moments when I was taken in spirit and shown sections of humanity and stopped them. No matter what they were doing, just stop them, and they could go no further. And then I released it, and they completed their actions. I stopped them again, and they could go no further. A bird flying, I stopped it, and it didn't fall, but it could go no further. A leaf falling, I stopped it; it could go no further. And then you ask fantastic questions in the depth of your soul, "What's it all about?" And you come to the conclusion that the whole vast world—all the men, women, and children and everything in it—is the resultant state of God's first creative act, and all this was brought into being like a resultant state. And you are not these garments of flesh at all. Something is being formed in this garment of flesh. What is being formed? It's called the Son of man. But God calls it his Son, and his Son and himself are one. So God is begetting himself in man, his very own self. And the day will come that the individual will be able to say to himself, he's not only begetting his Son in me, he *begot* his Son in me, and I and my Father are one. For when you are awakened, there's no other being; it's you. You awaken *in* yourself to discover that you've been sound asleep and really dead for these unnumbered years. So when he tells us in his letter to the Colossians, I will tell you a secret, "a secret hidden for ages and generations . . . Christ *in you*, the hope of glory" (1:26, 27). There's a way in man that leads him to God, but man doesn't know it. He thinks he's completely awake and independent.

I can go back, oh, maybe thirty years ago and I would walk up Broadway, and it happened to me so often. I was young and strong; I was a dancer, a professional dancer. Not a thing was wrong with me. And yet I would walk up Broadway, and all of a sudden I knew that someone was arresting me, and I couldn't walk. I would stop in the street, and I couldn't put one foot in front of the other. I didn't understand it then. Then I would be released, and I'd walk on. Then it would happen again; on the sidewalk I could not move, and I was fully alert, conscious, seemingly, but I was still. And I know now that someone was doing to me then what I, years later, was taken in spirit to do to others. I was being trained and prepared to do the same thing to another that was done to me: I could not move. And yet I was playing on Broadway. I had my four little shows. I played every theater east of the Mississippi. I had my six Broadway shows. I was a strong, strapping fellow, dancing for a living, a professional dancer. And so not a thing was wrong with me, and yet I couldn't move. Walking up the street, all alert, and suddenly I am still. I could feel something holding me, not embracing me, but I could feel something binding, and I couldn't move. I stood there paralyzed. Then after a few minutes or so, whatever it was released me and I moved on.

So I was used as the guinea pig by someone who was being introduced to this power in himself, just as I, years later, used others as a guinea pig when I was being introduced to that same power. "For as the Father has life in himself, so he grants the son also to have life in himself"—as he is about to awaken *that* son (John 5:26). And he knows it who is being ripened, for we all must conform to the image of the invisible God. When the image is coming into view in the eye of God, then he introduces that being, who's going to be his son, to the power that he will exercise tomorrow. And so he takes him in spirit and shows him this fabulous world, and he has control over it.

And so what is the world? The world is a stage. And you are not the garment you are wearing, but I'll recognize you. There's a certain identity, a sameness of identity, and you and I will know each other in eternity. But for all this sameness of identity, there's a radical but *radical* discontinuity of form.

So this body of ours—face, yes; hands, yes; feet, yes, but not the body. You're beautiful beyond your wildest dream!

Now let us go into the Silence.

*   *   *

Q: ___(??) the Bible calls perfect love will cast out all fears?

A: The Bible speaks of perfect love casting out all fear? Well, my dear, if you came into a world, like this room for instance, and you could multiply this to encompass the entire world, but should you come into a place, say, as large as this with an audience like this; and suddenly you knew in the depth of your soul that you by stilling not them but by stilling an activity in yourself that everyone would be still, and you did it and proved the truth of your intuition, who then could disturb you? If you were faced now with the most horrible thing in the world, and you by stilling an activity in yourself made it still; and it is so still it could outlast marble, if you didn't release that activity in yourself, you wouldn't have to embalm it. It wouldn't decay. It would stand just as it is.

Suppose you were faced with an army of millions armed to the teeth with their earthly might, and then you still the activity in you that gave them motion. Then suppose in you, you could change their intentions or direct them, you could by changing their direction march them into the ocean; and when they got beyond sight, you released the activity within you, then what would happen to them? They would be once more flesh and blood, and they would drown. Do you know that? But you wouldn't do that because you would not be afraid of man, they're only men.

So all this processing that God is extracting his Son from man, so it is from man; therefore, it is man's son. "I will raise up your son after you, who shall come forth from your body. But *I* will be his father, and *he* shall be my son." So God is begetting his Son in man, bringing him out of man. You can't deny he came out of man; therefore, it's man's son. It's man's offspring, but it's *God's Son* now. For this is going to be done differently. This that comes through the world, my son, came from the womb of my wife. But when my son in this world, who came from the womb of his mother, is brought forth from that body, he's brought forth from his skull; that's the second birth. There are two births: one from the womb of woman, and one is from the skull of man. As the second brings him forth from the skull—that's God's Son. But he brings forth garments from the womb of woman.

Now the question is asked in the Book of Timothy, "And how will woman be saved?" because man can't quite understand "generic" man. So the question is asked, "Well, how will woman be saved?" It's wrongly translated (the answer): "And woman will be saved by the bearing of *the* child." Unfortunately, they put that in the footnote, and they give as the answer, "Woman will be saved by bearing children." Hasn't a thing to do with any bearing of children. Woman will be saved by the bearing of *the* child, just as *man* is saved. But they can't believe that man could bear a child. He can sire one, but he can't bear one. Yet the question is asked in the Book of Jeremiah, "Can man have a child, can he bear a child?" The question is not answered. But God answered it by stating what he has seen, having asked the question. So the Lord asked the question, "Can a man bear a child? Why then do I see every man with his hands delivering himself, pulling himself out of himself, just like a woman in labor?" So that is posed in the Book of Jeremiah, the 30th chapter, (verse 6). And in the 2nd chapter of 1st Timothy, "How then will woman be saved?" and I tell you the true translation of that Greek phrase "by the bearing of the child"—the footnote uses it—it tells you the literal Greek is "the bearing of the child." But they cannot understand it anymore than they could understand Jeremiah when they say, "woman will be saved by bearing children." Hasn't anything to do with bearing children.

Salvation is something entirely different: out of the skull of generic man, male or female. The symbolism is the first step in the great Way, called Christ. Christ is the Way. The first is the birth of the individual, while being resurrected, symbolized as that of a child. They find the *sign* that they were told they would find when this event takes place in eternity. *They* will find the sign, and the sign is a child. They will tell you it is your child, and they'll give it to you. You'll hold it, as told in the Book of Luke, and you'll have a joy in seeing the Way of salvation. There's a definite Way, and there's no other Way.

People say, "Well, there must be another way." I swear there is no other way. The foundation is the only foundation. Don't try to get away from it; it's the *only* foundation. It's all in the Hebraic world as a promise. So it is said, "He opened unto them the scriptures." Then they said within themselves, "Did our hearts not burn when he opened to us the scriptures? And beginning with Moses and all through the prophets and the Psalms, he interpreted to them all concerning himself" (Luke 24:27). The whole thing is about himself. That's you.

Moses rejoiced. He rejoiced for what? Why, he endured all the fires of Egypt and gave up all the treasures of Egypt because he considered the wealth of Christ far greater, having endured as seeing him who is invisible. He endured. Well, now you read the story of Moses, how would you say Moses, who preceded him by thousands of years, endured as seeing him? Well, that's told you in the 11th chapter of the Book of Hebrews (verse 27), "Moses endured as seeing him who is invisible." Now we are told, "Abraham rejoiced that he was to see my day; he saw it and was glad" (John 8:56). How could Abraham rejoice?

Everything was in preparation and then came that moment in time when the *first* could be brought forward. But from that moment on, all are being brought forward. How many in this world, I don't know. But all are being brought forward and not one will fail. So God is doing it: "He who began a good work in you will bring it to completion at the day of Jesus Christ" (Philippians 1:6). And so the day is coming when that moment in time you're the image of the invisible God that's bringing you out. Can't bring you out before you conform to the image of the invisible God, for you must be one with your Father that you may be one with him in the true essence of the word: "I and my Father are one."

Q: (inaudible)

A: Well, we have that in the gospels. Two of them, John and Luke, give the first words of Jesus concerning a search. John will give you the first words of Jesus, "What do you seek?" and the two disciples, not yet named, answered, "Where do you live? Where are you staying?" He said, "Follow me" (John 1:38, 43). So these are the first recorded words. But then Jesus is a man fully grown. Luke records the first words of the character called Jesus as a child in the temple, which we quoted earlier, "Did you not know I must be in my Father's house?" Mark quotes it: "The days are fulfilled and the kingdom of God is at hand; repent, and believe the gospel" (Mark 1:15). That's Mark's presentation. Matthew brings it in—in a conversation with God. John recognizes it's the Lamb of God, who takes away the sins of the world. And then the first words given into Jesus' mouth, "Suffer it so to be now" (Matthew 3:15). In other words, not suffering as we use the word suffer—suffer means "to allow it"—to allow a thing is to suffer it. I will suffer it; I will allow it. And so, "Suffer it so to be now."

So he will assume the physical limitation expected of man because he *is* man, for here is a man that is now about to be awakened, completely awakened. But he's still man, and he doesn't deny in the true sense that you will bury me. They will look at him and see him buried and to his social background, his intellectual background, but he had an experience to take him completely out of this way. And so allow it, this is what man demands. And so if man demands these physical things, I would allow it. I'm not going to disturb society, and think they shouldn't go to church; allow it. But these marvelous things when they lose their understood meanings or they make rituals for the churches, then they crystallize into, well, ___(??) symbols, really.

So allow it now. For this baptism, which is not mentioned in John, the most mystical of all, is mentioned in the others. So he allows it. It's part of the mystery. You were baptized. I was baptized. Mother allowed it. Yet before she baptized me, a voice spoke to her out of space and called me by my name. She knew in some sense that he was destined for something different, but she had to allow it. And so they threw water in my face. It may have given me a cold, I don't know. ___(??) do in this world. I was baptized and therefore christened, and yet she had the voice speaking to her prior to that physical act. But she had to go through the physical act because she would have thought for one moment that Neville would never be saved. That was her concept of life: physical baptism meant saved. That if you were not baptized, you couldn't be saved. So she was determined to save her child. When she came to this country and saw that I had a little boy, who was then two years old, and she had to have him christened. She said to me, "Is he christened?" I said no. I said, "No, I see no reason for it." She said, "Neville, if he dies tonight, he can't go to heaven." So to satisfy Mother and to satisfy her feelings, I took him the next week down to the church and had him baptized, and Mother was satisfied. Now he's baptized.

Q: Neville, would it be correct to say that sensory perception is merely an illusion? Is that correct?

A: ___(??) then she told me that she had a vision, and at the end of the vision, she realized this play, and realized that when the curtain really comes down on the final act, you will thank every being in the world for playing the part they played relative to you, even those who murdered you. For without all these parts being played, you could not have been awakened. So those who imprisoned you, those who hurt you, those who accused you wrongly, those who spat in your face, and those who did everything in this world to you contributed to your waking. And she said, I thought at the end . . . (Tape ends.)

IN THESE LAST DAYS BY HIS SON

March 19, 1963

___(??) "In these last days by his Son." I know from my own personal experience across this country that scientists and philosophers that I meet or are introduced to me as brilliant minds are unwilling to accept as explanation anything beyond and above this world of nature. I begin to discuss with them my personal mystical experiences; they want me to bring it down to this world—I'm not a physicist, I'm not a scientist, and I'm not a philosopher—but bring it down and explain to them in terms of the structure of this world. So I can't do it. I can only tell what has happened to me.

So tonight's subject, which is "In these last days by his Son," and this is taken from the epistle to the Hebrews. The author is unknown, it's unsigned, and it's really not addressed to anyone in particular. He doesn't address it to the Corinthians, or this or the other; it's simply an epistle to the Hebrews. And so, *we* are the Hebrews; he's addressing it to us. This one begins his letter: "In many and various ways God spoke of old to our fathers by the prophets; but in these *last* days he has spoken to us by his Son" (Hebrews 1:1). A few verses on, which is the fifth verse, he pinpoints the Son by quoting scripture. For this author bases his entire argument upon scripture, which he quotes or refers to in every chapter. So in the fifth verse, he pinpoints the Son for us by quoting scripture. He's trying to prove to his own satisfaction the superiority of man over everything in the world, for man bears the very stamp of the nature of God; he makes that plain. And now he comes to this quote, and he quotes for us first the 7th verse of the 2nd chapter of Psalms. He asks the question, "To what angel did God ever say, 'Thou art my Son, today I have begotten thee'?" Or again, now he quotes 2nd Samuel, the 7th chapter, the 14th verse, so he makes the statement, ___(??) again, "I will be his father, and he shall be my son." Now, these two

130

are addressed—and anyone reading the Bible can see it—these are addressed to *David*. So he pinpoints the Son by whom he will speak in these last days. Now this is the letter to the Hebrews. Now how did he speak in many and various ways to our fathers by the prophets?

But first, the nineteenth Psalm: "The heavens are telling the glory of God; and the firmament proclaims his handiwork." I think anyone who has ever seen the heavens, even with the naked eye, would see the glory of God. But when we ask the physicist to look at it through the mathematical eye, trained as they are with the aid of telescopes, what a joy would be ours were we to look at it through *that* eye. But then we come down to the geophysicist, and the firmament proclaims his handiwork. And here we see this fantastic world in which we live today. Because here, only in our century, here, a young man in 1905 had a different concept of the world; his name was Einstein—an entirely different concept of the structure of this world—and gave us his famous equation. It startled the physicists of the day, and it still startles them, but we're living in that world today, a world of nuclear energy. And he gave that to us in 1905.

Here is a statement in Paul's letters written 2,000 years ago. You read it in the the 1st chapter, the 20th verse of his letter to the Romans: "Ever since the creation of the world, his invisible nature, namely, his eternal power and deity, has been clearly perceived in the things that have been made." Doesn't mean the chair, this building, but the elements, the eternal elements of the world. "Ever since the creation of the world his invisible nature, namely, his eternal power and deity, has been clearly perceived in the things that have been made." After 2,000 years, no one saw the structure of that basic brick of the world. But Einstein saw it and revealed it in his famous equation.

In 1928, Professor Dirac, studying his great theory, that is, Einstein's theory of relativity, postulated the existence of a little particle that he named the positron. He said, "*If* the equation is true, this *must* exist." But no one else heard of it; no one ever saw it. But he predicted the existence of that positron. Four years later, Professor Anderson proved it experimentally in his experiments with cosmic rays and had them photographed. When it first appeared, it disturbed our theoretical physicists. They never heard of it, they'd never seen one, and what to do with it? It completely upset all of their thinking concerning the structure of the universe. But now they saw it, and although they were skeptical when it was first told them by Professor Dirac, they could not now discount it. In great scientists and great physicists, they had to accept it, so they accepted it, but what to do with it? It was a great embarrassment. For this thing didn't act like anything ever heard of by man before.

And so in 1949, another great theoretical physicist by the name of Feynman, he's now at Cal Tech, and he wrote a paper on it that came out in the *Physical Journal*, a scientific journal. And this is what he said, "It's a wrong-way electron. It's upside down, so completely wrong-way its charge is positive instead of negative." It's an electron, but it's completely opposite to all that they knew concerning the electron. Then he said, "When a speeding electron hits something, it is usually deflected and continues on its way. If it is hit too hard, its time sense is reversed, and then it moves backwards in time, and *it* is a positron." It goes backward in time. If I started from here to the end of the room, and someone got in my way and deflected me and then others got in my way and deflected me, at the end of an hour, by all of these detours I found myself back here, I still am not moving backward in time. I come back here in space, but I kept on moving in the right direction of time; an hour later, I'm still here. The clock didn't go back to find me starting at eight and then finding me here at seven; they found me here at nine, with all my deflections. So an electron when speeding, if it hits something, it's deflected but continues on its way. But if it's hit too hard, its time sense is reversed, and it moves *backward* in time, something entirely different. And no one knew what to do with this ___(??).

For now we go back to the book of books, the Bible; and you listen to it carefully, for these are based upon my own experience. You've heard the story of the prodigal son, haven't you? Every minister in the world has used it and tried to explain what it means, but I don't think they come near the point. So a prodigal son went into a far country. One day, he became hungry; and when he was really starving, he came to himself and said to himself, "I'll return. I'll go back to my father's home, for he has everything." And so he made his journey back to his father's home. The father seeing him afar off ran and met him and commanded the servants to bring the *best* robe, not just a robe but the best robe, and put it on him and give him a ring and put the ring on his hand—the symbol of authority, of power, and of a princely being forever—and put shoes upon his feet. "For this my son was dead and he's alive again; he was lost and he's found" (Luke 15:11-24), when he came to himself.

And may I tell you from experience that we're all on a journey. I saw it, all of us moving in a negative direction, like the electron. An electron is a negative particle. It's proceeding without noticing that it precedes, as we do. And here we move forward in one negative direction, regardless of all the details of life. So if today you're disappointed, and you move all around and come back spatially to where you were, but you're still moving negatively in the right direction, the clock didn't turn back. But there will come a moment in time that God will hit you and hit you so hard that you will jump back in time to the one thing that begins the whole vast unfolding of God's wonderful play.

For when I was struck, may I tell you, it's an experience that no one can describe in words adequately. When you are struck from above, it's a peculiar sensation—that you think you are going to die. This is it, there's no possibility of coming out of this. But at that moment when you are struck, you are struck so hard that you are turned around, and you go back in time to an experience that took place—if today is 1963, 1,963 years ago. Were it 1959, as it was in my case, 1,959 years ago. And you jump back over that section of time, not space; and now instead of having *heard* of the story, you are the star in the drama and you enact the drama. You are the star performer of the entire play as you jump back in time.

And then here you move forward negatively with the whole vast world for another five months, and he hits you again. He hits you so hard that your time sense is reversed; and this time, you jump back not 2,000 years. You jump back 3,000 years and encounter a scene recorded 3,000 years ago. Suddenly, before your eyes comes his Son, and he speaks to you as *your* Son. You have no doubt in your mind who he is. The whole thing is so *vividly* clear to you and you've always known him. But you knew him negatively as you journeyed through these far, far countries over the ages. And then God hits you, and at intervals you jump back and jump back and jump back and enact positively God's eternal drama.

So here, we are told this is a particle discovered only in the year 1928, postulated in '28, discovered experimentally in 1932. But God is one and his name is one: The first great commandment, "Hear, O Israel, the Lord our God is one Lord." So God is one and his nature is one, so the physics of the mind cannot differ in any respect from the physics of the rest of nature. If the little particle behaves this way in this cloud chamber when they bombard it with cosmic rays and discover and photograph it, it cannot differ in any respect from that same particle in the mind of man. So God and God alone knows how to hit that mind at a moment in the journey, as we journey forward into the far country. As we are struck at that moment, it is so intense we are turned around in time, not in space, and we move back across time in the twinkle of an eye as we encounter and begin to unfold God's eternal drama.

So we are told in the 33rd chapter, read it from the 18th through the 25th verses of the Book of Exodus. Moses said to God, "Let me see thy glory" and God answered, "I will let my goodness pass before you . . . but my face you shall not see. I will cover you with my hand as I pass by; then I will take away my hand, and you will see my back; but my face shall not be seen." The face of God, everyone in the world would like to see the face of God.

They would like to see the tomorrow—that's the face of God. He shows you the back—his eternal play, all that is taking place. But everyone would like to see the face of God, and should they see the face of God, man uncivilized as he is would hurt man all the more.

I'll give you a story. Seventeen years ago, I gave a Bible class in New York City. I give them here, but this was seventeen years ago. A couple flew in, or rather they came in—whether they came by plane or train, I do not know—but they came in from San Francisco. Checked in at the Plaza Hotel, where they had a suite of rooms and lived there for six weeks while they came to my Bible class. That's not a pretty penny, may I tell you, when you check into the Plaza and take a suite of rooms. I learned afterward that they had nothing but money. They were millionaires on both sides; they had no children, were fabulously wealthy, and had this huge apartment in San Francisco up on Nob Hill. And then they had eight acres with the most fantastic home, which I saw on many occasions, here in the Holmby Hills. And so money meant nothing to them. Well, what do you think he wanted in my Bible class? And this is a Bible class; he came all the way to New York City from San Francisco to attend my Bible class, he and his wife. No children. She had one brother who was one of the huge, big financial giants in Bay area, up in San Francisco, no children. They came from a family of no children, all of them, but all had millions. And she wanted more millions. He wanted to see the face of God: if he could only see tomorrow's closing stock market quotations. And so he would sit in the hope. He read one of my books, which is now out of print and called *Out of This World*, in which I stated in this so-called *Out of This World* what someone could do.

On the strength of that they came. Money meant nothing. If they could only find out the closing prices of the stock market on Wall Street twenty-four hours before, he could make another, what, 20 million in one day. He could sell short, he could depress the market, and he could raise it; he could do anything if he could only see the face of God. But suppose he bought the paper that was printed twenty-four hours in advance and as he's moving forward quickly toward the stock market quotations, his attention is arrested by a little notice on the obituary column, and it's his. He could. He's turning quickly to make another billion; and finally, his attention is arrested, and he reads his own obituary notice that is printed for the next day, but he reads it. What do you think would happen to him? He would die at that very moment. Well, that's what he wanted to see, the face of God.

And yet I tell you it's already done. For tomorrow is all done, yet you can modify and change within certain spheres. You can do it, but it's done. Listen to these words, the 10th and 11th verses of the 1st chapter of Ecclesiastes: "Is there a thing of which it is said, 'See, this is new'? I tell you it has been before. But there's no remembrance of former things, nor shall there be any remembrance of later things to come after among those who will follow." Man can't believe that because he only has a memory of the past, and he can't see the future until one day when he is struck hard enough for his time sense to be reversed, and then he goes back. And then everything said of God in that fantastic verse that's recorded in the Book of Matthew and the Book of Luke he experiences. And now he knows who he is.

Then he is struck again, and he's brought into the presence of the Son of God, as told you in the 1st chapter, the 5th verse of Hebrews by the two quotes. You can't get it any clearer than the author—whoever he is, he's the unknown author of the epistle to the Hebrews—when he quotes that 2nd chapter, the 7th verse of Psalms: "And to what angel did he ever say, 'Thou art my Son, today I have begotten thee'?" These words are addressed to David. Or again, "I will be to him a father and he shall be to me a son." These words are addressed to David. I tell you David is humanity. The whole vast world—all races, all nations—altogether form David. But when you have the experience, all together are coalesced into one lad, and he's David. The whole vast world of humanity is David, God's only begotten Son. But when you have the experience of seeing God's only begotten Son, you don't see it as a nation, as races, one wonderful lad about twelve years old, and it's the *only* David. And it's *your* son.

So, "In many and various ways God spoke of old to our fathers by the prophets; but in these last days he has spoken unto us by a Son." It's the finality of God's revelation to the individual when he speaks to that individual by his Son. And when he speaks to him by his Son, it is then that God succeeded in giving himself to that individual. For he gave you his only begotten Son as your Son, so you are the father of God's only begotten Son. And there's nothing but God. So he gives you his Son, then you know you are truly the father, collectively, of humanity. And what aspect of your own being you wouldn't forgive? If this hand began to itch, it's easier for me to take the hand, over here, and ease it, than to take the hand and compel it to release itself. It's all part of my being. If my back began to itch and I can't reach it with my hand, I will scratch it with the door, but it's my back. So the whole vast world is my body and collectively they form one being, and that being is personified as David. And when you are struck hard enough to go back in time, you see it all as *one* man. It's your Son, and he's David.

So here, our scientists in this generation, in our generation, they have found this peculiar particle. Well, I am not a scientist, but I have found that I can use it in a way that maybe they will not admit, and you can use it. I was struck, and I jumped back in time 2,000 years in the twinkle of an eye after an enormous blow in my head delivered by God to have the experience as described in the Book of Luke. And then five months later, another blow, terrific blow, and I jumped back another thousand years in time, not in space; and then, four months later, another thousand years, where the stories are buried. It's a true story of the brazen serpent. All of these are true, that man can only encounter, for they took place unnumbered thousand years ago. You encounter them, as the star of the role, as you move backward positively in time. For we are all moving forward negatively, like sleepwalkers . . . forward.

I saw it so vividly one night, that all of this enormous crowd moving toward some invisible Mecca. And yet that very moment, it was revealed to me that I would reach six hours. I didn't know then my journey would be *backward* in time, for I was walking with them toward some invisible goal in the future, in the negative direction of time. And I had to reach six hours and go *back* in time, for God's history is completed; it's all done. And man takes God's eternal history, and he himself after his journey into a far country, like the prodigal son, and the prodigal son comes to himself because he was hungry. What is the hunger? Physical hunger? No. You're told in the 8th chapter, 11th verse of the Book of Amos that "I will send a famine upon the land; it will not be a famine for food or a thirst for water, but for the hearing of the word of God." When that famine comes to man, nothing in this world can satisfy that hunger but an experience of God, but nothing.

And so until that hunger comes, all right, we walk forward negatively, hoping we'll see tomorrow that I could take advantage of my brother. But I can't see tomorrow, not really. But I'll show you in a way how you can apply this same technique toward tomorrow. You can stand here today and assume that it is not this day, this month; you can assume it's another day of this month, forward in time, or another month, and then in your mind's eye build a world around you that would imply it *is* that day. You can go to the calendar in your mind's eye and cross "this is the day." Do anything to make it natural. When you make it natural to your mind's eye, see that things are as you desire them to be on this day. Today is Tuesday. Suppose you went forward in time and this is now, say, not March but April. Go forward into April and take a day that would mean something to you, and see that what you want today, in the month of March on this day, you now realize. Look at the calendar, see it, and talk to your friends about your accomplishment. Then open your eyes, and you're back on this day, Tuesday, on this day in the month of March. You were shocked when you came back to discover that here you are. You're like someone else turned around, and now you move forward across a series of events leading up to that day in April. When you arrive there, things will be as now you've imagined them to be. That's how you can use God's law. That was only recently discovered in the negative world we call the world of nature. You try it.

When I first read with understanding the 14th chapter of John, something in the depth of my soul told me I could apply it in this manner and I did and it worked. Then I told my audience in New York City many, many years ago what I had proven to my satisfaction and asked them to join with me in an experiment. A lady in the audience, a Mrs. Bower was her name, was a widow, and she had two homes in Brooklyn that were not in the best district to bring in money, but they were all the things that she had in this world, and no ___(??). She wanted money to repair them. She couldn't go to a bank and ask for a loan unless there were tenants. This is what she did in the month of October, in the first week of October. She assumed it was, she named a date, the twenty-ninth of October, and they were completely rented. And she felt all that she would feel were it true that they were rented. Then she opened her eyes; it's only the first week of October. By the twenty-ninth of October, every room in her two apartment buildings were rented. Every room was rented.

I said to her, "Mrs. Bower, why did you take the twenty-ninth of October? Is it an anniversary? Is there some reason for it?" She said, "No. I wanted to get a loan, but I couldn't get a loan. I didn't think I could, unless they were filled. So I wanted to get a loan on the first of November, so I took the twenty-ninth of October just to feel sure that if they were rented on the twenty-ninth of October, I could go to the bank on the first of November and get my loan." And by the twenty-ninth of October, every room was rented. She went forward in time and actually saw that it was the twenty-ninth of October. She opened her eye, and she bounced back to that day on the first week of October. She went back in time, not in space. Then she moved across a bridge of incidence, and people began to come in and rent the place, and they were all rented. So by the twenty-ninth of October, her two buildings were rented.

I discovered *that* by an experiment, just as Professor Anderson discovered the existence of the little positron that was mathematically predicted, for it fitted in with the theory of relativity. And so Professor Dirac discovered that if Einstein is correct in his theory this thing must exist. But nobody wanted it. What to do with it? It was an embarrassment because everything about it was backward. It moved backward in time, where electrons always moved forward, as they should ___(??) electrons, in time. So all of us are the electrons of God's world, and we obey willingly; we move forward in time. We think we're so free. We don't know tomorrow is already completed. And we want to see the face of tomorrow, if it does exist; and God said, "No, you can't see my face, but I'll put my hand over you, and as I pass by I'll take

away my hand and you will see my back; but my face shall not be seen."
And so he takes away the hand and shows the back, and the back is God's
eternal play.

And man when he hits us over the head, we then, at that very moment,
we move back, not in space, we move back in time and cover 2,000 years in
the twinkle of an eye. But we think at that moment we are struck that we're
going to die. We think this is it. But instead of dying, we go back and enact
God's wonderful drama, where the whole thing begins at that point in time.
Then we have access to both the past and the future. Then he strikes us
again and strikes us again. But every time he strikes us, just as we are told,
an electron speeding if struck is deflected in a new direction but continues
on its way in the right time direction. If it's struck too hard, its time sense is
reversed.

Now, this is what Professor Feynman concluded. It changed the entire
concept of man's picture of the world. Up until that moment in 1932,
people believed that the future is continuously developed out of the past,
and we still do. The whole vast world stops and plans its future based upon
that concept. He said, "No one now knowing the structure of the atom
can hold that view. We must now believe the entire space-time history of
the world is laid out, and we only become aware of increasing portions of
it, successively." I am quoting Professor Feynman. The entire space-time
history of the world is laid out, and we only become aware of increasing
portions of it, successively.

So if man could see as my two friends who came out from California
to New York to take my course. If they could get their wish by taking
my class—so they sat listening just for twenty-four hours to make more
millions than they already possessed—then they would have seen the face of
God. But you don't see the face of God; you see the back. "I will show you
my back; but the face you shall not see." And so he shows us that divine
history is completed. And divine history begins with Christ Jesus and ends
there too. Everything prior to that was all prophecy about him. So it *begins*
there.

And then he is the father of God's only begotten Son, for the Son
calls him Father in fulfillment of scripture. He is the one who ascended, in
fulfillment of scripture again, in the Book of Exodus, where he ascended
as the brazen serpent. And the whole thing unfolds *backward* in time. But
when you move backward in time, you are positive; when you move forward
in time, you're negative. And so the prodigal son goes forward in time into
a far country until he becomes hungry and that hunger was for the word of
God. At that moment, he was struck and returned to his father's house; and
he was given the best robe and the ring upon his hand to signify his princely

power, forever in the kingdom of God, and shoes on his feet. Only slaves went without shoes, so the shoe was the symbol of sonship. But here he goes back into his father's kingdom, and everyone will.

But collectively, humanity is David. When you are struck the second blow after you are born from above, you will encounter David in one piece, not scattered all over the world, personified before you as one *heavenly* boy. And he's your son, and he calls you Father. You don't ask anyone who he is; you know who he is. The Father of David is I AM. In the Bible, he's called Jesse, but the word Jesse in Hebrew means I AM, and God's name is I AM. And Jesse has no forefather in spite of the Book of Ruth and the Book of Chronicles. These were later insertions as now admitted by all scholars. But Jesse has no forefather, just like Melchizedek, because God has no forefather. God has no origin outside of God. And so when he calls you Father and his father is Jesse, you know who you are. And everyone will become that Jesse, that I AM, and all will be redeemed. All the races and nations of the world will one day look into the face in that second blow from God and see God's only begotten son as *his* only Son. So God speaks to man in the last days through his Son.

And so we have all the characters of the Bible; they're all states. And the day will come that you'll see how true this story is in spite of our scientists and our philosophers. And I know the arguments that I've had. If I tell them the story or they've read about it before I've met them, they invariably will ask me to give them some philosophical or physical reason for these things. Can't do it. How can I do it? I can't present anything known to science to support my claim. I can only do what the author of Hebrews did. His entire argument is supported by passages from scripture. He either quotes them or refers to them. In the ___(??) chapter of the thirteen chapters of the Book of Hebrews, he supports his theme by quoting scripture because as some wonderful rabbinical principle has it, according to this principle what is not written in scripture is nonexistent.

God's play is over, God's entire plan is over, and we're on the journey. No matter where we are on that journey negatively, it doesn't matter what's happening to us at all. You're struck, and when you're struck, you go back to where the real play and start it from there. And the first is the birth. And then, it gives himself to you by giving you his Son. And then comes the great brazen serpent, which you are. And all these are backward in time. So we're all moving forward, seemingly in a negative state, just like the electron. And so we have money today and none tomorrow; we're famous today and not known tomorrow, and all these things; doesn't matter, it's all a journey in a negative state like a sleepwalker. And then who knows his great secret of elective love? So he hits this one tonight and that one tomorrow night. And each one as he hits it, there is a power. You can't conceive of the power that is used to turn you around, but you are turned around in time, not in space. As he hits you, just like that little negative electron, if it's struck too hard, it's turned around in time and its time sense is reversed.

Now here is something that's said of this little thing. "It starts from where it hasn't been and speeds to where it was an instant ago." Can you figure that? I'm quoting Professor Feynman: "It starts from where it hasn't been and speeds to the place it was an instant ago." So I stand here, and I put myself elsewhere, say, New York City. I'm physically here, but now I will imagine that I'm in New York City. So I will think of California, and I will see it to the west of me 3,000 miles. If I really see it that way, I must be then 3,000 miles to the east of me. If I see it still under me, I haven't succeeded in the journey. If I see it around me, I haven't succeeded in the journey. But I will remain perfectly still until I can think of California and see it 3,000 miles to the west of me. Then I will hear and see my friends all around me in New York City, those I would know in New York City. And now, seeing it naturally where I'm shaking the hand of a friend who lives on, say, Fifty-seventh Street, I'm embracing her; I know her so well and am talking to her. And while in the midst of talking to her, I open my eyes, and she isn't there and I'm here, haven't I started from where I haven't been, and didn't I speed to where I was an instant ago? And arriving there I am struck so hard, my time sense is reversed, and then I go back to where I haven't been.

Is that clear? I hope so. That's the story of this little particle. And remember what I told you earlier; God being one and his name one, well, that's the first commandment: "Hear, O Israel: The Lord our God is one Lord." His name is one and they ____(??); he is one and his name is one. Therefore, the physics of the mind cannot differ in any respect from the physics of the rest of nature. If this is how the positron behaves, that an ordinary negative particle known as the electron, if it's hit too hard, its time sense is reversed and then it moves *backward* in time. Is that clear? Well, now, it cannot differ from the structure of your mind. You can put yourself any place in this world and make it natural, make it real; and when you make it natural and make it real, suddenly you open your eyes, and you aren't there, you're back where you were. So you start from where you haven't been and speed to where you were an instant ago. Arriving there, you're bumped so hard your time sense is now turned around, and now you move negatively across a series of events leading up to where you had been only in your consciousness, only in your Imagination. I've done it, it works.

And don't be concerned about losing your mind. Because if you read the modern scientific journals, you would think they're stark mad if you could follow them. Luckily, you can't follow it. But these are men who live in an entirely different world, especially the great theoretical physicists—men who are quite willing not to come down into the practical world and execute their dream, but just simply to dream. And when you read their papers, you think they're completely mad. For these words are the words of one of the truly great present-day theoretical physicists. He's over here at Cal Tech. He called it the upside-down, wrong-way, twisted-around, electron, where everything about it is reversed. Instead of having the negative charge, it has the same mass as the electron, but its charge is positive instead of negative. And then it moves backward in time.

And I tell you, from my own experience, I was struck a blow from above in my head. The one who administered that blow was God, and he did it because of his infinite mercy. He took me out of that enormous sea of humanity as we're moving negatively forward toward what we thought to be the goal. The goal wasn't there; it was back in time, right back in time to where the whole vast thing started. And everyone must go *back* in time and replay that scene as the star performer in the drama, but *everyone* will, all that you now read about Christ Jesus. But may I tell you, *you* are Christ, the Lord, the Son of God, the Son of man, and that human life has its significance *only* in the relation to these eternal visions. Everything here in this whole vast world has significance only in relation to these eternal visions that are already spelled out for us in the drama of Christ Jesus. Everything that preceded him told about him and his coming. That very moment in eternity when God is born is going to happen to you, and he'll be born. And then you don't move forward, but you jump backward.

It took many blows, all administered by God. The second blow, he reveals his Son as your son. And then the third blow and all the blows come, all from above, and each new one seems like the end. It's not the end. The end is that moment in time when you jump and you reverse this interval of a thousand years in the twinkle of an eye and relive the scene as before in scripture. So we're moving forward negatively given us now, for man has discovered about this peculiar particle, and it all is in us.

So you can sit here this night and dream nobly and put yourself forward in time and give yourself a shock when you open your eyes and see you're not actually there. But you went forward in time. And read the first two verses of the fourteenth of John: "In my Father's house are many mansions; were it not so, would I have told you that I go to prepare a place for you? And if I go, I will come again and receive you unto myself, that where I am there ye shall be also." So you go forward in time and prepare the place, and having prepared it, it seems so natural that it's taking place now. Then you open your physical eye to find you're not physically there, and so the very opening of the eye is a shock, bringing you back to where you were. So you start from where you haven't been, physically, to where you were the first time, and you're turned around: and then you move forward now negatively across a bridge of incidence, which leads you up to that very moment where it seemed so natural to you ____(??). (Tape ends.)

IS CHRIST YOUR IMAGINATION?

March 22, 1963

Tonight's subject is in the form of a question, "Is Christ *your* Imagination?" When we ask the question, we expect the answer in terms of our current background of thought, and quite often, that is not adequate to frame the answer. But I'm asking the question, and in order to answer myself, I should really clarify the terms *Imagination* and Christ.

I think there would be no problem tonight if I define, say, Imagination. I think you will agree with me. But you may not agree with me when I define Christ. If I say to you that Imagination is the power of pre-deforming mental images, you wouldn't quarrel with that, the power that pre-deforms mental images. Sitting here tonight, you can think of anything and see it mentally. You may not see it as graphically as you see it in the present forms in the room at the moment, but you could see it vividly in the mind's eye and discriminate. Think of a tree and think of a horse, and you don't think that one is the other. They are two separate objects in your mind's eye. Well, that's the power of Imagination. But when it comes to Christ—and there are hundreds of millions in the world who call themselves Christians—the very use of the word instantly conjures in the mind's eye a person. They think of Christ as a person, and no two have the same mental picture of this person.

I know many, many years ago, in New York City, this French artist went to the library on Forty-second Street and brought up forty-six different pictures of Christ and threw them on the screen with his little lantern. No two were alike, and each artist claimed that this was an inspired picture and it was presented to him, and he painted the picture. There were blond and blue-eyed pictures; dark swarthy skin; there were those with a very black skin. There were forty-six pictures all projected as so-called originals. So man has been conditioned to believe that Christ is *a* person.

So I ask the question, "*Is* Christ your Imagination?" Can I personify Imagination? I will. But let us go back to the book, the Bible. What does the Bible say of Christ? Here, in Paul's first letter to the Corinthians, the 1ˢᵗ chapter, the 23ʳᵈ and 24ᵗʰ verses—I'll just give you the highlights. It is, "Christ, the power and the wisdom of God." He defines Christ as the power and the wisdom of God. In the 1ˢᵗ chapter of the Book of John, which brings Christology to its height as far as the Bible goes, there is no single book that takes this secret of Christ and brings it to the heights as you'll find in the Gospel of John. So in the gospel of John speaking now of this presence that was *with* God—*his* meaning, his power—that by him—now he personifies it—"by him all things were made, and without him was not anything made that was made." It's the power, and yet it is wisdom, for *all* things were made by him, and without him was not anything made that was made. So here is a creative power.

If I take that now and analyze myself with another word from Paul, this time he goes to the end of his second letter to the Corinthians, and he calls upon all of us who would read that letter: "Test yourselves. Do you not realize that Jesus Christ is in thee?" Now here I'm told all things were made by him; he is the power and the wisdom, he is the power of God and the wisdom of God. But every attribute of God is personified, every attribute. And so his power is personified; and may I confess that I have seen that power, and it *is* a man. I have seen that wisdom, and it *is* a man. And when you stand in the presence of that personified aspect of infinite being, you know you are standing in the presence of infinite might. It's not just power; it's almightiness. You stand in the presence, and yet it's man.

So here he calls it the power and wisdom. Now he asks me, asks you who read his letter to test ourselves. "Test yourselves"—this is the 13ᵗʰ chapter, the 5ᵗʰ verse of 2ⁿᵈ Corinthians—"Test yourselves. Do you not realize that Jesus Christ is in thee," and he made all these things? Well, then, let us put him to the test in us. I say he is our Imagination. That's the power; that's the creative power of the universe. Look around the world. Do you know of anything in the world of man that man has created, from the clothes that he wears to the homes that he inhabits, that wasn't first imagined? Do you know of anything in this world that is now proved as fact, as a concrete reality, that wasn't first imagined—only imagined—and then externalized? Yes, using hands, using implements of the world, but it first began as an image. And an image is simply the product of this pre-deforming, image-making faculty in man, which is man's Imagination. So if all things were made by him and without him was not anything made that was made, I can't come to any conclusion other than the fact that Christ of scripture is my Imagination.

Now, who is Jesus? If Christ is the power and the wisdom of God, and God sunk himself in us, that was his sacrifice. He actually became us that we may live. For were it not for this sacrifice of God to actually limit himself to the state called man, man would, like the earth, wear out like a garment. As we're told in the 51st chapter of the Book of Isaiah: "Lift up your eyes into the heavens, and look down to the earth beneath; the heavens will vanish like smoke and the earth will wear out like a garment, and they who dwell upon it will do likewise; but my *salvation* will be forever, and my deliverance will never have an end." My salvation will be forever. Well, that word salvation means Jesus; the word Jesus is "Jehovah saves." That's salvation; that is forever. Were it not that God became man that man may become God, and he would save man and lift him up to immortality because the promise is that earth will wear out like a garment. Our scientists tell us today that the sun is melting in radiation, and it took unnumbered billions of years if it started the process of melting; no matter how long it takes, it has an end; and with its end, we have our end as part of the system. So we, walking the earth, all would have the end. So to stop that process of bringing man to an end, "My salvation will be forever and my deliverance will never have an end."

So God became man that man may become God. In becoming man, and God is the only creative power in the world, what in me creates? My Imagination. I may not have the talent to put it on paper. I may not have the ability to execute it as great artists who did it, but I can imagine it. I can imagine the book. I can imagine the joy of having a book. I can imagine a picture. Without being an artist I can dream. And I cannot conceive of a picture that a man can paint on canvas that's more alive than my dream, and yet I can't put a thing on canvas. But I go to sleep, and I can dream. What is doing it? It's just my Imagination. And here, when I lose the conscious faculty, this restricted area, I can actually dream, dream as no artist in the world can paint. Put color upon it, put motion upon it, and have the most wonderful drama. And that's my Imagination.

But now, this is not only the power and the wisdom of God. In the greatest of all the New Testament, which is John, John does not emphasize the power. He states in the beginning, yes, he declares Christ as power, but the emphasis is not on power; it's on redemption and revelation. Revelation, in John's gospel, is an act of God in self-revealing. So in the very first chapter now he tells us what this power will do for us. First of all, there are two endings to John. Let us take the real ending, which is the twentieth chapter, the first ending. Whoever the writer is who calls himself John, "Now Jesus did many other signs that are not written in this book; but these are written that you may believe that Jesus is the Christ, and *believing* have life in his name" (verse 30). He is the power and the wisdom of God, that's what the author is telling us in the very end. Many signs he did, but in spite of the number of the signs and the character of the signs, it did not evoke faith. And the whole teaching of the gospel of John is based upon faith and unbelief in him, either one or the other. I have faith in him, or you disbelieve him. Few believed him, few, we are told; even among the disciples, only a few believed, and they imperfectly.

Well now, who is Jesus? If Christ is the power and the wisdom, but now who is Jesus? So here we have this wonderful thought as expressed in the second chapter of Paul's letter to the Philippians: "Though he was in the form of God, he did not consider that he should be equal with God as something to be grasped, but he emptied himself, and took upon himself the form of a slave, being born in the form of man"—that identifies man with a slave, every man—"And being found in the fashion, human fashion, he humbled himself and became obedient even unto death, death on a cross. Therefore God has highly exalted him and given him *the* name." Not the indefinite article, the definite, "given him *the* name that is above every name, that at the name of Jesus every knee should bow, in heaven, on earth and under the earth, and every tongue confess that Jesus Christ is the Lord, the glory of God" (verses 5-11).

He gave him the name that is above every name, and at that name, every power in the world must bend. It's the name of names. That's the name called Jesus—but this is Jehovah—Jesus simply is "Jehovah saves." Every child born of woman in this world will one day wear that name. There's only one name, only one being—Jesus. You go through the same story as told us in the gospels, everyone will. And when he passes through this series of events outlined in the gospels, that name is conferred, conferred on the *risen* Christ. That power that is latent in man—that's man's Imagination—when it's lifted, on that risen Christ, the name Jesus, the divine name Jesus, is conferred. And that individual then enters a new age, an entirely different age, an age that is immortal, an age that is eternal, because until the end of that age, we are still subject to being worn out like a garment, as told us in the fifty-first of Isaiah. So everyone, moving on the wheel that is being worn out, wearing out the garment, and vanishing like smoke ___(??) heaven.

But not one will fail, for God redeems us. God resurrects us one after the other, lifted up, and confers on that *risen* Christ the name, the name Jesus. So you're told, in the end, they looked up, and there was Jesus only. When Blake was asked quite innocently but in a serious vein, "What do you think of Jesus?" Without batting an eye, Blake replied, "Jesus is the only God" and then hastened to add, "But so am I, and so are you." So in the end, *all* receive the name, where the power called Christ in man is lifted up, lifted up so the whole vast wonderful being that was sunk in man is now awake. What that body will look like, I can't describe it to anyone. I can't find words to describe the glory that is yours, but everyone. It certainly isn't this I am ___(??), yet I will know you and you will know me in eternity. But for all the sameness of identity, where we actually know each other, there will be a radical discontinuity of form. Not the form that I now wear and walk here this day and have been wearing for the last fifty-eight years, not this form. But identity, yes, you'll know me. But how to display the glory of the being that you are when you're resurrected?

Now, this is shown us by the Sadducee, who does not believe in the resurrection. They are the modern scientists. The Sadducees of 2,000 years ago were the wise men; the Pharisees were the priesthood of the world. The Sadducees were the intellectual giants of that day; and they, any more than today, could believe in not even survival, far less resurrection. Like today, the world puts the two words together, and they think of survival as resurrection, and they are not. Survival is continuity; resurrection is discontinuity—you leave the field completely and enter the world of eternity. So they asked the question, based upon the law of Moses, and Moses said, If a man married, died, leaving no issue, and has a brother, the brother should marry the widow. And if he dies leaving no issue and has a brother, he should take the widow, to raise up seed for his brother. Well, there was a man who married, and he was one of seven brothers, and he died without issue. The second married her, but he died. The third married her and he died. Finally, seven brothers married her and left no issue, and finally she died. So, whose wife will she be in the resurrection?" (Luke 20:27) It was a bait, because they did not believe in the resurrection. And he said to them, "You do not know the scriptures. For the sons of this age marry and are given in marriage, but those who are accounted worthy to attain to *that* age, to the resurrection from the dead neither marry nor are they given in marriage, for they cannot die again, for now they have become sons of God and sons of the resurrection" (Luke 20:34). They are completely above the organization of sex. What we call sex here, these garments of sex are shadows thrown by this fabulous being above. And the body that you really have, as you're told, I quoted earlier, Being in the *form* of God, he didn't consider equality a thing to grasp, but emptied himself of that form and took upon himself the form of a slave; and being born in the form of man, didn't think it strange, humbled himself in the image of a man. And then, finding himself with all the limitations of man, all the weaknesses of man, everything that is man, then God exalted him at the end when he resurrected him, and gave him the name. That name is conferred only at resurrection.

So here, everyone will get it, for everyone will be resurrected. Then you will not be wearing this. These bodies, wonderful as they are for us, filled with all the passions of the world, that's all wonderful, but it's not the body that you will wear. You will be completely above the organization of sex. No need for this kind of creativity. Imagination will be completely awake and you create at will. Your imaginal act will be an immediate objective fact. What we call reality today, all this fabulous world of ours—may I tell you, and I've seen it—it is all Imagination. When it has played its part and God has completed his purpose, which is to bring forth from *us* himself and make us all God with him, then these garments, made up of all the elements that seem so permanent and so wonderful, they will vanish like smoke. Vanish like smoke. There isn't an element that wasn't brought into being by the creative power of God, by his own wonderful divine imagining, and it's sustained in being because he sustains it by his imaginal acts. When he ceases that imaginal act, all the elements will melt, all vanish; and the world will be as though it never existed. But you and I will be lifted up above it all into an entirely different world, an eternal world.

So is Christ your Imagination? I say Christ is the power and the wisdom of God, and this power and this wisdom create everything in the world. I can trace to my own being an imaginal act that became fact; then I repeated it and it becomes fact. But if I can repeat it and repeat it and these imaginal acts externalize themselves in fact, then I've found him. I have found that power in myself. Well, the Bible calls it Christ, and personifies it and speaks of the presence of a man, and that man is Jesus. Jesus Christ is simply the *resurrected* being that is God now because he's resurrected the *power* within him, which is Christ, and that's Jesus Christ. Now he's called the Lord, and everything should bow before him when it happens.

Well, I say to you, the day will come, you will have the experience and you'll be startled. No one's going to believe you, may I tell you. They aren't going to believe you any more than they believed that first person to whom it happened. He is the first that rose from the dead, but no one believed him. Up to the very end, who would believe the story? They were looking for a different kind of Messiah, a conquering hero that would come just like a man, out of some glorious background of warriors, and then conquer the enemy of Israel and then lead Israel to some victorious end. And they always look for that kind of a Messiah. We have them all over the world today, these false Messiahs who promise their nations to lead them to some victory, even though a little temporary victory. That's not Messiah. Messiah hasn't a thing to do with this world. He's resurrected out of this world. This world is vanishing; this world is wearing out just like a garment.

So Christ *in* man is the power and the wisdom, and when *in* that man, that Imagination becomes alert because he exercised it lovingly. So if I read John correctly, not only my salvation is dependent on it, I must actually believe in him. Well, who is this being? My own Imagination. If I don't believe in my Imagination and test it, even though I fail, well, then I don't believe in Christ. For Christ is really my Imagination, your Imagination. So you imagine something lovely of another, and you don't believe in the reality of that imaginal act, you don't believe in Christ. So you go to church every day and give ten percent of your income to the church of your choice—all these things are lovely, therefore, if you feel that way about it, give them—but that's not Christ. That's not believing in Christ.

To believe in Christ: If you see someone in this world and have a sweet feeling toward that one, that he hasn't yet realized something lovely, something without his knowledge, and then represent him to yourself as though it were true, and believe in the reality of what you've done mentally. Believe in it; believe in Christ, for all things are possible to Christ. And so bring him before your mind's eye and see him as he would like to be seen by himself, as he would like the world to see him. But *you* do it, and then you believe in the reality of what you have done. That's believing in Christ.

And may I tell you, you'll be surprised beyond measure how it works. At that very moment, because all things by a law divine in one another's being mingle, at that very moment that you interfere with his life, you reshuffle the entire deck, and all things will completely rearrange to mirror the change that is going to take place in him. And everyone in this world who can aid that change will be used to bring about that change, without their knowledge and without their consent. You don't need the consent of any being in the world. If they can be used to externalize what you have imagined, they'll be used. So leave them alone and simply imagine the best of every person in this world, and *believe* in what you have done, and you are believing in Christ.

When you least expect it, because you believe in him, then God resurrects you, then you are lifted up and you stand bewildered when you see what God did for you. Of everything claimed of him that you thought, that your mother taught you as mine taught me, happened 2,000 years ago, and it is happening. It didn't stop. You go back and read the Bible, and here we are told in Paul's letters to Timothy, "Those who teach that the resurrection is past are misleading the faithful" (2 Timothy 2:18). Those who teach it's *past*, that it's over, they are deceiving. It isn't past. It *took* place in one, and it's taking place in unnumbered. But it's *taking* place; it isn't over. The crucifixion is over, yes, but not the resurrection. The resurrection is taking place in everyone that is called and lifted up. And so, as we are called, God's mightiest act is performed, and we're lifted up, and pass through the series of events leading into the kingdom of heaven, although we seemingly remain here still wearing this garment for a little short while. The garment will be shown you that you'll occupy, and you can't describe it to anyone even to your own satisfaction. It's such a living thing, it's so luminous, and it's such light, like the rainbow. And you can't describe it to the satisfaction of any being in this world who lives only in terms of a God of the flesh.

Now we are told—and you read it in the 1st chapter of John, the 11th through the 13th verses—for he's speaking of an entirely different kind of a birth. "Those who believe in his name will be born, not of blood nor of the will of the flesh nor of the will of man, but of God." Not born in any way that this [body] is born. This was born just as you were born from the womb of woman, flesh and blood. But flesh and blood cannot inherit the kingdom of God, only Spirit. So this is going to be born not as this was born. It's born differently: not of blood nor the will of the flesh, and not of any human passion nor of the will of man of human parentage but of God. And may I tell you, when you are born you are *self*-begotten. You have actually no parents; you are self-begotten. You come right out of a grave, the mystery of the grain of wheat that falls into the ground. If it doesn't fall into the ground, it remains alone. If it falls into the ground, it bears much fruit, the mystery of life through death. For God died, actually died, to become you and to become me. And God is divine Imagination. He limits himself to the very limit of contraction, called human Imagination and actually dies in the sense that all the power and all the memory of his glorious being had to be completely forgotten.

So that cry on the cross is true, "My God, my God, why hast thou forsaken me?" (Matthew 27:46) He, *himself*, is crying out; because he so completely gave himself up, he suffers from total amnesia, complete forgetfulness of his divinity, as he became us. And that was what? Divine imagining becoming human imagining, and then we building our little world. Now ___(??) to many of us, it's so different, and the power we exercise is so fragile compared to that same power when it's raised up, when lifted up, and the name, this great name, above all names, is conferred upon us. And the day will come, without loss of identity, that you will bear the name Jesus, no loss of identity. Everyone is *destined* to be Christ Jesus, that risen power with the name, exercising infinite power, without loss of identity. So we all know each other and all glorified, but everyone. There is no limitation of the gift; some exercise it more than others, but certainly the gift is the same, the gift of Christ Jesus.

So my question, as far as I am personally concerned, "Is Christ your Imagination?" I said yes. And yet you're limited only to power and wisdom, for the emphasis is not on power and wisdom, it's on redemption, revelation. And so he *reveals* himself. In that same first chapter of the prologue—the first eighteen verses, not a prologue—and the very last, the eighteenth verse, he shows you the revelation: "No man has seen God at any time, but the Son, in the bosom of the Father, he has made him known" (John 1:18). No one has seen him, but in the bosom of the Father, there's a Son and the Son reveals the Father.

Then we are told in the tenth of Luke, "No one knows the Son except the Father; no one knows the Father except the Son and any one to whom the Son chooses to reveal him" (verse 22). There will come that moment in time when the Son reveals you, and you will know your name is Jesus, Jesus Christ the Lord. For the Son is going to call you "my lord" and actually going to call you his Father, his Lord, and the Rock of his salvation; and then you will know who you are. I could tell you from now to the ends of time, but it can't carry the conviction that the experience would carry when it happens. When it happens to you, it will make no difference to you if all the wise people in the world rose in opposition and told you that you're suffering from some grand hallucination. It would make no difference whatsoever.

This is revelation, and the whole thing is lifted, the veil is lifted; and now you know why you couldn't see the face of the Father. You can see him only reflected in the Son. There was no mirror to reflect it but the Son. Can't see your face. You go to a mirror on earth, but that's not the face. And you'll only know your face in the beauty of your Son. That Son can't be described he's so beautiful. When you look at him, you sit there amazed that you would produce such beauty. It took the Son to reveal the beauty of the Father, for the Father is invisible, and yet more real than the whole vast world that seems so real that is slowly vanishing like smoke and wearing out like a garment. So everyone in the world is destined to bear the name of Christ Jesus the Lord but everyone. And all will then be the first fruit of those who slept because it's only God resurrecting himself. All will be resurrected, all individualized, and all one. All being the Father of the same beautiful Son, reflecting himself, and yet he's individualized.

So you try this tonight. I told a friend of mine before taking the platform that many years ago, in the war, I was invited to go through this huge plant, Alyce Chalmers. The man who was the head of the chemical department, Professor Inmar, came to my lectures. And in my lecture, I spoke of a certain motion in time that produced physical results. If I could move forward in time and imagine something taking place at that moment in time, and open my eyes upon this world to find that it was not that time at all, I came back here. But, strangely enough, I would then be led across a series of events, which I did not consciously devise and as I moved across this series of events, I came upon what I had only imagined that I had done at a point in time. He said, "That can't work, Neville. After all, I am a chemist, I am a physicist, and we have a laboratory bigger than this room, where there were unnumbered little vials, little bottles of water. For they make these huge, big turbines; and all over the world, they're shipped. And as the water comes down the rivers, they're ___(??) differs with chemicals because the world differs. And so, certain turbines were caking, enormous caking on the inside, so this was a problem. They would send samples of water, and all day long, he analyzed the sample of water and then he would give the solution. Because you can't change the water, the water is coming through certain mineral deposits. And so it's a very exciting thing to sit down and analyze these little sample things of water." And they would write back to Australia, New Zealand, all over the world and suggest something to do to prolong the life of the turbine.

And then he took me into a thing and he showed me what they used in the lab and he called it entropy. He said that we have to have this in every lab in the world. And then he explained to me that entropy is based upon the *unalterable* past. Can't change the past, said he; the past is unalterable. So you make a test and then you move forward; you know what you've done, and that is so. If you repeat that test, the result is the same under the same conditions. And so Larry said, this is something that we know, and we're all scientists. And you come with this crazy idea? I can't see how it could fit in with what we know about entropy. Well, he explained entropy for me. Then he said, "Of course, the future is in a state of flux. We do not believe in the future as something existing. It doesn't exist. We simply weave these strands, as it were, likening the whole thing to a rope—the past is already woven, and the future not yet woven, and we are weaving it moment by moment as we go forward to the future. And I said, But I went forward to the future that you say doesn't exist and I wove it there. And then whatever I did, I know it worked because when I came back here, I moved across a bridge of incidence that led me to what I wove before I arrived there.

Well, he didn't believe that, but a very sweet man, an honest man. And then, about two months later, I was in New York City, and he sent me this wonderful clipping from the *Science Newsletter*, the story which I told you the last evening you were here, which was the story of the positron. In his letter to me, he apologized for taking that adamant position that he did as a scientist. For he said, here one far greater than I am, Professor Feynman, has just delivered this lecture at Cornell University wherein he makes these fantastic claims for a little particle just discovered, that is, a few years before, called the positron, and the same behavior of the positron, that it can meet itself coming back from where it hasn't been. And so he said, "Now I apologize because here is the behavior of the positron. It starts from where it hasn't been and speeds to where it was an instant ago, arriving there it is bounced so hard it's time sense is reversed, and then it moves back to where it hasn't been." Now these are the words of Professor Feynman.

And so I would say it in my own simple way. I close my eyes on the now: for today's the twenty-second, so it's the twenty-second, and not a thing happened that I wanted today. So it's the twenty-second. This is the first of April; make it All Fools' Day, and so as to the calendar, it's All Fools' Day, the first of April, and then I feel emotionally excited because something just happened, and it's so altogether wonderful I could not have foreseen back on the twenty-second of March how it could have worked. But it has worked! Look! It's the first of April and it worked. Then I open my eyes; I'm back on the twenty-second of March. Not a thing has worked. But all of a sudden, I move forward the twenty-third, twenty-fourth, and twenty-fifth, and things begin to change. When I get to the first, it has worked!

Now, *he* put it in his own wonderful technical language and called it the positron. And then he also gave me this principle of entropy. But I never heard the word before. Entropy is the unalterable past, which you must have in the laboratory, or else it would be all confused. You couldn't make any tests and be sure that you could repeat it. It's a fixed fact. Well, I said, as far as I am concerned, I knew a point in time, if you dwell in the future as though it were true and shocked myself so severely when I opened my eyes to think that I'm not there. It's a little trick that my old friend Abdullah taught me in New York City.

I had a telephone that I couldn't possibly see, unless I could see around corners. If I sat in my living room, I couldn't possibly see where my telephone was. It was down the hallway, and I couldn't look around a corner unless I got off the chair and looked around the corner. But I would sit in my living room in my big easy chair, assume that I was sitting at the telephone, and then I would think of the living room and see that chair, on which physically I sat, and see it empty. Then I would, while at that place, open my eyes and feel myself bounce this way. Then I knew that man was where he was in Imagination, that man being all Imagination, he had to be wherever he was in Imagination. And so in that twinkle of an eye you would feel a change, a motion. That was a little exercise that old Ab taught me.

So try it now on other things, more important than that. Do that just as an exercise and feel it. Now, try it in other things. I began to try it and things worked. Well now, if we have evidence for a thing, what our scientists think or wish about the matter is nothing to the point, is it? If I can produce the evidence for anything in this world, although I can't explain it, if I can produce the evidence, what anyone thinks about it or even wishes for it is not to the point. So I ask that you try it and see if Christ, as stated in that wonderful John 1:3, is the creator of everything in this world. "All things were made by him, and without him was not anything made that was made." All right, let him try this and see if you don't come to the conclusion that if that is true, Christ, that is called the power of God and wisdom of God, is not your Imagination.

I don't see how you can come to any other conclusion than that—if he is the creator of *all* things; and you set a goal, and without raising a finger to make it so, it becomes so, because you know what you did in Imagination—then you go right back to the cause, and the cause was your imaginal act. And if Christ does *everything*, and you know what you did, then you've found him. You've found him as your own wonderful human Imagination. And the day will come as you trust him and believe in him and test him and bring these things to pass, when you least expect it, ___(??) the resurrection. And that power will rise within you, and then you'll move into a world completely subject to your imaginative power. And although you come back here to wear this garment for a little while, still limited; and with all the weaknesses of the flesh, you know when you put it down you are already numbered among those who are resurrected from the dead, dying no more, for now you are the son of God. And the Son of God is one with God, for the Son of God is also God the Son. And he said, "I and my Father are one." Even though my Father is greater than I, we are one, one in nature.

And so you'll be resurrected. But trust in him. It seems we have our salvation, and its origin in God's faith, but it's bestowed in proportion to *our* faith in *him*. And we have found him to be our own wonderful human Imagination.

Now let us go into the Silence.

*   *   *

Q: (Inaudible)
A: I knew Mr. Burns only in Barbados. He came here as a young man, in his twenties or thirties—made his exit at a very mature age, at eighty-five or eighty-six. But I visited the old boy quite often, but I wasn't impressed. He was a prolific writer. He wrote volumes. He had logorrhea, just in a poem, word after word after word, and voluminously. But personally, I was not impressed. But he had a certain

following who thought because he could write these unnumbered books that he was a very wise man. But I, personally, I wanted to feel deeply about him because we are all tied to the little island where we were born. I was born in Barbados, and I would be very happy if a Barbadian made it, one of those things, but I just couldn't. ___(??). He wrote so many books. Then he made his exit; and of course, a very close friend of mine attributed his exit from this world to the fact he used copper pots instead of aluminum pots or something, and so they got all mixed up in the strangest things based upon this level.

No, I'd rather go for the poets, the Blakes, the Shelleys, and the Bible. You read the Bible; really, if properly interpreted, the whole thing would be poetry. We call it prose, but how can you say what I quoted tonight from Philippians and call that prose? It's just sheer poetry. These are the inspired giants of the world. And the poets to me are nearer reality than anyone else because you can't rationalize God's Word (and Percival tried to do it). When you sit down to rationalize the Word, you can't do it. It's revelation. It's a tremendous ___(??), coming only by revelation. Our prophets and our evangelists, they were not speculating trying to set up some workable philosophy of life; they simply told what had happened. Couldn't possibly speculate; you just tell your own experience. And what more can you say than your own experience? What you've experienced you know more thoroughly than you know anything else in this world. And so I'm sorry, I cannot give you a good answer about Mr. Percival. He's now on the wheel telling it elsewhere.

Q: (Inaudible)

A: Well, in Revelation, you have the seven. Well, I couldn't put my finger on it, but you have the seven stars; you have so many sevens in the Bible. Well, David was a dancer, and Saul's daughter criticized him for dancing and displaying himself seemingly in the nude before the servants. And so he displayed himself in the nude, and she criticized him for being a king and still acting that way before the servants. And he said, The Lord God chose me; he didn't choose your father. He denied your father, King Saul, and chose me in his place, and I will dance forever before the ark of the Lord. And so he kept on dancing. And then, in his infinite power said to her that she was ___(??), and to the day of her death she bore no child. That's how the story ends with her. So you can use or misuse this power. But she was speaking to the Lord's anointed, and the Lord would never take his steadfast love from his anointed, no matter what David did (2 Samuel 6:16). (Tape ends.)

BLAKE ON RELIGION

March 26, 1963

Tonight's subject is "Blake on Religion." When you discuss Blake, you are discussing one of the great spiritual giants of all time. You might just as well discuss St. Paul, for they had the identical vision, the vision of reality. So tonight we can cover only a portion of his gift to the world.

> In his *Auguries of Innocence*:

> To see a World in a Grain of Sand
> And a Heaven in a Wild Flower,
> Hold Infinity in the palm of your hand
> And Eternity in an hour.

What's the sequence? The most inanimate thing in the world, a grain of sand, and in *it* to see a world. Then he moves to the first animation, a flower, and then to see harmony, which is heaven, to see a heaven in a wild flower. Now he comes to space: "Hold infinity in the palm of your hand"; and then to time: "And eternity in an hour." Then he moves on now to the bird world to show us the relationship of the whole vast world, the *unity* of the world, that we are all actually related. That you can't disturb anything at this moment in any way and not actually affect the whole.

> A Robin Red breast in a Cage
> Puts all Heaven in a Rage.

So we think we can catch the little bird and cage it for our own amusement, that which should be set free. For he said in *The Marriage of Heaven and Hell,* (Plt.6);

> Who knows that what every bird
> That cuts the airy way,
> Is an immense world of delight,
> Clos'd by our senses five.
>
> So, the little "Robin Red breast in a Cage
> Puts all Heaven in a rage.
> The dove house filled with doves and Pigeons
> Shudders Hell thro' all its regions."

Then he moves on to the *next* stage, what the world would call evolution, but he doesn't call it that. Now into another aspect of the animal world:

> A dog starv'd at his Master's Gate
> Predicts the ruin of the State.
> A Horse misus'd upon the Road
> Calls to Heaven for Human blood.

And he takes the stages right through. You will read it as you go home, *Auguries of Innocence.* It's his *The Pickering Manuscript,* if you have his book, for here is this mental giant who saw the complete relationship of all of us. So I think I could be isolated. Were I in a dungeon and I thought of you, my thought is affecting the entire universe. I thought of you with envy or with hate or with love—whatever the thought was, as I conjure you in my mind's eye and represent you to myself as I want you to be, whether it is in hate or in love, I am affecting the whole vast world. And if I believe in the reality of what I've done, it will come to pass. Because we are all one, all interwoven, I will use you without your consent, without your knowledge to fulfill that which I have imagined at that moment.

Then he makes this statement:

> What seems to Be, Is, To those to whom
> It seems to Be, and is productive of the most dreadful
> Consequences to those to whom it seems to Be, even of
> Torments, Despair and Eternal Death; but the Divine

Mercy Steps beyond and Redeems Man in the Body of
Jesus. (*Jerusalem*, Plate 36)

He steps beyond. Because of this principle, man could be lost forever,
not knowing what he's doing; but "Divine Mercy steps beyond and Redeems
Man in the Body of Jesus."

Then he makes the statement, "God is Jesus." There was no doubt in
Blake's mind that Jesus is God, not one of many gods but the only God.
That was Blake's concept of Jesus. God is Jesus, and we are but members in
this divine body and therefore only one name; we are he. So he made this
statement:

Man is all Imagination. God is Man and exists in us
and we in him. (*Annotations to Berkeley*)

The Eternal Body of Man is The Imagination, *that* is, God
himself, The Divine Body, Jesus: we are his Members. (*The
Laocoon*)

And he meant every word of it.

Now he asks us to join with him in putting this to the test. When you
read his work from beginning to end, he never wavered from this premise.
One thing he asked us all to do and to always bear in mind at every
moment in time was to distinguish between the immortal man, which he
saw; he said, "When I first did descry the immortal man that cannot die"
and that immortal man was Imagination. Imagination has a body, and he
describes that body, but he begs us to please always discriminate between
this immortal man, your wonderful human Imagination, and the *state* into
which it has fallen. So you may this night be in the state of love—I hope
you are—the state of tenderness, the state of affluence—I hope so. But you
may not be. You may be in the opposite state. But were you in the opposite
state or some friend of yours or some total stranger of yours in the opposite
state, he begs you and begs all of us to always bear in mind the distinction
between the occupant of the state and the state; and lift everyone out of the
state, if it is an unlovely state.

For man is like a pilgrim passing through states, as though I pass
through the states of this country. If I pass through this night in Chicago,
Chicago remains; but I, the pilgrim, pass on. If I pass through any state, say
the state of poverty, when I leave poverty, it doesn't really dissolve; it hasn't
disappeared; I have left it for anyone to enter. I hope they will avoid it, but

anyone may fall into it or deliberately go into it by feeling sorry for himself and feeling unwanted. And so he tells us of these enormous states, infinite states in the world, that everything possible to happen to man is already created in the form of states. When man enters the state, the state unfolds because he, the operant power, has entered the state; and unknowingly, he simply unfolds the state. If the state is one of wealth, in a way he does not know, everyone in the world that can aid the unfolding of that state must aid it. If he enters any state, the state of poverty, although at the moment, when he enters it he may have everything in the world, in no time he will grow the fruit of poverty in his world, for he's in the state of poverty. But he, the occupant of the state, is neither rich nor poor.

So he calls upon everyone to bear this in mind constantly and forgive every being in the world. For he said, "Mutual forgiveness of each sin, such are the gates into heaven in our world." If I could only remember at every moment of time when I see someone that I dislike that he is only in a state. That's why I dislike him: I dislike the state. I identify him with the state, and I dislike the state, but I think it's the occupant of the state. It's not the occupant. He could come out at any moment of time, or I could get him out of it. If I pulled him out of it and put him into another state, I wouldn't dislike him. It's only the state that I dislike. But not knowing the difference between the occupant and the state, I think I dislike *him*, and I don't dislike him at all. He is simply in a state. If I bear this in mind, knowing my power to pull him out of a state, I could save him, at least temporarily, until he's actually redeemed by the "Divine mercy that steps beyond and redeems man in the body of Jesus."

And that's a true vision: we are redeemed in the body of Jesus. The day will come that you will actually be pulled into his presence, for it is he, divine mercy, that steps beyond, in spite of what we have done, and pulls us right into his presence. Then we are asked a very simple question. The world will answer correctly, or he would not have pulled us. It's automatically done. We are divinely prompted what to answer, what to say, when the question is asked. We cannot make a mistake, for we are actually prompted from the depths of our souls, and we answer. At that very moment, he embraces us and we become one with Jesus. We are fused into the body of Jesus. And you say, "Well, is Jesus a man?" This is a man. So Blake makes the statement:

> If you humble yourself, you humble me;
> You too dwell in Eternity.
> Thou art a Man, God is no more,
> Thy own humanity learn to adore.
> (*The Everlasting Gospel*)

So when you stand in his presence, you're standing in the presence of man; and it is infinite man, and infinite man is Jesus. And you are actually saved in the body of Jesus because he embraces you and you are locked in his body, one with the body. You *are* the body. You aren't locked in the sense that you disappear; you are one with that body, and you *are* that being. You become one with Jesus, yet you do not lose your identity. No loss of identity and yet one with God, for God *is* Jesus. Now this is Blake's teaching, and I have proven much of it to my own satisfaction by my own mystical experiences.

Now he comes to discuss the story of "The Virginity of the Virgin." For are we not told in the 7th chapter, the 14th verse of Isaiah, "And the Lord himself will give you a sign. A virgin shall conceive and bear a son, and shall call his name Emmanuel." The word *Emmanuel* means "God is with us." Listen to it carefully: "You will conceive and bear a son, and call his name Emmanuel." The child will be given a name as a token. The child is not the great event. The child will be given a name and a token of deliverance. The child himself is not the deliverer; the child is simply the *sign* of an event taking place. Now Blake writes one single little verse, and he speaks of it as "The Virginity of the Virgin." *You* are the virgin, whether you be male or female; I am the virgin; we are all the virgin. I didn't know what was happening to me anymore than you will know what's happening to you. And so he puts it in four little lines:

> Whate'er is done to her she cannot know,
> And if you ask her she will swear it so.
> Whether 'tis good or evil none's to blame:
> No one can take the pride, no one the shame.

So it is said in the story, "How can this thing be, seeing that I know not a man?" And through the centuries, thousands of volumes have been written condemning the act, for it was out of wedlock. And they take it on this level. It's not on this level. *You* are the bride of God, as told us in the 54th chapter of the Book of Isaiah, "Your Maker is your husband, the Lord of hosts is his name." So the one who made me is going to sire me, without my knowledge, without my consent; so whate'er is done to me, I cannot know, and if you ask me I will swear it so. Now, whether it's good or evil, there's none to blame, no one to take the pride, and no one the shame. No one can take the pride when I confess openly that I gave birth to a child out of wedlock, for no one sired *that* child and no one can claim he sired it. Whether it was a shameful thing to perform, well, the world will judge. Whether it be good or evil, well, who knows? But one thing I know is that no one can claim they did it; therefore, no one can take the pride and no one the shame, if it's a shame.

So the prophecy was made, and then he writes in four little lines the story of "The Virginity of the Virgin." He is telling every being in the world that they are that virgin, and you *will* be sired by the Holy Spirit. And you will produce in visible form an infant, just as told us in the gospel. And having produced it, you stand amazed because how could you produce it in such an unnatural way? For it happens so unnaturally, it doesn't happen in a natural way. Therefore, you were the virgin who conceived unknowingly, for she said, "How can I conceive, how can I have a child, seeing that I know not a man?" And then you are told that the Holy Spirit will come upon you and the child will be the child of God. But it will only *symbolize* an event that is taking place, and *you* will be the Son of God (Matthew 1:23 and Luke 1:34) In that act, *you* were the child who symbolized your acceptance. But the Son of God is also God the son, and the Son of God is made to say, "I and my Father are one." So Blake saw the whole vision so perfectly and so clearly, and told us in his fabulous works.

So said he of the Bible, "I know of no other Christianity and no other gospel than the liberty both of body and mind to exercise the Divine Arts of Imagination, Imagination, the real and eternal world . . . into which we shall all go after the death of this vegetable mortal body" (*Jerusalem,* Plate 77). He would accept no other form of Christianity. And he said all rituals and all creeds—everything external in the form of a ritual was anti-Christ. Now, religion means by definition a tithe, a devotion to the most exalted reality that one has experienced; but religion as practiced is simply artifice, creed, ceremony, confession, and all outward show; and Blake would have none of it. The whole thing to him was anti-Christian because to him the whole thing was from *within,* something that the individual experienced that no one by argument could shake.

Years later, another brilliant mind, William James, made this observation and wrote it in a letter, not in a book; he wrote it to his son, and the son allowed it to be published in 1920 in the *Atlantic Monthly.* In this James said, "The mother seed, the fountain head of all religions begin in the mystical experience of the individual. All theology, all ecclesiasticism are secondary growth, superimposed. These experiences belong to a region that is deeper, wiser, and more practical than that which the intellect inhabits. For this they are indestructible by intellectual argument and criticism."

Blake would have endorsed that 100 percent. You couldn't disturb him. They called him a mad person. Even to this very day, they speak of him as one who was unbalanced. And he confessed in one of his letters that William Cowper was one of the great poets and himself considered one of the six greatest of all writers of letters in the English tongue; he was a contemporary, died in 1800 and Blake in 1827. He was a much older man than Blake, and Blake did not say in his letter whether Cowper came to him while he walked this earth or after he made his exit from this earth. Because Blake could not conceive of death in any sense of the word: nothing died, and all things survived. He said, "Cowper came to me and said to me: 'Would that I were mad always. I cannot rest. Would you not make me truly mad?" Then he said, "Look at you, you are healthy and yet you are more mad than all of us. Would that I were as mad. I cannot rest until I am as mad as you are." Now he claims that's what Cowper said to him, that he would now be a "refugee from unbelief."

We think that we are sane when we believe in the evidence of the senses, when we believe in some mathematical state that proved itself in performance. And he spoke of Blake as one who was a real refugee from unbelief. So I tell you a fantastic story, and you don't believe it. Would that you would believe! Believe it though reason would deny it and your senses deny it, just to believe it and become a refugee from unbelief. Because true religion cannot be analyzed, you can't rationalize it. It's based upon these mystical experiences in the depth of the soul.

And so Blake said of the Bible, the entire Hebrew Bible—he did not mention a few of the works but just a few; he didn't mention Ruth, Nehemiah and things of that sort. But he said the Decalogue, the first five books, and then he said, Joshua and Judges, 1st and 2nd Samuel, 1st and 2nd Kings, the Book of Psalms, and the prophets, without naming the prophets. So he just simply named "the prophets," which he called the lesser prophets and also the major because he called Isaiah and Jeremiah and Ezekiel within the prophets. He said these are true visions, as well as the four gospels and Revelation. He did not mention the epistles. But he said the four gospels and Revelation and the Hebrew Bible are *eternal vision* of what really exists. He saw it so clearly.

So all these characters are personifications of eternal states. And commune with these states, for when you commune with them, they seem as real as you are. But they are personifications of God's infinite mind. Every aspect of his mind is personified. But you are not an aspect of the mind, something entirely different; you are one with God.

Man is All Imagination.
God is Man and exists in us and we in him.

The Eternal Body of Man is The Imagination, that is
God himself, the Divine Body, Jesus; we are his Members.

Part of the body of Jesus, and because there's only one name, we are he. So we pass through a process, a simple process, which we can't evoke; you can't hasten it, but when you least expect it, the divine mercy steps beyond and redeems man right into the body of Jesus. Then he passes through these stages where he is born from above, where suddenly he beholds the divine Son as *his* Son, and then the great woven structure of the body, the temple, is torn from top to bottom. And then he ascends to be one around this infinite throne of Jesus who is God.

I actually believe it. I can't prove it to you, and I can't take you with me into that moment of time where I experienced it. I can only tell you I have experienced it and ask you to believe it and share with me in belief that you yourself may become a refugee from unbelief. For the man who cannot leave what he can touch with his hands and rationalize, cannot believe. And this is something that you are called upon, although you have not seen it: "Blessed is the man who has not seen and still believes." That is how the gospel of John ends, chapter 20, verse 29: "Blessed is the man who has not seen and still believes." Those who heard about it, who would eventually experience it, like Job, he said, "I have heard of thee with the hearing of the ear but now my eye sees thee" (Job 42:5). And so he heard about it and then came the experience, and he saw exactly what Blake is talking about because Blake saw it.

So I ask you to believe with me and take his works. I wouldn't attempt to interpret for you. I have so many commentaries of Blake at home, and they cost much more than all of Blake's works put together, any one of them. You can buy Blake for five dollars, for four dollars—all of his works, including his letters. And I have invested in Blake's works at home close to a thousand dollars in commentaries, and no two agree as to what Blake means by these fantastic experiences. But you see, I bought all these commentaries of Blake before I had the experiences. I could have saved a thousand dollars. I don't regret it. I have them at home, and there they stand in my library. Three volumes I paid $100 for, published by a dealer whose name I don't know and don't care, said he just got back from England and these are rare volumes—it's by William Butler Yeats. And so I have these three on credit, and he made me pay $100 for them. Others, he made me pay fifty-five dollars and sixty-five dollars for them, similar volumes. And I have the whole of Blake in a small little Nonesuch volume.

So you read him, and all of a sudden, you see exactly what he's trying to tell you because you had a similar experience. And then comes the unfolding of the flower within you, the tree within you, and you have the experience, the same thing. So all will have the identical experience, colored a little bit differently because we are all unique in God's eyes. Not identical, a little bit different, because no two are alike in God's eye. But we have the same experience as we unfold on this great tree of life.

So just think of it. If I could tell you what I would feel from Blake . . . someone said of Blake that he was the last civilized man. Well, I hope not, but that's what was said of him. He was the last civilized man. For Blake had no venom in him, no impulse to hurt; he didn't have to restrain the impulse. Being all virtuous, he acted from impulse and not from rules. He was simply a virtuous man in the sense that he loved people.

So if I would take the summary of Blake and tell you what I get out of it, I would say, tell your children while they are still tots, all the little children, and teach them never unnecessarily to hurt a creature or desecrate a flower. That is the beginning of reverence, and reverence is the beginning of wisdom. If you couldn't hurt a flower, you couldn't desecrate it. Have you seen little children, not knowing what they're doing but in the presence of adults who should know better, and they will simply take a lovely rose and tear it and desecrate it. Well, if the parent at that moment, or the adult, whether it be parent or not, would stop the child and explain to the child not at any time unnecessarily to hurt a creature, take the wings from a butterfly (I did it myself), to take the wings from a fly, or to take the wings from something else. No reason for it, but I did it; as a child I did it. But I did it when possibly there was no one around, like my father or mother, to stop me in the act. But I did it—maybe you did it—but I did it. But I know today from experience that if you can take a child and in its youth, in its infancy, teach it never unnecessarily to hurt a creature or desecrate a flower, that would be to it the beginning of reverence, and reverence is the beginning of wisdom.

Take George Washington Carver, who would take a flower in his hand and talk to it. He couldn't hurt; the man couldn't hurt. He was incapable of hurt. He would talk to a sick flower and ask the flower what was wrong with it and try to tell him that he, in turn, may bring the solution to that rose bush, which he did. And he gave us because he couldn't hurt, this synthetic world of ours today, really. He took the ordinary little peanut; he talked to a peanut and wondered, "What are you for? Why did God make you? He made you for a purpose. Tell me, why did God make you?" Then the peanut communed with George Washington Carver. Today we have 300 by-products from the peanut and hundreds of by-products from the southern pine and from other things.

I heard that gentleman the year he died. Just before he died, he spoke in New York City at a forum held every year by the *Herald Tribune*, always held at the old Waldorf Astoria. He said—and I heard him and saw him—about this concern about tomorrow not being able to feed the world, he said, from the southern states of this country, forget the northern states, from the southern states, we could feed the entire world and clothe the entire world from by-products. What we could extract from the southern pine, the peanut and all this, the synthetic world—he called it the synthetic world—we could feed and clothe the entire world from what could be produced out of the southern states of America. Forget the northern states, just from the southern states, I could clothe and feed the entire world.

Now today, you go into a store and they brag about the synthetic garment. They call it Dacron, or they call it by some other name, and tell you how much better it is than the so-called natural thing, which you would normally wear. All these are synthetic products, and they claim they are better in feeling and in lasting wear and in everything else. All that goes back to a man who couldn't hurt. He was born a slave. I think he was sold for a horse or something. Someone had to redeem him, and here is a man born to slavery, who just couldn't hurt. And he is one of the mental, spiritual giants of the world. If you met him beyond the grave, you would see a glorious being like a Blake because he couldn't hurt.

So I would say to everyone here who is in contact with tomorrow's children, start it. If you start the child and tell the child never, unnecessarily—and by that I mean, if a horse breaks its foot, then you have to destroy it. You can't mend it, and the merciful thing to do would be to blow its brains out. That would be a merciful act. But then you would do it not unnecessarily. So Blake said,

> A Horse misus'd upon the Road
> Calls to Heaven for Human blood.
> A dog starv'd at his Master's Gate
> Predicts the ruin of the State.
> A Robin Red breast in a Cage
> Puts all Heaven in a Rage.

To take this wonderful thing and cage it for your own amusement when it should cut the airy way. And then he said,

> The Skylark wounded in the wing,
> A Cherubim does cease to sing.

You wouldn't think a cherubim, one with the seraphim around the throne of God, would at that very moment when we wound the skylark in its wing would be silent. But that's the interrelated world: "All things by a law divine in one another's being mingle." So you could not wound the skylark in the wing and expect a cherubim to continue to sing. And so all of a sudden, things come to an end by our misuse of this fantastic power that is ours. For being *all* Imagination, as we misuse the power that is Imagination we cause cherubim to become silent. We cause the whole of heaven to cry out when we cage something that should be set loose and free in this world.

But you start, and I'm quite sure it wouldn't take more than one generation, if the world would believe it, if you start it in the home with children. Take them into the garden and let them see, and just watch their reactions. Some may be more violent and tear it off, but stop them right there. Don't hit them, just stop them and explain to them that it is a creation of God. The one who made the stars made this for your enjoyment, not for your destruction. And explain they should not desecrate the flower. Then, if you see them taking off the wings of the butterfly because they are given that way, then explain that they should never unnecessarily hurt a creature. They would suddenly believe it, they trust you, and then suddenly that's part of their structure. They couldn't then violate that conditioned mind. Why, it wouldn't take any time to really become a world like a Blake. What a world that would be!

So I say to you, Blake, read him. I could talk about him from now to the end of time and never exhaust him. He lived to be seventy years old. He never went to school. His visions began at four, and he thanked his father for not sending him to school to be flogged into memorizing the works of a fool. And even in today's paper, the *New York Times*, ___(??) edition, a science editor told the story of man's *new* concept of the Universe—a radical departure from what it held only last year. Well, this is not final you know. This will be a radical departure from what it will be called next year. And that is man's concept. Whether the thing is really expanding to the limit of complete explosion, or whether it is like a breath, where it will go to a certain point and then once more begin to contract, taking unnumbered trillions of years, they don't know and they hope to find it out through telescopes. So they are experimenting with their telescopes, and their mathematical concepts.

But Blake made this observation that "God is not a mathematical diagram" (*Annotations to Berkeley*). You'll never in eternity discover God through mathematics. Not in eternity will you find him as a mathematical diagram. When you find him, you'll find him as man. And so he said,

> God Appears and God is Light
> To those poor Souls who dwell in Night,
> But does a Human Form Display
> To those who Dwell in Realms of Day.
> (*Auguries of Innocence*)

When you meet him, it's man. But how can I describe him when he himself describes the body and the form is love? How do you describe love? Yet I stood in the presence of love; it was human. But he said,

> Mercy has a human heart,
> Pity a human face,
> Love, the human *form* divine,
> And Peace, the human dress.
> (The Divine Image, *Songs of Innocence*)

But how are you going to describe love? Love is the human form divine. When I stood in the presence of love, it was human, and it was Jesus, and it *is* form, but it's infinite love. I couldn't think of anything but infinite love as I stood in his presence. Then you understand the words concerning forgiveness that "In Heaven the whole Art of Living Is Forgetting and Forgiving" (Notes, Plate 81). And you stand in his presence, and you hear these words ring out, "Forgive them, they know not what they do" (Luke 23:24). "Mutual forgiveness of each vice; such are the Gates of Paradise." No one can get through holding any resentment because you are holding it against a being when it should be a state, and the states are fixed forever through which we pass.

So I would encourage everyone to read Blake. He grows every year bigger and bigger in the minds of men, yet he died and is buried in the unknown grave. I doubt if anyone truly knows where he's buried, possibly, because he was poor, and in those days in England, they buried paupers four and six to a grave. So who knows where he's buried? At least we have his works, those that survived. And so, after two hundred years, here is this giant. And in his day, we had men who were only remembered because of a certain violence, like George III, who reigned when he lived, when this was a colony. And here, this mad George, *truly* mad, and nothing was more sane than Blake. And so George, who was then king of England, who founded this colony, would give away sections of it, vast areas to those that he favored. He was mad as a hatter, and they called Blake the madman. Yet Cowper, who *did* go mad—three times he was put away—appeared to Blake and asked Blake to make him "truly" mad. Not mad as the world judges it because there are unbalanced mental states, no question about it. But he called upon Blake to make him truly mad, "Make me so mad, Blake, till I become like you, a refugee from unbelief." He was torn between the two.

If I could only go all out and believe in the reality of my imaginal act and not look back, just go all out and believe that things are as I desire them to be. But don't look down now to my understanding to see if it is really happening, like pulling up the little seed to see if it's taking root. Really believe that it is going to take root and, in its own way, it unfolds within itself and grows. But don't pull it up! Walk right out in the belief that things are as I desire them to be, even though at the very moment, it seems darker than ever. Walk right out in it, just as though it were true. And if I will do that, that's what Blake did.

They said that many a day, he had not a potato in the house and no money. And his wife must have been an angel of angels. To remind him that there was no food in the house and that he would have to go out and sell one of his paintings or get a commission to make a painting, she would put before him at the bare table an empty plate and a spoon. So when he came to dinner, well, that's it. Then he took the hint, and then he would go out and try to borrow a pound or a few shillings or try to get a commission for a picture that he hadn't yet painted. He lived in that so-called dream world.

But what he has done to posterity! How he has affected the entire world! And when you think today that, no one who understands the English tongue called upon to make a list of the six greatest users of the English tongue of all time could, if they understood it, omit the name of Blake. They may not have the same order of value, but within six, they could not omit the name of Blake. And he never went to school, just that *inspired* mind, the greatest, wonderful mind. He said he talked to Isaiah, he talked to Ezekiel, and he asked them about Imagination, and they said, "Why, in the days of Imagination, Imagination moved mountains; but in this day there are very few who are capable of removing mountains because they are not imaginative. They don't imagine anymore. But in the days of Imagination, Imagination would move mountains," said Ezekiel to him. You must read it, that's in his *The Marriage of Heaven and Hell* (Plate 12-13).

Well now, I could not, as I told you, for the rest of my days exhaust or do justice to Blake, but just enough to encourage you to read him for yourself. And take my experience, having spent a thousand dollars in the works of Blake—who can afford that these days?—you buy less and omit the commentaries. I have them at home and I read them and they remain read but not to be reread they remain. But I make Blake my daily companion; I read him daily as I do my Bible. So take Blake and take the Bible and read it. If you don't understand it at the first reading, reread it and keep on rereading. I'll tell you one thing it will do for you; it will increase your vocabulary and lift your use of words to the heights.

Now let us go into the Silence.

*   *   *

Q: What is the symbol of the lark?

A: When he said, "The Skylark wounded in the wing, a Cherubim does cease to sing." So he identifies that skylark as but the externalized shadow of the song of a cherubim. He calls this world the world of shadows, faintly reflecting an activity that cannot be seen by mortal eyes, that the heavenly world enacted and throws its shadow to interest man in some strange way in this world. For man is in a world of sleep; it's sound asleep. His greatest poem, *Jerusalem*, begins on the theme that "The Sleep of Ulro"—this fantastic world is called Ulro by him—where we are so sound asleep it is likened unto eternal death. Then he calls upon us to awake. So all these will aid us to awake.

And so it's the cherubim by his song in this world through a shadow of a bird called a skylark. But we go out and shoot doves, for instance. I have friends of mine—and I call them my friends—and they wait eagerly for the dove season. Of course, I've always refused their dinner invitations to come and dine on doves. Well, I just love the doves; they come all over my place and the mourning dove when it begins to coo. And of course, coming from Barbados as I did, we have a certain native feeling toward the dove, and so they're fed ___(??). The male dove is actually saying, and you listen to him carefully, "Moses spoke God's Word" and then the female answers, "He did, he did." ___(??). You listen carefully, you will hear that male bird in his coo saying, "Moses spoke God's Word." You listen to him. I listen to him every morning. And then someone shoots him and asks me to come and dine? No.

He tells us of the little lamb: "A Lamb misus'd breeds Public Strife, but yet forgives the Butcher's knife." For that purpose, to feed these vegetable bodies, the shadows, the mortal bodies, you forgive them that use of the knife. But to abuse it, "The Lamb *misus'd* breeds Public Strife, but yet forgives the Butcher's knife." Goodnight.

YOU CAN FORGIVE SIN

March 29, 1963

You can forgive sin. That to most people will be blasphemy, as you will hear later on, quoting from scripture. It is so common among all of us to ascribe our ills and our troubles to outward things, like the present conditions of the world, to our environment, or simply to things. And these things may be things that are absent from our world, or they may be things that we have in our world but still things, while all along the real cause of our ills is sin. So we're told he was called Jesus because he came to save men from their sins. His only concern was the saving of man from sin. So what is sin? Sin means missing the mark, missing the road, and missing the goal in life. If you haven't a mark, you can't sin. If you have a goal in this world and you do not realize it and you missed it, then you've sinned. So his purpose is to show man how *not* to sin in this world. No condemnation. Tell me your aim and tell me your goal, and I'll tell you God's Word; that's what he said. He's come only to show a man how *not* to miss his objective in this world.

Now we turn to the Book of Mark, the 2nd chapter, or we can read the same thing with a little different twist to it in the 9th chapter of Matthew—it's the story of a paralytic. As we are told, he was preaching the word, that is, the story of salvation, and they brought in a paralytic carried by four men. Seeing their faith, he said to the paralytic, "My son, your sins are forgiven." Scribes sitting around thought in their hearts, "What is he saying? It is blasphemous! Who could forgive sin but God alone?" And discerning in their hearts what they contemplated, he said, "Which is easier, to say the paralytic, 'Your sins are forgiven,' or 'Rise, take up your bed and walk'?" And so he said to him, "Take up your bed and walk and go home," and he rose and went on his way home. Then we are told those who saw him were afraid, and they glorified God who would give such authority to men, for it was a man who did it. *We* are that man. It is to us that this authority to forgive sin has been given. But the world thought it was simply the exclusive power of some being *outside* of man. You read it in the 2nd chapter of Mark and the 9th of Matthew.

Now, what is this ability to forgive sin? We know that sin means "missing the mark." The one that forgave it called himself "the truth." He said, "I am the truth. If you know my word and you abide in my word, then you will know the truth, and the truth will set you free" (John 8:32). For the whole story begins, he was teaching the truth, teaching the word. Now he calls himself "the truth." And "if you know the truth and you abide in my word, the truth will set you free." If I said to you tonight, "What would you like to be in this world?" and then you name it, "I would like to be . . . ," and you name no matter what it is in this world, then I would turn to you and I'd say, "You are that. But you are it, right now you are it." You would say, "I am it? Well, I can't believe it. I am not that," then you are denying the truth. "I am the truth." I am everything in this world. Everything that man could ever imagine, I am.

All right, so you imagine what you would like to be. If you cannot remain faithful, remaining loyal to that vision of yourself, then you are sinning. And not to sin is to have a goal. You have a goal, what would it be like were it true? Were it true that I am and then I name it, what would it be like? Then I would see the world as I would see it *were* it true. If I remain faithful to that vision of the world just as though it were true, no power in the world could stop me from realizing it but *no* power. I'd realize it. How? Don't ask me. But I would realize it. If it took the entire world of three billion to play different parts to aid me in the fulfillment of my vision, they would play it without knowing that they played it. Makes no difference if they knew it or didn't know it; they would all have to contribute to the fulfillment of my vision if I remain loyal to that vision.

So what would it be like were it true? And I ask, "What true?"—that I were the man that now I would like to be. If I said to you right now, "Is there a man in this room who's rich?" and no one said, "I am rich", well then, that's not your goal. Or if it *is* your goal, you are missing it if you didn't reply. But "Is there a man in this room"—by man I mean generic man—"who is known, who is contributing to the world's good?" and no one replies "I am he," well then, either it is not your goal or else if it *is* your goal, you're missing it. So the name is "I am he" as told us in the 24th verse, the 8th chapter of the Book of John, "Except you believe that I am he you die in your sins." You remain just where you are, missing the mark, unless you believe that I am he. Not a man talking to me; this is taking place in the depth of the soul of man. If you don't believe now that I am the one that I *would* be, well then, you're going to miss your goal. You are sinning.

And so it doesn't come from without at all; it isn't caused by anything on the outside at all. My ills, my troubles, and my problems are *not* caused by conditions and by environment and by all the other things at all; it's caused *only* by sin, and sin is missing the mark. There's only one person, one being in the world, that could hit that mark, and it's God. God forgives sin, as we're told in the 43rd chapter of the Book of Isaiah, "I am the Lord . . . I am thy Savior, and there is no other Savior" (verse 3). "I, I am he, and there is no other Savior" (verse 11). No one was formed before me, and no one will be formed after me. I am the Savior." So you'll be saved from what you are. There's only one being in the world that can save you and that being is I AM.

So you say to yourself, "What would it be like were it true that I am now the man that I would like to be?" *Assume* that you are it. Dare to believe that you are it. Walk in that belief just as though it were true and no power in the world can stop it, but *no* power. There is no one greater than God. Say "I am"; that's God. There's no one greater than God. You stand in the presence of a being; and because he has a little tag and he may be a premier of a certain country or maybe a queen of a certain land or maybe the president of a certain land, and you think that because of that title, he's greater than you are? You're missing the mark. You can't stand in the presence of anyone who is greater than you are if you *know* who you are. You aren't going to laud it over them, no, but no one is smaller either, all God.

Then you are told, "Go and tell them all." So here we are told in the Book of Ezekiel, I think it is the 3rd chapter, the 18th verse, and 33rd chapter, the 8th verse. But you can read it; they aren't long chapters. "Go and tell them. If you do not tell them and they sin, and you do not tell them, they will die in their sins, but their blood will be upon your head. If you tell them and they do not repent, they will die in their sins, but their blood will not be upon your head. So tell them." And so Jesus is made to confess that he told them that their blood may not be upon *his* head. In the Book of Acts, Paul makes the confession, "I have declared it. I did not stray from the declaration of this truth; therefore I am innocent of the blood of all of them." He told them that he may not carry with him that secret to the grave and did not share it with the world. And so I told them all that this is a principle that cannot fail.

Now let us come back to the paralytic. You came here tonight under your own steam, as it were. If I told you that *we* are the paralytic of scripture, maybe you'll be surprised. They were brought into the place by four men. Know who the four men are? The ancients always called by the four senses, spoke of the four rivers that ran out of Eden. They didn't think of five senses, they always spoke of four senses. They joined taste and touch together because they depended upon contact. To taste something, it must be contacted; and to touch something, it must be contacted. But they separated sight, sound, and scent. These three were separate in the great symbolism of scripture. But taste and touch were joined, so they called them the four senses.

We came here tonight borne by these four men, the four senses. I know my bank balance, all right, in two weeks, Uncle Sam wants part of what I've earned. He didn't ask me to consider anything at all; he told me what I owed him. I don't even know Uncle Sam, but they tell me he exists somewhere, where I don't know, but he exists. So I'm supposed to pay on the fifteenth of next month x-number of dollars. Regardless of how I live, I must save something to pay him that much. Perfectly all right; it's the land of Caesar. So I am fully aware of that; I can see my bank balance. I know what's in my world. I can take all of my senses and bring them to play upon what I must meet tomorrow. I was brought here tonight on the shoulders of these four men. Now he tells me, "Your sins are forgiven you. Rise and walk." How can I do it, knowing that I must pay on the fifteenth? Knowing what I must do between now and then, how must I do it? "Your sins are forgiven." But who can forgive but God? Only God can forgive, and God is what?—I AM. All right, I will now see the world as I would see it were it now May 1, with all things behind me, completely paid and paid in full.

Suppose I were unemployed. I would walk here tonight on the backs of these four men. I know I'm unemployed, and I have rent to pay, food to buy, all these things, and he tells me that my sins are forgiven and to rise, take up my bed, and walk? How would I do it? I was brought in here on the backs of four men. I'm called upon to rise, ignore these four men, walk on my own steam now. Don't walk based upon what before allowed you to think and to hear, and to smell and to taste, and to touch. Walk out of here not aided by these four at all. Walk on my own.

Well, how would I walk on my own? I *would* ignore the evidence of the senses. They brought me in here. I completely ignore what they tell me that I really have in this world, and I see what I would like to see. I assume that things are as I would like them to be. I would influence every being in this world to play their part to fulfill what I am assuming that I am in this world. So I came in as a paralytic and walk out on my own steam. So that's the story.

Every being in the world is called upon to rise and to walk out, for he forgives your sin. He comes into the world only to free man of sin. I don't care what you've ever done in this world. Don't look back. Don't look upon the things as they are. Look upon things, as they *ought* to be. The man that you would like to be, assume that you are it; the woman that you would like to be, assume that you are it. And see that, and see that only. Then you will know what it is to forgive sin. Well, who forgives sin? God forgives sin. Who forgave you? Well, I assumed. Who assumed? I assumed. Well, that's God. I AM is his name. So I am assuming that I am the man that I would like to be. Well, that's God. There's nothing impossible to God. So I am assuming that I am—that's God. Then I begin to name it, and I walk in that state—and that's God. There's nothing but God. So forget what you have done, what you seemingly are doing, and dream of the man or the woman that you would like to be and dare to assume that you are it.

Now we are told by the great Blake, "The Spirit of Jesus is the continual forgiveness of sin," every moment of time forgiveness of sin. Tonight, when we go into the Silence, we can sit here at this moment for a minute and forgive each other. Suppose now I could actually hear everyone rise and tell the most fantastic story in the world about themselves or about a friend of theirs, a relative of theirs, someone. Suppose I really *wanted* to be told from this platform, from this audience, that I would sit in the Silence and listen to that and *only* that, just as though it were true—the most fantastic story in the world that you could tell me, individually, all of us. And if I walked out of here tonight convinced that I have heard it and you heard it and remain loyal to what I have imagined that I have heard, I *must* hear it. No power can stop it if I remain loyal to it. If anyone should say it hasn't worked, I am not asking any questions why it hasn't worked, as far as I am concerned, it *has* worked; I have seen it.

But I know that the vision that I will hold now concerning you, individually, will have its own appointed hour. I know it is ripening and it's going to flower. If to you it seems slow, I ask you to wait, for this thing is *sure* and it will *not* be late (Habakkuk 2:3). If I actually assume that things are as I would like them to be for every being here and I remain loyal, I either know that this story is true or it's false. *I* know it's true. It can't fail. But there's no power in the world to make it fail. It can't fail!

But if . . . for instance, another word for sin in the Bible is trespass. In our wonderful Lord's Prayer, "Forgive us our trespasses as we forgive those who trespass against us" (Matthew 6:12). It's a minor infraction of this principle. *Trespass* means the "individual lapse, just a temporary lapse." So that tonight, you and I begin to discuss a personality. What am I doing discussing a personality? He's only in a state. So I ___(??) think he's unemployed; and you and I get into a discussion and discuss a man who is unemployed and we see him as unemployed and begin to say, well, the conditions are bad or maybe he wasn't good enough for the job, and suddenly I am trespassing. I am not applying this principle. I am seeing him as the state. He's not the state. But I may fall into that little trap. We all do it every day and all day long. We read the paper, and a man is called a great man because he happens to be President or he may be some other person in this world and you read some columnist about him and then you're carried away with what the columnist tells us, the arguments presented to us, and suddenly begin to think as he would have you think and you're trespassing. "Lord, forgive us our trespasses as we forgive those who trespass against us." It's a slight departure from our goal. We were moved aside by what we heard, by what we read, by what we saw in this world—and that's trespassing.

And so I discuss someone who can't find a job, and suddenly I think, "Well, what is his salary? Is he qualified? What did he earn in the past?" I'm asking all these things, and they are *irrelevant*. Not to this principle do they have any value whatsoever. What does he want? He wants a job? Well, how much do you want? And he names a figure. I don't care what he names.

Now, were it true—suppose it were true that he had it. Well then, let me assume that it's true. I begin to see the world as I would see it for him were it true and feel the joy that should be mine were he now gainfully employed earning that sort of money. Now this thing is either true or it's false. I tell you it's true. And so every day, you and I can say the Lord's Prayer, but really saying it asks for forgiveness of our trespasses. Then he shows mercy upon us to forgive us for having trespassed this day, for having gotten off the beam as it were.

So here is the story. He's brought in on the backs of four men. He himself had no faith. He's saying not to the man; he's telling it to those who brought him in, the senses. In spite of what they knew, there was still a certain faith and brought him into the presence of God, knowing that God could forgive sin. He said, "Because of your faith"—he speaks now to those who brought him; he didn't speak to the man at first, and then he addresses the paralytic—"My son, your sins are forgiven you." Here is a vicarious faith. So I can have the faith for you if you don't have it for yourself. You can have it for me if I don't have it for myself. And quite often, vicarious faith is easier than the direct faith. That, if I can turn to you, if you really believe that an imaginal act is fact, and if you could actually believe that I am now what I would like to be and although at the moment I doubt and I am unfaithful, you can save me. It's such a wonderful story. In spite of myself, you can pull me out of it. For the man had *no* faith. Those who brought him on their backs showed faith in bringing him into the presence of God. God commended them for their faith and then turned to the paralytic and said, "My son, your sins are forgiven." And those who heard said, "What sort of blasphemy! Who can forgive sin but God alone?" Well,

God did forgive sin, for he was the I AM. He said, "Unless you believe that I am he, you die in your sins."

So I ask you tonight, turn to your neighbor, turn to all, and maybe *you* could hear what the other one wants and rejoice in his good fortune, and he or she hear what you want and let them rejoice in your good fortune. And actually *feel* that it's true. See the world as you would see it were they as they would like to be, and may I tell you, they'll become it. So this is the story of our ability to forgive sin.

So they were afraid when they saw what happened, and they glorified God who had given such *authority* to men. For we are told, if you retain it, it's retained and if you release it, it's released. So I see a man, and I judge him by my senses. I say, all right, so he's no good, and so I retain his restrictions, his paralytic state. But I could release him by seeing him standing on his own feet and moving in this world in a glorious manner. And so the material that formerly I would discard as no good, having heard the story, I don't discard it anymore. I take it and use it. I take the same man that formerly I would discard as hopeless in this wonderful world of ours and see him as gainfully employed, loved, and loving. And believe that the thing that I am seeing for him is true. To the degree that I am faithful to that concept that I hold of him, it becomes true in his world.

So that's our power. We have power to forgive sin, and sin only means missing the mark. If you don't have a mark in this world, you can't sin. It doesn't have anything to do with some moral issue, no, do you have a goal? Do you have some objective in this world? If you have an objective, then this is how you realize it: suppose it were true. Now he tells us in the 8th of Romans, "Let us walk now not by flesh but by Spirit." The flesh would be my senses. My senses deny that I am what I would like to be—let us not walk by flesh, and let us walk by Spirit. Well, Spirit is, well, to see it now in my Imagination just as though it were true. Well, tonight I may go home to find an empty cupboard, perfectly all right. To find that there's a notice under my door that tomorrow or else. That's perfectly all right. If I believe what I've imagined, it wouldn't make any difference what threat was given me. It would make no difference whatsoever if I really believe in it. Now believe it, we're told. If you believe it, it will crystallize into fact. It doesn't really matter what threat at the moment, what my senses tell me, I will ignore the four who brought me into this place. I will not now anymore be borne by these four; I will simply walk by Spirit and not by flesh.

So I ask you to try it. If you try it, you can't fail. And realizing your objectives, may I also ask you to share it with me that I may tell others of your wonderful stories. A man sat in this audience, he and his wife, a little while ago, well, it is now about three months, and he wrote me a sweet, wonderful letter, which I got this morning. He expected a big bonus. He had worked hard; found a good job, with all the promises; and then came Christmas and all the bonuses. One who was never on the job, one who was always off, but by his estimate, one of the girlfriends of the boss, and so she got the great big bonus. She was never on the job. He who had done all the work got practically nothing. He and I agreed just mentally that he would have the most wonderful job, with more money, with everything. This is now going on April. It seemed a long while, but today he *is* on that job with more than he had, more than he expected—more responsibility, more opportunity, and more of everything.

And I received that letter this morning. I remained faithful to that letter that I knew would come from him when he would write it. Maybe he could have written it two weeks ago, maybe he could have; I do not know. I see his mother-in-law in the audience tonight. Maybe she can tell me after the meeting. But I got the letter today, and I can't tell you the thrill that was in our household this morning when we read the letter from this man, who told us of this wonderful thing that had happened to him. Within the area that he wants to work, just what he wants to work, just what he wanted, everything. And all that I did, I heard him tell me what he would tell me were it true, and I never wavered. So I haven't heard and didn't hear, but this morning's mail brought it.

So I only ask you to be as faithful to any imaginal state in this world; I don't care what it is. Take anyone but anyone, because in everyone God resides. Everyone has to say, "I am"—that's God. So you may say, "Well, I am an Einstein." Wonderful! But you still say, "I am" before you say Einstein, and I AM transcends all the Einstein's of the world, for I AM is God. When I say, "I am Neville," Neville is a tiny thing resting upon the foundation that is God. If I say, "I am rich," I don't care what you call wealth, that's a little tiny thing on the foundation of God. And God is infinite; God is everything. Therefore, whatever you say, before you say it, you say, "I am"—that's his name; that's God's name. "Go and tell them I AM has sent you. When they ask, just say I AM. That's my name" (Exodus 3:14). And so before you make any claim, you say, "I am," and that's God's name.

And so no matter who the being is, suppose now he would say to you, "I am . . . and ___(??)," and you listen. At the moment the four men who brought him into your presence brought him in paralyzed. He isn't that at all because they deny it. For the four senses are bringing him, and his four senses *deny* that he's that, that he's ___(??) that he would like to be. So he's called upon the name of God. And when you call upon the name of God, you don't say, "In the name of God so and so." You ask *with* the name of

God, and to ask *with* the name of God, and God's name is I AM, you say, "I am," and you name it. I'm known, I'm wealthy, I'm secure, and I am healthy. Whatever you claim, ask with the name of God, and then *believe* it. If you ask with the name of God and believe it, mentally you will see the world as you've never seen it before you made that claim. And then seeing it as you would see it were it true, remain faithful to that claim, and it must crystallize in your world.

This is this principle. And it goes for every being in the world, regardless of nationality and regardless of the pigment of the skin. It's all God because everyone in the world has to say, "I am," before he says, "I am this." He said, "Who are you?" "Well, I am a man." All right, but you said, "I am" before you said man. You said, "I am an American." But you said, "I am," before you said American. You said, "I am an Indian. I am a Japanese. I'm a Chinese." But before you said anything you said, "I am." That's God. Now what kind of a being would you like to be? Well, I would like to be, and you name it. I would like to be loving. I would like to be loved. I would like to be sexy. I would like to respect. I would like—and you name all these things. All right, but it's I AM doing it. Well, then, take this fabulous world of yours, and take all your dreams and put it on the only foundation in the world. There is no other foundation than God, and God is I AM.

So here, the paralytic came here tonight in all of us, and we were borne on the backs of four men; and the four men are our four senses: sight, sound, scent, taste, and touch. Taste and touch are joined into one because they depend upon contact. So these are the four streams, the four rivers of life that come out of the garden of Eden, and they bear us all over this world. But every moment of time we are in the presence of I AM. Let them put me down, and let me forgive me my sins. And so I forgive myself by daring to assume that I am what I would like to be. Assuming that I am what I would like to be, I walk in that assumption and that assumption slowly crystallizes into fact. So you try it. Try it and you'll be able to share with me as this gentleman shared with me today his wonderful story of his good fortune. No power in the world can stop it, but none.

But here, when we speak of sin, don't let anyone scare you about sin. He comes to forgive the sinner. His only interest is in the sinner. And so the so-called moral violations and all these violations, forget them! I'm not asking you to go through violations, but forget them. Everything will be wiped out, but everything. But it is my duty having heard the story and having proved it to tell you. For I am told through the confession of Paul, through the confession of Ezekiel, through the confession of Jesus, that if I don't tell you what I know of God's law, well then, your sin is upon my head. But if I tell you and you still do not believe me, you will die in your sins, but your blood will not be upon my head. So Paul said, I will tell them. I have declared the entire counsel of God to them, so I am innocent of their blood. Read it, the 20ᵗʰ chapter of Acts, the 26ᵗʰ through the 28ᵗʰ verses: I am innocent of their blood. I told them, they didn't believe it, and I am innocent of their blood, for I declared the entire counsel of God to them.

Infinite states . . . a man falls into a state, so he's in a state, but he is not the state. Take him out of the state by saying to him while he's in the state, "What would you like?" He says, "I would like to be" completely opposite to the state he's in. But he names the state that he would like to enter, and you put him into that state by asking yourself, What would it be like were it true that he now . . . and you name the thing that he would like to be. Then, as you name it to yourself, you see the man as he would be seen were it true. Then you remain faithful, leaving him just where he is, but you remain faithful to this concept that you hold of him, and he comes out of it. On reflection, he may say, "It would have happened anyway." Perfectly all right, you know how it happened.

So you tell every being in the world the story if you have the chance to tell them, and telling them, it's entirely up to them. They either believe it or disbelieve it. As we are told, "If you do not believe that I am he, you die in your sins." Read it carefully in the 8ᵗʰ of John, "If you do not believe that I am he." Well, those who read it, you might think a man is telling you that I am God and you are not. If you don't believe that I am God and you are not, well then, you die in your sins. That's not it at all. The whole story is taking place in the soul of man. If *you* don't believe that yourself saying "I am" is the being that you would be, well then, remain as you are and die in that limited state. That's the story. So, "Unless you believe that I am he, you die in your sins."

Now, he tells you the truth: "Know the truth and the truth will set you free." And they complain, "Well, we *are* free." Here they are enslaved, and they thought they were free. That's the whole vast world; you and I say, "We're Americans. We're free!" Can't pay rent, to what state are we free? Can't buy the soup, to what state are we free? By saying that I'm an American? These are all words. I must be *free* to move across this world. I can *only* be free if I know the art of forgiving sin, and the only one who can forgive sin is God, and God's name is I AM. In this world today, right in our wonderful land, there are hundreds of thousands who are imprisoned physically, but they are Americans. There are hundreds of thousands; in fact, they said six million who are unemployed, who can't pay the rent. Free? They're Americans.

I say, go tell every being in the world of the story of God, as told us in both Old and New Testament, and set them free. They can be free if they know who they are. There isn't one being in jail tonight who if you ask him "Who are you?" before he tells you the name says, "I am John." I am John what? "I am John Smith. I am so many years old." But before all these things, he tells you "I am." For I have seen this; you see, it frightens people. As you're told in that 9th chapter of the Book of Matthew, they were frightened: "When they saw what happened, they were afraid, and they glorified God, who had given such authority to men."

In San Francisco, when I told this story, a lady sat in my audience who had just received notice from the army that her brother had been tried, court-martialed, and sentenced to six month's hard labor. She went home and said, "If this man is telling the truth, I can set my brother free." She sat upstairs in her apartment. She had to go down the stairs to the door if anyone came to it. And sitting alone upstairs, she lost herself in this imaginal state that the bell was ringing, and she ran down the stairs, threw the door open, and embraced a brother who was waiting there. And she did it. And she did it. For one solid week, she sat there in the morning when she had breakfast and imagined that the bell was ringing, and she ran mentally down the stairs, threw the door open, and saw her brother; and she embraced him. The next Sunday morning, before she came to my meeting, it happened. And when she came to my meeting, she couldn't restrain herself any longer; she couldn't restrain the impulse to rise. She jumped up in the audience, a thousand people present, and she jumped up and said, "I *must* tell this story." And she told her story of redeeming and setting free her brother. He was honorably discharged. Although he had been court-martialed and sentenced to six month's hard labor, it was retried, and he was honorably discharged, and he came home that Sunday morning, one week later.

I say everyone can be forgiven. He's not the same being that he was. Whatever he did to warrant the court-martial, why must he, so called, pay the last ounce? If she could redeem him by pulling him out of that state that caused him to do whatever he did, he's not the same person. If I pull out of a state into another state . . . if I had tonight someone that was a horrible beast in my world but I determined to make him a loving, kind person in my world, and then he comes into my world and he demonstrates his kindness by his acts, by everything; he isn't the same being he was when I disliked him. The same immortal soul, but he's in a different state. Formerly I was judging the state. But I keep him in that state and make him pay a price that only belongs to that state? You see, there is such a thing in this world as God's mercy. All sins must be expiated unless God intervenes and is merciful. Well, you are God; you can intervene. He gave it to you. Only God can forgive sin and *you* could forgive sin; therefore, are you not he? And God is merciful. But can't you be merciful and completely transform any being in this world? Oh, what a thrill it is to be able to transform a being and see them differently at the end of a little while! So I ask you to try it, just try it. And you will share with me your good news and tell me how you've done it. It works, may I tell you it doesn't fail. It can't fail.

But believe that statement in the Lord's Prayer, "Forgive us our trespasses," for today we trespass; we actually trespass. We heard a rumor and we got off the beam and we simply went upon the other land, as it were. We see the sign No Trespassing all over the place, and we step on the other fellow's land; well, that's the way we trespass: we step upon it. Don't! No matter what you hear of anyone, just have no ears to hear it if it is not something that is lovely. Because they're only discussing a state, and they're seeing that being in a state. So just don't listen to it. Pull everyone out. But don't forget to pull yourself. Put yourself right into the most glorious part in this world and be successful. Not a thing wrong with being happy, being successful, and being wanted, one who contributes to the world's good.

You try it. I promise you it will not fail you. And then do me a favor and share with the platform your success that I, in turn, may share with those what happened to you. (Lady interrupts from audience.) "Neville, may I say something? Many years ago, in New York City, the old ___(??) church, and I was very, very new in all of this. I would sit there and listen to you, and I was going through a very, very dark picture. Only the soul listened to the good news of the kingdom. I had a son that was in the service at that time, and how it was not a crime or anything like that, but it was a very, very dark picture. It looked so dark. Well, it was one of the things where it seemed that everything wrong happened to him besides the fact that he had ___(??) and everything else. But he was on a ship that was sunk, and everything was wrong. I asked you about it one evening, and you said, 'Will you let me hear good news of his deliverance?'" Of course, I was overjoyed.

"And I sat for one day . . . on George Washington's birthday, I got up early in the morning, and all day long I just sat there and I did just what you told me to do, to hear this good news. I hadn't seen my son for three years. Every time I'd get a letter from him, it used to—well, I'd almost quiver all over. He was ready to commit suicide, and the boys were leaving the ship, and everything was, well, in a condition that was almost impossible for any human to take. And I sat there all that day knowing and knowing and knowing and feeling just the truth that you had told me to try to impart to myself—when all of a sudden, something happened and such a thrill, a joy went over me, and I cried with gratitude. The next day, I received a letter from him, and it was another one of these indigo letters and I could look on it and destroy it and just laugh because it doesn't mean anything. Within four days, I received a cablegram saying that he was coming in on a luxury liner and was coming into the States, returning home."

Thank you, my dear.

"I'll never forget you, Neville Goddard. You don't remember me, but I'll never forget you."

May I tell you, thank you! It doesn't fail!

Q: (inaudible)

A: No, that is, "Do not cast your pearls before swine." If I got into an argument . . . I'll tell you the story, but I will not argue with you. These are pearls, and I would not cast them. I would not try to *persuade* you against your will to believe me, but I would tell you. I would this night tell any person in this world what I've experienced. They may laugh at me because of their position in the world. If I stood this night in the presence of, say, the outstanding religious leaders of the world, say, the pope, the archbishop of Canterbury, the head rabbi of the world, and I'm telling them what I told you, what I've written in my books, they may smile and they may turn their backs. Perfectly all right. But I would tell them. And I would not feel that because they didn't follow me that in any way that they were wrong. They haven't had the experience.

I know, many years ago, I met Walter Damrosch ___(??) when he came to New York City. They met every month at the Harvard Club, the first Monday of the month, the Harvard Club. Well, I was introduced to him as a great metaphysician, and he said to me, "What is your school? Germanic? French?" Well, he named all these different schools of metaphysics, and I said to him, "None of these. It came through revelation." The old gentleman just took one look at me, thought he was in the presence of madness, and walked away. He would have not a thing to do with me because I couldn't give it a tag of authority that he could find a school authority. So the men got together, and they rationalized the Word of God. And here they studied the Germanic school, the French school, and all these schools; and their concern was simply to build a certain philosophy of life that to them seemed reasonable. And ___(??) would be very unreasonable concept. Mine wasn't reason at all. Mine was all by revelation, when the veil was lifted and God showed me his secret. He took away the veil and revealed the secret.

And so I met the great Damrosch, and that night he brushed me off completely. If had I said to him it's Germanic, he would have loved it. Had I said it was something else, he would have loved it. But I simply told him the truth that I didn't get it from any school of men. Like

Paul, "I didn't receive it from a man, neither was I taught it, but it came through revelation of Jesus Christ." Well, had he stood in the presence of Paul and heard the same words, he would have turned from Paul too. So he went blindly on his way, the blind leading the blind. Perfectly all right.

Q: (inaudible)

A: Blake was a man of complete ___(??) vision. It happened when the boy was four years old, and he never lost his vision. For one short little interval, he felt he lost the vision, but then it came back. But through his entire seventy years, just a short little interval when there was no vision and he couldn't see the ___(??). But prior to that and after that, it was always an open vision and he saw God's symbols. All these are symbols. And so he started, as we quoted last Tuesday night, ___(??), and he moved forward in a perfect progression of these more and more animated forms. He shows you everything is related, that there isn't a bird that splits the airy way that isn't in some way related to a heavenly being. That the very dog that is starved at the master's gate is crying out ___(??). It's all related. There's not a thing that's unrelated in this world.

So to me, Blake is like Paul. I put them in the same category. To me Paul is this giant but truly the giant, a spiritual giant. Well, I put Blake, along with Paul, with Elijah, with Ezekiel, and with Jeremiah. I put all these mental giants in the same sphere. They're all God, God awake. Blake is *definitely* God awake. So are all these mental giants and spiritual giants. (Tape ends.)

BELIEVE HIM IN

April 2, 1963

Tonight's subject is "Believe Him In," which begins with believing in him. Believe him in only as you really believe in him. When Paul tells us in Romans, the 10th chapter, the 13th through the 17th verses, he makes the statement that everyone who calls upon the name of the Lord will be saved. No one is excluded. "Everyone who calls upon the name of the Lord will be saved." Now you might think, based upon your training, your conditioning, that it means calling upon Christ Jesus or calling upon a name called Jehovah or calling on some other name. May I tell you, it is not. There's only one name for God, and that name is I AM (Exodus 3:14). When you speak of the word, when you use the word Jesus, Jesus means I AM; *Jehovah* means I AM; *Jesse* means I AM. It's his *only* name forever and forever. So everyone, not just a few special individuals, but everyone who calls upon the name of the Lord will be saved.

But now he goes on, he makes the statement, "But how can men call upon him in whom they have not believed?" Well, I promise the whole vast world would come under that heading. They have never believed, really, in I AM. How could men call upon him in whom they have not believed? They believe in God, they believe in the president, believe in the power of this country, believe in their money in the bank, and believe in everything outside of I AM. So how will men call upon him in whom they have not believed? And how can they believe in him in whom they have never heard? The average person never heard that this is the name of God. And how can they believe in him of whom they have never heard?

I could take my own family. Go to Barbados tonight, and they are an enormous family, with three generations, and they all believe in God, but they'll call him by some other name. They will never think of him as I AM, so how could they believe in him in whom they have never heard? They have read about it. My books are home, closed, completely closed, never opened. Neville wrote it, so what would I read of—Neville wrote it? So we'll keep it here as a little memento because he did write it. But they've never read it. So there it is. Multiply them by the entire world. You sign the name Neville . . . one chap in Australia, he signs five or six degrees behind his name, and so when he received my book just simply signed Neville, he closed it. There was no power of authority behind that name. He wasn't a man of letters, just plain Neville. What could he say to me, a man who was a great professor, the head of a certain great university? So he closed it. And he was offended when he saw all through that book, which was *Your Faith Is Your Fortune,* just the words I AM, I AM, I AM, page after page. That meant nothing, so he closed it. But he would pray to God and address him as "Thou art" and speak of him as "He is," and then in conversation use the words Jesus Christ, cross himself all over, and bow. But he doesn't know the name that he would call on.

So let me go back, "*Everyone* who calls upon the name of the Lord will be saved," but everyone. No one is left out, everyone, if he calls upon the name of the Lord. But how can men call upon him in whom they have *never* heard? And how can men *believe* in him of whom they never were taught about this being? How can they actually call upon him and believe in him? And how can they believe without a preacher? And how can there be a preacher unless he's sent? Therefore, faith comes by hearing and hearing comes by the preaching of Christ. So I tell you, I'm speaking to you from experience. No one can be called and ___(??) and become one with the body of God and remain there. He's sent. To be called at the same time involved as it were being sent, for to be called or to be rescued from something carries with it being sent to do something. And the being sent to do that is to tell you who he is, and he's your own wonderful I-am-ness. That's God.

So everyone in the world who calls upon the name of the Lord is saved. Saved from what? Saved from everything in this world. Here we'll take it on this level. If there's anyone here tonight who is in need of something, call upon his name. His name is I AM. And then you say to call, not call *upon* his name; you call *with* his name. That's how you call. Don't say, "In the name of I AM give me bread" but "I am filled to overflowing!" That's asking for bread. Say, "I want a job. In the name of God, give me a job"? No, "I am gainfully employed." Call *with* his name for everything in this world, and you'll be saved from your present state. You'll be lifted out of your present state into the state where you are affirming *in his* name, and his *only* name is I AM.

If you faced the court tonight and all the things of the world were against you, call in his name. Don't say that in certain cases it can't work. There is *no* case where it doesn't work. Try it. If tonight you are faced with some court case where everything is against you, listen to the words—I am quoting now the 13th verse of the 10th chapter of Romans—"Everyone who calls upon the name of the Lord will be saved." The next verse, "But how can men call upon him in whom they have not believed?" Well, that's so obvious. The whole vast world, how can I call upon my own consciousness when I never thought I was any more than a simple little man, that everyone was bigger? The President is bigger—he exercises enormous power—and the great churches of the world and society and the banker. We go into all these places and all seem so big, and so you call upon them. You go into a bank and ask to see the banker, feeling close and feeling nervous. And so you have no collateral, but you feel like a stuck pig; and he seems so big, a giant in your mind's eye. You call upon *that* name.

So we are told in that fourteenth verse, "How can men call upon him in whom they have not believed?" What man really believes in himself, that resident in his own being is God, and God's name is I AM? So after that verse comes the next, "And how can they *believe* in him of whom they have never heard?" But may I tell you, how true that is. What priest in the world tells those who listen to him that the name of God is I AM. No, they will say the name of God is Jesus Christ. Instantly you think of someone who was born 2,000 years ago. And others will say his name is Jehovah, and that goes back thousands of years ago. But others will call him by some other name. So how can we believe in him of whom we have never heard? Who is telling you the name of God, who God really is? And "how can we *really* believe unless there is a preacher? And how can there be a preacher unless he is sent? And so faith comes from what is heard and what is heard comes from the preaching of Christ." Well, Christ means the power and wisdom of God, and God is your own wonderful I-am-ness. Now you try it. You try it and see if it doesn't work in the immediate present.

In the Book of John, there are only a few case histories. They're all called signs. Yet that book has been in print for 2,000 years, and people read it and are *thrilled* beyond measure. Only a few. You have hundreds of case histories that you have given to me, and I have given back to you in the written form in the last few years—same signs. Where a man had nothing and a woman had nothing and they dared to believe that "I am" and they named it and lost themselves in calling in the name of God, it happened.

A little lady had a little home in need of repair—it needed painting—and she dared to believe this story and she called upon the name. How did she call upon the name? She went to sleep, smelling paint. Who is smelling paint? "*I am* smelling paint." Well, who is seeing the thing repaired? "*I am*," before it was repaired. Who is paying the bills? "*I am*." She paid the bills. So she is calling upon the name. In the *true* way, she is calling *in* the name, *with* the name. And in a matter of weeks, a letter comes bringing $7,500 from one she had never seen. You read that case history. She had never seen this party. She did a little tiny favor, investigating the cause of her brother's death and where he was buried, and she wrote three letters in the course of a year, giving all that she found out about the brother's death. And then years went by and she died. Then a bank notified her she was mentioned in her will to the tune of $7,500, where the repairs and the painting only came to about, say, $800 or $900. So she had almost $7,000 left over because she dared to call upon his name. Multiply that by the hundreds that I have told you from this platform. It's the same, really.

So believe in him. How could I do it when I've never heard of the one in whom I must believe? Well, I'll tell you in whom you must believe. Believe, not in Neville, don't believe in Neville—I'm just as fallible as you, the same being that you are—but believe in *him*. Well, who is he? I AM. Not Neville; you're saying it, "I am"—that's the being. And so everyone, believe in him. But how *can* I believe in one in whom I've never had faith?

What man believes in himself? Today, the President believes in the mighty power of his office and not in himself. He believes in the political power that he wields. And so someone who's the head of the army or the navy, they believe in the power they hold by reason of that position, but not in themselves. Tomorrow when they reach a certain age, and they are let out to pasture, overnight they're not the same person. Twenty-four hours before they are writing all these things and dictating policy and putting out billions of dollars of our money and overnight when they are sheared of that, they don't believe in themselves. They believe only in themselves when they fill a certain office. They believe in the office, not themselves.

So you have no office, but you do have a name, and you can call upon that name and that name is I AM, the only name by which I am to be known forever and forever. You read it in the 3rd chapter, the 14th verse of Exodus: "This is my name forever. I have no other name. Go tell them I AM has sent you. I AM that I AM." I AM what I will be. I AM who I AM. This is my name; I have no other name. And so ask in this name and call upon this name forever, and no power in the world can stop you because it's the *only* power. You read it carefully, and see who you really are.

Now this is the being of whom I would speak this night. On this level, we can take it and transform our world. When it comes to being saved in the ultimate sense, forget it; you *are* saved. No one can be lost, but no one.

"No one is lost in all my holy mountain," as told us in Isaiah 11, but no one. I don't care what you've done, what you're contemplating doing. If you contemplate hurt, you're simply blind, you're simply asleep because no one could contemplate the hurt of another unless you were asleep, really. And so no one ultimately will be lost, but no one.

That comes in the most wonderful way through a series of events, all foretold in the beginning of what is known as sacred history. That's the 17th chapter, the 17th verse of the Book of Genesis—that's where it begins. Sacred history and divine history begins there. And you and I are brought into that state of consciousness called Abraham, and there we are shown, only in words. But if I painted a word picture for you, you would say, I see it, but you don't actually see it as you see me now or I see you. Well, you would say to me, I see it. I would paint the word picture to the best of my ability, and you would see what I'm talking about. So Abraham saw, but he only heard; he heard it in words. But he saw it, as you will see it, if I now paint it, what was promised. So it was said of him, "Abraham rejoiced that he was to see my day; he saw it and he was glad." The word *laughed* in that 17th verse of the 17th chapter of Genesis when translated in Aramaic is "rejoiced." He rejoiced. Well, it says he fell upon his face and laughed because it is the most ridiculous promise in the world. And the promise is the promise—it's called a child—but it's the promise of resurrection, when everything round about him died. All things are dying, and he is promised a child which would survive and seemingly extend—that's all symbolism. What he's really promised: that in spite of his seeming death, he will resurrect. All things will be resurrected; nothing will die in God's infinite world. Nothing dies.

He's promised this resurrection, and to him, it's the most ridiculous thing in the world. But he believed that all things are possible to God. With God all things are possible, and so he believed. He fell on his face and he laughed, which is a play on the word *Isaac*. For the word *Isaac* which is promised him means "he laughs." And so you're told in the story, which is all symbolism that he sired the one who is already beyond bearing a child, and the name was called Isaac. For the Lord demanded that the name should be called Isaac; he was called Isaac. The symbolism is perfect; it's true. May I tell you, I've had it and I know this experience. The whole thing is completely true.

Now, in the epistle of John, and here comes the great first epistle, the very first and third verses: "That which we have heard with our *own* ears, that which we have seen with our own eyes, that which we have beheld and handled with our own hands . . . this we declare unto you." Here comes now experience: "I *heard* of you with the hearing of the ear," said Job, "but now my *eye sees* you" (Job 41:5).

I tell you tonight what's going to happen to you, as I was told what would happen to me. I only heard it. Then came that moment in time when I would handle the word of life with my own hands. It's only a symbol. It's a child, an actual, simple, wonderful child, Isaac, and you hold him. He's solidly real to you. But you are told it's going to happen to you, and you believed it. Who told you? God told you. Well, who is God? I AM. I told myself? Yes. In the depths of my own being, I told myself *this* is going to happen to you. And then you and I who now tell you the story will be one.

But you can't become one with me until this series of events takes place. And the first one is going to be a child. You will be born from above out of your own being. It's going to be symbolized to you as that of a child. And then I'm going to show you another. You're going to find a son. He will be my son before he's your son. I'm going to give him to you as your son; and therefore, if he's your son and he's already my son, then you and I are one. Then I'm going to resurrect you. I'm going to lift you up into heaven. You'll be lifted up just as I promised in the symbolism of the serpent, lifted up just like that, and you'll be one with me. That is told us in scripture. You go through this entire series of events just as I've told you and you are saved, completely saved, from this wheel of recurrence that goes on here.

But even though we are still locked on the wheel, call upon my name and you are saved from any state in this world. While you're locked upon it, call upon my name. My name is I AM. So at any moment, when you're in prison, say, "I am free." If you're now not feeling well, "I never felt better." Let the weak man say, in the Book of Joel, "Let the weak man say, 'I am strong!'" (3:10) Let him say, "I am strong," while he's not feeling well. Let him call upon my name in everything in this world. And while we move upon the wheel of recurrence, call upon my name. And externalizing all the states as you call upon my name, I will one day stretch beyond and redeem you and lift you into my own being, and you become one with me, completely freed from the wheel of recurrence.

So I bring him into being by believing in him. So I tell you the story, well, here is the story. The first series of parables in the 13th of Matthew, and here they're listening to the parable of the sower. "A sower went forth to sow. And as he sowed, some seeds fell upon the wayside, and birds ate it up. Some fell upon rocks, and it quickly grew, but it had no root; there was no soil, no depth of soil, and so when the sun came, it scorched it. Some fell among thorns and it was quickly choked by the thorns. But some fell on good soil, and it brought forth a hundredfold, sixtyfold, and thirtyfold." And they said to him, "Why do you always speak in parables? Why can't you speak clearly?" He said, "To you it's given to know the things, the secrets, of the kingdom of heaven, but to others it is not" (verse 3-11).

Then he explained to them the mystery of the sower. He said, "The things sown, the seed, is the word of God." Now, the word of God is the message of Christianity. The promise made to Abraham would be fulfilled in what we call the coming of Christ, that God himself comes into human history. He not only came, but I use the word *he comes*. The world thinks that God himself came. I say God himself came and *comes* into human history in the person of Jesus Christ. Not only came but he *comes*—everyone who has the identical experiences as recorded is Jesus Christ. For there's only Jesus Christ, who is God, who is I AM, but then awake.

So here, he tells us the story of the sower. The seed is the word of God. And so it's planted. There are those who do not even hear it and use the words "they do not understand it." The evil one comes and snatches it away. Well, the *evil one* in the Bible means "unbelief." First they don't understand it. It's incredible. It's the most impossible thing in the world, so they don't believe it, they don't understand it. So it's completely removed from them, from that soil, that mind. Then comes the second planting, and that falls among rocks. The individual has no preparation in himself; there's no depth in himself. So when he accepts it, he accepts it with joy; but overnight, when the sun rises and the facts of life present themselves, it scorches that little thing that he received with joy. That was simply, "Last night's lecture means nothing. I must now face the world with today's *facts*," and so the whole thing is rubbed out. Then comes the third, and this is an interesting one, for I've seen it. It falls among the thorns, but the cares of the world and the greed for riches choke it, and then it doesn't grow.

How I have seen that! In 1925, ___(??) in London—I was then twenty years old—I said to my friend, who was my age and whose name was Matthew Bentley, "Matt, why don't you show some interest in your father's philosophical approach to life?" His father was then what I am today, fifty-eight years old. Well, when you are twenty and your father is fifty-eight, he looks like Methuselah. And so he said to me, "Well, Father's an old man. He's retired." He's a mining engineer, and he's retired. So he and his wife lived in a very small, modest little home in Hammersmith. Matt said to me, "Let me live first. Let me make a million. Let me earn some money and stand on my own feet before I become interested in what my father today finds so interesting."

But after four months in London, I returned to New York City, and then a few months later Matt went off to India in the service of some tea company. And three months later, Matt died. He contracted malaria, and Matt was gone from this world. He had to make a lot of money first before he could show any interest in things spiritual. Money was the only thing that to him would symbolize success in his world, not an experience of God but money in the bank or things in his house, or things. And so the third seed fell upon soil, and the soil was among the thorns and the thistles of the way. Then he describes for us what he means by it, by the thorns: those who must have riches in this world, and the cares of the world and the desire for wealth overpower what he heard about this story, and so he simply stifled the word of God.

And then comes the fourth one. It fell upon good soil, and it brought forth a hundredfold, sixtyfold, and thirtyfold. So let me tell you, when it brings forth thirtyfold, you are born above. When it brings forth sixtyfold, you are the Father of God's only begotten Son. When it brings forth a hundredfold, you have completely ascended, *completely* ascended in that serpentine form, right up into heaven.

Now here he tells us, "You see John the Baptist? No one born of woman is greater than John, but I tell you, the least in the kingdom is greater than John" (Matthew 11:11). John was the greatest born of woman. If I could put John, without being offensive, put him into the modern world, he would be the head of the welfare state. John said to those who listened to him, You have two coats, give one to one who hasn't. You have more food than you can consume, give some to those who haven't yet. He said to the soldier, be satisfied with your wages. No disturbance and no strife, take what you are given and be satisfied with it. And that is John. John is represented in our world by those who would take all of our earnings and share it with the whole vast world, whether they want it or could even use it. They are the ones who would share everything in the world—but not their own, ours. They don't share theirs; they share ours.

So he said, "You see John? John is greater than anyone born of woman, but the *least* in the kingdom is greater than John." John hasn't the slightest concept of the kingdom. He proclaimed it, but he didn't know what the kingdom was all about. He thought it meant doing good. He was the do-gooder. And that's the whole vast world trying to earn the kingdom by doing good, and the kingdom is entered not by any doing good; it is God's most mighty act. He singles us out, one by one; and God's mighty act, he lifts us out of the wheel of recurrence into this kingdom. And the first act is birth from above. His second mighty power, lifting us higher still, is to make us one with himself, and we are the Father of his Son. The third, he lifts us up into heaven itself, in that serpentine glorious form of luminous gold as it were, one with him, pure gold.

Believe it. I am telling you this that you may believe, for just as you must believe that you are rich to be rich, you must believe this story to be eligible to be lifted up. For man's salvation has its source in *God's* faith, but it is bestowed upon man in response to *his* faith. And so he can't be qualified until he hears the story. I am telling you the story, for it has happened to me. If the whole vast world rose in opposition, it would make no difference to me: I have experienced it. You can't take it from me. If tonight you shot me full of holes, if you annihilated me, you could only annihilate this garment; you can't annihilate the experience, for I have already been lifted up into that sphere, and I'm sharing with you what I have experienced.

And so to be salvaged, to be rescued *from* something carries with it being sent to *do* something; and so one is sent because one has been called and rescued. So somewhere along the way, I was told this story as I'm telling it to you and somewhere along the way, I believed it. It was mixed in me with faith, as told us in the 4th chapter of the Book of Hebrews. Here we are told the word spoken to us was also spoken to them. He calls it the good news, the good news given us was also given them, but it did not benefit them because it was not received by the hearers with faith (verse 2). They rejected it; it meant nothing to them. Therefore, they did not enter into the rest of God. So here, you and I hear it. I am telling you, you can prove it on this level, and proving it on this level you may be encouraged then to prove it on the higher level. You can't on the higher level do anything about it. Simply live on this level *fully*, calling upon the name of God, in the hope that this that was promised our father Abraham—and we are he—would someday, in God's own good time, be given to us.

So now we come to the great one who first proselyted the idea. He said, "O King Agrippa, here I stand before you on trial for the *hope* that was given to me as made by God to our fathers. I stand here on trial for hope in the promise made by God to our fathers." Then said he, "Why should any of us think it incredible that God should raise the dead? Was that not the promise that he made our father Abraham?" (Acts 26:6-8). When you read it carefully, you might think that it refers to some other promise, which was the child, but the child all through scripture is only a symbol of resurrection. The birth and resurrection are the identical experience. So why should any of us think it's incredible that God raises the dead? And then, he stood before the king, and when the king said, "Are you going to make me a Christian?" He said, "Would that you at this very moment were as I am—save the shackles, the chains on me." Just as I am . . . would that you were as I am, minus the chains. Then, said he, from morning to night, he expounded this mystery of the kingdom of God and tried to convince them of Jesus, using all the law of Moses and the prophets. Some were convinced by what he said and others disbelieved.

I hope that if this is a repetition of Paul that in this audience tonight there aren't any disbelievers, but I have no way of judging. I can only tell you that it's true. I tell you, you can prove on this level that you can call upon the name by calling with the name and prove anything. The other, believe it. In God's own good time, after the seed has been prepared and the field has been prepared, he's going to call you and call you into an entirely different world. It's not this world; it's an entirely different world where your body's different. You haven't this body. This body belongs to this world. But it's *not* this body; it's an entirely different body. You can't describe it. I have tried to describe it, but I can't. I can't describe the body. It's something that is immortal, something that never dies, eternal. Something that when you are housed in it, you'll be an immortal being housed in the eternal body. Everything then is subject to your imaginative power, but everything. In this world you wait for it, confident that it will work and it does, but *then* it's an immediate creative fact.

So here, I share with you that which has been experienced by me. The seed falls on four soils. I do not think tonight in this audience, unless you're here for the first time, that it would fall on the first soil, where the evil one comes and snatches it away, which means complete unbelief. I hope I have not been that cloudy and dark in what I'm saying that you would not understand it. For he uses the word, "They did not understand it"; and then because they didn't understand it, it was snatched away.

The second soil, I hope you aren't that one; but if you are, listen to it carefully that you may overcome it. For the second soil is the rocky soil, not yet prepared, and you take it joyously, but the sun will rise tomorrow, you face the facts of life, and then having no depth in yourself, it will quickly be devoured by the sun and be scorched.

And the third—and that is a warning that Paul gives us in his letter to Timothy when he said to Timothy, "The love of wealth is the root of evil." The love, not wealth—you can have all the wealth in the world—but the love of it, when someone has to be wealthy first before he can listen to the word of God. Let him get wealth *first*: when I get all of that and I'm well cushioned, then I'll listen to you. Then they'll be so fat mentally they couldn't listen to anything. The brain would have no muscle whatsoever, just all fat, all cushioned. And so let me get it all first, and then I will listen. And that chokes the word. They couldn't stay awake long enough to listen to it anyway.

But then comes the fourth one, and that soil is well prepared. It brought forth three different measures, a hundredfold, sixtyfold, and thirtyfold. And so the thirtyfold is the first, ___(??), and that is the birth from above. Then when the second wonderful experience comes and you are the father of

God's only begotten son, you have brought forth sixtyfold. Then comes the third when you are lifted up in the serpentine form right into heaven. Then you've brought forth the full measure, a hundredfold. But even though you only bring forth the thirtyfold, may I tell you, you are greater than anyone born of woman. So John was the greatest of all born of woman, but the least in the kingdom is greater than John.

So here, you try it tonight. You take this name and call upon it tonight if you are facing any problem in the world; I don't care what it is. Listen to the words, I'm quoting correctly, "Everyone"—no discrimination—"Everyone who calls upon the name of the Lord will be saved." And we know tonight that millions are calling upon other names—"In the name of Jesus Christ," so and so—not a thing is going to happen. They'll go to church and light their candles, do all these things, cross themselves, and not a thing is going to happen. But you call upon the name, and you'll be saved from any condition that now faces you. And his name and his *only* name is I AM. Don't call with any other name, just I AM. So what would it be like?

Now I tell the story over and over because it's a true story. I did not incorporate it in my book because my friend who read my manuscript (he has never had the experience) and he said to me, "Neville, if you tell this experience people will think that they must have that experience in order to be saved. And so let us eliminate the experience." So I did. So I did not tell it in my story. But when I, imprisoned as I was, called upon the name, this is what I did. Two thousand miles from my face, for I was in the army, and 2,000 from my home, I simply sat on the army bed, but in my Imagination, I said to myself, "I am sleeping right now in my own home on my own bed in New York City." And there I remained until it seemed natural. It took on all the tones of naturalness, all the tones of reality. And then, I got off my imaginary bed, looked through the window, saw the things that I would see were it true, looked to east of me, looked to the west of me, saw what I would see, walked all over my apartment, all in my Imagination, and went back to bed. Who's doing it? I'm doing it. I went back to bed. Who's going to sit on this bed? I am. So I got back into bed, and I lost consciousness in that state.

And then suddenly, sleeping in that state, a thing came before my mind's eye, a smooth big sheet of paper and a hand from here down. The hand held a pen, and the pen scratched out the word *Disapproved* and it wrote in the word in big bold type *Approved*. Then the voice said to me, "That which *I* have done *I* have done. Do nothing!" So I did nothing. Nine days later, the very one who disapproved my application called me into his presence and asked me ___(??) of me wanting to get out. And then among the things he said, he approved it, and he wrote in the same bold type *Approved*. But nine days before he confirmed it in his own writing, here it was confirmed in the depth of my soul. The voice spoke to me and said, "That which I have done, *I* have *done*. Do nothing!" So I did nothing.

So I tell you, I called upon the name. I didn't say, "O God, get me out of the army." I didn't say, "O Jesus Christ, what am I doing here? Get me out of the army." I did none of these things. All I did, I simply went to bed, sat on that cot and assumed I am in New York City. I slept in New York City just as though I were there. Then came this vision from the depth of my soul, speaking in the first person, saying, "That which I have done I have done. Do nothing!" And I did nothing until I got out, honorably discharged. And so I eliminated that in telling my story only because the man who corrected my manuscript for me, never having had a vision himself, he thought had he read it, never having had vision, people would think you had to have one in order to make it work. That's why I eliminated it from the story when I told it in my book.

But I tell you, it works. Listen to the words, "*Everyone*"—not an occasional one but—"everyone who calls upon the name of the Lord will be saved." I was saved, saved from what to me—maybe you don't think it's horrible—but to me it was a horrible life. The whole vast world is a world of freedom. God has made us to be free. And so that to me was the most confined, restricted state I had ever experienced, save for school; but there I didn't go too long anyway. And so may I tell you, you call upon his name and he will set you free. But his name is I AM; there's no other name. Let no one give you some other name. It's all over the world. Listen to it and read it carefully when you go home because how true these words are.

After he makes the statement that everyone who calls upon the name of the Lord will be saved, he goes right in to the next verse, "But how can men call upon him in whom they do not believe? And how can they believe in him of whom they have never heard?" Well, do you know today in the world of three billion of us you could almost say three billion never heard that name for God? Three billion never heard the name. How could they believe in him of whom they have never heard? And how can they hear of him without a preacher? And how can there be preacher unless he is sent? Those who are not sent tell them his name is Christ or Jesus or Jehovah or Moses or some other name. And they use all kinds of names because they have not been sent. They do not know the name, yet they say the Bible for us. But when you're called and enveloped in his being and you are one with him, you know his name. His name is I AM. And so you call upon his name and you are saved from any state in this world.

But how can you call upon one in whom you do not believe? Well, you can't believe in one of whom you've never heard; and if you haven't heard about him, how will you hear about him unless [you] have been told? And how could you be told unless someone is sent to tell you? Therefore, you're told faith comes by the hearing of the word; and this is by the preaching of Christ, and Christ is the power and wisdom of God.

So tonight, I ask you to join with me and prove it. You can't disprove it, I know this much. It took me nine days in that state, and I did nothing in the interval of nine days. I simply went to that state. And when it happened to me at four fifteen in the morning, I couldn't disturb the other soldiers. I waited until the sun began to show, and then I went down to the men's room, shaved and bathed, and got ready long before anyone was up. I was so excited, and the whole thing was so vivid in my mind's eye. So I tell you, everyone who calls upon his name will be saved. I was released, honorably released, in nine days.

And now, you may or others would, as they have, criticize that attitude of mind. Makes no difference to me if the whole vast world criticized it. They'll say, "Well, we must have soldiers." I'm not denying that to have soldiers. Let's have morticians too. Let's have, as long as we believe in burial grounds, let's have Forest Lawn. I'm not denying that. The day will come that all will be the most ludicrous things in the world—burial grounds and morticians and all these things will be the most ludicrous things in the world when man completely awakes.

And so I was awakened, and God did not restrain my right to awaken but granted my life based upon his holy word, "Everyone who calls upon my name will be saved." And I wanted to be saved from what to me at that moment was the most frightful confinement and mental restriction. But the only books that are safe ___(??) you know are those that nobody wants in the library. You start collecting books for the navy or for the army, and you see that people only give away what they don't like. No one saves one decent book in the world. ___(??) go to the library and see what you're going to find—all the trash in the world. So that's your library plus all the other mental food. What mental food would you get?

So I ask you to believe what I've told you. When it comes to being saved in the true sense of the word, you forget it. You *will* be, because that is in the hand: God's mightiest act is the act of resurrection. And no one will fail. But you can't earn it. If you could take the greatest president in the world, the wisest president in the world, you cannot earn *that*. But you can prepare for it, but you can't earn it. It's something beyond the wildest dream of man, and God gives it to everyone in God's own good time. When he does it, he does it without notifying you. Suddenly! And then you are resurrected and you awaken from the deep. And you didn't realize 'til that moment in time that you had been sound asleep all along. You had no idea that all through the ages you were asleep, dreaming this fantastic dream. It was a dream until that moment in time, and then you awoke. And that was God's resurrecting power. His birth, which was *your* birth, is your resurrection. And then comes the other, the sixty percent, and then the one hundred percent because a seed fell on good soil. (Tape ends.)

BARABBAS OR JESUS

April 5, 1963

Tonight's subject is "Barabbas or Jesus." This is the greatest trial that ever took place in eternity. You and I have read of trials where countries and countries where billions are involved, it means *nothing* compared to this trial. This is the greatest of all trials.

When we read the scriptures, we find the thing says the raising of Lazarus, which is the most fantastic thing you can imagine. A man who is dead for four days and his sister said, "By this time there's an odor." And so he raises Lazarus. And yet only one evangelist recorded it; only John tells the story. Matthew, Mark, and Luke do not mention the story of Lazarus. How could you tell the story of a man in this world who could raise someone who has decayed and bringing him back to life, as we understand life, and not tell it as part of his biography? Yet it is only mentioned in the gospel of John.

So I could take you through the many stories and show that one story is told by two, sometimes three, and only by one. But here, in *this* story of the trial, all mention it. It has tremendous significance, this story of the greatest trial that ever took place in eternity. And may I tell you, it's taking place here tonight, and you are the witnesses. You are the ones who will either cry out for the release of one or the other. It's entirely up to you, for this is the story; it must always take place in this manner. The supreme effort of God to reveal himself in the present tense was the coming of Jesus. Jesus came to reveal God as the eternal contemporary. That's the trial. One believes it or they disbelieve it. But here is this supreme effort to reveal himself in the present tense, for the present tense is "I AM. That's my name forever. I have no other name" (Exodus 3:14). Man either believes it or he disbelieves it, and this is the trial.

Let us turn to the gospels, the 18th chapter of the gospel of John. Here, a man is on trial. He knows who he is, for he's had all the experiences to reveal the being that he is; sent into the world to tell the world who *he* is; and tell them who *they* are, for they're one. So he comes to tell the world who he is. He's brought in to trial and Pilate, the arm of Caesar, is trying him. Pilate said to him, "What is truth?" but he doesn't reply; he doesn't answer. Pilate said to the crowd, "I find no crime in him. But you have a custom that I should release a man to you at this season of the year, at Passover; will you have me release the King of the Jews?" They cried out, "Not this man, but Barabbas!" And then it simply states, "Barabbas was a robber." That's all that it states, "Barabbas was a robber." Not this man, release Barabbas.

Well, here is the trial. Who is Barabbas? Because Barabbas was a robber, he's only mentioned in one little statement but in four gospels. It's *very* significant. To find out who Barabbas was let us find out who the thief and the robber is in scripture. We go back to the 10th chapter of the gospel of John, that anyone who enters in any other way than through the *door* is a thief and a robber. They did not understand it. So he said to them, "*I am* the door." There is no other way into the sheepfold: "I am the door." Anyone who attempts to come in any other way is a thief and a robber (verses 1 and 9).

Now, you present the case to the world. Will you believe it? Will you believe, as you are seated here tonight, regardless of your present limitations, the only door into your success, into your future that is as you would conceive it or desire it to be, there's only *one* door, and that door is I AM? There is no other door into that sheepfold? And if you go through that *only* door, the sheep will hear your voice, they will recognize your voice as the shepherd, and they will respond and come out? So I decide that I would like to be, and I name it. I would like to be healthy if I am unwell at the moment. I would like to be gainfully employed if I am unemployed. I would like to be and I name it—to be happily married. And I name all the things that I would think would constitute a lovely life in my world. Do I really believe there's only one door into that sheepfold, where I could bring all these unseen things out into my world? And these things can only respond to the voice of the shepherd, and the shepherd is I AM?

So he asked the crowd and the crowd shouted out, "Release Barabbas!" They would not have Jesus released; they'd have none of it. So they chose the robber, and the robber rules over them to this very day—that's the world—I chose the robber. My senses rob me of all that I could be. So I see my bank balance. I know the world, as my senses allow it, I know what reason dictates in my world, and yet I want to be other than what they dictate. Yet I can't bring myself to believe the only way into that sheepfold is by the only door in the world, and the world's door is I AM.

So here, Jesus comes to reveal God in the present tense and man refuses it. So they speak of God in the past, he was or he will be, but few people in world can believe in the reality of I AM. And that's the great trial. You are on trial tonight because you're asked the question: Will you believe that your own wonderful I-am-ness is the one and only God? Or do you believe because of your present social position, intellectual position, financial position that you are less than someone else, and you allow your reason to dictate this as something that is final? Can you believe tonight in this trial and really believe that I am . . . you name it . . . and dare to believe it?

I could tell you unnumbered stories where it has worked. I could tell you unnumbered stories if people would believe me. In this audience tonight, there sits a man who, only a few weeks ago, was let out of a job. I told him it would make no difference to me if he was let out of a job and they told him it was forever and permanent and that I would hear good news for him, good news. And so I heard exactly what he would tell me were it true. Tonight, just before I took the platform, he could tell me that he's been transferred to a new job, completely new job, where his income is in excess of what it was before. All things being relative, when you make $13,500 on a job, that's not hay, yet it could be a hundred thousand. And I'm telling you right now, I don't care what he's ever done in the world that exceeded $13,000, it could easily be, if that's what he wants. There's only one door into the sheepfold and that door is I AM.

The supreme effort that God has ever made to reveal himself to us in the present tense came through Jesus. So Jesus comes affirming God as the *eternal* contemporary, forever and forever. If tomorrow you have a child, or a grandchild, they are going to say "I am"—it's contemporary, it's forever contemporary, *eternally* contemporary. And there wasn't a "he *was*"; it's always "I am." And so for one to declare "I am" and just simply name it and sleep just as though it were true, there's no power in the world that can stop it.

Now, this is one level of this fantastic trial. There are numberless levels to this trial. First of all, the word *Barabbas* means "son of a father." *Jesus* means "savior." *Barabbas* means "son of a father." For every child born of a woman is the child of a father. *Bar* usually means "daughter"; and *Ben*, son, but they're interchangeable depending upon the context. And so, Barabbas is now known as "son of a father." And they chose the son and denied—it doesn't say "the father"—but I will show you how they denied the father. For Jesus said, in the same gospel of John, "When you see me you see the Father, how can you say, 'Show us the Father'? He who has seen me has seen the Father," so he declares, "I am the Father" (14:9). I go back just one verse before it, the 6th verse of the 14th of John: "I am the way, the truth, the life;

no one comes unto me (my Father), save by me. But no one comes unto the Father, but by me. Then they said, 'Show us the Father, and we will be satisfied.' He said, 'I have been so long with you, and yet you do not know me, Philip? He who has seen me has seen the Father.'"

Now they deny the Father to fulfill prophecy: they will kill you, excommunicate you, and this they will do because they believe that they are pleasing God; and they do it because they know not the Father (John 16:2). For there's a prophecy that when a son destroys the enemy of Israel the Lord will set his father free. But they didn't choose the father to set him free; they set the son free. The one that robs them morning, noon, and night, they set him free. They wouldn't set the father free. This I am quoting from the 17th chapter, the 25th verse of 1st Samuel, "He who destroys the enemy of Israel I will set his father free in Israel." The *father* of the one who destroyed the enemy, his name was I AM, called Jesse, but the word *Jesse*, the word *Jehovah*, and the word *Jesus* are identical in meaning: they mean simply I AM. I will set that being free, and his name is I AM.

Now, if tonight you could do what dozens of you or hundreds of you have done and believe that this is not a little trick, it always works and really believe in it, you'd believe in God. When a lady sits in this audience and she's in her seventies she has no money and she dares to sleep in a home in need of repair—and she has no money—and then she looks at the unrepaired, unpainted house, and she could smell the paint, and she could see the whole thing as it would be seen were it true that things are exactly as she wants them to be, and she sleeps in that assumption, what is she actually saying? If I said to her, "Who is smelling anything?" She would say, "*I am* smelling paint." She said I am. And "What do you see?" "*I am* seeing a repaired house." "What else?" "I am seeing that the whole thing has been paid for." So she falls asleep in the assumption of seeing from her own wonderful center. "I am seeing it. I am smelling the paint," all of these things she's doing; and in one month, it's all repaired and painted and paid for, with a surplus of $7,000, a gift from one she had never seen in this world, only communicated with her two or three times in the course of a year.

And here, she saw it. Whether she's here tonight or she's been coming recently, I do not know—her story I've told in my latest book. She may even have forgotten the name of God. Who did it? Well, she might point across the water to a lady in England, 8,000 miles away, who died and left a certain will where she received $7,500 in US currency, which allowed her to do all these things, with something left over. A considerable amount left over. She might think the cause of it all was one who died. I tell you the cause of it all: she called upon the only name of God in this world. She went into the sheepfold through the only door in the world, and that door is I AM. So she fell asleep in her bed. But before she fell asleep, she saw and could smell the paint; she saw the repaired areas all painted over, and she felt herself giving a check in full payment for all work done. And then she slept. Because it was so much fun she did it for, maybe, nine or ten days. Then came this wonderful draft from England and a letter from the bank, Lloyd's Bank it was, telling her of the story.

She entered the sheepfold; and they all heard her voice, and they all came out. The sheep happened to be the money. Everything in the world responded to her voice. She was calling them out, calling out paint, calling out the repair job, and calling out everything. They only respond to the voice of the shepherd. Well, who is the shepherd? "*I am* the shepherd." There is no other shepherd. If you think he will shepherd you and put your trust in our president or our mayor or our governor or your father or mother or some uncle who's about to die, and so you are now giving him the most marvelous meal in the world because he's going to leave you in his will, so he is your shepherd; and all these you think are the shepherds, you are simply looking in vain. There is no other shepherd, and no other door into eternity save the one door and that door is I AM.

So here is the greatest trial that ever took place in eternity, and you are called upon to scream out the one you want released. And the world invariably screams out—but not all; there's always that minority who will scream out, "Release Jesus!"—but the majority invariably will scream out "Release Barabbas! Release the robber!" And so they chose the robber, and throughout the centuries, the robber has ruled over them, right down to this day. So you and I will go to bed tonight and our senses will dictate what we ought to believe to be true in this world. Read this morning's paper and ninety-nine percent of the morning's paper, including the ads, all paid for. You read an ad—that's obvious it's been paid for—and there may be something you would like to buy. It's perfectly all right; it has been paid for and you know it.

But you don't know all the *news* items were paid for. That has been concealed. They're *all* paid for. All the press agents all over the world; there is not one person in this world who is in the public eye who does not maintain some press relationship. They call them—these, not "press agents"—they've been glamorized into some other name. But it's still—they take your money month after month, and they put these little items into the story, and you read it morning, noon, and night. So you go to bed tonight, and you *know* all these things because you read it. That's what you know. And you are fed morning, noon, and night on all this, and you believe that to be true.

I tell you: forget the entire vast world, and ask yourself a simple, simple question, "What would I like to be?" Just look at the world, "What would I like to be?" Forget Cuba, forget Russia, forget China, and forget all this stuff that is going on in the world. What would I like to be? A decent, wonderful being that contributes to the good of the world? To be happily married? Yes, to be in this world and contribute to the *good* of the world but really contribute, so that when I am gone and my children's children are gone that they will say, "He gave a thought to the world that has fed the world." The unborn tomorrow could be fed by what I have left behind me.

Would I like to do that, at the same time not neglecting my obligations tonight? For I am married—there is a husband, a wife, a child, a father, a mother, and all these things in this world—and they must all, if I love them as I think I do, take care of them. And so I want *enough* to leave them cushioned. Regardless of all things, but maybe they didn't hear me. But they don't need my cushion, but maybe they didn't hear me. I'm selfish enough that if they didn't hear me—that there's only one door in the world into the great kingdom—that I could still leave them a cushion so that they'll be cushioned against tomorrow's blows. All right, I want that. Well, then, regardless of what the world will tell me, I will assume tonight that I am what I desire to be and dare to fall asleep in the assumption that it's true, just as though it were true. Regardless of what the whole vast world will tell me, I will actually believe in it. So I will cast my vote: "Release Jesus and you hold on to Barabbas," or else I will say, "Release Barabbas and hold on to Jesus." And so it is entirely up to us. I either believe it, or I don't believe it. The one called Jesus, his name is I AM.

Now let me quote you from the 4th chapter of Galatians. Whoever added one little phrase in it, all right, maybe they had reasons for it: And he had a physical handicap. It is Paul speaking. "When I came to you, I was a trial to you." He said, "I was a trial, yet you accepted me." And then one little phrase divides the thought—we will omit the phrase; it's the tenth verse. You read the tenth and eleventh verses of the 4th of Galatians. Omit the phrase. "And yet you accepted me and received me as *Christ Jesus*." He's telling you who he is. You accepted me, now are you going to turn back like those in the desert who disbelieved?

And then he said, "I see that you are observing days and months and seasons and years! I am afraid I have labored over you in vain" (Galatians 4:10). Here we are in what is called a season, the Lenten season, and then we have another season and another month. We had a few years ago the Marian year, and all this goes all the way back. I see that "you observe days, and months and seasons and years! I'm afraid I have labored over you in vain." That man could turn outside of himself when the whole thing has been revealed to him—who he really is—and believe in the sacredness of a certain day or a certain month or a certain season or a certain year! He is trying to tell the whole vast world who he is: and they received him as Jesus Christ.

There's only Christ. There's only Jesus. Jesus Christ is God, and so are you and so am I, if I *believe* it. I am it even if I *don't* believe it. But if I don't believe it, then I go through all the fires of hell in this world. If I believe it, there's no being in this world that can stop me from sleeping this night in the assumption that I am the man that I would be, just as though it were true. Falling asleep in that assumption, just as though it were true, I will bring it to pass in my world because I call all my sheep out, and my sheep are the *invisible* realities. No one sees them. They come right out and follow the voice of the shepherd whose voice they hear. They will not obey the voice of a stranger, only the voice of the shepherd. And the shepherd is "I AM."

So here is the greatest trial in the world, and you are the one to judge. You sit as though you sat in a jury, and you bring in your verdict. And so he rises and asks those who hear the testimony. "And it is customary," and may I tell you, there is no evidence as far back as man can go, there is no evidence to support this claim, whatsoever. There is nothing that we know of save in scripture. There is no custom to support this amnesty, where you forgive someone at this season of the year, none whatsoever. As far back as man can go, no scholar, and no historian can find any such custom, where there was an amnesty at Passover. It's only attested to in scripture. So you can see it's a *play*. It is a fantastic play and here is the play and every moment of time the play is taking place. "It is your custom that I release to you one man. Would you have me release the King of the Jews?" For he *is* the king of the Jews, and who is he? Jesus. Who is Jesus? I am and so are you and so is every being in the world. That's Jesus. And his name is "I AM," so the name is one with Jehovah: "I and my Father are one" as told us in John 10: "I and the Father are one." His name is what? I AM. If I'm one with him, well then, what's my name? I AM. And there is no other way in no other door, just one.

And so who will you have me release, the King of the Jews, whose name is I AM or release Barabbas, who's a robber, a man based purely on the senses of the body? "Release Barabbas!" So they released the robber, and he to this day rules them. For man cannot believe, or is unwilling to believe, that something is real that his senses cannot confirm. He must have it confirmed by the senses. If reason allows it or my senses allow it, then I will accept it. But to sleep this night . . . I'm unemployed. They tell me there are six million unemployed and I'm not as qualified as I think they're looking for certain qualifications, and I'm to believe that I *am* gainfully employed and put it up beyond what I made before, more than I ever made before? And go to sleep just as though it were true, in the conviction that it *is* true? And then I am employed, and it is beyond what I make."

So when he told me I can't tell you my thrill. He will not be here because this takes him away a hundred-odd miles. I say to him "Good!" Go and tell it. Tell it to those in your sphere. Tell it to everyone that you meet. If we never meet physically again, it really doesn't matter. I like him personally, he likes me personally; but the physical contact, that's not important. We are forever one in eternity, and so he can't get away from me and I can't get away from him, not in eternity. He heard the story, and he knows it works. Now go and tell it, tell it to every being in this world, whether they believe it or not, tell it. That's the story.

So here we are, at every moment in time, we're called upon to pass judgment upon the eternal drama—the greatest trial that ever took place. God is on trial, and he is presented to the world, and yet the sense-man that he wears is presented. Because the sense-man is what he wears, and so he presents it. Would you believe in me that you cannot see? Well, you can't see I AM. You can see I am a man, that you can see, that's the sense-man, a being of sense. But man cannot believe in the reality of I AM, something entirely different.

So here, this great trial will be presented this coming Sunday, called Palm Sunday. But they all will tell the story of how they placed the palms before him. If you have the *Apocryphal Gospels*, may I recommend that you read, if you have it, the *Gospel of Nicodemus*; it's called also *The Acts of Pilate*. In fact, it's a combination: the title is *The Gospel of Nicodemus and the Acts of Pilate*. What a fantastic story! It is all about this trial. It's in the Apocryphal New Testament. I think many of you have the James' combination of all the Apocryphal books. Why they deleted them I will never know, because they add so much to the thought. But here in this story of the great trial, where they placed the little piece of cloth before him as he came in to trial, and all the standards and all the images bowed before him. And they couldn't believe that such things could happen, so they did it over and over and over again. Every time he was brought in, they all bowed before him. Every inanimate object bowed before him as he came into the building on trial.

How true that is! May I tell you, you are going to have the thrill of your life one day, when suddenly the whole vast world's going to stand still before you. And it will be dead but really dead. You'll look at it and then you'll release it and it will move on; and you stop it, right in its motion, you'll stop it, to prove that you truly are life and life itself. So when you read these words, "I am the way, the truth and the life" you'll know how true that statement is. When he said, "I am the truth," can't you see what marvelous thing he's telling you: a true judgment need not conform to the external fact to which it relates. Today I will say what is true concerning my world. Well, I pay so much rent and I have an average income of so much and I have certain obligations to life and these seem to be the facts, that's true. I tell you, that *isn't* true, for a true judgment need not conform to the external fact to which it relates. Truth depends on the *intensity* of imagining and not upon fact. So I will imagine that I am and I'll name it that which I want to be. Believing that I am that which I'm assuming that I am and remaining loyal to that assumption, I become it.

I have done it or I wouldn't be here tonight. I have actually done it, time and time again. But man will always slip back into Barabbas, the man of sense. We must ever remember the trial and always move out. In spite of all of the facts that would deny it, live in the dream just as though it were true, and no power in the world can stop you from becoming the fulfillment of your dream. But no power! You don't need any other being because God's name is not "he is" or "she is" or "they are"; his name is "I AM." Before you say anything in this world, you have to say, "I am." You don't pronounce it. If I ask, "Who are you?" you'll say, "John." But before you say John, you say, actually in the depths of yourself, "I am John." Before you said anything you actually were aware of being, and that awareness of being was actually declaring in the depths "I am." And that is God. There is no other God.

So God stands on trial, and he will be tried in all the churches of Christendom this coming week. They will all weep and carry on, how God was tried, and the crowd shouted out release a thief and a robber, one who was an insurrectionist, and they do not know who he is. They'll make some mental picture of a horrible beast, who was an awful, awful man. And that's not the man at all. *They* are the man, for they are calling to release themselves of sense and make that the *real* being in the world and hold on and deny Jesus.

So listen to these words in the 16th chapter of Acts, "Believe in the Lord Jesus and be saved, you and your household (verse 31)." Well, the only Jesus that you could ever believe in that could save you would be I AM. Well, that's his name (Exodus 3:14). Believe in the Lord Jesus and be saved, you and your household. He has only one name in this world, for the word *Jesus* simply means I AM. It is spelled Yod He Vau Shin Ayin. The root of the name of Jehovah is Yod He Vau. The Shin Ayin put into the name of Jesus, which is Jeshua, is for a definite purpose. Shin is made in three little prongs like that, and it's called "a consuming fire; a tooth that devours, that consumes." An Ayin is an eye. Were it not for that in the name of Jesus, I would have to accept as final everything that I see. But in the name of Jesus, which is called Savior, what I don't want I can consume. So it's Yod He Vau Shin Ayin. So the Yod He Vau is the root; that's Jehovah, that is God, and that is I AM. But a Shin is put into my name, so is an Ayin, but a Shin. I can just see the world. I don't like the way you look. "Don't you feel well?" No. Well, then I will consume it. I will see you as you ought to be seen by me and the world, seen by yourself; therefore, if I actually see you differently, I am consuming what formerly you *appeared* to be.

How would I do it? The Ayin is an eye. So what is his name when he comes into the world, and how does he operate? Listen to it carefully, the 11th chapter of the Book of Isaiah: "When he comes into the world, he will not judge by what his eye sees or decide by what his ears hear (verse 3)." So I see . . . go to the hospital; you're going to die. Go to anyone else, and you see it's fatal. Regardless of the nature, it's all—they can't get a job, there are too many unemployed, this, that, and the other. There it is, the fact. I will not judge by what my eye sees, neither will I decide by what my ears hear. So what would I do then? I will see what I want to see. But now a Shin is present—it consumes the former state, completely consumes the fact as it seemed to me to be real—and I will put in its place what I want to see and what I want to hear.

So then they tried to quench the voice of Peter and John, and they said what they would do to them if they continued to teach this story. This is the 4th of Acts, and they said to the Sanhedrin, the great wise men of the day, "Whether it is right in the eyes of God to believe in you and not in God, you must judge; but we cannot speak other than what we have seen and heard." So whether you think I should do what you tell me I should do, all right, you judge it. The wise men of the world, who were called the leaders in politics or in religion, they will tell you, without vision, what you should see and what you should preach. They had no vision, none whatsoever and never had one in eternity, but they're going to tell you how you should tell the story. But "whether it is right in the eyes of God to listen to you rather than to God, you must judge; for we cannot preach other than what we have seen and heard" (verse 19). So I cannot preach other than what I've seen and heard.

And may I tell you: I have *seen* this story. When you see it from afar, it's one man, just one man; and as you approach it, it becomes unnumbered races and nations of people. I saw it so clearly one night when Blake asked me to fall backward and I did exactly what he told me to do to produce the vision. And here was one man, a glorious man, a radiant man, and his heart was all like living ruby. I approached him. I moved forward. I fell through space like a meteor, and when I came to a standstill, here I saw one man. Then at Blake's suggestion, I moved forward. Well, this was one man, a radiant being. As I came closer, I noticed the heart was like a ruby; and there were unnumbered, innumerable beings, making up the heart. The whole body was made up of nations and races—the whole body. When I came close enough, I recognized myself. I was he, containing within myself the whole of humanity. So I know from experience that when you see God, you'll see yourself. At a distance, it's one man; and as you approach, it becomes unnumbered men composed of races and nations—all one.

So this whole vast thing is the most wonderful play, and the final drama leading up to that very exit from this sphere is this trial. So I hope that you will bring in your verdict tonight and your verdict will be "Release Jesus!" But if your verdict is no, I must accept my senses more than I will accept the invisible reality; well, then, it's your choice. You're free to bring in your verdict. But your verdict will be brought by you. I can recommend the spirit if you dare to believe in the reality of your own wonderful I-am-ness, believing that *it is* God and there is no other God. Listen to the words, "I am the Lord thy God, the Holy One of Israel, thy Savior . . . and besides me there is no savior" (Isaiah 43:3, 11). There is no other savior. "I am the Lord thy God, the Holy One of Israel, thy Savior . . . and besides me there is no savior." Believe that and rather *die* than turn back, and you are moving toward being born from above.

Now let us go into the Silence.

*   *   *

Q: (inaudible)

A: Is there a fixed guide? Well, some believe that all of us present here have a certain code of decency, and I would go along with it, but I would put into practice what I told you tonight. I would guide myself with my code of ethics. I couldn't, if you asked me tonight—although all things are possible to God—if you asked me to join with you in knowing that someone was dead for your good fortune, I could not. I would not deny you the right to want it, but I would say go elsewhere. I could not actually dream with you that someone died because you were left in his will. But I would not deny you the right to want such a thing. I would leave it alone up to your judgment. So we all have a certain code. And I think that anyone who would come to a meeting of this nature would have a code of decency—what I would call a code of decency. And so I'm always right if whenever I use my Imagination I use it lovingly on behalf of another. If I ever use my Imagination lovingly on behalf of another, I am on the right track. So that to me would be the guide: Is it a loving thing to do?

We have that wonderful statement in the Bible, "Do unto others as you would have them do unto you." So would you have someone, because you have wealth and you've named them, see that you make your exit tonight because it would be easier for them tomorrow? Would you want that? No, well then, ___(??) the state today. So do unto others as you would have them do unto you. It is the simplest code in the world. It is done in the positive manner: do—not do not do. But it is written in the positive in the New Testament. In all other religions, it is written in the negative: "Do unto others as you would have them do unto you." So what would I like in this world? Something lovely? Something wonderful? Well, do the same thing to anyone in the world; and every time you use your Imagination lovingly on behalf of another, you have done the right thing.

Q: (inaudible)

A: Read Galatians, the 4th chapter, the 14th verse. That one little thought that is "as an angel" is superfluous because the next phrase is "as Christ Jesus." But "as an angel," it might stop right away. That is all inserted to cushion him because they actually saw him as the central being himself: they "looked upon me as *Christ Jesus*." But if you put the little phrase before it, "as an angel," that arrests the mind and you don't associate Paul with Christ Jesus. I tell you, he was the one in whom the whole thing awoke. It was Paul. Everything has to come right out of the Jew. The world will not believe it. It is the most fantastic story in the world.

Now, Bishop Pike, who was born a Catholic and became a priest, gave it up and became an agnostic. Then he became a most brilliant lawyer in New York City, practicing corporate law. He then rejoined the church as a Protestant priest. He then rejoined the church as a Protestant, and rose in no time—he was only in his forties—to Bishop Pike of California. If you have ever heard him, he is an able speaker. He has a wonderful brilliant mind. Bishop Pike made the statement "I am a Jew." Remember, he was born and raised a Catholic, became a Catholic priest, gave it up, became an agnostic, became a lawyer, and went back into the priesthood, this time as a Protestant priest. Now he is the highest in the Protestant world. You can't go beyond that. You may move from one section to the other, but he is tops in Northern California. And he said, "I am a *Jew because* I am a *Christian*. I *could* be a Jew and not be a Christian, but I can't be a Christian and not be a Jew."

You think about it. Meditate upon that thought. It's true! The whole thing comes out of Israel. It's a mystery, the most fantastic mystery in the world. So I am proud to say I am a Jew because I am a Christian. I have been born from above. I couldn't possibly be unless I were the Jew. And I know when the veil is lifted and the whole thing is revealed, well, it's fantasy beyond the wildest dream.

Good night!

THE CRUCIFIXION

April 9, 1963

Tonight's subject is "The Crucifixion." In the history of man, our human history, life begins with birth and ends with death. In divine history, it begins with death and ends with birth. There's a complete reversal of these histories. So here we begin in the womb and end in the tomb; but in divine history, we begin in the tomb and awaken in the womb, where we are born.

Now here, in this fantastic drama, I think that we have misconceived the part of Jesus Christ and made of him an idol. Having made of him an idol, he hides from us the true God. So here, let us turn to the Book of Luke, the 18th chapter; he turns to the twelve, "And taking the twelve he said to them, 'We're going up to Jerusalem and everything written of the Son of man by the prophets will be accomplished. He'll be delivered to the Gentiles and they will mock him, and shamefully treat him, and spit upon him; they will scourge him, and kill him, but on the third day he will rise.' And they did not understand what he said; this saying was hid from them, and they could not grasp what was said" (verses 31-34). We're told that no one understood it.

Now believe this, I am speaking to you as I try every night from experience. I am not theorizing. I have no interest whatsoever in trying to set up some workable philosophy of life, I really haven't. If I made my exit tonight, it would make no difference to me personally—maybe to my wife and my child, my family, but not really to me. I am not speaking from theory; I'm speaking from experience. The drama begins with the crucifixion. "Unless I die thou canst not live; but if I die I shall arise again and thou with me. Wouldest thou die for one who never died for thee?" (Blake, *Jerusalem*, Plate 96). This is the story of every being born of woman. No child in the world could cross the threshold that admits to conscious life unaided by the death of God. It's God's purpose to give us himself, as though there were no others in the world, just God and me, God and I. Believe this, really. If you believe it, then the most unbelievable gospel in the world becomes possible and believable. And it takes the Son to reveal it to be true.

Now this is the story as revealed to me. You may think, well now, that was just simple, wonderful—exciting, yes!—but just a dream. May I tell you, it was not a dream. It was an experience more vivid than this moment here in this room. For a true vision is far more alive than anything you've ever experienced in this world, but anything. This night in question, I was walking with an enormous number, as though the whole of humanity walked in a certain direction and I was one of the unnumbered. As I walked with them, they were all dressed in very colorful Arabic clothes and a voice shouted out of the blue; the voice said, "And God walks with them." A woman to my right—a woman I would say in her thirties, maybe forties, a most attractive Arab—asked the voice, "If God walks with us, where is he?" The voice answered from the blue, from the deep, "At your side." She took it literally, as the whole vast world takes these things literally; and turning to her side, she looked into my eyes and became hysterical. It struck her so funnily. It was the funniest thing she ever heard. God walks with us, and she turns to a simple man, with all of his frailties, all of his weaknesses, the ones she knew well; and having looked into his face, having heard the voice, she said, "What? Is Neville God?" And the voice said to me, "God laid himself down within you to sleep, and as he slept, he dreamed a dream, he dreamed . . . ," and I completed the sentence: he was dreaming that he's me. How else would I be in this world if he didn't dream? And you awake from sheer emotionalism.

May I tell you that this is the sensation of the crucifixion. It's the most delightful sensation in the world; it is *not* painful. My hands became vortices, my head a vortex, my feet vortices, and my side a vortex. And here, I was driven into this body on the bed through my emotionalism, held by six vortices: my hands, my feet, my head, and my side. And the delight and sheer joy of being driven upon this cross, this body! So I speak from experience that it is not a painful act. But it happened in the beginning of time. This was only a memory image returning when I was about to awake. But in that interval, how long? Who knows? Blake calls it six thousand years. The Bible speaks of three days between the crucifixion and resurrection, but that's all symbolic. Blake calls it 6,000 years. He said, "I behold the visions of my deadly sleep of six thousand years dazzling around thy skirts like a serpent of precious stones and gold. I know it is my Self, O my Divine Creator and Redeemer" (*Jerusalem*, Plate 96, Line 11).

Now, here we turn to the drama of this coming Friday that all the Christian churches will reenact. And they differ. Matthew and Mark give the last cry on the cross as the quotation from the 22nd Psalm, the 1st verse, "My God, my God, why hast thou forsaken me?" John gives it in the cry, "It is finished!" (John 19:30). Luke substitutes the 31st Psalm, the 5th verse for the 22nd Psalm, because he was using Mark's script. Perhaps he elaborates on Mark's script, and he substituted Psalm 31:5 for Psalm 22:1. This is what he quotes, "Into thy hand I commit my spirit." That's all that he quotes. But the completed fifth verse is fantastic. This is the verse, "Thou hast *redeemed* me, O Lord, faithful God." "Into thy hand I commit my spirit; thou hast redeemed me, O Lord, faithful God." He kept his faith, for he told me, "Unless I die thou cannot live; but if I die I shall arise again and thou with me." There came the very act of crucifixion that was in itself resurrection. Yes, at an interval of time between, yes, no question about it. But may I tell you, no one in this world can fail, for quoting in the 6th of Romans, "If we have been united with Christ in a death like his, we shall certainly be united with him in a resurrection like his (verse 5)." And everyone in this world will be resurrected, but it takes this interval of time and all the blows in the world to make the immortal garment.

Now listen to this carefully. It has been given to me and you; take it for what it's worth. The promise of this begins in Genesis, the promise of an infant called Isaac. The whole vast world has the strangest concept of Isaac. The Lord begot Isaac. Isaac is to be ___(??) not as the *result* of generation but the *shaping* of the unbegotten. Here is God, the unbegotten, shaping himself upon us; and when he completes that shape and it's perfect in *his* eye, then we are born from above. So Isaac is the shaping of the unbegotten. For God is not begotten. He is begetting himself on man, individual man.

And when he begot himself in me to *his* satisfaction, I was born from above and went through the entire series in the interval of five months, judged by Caesar's calendar. How many thousands of years prior to that, I do not know; I cannot tell you. I would if I knew, for I have no secrets. When I get it, I'll tell you. But I do not have it; the veil has not been lifted to that extent. But I do know that when it pleased him, that which he begot in me, and then it took nine months for the entire series of mystical experiences, as described in scripture, to completely unfold within me. And so I can tell you it's going to happen to you.

And so there's no time; it took nine months from the moment of the birth, but when that birth takes place, it's all in God's keeping. You and I are put through the furnaces of affliction. Let no one tell you that you're not going to. "As I have planned it, so shall it be, and as I have purposed it, so shall it stand" (Isaiah 14:24). And no one will thwart it, but no one.

I'm inclined to believe that in spite of the pain, in spite of all the things that man plots and plans in this world, there is a definite period. I'm inclined to believe it. The Book of Habakkuk tells me—but they won't tell me what the period is—"The vision has its own appointed hour; it ripens, it will flower. If it be long then wait; for it is sure, it will not be late" (Habakkuk 2:3).

If it will not be late and the vision has its own appointed hour, then whether Blake is right or someone else is right, I do not know. But I assure you that the last section takes only nine months, even though you linger for years beyond that nine months, for you came into your inheritance at that third experience. But the glory of your heavenly inheritance cannot become actual or is not fully realized in the individual, so long as he's still in the body. But the moment that he takes off that veil called the body, he is clothed in that garment that God and God alone made. God was actually shaping himself upon this garment, without my consent and without my knowledge, molding that unbegotten being that he is and giving me himself. So then he succeeded in giving me himself, so he satisfied him, that immortal garment that *he* would wear. So *he* wears it, for his name is I AM.

And may I tell you, in all of my experiences, I have never had a change in identity, never. I have always been aware of being I am. I have never had any feeling of being other than who I am and something taking place in me, and it was God. As we are told, "He who began a good work in you will bring it to completion at the day of Jesus Christ" (Philippians 1:6). Jesus Christ is the perfection that is God, and he will not stop it until he brings it to Jesus Christ *in you*. But now we have taken Jesus Christ and made of him an image, an idol; and having made of him an idol, he now hides from us the true God. It is God, the only God that is actually shaping himself upon you. When that is shaped upon you—this is a form, a mold, but this cannot inherit the kingdom of heaven; this is flesh and blood—it takes this that is molded upon it. For what is being molded upon it is God, the unbegotten; and God, being Spirit, is molding himself as Spirit, the immortal you. And then you, as God, are clothed. Well, how could you clothe God in form? He's clothing himself in a shape. That's you. So he begets us.

But it begins with the crucifixion. The crucifixion does not end the drama; it begins the drama. And so everyone becomes a breathing, living, conscious being because God died for him. It's the mystery of life through death, as told us in 12th chapter of the Book of John, "Unless a grain of wheat falls into the earth and dies, it remains alone; but if it dies it brings forth much fruit." It has to fall into the earth and die, and this [body] is the earth in God's kingdom. God falls into this earth and dies: He forgets that he's God in his *belief* that he's man. God actually becomes man that man may become God, and he molds himself, this unbegotten being, upon man. When he is satisfied with that molding process and in the eye of God that it's perfect, therefore if it is perfect God is born in that man. So God actually gives himself to us, to *each* of us, as though there were no others in the world, just God and you, God and I. Believe it. The whole story of the gospel is this story.

So the crucifixion, from my own personal experience, is not as the churches depict it. The sorrow comes in between. That interval, be it 6,000 years, I do not know, but in that interval we have to be molded. As we are told in the 48th chapter of Isaiah, (verse 10), he has put me through the fires of affliction. For his own sake, he did it, for his own sake, for there is no other way in the world of bringing me into that state of perfection and to weave me into an immortal body to receive God himself as my own being, unless I went through all the fires of affliction, all these fiery, fiery ordeals. But don't be concerned. "Whom God afflicts for secret ends, he comforts and heals and calls him friends" (Blake, *Everlasting Gospel*).

So when you and I entered Golgotha, as we are told, "And when they came to the place which they called The Skull, there they crucified him." Read it in the 23rd of Luke, "When they came to the place which they called The Skull, there they crucified him." The word *skull* is translated as Golgotha; another definition is the Holy Sepulcher, so now we know what the Holy Sepulcher is: it is our own wonderful human skull. That's where he is crucified. But he is also nailed upon the cross. He is nailed through the feet and hands and pierced on the side.

Now here John gives so much time to the piercing of the side. He does not give the cry of dereliction, "My God, my God, why hast thou forsaken me?" John only claims, "It is finished!" and then came the soldier's shaft into the right side and out came blood and water. Down through the centuries, they are in some way trying to explain it. They can't explain it on anything that is biological, save that a birth always has the phenomena of blood and water. When a child is born, the water is broken, and there is a flowing of blood and water. This is birth. To understand it, we go back to the 31st Psalm: "Into thy hand I commit my spirit; thou hast redeemed me, O Lord, faithful God." So he promised it and he did it. That is only a symbol of one's birth which is redemption.

So I say to you, don't weep when you see it. Rejoice! It was God's sacrifice of himself because he desired to individualize himself in unnumbered garments, in all of us. God can't beget anything other than God. So we are told in the 82nd Psalm, "God has taken his place in the divine council; in the midst of the gods he holds judgment." One God in the midst of the gods—all is God. He is ___(??) and begetting this unbegotten being. The cue is given us in the Book of Hebrews, the 5th chapter, 6th verse. It is called by a different name; it is called Melchizedek. He has no father, no mother, and no genealogy. He is telling you who he is. Everyone who is born from above, because God succeeded in giving himself to that individual, that individual has no genealogy. He is God the Father. Believe me.

- (Hiatus in tape required text from previously typed lecture.)

For the son ___(??). Well, how could he give me himself as if I'd known him? He gave me his Son. I tell you, the whole vast world of humanity is symbolized in a single youth called David. David is the whole vast world of humanity in the language of symbolism. And the day will come in the second mystical experience in the nine-month period, and there you look at David. David is your Son, and you know it more surely than you know anything else in the world. There's no uncertainty when you look into his eyes and you see David and he calls you "my Lord, my Father." He *calls* you "my Father." And so then you know for the first time who you *really* are. You tell this to the world and you tell them what happened; but you're told, as I quoted earlier from the 18th chapter of the Book of Luke, they did not understand the saying. This saying was hid from them, and they could not grasp the meaning.

How can you persuade the individual that the day will come . . . that even at this very moment, I could take the most orthodox Jew in the world . . . if I went to Israel tonight and talked to the head rabbi and asked him if he feels any relationship to David, he would say, "Only as the greatest of the kings of Israel, but relationship as to myself, no." But he respects the great king of Israel and hopes someday to rebuild the dynasty that is now gone. But he could not feel a relationship. And if I, in his eye a total stranger, a gentile, would tell him I am his father, he would spit in my face. To him that would be blasphemous—he would spit in my face. And yet I could tell him I am his father. I'll go further and I'll tell you *you* are his father and the day is coming that it will be revealed to you. And when the whole vast world is completed God's work is finished, and he's given himself to every being in the world because he *is* the father of David. To give me himself, he has to give me fatherhood of David. Not just fatherhood. There's no need to give me fatherhood and not the father of his son. His son? Yes, the 7th verse of the 2nd Psalm: "Thou art my son, today I have begotten thee." And then he takes this only begotten son to prove his gift to us by giving us *that* son as *our* son. You look right into his eyes and there he calls you Father. He calls you Adonay, my Lord.

So I tell you that the day will come that you and I will be the same father of the same child, the everlasting eternal youth, that God in the beginning put into the mind of man and molded man into the likeness of him. Read it in the 3rd chapter, the 11th verse of Ecclesiastes: "And God has put eternity into the minds of men; yet so that man cannot find out what God has done from the beginning to the end." The word called *eternity*, translated eternity, is the Hebrew word *olam*, and *olam* is translated "youth, man, *stripling*."

Listen to the words, and see how we know who he is. The king wants to find out the identity of this fantastic youth that conquered the entire enemy of Israel—he brings down the giant. And so the king said to his lieutenant, "Abner, whose son is that youth?" and Abner said, "As your soul liveth, O King, I cannot tell." He said, "Inquire whose son the *stripling* is." No one knows. Now the stripling comes in with the head of the giant in his hands, the head of Goliath, the enemy of Israel, and the king said to him, "Whose son are you, young man?" He said, "I am the son of thy servant Jesse the Bethlehemite" (1 Samuel 17:56-58).

Now, prophecy was made in the 17th chaper of 1st Samuel, the 25th verse, that the father of such a lad would be set free in Israel. Not the lad—the lad is buried in every being in the world—but the *father* of that lad, who *knows* he is the father; he is set free in heaven, free in the New Israel. And so when one *knows* he is the father by actual experience, at that moment, he is free in Israel. The 6,000 years of turmoil is over for him. But David is still to be redeemed, to be discovered in the minds of all, and everyone is going to find him. Finding him, they'll find the relationship of himself to that lad. We all will be one, and our name one when the curtain comes down on the final act of this marvelous play.

Blake said, "Do not let yourself be intimidated by the horror of the world. For everything is ordered and correct and must fulfill its destiny in order to achieve perfection" (To M. Beckman, *Modern Painting*). *Everything* is ordered; everything is perfect. God planned it just as it's come out and it will be consummated and no tyrant in the world is going to stop it. He will take all the tyrants in the world and use them for the fulfillment of his purpose. As we are told in Proverbs 16:4, everything, not just a few, "God made everything for its purpose, even the wicked for the day of trouble." Yes, even the wicked for the day of trouble. For if it takes the wicked being to cross your path to add a little more fire to bring you closer into the image of God, then he'll cross your path. If it takes many to cross it, they'll cross your path.

And finally, one day will come that in the eyes of God, not man, what man looking at this garment that wears out could ever see you in the image of God? But this is not what is molded. This is only a form in which he is molding himself. And when he's finished that molding, then comes this fantastic experience *in* you, and you awake. You awake in a tomb, and the tomb all along was the womb. That was where you were crucified, but you didn't know it. One day, you awake in a tomb and the tomb is your own wonderful skull and that is the Holy Sepulcher.

But this week, thousands of pilgrims will go to Jerusalem to the Holy Sepulcher, and some priests, quite innocently, will point out a place and say, "That's it, that's where he was buried." He wasn't buried there at all. There is no holy place in Jerusalem. The holy place is your own wonderful skull; that's the Holy Sepulcher; that's where he's buried. That's where he's sound asleep, dreaming with you these visions of eternity until you awake. But when you awake, you are he and he is your very being. It's his purpose to *give* you himself. There is no way in eternity that God can give me himself and prove it unless he also gives me his most precious possession in the world, and that's his son. He doesn't give me his son to walk the street with me as a companion; he gives me his son *as my* son. So I look right into the eyes of the Son of God and know him to be *my* son.

Then I wonder, "How can this be? Here a man, a few years old, weak and limited, with all the frailties of the world and all the weaknesses of the flesh, and yet God so succeeded in his purpose for me that he, the unbegotten, gave me himself; therefore, I am unbegotten?" So I who seemingly had a beginning in time, with the gift of God, the unbegotten, I now cease to be begotten. I have no genealogy. I have no father. I am Father, the father of his only begotten son. I tell you, it's a mystery. But mysteries of this nature are not matters to be kept secret but truths that are mysterious in nature. They are not things to be hidden. The minute they happen to you you tell them to encourage every being in the world that in spite of the furnaces of the moment to continue and keep on moving, for you'll move anyway.

But the end, listen to the words, "Thou hast redeemed me, O God, faithful Lord." He has kept his faith. He promised me in the beginning that he would do it and then sent me through furnaces, without my consent, without my permission, just sent me through furnaces. The story of Job—for here is one subjected to all the most horrible experiments in the world produced by God. And in the end, he said, "I have heard of you with the hearing of the ear, but now my eye sees thee" (Job 42:5). He's sees the only thing in the world that could reveal God to himself. Because God is invisible to the world—but his Son reveals God. "No one knows who the Son is except the Father, and no one knows who the Father is except the Son and any one to whom the Son chooses to reveal him" (Matthew 11:27). And so how will I ever know God? When his Son comes into my world and looks me in the face and calls me Father, then I know God.

And yet in spite of this, may I tell you, the day will come that you will still be taken into the presence of infinite love. You don't have to ask who you are or anyone in the world who he is. You stand in the presence of infinite love; he embraces you, and you know who he is and who you are. For at that moment of the embrace, you become one with the body of infinite love. Yet that God is almighty, no question of that, but almightiness and omniscience are but attributes of God. God himself is love, absolute love. I can't describe it save to tell you it's man. When you look at him, infinite love, he embraces you and you are lost in the body of God and yet one with—it's your body.

And then comes the final journey. "I tell you these things before they take place in you, that when they do take place, you may believe" (John 14:29). So I share with you my experience and remember it because it's going to happen to you. When it happens to you, you will not differ from any other being in the world to whom it has not *yet* happened, for it's going to happen to every being in the world. But you are one with those to whom it has already happened. And when it happens to you—it may happen tonight—you'll wear the garment for a little while, and then you'll take it off. In the normal process of time, you'll take it off. And then, at that moment of the discarding of this mold that God used to mold himself, you'll be one with the gods. In your entire inheritance it is to inherit the kingdom of heaven. Believe me.

What that garment looks like, if I can describe it, I can't tell you. I can describe the sensation, but it doesn't make sense to anyone in the world. But the final act, when he ascends into heaven and *you* ascend as it, I can only describe it as the seraphim, a golden, golden liquid being; and you ascend as a serpent. It doesn't make sense, does it? A human serpent, as described in the 6th chapter of the Book of Isaiah (verse 2). The face, the hands, and the feet were human, but he couldn't describe the glory of the body. It's simply golden liquid light. Because in the resurrection, man is above the organization of sex—the garment he used by which to mold himself and to give man himself.

So Blake brought it out in his wonderful thought, called *The Gates of Paradise*: "When weary man enters his cave, he meets his savior in the grave, some find a female garment there, and some a male, woven with care, lest the sexual garments sweet should grow a devouring winding sheet, one dies! Alas! the living and dead, one is slain and one is fled." If this is slain, the mold is over. No need for the mold anymore, for he wove upon this divided image, male and female, the garment that is immortal that is above the organization of sex. So he discards then this divided image as far as that individual goes. He's now clothed in his immortal, eternal body, and no need for the divided image on which God molded himself and gave himself to us. That being means Jesse, which simply means I AM, the same being named as Jehovah, which is I AM, the same name of Jesus, which is I AM.

And so I tell you that this fantastic mystery of crucifixion is true. It *begins* the play of God. If I went to a play tonight and saw a three-hour play move before me on the boards, I could, as so many people do, misconceive the role of the actor and make of him, as people do here, a movie actor or a stage actor, and make of him an idol. Ask him for his signature, do all kinds of things, and make of him an idol. And then making of him an idol, he hides from me the message of the play. Here is a play condensed into a few hours that took 6,000 years to unfold. And so man's misconception of Jesus Christ has made of Jesus Christ in the eyes of all Christians an idol. And that idol hides from that man who holds him up as an idol the true message of God.

For God's purpose is to give himself to us without an intermediary—no intermediary between God and you. He's actually begetting himself *on* you; and because *he* is without origin, the unbegotten, when he begets himself, that very being still has no origin. So when he begets himself on you and gives himself to you, completely individualized as you, you have no origin. The reason you have no origin is the child, and you see God's Son as your son. Then you will know who you are—the being without father and without mother. And it's a strange thing to say that I, a little thing, a few years old, that some fantastic mystery could take place here. And here, undoubtedly this garment began fifty-eight years ago, and yet on this garment and the garment that preceded it, something was being molded that was unbegotten. When it was completed in its perfection, and then I wore that garment that was molded on me with all the pains I went through, that *I* am the being who molded it; and so I am unbegotten. So the garment I wear, the immortal garment, though begotten, it's being worn now by the unbegotten, God the Father. You dwell upon it.

But what I've told you this night may seem strange if you're here for the first time—maybe you're here for the hundredth time and it still seems strange—but it's true. Everything I've told you is true. I've spoken to you from my own personal experience. We all are on a fabulous pilgrimage moving toward some invisible shrine, and God is awakening in us. The world round about us will go on to their journey. And when we are singled out, one by one, they laugh at the very thought that he who dies a normal, normal death as any other man, was in that exit—his final exit—and he by that experience is immortalized, eternalized? And they smile and continue the journey that they're on.

But I tell you, ___(??). You too will be called out of the pilgrimage, and the voice will speak out of the vast sky: "God walks with them." Someone will question the voice, and the voice will answer, yes; and they will turn to you, and they'll be just as hysterical as they were with me. The voice in the depths of your own soul will tell you, "God laid himself down within you to sleep, and as he slept he dreamed a dream: he's dreaming that he's you." Then you will feel the wonderful thrill of being nailed upon this body. Oh, what a thrill! These whirling vortices—no pain, just joy, ecstatic joy! And then you are on the bed alone, and this journey continues in the soul, still moving on.

But now you cannot rest; from that moment on, everything changes. You see people as you saw them but still they differ. You know their future. You know what they are destined to be, that everyone is destined to have the experience and to remember in that ecstatic moment, where unnumbered ages before, he was nailed upon the cross through God's love. "Unless I die, thou canst not live; but if I die I shall arise *again* and thou with me. For if God dieth not for man and giveth not himself eternally for man, man could not exist." So God dies. And this is the wonderful mystery of *life* through death. But here is our story for you this night on the crucifixion.

Now let us go into the Silence and hear the ___(??), and believe, when we break the spell, believe in the reality of that imaginal experience.

*   *   *

Q: (inaudible)
A: Yes, my dear. If you really believe that God planned this thing as it's going to come out and it will be consummated, you can accept what without this knowledge you would be unwilling or unable to accept. When you read the horrors, man's inhumanity to man, and if you bear in mind that God will use it all toward his purpose, use it all. Nothing is wasted, not in God's kingdom. And so he's using everything toward molding himself, the unbegotten, molded upon us.

Remember what I said earlier concerning Isaac. The Lord begat Isaac, and Isaac must be thought of not as the result of generation, as this body is generated, but think of Isaac as actually pruning or shaping the unbegotten.

Q: (inaudible)
A: Well, the Sermon on the Mount. The Sermon on the Mount takes the entire law of Moses to a mental level. A very simple one, "You've heard it said of old, 'You shall not commit adultery.' But I say unto you that anyone who looks on a woman lustfully has already committed the act in his heart with her'" (Matthew 5:27). So he lifts it from a physical level to a mental level. That I may have the impulse to commit adultery, and then I contemplate the act that may seem to me pleasurable, but I

contemplate it along with its consequences to myself and to my family and to society; and fearing the consequences if caught, I restrain the impulse. For I am told in this principle that that's not good enough. To restrain the impulse does not in any way exempt me from having committed the act. The act was committed in the imaginal state, when I imagined myself in the act. So that although my desire was thwarted by my contemplating the consequences, that wasn't good enough. So he lifts the entire act of creation from a physical level to a mental level.

And so as I walk the street and I think, "How would it be were I . . . (and I name it)?" That's ___(??) based upon the evidence of my senses, and these tell me I am *not* the man, that I could not be ___(??) in this world, well, then I'm not going to occupy the state. But I am actually within the limitations of my senses; therefore, I only perpetuate the present state in my world. So he invites us to step out of these sense-limitations and live in Imagination as though things were as we desire them to be. That's what he's asking us to do.

Listen to this 11th chapter, the 24th verse of he Book of Mark: "Whatever you ask in prayer, believe you have received it, and you will." It doesn't say it's good for me. It doesn't say that I got the permission of the church or of society. *Whatever* you ask in prayer, believe you receive and you will. Now these are words put into the mouth of the central character, Christ Jesus, telling all within earshot of his voice: apply it.

Now I know that many people will say, "He didn't mean that. Then what did he say?" They will say, "You've got it all wrong, Neville. That's not quite what he meant. You tell us what he meant. ___(??) within the framework of the moral code of the priests ___(??) moral code. So which code must I adopt?" He didn't ask you to adopt anything in this world. In fact, he ___(??) and he had no kindly word for the Pharisee. He said you would circumnavigate the entire world to make one convert, then you throw away the key. So you do not know yourself how to get into the kingdom. After having converted him to your way of thinking, you don't know how to get in. You are ___(??), and you've converted one by circumnavigating the entire world to make one, and you can't *yourself* get in. You throw away the key; you don't know the key. ___(??)

Q: (inaudible)

A: My dear, the word *prayer* in the Bible is defined as "motion toward, accession to, nearness at, at or in the vicinity of." So if I would now pray successfully, I must actually move toward the fulfillment of my dream in my Imagination and make natural all the things that would be natural were it true. Only through such action in my Imagination are my prayers really answered. (Tape ends.)

THE RESURRECTION

April 12, 1963

Tonight is "The Resurrection." Although the resurrection is not described in the scriptures, it stands at the very central point of the Christian faith, for if he is not risen, our faith is vain. We are told if the dead are not resurrected, then Christ is not risen. The Christ, we are told, is the power and the wisdom of God (1 Corinthians 1:24). Every child born of woman is crucified with Christ—with the power and with the wisdom. In God's good time, he resurrects that individual when the individual has completely absorbed Christ—when that wisdom and that power is one with the individual who is actually crucified on that cross. No one can resurrect himself. It is an act of God. God's mightiest act is the resurrection, to save mankind and establish his people.

So we are told in Paul's letters to the Corinthians, "What you sow, unless it dies, it is not alive. And what you sow is not the body which is to be. But God gives it a body as he has chosen" (1 Corinthians 15:36). For the resurrection body is determined entirely by the gift of God as *he* has chosen. Don't try to even visualize it; you couldn't visualize it. Don't speculate. It's an immortal body, an eternal body given to the individual as that individual is resurrected.

Now let me share with you my experience of the resurrection. It's a true experience. Everyone will have this experience. Resurrection is a privileged new birth in a new creation. You did not earn your physical birth; you were born by the action of powers beyond your own. You'll be born spiritually by the action of powers beyond your own. So let no one tell you that you earn it. You don't earn it; it's a gift. It's all grace and still grace. Because it *is* a gift, everyone will be born from above. So though it's not described in scripture, I can describe it for you, for I've experienced it. We are not born *from* the body; we are awakened *in* it. We aren't awakened from it; we are awakened in it. It's something entirely different.

Now we are told that they came to the tomb, but bear in mind that only one person saw him placed in the tomb. Joseph placed him in a new tomb, but no one saw him in the new tomb. So they came early in the morning, and they said they looked in. These are the words, "They've taken away the Lord from the tomb and we do not know where they've laid him" (Mark 16; Matthew 28; John 20). They looked in, and they saw what appeared to them to be angels seated where the body of Jesus had laid, one at the head and one at the feet. Now no one saw how that body had been placed, for it was placed by *Joseph*, not by the women who came early in the morning and not by the disciples. And yet they claim that they saw what they thought to be angels in radiant light, seated where the body of Jesus had laid, and they said to them, "He is risen." "But these words seemed to them an idle tale, and they did not believe it" (Luke 24:11). That's how the story is told, it seemed to them an idle tale, and they did not believe it.

But now let me share with you what I have experienced. That record of the 20th of John and the 24th of Luke is not correct, but they do not describe the event. No attempt is made to describe the actual resurrection. I tell you, the resurrection is simply a new birth into an entirely different world. Don't try to visualize the world. Here, I tell you, you rise into a world completely subject to your imaginative power. There will be no such thing as systems as we have systems. *Everyone* will be God, but everyone. You will not have to contend with politicians or men in the churches who call themselves your superior, or anyone in this world who thinks himself greater. You are *God*, and everything in the world is subject to your imaginative power.

You enter *that* world where God is the substance of that world by taking us one by one into that world. And we do not have a thing to do with this body. In other words, it is as *he* has chosen. As we're told, "And what you have sown is not the body which is to be, for God has given it a body as he has chosen." You read it, the 15th of 1st Corinthians, read the 36th through the 38th verses. The entire thing is given to us, and he simply lifts us from this world into that. So I tell you from experience, resurrection is a new birth into *that* age as against *this* age. It's a privileged birth given to us by God.

Now when it happens, this is exactly how it's going to happen. You will awaken not *from* the body, as people teach; you will awaken *in* it. And when you awaken in it, you will be the most startled being in the world because until then you had no idea that you were asleep. You had no idea that through the ages you'd been sound asleep, dreaming this fantastic world. All this is man's dream, a nightmare. He dreams wars, revolutions, and convulsions, and sickness and poverty. Everything in the world he dreams here because he's sound asleep.

Resurrection is God's mighty act to awaken him in you, the body, from this dream. He awakens and the whole of him is in his skull, but the whole of him. The whole being finds himself completely sealed, entombed, in a skull. And then he comes out. He knows, seemingly, that he is unaided because he makes the effort to get out. He pulls *himself* out of his skull, so he can't say that anyone pushed him out or even aided him. He is self-begotten. He absorbed Christ in that state of dream, exercising unwisely that power. For Christ is the power of God and the wisdom of God but the *power* of God. And he made this fantastic dream, these horrible things come true by the exercise of that power that is Christ. And then suddenly, in God's own time, he saw him absorb Christ; he became one with that power, one with that wisdom. God of old, sound asleep.

And then the drama begins to unfold, and the tomb *is* empty; he comes out of it. As he comes out of it, there are men to meet him. Call them by any other name but they're men to meet him. The men cannot see him because the men present are men ___(??). They cannot see that heavenly being that is born. He belongs to an entirely different realm; he belongs to the kingdom of God, and mortal eye cannot see him. He doesn't even see himself because the body given to him is yet to be given, as God has chosen. What he sowed in this world is not the body which is to be. For God has given him a body as he, God, has chosen. And so that glorified body that is his to be worn in heaven, he doesn't see it at that moment, and no one sees him. He's simply aware, more aware than he's ever been before, *completely* awake. And then the drama unfolds. And they don't believe it either. Let me quote the words, "And the words they heard seemed to them like an idle tale, and they did not believe them."

So here is the story; one makes the fantastic, incredulous announcement that an event has taken place that is impossible to mortal mind. And so they didn't believe it. They asked in the most incredulous way, "How is this thing possible? It can't be!" He doesn't argue the point; he presents the evidence that this thing *did* take place. This is a birth unknown to any mortal man. This isn't the kind of a birth that takes place in this world, in this age. An entirely different birth, something that is self-begotten, out of his own fantastic skull he comes. And once you see beyond the symbol, it's a symbol signifying *that* birth. They did not believe it. I can hear the word now, *Impossible*! As far as they are concerned, they can't believe it. But he doesn't argue. The one who found the insignia, who found the little symbol called "a babe wrapped in swaddling clothes," puts it on the bed. And they look at it in amazement, but they still will not believe it. No little child is born;

that's only the signal, the symbol of an event that no mortal eye can witness. They accept it on faith, or they don't accept it. And they didn't accept it.

And so here, it's presented, and no one believes it. Even the one who finds it and finds it difficult—not only announced it but also finds it difficult, being human, to accept the evidence about the symbol as coming or signifying a completely new birth, a privileged birth into an entirely different world. But there it is. That is the insignia. That is the resurrection, resurrection in a new birth into the kingdom of God. Listen to the words from the 20th chapter of the Book of Luke, speaking of this world, "And whose wife will she be in the resurrection?" You do not know the scriptures, said he, for "in this age they marry and they are given in marriage; but those who are accounted worthy to attain to *that* age and to the resurrection from the dead neither marry nor are they given in marriage, for they cannot die again . . . they are now sons of God, and sons of the resurrection," something entirely different (verse 34).

But no man can see that. They can only see things based upon their experience here. And I can't blame anyone for it, for, may I tell you, I hadn't the slightest idea, certainly not any conscious idea, of this experience until it happened. Not the slightest concept that such things were possible until it happened, for I can stand today before the whole vast world; there are three billion of us and not bat an eye when I tell them I *know* the mystery of the resurrection. Although it's not described in scripture, I know exactly what the individual must go through to be resurrected, and he does not do it of himself; it's a gift from God. God, in his own wonderful time, resurrects us individually into an entirely different world, and he clothes us in this immortal body that cannot be seen with human eye and no one can describe it. It's fantastic beyond the wildest dream; that's the being that you are, clothed in this body that is forever. It's immortal.

And so that's the first act in the great scene of the resurrection, the birth. And then comes the series as it unfolds, and no one understands it. Conferred upon the risen Christ in the experience of man is the divine name, Adonay, which means "my Lord, my Father." That's conferred upon the Christ that is risen *in* man in that individual's experience and conferred upon him is the divine name, Adonay, which is "my Lord," which means "my Father." Well, how will you know it? Well, then comes the experience, which is just as exciting, just as unexpected, just as perplexing and bewildering as the first. You have no idea of this relationship; and suddenly it happens, and then he calls you, "my Father, my Lord." You look at him and here is this wonderful relationship and there it is.

Then comes the third. The third is the ascension, where man actually ascends. He is not man, yet he is man. He hasn't any loss of consciousness and no change of identity, but here is a golden, liquid being that he is. And just as described, an earthquake takes place. You don't get out; this whole thing takes place *in* the body, not out of the body. For when you rise up, after having been split right down the middle, from top to bottom, and then you rise into Zion, which is your skull—that's the great holy sepulcher—you make an Herculean effort to get out. You can't get out. You are around the throne of God. That's where he dwells. And you *try* to get out. You've never made such an effort in your life, but you don't get out. There you are *in* the holy city, the New Jerusalem, clothed as he had prepared it for you in that area.

So I tell you, the story is true from beginning to end. This coming Sunday, they will think a peculiar survival of death. It isn't that at all. It's entirely different. Resurrection is not that Christ survived death according to some general capacity for survival inherent in the human soul. No, it's the mighty act of God to save mankind and establish his kingdom. Hasn't a thing to do with survival—everything survives. I have said good-bye to my father and mother in this sphere, to a nephew in this sphere, and dozens and dozens of friends in this sphere. They've all survived. Nothing dies. But they are on the wheel of recurrence, and they're playing their parts over and over and over on the wheel of recurrence. And then in a moment that they do not suspect and no one knows, God redeems them and lifts them one by one. Not collectively, for we are known individually and loved individually by God. You are unique and can't be replaced; not one person in the world can take your place. You are completely unique and desired and loved and wanted by God to complete his purpose in this heavenly kingdom. So no one can replace you. Not one person in the world can take your place. So in God's own time, he lifts you up by the mightiest of all acts, the act of resurrection, which is the redeeming power that saves man from this wheel of recurrence.

So here, on this occasion, let me show you some of the power that will be yours. I tasted it. I tasted the power of the new age. It didn't happen in the last few years; it happened back in 1946. Therefore, the one who wrote the story, whether it be in Luke or in John, they rearranged the sequence of events. For before this happened to me in the ascent, I had this fantastic experience back in 1946. And it is said they said in the tomb, "He is risen." They said in 1946, called me by name, called me Neville. "Neville is risen." And then came this heavenly chorus singing, "Neville is risen!" and they kept on filling the whole heaven with this wonderful heavenly chorus.

Then I moved upon a sea of human imperfection—blind, lame, halt, withered, shrunken, everything that was imperfect. And here is the power that you exercise: as I came upon this enormous sea of humanity, without eyes, without arms, and without feet, sections of the face missing and sections of the body missing, I simply became a luminous being, made of light and air as it were, and I simply glided. I didn't walk in some labored manner; I glided by. They seemed to be waiting for me. Without effort, I molded eyes—I didn't do it consciously—but eyes that were molded into these empty sockets and ears that were missing came back. No scars, no surgeon in the world—put all the surgeons in this world together, they could not have molded one eye as I did with thousands in that sea. They could not have put one hand back as perfectly as I put it back. Arms that were missing came right back, legs that were missing came back, everything without a scar. There wasn't a scar, but it was perfect. When the whole thing was done and completed; this chorus exulted, "It is finished!" And then, I, of whom they sang and to whom they addressed every remark, crystallized, actually crystallized once more into this garment. I could feel myself becoming smaller and smaller and smaller into this little, tiny garment, on a ship at sea as I plowed through the Caribbean Sea, moving from Port of Spain, Trinidad to Mobile, Alabama.

And so here, I can tell you the story is true. When they said, "He is risen," in my own case, they called me by name. I'm quite sure the translators would have found the word there, but now they use the pronoun *he*. So in telling the story, not to offend those who might think me arrogant, I too used the pronoun *he*, when I wrote in my little book *The Search* when I told my experience. But they didn't say *he*; they said, "Neville is risen." Here this experience, and then through the years, it dawned upon me, for the 9th chapter of the Book of John: "Master, who sinned, this man or his parents that he was born blind?" He said, "Neither this man nor his parents, but that the works of God be made manifest." Then I realized over the years that this sea of human imperfection these are the things that I have played. Always Neville but blind Neville once, lame Neville, drunken Neville—everything in this world that would be distasteful I dreamt. They were all my broken body, and I rebuilt my broken body. And so no more eyeless in Gaza; the eyes came back. No more the lameness and the armless, and all these, they all came back. So, "Nothing is lost in all my holy mountain."

So I fell, and that was my broken dream. The whole thing that was there was my fall into the state of sleep, and I dreamt all the unlovely things in the world and played them too. So in the end, you are lifted up, and being lifted up everything returns to its divine perfection and nothing is imperfect. And every being in the world is going to have that experience. You and I will meet in the *new* world, called *that* world in scripture. We will be in control, completely in control, of a power that would dwarf any power known to mortal mind. So we are creative, creative in the true sense of the word, without the aid of any being we create. But we will create in concert.

You and I will agree to create in concert, and all of us will agree to create. No one will be greater than the other. All will be glorified in the eye of God.

So fulfilling scripture, in the Book of Hosea, the 6th chapter, the 2nd verse, And on the third day he raises us up, that we may stand before him, on the third day. I say that everything in the New Testament I could find it in the Old, but the Old is prophecy, the New is fulfillment. So it was there in the sixth chapter, second verse that he tells us on the third day he raises us up that we may stand before him to receive his glory and that we may know him and go on to *know* the Lord in his fullness.

So I tell you, the resurrection is an actual fact, although not described in the scripture. There isn't one passage in the scripture that describes it. I know it, for I have experienced it, and I tell you exactly how it happened. The resurrection is not from some little tomb; this is the tomb. And you don't resurrect *from* the body; you awaken *in* the body, right in it. You awaken in the tomb; the tomb is your own skull. The word skull is Golgotha, it's Calvary, the Holy Sepulcher, and you awaken in it and never had an idea that you fell asleep in this. It never occurred to man that he actually fell asleep, in a profound sleep, a sleep so deep it was likened unto death. And one day, God's mightiest act, the power of resurrection held him and awoke.

And may I tell you, when that power is applied to you, that night that you are sound asleep and it's applied, you think you are going to die. And then you are going to be awakened. But at that moment when it's applied to you, it's so intense you feel you can't stand it; it means this is the end. You explode. But you don't explode; you're awakened. And suddenly you awake. You have no doubts where you are. You are all together but in your skull. The skull is a tomb, and you know it's a tomb. You're sealed, completely sealed in your own skull. After one moment of panic, you push and something gives at the base of your skull and out you come, just like a birth. And it is a birth from above. "For except you be born from above you cannot in any wise enter the kingdom of heaven" (John 3:3). So man has to be awakened by God and come out himself, out of his own skull, born from above.

Then we are told, "And as Moses lifted up the serpent in the wilderness, so must the Son of man be lifted up" (John 3:14). That act takes place in the same manner. All these statements, they don't describe the act because who by reading it could see that as a description? I read it; I know my Bible, but I read that time and again. I never once related that to an actual mystical experience in me. But I would read the Bible, and the Bible uses the word ____(??) and translates it not as "from above" they translate the Greek word *anothin* as "again," implying that millions believe in reincarnation. It isn't any reincarnation. No, you are born from above. The word means "from above." But the translators can't believe it, so they put the word "again."

So you must be born again. It is again but not as the world would see it. You are actually born out of your own skull from above, and you come out self-begotten.

And here, the very symbol that you're told you'll find, you wouldn't find it; they find it for you. For the angel doesn't speak to you; the angel speaks to the men watching the flocks at night, and they come looking for the event. "For unto you this day is born in the city of Bethlehem, the city of David, a Savior" (Luke 2:11). Well, who is the Savior? Jesus is the word Savior, the word Jesus means "savior." "For unto you is born this day in the city of David *Jesus* the Savior, who is Christ the Lord." "Christ *in* you is the hope of glory" (Colossians 1:27). And Christ in you is that Savior; that's Jesus Christ in you. He's born. So the story is true from beginning to end, and you cannot alter one little dot; it's all true.

This coming Sunday, when they sing out the Hallelujah chorus that he is risen, you who hear me tonight you know how true it is. They don't know that city means "survival of the grave." It hasn't a thing to do with that. No survival? My father survived; I see him. My mother survived; I see her. My secretary, Jack, talked to him; he's as solidly real as he was here, I see him. But they survived; that's not resurrection. Resurrection is an act, a creative act, a *new* creation into an entirely different world—God's purpose fulfilled. The resurrection really in the true sense of the word is the fulfillment of the eternal purpose of God. All this is preparatory to the act of resurrection. So no matter how big you are in this world, how wise you are, may I tell you, the sum total of all the wisdom of man while he dreams this world will be as nothing compared to the power that is his when he awakes. All this is the dream of man.

But while we are in the world of the dream, learn how to dream wisely. And so I will take it up for you, and so next Tuesday, I'll show you how to dream wisely while we're still in the world of Caesar, waiting for that mighty act of redemption. How to really dream it into being in this world! Everyone can do it. I think I know how to do it, and so I will show you and teach you from now on until we close in the end of May how we dream it, even though we are sound asleep. Dreaming, we've got to be asleep, and this is the world of dream. We must dream lovely things for each other and realize them in this world, hoping for God's mighty act to take place in us. But until it takes place, why not learn how to dream constructively and dream wisely and dream lovingly. It's just as easy as to dream the other things, for we're dreaming anyway. While we are asleep, we can't stop the activity of the dreaming mind, the dreamer.

But here, our resurrection unlike what will be said this coming Sunday morning . . . and undoubtedly the service will be beautiful. Last Easter, I turned on the TV and had the most delightful service at home, watching and hearing Nat King Cole at St. James. He sang beautifully with all the depth of feeling in him. He hasn't much of a range, as you know, a very small range, but what he did with that range! I thought the whole thing was so all together wonderful. I learned only a few weeks later, or a few months later, that the minister, Dr. Terwilliger, was relieved from his post. But now I do not associate it; but in the world of dreams, there are such prejudices, such stupidities. So I do not say that because of that, he was relieved because Nat King Cole was a member of the congregation; he's a member of the church. Why should he not be spotlighted, known as he is with the opportunity to reach unnumbered millions across the country, really, if it went beyond our sphere here? But if it only went to this sphere at least three or four million could reach him and the church could be publicized beautifully. For the service was wonderful. The doctor himself, Dr. Terwilliger, gave the most *wonderful* sermon, and then he was so dignified, so altogether wonderful. Then to my surprise, he was sent elsewhere.

So I tell you, the congregation who would ease him out because of certain little prejudices, they haven't the slightest concept of this mystery of resurrection, not the slightest. First of all, they think they're going to be resurrected with the body that they wear. And that's not it. Let me quote it for you again, the 38th verse, the 15th chapter of 1st Corinthians, "And what you sow will not be the body which is to be . . . for God *gives* us a body as *he* has chosen." For the one wearing the garment today will not be like that. Yes, I will know you, but for all the identity of person there's going to be a radical discontinuity of form. So you can't envision that form, which is the *new* body, attuned to an entirely different world, where everything is subject to your imaginative power, where you are God. I mean that seriously, you *are* God! But at the present state of the dream, you can dream fantastic things, all the things that we do, like we've all done it.

But the day will come . . . and may it happen to you tonight. But I have no prophetic view; I do not know. It happens unexpectedly. It happens so suddenly. It happens, and you are bewildered. So I cannot tell you by looking at you with my mortal eye how close you are to God's mercy when he steps in and redeems you in the body of Jesus. I cannot; I do not know just how soon it ___(??). May it be, for your own wonderful sake, tonight. But you can't hasten it; it's an act of God. God's most wonderful dramatic act, his mightiest act, is the resurrection.

The resurrection and the birth of Christ in man are identical; they're one and the same thing. The beginning and the end are tied together under one act. When one awakes within himself, it's Christ awake; it's Jesus Christ awake. And that awakening within himself is one with his resurrection because you resurrect from the dead. You had no idea you were dead until that very moment when you find yourself entombed. Who goes into a tomb and has it sealed upon him if he isn't dead? And so, when you awake to find yourself *entombed*, you must have been dead or you wouldn't be there. Then you realize the words *until the end when Christ awakens in us*. We go through a cycle, cycle after cycle, having been placed into such a profound sleep, and then comes God's fulfillment of this promise, and he awakens from a sleep so deep that the world thought he was dead. Then he awakens, and when he awakens, he's the very being that is God.

Then he tells his story to those who will hear it. Listen to the words carefully, "And these words seemed to them to be a idle tale and they did not believe it." And then we are told in the same passage, which is the 20th of John and the 24th of Luke: "Behold, they did not know"—and the word translated "know" means "understand": "they did not understand the scripture—that Christ must rise from the dead." He told them, but they could not understand it. What does he mean by "rising from the dead"? And where did they lay the body? There is no body? Yet they see people sitting where the body *had* lain. How did they know the body had lain there when they never even saw the body? See the mystery?

It happens *in you. You* know where the body was, for *you* see it when you awaken within yourself. It's exactly the thing out of which you came, ghastly pale, and you look at it. And then comes the mighty wind that is the Holy Spirit. You hear it and you are disturbed and you look away just for a moment because you are disturbed. Looking back a moment later, the body is gone. But in its place, men are seated where the head was and where the feet were, but the body is gone. They are actually seated just as told in scripture, "Where the body of Jesus had lain" (John 20:12). Out of that he came, he's born; but first he awoke in it, and then it disappeared.

And they carry on this *incredible* conversation and unbelievable; they would not believe the tale. So one said, "It is" calling you by name. Whatever your name is, they'll call it and call you as the one of whom the angels spoke this night that a Savior is born. And then the symbol of that birth is on the floor, and they will say, "How is this thing possible?" And calling you by name, they will think it's the most stupid statement in the world. And whoever makes the announcement will present the evidence. They will see the evidence, but still they can't believe it.

So who will believe that you—a frail mortal subject to all the vanities of the world, subject to all the weaknesses of the world—could be so singled out for such a blessing when they know your background and they know your parents, your weaknesses, moral weaknesses, all kinds of weaknesses? And that *you* could be lifted up into an entirely different world and given such glory? No, they don't believe it. And so it seemed to them like an idle tale, and they did not believe it. That's what the world does.

So it happens to every one of us. But may I share with you my experience. And I am just as you are, with the same frailties today that I had before the event, same frailties—subject to all the weaknesses of the flesh. Over-eat, I did it; over-drink, I did it; and I still do both. So in spite of all of my weaknesses, it happened to me. So you don't become a goody-goody person after the event, and so you're the same person. It is said of him, why do you listen to him? He's mad. First of all, he's a glutton and a winebibber. He's a drunkard, and he loves harlots and tax collectors and all the people that are not socially prominent. He seems to make them friends of his. "Why do you listen to him?" And so he went about his way until the very end. No one believes that this has happened. That's the story.

He goes to his exit from this world, knowing exactly what has happened to him, leaving others to write it up after he has gone and tell it as best as they can. For he knows the New Age has been inaugurated; and then from that moment on, all are being called, one after the other, into the New Age, an entirely different age, from the state of sleep into the age of fully waking beings, all God. He knew that he simply opened up the door. And no one believed him, not to the very end. Because they were looking for some peculiar return in this garment and you can't return in this garment because you're not there. Yes, I'll recognize you, you'll recognize me, but we will not be clothed in these garments at all, for which I am most happy, because after fifty-eight years of wearing this, it's burned out. I'm very happy that God in his infinite wisdom at least gave us such things as dentists and barbers and tailors, for which I am most happy, because they can cover up so many mistakes. But the garment that you and I will wear tomorrow will need no patching up. It will need no tailor to put a suit on it. It will need no barber to cut its hair. It will be an immortal body, glorified beyond the wildest dream of any man in this world. And so that will be our body.

So this night, I've tried to share with you that which I *know*, not from a book, that which I know from experience. And so I show you the resurrection is a fact, it is *true*. And the resurrection means the resurrection of Christ Jesus; therefore, Christ Jesus *in* man is the hope of glory. Christ Jesus in every man is waiting to be resurrected, everyone. And a body is waiting for you that is God's own choice for you. Don't try to visualize it, but you go back and read it. *Everyone* has it already prepared for him, waiting for God to waken him and then clothe him in his immortal body.

Now let us go into the Silence.

*   *   *

Q: (inaudible)

A: My dear, when one is resurrected, clothed in his immortal garment, the entire world is exposed to him, not shut out, and ___(??) eagerly the kingdom. How could I ever forget my earthly father and mother who loved me, and she, the female, wove this linen sheet that I now wear? My flesh was woven by my mother, and I wear it. And so she who actually wove it for me in her womb, building this tabernacle out of a figure of nine months, how could I forget her? But I'm eagerly waiting for that moment when she too will be awakened.

Q: (inaudible)

A: Grant her complete freedom. She must be completely free to dream all the horrible dreams in the world, as we have been ___(??). Her freedom must not be inhibited. And God, in his infinite mercy, will step beyond and redeem her. But her garment is waiting for her, as it is for you, as it is for every being in the world.

Q: (inaudible)

A: Do what you want to. Infinite Love is in control. God has not abdicated in spite of the ___(??).

Q: Would you explain "Touch me not as I have not yet ascended."

A: "Touch me not as I have not yet ascended." That statement . . . I heard it by Wilberforce, who was once Dean of Canterbury. He said the true translation of the phrase is, Hold me not back by your tears and your sorrow because of my going. That you, by your emotional upheaval because of my exit, are holding me in your sphere. So do not by your sense of loss of me hold me back because mind communes with mind. So free me. Let me go. For if I do not go, the Holy Spirit cannot come, so let me go. But if by one's sense of loss you're always thinking of the departed with a sense of heavy loss, you're binding, you're holding him here because mind communes with mind, and you're putting a heavy weight on them by your sense of loss because of their departure. That was Wilberforce; and to me, it's the most satisfying interpretation of the phrase, "Hold me not back, for I have not yet ascended to my Father."

But I know the glory that is mine today, which I have inherited by these acts. For this series of mystical experiences in me is confirmed by scripture and by my own experience that I now have inherited the glory of the kingdom. But it cannot become *actual* to me, or at least not fully realized in me, so long as I am in this garment, this body of flesh, only when I take it off at the very end. But there is unfinished business. I can't lock it within myself or keep it to myself; I must talk about it and tell it and tell it to as many as it were who will listen.

And so far, since the experience, I've had the opportunity from a platform, on radio and TV, to reach maybe millions. I do not know how many. Because last year, in New York City, I had a six-hour marathon on radio, from midnight until six in the morning. And then I went on the night before the clocks were turned back, and that night it was seven hours. At midnight, and so what would be six when the clocks back, it really was midnight to seven. They cover twenty-six states in our country and most of Canada. They say back East that it's the most listened-to program; it's a popular station, WOR. I had a panel of four challenging my right to say what I did, which was exciting. And then there were ___(??) coming in asking all kinds of questions. And then the caravans are arriving. It was a very exciting two separate nights. And they claimed that people all through the night would listen to it. But I must have reached that night twenty million or close to it, and twenty-six states in the heavily concentrated areas in the East, not the far West ___(??), and in the really heavily concentrated states, and they must have heard it. So how vast an audience I don't know, but it ran into millions. ___(??), so at least I told it.

They may not believe it, or they may not want to hear it. One lady called in—the phone was ringing like mad—and she said, "Tell that man to read the 13th chapter of Mark!!" Of course, I knew exactly what she's talking about. In that thirteenth chapter, "If any man should say to you, 'Look, here, there is Christ!' or 'Look here!' believe him not" (Mark 13:21), ___(?? a liar. And then I said, Quite right, my dear. If anyone should ever say, "Look, there he is," don't believe him because unless you find him in yourself *as* yourself, you'll never find him. Then I quoted her the 1st verse of the 3rd chapter of the 1st epistle of John: "It does not yet appear what we shall be, but we know that when *he* appears we shall be like him."

But I said to her over the phone, "Do you look like him? Well, if you don't look like him, then you haven't found him, not as yet. Keep on looking until you are just like him. Because if you don't look like the one you now think that he is, then you haven't found him. And so you're quoting me scripture by having me read the 13th chapter of Mark? I'm going to quote to you now from the 1st epistle of John: "And so, it does not yet appear what we shall be, but we know that when *he* appears *we* shall be like him; and see him just as he is." Well, my dear, if you don't look like him in the mirror, keep on looking because you aren't going to find him unless you find him as yourself. Christ *in you* is the hope of glory (Colossians 1:27).

Good night.

THE PEARL OF GREAT PRICE

April 16, 1963

Tonight's subject is the "Pearl of Great Price." This is taken from the 13th chapter of the gospel of Matthew, 45th and 46th verses. It's all about the kingdom of heaven. First of all, let us say that the kingdom of heaven is simply that state into which man rises, where everything is completely subject to his imaginative power. He is destined to be an heir, one with his Father who is God, where everything is put under his power. Now, here is the quote from this 13th of Matthew: "The kingdom of heaven is like a merchant in search of fine pearls, who finding one pearl of great value, went and sold all that he had and bought it." It is my hope that I can bring you to that pearl tonight. You may not value it to the point where you're willing to sell all that you have to buy it, but I will tell you of this pearl. Very few are willing to sell all and buy the pearl.

But let me now quote from another passage of the gospel, the 11th chapter of the Book of Luke, the 21st through the 23rd: "When a strong man, fully armed, guards his own palace, his goods are in peace; but when one stronger than he assails him and overcomes him, he takes from him the armor in which he trusted, and divides his spoil." The very next line, as though it's an afterthought, throws all the light in the world upon that statement, "He who is not with me is against me." There is no benevolent neutrality, none whatsoever. He who is not with me is my enemy; he is against me.

So we find the one who is completely in control of this kingdom of heaven, and I tell you that being is called in scripture, Christ. But Christ is defined as "the power and the wisdom of God." In the first chapter of the first letter of Paul to the Corinthians, "Christ is the power and the wisdom of God" (verse 24). Don't look for a man. A man is only the instrument through which this power and this wisdom is exercised, but Christ himself is the power and the *wisdom* of God. You and I are the instruments through which this power and this wisdom is exercised.

So Paul makes the statement, "From now on we'll regard no one from the *human* point of view; even though we once regarded *Christ* from the human point of view, we regard him so no longer." You who are taking notes, that's his 2nd letter to the Corinthians, the 5th chapter, the 16th verse. "From now on we regard no one from the human point of view; even though we once regarded *Christ* from the *human* point of view, we regard him thus no longer." And then he, the author of that statement, defines Christ for us, "Christ is the power and the wisdom of God" (1 Corinthians 1:24).

Now we are told, "By him all things were made and without him was not anything made that was made," but nothing (John 1:3). And so we invite you now to test Christ *in you*. Again from the letters of Paul, the 13th chapter, 5th verse—in fact, read it through to the 7th verse—but I'll quote you the 5th: "Examine yourselves, to see whether you are holding to the faith. Test yourselves. Do you not realize that Jesus Christ is in thee?—unless of course you fail to meet the test. I hope you will discover that we have not failed" (2 Corinthians 13:5). And then he gives us a warning, for now he's speaking only of power, power and wisdom personified in the form of one called Christ Jesus. And now he warns us, "I hope and I pray to God that you do not use it in the wrong way" (verse 7). Even if you think—he's implying now that I have not used it to the full of my knowledge—I'd rather that you hear and feel that I have made a mistake or I have failed than that you use it evilly, implying, stating quite openly, that you *can* misuse power.

Everyone in the world is using this *only* power, but they don't know it. And so, he's trying to bring us to the knowledge of this power and the wise use of it. It's called, as we first quoted it, the pearl of great price. So great is this pearl, so valuable, that it takes everything that you own to buy it. Now you don't go and liquidate your stocks and bonds; you don't sell your homes; you don't sell anything in the world of Caesar. But it takes everything that you now believe in other than it to pay for it. You believe in authority? You've got to sell it. You believe in numerology, in teacup leaves, in astrology and all these things? No matter what you believe in as a power to control you, you've got to sell it. It takes all these beliefs and you've got to sell them. No one will buy them from you, but you give them up as valueless. Therefore, there's no price attached, no value whatsoever.

But you can't hold on to one thing you now believe in as a power that controls your life and still hope to buy the pearl of great price. Everything you now believe in, whether it be even the drugs that you take; even the things of diets—if you're a vegetarian and you think that's the way to

God; if you're a meat eater and you think that's the way to God; if you're a nonsmoker, nondrinker, and that's the way to God; or if you are a smoker and a drinker and that's the way to God. There is no way to God but Christ: "I am the way." There is no other way, way to what? To everything in this world, but *especially* to the Father. "No one comes unto the Father but by me." And here he defines it: he is the only way in the world to everything in this world that you and I seek. And it takes everything that we own as to beliefs that we think are powers to guide our life to pay for that pearl of great price. If you think for one moment you can hold on to one little thing in the event this doesn't work, you can't buy the pearl. So when I buy the pearl, I go all out and live by it. And there is no other being in this world, just this pearl, and I live by it. This pearl is your own wonderful human Imagination. That's Christ.

Now I see her in the audience tonight. Last Friday night, this sweet lady told me this story. She went into the baker to buy the usual things that we buy when we go to a bakery, and the lady who waited on her didn't look well. She, without asking the reasons for her present appearance, in her own mind's eye, when she got home, talked to her as though she stood before her physically. She didn't sit down, she didn't relax, didn't go into a trance, just brought her before her mind's eye and heard her say that she felt so well, and she complimented her on the way she looked. She looked so well. This was a communion between two souls, how she looked so well. And she believed in the reality of her imaginal act. One week later, she goes back into the same bakery, and here is this lady, same lady but radiant. So radiant it prompted a response from this one, and she said, "But you look so well! What has happened?" Well, she said, "This past week I inherited some money, and I paid all of my bills. I paid everything that I owed in this world, and so I have no debts and I have money." Now, this lady is totally unaware of the gift she received from the lady who is present here tonight, totally unaware of it.

Now listen to these words and try to put any other interpretation upon them in the world, and then tell me if you can. This is from the 25th chapter of the Book of Matthew: "In as much as you did it to one of the least of these my brethren, you did it unto me." You don't need the consent of any being in this world to hear good news for them. You don't have to say, "Do you want me to hear it?" Do you want praise? If you ask them in advance, "Should I hear good news for you?" you are only asking in the event that it works, they'll praise you or in some way give you something. You don't ask anyone for their permission to hear good news. For, "In as much as you have heard it, as you have done it to one of the least of these my brethren, you did it unto me. And when you did not do it, you did not do it unto me" (verse 45).

And so every moment of time, there's the opportunity to do it unto Christ Jesus, Christ Jesus being your own wonderful human Imagination. To see man in need and not act in your own wonderful Imagination, like she did, is to keep the wounds open and to bear more and more stripes upon the body of Christ Jesus, for the *only* Christ Jesus is in you as your only wonderful human Imagination. "Christ *in you* is the hope of glory. Come test yourself and see." What a wonderful invitation, "Test yourself"! How would I test myself? Well, this is how you test yourself. I tell you that if you imagine, as this lady did, that someone stands before you in bodily form, although they cannot be seen with your mortal eye, but actually you imagine they are standing before you and you carried on a conversation with them from the premise of your *fulfilled* desire for them, and then you feel them as you would feel them were they now solidly present, and you believe in the reality of that imaginal act, it's done!

And how it happens you need not be concerned. It has its own manner of externalizing itself within their world. All you need do is do it. As told us in the 1ˢᵗ chapter of the Book of James, "Receive with meekness the implanted word"—and the word is called Christ Jesus, the power and the wisdom of God—"But be ye *doers* of the word, and not merely hearers, deceiving yourselves" (verse 22). So when he tells me to be the *doer* of the word, the world thinks it means to go out and make some physical effort. No, James is not telling me substitute works for faith. Works are the evidence as to whether the faith that I profess is alive or dead. Is it alive? If it's alive, I will act upon it; if it's not alive, well then, I won't act upon it. I haven't yet bought the pearl of great price.

When I buy the pearl of *great* price, there is no other pearl like it. I sell all in this world to buy it. I sell all beliefs in powers other than my own wonderful human Imagination. Everyone, because he has Imagination and everyone can imagine and everyone can believe in the reality of his imaginal act, is free. It sets a man free, for we are told, "If you believe my word and abide in my word, then you know the truth, and the truth will set you free" (John 8:31). Well, how does he define the truth? He said, "I am the truth." He said, "If you know my word, you know the truth" and "I am the truth." So if you abide in this, then you'll be set free. You mean that if I simply imagine that I am the man that I would like to be, that's all that I need do? Just try it. Imagine that you are already the man that you would like to be, the woman you'd like to be, your friends are and total strangers are as you would like them to be. Just imagine it. Try it. Test yourself and see. As you test yourself and it happens, well then, can you turn back to the belief in any power outside of Christ Jesus? It's finding who he is, and I tell you Christ Jesus is your own wonderful human Imagination.

Christ in you must resurrect. And so you start to exercise him, believing in him. Believe in the law of Christ Jesus and be saved. So I begin to believe in him, put all my trust in him. It doesn't matter where I start in life. Behind the eight-ball? Makes no difference. I start believing in him and only in Christ Jesus. Then I take off from there, giving my entire life to him, just as though there were no others, just Christ Jesus, and I have found him: he's my own wonderful human Imagination. When I believe in him to that extent, things happen.

Now she tells me, the same lady—that's why I named this tonight "The Pearl of Great Price"—that she had a dream. And here is all mud, nothing but mud, whirling mud. As it whirled and whirled and whirled before her mind's eye in her dream she noticed a small, perfectly beautiful, perfect pearl. She picked it up and held this perfect pearl—wasn't big but it was a perfect pearl—in her hand, and then she woke. Now, this pearl she found in the series of experiences that she conducted. For a boy came east, came from the East to the West, with instructions that if he couldn't find a job in the immediate present, he had to return to the East. And so she simply, on a Friday night, saw him, not physically but in her mind's eye, as though he stood before her physically and congratulated him on the job, just as though it were a true *physical* contact. On Monday, the boy got the job and therefore did not have to return to the East Coast.

Now, here is a young lady—I call her a young lady, as she can't be more than her early twenties. If I looked at her through my eyes, all things being relative, she has three little babies, but I wouldn't think she's more than her early twenties. I'd be surprised if she's past beyond the middle twenties, looking at her. Born in Italy, of a Catholic family, Catholic faith, brought to this meeting of ours by her mother-in-law, and adopted this concept of Christ Jesus. Her family despairs because they think unless you have their concept of Christ Jesus, there is no entrance into the kingdom of heaven as *they* understand it. But I tell her she is well into it. She's exercising the only Christ Jesus in the world.

He calls upon us to test him every moment of time. But you can't buy him unless you pay the price, and the price—it takes everything that you have to buy him. Listen to the words, "The kingdom of heaven is like a merchant in search of fine pearls, who, finding one pearl of great value, went and sold everything that he had and bought it." Everything, not a few things. The average person would say, "Well, after all, I know that's all well and good, but Sanka does keep me in a state of sleep when normal coffee keeps me awake. And I know that an extra martini does so and so to me, and I take none. Or maybe, I could take vodka because it's good for my breath and not the martini. And a thousand things in the world people have concerning what they should do. Every belief in a power outside of Christ Jesus you give up, and you give it up and hold onto him and *only* to him. Then you've bought the pearl. Then you exercise it, the greatest value in the world, and that's Christ Jesus. So here, she has tonight—*I* think she has—the pearl of great price.

I hope you, tonight, will accept it. You know, not everyone who finds Christ Jesus sought him; they're brought to him by one who found him. In the gospel, Philip found him, and then he brought his friend Nathaniel. Nathaniel wasn't seeking him. Nathaniel was waiting for things to happen, for he knew the scripture backward. For when Nathaniel heard that the Messiah had appeared, he said, "What? Can any good thing come out of Nazareth?" (John 1:46). And Jesus said of him, "An Israelite indeed, in whom there is no guile" (verse 47). He knew his scripture. Peter wasn't seeking him; his brother Andrew found him. Andrew went and called his brother Peter and said, "We have found him of whom Moses and the law spoke and all the prophets spoke." So they were not looking for him, but they found him because someone found him and was so interested in what they found they wanted to share him with those that they loved. For if he is all that we claim that he is, we can't keep him to ourselves; we have to share him.

And so maybe this night a total stranger may be here who is really not overly eager to change their concept of Christ Jesus. They aren't seeking another concept of him at all. And maybe you will be interested enough to test what I'm talking about and see if this is not Christ Jesus, for listen to it, "By him all things are made and without him there was not anything made that was made" (John 1:3). Well now, here, a lady brought into being something that she had imagined without devising the means by which it would happen. She simply imagined it. Didn't she make it? She certainly made it, without the consent of the one for whom she made it. Well, if she made it and all things are made by him, she didn't say to herself, "Well, how can I make it? I only imagined it." Therefore, he must be Imagination, and this being in action must be imagining. And there it is. So she found him. She tried it again and it worked. And someone tried it a third time, a twelfth time, a hundredth time, and it works.

But if I say this to someone in the world and they won't even try it, well, you know in science to demand a proof before you are willing to make the experiment is nonsense. It's only through the experiment and its working out in performance that proof can be received by us. So to demand proof before I make the experiment is stupid. So I say to the world, if there is evidence for a thing, then what the world thinks about it or even wishes for it is nothing to the point. Makes no difference whatsoever what the world thinks about this if I can prove it in performance.

So I say to you, take a friend who is now unemployed and bring him before your mind's eye, as the lady did, and see him now *gainfully* employed. He need not be physically present—in fact, he's not physically present—but you treat him as though he were and put your mental hand upon him and give him the solidity that would be there were it true. Then carry on a mental conversation with him from the premise that it is true, and let him tell you that he's gainfully employed and that he loves what he is doing; there are such opportunities, such growth in what he is doing. And do nothing outside of that, for listen to the words of Paul concerning Christ, "Christ is the power and the wisdom of God." It's not only power, blind power; it's wisdom, the wisdom of God. If it's the wisdom of God, it knows how to navigate the whole vast world and move it to bring this one into a gainfully employed state. All you need to do is believe in Christ Jesus, and that is the pearl of great price. No power in the world can stop it. All it needs is acceptance on the part of us.

So here, "When there is a strong man, and he's fully armed, and he guards his own palace, his goods are in peace; but when one stronger than he assails him and overcomes him, he takes from him the armor in which he believed, and then disposes of the spoil, divides the spoil." Now that wonderful statement, "He who is not with me is against me. He who does not gather with me scatters." It's so irrelevant to that scene that preceded it, and it throws all the light in the world upon that statement. Some power in the world comes into man's mind; it's Christ Jesus. You don't need a social standing, a financial background, intellectual background, any of these backgrounds to feel secure in the world; you've found him. And this is the one who can overcome all the powers of the world, and if you are not with him, then you are against him. You wouldn't think that.

In this world today, we have countries that are called neutralist countries, benevolent neutralist. Not in scripture—you're either with me or against me, and either you're with me or you're my enemy. Can you imagine that? I'm either for him or his enemy. Can't be neutral. I either believe in it, or I don't believe in it. And of the nine hundred million Christians in the world, how many really believe in the *true* Christ? They believe in lighting a candle; they believe in genuflection and all the other things in the world, and I wouldn't criticize any of them. Leave them, until they find the true Christ. When they find the *true* Christ, then it doesn't really matter whether you eat meat or don't eat meat, whether you drink or don't drink, whether you smoke or don't smoke, and whether you do any of these things. It has nothing whatsoever to do with the true Christ, for you do not give power to *anything* outside of Christ, and Christ is your own wonderful human Imagination. That's Christ. So when you go before anyone, don't even take thought as to what you're going to say. Just imagine the end, and having pronounced his judgment based upon the end you have predetermined, do that.

Live this way in the world, trusting 100 percent in the pearl of great price. May I tell you, it will not fail you, but you can't modify it. You can't hold back one little reserve thing. I'm speaking from experience. Not knowing that it was my own Imagination that predicted accurately, through the medium of the cards and the medium of the stars, I held back a little reserve note in my mind's eye when I found Christ. I would still have in my mind's eye my old horoscope and I could quickly arrange its progression and I would know the day and justify failure. For the rule of my second house in conflict with the rule of my sixth, can't get the job. There's no money to it. So it's all there; it's all in my mind's eye. I had to completely give it up and so tear up my horoscope in my mind's eye it doesn't exist. I had to completely destroy it as a power that guided me.

But I held it because I successfully foretold events for unnumbered people in New York City. I had almost the entire Metropolitan crowd. The entire Metropolitan Opera, they came to me. I so believed in what I did that I predicted with conviction. It worked. And they were so sold on it. Then I had to have an experience one day to show me it was only my own intense belief in these little symbols that made them work. I came into my friend's home, and I taught her how to read charts and how to set them up. Her name was Carpenter, Norma Carpenter, and I taught her. Then, having retired from a teaching profession in Scranton, Pennsylvania, she had a small pension from the railroad where her husband worked, plus a small pension from her former job, so she eked out a living. But she could augment it in a nice way by telling and reading charts, and I taught her how to do it.

When I came to her place one day—she lived in a hotel—Norma was in tears. I said, "What's wrong, Norma?" Well, she said, "A man called me up—he was recommended by a friend of mine—and he was very eager to see me right away. He had this fantastic deal on. So over the phone, before he arrived, he gave me his birthday, his hour, everything about it, and so I erected the chart. When he came, I told him, 'I'm so convinced of this good fortune falling his way *today* that I can close the book on it.' He said to me, 'Mrs. Carpenter, if you're telling me the truth, I will give you a hundred dollars.' She said so confidently, "Well, give it to me now because it has to work today." And she gave me all the reasons, which I knew—I taught them to her—how it had to work today because of this transitive moon over these certain aspects of the chart. He said, "No, if it works, you will get it today, but I'll not give it to you now."

I said, "What's wrong with that?" Well, she said, "I made up this chart from a bound volume of Ephemerides. I was sitting at the open window—it's hot—and so I turned away, I was diverted. And when I went back, I didn't realize the wind had blown over the pages, and I erected the chart of a man who was born ten years before this man. This man wasn't even born. I progressed my chart from this horoscope, made up ten years before the birth of this man." I said, "Norma, did you believe it when you spoke to him?" She said, "Certainly I did!" I said, "Forget it! Just completely forget it. It's done!" I was in her room, her suite of rooms, that night, around eight, when a Western Union boy came upstairs and delivered a check, a Western Union check for one hundred dollars. And the chart was drawn on a man who wasn't born. He was born ten years after this chart of a man. But Norma cannot sell that because she feels "they all believed in me." She cannot buy the pearl of great price because she feels her only security is to get her little, small check from the railroad in Pennsylvania and a small check from the schoolhouse in Scranton, Pennsylvania, and eke it out with this. So she cannot give up and buy the pearl.

You've got to give up every belief in this world in a power outside of Christ to buy Christ. There is *nothing* but Jesus Christ. So you either believe in him or you don't believe in him. And any reservation for a rainy day—it'll rain. So you hold back the belief in stars? Well, I'm confessing, having done it so successfully over the years, that I still carried in my mental furniture my chart. And so you see you could always justify failure. As Blake said, "Self-justification is the voice of hell." I didn't know it . . . in hell everyone is justifying himself. No matter what he does; if it's a failure, he justifies it. He gives you all the reasons in the world. But hell is not a place outside of earth; it's right here. So we are in the hell justifying failure. We say, I couldn't do it because look at my Venus. And then as soon as Venus gets beyond the point where it interferes with me, But I still have Mercury. And so there I go. And when in spite of Venus and Mercury something happens, Oh, why didn't I see this? Well, there it was all along.

A man goes back, and reflects and then again justifies. No. He went and sold all that he had and bought it. *All* that he had, not a few things. You can't just buy it with a few of the things that you will dispose of. Yet you can use it, use it wisely and successfully, but you don't really possess him, that pearl, unless you buy him. And you can only buy him when you've sold everything that you have. Well, then buy him. And so that it's all out or nothing, so he who is not with me is against me. I know it's a difficult thing, but is it worthwhile having when you consider by having Christ Jesus you are rising into a world of an entirely new order, where everything is subject to your imaginative power? You're not here at all. You're moving from the world of death into the world of life when you find him and make him one with you.

So you take it. And let me tonight in a quick summary—it will take me no more than one minute to do it, two minutes at the most—you take this pattern, it's going to happen to you. Crucifixion is over for *all* of us. You aren't going to be crucified. "I have been crucified with Christ; it is not I who lives, but Christ who lives in me; and the life I now live in the flesh I live by the faith of the Son of God, who loved me and gave himself for me." That is Galatians, 2nd chapter, 20th verse. The 6th of Romans, "If we have been united with Christ in a death like his, we shall certainly be united with him in a resurrection like his." Listen to the tenses, "If we *have been* united with Christ in a death like his"—that's past; then a change of tense—"we *shall* certainly *be* united with him in a resurrection like his"—that's to be. Now we are told that those are misleading the people by teaching that the resurrection is over and past—the resurrection is not. It's to be. It's taking place one after the other. So believe me, the crucifixion came first. That's over.

The second stage in the unfolding drama is resurrection. The second stage when man awakes in a grave to find that he was all along dead or he wouldn't awake in a grave. You don't put anyone in a tomb unless he's dead. So you awake in the tomb of your skull to find that it wasn't what you thought it was; it was a tomb. And then at that very moment, that you discover, in the act of resurrecting, it now is converted from a tomb into a womb. And then comes the birth. So it's crucifixion and then resurrection, birth from above—these are the three stages.

Then comes a fourth stage. The fourth stage is when the title of titles is conferred upon the one who is born from above. For conferred upon the risen Christ in the *experience* of man is the divine title, Father. No one can utter the word *Father* but the Son. So the Son, God's only begotten Son, calls you Father, and then the title is conferred upon you and you are Father; one with God because he is God's Son and he calls you Father and you know it (Psalm 2:7; Psalm 89:26).

Then comes the next stage, the final stage, when the temple and its wonderful curtain that separated man from God, is torn from top to bottom. So that now you have *direct access* to the being that you were and are, the being that is God. No intermediary between yourself and God. Go straight to the being that you really are, which being is God.

So these are the five perfect stages. And all the others told about him will happen in their own wonderful way, regardless of the order in which they happen. But this series, as I just gave it to you, this is the sequence. We're all already crucified and all will be eventually individually resurrected. Then after the resurrection will come a spiritual birth, where he is born into an entirely different sphere. And then on him is conferred, in that sphere, the divine title of Father. And it takes God's only Son to confer the title, for the Son comes and calls you Adonay, my Lord, my Father, in fulfillment of scripture, in fulfillment of the 89th Psalm.

And then comes the final one when the curtain of the temple is torn from top to bottom and everything is split, all the rocks are split, and all the earth quakes. Then *you* rise, as you're told you must rise, in this form that cannot be described. It's called in the scripture, the Elohim, a celestial being, and the closest they can come to describing the Elohim is a fiery serpent. That's exactly what you are and feel and see when you rise. Human, yes, but for all the identity of personality, a radical discontinuity of form. Then you rise and the whole world quakes. It's all within you. The whole drama takes place *in* the individual. You do not rise *from* the body; you rise *in* the body. You do not awaken from the body; you awaken *in* the body. And the whole thing takes place within the individual.

But tonight, you believe me. And if you didn't know this was the pearl of great price, and I brought it to you this night, I hope you'll buy it. But like all the great things of scripture, "Come buy wine, buy milk, without money, without price." The only price you pay for it—not dollars and cents—you give up your belief in powers outside of Christ Jesus, and Christ Jesus is your own wonderful human Imagination.

Now let us go into the Silence.

*　　*　　*

Now are there any questions, please?

Q: (inaudible)

A: Did I say that? No, my dear. No, no, no, Shin is made like you would a big W, and there are three prongs. It's like Neptune's staff. You know that three prongs of Neptune? You make it that way. The symbol of a Shin is a tooth that consumes, that devours, and it's also called a flame, a fire; a fire consumes. Well, a Shin is in the name of Jesus. The first three letters of Jesus are the first three in the name of Jehovah, which is Yod He Vau; then you put a Shin, and then you put an Ion. Because, Jehovah, everything *is*, nothing passes away, but to be a Savior one would have to be able to change. If you could not be changed from what you are, you could not be saved. So the Savior, when Jehovah comes as Savior, a Shin is in his name. That he could transform the lady; she took the Shin and used it in her power when she saw a depressed lady. Could have been that her feet were hurting; she didn't know what was wrong. Could be standing on her feet all day long. But didn't ask her what was wrong; she just saw a lady in need of help, and in her mind's eye, she just saw her radiant and saw her happy. One week later, she could confess in that interval she got some money, a gift out of the nowhere; she inherited it and paid off all bills. If she didn't have the Shin in her name, then that woman forever would be as she is. But a Savior must have the Shin. So, it's really a big W.

Q: (inaudible)

A: Well, no, that would not be significant in that sense. No, no, they're thinking of the trinity, but this is all churchianity. When you see that of the Christ, this is all churchianity, for it's not in the Bible. But our churches through the ages have developed the most fantastic traditions, which they keep alive. They will die to protect their position, but that's not scripture. But a Shin is in the name of Jesus, as it is in the name of Jeshua, which is Joshua, which is the same thing as Jesus. Because the last one, Ion, in the name is an eye. It's the sixteenth letter of the alphabet, which has the value of eye and the numerical value of a seventy. So he sends seventy into the world to really do this work. Not seventy people; that's eye: to see it seventy times seven. To see it so clearly that you see it and not a power in this world could move you from it. I saw it, I am still seeing it, I will continue to see it until that which I have seen—and I am seeing and will continue to see—is externalized. No wavering. I believe in the reality of the imaginal act, and the day will come that you will see it as something objective to your mortal eye. It will be so vivid in your mind's eye that you will objectify it.

But the Shin is a flame. It's a tooth that consumes. And could I not consume in my own mind's eye unlovely things I see in another, I couldn't help them. But my ability to completely forget all that I saw them to be and put in its place what I want them to be allows me to save them, to be a savior. And Jesus is Savior. And Jesus Christ is the one who actually has lifted up within himself the power and the wisdom of God, which is Christ. And the day is coming that everyone will move into this world completely subject to our imaginative power. All of us will recognize each other, although the bodies will be trans . . . in fact, you can't describe the body, you can't . . . completely above the organization of sex. There's no need for sex as we understand sex, for we create without bodies of this nature. Yet we have a body. As Paul said, "But the body you sow . . . or, what you sow is not the body which will be, but God gives us a body as he has chosen." And so the body will be as different from this as the butterfly is from the caterpillar, something attuned to an entirely different realm and yet luminous. I've seen it. I became one with it.

Someone said to me, "Neville, how can you dare say that infinite power, infinite wisdom, can be conceived as personal?" Yet in Romans 8 are we not told, "The whole creation waits eagerly for the revealing of the sons of God." God is this power, this infinite creative power, and yet he has sons. And are we not personal? If he's waiting eagerly for a revealing of his *sons*, then is he not a person? But I don't have to rationalize it; I've seen him, and God *is* a person. And the infinite power, how could you personify it and call it a person? I have seen it, and it is man. Infinite power is man. Infinite wisdom is man. I've seen them. Stood in the presence of infinite love, and infinite love isn't some intangible little thing; it's man, and it's infinite love. Stood in the presence of infinite power, almightiness, and he talked to me, ordered me, commanded me, and sent me on my way. It was man.

So they will say to me, they've asked me, "How are you speaking of God? We speak of the exalted God. How *can* he be this exalted God?" They couldn't see him as personal. Well, I tell you that he is. And then one said to me, "Well, tell me, was your Christ once a man?" What can you say to that when you have heard me this night? But to say *was*? He *is* the heavenly man. I saw the power: It's man. And Christ is the power and wisdom of God, and I saw infinite power and infinite wisdom as man. So Christ is the *heavenly* man. As we are told in the 15th of 1st Corinthians, "Just as we have borne the image of the man of dust, so shall we bear the image of the man of heaven" (verse 49).

Good night.

LIVING WATER

April 19, 1963

The very first symbol given us in the Bible is that of water. You find it in the 2nd verse, the 1st chapter of Genesis. Before his first creative act, we're told that God moved upon the face of the waters, and God said, "Let there be light, and there was light." Before his first creative act, he moved upon the face of the waters. Water is a very precious symbol to me because of my first vision at the age of seven.

But what is this water that he is speaking of? Here we are told in the 2nd chapter, 13th verse of Jeremiah, "My people have committed two evils: they have forsaken me, the fountain of living waters, and hewed out cisterns for themselves, broken cisterns, that hold no water." So here, he now defines himself as living water. In the 4th chapter, the 10th verse of John we are told, "If you only knew the gift of God, and who it is that is saying to you, 'Give me a drink,' you would have asked *him* and he would have given you living water." Here we find the same living water. He's telling you he has the power to give you living water, which God defined as himself.

So what is the living water? Here, you listen to it carefully, for now we have the truth. And this is in the Book of Proverbs, the 27th chapter, the 19th verse, "As in water face answers to face, so the mind of man reflects the man." Now we see what the water is: as in water face answers to face, so the mind of man reflects the *man*, not the mind. The mind is but a reflector—it reflects the man, the operant power. He *has* living water.

Blake, of whom I am very fond and speak about all the time, his first vision was that of a tree of angels, at the age of eight or nine. So he came into the family, and he told his parents he'd just seen a tree full of angels. His father, to make him a sensible boy, prepared to give him a sound thrashing. Fortunately for Blake, his mother interceded and saved him. Maybe that's

248

what mothers are for, to protect us from our violent fathers. Nevertheless, he wasn't thrashed, but the father wanted to make him a reasonable, sound, solid citizen; and he was seeing angels in a tree. That's the earliest thought we have of Blake, of anything said about Blake, and the last thought is said about a neighbor woman who was present at his deathbed. Then she went home, and she told her relatives she had just been at the death not of a man but a blessed angel. That's what Blake taught all his life: "We become what we behold." And here a neighbor could say she saw the death not of a man but a blessed angel.

No, he didn't become it immediately. And undoubtedly there were unnumbered moments in his life in the seventy years that he lived where there were many, many an unangelic moment, if you read the story of Blake carefully; but in the end, he fulfilled what he beheld. All through his greatest poem, *Jerusalem*, that one thought permeates the entire hundred plates. "They become what they behold." We do, every one of us. And so what is your concept of yourself today? Is your concept truly what it ought to be? A child of God or a child of Mrs. Brown? Sweet and lovely as Mrs. Brown is, sweet and lovely as your parents are in this world, it can't compare to the concept you could hold of yourself, which is "I am the child of God." If that truly is your concept of yourself, and you look into the mirror of your mind and behold such a concept of self, it may not appear immediately in your world, but it will appear. For by this law, we become what we behold.

I know that when I was seven, my first vision was that of water. It used to frighten me. It happened once a month until I reached the age of puberty. I could always tell when it was coming because of that mood that would build up in me during the day. And it always repeated itself. I would become an infinite ocean, and yet I was a wave moving upon the breast of that ocean. During that interval of the night, I was both ocean and wave. And as wave, I was tossed into the air and then received back unto myself on the bosom of that ocean. It was a frightening experience. But the ocean was a very angry ocean, a turbulent ocean. And then it passed when I reached the age of puberty.

Then it was taken over by another concept of an ocean; and this time, the ocean was living water. That was when I was in my early twenties, maybe twenty or twenty-one, in the city of Larchmont, in New York City. This night in question, as I faded from this world, I became one with an *immensity*—I had no circumference—and it was all liquid golden light. But not an angry light, it was a soft, pulsing light. The whole thing was soft and pulsing, and I was it and there was nothing but. There was no wave now; there was integration, complete integration. I was one pulsing, living, golden liquid light. It lasted through the night. For when I woke in the morning, my book that I was reading was on my chest, a very big heavy book, proving that I had not turned in my sleep. I must have been in trance. I must have gone into some cataleptic state sometime in the early evening, for the bed was practically unmoved, untouched. The sun was up, and the reading lamp was still lit. So I must have had eight or nine hours of a deep catalepsy, in this infinite ocean of golden, pulsing, liquid light.

But now, the mirror took on a different form. In such a mirror, you could see what you want to see. In such a mirror, it's not a broken image, as when I was a boy of seven; that was a broken image. I couldn't see anything in such a mirror; it was too turbulent. But then came that moment in time when I truly sought him. As we are told in Jeremiah, "If you seek me with all your heart, I shall be found by you . . . and then I will restore your fortunes" (Jeremiah 29:13). If you really seek me with *all* your heart, I'll be found by you. Then all your fortunes that seem to have gone will all be restored. And so everyone can find him. Everyone *will* find him, when they're thirsty to find him, for there's a thirst that only an experience of God can quench. Nothing in the world can quench it but an experience of God.

So here tonight, this living water is your mind. You are not mind; you are God. God moves upon the face of the waters, and we are told in that 27th chapter, that 19th verse, which I just quoted, that as in water face *answers* face, so the mind of man reflects the man. And that man is a mind; the mind reflects the man. The man is God. God became man that man may become God. So when you look into the mind of self, what are you seeing yourself to be? Whatever you behold yourself to be, although it may not in the immediate present externalize itself in your world, if you are faithful to the vision, no power in this world can stop you from externalizing it within the world. But no power!

So in the words of Blake . . . and he was faithful to the divine vision in time of trouble. All the troubles of the world, the turbulent seas of the world, did not disturb the vision. He beheld the vision of an angel, a true angel. So they say he's mad. I heard it here only recently. My wife said someone who came here asked one of the teachers in the city what he thought of Blake, and he replied, "Oh, well, that man was mad. He's insane." Now, Blake had all of the attributes of insanity, all the assets of insanity, but none of its liabilities, none. Would we were all as mad as he was mad. If we were as mad as he, then we would see what he saw. He wasn't mad. He actually saw the twofold vision. He saw the threefold vision. He saw the fourfold vision.

The fourfold vision I will touch on Tuesday night, when I speak on the power, the wonder working power of attachment: for that's the fourfold vision. But he was always twofold vision at all times. Nothing to him was simply what it appeared to the senses. A tree was not just a tree. That is what he called a single vision, Newton's sleep, the sleep of the scientists, where, well, the moon is not a moon, the sun is only a sun, a burning body. To him it was simply angels proclaiming the glory of God. So he looked at a thistle—wasn't only a thistle, "an old man gray." No matter what he saw, he saw it doubly: everything had another image contained within it, until finally he could reach the fourfold vision, and that's the perfect vision.

But here, when the mind you accept it not as some little thing that the outside world would train, just as a mirror; leave it just as a mirror, and you determine what you want to see yourself as you look into the mirror and conceive yourself to be one with God. And as you look into the mirror of your own mind, fully believing that you are he, like all mirrors, they won't change the image, it will reflect it. And the day will come that you will be rewarded with actual experiences to prove to your own satisfaction that your image is true. You have all the experiences as recorded in scripture. For the mirror only reflects you. So if your concept of yourself is a little person, beaten, poor, and insecure, as you looked, you are going to get only confirmation of it.

Tonight you can give to yourself any gift in this world. If you only knew the gift of God and who it is, saying to you, "Give me a dream," you would ask of him and he would give you *living* water. Not just water for which you would now thirst again but *living* water. If you really believe this is how it works, that you don't need any being in this world, you have the mirror. Just steady it. As told in the 23rd Psalm, "He leads us beside *still* waters"—not stagnant water; it's still and it can reflect. He restores my soul this way. So he leads me beside the still water. And so the mind is brought still. I'm not anxious, I'm not concerned, and I know if I look into my mind and see you as I would like to see you and convince myself and persuade myself of the reality of that image of you. I need do nothing to *make* it so; it becomes so. It unfolds in its own specified time, and then you conform to the image that I hold in my own mind's eye concerning you. So the mirror only reflects the concepts I hold in myself. Not you, it's my *concept* of you that I should be faithful to. If I hold the most noble concept of you and others in my world, and I remain faithful to my vision, there's no power in the world that can stop it from externalizing itself in my world.

So here, this symbol of water is really very, very close to me. For I go back in time, the very first . . . we recapitulate all the things said in scripture, and the first image is water, and my first vision was that of water. I can't tell you how frightening it was until I reached the age of puberty, and then it vanished. Then it returned as I turned into my twenties, but this time the water was not turbulent it was living, really living water. I was the only thing: I was it. And yet there was no world, there was nothing, just living, pulsing, glowing, golden light, infinite light. And then I knew, later on, that into this I could see anything that I wanted to see; and seeing it, no power in the world could stop it from coming to pass. And then because you're not a wise man, you haven't the scholastic background, you haven't these things to support your claims, but no power can disturb it. For these experiences belong to a region that is much deeper and more real than that which the intellect inhabits. So all the arguments in the world that they throw up cannot disturb it, no matter what they tell you.

And so the eternal question, "Which came first, the chicken or the egg"? And so it has shattered the minds of unnumbered people trying to figure out which came first. For reason tells us you couldn't have a chicken unless you have an egg, and how could you have an egg unless you had a chicken? So which came first? The eternal problem. You can resolve it in no time with Imagination. That's a foolish question and any attempt on the part of man to answer it is a foolish answer. They came from each other. I came from God, and God came from me. I'm just like the egg. And God, *from* himself I fell. He caused me to fall as the hen causes the egg to fall. That's the end of the doctrine of the fall, no other fall. And then from that state I simply rose, like a chicken out of the egg. And that's the end of the doctrine of evolution: I am one with the very being in whom I was before I fell from him.

So we all fall, predetermined setup, as told us in the 1st chapter, the 4th verse of Ephesians, "And he chose me in himself before the foundation of the world." Yes, he chose me *in* himself before the foundation of the world. And then when all things were prepared, just like a nest—for that's what the world is, all these galaxies, just like a nest—he drops me. I fall upon God, right into the nest; and after incubation, I, by an effort within myself, come out. And so that eggshell is just like your skull. It's sealed, just as your skull is sealed, and within it is all that was its seeming Creator, no more, no less. When it's all complete, you will come out. When it comes out, you will be one with God, just like God, containing within itself the same power to beget itself and drop its own being into the galaxies and let gods appear.

And so only Imagination can bridge that gap between, which came first, the chicken or the egg? No, they are one; they come from each other. As told us in the 3rd chapter, the 16th verse of Galatians: And so out of *man* comes Christ . . . "and *your* offspring who is Christ." I know the whole vast world teaches something other than that. But to me, religion begins in revelation, and then it falls into dogma, into ecclesiasticisms, into rituals, into all these outer things; and there remains bound. But that's not the truth. The truth is vision. Tell the vision just as it was given to you. If it doesn't make sense to those who hear it, tell it without distortion, tell it just as it came. If they don't understand it, do not modify it that they may understand it. Tell it just as it came. And so this is exactly how it happened.

So just as you're told, "We become what we behold," I'm trying to encourage you to take an image this night. It may be that this image you will take tonight would need no more than, say, a day, a week, or a month to materialize. I do not know the interval of time. But take a lovely, noble concept of yourself where you are contributing to the world's good. Where you really contribute and feel clean and wholesome in that contribution. What would it be like were it true? Well, now look into your mind's eye and see yourself *as* that being who contributed. For you can conceive yourself as that being. If you can, look until actually you feel the thrill of being such a being. Now, in a way that no one knows it will hatch out because out of that very vision of yours will come all that it takes to externalize it in your world.

You can be anything in this world that you want to be if you know how to move upon the face of the waters, and the face of the waters is simply moving upon your own mind, that's all. You don't argue with anyone. You ask no one to help you. You simply look at your own being and conceive yourself to be the man, to be *already* that man or that woman that you want to be. And ask no one if it is possible. If it is wealth that you want, well then, let it be wealth. If it is recognition that you want, then let it be recognition. If it is an increase in talents that you're now expressing, then an increase in talents. I don't care what it is. Conceive yourself to be *already* the being that you would like to be, and conceiving it, look for confirmation.

Were there not a reflection in this world, no one would know what he looks like. So God creates a reflector right away. It's a mind; it's called water. But then it's explained to us in Proverbs what he means by water, and he tells us, "As face in water answers itself, so the mind of man reflects the *man*" (27:19). Not reflects the mind but reflects the *man*. So what is that man to himself? Then look into his mind. As he looks into his own mind, you will see reflected in that mind—it's only a mirror—what he is to himself, and by the law that all things become what they behold, he can't help becoming such a man. He can't help it! So I tell you, dream nobly, dream the most idealistic states in the world, and then remain faithful to your dream, just as though it were true. And if you do, it'll come to pass without the help of any being in the world. You don't need it. You need no one to assist you—you'll become exactly what you imagined yourself to be.

So this living water is not some strange thing that he's going to give you. He'll give you the message, that's what he's going to give you. He'll tell you all about yourself. If you are thirsty to be other than what you are, ask of him—he's within you—and tell him. He will give you living water, something so alive that it reflects exactly what you are. Nothing turbulent;

I went through the turbulent state. Undoubtedly, that's exactly what man in his earlier stage went through, where he couldn't see anything reflected. He only saw confusion and turbulence. Then came that moment in his time when he could steady the mind, and the mind took on a *living* quality and became *living* water. But you take primitive man: he can't conceive that anything that he is doing is causative of things that are happening in his world. He can't conceive because he can't see any reflection in his mind; because the mind isn't still, the mind is too turbulent. But when man controls that mind, he turns from that violent stormy sea, which I experienced as a boy of seven, into that living, pulsing but reflecting light where he sees himself as he looks into it.

Because, looking into it, the strangest things happen. One day, reading or contemplating a similar image that was in the book that I read that night when I fell asleep—for I was reading *The Life of Buddha* when this first happened to me. And then this night in question—not reading the book of Buddha but contemplating Buddha—as I did so, before my eyes came this huge big flint. And then without effort on my part, it broke into many small fragments, and then invisible hands molded it into the most beautiful meditating figure that was like a Buddha, meditating. As I came closer and looked at it, I was looking at myself. I *was* the thing that I'm contemplating. And the thrill that was mine! Here I saw this Eastern figure sitting in the same posture as you find a Buddha, the little statue of Buddha, made of this flint. As I looked at myself and saw I *was* the figure that I contemplated, it glowed and glowed and glowed. When it reached the intensity of light it exploded, and then I was back where I was before.

This mirror of the mind reflects perfectly what you do. And so I tell you, try it. Try it this night. Take a glorious concept of yourself; take it of a friend; take it of your father, your mother, and your child; and you remain faithful to the image you hold of them. Do it without their knowledge, do it without their consent, and just hold it in your mind's eye until you can see it, see it clearly. You don't have to do anything beyond that, just see it clearly in your mind's eye, and then leave it. In a way that no one knows and you could not consciously devise the means to bring it to pass, it will come to pass.

Now, in the very end of the book, the 22nd chapter of Revelation, brings us back as it started the Book in Genesis. We were all invited to come, those who are thirsty, come and take it without price. Take what? Take this living water. So the entire sixty-six books are permeated with this living water. And when you come to the very last chapter, almost the last verse—it's the 17th verse of the 22nd chapter of Revelation—once more he brings in the theme of this living water. So everyone is invited to come and drink without price, buy it without money, and take it. Anyone who hears me this night, you have it, so it will cost you nothing to try it. You need no more than a determination to be something other than what you are and something great, something noble, something wonderful. Then, in your mind's eye, see yourself *as* that person.

A nice way to see yourself as that is to bring a friend into your mind's eye and have your friend by his expression and the sound of his voice and what he is saying confirm that he sees in you such a being. Let him see you, and then in your mind's eye, see his expression, one of complete satisfaction if he's a *true* friend, no envy on his part if he's a real friend but pride on his face because he has you as his friend and he's so proud of your accomplishments. If you want to add to it, carry on a mental conversation with him from the premise that he actually sees and approves of this you that you have become. That will tell you what you would see if you didn't have that to reflect against your mind, what you would see in the depths as yourself. You will see the same being that he is seeing. So take a friend and use a friend to confirm that image of yourself. And may I tell you, you will be surprised how it works. But you must want him. Even "he who seeks me with *all* his heart, he shall find me and I will restore all of his fortunes." But you must seek him. But all . . . I must really want him with *all* my heart. When I want him, but really want him, I'll find him.

Then you have that enormous satisfaction that it doesn't really matter if all the wise men in the world rose in opposition, it would make no difference whatsoever. You're not speaking of this sphere. Not speaking of something you can see with a telescope or a microscope; it can't be seen by any instrument made by man. It's something entirely outside of the range of telescopes and microscopes. So you simply look right in and see it. When you become it, reason will step in and try to justify it, and all the wise men will say, "But you know that it would have happened anyway. Look, you met so and so, and then he in turn introduced you to so and so, then you got the breaks. And because you got the breaks you'll become it. But don't expect someone else to do it." And then they'll always try to minimize the working of this wonderful power. But I tell you it never fails. It *never* fails.

Everyone is invited—the 55th chapter of Isaiah, the very 1st verse—"Ho, everyone who thirsts, come to the water," but everyone. No limitations, not just those who are of a certain race or who belong to a certain tribe but *everyone* who thirsts, come to the water. And there's no price to it. Come and take it without money, without price. So everyone is invited if he's so thirsty to come to this water. So throughout the entire sixty-six books, it's permeated with this fantastic water, and the water is your own wonderful mind. The one who's looking into it morning, noon, and night is the man that you really are—and that man is destined one day to awake to find himself God.

Yes, you fell, deliberately. God allowed you to fall, for the name Yod He Vau He, the verb He Vau He, ___(??), means "to fall" or, causatively, "to cause to fall"; or "to blow the wind" or, causatively, "to make the wind blow, or make it move." And so it was God, for that's his name, Yod He Vau He, who like the chicken allowed the egg to fall. But in that egg which was fertilized by God is himself; and then after incubation, it from within makes an effort—for the plan is all there—and breaks it. Then it rises as [does] a chicken, capable of the same creative power, the same creation, that that which seemingly brought it into being, one with God, its own begetter.

So tonight, if you have a concordance and you want to pursue it beyond the hour, just take it and take the word *water*, and go through chapter after chapter and see what is said of this wonderful water. First of all, the argument in the 4th chapter of John, the minute he tells of this water, "Well, how can you do it? You have no bucket, no rope, and the well is deep. You mean the water you would give us is greater water than I can get from this well that our forefather Jacob dug for us?" And he tells you, "With this water you thirst again. The water that I'll give you will be a newer well of water, springing up into everlasting life. It will never change." But she couldn't quite understand him, and then he revealed who he is to her.

The first miracle performed in the gospel of John is turning water into wine; in other words, into *living* water. From a turbulent state, you turn it into something alive, a living water. So we are told, in the first letter to Timothy, the fifth chapter, "Drink no more water; use a little wine for your stomach's sake and your many afflictions" (verse 23). It hasn't a thing to do with wine that you and I would enjoy with a good meal. But you stop simply absorbing what to do and you become a *doer*, and you do it. So stop drinking water: stop simply absorbing news morning, noon, and night as to *what* I should do to become what I would like to be; and then become a doer, and do it. So you turn water into wine.

So the first miracle performed in the gospel of John, which is in the second chapter, he filled stone jars with water and drew forth not water this time but wine, living water. For that's what wine is. It's something alive. And so he turned it into something that is really living in the life of man. So if anyone goes out of here tonight, using wine for your stomach's sake and not simply absorbing the news, to hear what you heard this night and not do it, you are still drinking water. But if you go out and you never return here again because your pattern changes in the world and you go elsewhere, but you don't forget what you heard, and not forgetting it you apply it, then you are drinking wine. You are putting it into practice no matter where you are in the world, and as you put it into practice, you'll get the results to fulfill James' statement to us, "Be ye doers of the word and not hearers only, deceiving yourself" (James 1:22).

So become a doer, and a doer is to put into practice what you heard this night. Start with a friend. Take any friend in your world who you think tonight could really be helped financially, socially, and physically. But can he be helped? You *think* he can be helped, well, then you help him. Bring him before your mind's eye, represent him to yourself as he ought to be seen by the whole vast world, and you believe in the reality of that image of him. You're moving like God upon the face of the waters, and you're creating just as God created in the beginning. "And the Spirit of God moved upon the face of the waters . . . and then God said, 'Let there be light' and there was light" (Genesis 1:3). But he did nothing until he moved upon the face of the water.

So you can walk the street and move on the face of the water, ride the bus and do it, sit quietly and do it. But still the mind. No matter what formerly he or she *appeared* to be, that's a very disturbing thought if you must fight with it. No matter what they were, that's like a stormy ocean if they aren't pleasant, if things aren't right for them. So you don't try to do anything about it. You just bring them before your mind's eye, as they *ought* to be seen by you and by the world and by themselves. And so you put *that* as the image to be reflected from this wonderful moving water, which is your own mind.

So you read it when you go home, "As in water face answers to face, so the mind of man reflects *the man*." How can you get around that? The mind of man reflects the man. So a man is complaining that society is not kind to him, that the boss on the job is too cruel, and he's not making enough money? He's reflecting only the being that he conceives himself to be, and they in his world are only mirroring what he within himself has set up as a pattern. If he doesn't like what is happening because they are only mirrors, well, then let him reshuffle the deck as it were and change the concept he holds of himself. Changing it, just let him be faithful. For remember that interval of time, as told us in the Book of Habakkuk, that second chapter: "Every vision has its own appointed hour; it ripens; it will flower. If it seems long then wait; it is sure and it will not be late" (2:3). So every egg has a different interval of time in which to hatch out: that of a chicken, three weeks; that of some other bird, maybe a shorter interval; another bird, a longer interval. The same is true of the eggs that bring men into the world, and sheep and cattle into the world. There are intervals in time. And so your image tonight of a friend or yourself will have its own appointed hour, and if you are faithful to it and not addle it, it will ripen and it will flower.

So I invite you to try it. And then you will know this mystery of the water; for I've told you the Bible is a mystery not to be kept secret, but a matter that is really mysterious in character. There's no reason to think for one moment that it should be held as a secret just for a few of us; tell it to anyone in this world. But the Bible is not what as we're told in that passage from Jeremiah, that 2ⁿᵈ chapter, when he said, "My people have committed two evils"—and then he states the first—"how they turned from him, the fountain of living water, and hewed out cisterns for themselves, broken cisterns that hold no water" (verse 13). And these broken cisterns are simply all of the isms of the world, but all of them. They're trying to get something out of this broken cistern and you can't get it.

For the men who wrote our Bible . . . and no one knows the authors, no one. This one we quoted this night from Genesis, there isn't a scholar worthy of the name who writes on this book that has any manuscript that is signed. There are three letters. One he speaks of as the J manuscript, the E manuscript, and the P manuscript; and that's all they have to go by, completely unsigned. There is no identity to the authors. Who were they? How did they come into the world? Were they born as we were born? Did they really come as you and I came through the womb of woman? Or did they appear in our world, as I, one night many years ago, stepped into another world, without going through the womb of a woman in that world. I was just as real as this world, solidly real. And so stepping from my bed into that world and it wasn't this earth, but a solid world just like this, with people clothed as you are clothed. And if anyone had arrested me there and compelled me to give a birth certificate or give an identification card that would be understood in that world, I could not have done it. So I was not there through any normal channel of physical birth. I returned here, without returning here in any known way.

So who is E and who is P and who is J? They give us symbols and letters, but we have no way of knowing who the author of Genesis is. As far back as we go, you can't find any manuscript that these scholars would in any way catalog, save it's the J manuscript, it's an E manuscript, or it's a P manuscript. So who are these fantastic authors? Because if you treat it even as literature, you wouldn't find anything greater than Genesis. And as far as vision goes, where would we find something greater? But who are the authors? Completely unknown to mortal mind. But there it stands, those fifty wonderful chapters. And the whole thing is permeated with water. Our historians and teachers of the Bible try to convince us that water was such a precious item in the desert, so precious where this whole thing was laid, that's why they made so much of water. Hasn't a thing to do with that. Hasn't a thing to do with it? So he comes into the desert to water his flock and the well was there and covered and he rolled away the stone and watered the flock. After he watered the flock, then he rolled the stone back and covered the well, Jacob's well.

So we are the sheep of his pasture, are we not? And so we are watered by anyone who knows how to water it and to feed all the sheep until they are completely satisfied. And then it's automatically rolled back. When one comes behind you and reads that same chapter, it's just like a closed book. He picks up the book, he turns to the 29th chapter of Gensis, he reads the story of the rolling away of the stone and the watering of the flocks, and he wonders, What is it all about? If someone knows how to roll away the stone and how to actually take that water of psychological meaning and give it to the world, after he's done it automatically the stone is rolled back. The one who comes behind him who reads the same chapter can't interpret it. It's always a sealed well.

But tonight, you've heard it, and I think that you will try it. So let me now clarify just in a few moments the water on which God moved—he said, "The Spirit of God moved upon the face of the waters"—that water is your own mind. If tonight it's too disturbed because you are too anxious, then that's like a stormy sea, a turbulent sea. But wait a while; it will become quiet, still water. Still running, for it is alive, but still enough to reflect the being that you want to see. And then the way to see it is to assume that you are what you'd like to be. Having assumed it, look and see the world reflect that man that you are because they all see it. Having seen it reflected on the faces of your friends, drop it. Just drop it. And that's the fall. That seed that came from you has its own appointed hour, and it will grow and come into this world.

So you try it. And may I tell you, after it happens—for it *will* happen—then share with me your good news by telling me how it worked that I, in turn, may tell it from this platform and let us all be mutually encouraged by our faith. If it works for you—which it will—then you tell me what you did and how it worked, and then I, in turn, will tell it to everyone present. They, in turn, will be encouraged to go on and be as faithful to their visions as Blake was, in spite of all the things that he went through in the interval. For his life, like the life of every great man, is really an allegory. Every person in the world, his life is really an allegory. People don't quite realize it.

In Blake's life . . . one of the outstanding things, this gentle, tender man who couldn't hurt a fly, and returning to his garden one day, he saw a drunken soldier and took him bodily and led him down the road. Then the man brought action against him and accused him of insulting the king, which is a frightful offense in England, and it was more so then, in his day.

This innocent man was accused because a drunken soldier wanted to get even. It was quite a trial in England. And then you see this wonderful story, a soldier is always a symbol of authority and a garden is always creativity, and here his garden. He was selling his soul at that time to a man who wanted him to become a portrait painter, and he didn't want any part of it. So Blake was selling his soul, his creativity, to this man who had money because doing this work, well, then his financial status would be eased somewhat. But he was selling his creative power, and so here, in his garden was the drunken man of authority. For the one who employed him had the authority and the power.

And then he broke it and refused not to make any portraits and not have one model in the world. He never used a model. He *saw* what he wanted to paint, as clearly as any model could ever be in this world. When he wanted to draw the soul of a flea, he saw the soul of a flea, and it was man. For the flea is a blood-sucking insect, but men are also blood sucking. Those who employ without *proper* compensation, are they not taking the blood of others? They don't care what happens to you when you go home. If you have a family of twelve and they're not well fed, they don't care once their profits are big enough. And if you saw them spiritually, just like fleas, for a flea is simply a blood-drinking insect. They are taking the blood of those without proper reward; they're bloodsucking.

When Blake painted his wonderful flea, the soul of a flea, the ghost of a flea, you should see that monstrous thing, but it's human. Everything is man in the world. And so the life of any great man, like a Blake, it's an allegory. So when he put his garden back in form, then the soldier went up. Blake won the case eventually. They all knew the man was perjuring himself. Blake would not say anything against the crown, and it was proven. But meanwhile, he just went through hell to prove it. But that was the turning point in his life, like the great allegory of his life. But here, his first thought in the world, "a tree full of angels"; and the very last thought, "I was at the bedside this day not of a man when he died, I saw the death of a blessed angel." So what he began as a vision, he fulfilled as a man: he saw an angel as a child, and he died as a blessed angel.

So tonight, you see a noble being. When you make your exit from this world, make your exit as it. But your true destiny is God, for we are one with God. He became you that you may become him.

Now let us go into the Silence.

WONDER-WORKING POWER
OF ATTACHMENT

April 23, 1963

Tonight's subject is the "Wonder-Working Power." I hope I can tell it tonight so simply that no one leaving this room can say I didn't quite understand it; that within the immediate present you can put it into effect and prove the truth of what I am talking about from this platform.

This wonder-working power is a showing in four different levels of vision. Blake made the statement:

> Now I a fourfold vision see,
> And a fourfold vision is given to me;
> 'Tis fourfold in my supreme delight
> And threefold in soft Beulah's night
> And twofold always. May God us keep
> From single vision and Newton's sleep!

Now here is the perfect description of single vision. Maybe you are familiar with this one little poem, just one verse:

> A primrose by a river's brim,
> A yellow primrose was to him
> And it was nothing more . . .

He looks at a tree, it's a tree—that's all there is. He looks at a man, it's a man; he looks at a rock, it's a rock, and it's nothing more. So, "A primrose

261

by a river's brim, a yellow primrose was to him, and it was nothing more."
That's single vision, and the whole vast world sees it in that light.

But now, we want to bring everyone here into a double vision. We are
all familiar with a fireplace. So we look at a fireplace and say something is
burning ___(??). And then one day, I see it was lit by something similar
to itself. A spark lit it and then it was fed and it blazed up, warming me,
radiating this wonderful heat; and then it cooled, and we had the embers
and then the ash. Looking at it you and I would say, well, you know, it
reminds me of my life. That's my life; my life is like a fire. It comes in, lit
in some strange way, and then it's fed and fed and fed, and it blazes up, and
then becomes an ember, and then an ash. And so I have a simile. Then I say,
"My life is a fire." Now I have a metaphor. One day I leave out the little "is,"
and I say, "Life and fire are synonyms." I can't see one without seeing the
other, without imagining the other. Then I have an image; I have a symbol.
And I do it with everything in the world, and I have many images. When
everything in the world is to me but a symbol, then I have double vision.

Double the vision, my eye can see now that nothing appears as it appears
to the world; everything is different. A man who appears to be a man, so
when I talk with him, and I get his moods, and while he takes advantage
of other men—he's in business, he doesn't pay good wages to anyone
who serves him—then I see that man as I would see any blood-sucking,
blood-drinking insect, just a parasite. He may be the head of society, he may
be the most powerful person in the world, a dictator, but I see him using
men for his own personal gain. And you see him now spiritually. And one
sight only sees the garment, and his name the little tag it appears, and they
bow before him. But you now with double vision and you see him and you
see him as a parasite, just like a flea . . . a flea that lives on the body of the
dog or the animal or anything in this world. He's only a flea. You see him as
a flea, although he may have billions of dollars; he may control the armies
of the world, but he's only a flea. And that's how God sees him. When you
begin your sight that way, all of a sudden, you see differently and he doesn't
offend you; you aren't moved by him. You see him just as he really is in the
eyes of God. That's the beginning of double vision.

Now comes the third vision. The third vision, when these images
interplay and they marry and beget other images; that's the threefold vision.
Now, here is what I want to talk about this night, the threefold vision. Here
is a little child; the child is three. This is a true story. The grandmother is
present here tonight. This story was told me before I took the platform.
She's now five and a half—but the mother knows this, as she's been coming
here over the years—so the child's now five and a half. When she was three,
the father and mother had no money. He was working on a job at a small

salary, and they dreamed of owning their own home, a wonderful home, but they had no money and they were in debt. So the little child, while in bed, was told by the grandmother and the mother, "Close your eyes and see this lovely home, a huge big fireplace right up to the ceiling, glass all around, two bedrooms for you, Pammie" (her name is Pamela), and then Julie, her sister, who was then only a year old. "So you see it clearly now. Go into the bedroom. Keep your eyes closed. If you open your eye, it's going to deny what I'm telling you. So keep your eyes closed, go into the bedroom, and go into the other bedroom—one is yours and one is Julie's—and a huge fireplace up to the ceiling."

In a little while, this firm was absorbed by a larger firm, and all the men were given aptitude tests. His came out with this kind of a test: you are a salesman. At first, he refused to accept the thought he could sell. He was going to quit. They said, "You may quit, but you can't work for us unless you become a salesman. That is what we see in this test. You must become a salesman." In the immediate present, he was making a fortune, and they bought the home—glass all over, two bedrooms leading off of this enormous fireplace, up to the ceiling.

Now he's making money. He was never given to spending money and was never considered a generous father or husband, possibly afraid of the future. When it came to Christmas, the mother wondered, "How am I going to get five dollars out of him to buy toys for my children?" So remembering what they did prior to getting this home, she said, "Pammie, do you remember what we did with the house?" Yes, she remembered the whole thing. "Now close your eyes and there's a huge, big playpen in the backyard filled with toys. And you go into the backyard and play. Remain here physically, but now you go right into the backyard. Don't open your eyes because it will then be single vision. Go into the backyard, and all these images are playing now."

Just before Christmas, she called her mother, who is here this night, and said, "I think he's gone mad. You know what he's contemplating? He's contemplating buying a hundred-dollar playpen for Pammie and Julie, and undoubtedly, he'll fill it with toys." But she said, "I was there Christmas Eve night and Christmas Day when we opened the toys. This enormous playpen—he paid a hundred dollars for it—and it was filled with toys." But said the grandmother to her daughter, "Have you forgotten what you did with Pammie only a week or two weeks ago?" And then she remembered. How could she now criticize the extravagance of her husband, who was always so mean, when she herself had put the child into the state of seeing this wonderful playpen filled with toys? Now that is threefold vision.

You take a vision. Everything is a symbol. Take me, I'm a symbol, you're a symbol, and everything's a symbol. And you interplay them to form a certain pattern, which will then give birth to another image. So I bring you before my mind's eye in a certain manner. I bring another party into the same picture. Then I add to these two a conversation between the two of them, which conversation would imply that you *know* I am what I want to be. I bring you, I bring another, and I eavesdrop and I listen. I hear them discuss, and they are discussing my good fortune. I listen until I actually hear what I would hear were it true. Everyone is discussing exactly what I want to hear, for if I heard it, it would imply the fulfillment of my dream. That is taking now symbols, taking images, and interplaying them. Interplaying them so that I marry them; and as they marry, they beget another image—the images that are bringing me forward in the image that I want to see myself express in this world. That's threefold vision.

Now, fourfold vision. I trust you have it. If you haven't had it, I can't describe the joy of fourfold vision. If I could describe it, it is dreaming, yes, or loving or imagining, and these are only three forms of the same thing. But dreaming with such intensity that it obliterates the daylight, just as daylight ordinarily obliterates the dream. You're sitting in a chair, and you're loving, you're imagining, you're dreaming, and *suddenly* it is no longer something that is unseen by you. For this little child, she saw it in her mind's eye, but not as I'm seeing you now and you see the speaker. She saw it, kept the physical eyes closed, and moved into the imagined state and made it real to her. But fourfold vision, something goes out, and suddenly you say to yourself, "I'm dreaming. No I'm not; it's real. I'm not dreaming, here it is; it's real, just as real as this." The curtain goes up on it, and then what began as a dream, just a daydream, but you did it with intensity, and suddenly the curtain goes up, and you step into the world of your dream. You are awake in what formerly began as a dream.

And now, let me tell you my first experience of it. I used the threefold vision unnumbered times to produce results, and talked about it, told all my friends about it, and all these things worked. Threefold vision produces the same results that the little child produced. It *never* fails. But one night, here in Beverly Hills, I suddenly looked up, my eyes were closed, and I was awake. I knew exactly where I was. I was in my home in Beverly Hills on El Camino, and I knew what I *should* see were my eyes open. I felt my eyes closed, and yet I am seeing more vividly than I'm seeing you now. I should see the familiar objects on the wall. I should see the familiar things on my bureau, for I was lying on my right side; but instead of seeing these, suddenly I am seeing the interior of a fantastic building. Consciousness followed vision, and I stepped into the state that I am seeing. I came back to my bed; and once more, I am now in a horizontal position. Then again, I stepped into my vision, and I am now vertical. I'm stepping right into what I see. I did it maybe a dozen times, and then I decided to explore. Regardless of consequences I'm going to explore. If it's the very end of my life in this world, I can't stop it; I must explore.

And so I stepped into this place with the determination to go on. As I did so, it closed around me. The room that seemed when I was on the bed, it seemed maybe thirty by twenty, it now became ten by seven. I discovered, as I examined it, that it's simply a dressing room. I left this room into a huge, big suite, an enormous suite of rooms, unoccupied but prepared for occupancy, but not occupied. It was just as solidly real as this room is. I was to myself just as I am now. Everything I touched was solid. My hands could not go through it; it was solid. I came out of this room into a huge hallway, which led to a huge, big public hallway. When I got there, I saw two ladies coming down the hallway. I knew how the whole thing started, and so I said to them, "Ladies, this is a dream." Well, they were just as startled as you would be if you met me, a total stranger, say, at a hotel, the Ambassador. You never saw me before, and suddenly you saw a man coming into this place who suddenly talks to you. You don't know him, and he tells you, "Ladies, this is a dream." Wouldn't you be startled? You would say, "Well, the man is insane. Let us get out of this place as fast as we can." That's exactly what they tried to do. They got as far away from me as they could, right next to the wall. But I insisted it's a dream because I remembered exactly what I did. But now I'm fully awake in the dream. My eyes are wide open, and I'm awake *in* my dream.

As they passed by, walking rapidly, I saw this ornate thing over my head, and I remembered a little visit a few months before in a friend's home near the hills of Hollywood, where he had a similar thing hanging from his wall. I remarked then, "How does such a thing remain up?" He said, "If you look closely, you will see an almost invisible thread supporting it from the ceiling," which I did. It was a beautiful cluster of leaves made of very thin copper. Well, this resembled that and reminded me of that. Again, because I saw this in my now waking dream, I said, "Now I *know* it's a dream because this is only a memory image of what I saw in my friend's home in the hills of Hollywood, there six months ago, so it *must* be a dream. Even though they're so real, and this is so real and I am so real, everything is so real, it *is* a dream." And so as I did this, I held one of the leaves, and I said to myself, "C'mon, Neville, you know it's a dream. Wake up! Wake!" and I came to, standing in that place more awake than I am here now.

Now, being a father, then my little girl was in high school. She had to go through high school; her desire was to go through college, and I said to myself, "Here, Vicki is unschooled, and she must be educated. If I make my exit now, I leave a wife unprepared for this problem and so I can't leave here now. I have unfinished business in that world—for I am completely shut out in an entirely different world." So while standing there, I closed my eyelids; and just as if I closed them here now, I wouldn't see you, so I didn't see the hallway. I opened my eyelids, and here is the hallway. I did it maybe a dozen times. I am completely locked out in this world. I said to myself, "They'll find the body tomorrow morning in Beverly Hills, and because of insurance policies they'll have to cut it up and say, well, he died of this, that or the other." But I still didn't want to terminate it in this way; I wanted to get back. And this is what I did.

Standing there, completely shut out in this other world, I simply imagined with the same intensity that brought me into that world, I imagined a pillow under my head. I stood there just simply feeling a pillow, that's all. Suddenly, while standing there, I could feel a pillow. And then to my great surprise, I am not vertical; I am horizontal, but I could feel myself on a pillow. But then I was cataleptic, and I couldn't move. I couldn't open my eyes. I went to the most enormous effort to open my eyes, and I couldn't open my eyes. I couldn't move a hand; I couldn't move a finger; I'm completely cataleptic. Then, maybe thirty, forty seconds later, I could navigate the little finger. We had a double bed, and so my wife slept on the other side. After a little while, I could move from the elbow and I pushed it over and I could feel that nice warm body of my wife and I knew I'm back. A little while later, I could move the other hand. And then with a tremendous effort, I opened my physical eyelids and saw the familiar objects on the wall.

So I tell you, when Blake said—he didn't claim it was his always—

> Now I a fourfold vision see,
> And a fourfold vision is given to me;
> 'Tis fourfold in my supreme delight
> And threefold in soft Beulah's night
> And twofold Always. May God us keep
> From Single vision and Newton's sleep!

So when you only see a man, when you look at a man, and he is no more than just a man, he's not a loving being or a hating being or a bloodsucking insect, he's none of these things, just a man, that's single vision. If a fire is a fire, and it means nothing else, if a tree is a tree, nothing else, but not a thing becomes a symbol or image to you, then it's single vision. And may I tell you: the difference between fourfold vision and single vision is the difference between normal eyesight and blindness.

One who was *born* blind—I don't mean going blind, with memories of what you once observed while you had sight—I mean to be born blind, where no one in this world could convey to you what it means to look at red. If you're born blind and you never had the experience of the color red, there's no word, not a thing in this world that man could use to convey to you the sensation of red or blue or any other color. A form, yes. You can bring your hands and you can touch a form. And you can say this is a symbol of that term, and then this is something different and this is something different and a bed and a chair and this and a cross, and all the materials. But you haven't *seen* color. There is no word known by man that could convey to you the experience of color. Well, the difference between fourfold vision and single vision is the difference between normal eyesight and blindness from birth.

So when one gets into it, I can't tell you the thrill. It's *supreme* delight. And you enter it, as I say, yes, dreaming or loving or imagining—three forms of the same thing—but with such *intensity* that suddenly you are awake in the state you contemplate. You're contemplating it, and suddenly you are awake *in* it and it takes on all the objective qualities that this room has now. That's fourfold vision. But for practical purposes in this world, we discuss and try to encourage you to practice threefold vision. And threefold vision, like this little child; here is a child, three years old, and "Now see the fireplace." So she sees it. "Don't open your eyes, Pammie, because if you open your eyes you aren't going to see it, and right away you're going to come right down to onefold vision. So a fireplace, do you see it? See the wall?" "Oh, yes." "And lots of glass all around?" "Yes." "And then over here, there's a room, it's your bedroom; and over there, there's another bedroom and that is Julie's bedroom." You get it?

And then out of the nowhere what seems like a disaster, for his firm was being absorbed, and all the jobs are uncertain. So they're all given an aptitude test, including the father of this child. He comes out on the top but not what he had been doing in the other job. He now must change jobs and become a salesman, which he doesn't want to do. But the aptitude test revealed he has all the qualifications for salesmanship, which he never thought of before. Now he becomes a salesman, and he's making a fortune. But now he becomes uneasy. He wants lovely things in this world but very penurious. However, they buy the home, the home of the child's dream, Pammie's dream.

Then comes Christmas. How to get out of him five dollars to buy presents for my children? He, on the other hand, comes home with a hundred-odd dollars worth of presents. And she, forgetting what she did, thought he's gone insane. So when she called her mother and said, "He's gone mad. He is contemplating buying a hundred-dollar playpen," and she said to her daughter, "Have you forgotten what you did with Pammie? Didn't you put Pammie into that lovely place where she actually played in the backyard with the playpen?" "Oh, yes. I completely forgot it!" Well, who did it? It's not *his* generosity; it's *Pammie* who did it. Pammie stirred him to go looking for the hundred-dollar pen. Because Pammie had played in it, it had to be there. Now she takes all these images and she interplays them and marries them, and it produces a result. And she is the result.

So I tell you, nothing is impossible to this wonder-working power. Christ is called in the Bible "the power and the wisdom of God." You read it in the first chapter of Paul's first letter to the Corinthians, the twenty-fourth verse, "Christ the power and the wisdom of God." For God is all Imagination, and his power is imagining—that's Christ. So Paul could say having once thought of Christ as a man, he then said, "From now on I regard no one from the human point of view; even though I once regarded Christ from a *human* point of view, I regard him thus no longer" (2 Corinthians 5:16). He now sees who Christ is. Christ is the power and the wisdom of God; and the power and wisdom of God is imagining, as God is *all Imagination*. And God became man that man may become God. So Blake said, "Man is all Imagination, and God is man and exists in us and we in him. The eternal body of man is the Imagination, and that is God himself."

Now you may not with your concepts of Christ and concepts of God accept it. But I suggest if there is evidence for a thing, what you think about it or even wish about it is nothing to the point. So this little girl and her mother remembered what she did and brings about this, and you may not relate her imaginal act to the fact and you may say it would have happened anyway. That's your right to say that. But if she repeats it, as she did, and you still insist in saying, "Well, it would have happened anyway." Then the third time she does it, all in the interval of two years, and the parents realize exactly what they did.

Now, we come to the crux of the story of the child. As happens in the lives of all people—especially in California, why I do not know—but in California there are so many divorces. Anyone who is married for ten years is the senior citizen. It's a more fantastic thing. If you remain united for more than five, that's really an accomplishment. Well, in spite of their two little girls, sweet children, they grew apart. He is Catholic, and he didn't want a divorce. He'd rather live in hell than have a divorce. But nevertheless, they got a divorce. The divorce was granted and finalized—using the grandmother's story and her very words, using the word finalized—it was finalized two weeks ago. And she began, so she said to me, to lose faith because she called me on this case when it began to develop a couple of months ago, say, three months ago. And she said, "I don't want them to be divorced. I'm quite sure they can reconcile the whole thing and become a loving, wonderful family as they were and must be." So I agreed with her, certainly they could be.

Well, in spite of that agreement here came a divorce, and the papers signed, the whole thing finalized. So the grandmother said to the little girl, "You want mother back, don't you?" and she began to cry. She said, "All right, you know what you did with the house and the fireplace and the grass and the two bedrooms?" "Yes." "You remember what you did with the playpen and all the toys?" "Yes." "Well, now, tonight, right now, you close your eyes, and mother is coming through the door. You hear the door open. She is coming in, in her nightgown—not in any suit, not in a dress where she's leaving this house tonight—she is coming here in her nightgown. She's sleeping here. So the door is opening, and it's mother. She's coming over, and she's kissing you. Feel the kiss; it's mother, and she's in her nightgown." She did it Monday, Tuesday, Wednesday, Thursday, and mother returned to that house on Friday. And mother is now back in the household, in spite of a divorce decree that has been finalized. Maybe in the eyes of the priest they are living in sin, but there they are, parents of the two little girls, and mother came back, just as the grandmother told her granddaughter that it would happen. And so, when she met the grandmother, she said to the grandmother, "You know, Grandma, you're mature, you're old, but with me Imagination works like thunder!"

For we are told in the Bible to never send a child away, for the child will lead us—in Isaiah, "And a little child shall lead them" (11:6). A little child brings back the grandmother's faith, for she called me, the teacher of this principle, and I agreed with her over the phone, yes, reconciliation is perfect. So I heard her say yes, not devising the means toward the end, simply the end. And then came what seems to be final and absolute, a signed decree of divorce. You can't go beyond that. Who says you can't go beyond that? *Everything* is possible to God. With God, nothing is impossible, if you know who he is. God is your own wonderful human Imagination, and God in action is Christ. Imagination in action is imagining.

So what are you imagining, on a threefold vision or a single vision? A single vision is right here, and these are the facts of life, and I can do not a thing about it. So I perpetuate my world based upon the single vision. Then comes that moment in time, I get a double vision, where things are not what they seem to be. They become similes. They become at first just a simile. I relate myself to the burning fire, knowing that as I began at a certain moment in time, it will come to an end, just like the fire. So I am a simile. Then I say, "Life is a fire," a metaphor. Then I rub out the little "is," and I say life and fire ___(??) are synonyms. And then I see it as a symbol. I can't *feel* one without thinking of the other. Then I have images. I take it with everything in my world then. And so I think of people, and there are certain—well, I saw them in my mind's eye spiritually, and they are all images. Then I begin to blend them, and I interplay the images. As I interplay them, they marry, and as they marry they beget other images.

And then I tested it. I would like to be and I named it. I would like to be, say, elsewhere. Well, elsewhere is an image. And so I assume that I am elsewhere. Were I there, I would see people that I couldn't see from this angle. And so were I there, I would have to see them, for they would be there; then I began to see them in my mind's eye. Seeing them would imply that I am there. And so I began to talk with them, just as though I were there. And then I found that things rapidly change in my world to compel the journey, and I move across a series of events, some bridge of incident, that led me up to the fulfillment of that journey, and there I am. But then I remembered what I did. I took images, just simple images, and so interplayed and intermarried them that they produced another image; and the image was the fulfillment of my desire for myself, and I made the journey.

So this is the threefold. He calls it "soft Beulah's night," the thing nearest to heaven in Blake's terminology. First of all, he has eternity; he calls it Eden, and he likens it to the sun. The sun is the symbol. Then he had next to that "soft Beulah's night," and the symbol of that was the moon, for the moon reflects the light of the sun, and this reflects the activity of heaven. Then he has the limit of it all—he had five worlds—the limit of it all he calls "Ulro," this world, for it was opaque; the limit of contraction; and the *limit* of opacity, where man has single vision.

Now, everyone in this world has single vision. But we are here for a purpose; this is for a divine reason that we are here. You and I didn't do a thing that was wrong to bring us here. We are here that we may be awakened as God. Just like a chicken dropping an egg and the egg contains the chicken; and by an effort from within, after germination, it comes out. The egg, giving birth to what it contains, is God coming out of this egg, and the egg here is the human skull. God actually comes out, and it's God. God became man that man may become God. So here, the fall, spoken of in the Bible, is no more than the fall of the egg from the chicken. That's the full doctrine of the fall; and then the chicken rises from the broken egg, and it's God. And that's the end of the doctrine of evolution. So God became man that man may become God. So I tell you, treat it seriously and become as the little child. This night, when you go to bed, put yourself into the state of the wish fulfilled. And then blend all the images that would imply the fulfillment of that state, and live in it just as though it were true. How it will happen, I do not know.

Another lovely story which I must tell you. For last Friday night, my wife came to the door and said, "Is there a gentleman in the room or a lady in the room who left a little dog in a car? Well, he is needed, or she is needed." So the gentleman jumped right up and went out looking for the dog. He called me late that night, said he hadn't found the dog. He said, "I love the dog. I know it's my own negligence; I left the door open because I was so eager to get to the meeting without missing any part of it, that I did not close the window." It was a little poodle. So he sought all over the neighborhood, and he couldn't find the dog. He was up very late that night and called me. He said, "What must I do, Neville?" So I told him what I would do were I he, I would go to sleep just as though the dog were in the house. Feel the presence of the dog and think only in terms of the nearness of the dog; it's right here. And so I am able to tell you tonight—not the details; I don't have the details as yet—he has the dog.

And so it never fails. You know the meaning of the word *prayer*? You're told in the 11th chapter, the 24th verse of the Book of Mark, "Whatever you desire, when you pray believe you received it and you will," for the word prayer means by definition in the biblical concordance: "Motion toward; accession to; nearness at; at or in the vicinity of." Now, you have a little dog and it's lost and now you are living miles and miles away from where it jumped through the window? No. Prayer means "nearness to; motion toward; nearness at; at or in the vicinity of." If you found him, where would he be tonight, in a kennel? No. He'd be home, wouldn't he? Well, now that's praying: he's here at home, and you feel his presence at home. That's praying. For if he actually came back, if you found him, you wouldn't leave him behind you; he'd be at home. Therefore, you would actually bring him into your house. Now sleep as though you can touch him and feel him and smell him and *feel* his presence. Then go to sleep. Well, tonight I can tell you he is at home, and the owner of this little dog has learned a lesson, not to leave the window open.

So here, I invite you to join me in threefold vision. May I tell you, it will not fail you. No power in this world can stop it from working. For there's only God; there's nothing but God. God is reconciling the world to himself through Christ, and Christ is your own wonderful human *imagining*—that's Christ. Christ is the power and the wisdom of God. You don't need to be any wiser than you are. What would it be like were it true? And then you go to bed in the assumption that it *is* true and sleep in that assumption.

Now, Friday night, a lady—I do not see her here tonight, but maybe she's here—but she gave me a letter Friday night. Pardon me, I now see her.

But on Friday night, she gave me this perfectly wonderful letter, a true story I told because she gave me permission to tell it. I told it last Sunday morning without using her name, without using the firm's name. So I didn't tell the firm's name or her name, but she's here tonight. Three weeks ago, she and I were in the back room here where I speak. She wanted to see me before my meeting to discuss her problem. Her problem was the filling of a position in a fabulous company with resources in excess of a half billion dollars. No lady had ever filled that position before. It was never considered that any woman could fill that position. There were many men, eligible, with ability to fill that job, but she wanted it. I simply said to her, "Were I you, I would just simply occupy it, just as though it were true." So she occupied that job, and three weeks later, she was appointed to that job. Now she is loan counselor in a corporation whose resources exceed a half billion dollars—the first woman ever appointed to such an office. She is here tonight. I'm not going to ask her to identify herself. But someday, maybe, in this wonderful world of ours, you will be in need of her services. So she will tell you what I told her, and yet she can be of service to those who need *her* services.

So here, join with me in putting into practice this threefold vision. It won't fail you. But may I tell you, you are the operant power. Knowing it is one thing and doing it is another. You either do it, or you don't do it. If you do it, it will not fail. If you say you know it and that you are a good person therefore, God, because you are good, is going to take care of you; I have news for you! So let us go into the Silence and put into practice this perfectly wonderful principle.

*   *   *

Q: (inaudible)

A: My dear, the difference between the fourfold vision and single vision is the simple difference between normal eyesight and blindness from birth. Normal eyesight, if it's a good 20/20 vision, sees objects just as they are. Colors are seen with the normal eyesight, except people who are color blind. I mean a normal eyesight, not a color-blind person, one who sees objects just as they are presented. Now, a child born blind, who has no organ of sight, could get by in this world because they do, but you could never convey to them the experience of color. They could feel objects.

Right now, we're having a few chairs re-caned. We got them at Sloans in New York City, and so we took them over here to Sloans; that would be ___(??) Sloans, and they said, no, we can't do the job. We'll take the job because you bought them from us in New York City, but we give them out to the blind. And the blind we're speaking of here are the best workers on this job, like re-caning the chair. Well, they haven't yet been sent back, but they tell us that there's no one better than the blind, for they can feel. And so undoubtedly, someone brings the regular cane to them, just what to do with it. But they can feel, and they're experts at putting it back in order, so that they have it that no one comes near the blind in re-caning chairs. So they have our two chairs for re-caning.

Q: (inaudible)

A: My dear, I'm just saying any person who dreams sees color, but you couldn't convey to them what *you* mean by color. A blind man who goes blind after he saw color, it would be easy for him to see color. But if you are born in this world wrapped in this little garment of skin without the organs of sight from birth, I'm not denying that you would still, in the depth of your soul, see color, but you would not relate it to anything the man is talking about concerning color. So the difference between fourfold vision and single vision is just as vast as the difference between normal sight where all things are seen and observed and one incapable of observing anything. So when one awakes in a dream and the dream is so real, until one has that experience it's difficult to convey the thrill that is one's. So he said, "Fourfold vision is my supreme delight." You contemplate an image and suddenly you are in the image and the image takes on objective qualities and everything in it becomes as solidly real as this, as you are, everything. You are in an entirely different world. The day will come that you, and I will be in a world completely subject to our imaginative power. A world only of images that we will enter at will, and it will be all objectively real to us.

Q: Would you please explain a little bit more about the fourfold vision. You're explaining your being in this building and trying to get out and back because you had your little girl to put through school. Well, would that be considered what we call death that you were in the state of?

A: Did you hear the question? To go back to my experience of entering into an image and the image closing around me and becoming a ___(??) of this whole fabulous world. Had I not succeeded in returning, the world would tell them the garment that I now wear, identifying me with the garment that I wear, they would have said, "Neville has died." I would not have died, but the garment would have been left behind, and they would have buried it, after examining it for reasons why I should have died. *It* died but I didn't, for I am the occupant of the garment, as you are the occupant of that garment. You never die, not in eternity, but you wear out garments. And this garment would have been, by my adventurous nature, have been declared dead. But I do not die. But I had unfinished business here. I had a wife that I could not in my own mind's eye ensure by Caesar's law. I had not seen that my little girl was properly educated, and she had the talent and the desire for higher education. So I had not completed that or left behind me the means for its completion.

So my desire then allowed me to experiment, and I did it with touching. I discovered the sense of touch is so important. And so by feeling the sensation of a pillow, I came back. For there's no man that moves that would have led me back here. There was no road from that world to this world. And touch brought me back. So I emphasize the sense of feeling, the sense of touch. If I could tell any person who was desirous of being happily married, and it's a lady I'm addressing, would you wear a ring? Yes? Well, then, feel the ring. Don't feel a huge, big nugget there. That doesn't mean that you're married. That precedes marriage, and it's no proof that you are married. But a simple gold wedding band there would imply to the rest of the world that you're married. And then put the mood with that you're happily married, that you're proud of the one whose name you bear. Although you do not know the name, just feel how proud you are of it and thrilled and clean and wholesome in this relationship. And touch it; go to bed feeling the ring, the one thing that would imply the fulfillment of the state known. So touch to me is so very important because I've proved it.

Q: Neville, you equated the activity of dreaming and loving and imagining, could you elaborate on that just a little?

A: Well, first of all, one cannot dream . . . in tonight's dream, I take the object of today into the day and rearrange the living pattern based upon my fears and my hopes. So my hope and my fear of this day will produce my dream of tonight. But I use the images familiar to me, and there I weave them into this living, living structure. Well, note the very word imagining implies using energy; and so to be loving, there must be an object. You can't just love unless there's an object of one's love. And so that's an image. And so I use the word dreaming; dreaming is simply imagining. Imagining is dreaming, and then dreaming is simply imagining. So I use the three terms, and I say they are only three forms of the same thing.

But now when I sit down to imagine a state by becoming ___(??) but really absorbed in what I am imagining, I tend to step into the state imagined. If I should succeed in making my consciousness follow my vision and step into it, it closes upon me. Then the whole world is just as real as this, as solidly real as this. And I'm speaking from experience, I am not theorizing.

Q: (inaudible)

A: ___(??) fourfold vision, then threefold vision, like the little child. Roosevelt went into office when we were in the deep of Depression and he couldn't stand on his own feet. We couldn't stand on our feet, and we wanted support from our government, so we voted into office one who couldn't stand on his own feet and had to be lifted up. Every time he stood, he had to be supported by someone other than himself. So he gave us the WPA, the CCC, and the ___, and all these supports outside. But this is a *symbol*. I am not now criticizing anyone that you and I vote into office. That's the highest office in the world, in the world of Caesar. I can't conceive of any political office higher than our office as president in this country. There's nothing compared to that when it comes to a political office. But don't let me because of the greatness of the position become blind to the symbol, the symbols in this world. Every man is a symbol. Every great man's life is an allegory. Every great man's life is an allegory.

And so when we brought him into office and repeated it for four times, we were in need of external support; we didn't stand on our *own* feet. We had a deep Depression. Until the war broke in 1941, we still had a fabulous unemployment. Not a thing was done to relieve that, in spite of all the years and all the millions that they used, the entire alphabet, trying to get things moving. Now comes this present chap and, undoubtedly, he's been doing—personally you would love him, no question about it; he's a brilliant, brilliant fella, a lovable fella, a wealthy fella—but what got me, knowing the symbols of the world, the minute he gets to office, he gets into a rocking chair.

Well, no more of that. Good night.

LIFE HAS A PURPOSE

April 26, 1963

Life has a purpose, and that is saying God has a purpose. You and I may have plans in conflict with God's purpose and God allows it for a short while and you and I can realize our dreams but only within the framework of God's plan. As we are told in the Book of Isaiah, the 14th chapter, the 24th verse, "The Lord has sworn: 'As I have planned, so shall it be, and as I have purposed, so shall it stand.'" No one will thwart God's plan, God's purpose. God's purpose is to give himself to us, individually, as though there were no others in the world, just God and you; ultimately, because the gift is complete, just you. That is God's plan, that is God's purpose, and he's mapped the whole thing out for us in the Bible. The entire story he told us in the Old Testament; the New Testament is the fulfillment of God's plan. Men will not believe this; even the hundreds of millions who claim themselves to be Christians do not fully grasp it, if they do at all understand it.

Well, it is his plan; it is his purpose. Tonight, it is my desire to share with you what I have experienced concerning God's plan. Night after night, I want to share with you the joy of a change in imagining, really. If I could take you with me and persuade you to believe that you are already the one that you want to be and that you could really believe that you really are and remain loyal to such an assumption that you really are the man, the woman, that you want to be, I know from experience that you would become it. I trust you will do it just as we are told in scripture within the framework of his purpose. You will not try to influence me, influence the other, but you will do it just as we're told in scripture, to alert him that I am what I want to be, and do nothing about it, just live in it just as though it were true; and I, in a way I do not consciously know, I will become it. That I know from experience.

But tonight's purpose is to show you to the best of my ability God's purpose, which we said earlier, is to give you himself. In the very last book of the Old Testament, the thirty-ninth book, the Book of Malachi, he said, "The son is the honor of the father, as the servant honors the master. If then I am a father, where is my honor?" (1:6). That's the end, the very last book. "If the son honors the father, as the servant honors the master, if then I am a father, where is my honor?" The entire thirty-nine books have prophesied such an honor, that God is going to give himself—God is God the *Father*—he's going to give himself to me. And I do not know that I am a father. If I really am a father, where is my honor, where is my son? So the book closes on that note, the Book of Malachi. The first book of the New Testament begins to express beyond: he *gave* the son. But people do not understand this great mystery.

So tonight, listen carefully and let me share with you the mystery, as I *know* it from experience. For you could be rich, you could be poor, you could be known, you could be unknown, and you could be anything in the world; it hasn't a thing to do with God's promise. God's promise is the most fantastic thing in the world, for he gives you *himself*. You actually become *one* with the body of God—it's your body. You *are* he. You contain all other beings. So whether you are in part a rich man, a poor man, a beggar man, or a thief, these things are really not important. They don't add up to God's promise. But God's promise is not given in ___(??) to any work of man. You can be the wisest man, the biggest man, or the richest man; it still doesn't entitle you to his promise. His promise is a gift; you can't earn it. It's a gift, it's grace, it's all grace, and he actually *gives* you himself.

The promise goes back to Genesis. We read the first inklings of the promise in his promise to Abraham. Then we find the promise coming through, evolving slowly, and we find it really crystallizing in his promise to David. Then we find it maturing; and finally, we find it in its fulfillment in the New Testament, in the story that we've been taught, the story of Christ Jesus. The story is true, but *not* as I learned it in my church. I was born and raised in the Episcopal Church. We had it in school. I had Sunday School every Sunday. We had it every Wednesday. Yet it was not the story that my minister taught me. It was not the story that my mother understood and she taught me. It was not the story that my father understood. And they were all Episcopalians. That's not the story.

It's a fantastic story, how God gives himself to us. Now listen to it carefully; it's true. I am speaking from experience. God becomes man that man may fully become God, one body. As we are told, "As there is but one body and it has many members, and all the members one body, so it is with the body of Christ" (Romans 12:4). The day will come that you will be brought into his presence, believe it or not, into the presence of God. And in spite of the year 1963, where our scientists could not conceive of God as man—to them God is a force, God is a power, God is a process—*I* tell you God is man. You will be brought into his presence, and he will ask you a very simple question, in your own tongue. If you speak only English, it's asked and you hear it in English. If you speak only Hebrew, you will be asked in Hebrew and you will hear it in Hebrew. You will hear it because it's thought you hear as words.

He asks a very simple question, "What is the greatest thing in the world?" and you will answer correctly, as though you are supernaturally prompted and you cannot fail in the answer, and the answer is love. You will answer in the words of Paul, "Faith, hope and love, these three, but the greatest of these is love" (1 Corinthians 13:13). And as you answer, *God* himself will embrace you and incorporate you into his body. And strangely enough, it becomes your body. *You* occupy as your own body the body of God, as though there were no others, just you. No loss of identity, but none whatsoever, and you're actually incorporated into the body of God. We are called this way, one by one. And after this incorporation, you are sent into this world to tell it to the best of your ability. You will never in eternity forget that incorporation. Although you wear a little garment that wears out in this world, subject to all the pains, all the limitations, and all the restrictions of garments in this world, you have the memory of the garment into which you were incorporated. And it is the body of God.

You have no doubt in your mind who asked you the question, none whatsoever. You have no doubt who addressed you when you answered correctly. And the whole thing is done in the most glorious manner, and you feel as you never felt before—well, or since for that matter—a delight beyond the wildest dream of man. A joy you can't describe when love, personified as man embraces you, and it is God. Then it's God's purpose to take each and every being in this world and save him by incorporating him into his body, and *the* body becomes *his* body. You are one with God. So it's God's purpose to give himself to us, individually, as though there were no others in the world, just God and you, and finally, only you.

But God is a father. Listen to the words of Malachi, "The son honors the father as the servant honors the master. If then I be a father, where is my honor, where is my son?" So the end of the Old Testament comes on that note. You'll read it in the first chapter of the Book of Malachi; I think it is the sixth verse. It is you asking a question, "All these promises to us through the ages have been made, where is my honor?" If God is going to give me himself and God is a father, he can't *give* me himself unless I am aware of being a father. My child in this world, I know I am the father. I fully believe that I sired my two children; I fully believe it. But millions and billions have done the same thing. That's not what God intended. God has a son, an only begotten son, and unless he gives me *that* son, I am not God the Father (Psalms 2:7). But God gives you that son.

It's the most fantastic thing in the world. I've talked since it happened to me to dozens and dozens of ministers, and they all turn away from me. They think they're in the presence of mad men because they were not taught it any more than I was taught it. I was raised in the same strict orthodox background that they were. I've talked to rabbis; I've talked to priests, Catholic priests; I've talked to Protestant ministers; and none of them see it. And it's true. God gives the individual his only begotten son, and that son is David, David of biblical fame. The *only* one, it's David.

And one day you will have this experience. There will be an intensity you've never felt before all possessing you; and then you'll explode, your brain will explode, and standing before you will be God's only begotten son, but he's *your* son. And you know it more than you know anything else in this world and he knows it. David, the symbol of humanity—for he symbolizes the whole vast world of humanity. But he is a single youth, beautiful beyond description, and he looks into your face and calls you Father. You *know* you are his father, and he knows that he is your son. And then the fulfillment of the 89th Psalm, "I have found David. He's cried unto me, 'Thou art my Father, my God and the Rock of my salvation'" (verse 26)

So here, you come to fulfill scripture, and God is fulfilling his promises. He's promising *in* man. He promised everything to man, which is himself, that's everything. And then he's a father, and the honor of the father is the son and "If I then be a father, where is my honor?" Well, from the Old Testament ends this note: It hasn't yet *fulfilled* the promise of God. Then comes the New who makes the claim—and men to this day will not believe that it happened because they were misinformed—it has happened and it is happening. At every moment in time, it is happening in every child born of woman. God is *giving* himself to every one of us, but actually giving himself. And then you will have the complete knowledge of being the father of God's only begotten son. He doesn't walk with you as a companion; he's your son.

So when we are told he *gave* his only begotten son, people misunderstand it, and they speak of Jesus Christ. And I swear I do not know anyone that will take his words, but when I quote the words of the 14th chapter of John, they'll say, Well, I've heard that, but it isn't literally true. And I tell you it is literally true. The day is coming that you will know who God really is. *You* will actually be that being, and his name is Jesus Christ, and you are he. You will be the father of David, as Jesus Christ claims in scripture if one reads it carefully, he is the father of David. It is said to him,

"Show us the Father and we'll be satisfied." He said, "I have been with you so long and you do not know the Father? He who sees me sees the Father. I am the way to the Father. No one comes unto the Father save by me."

But they didn't understand him—that *I am* the Father—and I said that after it happened. A man said to me, "Well, it's not recorded in scripture." You've got to go back in scripture; it's got to be recorded in scripture that he's a father." And when you quote him, he still can't see it. But now he goes further. No one asked him, if I said to you, "I am the Father," would you not normally ask me, "Well then, where is your son?" Wouldn't you? I can't be a father unless there's a child bearing witness of my fatherhood. There *must* be a child, so where is the child if I am the father? No one asked him the question, so he brings it up, "What think ye of the Christ? Whose son is he?" They answered, "The son of David." Then he replied, "Why then did David in the Spirit call him Lord? If David calls him Lord, how can he be David's son?" And they asked him no more questions thereafter. The word translated Lord is Adonay, which is "my father, my lord." But every child spoke of his father as Adonay, my father, my lord. So David in Spirit calls him "my father." He *revealed* who he is.

But who believes it? Who accepts it? It's a mystery. As I told you over the months, a mystery is a matter not to be kept secret, but a truth that is mysterious in character. How can I explain to anyone this peculiar, mysterious experience where David of biblical fame—go back now unnumbered centuries—and out of my own skull comes a child, David? An explosion and David looks into my face and calls me "Father"? I had no feeling prior to that moment of any relationship to any biblical character. I was taught it as you were taught it. Everyone was taught it just like I was taught it, and then suddenly to find the whole thing recorded in scripture unfolding in the individual, that God inwove the whole drama in man and then inweaves it and all these characters become personified, and there they are.

Now listen to this carefully, it's the 4th chapter of Ephesians, only three verses, the 4th, 5th and 6th. And the word "one" is repeated seven times in three verses. Each time it is attached to a noun. The first noun, "There is one body." Then comes the next, "one Spirit, one hope, one Lord, one faith, one baptism, one God and Father of us all, who is above all and through all and in all." One. Now, here in Zechariah, the one next to the end of the Old Testament, ___(??) Zechariah comes, the thirty-eighth book, and this is the 14th chapter, 9th verse, And the Lord will become king over all the earth; on that day his name one and he one. "On that day the Lord will be one and his name one." One body, one Spirit, one life, one king, one everything, just one. And then you are absorbed into his body because you answer correctly, "The greatest thing in the world is love," and he absorbs you. He incorporates you into his body, and you are he. The body of God you wear—it's your body—without loss of identity.

So today, there are three billion of us in the world, and they project billions to come. I wouldn't care how many billions. We're told in scripture, more than the sands of the sea, and yet the whole vast world and the sands of the sea, how many billions? It would make no difference, *each* is the one. That's the great mystery. God *gives* himself to us as though there were no others in the world, just God and you. And finally the gift is so complete, there's only you, and you wear the divine body that is God. That is the great mystery. And then we understand the story that is told in the very end of the 2nd of Genesis, for it is all God. It is God who is called man in that chapter. Man must leave everyone and cleave to his wife until they become one flesh. It is God who emptied himself and became man and redeemed man, became one with man and gave himself to man. That's the story. He gave everything up and became man and redeemed man.

So we are told in the great mystic's concept—the works of Blake—"And those in great eternity who contemplate on death said thus: 'What seems to be, is, to those to whom it seems to be . . . even of despair, torment and eternal death; but the Divine Mercy steps beyond and redeems Man in the body of Jesus'" (*Jerusalem*, Plate 36). You and I, and you prove it, what seems to be is to those to whom it seems to be. You can assume anything this very moment and rise to the very highest position in the world of Caesar, or you can go down to the very depth in the world of Caesar. What seems to be is to those to whom it seems to be. And you can't save yourself. No individual can save himself. He is redeemed because Divine Mercy steps beyond and redeems man in the body of Jesus. And that's the body. But when you are incorporated into the body, you *are* he. Now you know the second verse, "It does not yet appear what we shall be, but we know that when he appears we shall be like him" (1 John 3:2). It doesn't yet appear what we shall be, but we know that when he appears, we shall be like him. As he embraces you, you are the very being who embraced you; you are one with God, and no loss of identity, none whatsoever. You dwell upon it. This is God's purpose because life has a purpose.

But within the framework of *God's* purpose, you are free to be anything you want to be in this world. You can be rich, you can be poor, you can be known, you can be unknown, and you can be anything in this world, if you really believe God's principle. And God's principle is very, very simple, very simple. Whatever you desire, make it known to God and do nothing. That's what you're told, just do nothing. Sleep this night as though you were the man, the woman that you would like to be, just as though it were true.

Have confidence in that assumption, just as though it were so. And in a way that no one knows because all are incorporated into the one body and all things by a law divine in one another's being mingle, it will influence every being in this world that can play a part to aid the birth of that assumption. If you assume that you are (you name it), and if I can play the part, without my consent I'll play the part. Without my knowing, I am playing the part to aid the birth of that assumption; I'll play the part. Everyone in this world will be used if they can be used.

And God knows it all, for he ____(??) me it all, "All things by a law divine in one another's being mingle." So I can, without anyone asking me, if you dare to assume that you are what you want to be; and if I can be in any way instrumental in aiding the birth of your assumption—you don't need to influence me deliberately and consciously—I will be used. And I will be used totally unaware of the fact that I was used in the birth of your assumption. So you take anyone—leave them alone; you don't have to take any person and use them—you simply know what you want. And it may not come within the framework of his purpose; but in these short distances, it works anyway.

God will adjust it. As we're told in the 16th chapter of Proverbs, "He has made everything for its purpose, even the wicked for the day of trouble." But he tells us in the beginning of that third verse, "Commit your works to the Lord, and your plans will be established." You commit them to the Lord, and your plans will be established. If you start to work on them yourself, it may be in conflict but just commit them to the Lord. Well, how would I commit them to the Lord? If tonight I wanted (and I name it) without telling you, without asking anyone to help, I would this night see the world as I would see it were it true that I *am* the man that I want to be. I would see my friends, seeing me as they would see me were it true. I would see the world as I would see it were it true, and then I would sleep in the assumption that it *is* true. And I know from experience it would work. Everything in the world would move and adjust itself to mirror that which I am assuming that I am; and in the not distant future, I would externalize it. I would become it in my world.

I am not in conflict with God when I commit my work to the Lord. If it's not within his purpose, that's something entirely different. But he'll work it; he'll externalize it. And to show us how he allows it, the 18th chapter of the Book of Jeremiah tells us how he allows it. He warns us, and he tells the prophet, "Go and tell them to amend their way and change, and turn from their evil doings" (verse 11). "But they said, 'We will not. That's all vain! We will continue in our stubborn, evil way.'" And then God said you've plotted and planned the consequences of their acts. He isn't going to hurt;

their concepts produce what appear to be God's plan and the consequence of their misbehavior. God doesn't hurt; he'd be hurting himself because we are all God. It's all God. For he tells me to change my way, to amend my way, but man will not. You read it carefully in Jeremiah 18: Go and tell them what's going to happen *if* they do not amend their ways. And then man will not do it.

In that same wonderful chapter, he tells us how you and I should operate in this world, just like a potter. We take anything in the world and refashion that being in our mind's eye, just as though he or she were as we would desire them to be. Just do it and believe in the reality of that reshaped being. A man unemployed, see him gainfully employed; a man who is up against it, see him freed; a man who can't make the grade, see him already on the top, in your own mind's eye. Don't tell him what you're doing. Don't ask his consent. But do it lovingly. Whenever you operate this law lovingly, you are doing it wisely. So you aren't hurting anyone if you see him as a better person than formerly he appeared to be. And so take any person in this world without their consent and see them as a noble, glorious being—don't tell them that you've done it—and then be quite satisfied to see them become that being. And give full credit to other people, completely rubbing you out as something that had nothing to do with it, perfectly all right. You know God's law.

But within the framework of his purpose, these wonderful promises are made in the Old Testament. For he said to David, I'm going to bring forth out of you a son, and I will be his father. The very end of the book, it didn't happen, it didn't happen. The promise is made to David. Where is his son who could reveal me as God the Father? And no one understands it. I said it to this minister—a very prominent minister right here in this area, the head of his very, very large following, running, so they tell me, to over a million—and when I quoted the 2nd Psalm to him to tell him who David was, he confessed he never saw it in that light. In the 2nd Psalm, addressed only to David, "Thou art my son, today I have begotten thee" (verse 7). That is established in the beginning. But man never saw it.

Because as a speaker, I was misinformed; I was told that Jesus was God's son. I believed it. I was raised in that environment as an Episcopalian, and I did not know, even though I read it myself, that *he* was God the Father. I always thought he was the son. And yet, he tells the whole vast world who will receive his word, "When you see me you see the Father." But no one believes it. It doesn't make sense. How can the Father condense himself, empty himself, and become a man, a simple man, as you are? How could you and I plus individuals in billions in the world occupy one body, and that body is our body? It doesn't make sense. How can he so give himself to me that I am the father of his son and give himself to you to the same extent that *you* are the father of the son? If you are the father of God's only begotten son and I am, are we not one? How could I ever reach unity unless there's a son to unify us? Only one son, and if I am the father of that one son of God and *you* are the father, every being in the world is the father, are we not one? Can't you see this great mystery unfolding where all the people in the world become the only father of the only son? Not sharing, occupying the only body that is God. And is that one body? Listen to the words, "Divine mercy steps beyond and redeems man in the body of Jesus" and that one man we call Jesus the Christ, and you are he.

If you see him on the outside, you don't see the right one. The day will come you are he. You'll stand right in his presence and then the 82nd Psalm is fulfilled: "And God has taken his place in the divine council, in the midst of the gods he holds judgment." And you'll be taken in Spirit right into his presence, and he's just as he's described in the Book of Daniel. Believe it. Just as Daniel the prophet described the Ancient of Days, there he stands before you. You don't have to ask who he is; he's infinite love, but infinite love. And then you see an attribute of him and it's almightiness and it's man, everything is man. There's nothing but man. And then you see infinite wisdom is man. But God himself is love, infinite love.

When we are told in the letters of Paul that God is love and the letters of John that God is love, believe it. They didn't manufacture this; it *happened* to them. God is love, infinite love. And you will stand in his presence and he'll embrace you, incorporate you right into his body. And you don't see anyone else, just you. You are he and the body of God is your body. So go back in Ephesians, one body . . . it begins with the word body. "One body, one Spirit, one hope, one Lord, one faith, one baptism, one God and Father of us all, who is above all and through all and in all" (4:5). And then you will know what it means, he's ___(??) one, only one body, only one Spirit, only one hope.

So when Paul tells us, as he stands before the king, "Here I stand in chains, stand on trial for hope in the promise made by God to our fathers." What promise? He promised me *himself*. He promised to *give* me himself because he's going to draw from me a child who is his child. If a child comes out of me and it's my child and God makes it his child, so he brings out of me a son and calls the son his son, and then gives it to me as my son. Then I wait and wait and wait through the ages and wonder, "When is this thing ever going to happen?" And I was misinformed until it happened to me. When it happened to me, then I knew how it happened to everyone. And so I tell you, whether you be Christian, Jew, or Mohammedan, or you call yourself an atheist, it's going to happen to you. It's the only way in the world that we will ever be unified. And when we are completely unified in one body, it's the body of God. And each will be the father of God's only begotten son, the personification of humanity.

So in the 8th chapter of the Book of Proverbs, he is personified as wisdom, the very first act of God. As you are told in the 22nd verse, and it goes through the 36th verse, "God created me in the beginning of his way, the first of his acts of old." Before he brought forth the heavens, before he brought forth the earth, "I stood beside him as a little child." Now scholars are all agreed that this personification in the form of a little child is the personification of wisdom. All right, Christ is defined as the wisdom and the power of God. And so when Paul writes his letter to the Corinthians, the 1st chapter of 1st Corinthians, he said, "Christ . . . the power and wisdom of God." So all right, I would go along with the scholars that the teacher who wrote that 8th chapter of the Book of Proverbs *meant* wisdom, but he personified wisdom as a little child. But I still say the whole vast world of humanity is personified as a youth, just as you're told, and you look right into his face. It represents the whole vast world of humanity, and he's your son and it's David.

And so who would you hurt when every being in the world rolled into one makes one youth, and that youth is your son? Who would you hurt, who would you rob, who would you destroy when it's all going into one being, and it's David? A beauty beyond the wildest dream of man, you can't conceive of the beauty of David of biblical fame, when he symbolizes and personifies the whole vast world of humanity, and it's all your son. For humanity is the son of God, personified as a single youth. It's told so beautifully in the Book of Samuel, if one could only see it. And here is the one; if he succeeds, he will set his father free, and we're all set free by the son. So if he succeeds, the promise of God is "I will set his father free" (1 Samuel 17:25).

And so the king asks a very simple question, "Whose son is that youth?" And no one knows. Then he said, "Inquire whose son the stripling is?" No one knows. So he turns to the youth himself; he said, "Whose son are you, young man?" and he answered, "I am the son of your servant Jesse the Bethlehemite" (1 Samuel 17:56). Well, the word Jesse is any form of the verb "to be." In other words, I am the son of whom I am: I am self-begotten. That's what he's telling you. That's exactly what God does to us. God's name is I AM, "Go tell them I AM has sent you" (Exodus 3:14). So the father of David is I AM. So when you are embraced and you see him, that's your name, I AM. It's all in the Bible. Check me.

So you are the being spoken of in scripture as the one who has been promised this fantastic gift from God, and the gift is the gift of himself. He gives man himself. And there's no way in the world that he can prove to man that he gave himself unless there was a son, for God is God the Father. So to go back to Malachi, "The son honors the father, as the servant honors the master. If then I am a father, where is my honor?" And then the book closes. And no one can read the story other than the ___ (??) unfold in Matthew, Mark, Luke, and John. For the Old Testament closes on the question, Where is my honor? This promise is long overdue; if then I am a father, where is my honor, where is my son? And then comes the unfoldment: here is your son.

And who believes it? As I said, I'm testing the limits of the rabbis, the priests. Who can follow the reasoning behind the visions, an actual series of mystical experiences? They won't believe it. How can David be the son? How can David be Messiah? How can Jesus be the Father in spite of all the confession: "He who sees me sees the Father"? "And I tell you there is only one body, one Spirit, one hope, one faith, one baptism, one God, and Father of us all." No other, only one, "And in that day the Lord will be one and his name one," and you are that one. To prove who you *really* are he sends *his* son and gives him to you as *your* son.

Now, you believe it. But whether you believe it or not, it is true. And because not a thing that man can do to thwart it, I'll prophesy for you: you're going to have the experience. If you oppose him with all your might, you can't thwart God's promise to you, which is to give you himself. And God is a father, and he can't give you himself unless he gives his only begotten as your son. No other way in the world that he can give you himself unless he gives you his son. I am telling you in advance, before it takes place, that *when* it takes place you may believe. For I tell you, he gave himself to me. And although fragile as I am and wearing out this garment as all garments wear out, and it can't be too long delayed before it's worn out, I still know the body that I have inherited. There's only one body and that one body we call Jesus the Christ. It's my body; and it is your body, and it's everybody in the world, the one body. Man cannot, looking into this fabulous world, believe that God is man and that man is God. But I tell you it is true.

Now let us go into the Silence.

*   *   *

Q: (inaudible)

A: ___(??) within the framework of his promise for us, we can be anything we want to be. So take a noble dream, assume that it is true, just as though it were true, and relax into it, just as though it's true, and then let it work. It works.

Q: (inaudible)

A: ___(??) why Jesus cursed the fig tree? My dear, nothing should be barren
   in this world, nothing. If I come to a person who says, "But I've had
   this condition so long that no one can help me." And they'll tell you
   that, "You couldn't help me. I went to all the doctors, went to all the
   psychiatrists, went to all the people in the world, still none could help
   me," and they're feeling very sorry for themselves. They're in a state. But
   there isn't a state that man cannot vacate. There isn't a state in this world
   that a man is in, whether he did it consciously or unconsciously fell into
   it—he either entered it knowingly or unknowingly—but he can leave it,
   as I would leave the city. I am in this city, and I love it, but I don't have
   to remain here forever. I can leave it, so can you. So a city's like a state.
   If you go into a state, you must bear the fruit of that state and partake
   of all the experiences while you're in that state.

   So he comes to a tree that doesn't bear. Nothing should be barren
   in God's world. And so he cursed the tree, the state. That's the state,
   permanent to himself, but man doesn't have to fall into it and remain in
   it. You pass through it. Or not even go into it and avoid it. There's all the
   difference in the world between individuals and states that individuals
   occupy. The fig tree is only symbolical of a state of barrenness. That
   barrenness need not be of the womb; barrenness of things in my life,
   that I'm not bearing the fruit that I need to bear to support my family in
   the order that I would like them to see. ___(??) barren fig tree. So don't
   accept anything based upon the evidence of your senses—don't, unless
   it's in keeping with what you desire in this world.

Q: (inaudible)

A: No, my dear. I said that within God's framework you and I are so free.
   It's just fabulously free within the framework of his purpose. Men try
   to thwart his purpose. But he even allows that for a while, and then
   God makes an adjustment. If I ___(??) have a tension within a machine,
   you must release that tension. Well, the world builds tension, and then
   volcanoes, earthquakes, and wars—all these are the release of tension.
   Well, man does it. But God allows it, within the framework of his
   purpose. What I said when I first started, it is my desire to get more and
   more men, more and more often to assume a higher level of imagining.
   For if they do, without effort on their part, then things will follow
   normally and they will unfold these higher dreams in our world.

   Today we have a fear-crisis culture. Every morning's paper produces
   another crisis. If we don't have one, they're going to make one. It's crisis
   after crisis after crisis. If you read the papers, as I do, undoubtedly you
   do, they sell by what you read on this level, and they simply are stocking

themselves on that level. And so it is my hope to get everyone who will come here to more and more adopt a higher level of imagining. What would it be tonight, regardless of favors, if things were as you nobly would love them to be? What would it be like? If one could only more and more sustain that level of imagining, then things would follow normally in the world. But if tomorrow morning's paper is more important to us than our imaginal activity, well then, you come right back down with the ___(??). And it's day after day after day the same old thing, one crisis after the other.

You can see it plotted and planned, if you read the paper carefully. Some little ___(??) goes out, and we see they're going to follow through. It's all plotted and planned to keep us in a state of uneasiness, to make us feel that he or they are going to pull us out of it. They cause it in the first place and then pull us out of it. (Tape ends.)

THE KINGDOM

April 30, 1963

Tonight's subject is "The Kingdom." We're told in the Book of Luke, the 12th chapter, the 12th verse, "Fear not, little flock, for it is your Father's good pleasure to give you the kingdom." In the same book, we are told, "The kingdom of heaven is within you" (Luke 17:21). So here, he's going to give us something that is within us. So we must be locked out from something within us. Fear not, little flock, it is your Father's good pleasure to *give* you the kingdom, and the same evangelist, Luke, now tells us that the kingdom of God, the kingdom of heaven, is within you.

To get to the point, the earliest of the gospels, which is Mark, the first word put upon the lips of Jesus is about the kingdom. It's the 1st chapter, the 15th verse, and the evangelist has him say, "The time is fulfilled and the kingdom of heaven is at hand; repent, and believe in the gospel." That's the message, the whole beginning. Here we have four profound thoughts in that one verse, that 15th verse of the 1st chapter: the time is fulfilled. Everything prior to this moment in eternity was only preparatory, and he's making a declaration that everything the prophets foresaw, everything that they foretold, is now beginning to awaken. And he's the first one, the forerunner, of all that was foretold that would happen to man. For the time has been ____(??); it had to be filled up. At this moment in time now, it begins to unfold like a flower. Then he said, "The kingdom of heaven is at hand," which is a moment. He makes the statement, "Repent, and believe in the gospel." There are four distinct thoughts all buried in that one verse.

Tonight, we will take many passages of it, with an emphasis on repent. It is not said in this statement that if you and I repent that we will in any way be able to cooperate with God in bringing in the new order. No, the new order is coming whether we repent or not. You can't stop it. That's

God's purpose; that's his plan. So my repentance is not going to aid the new order at all. Yet I'm invited to repent. And we should every moment of time, if you know what it really is to repent. For repentance hasn't a thing to do with grief, feeling sorry for what we've done, feeling remorseful, and regret. That hasn't a thing to do with repentance. The word "repent" means "a change of mind, a change of attitude toward life itself." I don't care what the facts of life are; truth depends not upon fact but upon the intensity of imagining. And so if I repent, I simply change my attitude toward anything in this world. And if I am intense about the change and persist in that changed attitude of mind, I'll produce a corresponding external fact.

Well, go back to what we said earlier, "It is your Father's good pleasure to *give* you the kingdom" and "The kingdom of God is within you." I am shut out from something within me of which there is nothing but; for all things are in the kingdom and the kingdom of God is within you. Then how do I arrive at that inner state? He's invited me now to practice the art of repentance, just practice it. He doesn't tell me that if I don't practice it, I'm going to be shut out from the kingdom. He does not say that. He tells me to repent and believe in the gospel; believe the story, read it, and believe it. But do repent. But I do not bring in the kingdom by my repentance. For that kingdom is coming whether I repent or not. But it makes it so much easier while I'm still shut out to live in the world where I am shut out if I repent.

And that is called "the days of Messiah." For there are two ages discussed in the Bible, *this* age and *that* age, described in the 20th chapter of the Book of Luke, the 24th through the 36th verses. And these two ages are separated by the act of resurrection. Resurrection separates them. But around the resurrection, before and after, there is what is known as "the day of Messiah" or the "days of Messiah" as characterized as good days, joyful days, and the days where you can reap the harvest. And that is repentance. But it does not, if I repent every moment and owned the earth, it doesn't really matter as far as the kingdom goes. I'm getting into the kingdom, as you will, everyone will. But for our own sakes while we're in the world, let us master the art of repentance.

Now, ___(??) a week ago, I told you concerning a little girl. She didn't call it repentance, her grandmother didn't call it repentance, but she puts on an act, an imaginal act, and produced one after the other of these fantastic, lovely demonstrations. The grandmother went home that night and wrote me out the entire story in detail, and added one, which is a delightful story. The child was then only four, and she said to the child, "Now, Pammie, you know what you did to get the house for daddy and mother?" Yes. "And you know what you did to get the playhouse with all the toys." Yes. "Well, now I would like a stereophonic machine for my records, but Daddy won't give me one. He will not give me anything, and here I only have the same little radio that I had when I was a girl, when I was a child. That's the only means in the house. And so I would like, really, this wonderful instrument to play the records. I want a slow one, a long one that would almost fill that wall. But an enormous one!"

"Now, this is what we do, Pammie. You stand right here, close your eyes, but you don't physically walk across, any more than you did when we got the house. But you do walk across the carpet, you walk across the room, and you go over and you feel this wonderful instrument. You feel the lovely wood and you see it, but your eyes are closed. But now you're there physically. But you walk toward this instrument, and then you hear it. When you hear the music coming from it, you and I will dance. We'll dance all over this room together. And so now let us play our little game."

Remember this little girl, what she said to her grandmother, "You're old. You can't do it, but my Imagination works like thunder." Well, here is thunder. The divorce was already in the works; papers were signed. The month is August, and a week before her birthday, which was October 11, he said to his wife, "On your birthday there will be delivered to your home this stereophonic machine, to play all the records." "When it came, it was exactly as we had imagined it, a long one, a long one filling almost the wall, and it's perfectly heavenly. It's the one thing she wanted; that is, my daughter wanted because all through her life it relaxed her when she heard good music. She put the records on and simply relaxed. As we would relax with something else, she relaxed with good music. And here, he gave it to her on her birthday." A little girl four years old!

Now, you and I will teach our little children—I know I taught mine—to say thank you, and *how* to say thank you, and how to be gracious. But we don't have to teach any person in this world how to feel it. We can teach them how to say it, but we don't have to teach them how to feel it. They can *feel* it, and that is the *secret*. But man will not let himself feel what the senses will not allow. He may on his own try to feel what reason denies. So he's shut out from the fabulous world within himself. Where did she do it? She did it *within* herself. She remained physically stationary in the room, and mentally she walked forward and felt what was not there to be felt physically. But she gave it all the tones of reality; she gave it all the sensory vividness a little child of four can give it. And she brought all the senses to play on it: she touched it, she heard it, and she felt.

Well, you can't taste the wood, and you couldn't, well, I dare say you could, but if you brought three senses to play upon that imaginative drama—within six weeks that was realized in a household where this lady of the house was still using a little, tiny machine she had when she was a girl. Yet she was the mother of two children, and he never felt that that was something he should give her, because that to him was an unnecessary luxury. That was a luxury, an unnecessary luxury, why give it to her? And so she didn't ask him; the little girl didn't ask it. They dropped it having done it, and having done it, it was done.

That's the word repentance. Listen to it again, the beginning of the teaching of Jesus Christ in the Book of Mark, the very first word put into his mouth—if you have a red letter edition, you can see the first red-letter phrase, "The time is fulfilled and the kingdom of God is at hand; *repent*, and believe in the gospel." Believe the story, for the seed must be sown on man. For there is a certain moment in time when the time is fulfilled, when it's filled up; and man can't stop it, he's going to be moved right into the next world. He can't stop it. But I am convinced by that last statement in that 15th verse, "Believe in the gospel." Believe it. The sower in rabbinical tradition is the teacher. So you hear the man telling the story; he's telling you he's the teacher. And some will not believe it, some believe it, some hold it with a reservation, and some with a big question mark. Believe it implicitly. You can't understand it, but believe it. From day one he's trying to ___(??). And when that time is fulfilled, well then, the kingdom of heaven is at hand. But in the meanwhile, practice repentance and repentance is simply a change of attitude toward everything in this world. No matter what it is that denies the fulfillment of your dream, change it. Just as she, four years old, did it.

Now tonight, before I took the platform, another story by a lady who is here . . . and she, too, has gone through the usual thing in California, a divorce. It seems to be epidemic. So she went through it. She has two children, two sons. There was no settlement in the divorce for any car for a boy seventeen years old. But he would like a car. He wouldn't come to the meetings. She told me what the other brother has done using this technique. But he thought it would take too long. The divorce was granted, monies all settled, all arranged, and the judge said, "No, no seventeen-year-old boy would I recommend for a car." So that was not in the cards. She went home, and she said to the boy, "You know what (calling the brother by name) what he did, so why don't you try it anyway? It isn't going to cost you anything. Your father said no, the judge said no, everybody said no, but you still would like the car, why don't you try it?"

So last night, as he retired, he was in his new car. "With all the feeling that you would have were you in the new car, and it's your car." This is on Sunday. On Tuesday night, the husband called and said, "You know, in spite of what the judge said, in spite of what the settlement reads, I promised him a car and I'm going to give him the car." Now this is only this past week.

The car has not been delivered, but within three days, his imaginal act . . . then said he to himself, "It worked so quickly and so easily, now I'm going to work upon my skin and upon my own marks in school." It never occurred to him before to use this wonderful law of forgiveness. We call it forgiveness, the Bible speaks of it as forgiveness, but the first word was repentance.

How do you repent? Not to feel remorseful that my father and mother separated; if he wants his father back, he can bring him back, if he wants him back. She can bring him back, if she wants him back. But if she sees the paper all signed and that is the end of the picture, well then, you can't repent. I can't repent when I accept the facts of life as they appear on the screen of my world. For the whole thing is within me, it's not on the outside: All that I behold, though it appears without, it is within, in my Imagination of which this world of mortality is but a shadow. How can you deny the fact of the little girl producing the instrument? Who knew in that household that a little child, four years old, was the one treading the winepress? As William Butler Yeats said, "I will never be sure that it was not some woman treading in the winepress who started the subtle change in men's minds." Or in that household, the father's mind was changed suddenly. He thought he initiated the desire to buy this machine. He didn't; the little girl did, four years old. And who knows today what we are reaping because someone other than members of the household are imagining for him? We're doing it anyway, until that moment in time when it's all filled up and we enter a world completely subject to our imaginative powers.

So I tell you the kingdom is yours regardless because it's within you; it's not on the outside. And God is going to give it to you. He has to open up the way, and the way is very, very narrow. So we're not called collectively; we're called individually. The 27th chapter of the Book of Isaiah, "And you will be gathered one by one, O people of Israel." And you will be gathered one by one, O people of Israel. Well, Israel means "the pure in heart"; that's what the word means. Only the pure in heart shall enter the kingdom. But everyone is going to be made in the likeness of his Father, who is perfect, therefore, pure in heart. For to see him, one has to be pure in heart. "Blessed are the pure in heart, for they shall see God" (Matthew 5:8). "I behold an Israelite indeed"—his name was Nathanael—"I behold an Israelite indeed in whom there is no guile" (John 1:47), one incapable of deceiving another for personal gain.

A week ago, last Sunday, a friend of mine was home, and he told me this story. He said, "I have been to jail. I'm not ashamed of it. I ___(??) and for my abuses in that department, I went to jail. I met all kinds of types there. I met two men ___(??); they wrote a book. They were con men." He called them bilko artists. "And there was a book in which they confess in this book that they had never been able to bilk a man who himself was incapable of bilking another. Not in the history of their experience could they take from any man a dollar by selling him the Brooklyn Bridge. They set out an ethical code by which they operated. They were successful, and you couldn't take them over." No man who is incapable of bilking another can be bilked. It isn't his cup of tea. He doesn't know how to operate that way.

But if there are people in this world who will only buy what is repossessed, you can take them over. There are those who only wait until they repossess something, the repossess set. When it's repossessed—the man lost his initial investment—they can get it at x-number of dollars less than that. Repossess a car, repossess this, and what you can buy repossessed, well then, such people can be bilked. They don't realize they've got to go through all the fires of the world until the heart becomes the heart of Israel, where it cannot take anyone over. They'd rather die than do it. They'd rather starve to death than do it. But any man in this world who can bilk another can himself be the victim of a bilko artist. And these two men who wrote this book wrote it in jail, and they confessed in all their years—for that was their profession—___(??) their life was simply that, that's all gone. But they couldn't take one man who himself couldn't bilk another.

I can go back to my own personal experience in my father's life. A most successful businessman, very successful, incapable of taking advantage of another for personal gain, in a highly competitive society, little, tiny Barbados, very competitive; but he could not take advantage of another for personal gain. He could go around with him in a competitive bid for a job, but not in any way deceive you, so that he, personally, would get the contract. Not ___(??). So when he made his exit, he left a fortune for his family. And I know in my own family that was their ethical code. They're sharp dealers, very, very successful businessmen, and they buy at the lowest price, but they do not bilk. And there are people who will take anything in this world on that basis, and everyone can be taken over, everyone.

I went to the track with friends of mine the other day, and this gentleman who drove us out, as he walked out of the track, someone approached him with a watch and said, pointing to a car, "See that car?"—a lovely car, maybe a six- or seven-thousand-dollar job—"That's my car." Well, right away, my friend, who is a lawyer, noticed that behind the little glass he saw the Turf Club sticker. And the man is trying to sell him a watch for twenty-five dollars he claimed is one hundred fifty dollars in value. Well, he knew that any member of the Turf Club could go into the Turf Club and cash a check for twenty-five dollars if that's what he needs. But instantly, my friend couldn't possibly do that because he couldn't bilk anyone. He's a fine, decent gentleman. He couldn't take anyone over, yet he's a very successful lawyer. He couldn't possibly take somebody's watch. And so here the bilko artist was up against a stone wall with my friend. So he came back in and told the story, and he was just simply amused. He couldn't possibly be taken over because that's not the way he approaches life.

Now here in our world, we are given the chance to practice repentance. It works like a charm. I don't care what the facts are. You don't need to bilk anyone regardless of what the facts are. So this little girl did not go hit the father over the head to buy the instrument; she simply played a little game. She heard the music and she danced to the music and she felt the wood and she walked across and saw it and touched it and felt it and heard it. Then, six weeks later, seven weeks later, here comes a gift. He thought he originated the urge to give his wife something she had never dreamed of in the past he would give. Now who in the interval held him in the state of the giving in? The wife did. He never expressed it, and she accepted the facts of life. He never expressed that feeling of generosity. Because he never did, she took the facts of life and lived by the facts.

Imagination has many aspects. One aspect is the conservative aspect. It's fed by memory. If I feed my Imagination only images supplied by memory—he never did it; therefore, he isn't going to do it, and he never did it; therefore, he cannot do it—and so all day long, I feed my Imagination with these images supplied by memory, I perpetuate what is the conservative aspect of imagining and that is fed only by images supplied by memory. There is a transformative aspect—that's where repentance comes in—where I would take a scene that is already in being and modify it. And so I have the same room, the same living room. What did I do? I put against that wall an instrument that were it true, I would then hear the music I want to hear. And so I modify the scene. But the house is here, the whole building is here, everything about it, the same children, same husband, and same everything. But now I change the pattern of the living room and modify that scene of that living room that is the conservative aspect.

But the day is coming when you and I get into the kingdom of heaven, where everything is subject to our imaginative power, we create radically. We don't need any memory image to supply models to build our world; out of the nowhere we create. That's what you and I are destined to be tomorrow. And everyone will enter that world, that fabulous world called the kingdom of God. Because the kingdom of God is *in* us, and we're only shut out of something that's already in us. We're living on the surface looking out, not knowing that we are casting these shadows on the screen of space, shadows that are really prompted from things *within* ourselves.

I invite you to try it. Try this theme, which is the third statement as he begins his message to the world. He proclaims the fantastic thing that "the time is fulfilled," that what the prophets foresaw over ages and ages and ages has now come to its fulfillment. He'd be the first one in and he proclaims it. No one believes it because he didn't come as they thought he should come. He didn't come to conquer the outer world; he conquered himself. He overcame self. Not the outer world, for he knew there was nothing on the outside. The whole vast world reflected the harmony within himself. And so he proclaimed, "The time is fulfilled and the kingdom of God is at hand"—he's been waiting for this moment for unnumbered eons of time and now it's come—now "repent, and believe the gospel." Believe the story of your ___(??), the most fantastic story in the world.

What story? That God so loved man that he became man that man may become God. That's the story. He actually became us? Yes. How could he do it? He emptied himself, completely emptied himself and became us, every one of us. And then, as it's fulfilled, the time is fulfilled, the door opens, a very narrow door, for we go in one by one: "And you will be gathered one by one, O people of Israel." What, Israel? Yes, the pure in heart. Only the *pure* in heart can enter and the pure in heart is Israel.

And so everyone will come through because he's just like his Father. As you're told in the 19th of Leviticus, "You *shall* be holy";—no doubts about it—"because I the Lord your God am holy" (verse 2). You can't *avoid* it. If I put you through all the furnaces in the world, you can't avoid it, "You *shall* be holy; because I the Lord your God am holy." And, "Be ye perfect as your Father in heaven is perfect." You can't be less than your Father because he's given you himself. He's given you fatherhood. And when you enter that kingdom, you are the *Father*, the King of kings, and everything subject to your imaginative power, but everything. In the kingdom, you will create radically. You need no model supplied by memory. You don't modify scenes in being; you create out of the nowhere, out of nothing, something out of nothing. It's all your own wonderful Imagination.

But until the end of it, well then, let us repent. Everyone can take someone in this world and use that one to repent, as a challenge. Don't raise a finger to make it so. Use it as a challenge. So anyone can ask you because you know the story; you can ask me, I can ask you, and we can ask each other and then conceive a scene which would imply the fulfillment of the dream. Just like the little child. The grandmother, the mother ___(??). The mother said, "You know how we got the house?" "Yes." "You know how we got all the toys and the playhouse?" "Yes." "Well, let us play this stereo machine, and there it is against the wall. But you don't walk over there physically, you remain right here. Close your eyes, and you see it?" and Pammie said, "Yes, I see it." "Well, now do you know the color?" "Yes." "Do you know how it feels, if you could feel it?" "Yes." "What it would sound like?" "Yes." "Well now, you walk over mentally, not physically, and go over mentally and put your hands on it."

Because Imagination is spiritual sensation, that's what that means. If at this very moment I would imagine a ball here, but no one sees a ball here, but I could feel a ball there, couldn't I? And to prove that I am feeling the ball, let me now imagine after I felt the ball that I am feeling a piece of silk. Could I discriminate between a ball and silk? Well now, let me imagine something else. I imagine I'm feeling something steel. Can I discriminate between a ball and a piece of silk and steel? Well, if I can discriminate between these three imaginal objects, then they exist. You can't discriminate between that which does not exist. If they don't exist, there is no distinction; there's no discrimination. If I can feel one in my Imagination after the other, and no two feel alike, do they not exist to me? Well, they do. So ___(??) natural to this little girl, and she heard music and she danced, so she brought into play all these things based upon an imaginal act, and it came to pass.

Now you may not credit her imaginal act as the cause of it. But when the little girl, who is now only five, has four outstanding case histories to support her imaginal acts, are you going to discount it? As I said, if there is evidence for a thing, what the rational world thinks about it or even ___(??) for it, it's nothing to the point. She actually knows what she did when they got the house, even though it seemed to be a disaster. For the house came as a result of his little company being absorbed by a big company, and the big company putting him through an aptitude test and forcing him out of his job at the desk into a salesman job, where he made many, many times what he made at the desk. With all of his money, then he could buy the house. And it's exactly the kind of a house the little girl had imagined, with the aid of her mother and grandmother.

On the strength of this, they got this wonderful thing at Christmas, this playhouse filled with toys. On the strength of these two, they got the stereo. And then on the strength of these three, she brought her father and mother back together after the divorce had been finalized. Here, the papers were signed and delivered. She was living in Hollywood, and he was living in an apartment with the two girls. The grandmother said, "You want Daddy and grandmother back?" "Yes." She came back. A little girl—well now, if the little girl didn't know from experience what she did in the past, she would not have repented. She would not have known the art of repentance. She would have allowed this divorce to be final and cry her eyes out night after night because she wanted her mother, and her mother wasn't there. But she was not going to allow this after she had suffered it and was reminded of what she had done by the grandmother.

Do you know that you and I could be the most successful this night from repentance and then within a matter of a week forget it? Completely forget what we did to produce the result that we got, completely forget it, and start once more rationalizing time and space and arguments what to do, when we have done it without persuasion, without a thought of ___(??). We do it all the time. But let me encourage you; the kingdom is open, and you cannot be locked out indefinitely. For repentance, marvelous as it is, will not in any way allow you to work and cooperate with God in bringing the new order. The new order is coming whether you repent or not.

But while we're shut out, repentance is given to us to make life easier. For we're shut out, all of us, until that moment in time when we are resurrected. For the two ages are separated by the act of resurrection. In the 20th chapter of Luke, "The sons of this age marry and they are given in marriage; but those who are accounted worthy to attain to that age and to the resurrection from the dead, they neither marry nor are they given in marriage, for they cannot die any more, they are sons of God, sons of the resurrection" (verse 34). Lifted up completely above the organization of sex, where the individual is himself a unity, creating without the aid of any divided image. No matter what he imagined in the world he created, living in a world that is fabulous, all from within himself. And don't think some little, tiny world, it's magnified beyond the wildest dream of man, just like this. But he's not on the outside removed; he's on the inside creating. And that's God.

So tonight, you try it. Try it and see how it works, not *if* it works. Because not "I'll think about it"; try it and see how it works. Take every person's request, and then do it in feeling, not in words. There are millions of people across the country who will declare, "I am rich, I am rich, I am rich"; in the depths all they are feeling, where is the next dollar coming from? They are feeling poverty, but declaring in words, "I am rich"—doesn't work that way. As we said earlier, I'll teach one little child to say when someone gives you something, "Thank you." If someone is kind to them, say "Thank you." Teach them how to say "thank you," but I need not ever teach anyone how to feel it. So how do I feel it? Not the words, get below the words into the feeling. Well, what am I feeling? She felt that machine and she sang. She danced to the music she was hearing. Well, the music didn't come from anything but that wonderful stereo, and she danced all over the place. And then, they forgot it. Then he has the impulse to buy it for his wife's birthday. That's how it works. Two kinds of motion, one is done from the inside, and the outside is under compulsion. The one on the inside, ___(??); the one on the outside moved by compulsion to only bear witness to the inner motion.

You try it. Take a friend's hand, and congratulate him on his good fortune, on his wonderful job, on his success, on his—for anything in this world. But put your hand mentally into his hand and actually congratulate him and feel the thrill of ___(??) with a friend. How wonderful it is to have a friend who has been so successful because a friend would be happy for the friend's success. And *feel* it. Don't tell him a word. Say nothing to him and watch it work, just watch it work. And then the whole thing works in the world. But you've got to *feel* it. Ignore all the facts of this world, and then inwardly perform the act, and it will outwardly become the fact.

So I tell you, this book, the Bible, is the greatest book in the world. And just imagine what the prophets foresaw and those who wrote about it, for whom they searched and they inquired, asking what person and what time was indicated by that Spirit of prophecy within them when they predicted the sufferings of Christ and the subsequent glory (1 Peter 1:10). But they couldn't find him. No matter how they searched, they couldn't find him. And then one day, it happened. And when it happened, it happened so naturally that no one would know it. You can talk about it and tell others. Some will believe it, and some disbelieve it. But it happens in you, *individually*, and you are the same person you were before it happened. And they expect some fantastic being to come out of nowhere in a mysterious way. He doesn't come that way.

Everything that happens in you is mysterious. Oh yes, the birth is very mysterious. An unusual mystery takes place within you, as told in the 3rd chapter of the Book of John. For the discussion that takes place between Nicodemus and Jesus is the theme of this work. This peculiar birth that must take place is the only means of entry into the kingdom of heaven. There is no other way to get in unless this thing takes place first. And so, "Except you be born from above, you cannot in any wise enter the kingdom of heaven" (verse 3). But you *will* be born from above. May I tell you, all the precepts of Jesus are to be taken literally. People say, oh no, it couldn't be literal. I tell you every precept is stated as some literal fact to be understood in its literal manner. And I'm speaking from experience. I had no idea that this thing was so literally true.

So we are told, except you be born from above, Nicodemus, you cannot inherit the kingdom of heaven. You can't get in. And he said, well, how could this be possible? I am fifty years old, a man my age? And how could I be born a second time? He said, "Except ye be born from above, you cannot enter the kingdom of heaven. And you a master of Israel and you do not know this?" It all starts, a birth only in one way, from the womb of a woman. And it isn't from the womb of a woman. It's from the womb of God, and the womb of God is the skull of man. That's where God is buried. And out of that wonderful skull of man, generic man, comes the man, the individual man, no loss of identity, and he comes out born from above. It's literally true.

In that moment of awakening came the division between the two great ages: this age he left; that age he's entered. But he still wears the veil of the flesh; and therefore, he's not fully aware of his inheritance until the veil is taken off for the last time, for he can die no more, can't die. He's been resurrected from the grave, which is the skull of man. And having resurrected, he's inherited, but it cannot become to him actual, or at least, it is not fully realized in him so long as he wears the body. And so he plays his part teaching everyone who will listen, hoping that they will believe the story. For they must believe the story so that it may germinate as it were; for we are soil on which the seed is planted, and the seed in the Bible is called the word of God. And the word of God is called the gospel. So believe the gospel if you believe the word, the message of salvation.

So try it, try it tonight. Don't delay. No matter what the world looks like at the moment. And it's distressed for you—I trust it isn't—but if it is, you can't conceive of any more distressed state knowing it would be for a little child of five whose mother isn't coming home. How many nights she must have cried herself to sleep. And this night, she started the crying once more when she said, Now stop the tears. You know what you did. You did this, you did that, you did the other, and you can do the same thing. Then at the end of four days, the mother comes home and she could say to her grandmother, "You know that my Imagination works like thunder." Let our Imagination work just like thunder and make it all come to pass.

Now let us go into the Silence.

* * *

Q: (inaudible)

A: First of all, you couldn't stop influencing people. As you walk the earth your every imaginal act is influencing the world. As the poet said, "All things by a law divine in one another's being mingle." You can't disturb this and not influence the stars, all interwoven, all one. Like my ___(??) the morning's paper, and you're influenced. Ninety-nine percent of the paper is really a planned, controlled news picture. Everyone has a press agent—all the big ___(??) have press agents—and they want you to read what they *want* you to read. But they're influencing you anyway. People who aren't meeting you personally, they're influencing you by the written word. You're doing it without spending any money for a ___(??) as you walk the earth. You're influencing everyone. ___(??) saw this night that he was ___(??) someone other than himself, and the other influenced thought they had initiated the desire to do what they did. The boy at seventeen goes to sleep, driving his new car, a ___(??)

he hadn't tried before because he thought that that was hopeless. The father, now divorced, with the sanction of the judge—but he didn't have to do any car—he was paying so much a month for his keep and his brother's keep and so much for his wife and then so much insurance and all that___(??). But in spite of that, he calls up on Tuesday, three days after the boy begins to imagine the act and said, "I'm going to give him the car. I promised it to him a while ago, and I'm going to give it to him" and ___(??) give him his car." So the father thinks that he had a soft feeling toward his son. It's the son that did it.

Now the son may forget after getting the car how he got it and go sound asleep again. All through the Bible, it is one constant refrain: "Rouse thyself! Why sleepest thou, O Lord? Awake! Why cast us off forever?" and the command is to God in man. For this is the 44th Psalm: "Rouse thyself! Why sleepest thou, O Lord?"—not man. And then, in the New Testament, "Awake, you sleeper and arise from the dead"—the sleep is so profound it's likened unto death (Ephesians 5:14). And so man has to be constantly awakened from this state and go back to the exercise of repentance. He brings in the prize once, and then he forgets it. He has to be reminded, and he goes back again and goes back again until finally he lives by it—until that moment in time when he enters for the last time into the kingdom of heaven, which is within. For the kingdom of heaven is within you. And then he doesn't have to be reminded because he's completely awake, and he knows who he is. For God succeeded then in giving himself to the individual. But don't be concerned if you fail a thousand times, go back anyway. This is the way it works.

___(??) all of God's promises to Israel. It's not a new religion. Christianity is as old as the faith of Abraham. It's only the fulfillment of the faith of Abraham. And every word spoken in the New Testament if one searches the Old diligently they'll find the source of the quote. It's only fulfillment. ___(??) of the man's soul as it unfolded. He goes back into the Old, and there he finds what was foretold. (Tape ends.)

THE SHAPING OF THE UNBEGOTTEN

May 3, 1963

Tonight's subject is "The Shaping of the Unbegotten." We are told in Paul's letters to the Ephesians, the 5th chapter, the very first verse, "Be ye imitators of God as dear children." So we must find out what God did. We are told he called a thing that is not as though it were, and the unseen became seen. If you're taking biblical records, that's from Paul's letter to the Romans, the 4th chapter, the 17th verse. He calls a thing that is not seen as though it were.

The one who had the vision and I turn to one, that is, Blake. Blake said, "Many suppose that before Creation all was solitude and chaos. That is the most pernicious idea that could enter the mind, for it takes away all sublimity from the Bible and limits all existence to Creation and chaos." Now listen to the next statement, "Eternity exists, and all things in eternity, independent of Creation which was an act of mercy" (*Vision of the Last Judgment*, p. 614). Let me repeat it, "Eternity exists, and all things in eternity, independent of Creation which was an act of mercy." No scientists today believe that; they think we came out of chaos, so that the whole thing began to evolve out of something that wasn't. And here, one with the vision tells us eternity exists, and all things in eternity, independent of Creation, which creative act was a merciful act.

Now, what does he mean by it? Well, I have had the vision, and I know that Blake is telling the truth. For I am telling the truth based upon my visions. Everything in this world is forever. What you now see, what former people saw, what they are going to see, everything is forever. These are parts of the eternal structure of eternity. This body, this little lectern, this—everything in the world is but a little part of the eternal structure of eternity. It didn't come into being at all; it always was—all the stars, everything, everything on earth, all part of the eternal structure of eternity.

Now he speaks of Creation as an act of mercy. Here, you are as a body and I am as a body, and all these bodies, everything; and then God said, "Let us make man in our image, after our likeness" (Genesis 1:26). And here, man is . . . man is part of the structure of the universe. But here is God saying, "Let us make man in our image, after our likeness," and that is an act of mercy. So he takes man, as I would take a tree and say to you, "Let us make a tree and mold it into our image, after our likeness." Let us give to it the quality that we possess, our creativity. It can't create itself; it simply is a part of the structure. The whole vast world is simply the universe, and all part of the structure.

God is shaping himself now. God, the unbegotten, is begetting himself; and so he begets himself in me, he begets himself in you. When he completes the act of begetting himself in us, we are God. We are that which will now use the same structure to beget anything that we can conceive of. So God takes man, part of the eternal structure of the universe, and begets himself in man. When he begets himself in man, the state begotten is the one who begot it: God in man, or the thing that came out of man by God's act is God.

Now I'm told, let the individual imitate God as a dear child, and I'm told everything *is*: "Eternity exists and all things in eternity, independent of Creation." So I'm going to create. It all exists, independent of Creation. Well, how could I do it? I can't think of anything that then doesn't exist. I think of you in unnumbered states of mind—when you like me or dislike me, you're sympathetic or you're unsympathetic. I can think of you in unnumbered ways. But I want to create something now. I want to create something that is lovely for myself. So I bring you into my mind's eye and then I bring another into my mind's eye and then I have, in my Imagination, a little party—say, a cocktail party, a tea, a dinner. I control the imagery that I brought into my mind. You all exist in eternity. But I bring you, without your knowledge, without your consent, and I control the entire moment of time. Make it a minute or five minutes, anytime, not too long, I control it. But I so arrange the imagery that it implies something other than what it was prior to the arrangement. I bring you all into my mind's eye, and I allow you to hear something that is taking place. I allow you to see me as you would see me were things as I desire them to be. And so I am begetting something. I am actually shaping myself, the unformed, upon the formed. For all things in this world are already part of the structure of eternity—everything *is*.

So I bring a being from the structure. I bring another breath, it's a man; another breath, it's a woman, another breath ___(??), and I so arrange them in my mind's eye that when I put them into that form, then they see me as they would see me were my dream realized. It's my dream I am begetting. So I am begetting on the structure of the universe that which did not exist before. So you and I as living souls did not exist. But the structure, this garment, always existed. These garments existed, everything in the world existed, but these living souls did not. And God begot us, begot us just like himself, to be a creative being just as he is. So take the same structure, and then create and create and create.

So be ye imitators of God as dear children. How did he create? Well, this is how he created: "He called a thing which was not seen as though it were seen and the unseen became seen." That's how he does it. So let me go back and re-quote the brilliant Blake, and may I tell you, I can't read anyone in this world that I would put even near him. I go back into the Bible; yes, he's equal to all the great prophets of the Bible. He brought into our ___(??) today ___(??) understanding, and he said, "Many suppose that before Creation all was solitude and chaos. That is the most pernicious idea that could enter the mind, for it takes away all sublimity from the Bible and then limits existence to Creation and chaos. Eternity exists and all things in eternity, independent of Creation which was an act of mercy." Just imagine if God did not take that which is always eternal and through this wonderful intense desire on his part to create humans out of that which was, we would not be here as living sentient beings, creating, yes, miscreating but creating. If you miscreate unnumbered times, you can still create. A miscreation is still a creation. I bring war, revolution, all these horrible things of the world; it's still creating. And eventually, he who has started and stopped that will bring us into his own likeness, and we'll be one with God.

So just as he did it out of things that are eternal parts of eternity, that this body and this little thing here that will seemingly decay—and this will decay, the garment will decay, and all will decay—it doesn't really. That's the great illusion—it doesn't really; it is forever. Everything in this world is a part of the eternal structure of the universe. And out of all these parts God then said, "Let us make man"—for we already existed, like hanging on that tree—"in my image." We don't make man out of chaos; man exists, it's part of the structure of the universe. Well now, let us take man that's part of the structure of the universe and let us now make him into our image, after our likeness. And so he takes man and he makes man into his image.

Now we go back into the Book of Genesis and see what he's done with man. A word is used in the book, it's called the tree, the tree of life. The man in some strange way is expelled because he may eat of the tree of life before he's prepared. Well, if you have a concordance—I have James *Strong's Concordance*; it's an excellent biblical concordance—and the word tree is defined as "the spine, the backbone, the carpenter, the gallows." Who is hanging on the gallows? It's called the gallows, this word called the tree. It's the gallows; it's the spine, it's the backbone, and it's the carpenter; in other words, the builder, the potter, the creator, and there he hangs upon the tree. But the tree is the spine; it is the backbone. And after unnumbered ___(??) on this called man, he brings out of this something that is entirely different: It's himself. It is shaped because he is the unbegotten, and he's shaping himself upon a form. Just as I would take the potter, and I would mold the clay upon some form and mold it to my heart's desire, well, God is molding himself upon man.

When he has completed the act as he desires it, there are three definite stages where he reveals the completed work. He molds us and molds us and molds us, makes us ever more sensitive, ever more creative, and ever more like himself. And when he is satisfied that we are just as he is, he unveils his way. The unveiling of the work begins with the awakening of himself, and that is called the resurrection. He awakes within the individual in whom he has completed the work. That awakening, in the Bible, is the resurrection. Then, after the resurrection, he goes through a ___(??), like a bird; and he's born from above. He's self-begotten because the individual who is born cannot conceive of being sired by anyone other than himself. He can't for one moment when he awakens in the tomb of his skull believe that he's other than himself. When he comes out of his own skull, he cannot have any feeling, any sensation, of having any father or mother. So he's born—then he must be self-begotten. God is so begetting himself that when he begets himself, the thing begotten is God. And he comes out, just self-begotten.

Then comes a second stage where he has the experience of being a father. Until that moment, he didn't realize that he was. And now, strangely enough, when he sees the symbol, which reveals to him fatherhood, there is no mother. He is the father of God's only begotten Son. So he knows now who he is. It took the son to reveal to him who he really is. Then comes the third symbol, and the third symbol where the entire veil that separated the two is torn from top to bottom. From the top of his skull to the bottom of his spine, he is severed in two. And then the 10th chapter, the 19th verse of Hebrews tells you the purpose of that severing of ___(??). From that moment on, the two become one; they're not two anymore. They were separated by a veil, and the veil was the body of God, having torn the entire thing from top to bottom.

And then, strangely enough, you see yourself. And may I quote Blake again: "I behold the visions of my deadly sleep of six thousand years dazzling around thy skirts like a serpent of precious stones and gold. I know it is myself, O my Divine Creator and Redeemer" (*Jerusalem*, Plate 96). At that moment, you see the being that created you and you are the very being who created you. It's a self-creation. God begot himself on the mold called man. And at that moment, when you see it, after the splitting from the top to the bottom, you see this lovely liquid, golden light. It's you and you know it. You say, "I know it is my very self, O my Divine Creator and Redeemer." And then you, as the very being who created it, you, *as it*, move up now in serpentine form right into Zion. So all go into Zion, all go into the New Jerusalem.

So Creation is an act of mercy. This is—you can't claim ___(??) of a creator—it was always part of the eternal structure of the universe. As those who have taken certain drugs have seen a certain act and recorded it to those who would record what they were seeing, I am seeing a man emptying coal; and strangely enough on this level of my being he was always emptying coal. There was never a time in eternity he was not doing what he's doing, though at the moment it seemed to be he's doing what he's doing because someone ordered coal only at that moment in time. And yet, he was always doing what he's doing . . . part of the structure of the universe. That we are here tonight, and if you could see it on a higher level, we have always been here. We're all structures, part of the structure of the universe. But out of these structures, God, in his infinite mercy and intense longing, is begetting himself.

Now let me quote you the 4th chapter, the 12th verse of Job, "And a thing"—one book calls it a thing; the King James Version calls it a word; the New Bible calls it a thing; you can call it a thing or call it a word; I think a word conveys it—"a word was brought to me, it was brought to me secretly," said Job, "Which mine ear heard in a slight manner." It was brought to me, it was brought secretly, and my ear heard it in a slight manner. I wasn't quite sure, but I understood what I heard, what he had told me. And then the story of Job, in Job 10, he said, "You know that I am without guilt. Thou knowest that I am without guilt. Why then dost thou try by torture to extract from me a confession of guilt?" (verse 7).

You know I am without guilt—that's man. Here is man. I know I didn't do a thing to come into this world. But a priest tells me that I have sinned or my father and mother sinned because they begot me in this physical state. I know I didn't do a thing; I found myself here. And then my parents must go to church and pay a certain sum of money to the church and confess their mortal sin because they express the normal, natural function of the body? Yes, millions do that every day of this world, and the church gets richer and richer as they are made to confess their "sins." So Job makes the statement, You know I am without guilt, why then dost thou try by torture to extract from me a confession of sin? And then Job goes through the entire picture of horrors.

But in the end of Job, the 42nd chapter, I think it's the fourth or fifth verse, what in the fourth chapter he heard stealthily—a word came to him secretly, coming through the night secretly—and then he said, "I have heard of thee with the hearing of the ear, but now my eye sees thee" (verse 5). He has the experience, and he knows how true what he heard secretly was when he heard it, but he heard it so quietly; he only heard the word in the wilderness. To see is to know and to know is to experience, and so he knows it now by experience. I can tell you what I experience and share it with you and then you can say "I heard it." It was a secret that was revealed. I heard it, but I didn't see it, I didn't experience it, and therefore, I don't know it. I will trust him or will distrust, but I heard it. Then comes the power between the hearing of the word and the fulfillment of that word, where now I've heard of thee with the hearing of the ear, but now my eye sees thee.

And may I tell you: I have had a taste of the power in store for all of us when God fulfills his intention. He's begetting himself on us, actually begetting himself; and when he succeeds in begetting himself, we are he. When we are he, I'll show you what will happen because it happened to me. I have glimpsed and I've tasted of this power and the structure remains forever and forever. I came upon a scene, just like this, and it was all animated, all having or seemingly enjoying independent action. They all were at dinner. Dinner was being served. Birds were flying. Leaves were falling. Everything was in action, and it seemed completely independent of my perception. Then at that moment in time, I knew that if I could arrest in me an activity that then at that moment, I felt everything would cease. So I arrested the activity and it froze. The whole vast scene; it was arrested. And through the window, a huge big black tree, a tree—the leaves were falling, they couldn't fall, and they were arrested in space. The birds trying to fly, they were arrested in flight, and everything froze. And there I am observing this part of the structure of the universe.

Anyone prior to that moment would have thought they were completely independent of anything external to themselves. They could have ordered liver instead of duck. As the little Dennis the Menace said, "You mean that you can order anything in this world and you order liver?" They went into a restaurant, and the father had a wonderful menu before him and all of a sudden the father, who could never get it at home—because Dennis wouldn't have it, the mother wouldn't cook it—so in the restaurant he ordered liver. And Dennis' remark was, "What, you mean you could have anything and you order liver?" Well, here in this restaurant they could order anything, and whatever they ordered, if it was possible to be served, they would be served. Their thoughts were completely free to do anything. And the birds started from one limb to another, and they were free to make the limb.

When I appeared upon that scene, appearing upon that scene, I knew that nothing was independent of my perception of it, for I froze the activity in me that allowed action to take place in this world and everything stood still. The bird didn't fall out of the tree, which caused me after the experience to question seriously man's concept of gravitation. For a bird in flight if arrested would fall to the ground. A leaf if arrested would continue unless some sudden current of air takes it out. But all the leaves that were falling remained just where they were when I arrested them, and the birds in flight remained spatially without falling to the ground. The waitress—she was walking, and she walked not. Those who were dining, they dined not. Everything froze. He couldn't carry that spoon from his soup. He couldn't continue the action of soup to his mouth. And then, looking at them, amazed as I was, and then I released the activity in me, and they completed their intention. The diners dining dined. The birds, intending to fly, continued the action and completed their intention, and they didn't fall to the ground. All things moved on to their intention.

So I tasted of the power that is in store for all of us when God completes his intention in begetting out of these permanent forms something other than this form. This is not the being you're talking to any more than you are the being that I'm looking at. The Unbegotten is forming himself, shaping himself on these forms. ___(??). He needs a form, and I need form to beget something else. So I bring you tonight into my world, I bring another into my world, and then I talk to these two in my world from a certain premise, which if true implies I've realized my dream. And so, I say to him, "You know what's happened?" ___(??), but I am begetting something. I am using forms to form the unbegotten. Form what? Well, the Unbegotten's name is I AM; that's his name. And so I may be in need of a job. Well, the word job is something formed. I AM is unformed, the unbegotten. I want to beget something; I want to get a job. And so I bring you in my mind's eye; I bring another one in my mind's eye, and we have a little tête-à-tête. And then, whatever is taking place must imply I have what I want. When it implies, I am molded on these forms, myself the unbegotten, I'm begetting something. What am I begetting? I'm begetting a job.

So when I fulfill my act and I actually get the job, I am imitating my Father as a dear child. So, "Be ye imitators of God as dear children" (Ephesians 5:1). Imitate God! Just as he brought these entities into being by using eternal forms, then we take the same forms and we use them to bring in on a lower level what we want to bring into this world. So I want to bring in a job, not only for myself, bring it in for a friend, bring it in for another. So I take anyone, ask him what he wants. Know what he wants? All right, then test my talent to take from these eternal forms what I think. If I arrange them in a proper manner and then lose myself into this state, I would produce out of it that which in itself it doesn't have. So I take any gathering; you can gather anyone and gather it in such a manner that when it's gathered together and the conversation starts, the conversation plus those present would imply something other. The something other is what you are begetting. So you are begetting something in this world. So man can beget anything in this world by using these eternal forms.

Let me go back to Blake. When Blake wrote this, it's called *the Vision of the Last Judgment*, and Blake . . . I would put my head this night on a block that every word of it is true. Blake never had any ambition to be known in this world, only to transcend it, just to reveal God's vision. And when he said, "The Bible and the four gospels and Revelation"—he did not mention any of the parts of the epistles, any epistles—he said, "The four gospels, Matthew, Mark, Luke and John, and Revelation, these are the eternal visions." Then he mentions the Torah, Genesis through Deuteronomy, the five books. Then he mentions, "Read all of them." He implies without naming that these are eternal visions.

Now he said, "*The Vision of the Last Judgment* is not allegory; it is not mystery; it is vision." And he tells you exactly what he means by vision as against a myth, as against an allegory. For he saw the entire play as described in the Bible unfolded before his vision. And he tells it, exactly these characters, they're only states, but each state in God's play becomes a person. They're all personified. And so in this, let me now re-quote what I said earlier, "Eternity exists and all things in eternity, independent of Creation, which is an act of mercy." So I create from these eternal forms, and they exist forever.

Now, God is actually in you, in me, begetting himself. As I stand before you, and this is not arrogance on my part, for I did not do it, and yet in another way, I did. For when he begot himself in me, I am he. And so all the suffering that I have gone through throughout unnumbered centuries up to this moment, which in his infinite mercy, he keeps from me, so I would have no memory of the past, all the suffering. "For whom God afflicts for secret ends, he then comforts and heals and calls them friends" (*Everlasting Gospel*). So he puts us through all these sufferings. But, my Lord, the gift! The gift is the gift of creativity. He gives us himself.

So when I beheld at the base of my spine, this golden radiant light—if you want to read it, read it in Ezekiel 1:27 and 8:2—here, I beheld it had the appearance of man; but at what appeared to be the loins, there was a glow of light that rose; and then, at what appeared to be the loins, going down, was light, just radiant light. That's exactly what it is, right at the base of the loins, and you see it; and strangely enough, you know it is yourself. It would take that liquid golden light to take the impress of what God imagines himself to be when he began to create you in his image. He held you in his mind's eye and not a thing diverted him. But he had to bring you into that golden liquid state to take the impress of himself as he believed himself to be when he thought of you—all on the mold of man. And then you rose up, just like a serpent. Read the 6th chapter of the Book of Isaiah, "In the year when King Uzziah died I saw the Lord sitting on a throne . . . and then above it was the seraphim." Well, the seraphim are described as the most celestial beings, the highest of God's creation. Nothing compares with the wisdom, the might of the seraphim. They're called fiery serpents with human faces, with a power beyond the wildest dream of man. And we do go up, just as you're told, "As Moses lifted up the serpent in the wilderness, so must the Son of man be lifted up" (John 3:14). As Moses in the wilderness lifted up the serpent, so must the Son of man be lifted up; and you are lifted up, just like that.

May I tell you, when it happens to you, it will be just as I have told you, for it has happened to me. I am not speculating. I am speaking from experience; I'm not speaking from theory. And so all these forms, every form in the world, are forever. As far as the body goes, it's forever and doesn't wear out. Let it be cut apart and be buried; it's still forever. Everything this body has ever experienced, it will experience forever, all the bodies. But in it all, God is begetting himself, actually molding and shaping himself, the Unbegotten, upon a form called man. So, "Let us make man in our image, after our likeness."

Now we are told, listen to the words—is this the plural of majesty, "Let us make man . . . after our likeness"? Well, that's the plural of majesty. Or is it that God actually consults some divine society? Well, you can resolve it. Listen to the words in the 6th chapter, th 4th verse of Deuteronomy—the greatest of all commandments, said he. When asked what is the greatest commandment, he quoted Deuteronomy 6:4: "Hear, O Israel: The Lord our God is one Lord." Here, we find a compound unity. The word is, "Hear, Israel: The Lord"—that is Yod He Vau He, that's Jehovah—"our God"—that's Elohim, that's plural—"is one Lord." "One" is Achad. It's spelt in a way that you would almost hear the word "Zion." It's Achad, yes, Aleph, Beth, and Daleth. When you see it spelled and you are trying to use your Imagination, you can almost hear "Zion" coming out. But here is a compound unity, one Lord, maker of unnumbered gods. "Hear, O Israel, the Lord our God"—our Elohim—"is one Lord." So did he consult with those whom he had already brought into the divine council? Well, you be the judge. "Let us make man in our image, after our likeness." Either the plural of majesty or we go back to the greatest statement, "Hear, O Israel: The Lord our God is one Lord."

But you take me seriously this night and create as your Father is creating you. He is creating you on the mold of man. And you take man and be an imitator of God as a dear child. Create a lovely image of yourself by bringing into your mind's eye men, and so arrange them at a party that they are seeing you as they would see you were you now the man that you want to be. What would you like to be? So then arrange them. But if you were the man that you would like to be, would you have a certain circle of friends who would congratulate you on that achievement? Bring them all into that picture and let them see you as such a man. When you see them seeing you as such a man, you are actually shaping yourself on the forms that are forever. You are bringing in and creating as your Father created.

Now let us go into the Silence.

*   *   *

Q: (inaudible)
A: The day of the Messiah falls, the good day, in, well, not necessarily in the scripture but it's part of the tradition of the church, the good day. Well, the good day is when man discovers his own creative power, and he uses the Messianic power. There is only one power, and Messiah is your own wonderful human Imagination. Before you are actually born from above, before your resurrection, before the temple is split down from top to bottom, you are free to exercise the Messiah, the power of Messiah. And these are called the days of Messiah, and they come within, I would say, the moment of resurrection, before and after. And these are called the good days, when man knows of a power within him which is his own imaginative power so he can create without consulting any person in this world. He doesn't need to pull wires or do anything external to himself. And these are called the good days, the days of Messiah. But the days of Messiah are not the days represented as resurrection; that's something entirely different. But they come within the frame of that coming of Messiah in the individual.

So a man, given this thought today will challenge in the political world, financial world, hasn't the slightest concept of the days of Messiah. Their trust is in the enormous fortunes in the bank or the vault, and their political power. They have no concept. They cannot

___(??). There are men in our world—and you know them, know of them—that they play on prejudice, on superstition, and they were called honest. Well, the mayor of Chicago, he was a very honest man, and so when he died—he only got a few thousand dollars a year as the mayor—but when he died, they found in his many safe deposit vaults about $500,000 in cash. But he was called the honest one, ___(??). Because he had relatives who inherited all that money and ___(??) doing a very good job to overcome that. But he was elected year after year on the prejudice of the people. He said, "If the king of England came near, I'd spit in his face." Well, the people, they loved that because they were all Irish Catholics and Germans, and they hated everything English. "If he came to this city I would spit in his face." Well, they all cheered him for that, while he took their profits and ___(??). So they paid him ten thousand a year as mayor, but he got the half million dollars in cash in ___(??). And that's the entire picture all over the world. They have not a concept of the good days of Messiah. They have no concept of that ___(??) picture. But he as the mayor catered to a very large Catholic crowd. ___(??) well, that's all over the world. Have you seen any pictures recently of ex-president Eisenhower coming out of church? But he was for eight years. Every Monday morning, in New York City, there was a photograph of Mr. and Mrs. Eisenhower coming out of church. Now you find every Monday morning, Mr. and Mrs. Kennedy coming out of church. And so the whole world thinks how holy and sweet they are.

I'm not talking about that. I'm speaking of this eternal drama, where God is begetting himself on these eternal structures called man. And when he begets himself, it's like this is a cocoon out of which the great butterfly comes. It is giving birth to God. And the difference between what is coming out which is God and what hatched it out is the same difference between the cocoon and the butterfly, altogether different. You read it, the 1st and 8th of Ezekiel, and the 6th chaper of Isaiah, to see what faintly resembles what is being begotten in you. You read it. (Tape ends.)

I AM THE VINE

May 5, 1963

We're told in the 40th chapter of the Book of Isaiah, "The grass withers, the flower fades . . . but the word of God stands forever (verses 7 and 8)." The Bible is the word of God in its entirety. No matter how far it may exceed the limits of our logic, it still stands forever, and you and I will experience everything in that book. If at the moment we can't grasp it, don't try to change it, and leave it just as it is. It will prove itself in the most marvelous series of mystical experiences that you ever conceived. In fact, you couldn't conceive them. So don't even attempt to change the book, leave it just as it is. It stands forever. Everything will fade and wither, but it will stand forever.

Now we are told in the 84th Psalm, "Blessed are the men in whose heart are the highways to Zion. They go from strength to strength; the God of gods is seen in Zion (verses 5 and 7)." If you have the highway in your heart that leads to Zion, you will see God. And everyone is *destined* to go to Zion. Now the word Zion appears first in the 2nd Book of Samuel, the 8th chapter. I have yet to find a book written by anyone that can throw any light upon it. But you listen carefully, I am quite sure I can throw some light upon it. I'm not being arrogant: I have experienced it. So here in this book, the fifth chapter, beginning with the sixth verse, beginning with the first, for that matter, and you go through, say, ten or twelve verses of 2 Samuel. The word Zion appears for the first time. Zion was Jerusalem before occupied by Israel. The Jebusites occupied it—they were the lame and the blind—and it was *impregnable*, you could not take it. And they said to David, "You cannot come in here." Then said they, "The lame and the blind will ward you off." It would only take the lame, and the blind to keep you out of Zion. That's how perfectly arranged it was, impervious to any attack. But David took the stronghold of Zion and named it the city of David, which is the city of God, the New Jerusalem.

Then said David, "Whoever would take the Jebusites let him go up the shaft, the water shaft." The water shaft was a perpendicular shaft that led from the rock below to the rock above on which Zion was built. I have read unnumbered attempted interpretations of this, and they all conclude it doesn't make sense. Maybe the script is distorted, maybe someone changed it, but it doesn't make sense. For, said they, David is attempting to build a circular city at the same time he is building an inward city. So they conclude that no man can build in a circle and inward at one and the same time, unless of course he is attempting to construct this strange architectural feat in a *spiral* manner. For then you can build the circle and the inward at one and the same time if you are going to do it in a spiral manner.

Over the centuries, they have been trying to find just such a structure in the Near East, where we call Jerusalem, and it isn't there at all. It's all in us—the whole vast Bible takes place in man, individual man. And this is true. My entire circular world that I am building, and I am building the inner world. Here we are told, I look at it and it's made up of the lame and the blind, and they are strong enough to stop me from getting in to take the citadel. Yet I am told I *must* make the effort to take the citadel. And David takes it. Then he makes the statement, "Whoever would take this citadel must go up the shaft." From the bottom to the top, that's how he goes up. This is a perpendicular shaft that rests below, and it goes through all the rocks, right up to the top where Zion is built.

So let me show you how it's done. We turn now to the 15th chapter of the Book of John, which is related to the 18th chapter of the Book of Isaiah. Here we are told about a strange vine. He said, "I am the *true* vine, and my Father is the vinedresser. Every branch in me that bears no fruit, my Father takes away, and every branch that bears fruit he prunes, that it may bear more fruit" (verse 1). And you'll find a parallel in Isaiah 18. I look at my world, and everything seems on the outside but everything. It seems completely independent of my perception of it, everything in this world; I don't care what it is. This, the nearest thing in my world seems so completely detached and independent of my perception of it, and that is my circular world, as I look at the world; to the extent that I can take everything in my world and change it and make it conform to my ideal of what I think it ought to be, always using love as a motivation. Let me use my Imagination lovingly on behalf of every being in this world, and see them, as they ought to be seen were they now actually enjoying what they are doing. Let me persuade myself that it is true. As I bring about these changes in my outer world, this circular thing, I am producing that circular motion within me.

I'm binding it. And when I'm completely convinced that nothing in this world truly exists independently of my perception of it, but nothing; I have completed that circular motion.

And then will come that moment in time when I will have all these rocks, as told us in the 5th chapter of 2nd Samuel, they'll be split right down the middle, that which divided the land, and I will go up in circular motion into the city of Zion. For we are told in the 84th Psalm that crowds of people are eagerly waiting to mount into Zion to display themselves before God, eagerly waiting. The whole vast world is waiting, but they don't know how to get there. You get there in the same way that David builds the city. Said the critics, no man can build in a circle and inward at one and the same time, unless, of course, he proposes to build in a spiral manner. How else could he do it? And they can't quite understand it.

They have maps, all kinds of maps of the Near East, trying to in some way interpret this is where David did it. It hasn't a thing to do with modern Jerusalem or any Jerusalem. This is Jerusalem; this is Zion; this is Jerusalem. And I start from generation at the base of my skull. I go down into the base of my spine—that's where we generate in this world—and then I reverse the process. Someone told them, where I don't remember, but someone told them that nothing in this world truly exists independently of my perception of it. I may, at that very moment, have doubted it and then taken it under consideration. But maybe I experimented, and I proved at least to my own satisfaction that something worked. It seemed so completely independent of me.

And then I am told there are all the lame and the blind. Someone couldn't see his way toward a job, couldn't see his way toward something—he was lame, he was halt. And then I was told, he really is not independent of you, you know, that's your lameness, that's your blindness. He's in your world; that being is in your world, and that whole thing is in your world. He is unemployed, and yet he should be, because he has an obligation to life. He's unemployed? Well then, bring him into your mind's eye, because you are blind, you are the lame, and then do it. And you do it without his or her or their knowledge or consent, and it works. And up you begin to make this circular motion. As you change this fabulous circular world on the outside, you are moving up this way on the inside. As you move *up* by changing your world and making it conform to your dream, the ideal, as it ought to be, you move up.

One day, you hit the last point and then comes that enormous power of creativity, which was resting at the base of the spine. It was *enormous* power and you were it. It was God all along, God in descent. And there you saw it, and you can say to yourself, "I know it is myself, O my Divine Creator and Redeemer." And you, as it, moved up in a circular manner, in the most perfect manner, just like a serpent. But up you went in a circular manner right into Zion to present yourself before the Lord of hosts, the God of gods, and you are he. Everyone has to make the motion.

So I tell you, you started by seeing your world. And if you look at the world, everything seems in a circle. Everything really is blind. Who can see tomorrow? They're speculating; they're all plotting and planning tomorrow. All the great leaders of the world are plotting and planning for us. Our political leaders are plotting not tomorrow; they're plotting next year's elections. Not this November, but a year from November. They're more concerned about a year from this coming November than they are about any crisis in tomorrow, as far as they are concerned. They aren't concerned about that, they're thinking of a year from November. That's a year and a half away. They're more concerned about the results *then* than they are about things here now, all plotting and planning and scheming.

I tell you, forget it. Look upon your world, and you start doing it. Take a simple one in your world, maybe your servant, and maybe you have because of changes in your life you must let the servant go, let the employee go. But don't let him go or her go into the vacuum; see them gainfully employed before you let them go. When you give them their severance pay, bring them into your mind's eye and see them more gainfully employed than you employed them. As you do that, you are moving up this way on the inside. Let the whole vast world deride you; I don't care what it does. They will still be plotting for tomorrow's election unnumbered centuries from now. But you will be in Zion.

Everyone *must* move into Zion, and you move into Zion in a definite technique. Listen to the words, "I am the true vine and my Father is the vinedresser. Every branch in me that bears no fruit, he takes away, and every branch that bears fruit he prunes, that it may bear more fruit." And may I tell you, the true vine of eternity is the human Imagination; that's Christ. Christ is really your own wonderful human Imagination. It is he that is doing the work that must move up, and that's how he moves up. He moves up by transforming every being through the medium of love in this world, but every being, no matter who he is. And when I tell you the story, you may at this moment find this vine a wild tree. I found it a wild tree. Whenever I heard the story—whenever you hear it—at that moment it's a wild tree. And so the poet said, "I found it a wild tree, whose wanton strength had swollen into irregular twigs. But I *pruned* the plant and then it grew temperate in its vain expense of useless leaves, and knotted as you see into these full clean clusters to repay the hand that wisely wounded it" (Browning).

And so, if you look, it's a wild, wild tree. I had brought in everything in this world based upon the blind and the lame on the outside. They're all blind. They couldn't see where they're going. They're all complaining, doing all kinds of things, criticizing, and they were lame. They were in need of help, and I allowed it because to me that was fact. Then I was told it doesn't exist independently of your perception of it, all this blindness and this lameness; it's all you pushed out. And so when I found it, it was a wild tree. I hadn't pruned it, and I had allowed it over the unnumbered years of time to go into useless leaves.

Then I became the vinedresser, and then I would prune it. So it would start to bud, and then the bud became the blossom, and the blossom became the grape. As it ripened into the grape, then every branch that didn't have blossoms and grapes you cut it off. It isn't bearing? Well then, cut it off that it may not use that enormous power and sap these lovely clusters that could become bigger and bigger, and you cut it off. And so everything in this world becomes now something out of your own wonderful mind. There's nothing in this world but God, nothing. God is taking everyone here individualizing himself and *each* becomes God, with the *same* power; and so he has to do the *same* thing because my Father is the vinedresser. He is the vinedresser ___(??) and every branch that bears no fruit he takes it away, and every branch that bears fruit he *prunes* it that it may bear more fruit.

So someone will reach a certain level—there's no limit in this world—he's reached that. You can't coast in this world; there's no status quo. All right, push it up higher, something lovelier. And all of sudden, this thing is moving, and it's moving in a peculiar way, up your entire spine. And when you've done it, so that no power in the world could change it, there's no one who could convince you that this isn't true. You've proven it. You've had the experience. And you can say with Cathy of *Wuthering Heights*—which undoubtedly are the words of Emily Bronte, but she puts her own experience into the words of a character—and she said, "I have dreamt in my life dreams that have stayed with me ever after and changed my ideas. They've gone through and through me, just like wine through water, and altered the color of my mind."

Emily Bronte undoubtedly awoke in a dream one day. It could have been a daydream or night dream, but she awoke in the dream; and from that moment on, Emily Bronte never could be the same. When one awakes in a dream to find the dream not a dream, where you say of it, "I'm dreaming. No, I'm not, I am awake. It is *really* so," and the dream becomes as objective as this room is objective, then you can't think of anything in this world thereafter as you thought of it prior to that experience; you can't do it. So you think of a person, and you see the person as they would like to be seen by the whole vast world. You may not succeed in *awakening* in that dream, but that's a dream. That's a daydream. You may not succeed. But you can't deny the experience that once you were dreaming in a similar way and you awoke in it and there he was, the embodiment of what you imagined him to be. You can't deny that.

So whether you fail a thousand times, you can't deny that there is such a possibility of thinking of a friend, seeing him as you would like to see him, as he would like to see himself, and awakening in that state to see that he's *actually* in that state—and then it comes through this world. Well, whether you succeed or not, you can't deny the experience. So she said, "I have dreamt in my life dreams that stayed with me ever after and changed my ideas. They've gone through and through me like wine through water and altered the color of my mind." Like turning wine into water, you can't change it it's colored, and the whole thing remains colored. My life is colored, the pigment of my Imagination, having had these experiences, and I can't change it.

So I can tell you today, although the scholars will say it doesn't make sense . . . I was reading this day . . . and I went to my Bible. Here, these are the so-called greatest scholars on the biblical score in this world today, a hundred-odd. The books are only a few years old. So I opened up the book, and this is actually what he said, "Someone must have in some way disturbed the script, because one thing is certain"—and this is the word he used—"one thing is certain, this does not make sense." And there's no way they can rearrange it to give it sense. It makes all the sense in the world. For, said he, David is building in a circle and inward at one and the same time, and that can't be done; unless, of course, the accepted architectural feat, this unusual architectural feat, of building spirally, building in a spiral. That's exactly what he's doing. But the scholar did not have the experience of moving up in a spiral. And you move up in a spiral after you've been building and rearranging the circle. So you take every person in your world; I don't care who he is, who she is, and you represent them to yourself as they would like to be seen by the world, as you would like them to be, persuade yourself that they are, and then they become it. And you are rearranging and building your circle. As you're doing it, you are actually performing an inner action, and you're moving up.

Then comes that moment in time when there is a terrific severance of the stones. Bear in mind, David said, "Whoever will subdue the Jebusites, all these blind and the lame, let him go up the water shaft" (2nd Samuel 5:08). We must go up the water shaft, and that water shaft is *in you*. It's your own wonderful spinal column. As we brought out last Friday night, Moses discovered the dwelling place of Jehovah, in a tree that was aflame. And yet though aflame it didn't consume him. A flaming tree—well, I am the flaming tree; you are the flaming tree. It's an actual flaming tree, and yet it doesn't consume. Like that little poem—only in that case it consumed—two little moths were sent by their king to investigate the nature of a flame because the flame is to a moth its god. After a little while they returned with uncertain intelligence; one thought it was warm, and the other thought it was bright, but they didn't quite understand the nature of the flame. The third moth went and moved by true desire, he folded his wings beneath him and plunged headlong into the sacred fire, until he became one color and one substance with the flame. "He only knew the flame who in it burned and only he could tell who n'er to tell returned."

But unlike *this* flame, you *do* return; I return. I have plunged headlong into the sacred flame when I saw it, and I knew it to be myself as I saw it. I didn't hesitate for one *n*th part of an *n*th part of a second; I plunged headlong into the sacred flame and went right up in a serpentine form into Zion, into my skull. I have returned to tell it. So I can tell you exactly what's going to happen to you. Every being in this world is going to have the identical experience. And so we take the blind, and we take the lame and we take the halt; we take all these things, and we change them and make them conform to our ideal of men and women in this world. Regardless of headlines, regardless of all the things in the world, we do it and remain faithful to our concepts of others as they ought to be seen by themselves and by the world, and they will conform to it. As they conform to it, you, unknown to yourself, you are really building inward. Building inward. And finally, after unnumbered—how long I don't know—but there comes that moment when you least expect it—when these stones through which the shaft came are suddenly split from top to bottom. The temple is split from top to bottom, and you, plunging into the sacred flame, move up in this most marvelous way.

Then we are told: there will come before you a tall, smooth-skinned ___(??). Again, reading that, they said ___(??), for they're tall and majestic creatures. They can't get away from the outer flesh and blood. Hasn't a thing to do with the Ethiopian or any other majestic creature that he is. He is a majestic creature, no question about it, tall and majestic, but that's not the being. You are serpentine; you are seraphim, a being that is a flaming being. Yet you can't quite describe it; human face, yes; human hands, yes; human feet, but the form you can't describe. The best you can do when you come to it, it is serpentine, and it *is* smooth and it *is* tall and it *is* godlike; it is God. So that's the being we become as we move up.

You remain in this world, clothed once more in this little garment, to tell it to everyone who will listen to it, until you leave and take off the garment for the last time. For as you move into Zion, you inherit the kingdom of God. That's the kingdom of God. But the glory of your inheritance cannot be fully realized while still wearing this garment. But the day will come in the not distant future because what is life but three score and ten. And remember David in the story he started to reign at thirty; he reigned for seven and a half years, and then reigned for thirty-three years and made his exit at seventy. You ask yourself, who is this David? Who is this creature that conquered Zion, which is called God's living place? Whenever you see him, you will see him in Zion, for that is where God dwells. And David conquered it for him, and when David conquered it, then he sets the Father free. So everyone who finds David and sees him as his son has been set free. For he, as David, conquered. So he conquers by setting free the blind and the lame and the halt.

May I tell you, you will have an experience before the serpentine motion takes place, where you will anticipate the glory of that state. You will come upon a scene, but it will be preceded by a similar motion in you, a ___(??) motion, and a heavenly chorus will sing out. They will sing out, calling you by your name, "(You) are risen." And then you will see the blind, and the lame and the halt and the withered, and as you walk by everyone will be transformed into the most glorious creature you've ever seen. There will be no blind, no halt, and no withered, and you see them all and everyone will be made perfect. When the very last is made perfect, the chorus will *exult*, calling you again by name, and say, "It is finished!" And then, you will be encouraged to go on doing what you've been doing, tell everything you have seen, ___(??) not to really add up.

But you will do it, and you'll still do it. You may never hear from the unnumbered hundreds whose good news you heard, because only one in ten ever returns to say thank you. So don't expect two; they won't come. One will always say thank you, and the nine will go their way, saying it would have happened anyway. They could always justify the good fortune and never turn back. But one percent will always come back, one of ten, I should say, so ten percent. Ten will come back out of a hundred. You will hear it for hundreds, and they'll take it for granted and go their way. Because they think if they came back and thanked you, they should accompany the thanks with a bill, and you don't need their bill. They don't know you've inherited the kingdom of God. They're afraid to come back because ___(??) attached to their thanks some expression of thanks in the form of a gift, and you don't need their gifts. But they will do it and they'll go their way and the ten percent, only ten out of a hundred, will return. But as they return, it only confirms this wonderful—that you can set free the blind and set free the lame.

And as you do it, years later in my own case, because that happened to me in 1946, and it was in 1960 that this temple of mine was split from top to bottom, and I was moved up in a serpentine form into Zion, on the morning of April 8, 1960. So from 1946 to 1960, yet I went blindly on believing that I could transform people by simply believing in the reality of my imaginal act. And so I believed it. I imagined that you were so and so, convinced myself that it was true, went about my business, and ten percent wrote me letters or saw me in person or called me on the wire to tell me that it worked. The other ninety percent went their way justifying and thought that they had saved a dollar. That's the world. But there was no charge attached to it in the first place. However, that's the picture of the world.

So here, we are told it doesn't make sense—somebody in some strange way has changed the script. The script hasn't changed. They can't find any older manuscript or any other manuscript that doesn't say the same thing. But scholars can't understand it, so they conclude, "One thing for sure of which we are certain, this doesn't make sense." So they're sure. Because you cannot build in a circle and inward at one and the same time, unless, of course, said he, you're performing the most unusual architectural feat of building in, spirally. Well, you are building in spirally, of which you are totally unaware. But the spiral only begins when you're going to conquer a land where there are the blind and the lame. And that blind and the lame, it's Zion, ruled by the Jebusites. It is said it is so impervious of attack, it's so impregnable, you could never attack it. There's the smallest little garrison of the blind and lame to ward off the blows of David.

But David conquered Zion. Then he said, "Whoever would conquer Zion, let him move up this shaft," the only way to do it. They think of a huge big place, that is an enormous city, and down below where the water came that David and his men got under the ground, came down by the water's edge; and in some strange way came up the shaft and conquered it from within. Well, he did, but not as they planned it. Because the Zion that he conquers is his own skull, where, "All that you behold, though it appears without, it is within, in your Imagination, of which this world of mortality is but a shadow." There's nothing on the outside, even though everything tells you that it is. And so at that moment, when everything is screaming how real it is, independent of your perception of it, it is then that you've got to start applying this principle.

And someone who would not listen to you, but you love him. You're going to tell everyone, he will not listen to you; nevertheless, without his consent, you see him, as he would like to see himself. And maybe he will be one of the nine who never return. Because it's going to happen so naturally to him, he will never think that you in any way had any part in the doing. So leave him alone, perfectly all right. But to your own satisfaction, you saw a transformation: the blind is not blind any more. ___(??). And he wasn't lame any more. He didn't come home bringing excuses to his wife that things are bad, competition is horrible, and so he isn't lame any more. He comes home with his head up and it's *marvelous*. And so you heard of it; it doesn't matter, *you* heard it. And so, the lame is no more the lame, and you are conquering. As you conquer all the lame and all the blind in your world, suddenly up you go into Zion.

And may I tell you, I can't tell you the thrill and the joy that comes to the individual who moves up in that serpentine form right into Zion and becomes a member of the hierarchy. He knows in the depth of his soul that if he remains for another ten years or twenty years or whatever interval, ___(??) it's only until the garment for the last time comes off; for he has gone up. But he's hoped that he has told it so that they understood it to the point where they would believe it and practice it, that they too may start the process of building the city, starting, yes, in a circle but also inward at the same time. And so, it is inward; it's all done in silence, and up they go one day when they least expect it.

Now let us go into the Silence.

*   *   *

Q: ___(??) what about the other holy scripts of denominations?
A: What about other books other than the Bible? Well, first of all, the Torah is the first five books of our Bible, Genesis through Deuteronomy. When it comes to the others, I am not qualified to really pass a serious judgment on it.

I firmly believe that God's greatest revelation is given to us in what we call our Bible; I firmly believe it. I am not denying that he reveals himself in other ways at certain times, but I am convinced that what we call the Old and the New Testament are God's greatest revelation to man. And to me the final revelation would be that of a son, as told us in the Book of Hebrews: that "In many and various ways God spoke of old to our fathers by the prophets"—in the Old Testament—"but in these last days he has spoken to us by a Son" (Hebrews 1:1). And that is this fabulous revelation. No one understood it—the great vision of the prophets—until finally it happened. And it didn't happen as people thought it should happen. He didn't come as some conquering hero, enslaving others to set Israel free. Israel is *not* a race or a nation; Israel was the pure in heart. Every person, regardless of nation, regardless of race, regardless of everyone, an Israelite is the pure in heart.

And so he's come to ___(??) that in all these years, eons of time, to produce the pure in heart, where man could really see that it was not independent of his own perception of it, and therefore started to work on himself. And forgive and forgive and forgive. Regardless of what happens, you forgive him, because he's yourself pushed out, and transform him that he himself is set free; for he has conquered. And so when David conquers, he sets the Father free. You look and it's yourself, my Divine Creator and Redeemer, and I know it's myself and then go up. So you are he, the Father, set free by your own conquering as David, for David is humanity, and he has to overcome and overcome and overcome. But as far as the other books . . .

Q: ___(??) in Acts, where Christ was speaking through the Holy Ghost . . .

A: The Book of Acts? The Book of Acts is but an extension of the Book of Luke, written by the same author, and it introduces the truly great character outside of Jesus the Christ; it introduces the truly great character in the New Testament that is Paul. Paul ___(??) and then Paul begins with "the people of the way," for the Christians were called, at the beginning "the people of the way." Well, Christ was made to say, "I am the way." People thought before that it meant an individual. There were only the people of the way. What is the way? This is the way. The way to what? The way to the Father. He said, "I am the way. No man comes unto the Father except by me." So the Acts introduces the people of the way—those who will ___(??) as the way to follow. For fatherhood implies sonship, and so he brings in the picture of the Father and the Son.

So the very end of Acts, he's in chains, that is, in the 26th chapter he's in chains, and he comes before King Agrippa. He said, "Oh King, why should I be here chained as I am on trial for faith in the . . . (tape runs out). (The following is from a borrowed tape.)

Q: ___(??) psychological significance of . . .

A: Well, Mary is the Anglicized form of Maria. Maria is really the great sea, the great water. It can take any form. Water can take any form that you give it. We are told in the 2nd chapter of Luke, "Fear not; for I bring you glad tidings of great a joy to all the people; for unto you is born this day in the city of David a Savior, who is Christ the Lord." The city of David is Zion; Zion is your skull; that's where he is born. "Now this will be a sign unto you; you will find a babe wrapped in swaddling clothes, lying on the floor" (verse 10). And they go and they find exactly what the messenger of the Lord had told them. They found exactly the child, as a *sign*. The churches have completely confused the issue, and they say a little child was born in a normal way of a holy woman who didn't know a man. You are that holy woman, I am that holy woman, and the womb in us is our skull. That is the skull, that's the womb-skull that was in the beginning a tomb.

Out of that womb, *we* are born, but our birth is symbolized in that of a little babe wrapped in swaddling clothes and lying on the floor. The night it happens to you or the day that it happens to you, wise men will be present to witness the event because there *must* be witnesses to the event. In my own case, I had the witnesses, three, but even if I didn't have one, I would still have two—the inward testimony of the Spirit, for I can't forget it, and the outward testimony of scripture, for scripture records it. But I did have in my own mystical vision three who were present to witness the finding of the babe.

So Mary is no more than every child born of woman in this world. I am Mary, you are Mary, every person is Mary, and this birth comes not from the *womb* of woman; it comes from the *skull* of man. As told us in the first chapter of John, "Born not of blood nor of the will of the flesh nor of the will of man, but of God" (verse 13). It comes from above, this birth; it doesn't come from the womb. This body came from the womb, but my experience of the birth from above came from God. So everyone will be born from above, and from above out of your own wonderful skull. That's the actual birth. I mean it literally.

As we told you earlier this night, the Bible in its entirety is the Word of God, even if it goes so far as to completely go beyond the limit of our logic. Who can say yes to the question asked in the Book of Jeremiah, "Can a man bear a child?" And the one who asked the question is the Lord God of hosts. He doesn't wait for the response; he completes it, "Why then do I see every man drawing himself out of himself just like a woman in labor? Why does every face turn pale?" That's the 30th chapter of the Book of Jeremiah (verse 6). So he asks the question. Well, one could not answer yes to the question, "Can a man bear a child?" They'd have to say no. And yet, here is a prophecy that every man in this world is going to bear a child. It's going to be only a symbol of *his own* birth from above. He himself will be born out of his own wonderful skull, and he will be born in the city of David which is Zion. And this is a sign of his birth; for what was born is the Savior, and the Savior is Jehovah. The word Savior is Joshua, and Joshua is Jehovah, is Jesus. Everyone who is born that way is Jesus the Savior.

And so he'll find what?—the symbol of his birth. A symbol of his birth? A babe wrapped in swaddling clothes lying on the floor. Who said lying in a manger? I am giving you the actual fact: lying on the floor. But the churches over the centuries have dressed it up to give reason to it. You don't give reason to it; it's lying on the floor.

Good night.

INCUBATE THE DREAM

May 10, 1963

I promise you if you apply it in the immediate present, you'll see the results. It's based upon dreams. The Bible recognizes only one source of dreams and that source is God. But today, in 1963, our doctors, our psychiatrists ___(??), they know that the source of a dream is Imagination and so they will say, no, it's not God, it's one's Imagination. But they do not know that the word God and Imagination in the scriptures are the same. The word potter is Imagination. The word potter is God. And so we all agree there's only one source of dream and that source is God. But if it helps to change the name, I'm all for it, and to say it is human imagining, well, I'm all for that. By identifying God with human Imagination, we close the gap between God and man, and then we start from there. The Bible is simply filled with the secret of dreaming, and tells us that God speaks to man through the medium of a dream and reveals himself to man in vision.

Now, there are intentional dreams, and there are unintentional dreams. Most of us have the unintentional dreams. We go to sleep and we dream. Many of us do not remember the dream. The Bible tells us every dream has its own significance, that God instructs man through the medium of dream. Now the dream could be in a simple manner, told in very plain language that needs no interpretation. But quite often the dream comes in the form of symbolism, symbolic, and then it needs the real interpreter of the dream. The first grand interpreter of the dream in the Bible was Joseph. He rose from a slave to the second in command of the whole land of Egypt through the ability to interpret dream. So he took the dreams of Pharaoh, and because he gave them the true interpretation, he rose right under power of Pharaoh. It was through his dream that he was sold into slavery because of the jealousy of his brothers, for he saw the sun and moon and eleven stars bow before him. The father rebuked him and said to him, "You mean that I and your mother and your brothers will bow before you?" He saw his sheaf rise to its full height, and all the other sheaves bow before this sheaf. And so you know the story, I think you are all familiar with the story of Joseph, how he was sold into slavery because he was the dreamer. "Behold this dreamer cometh." He not only had the dreams but he could interpret the dream.

But here we find in the Bible not only these unintentional dreams, for we didn't plan to have them. And God prophesied through the medium of dream the seven years of abundance and the seven years of starvation, of famine, and it came just as he said it would happen. But there is one dream that was intentionally ___(??) and that we read in the 1st Book of Kings, the 3rd chapter, and then the same kind of a dream in the first chapter of the 2nd Book of Chronicles. And this is the dream that was induced by Solomon. So Solomon went up to the high hill, called Gideon. It was a holy place. For kings would speak in synagogue and the temple or some holy spot as they considered it, in the hope that they would in some strange way induce some communication between God and themselves. So Solomon went up for the purpose of inducing a dream where God would reveal himself to him. And so God appeared and God said to him, "Ask of me what you want." He asked for an understanding mind that he may rule his people, more numerous than the dust of the earth. And then, said he, and this is his prayer, "O Lord God, thy promise to David my father fulfill this day" (2 Chronicles 1:9). That was what he wanted above all things in this world: Thy promise to David my father, let it now, this very moment, let it be fulfilled now. And then God said to him, "Because you did not ask for a long life and riches and the life of your enemies, I will grant you all these plus."

Now the promise that God made to David was to bring forth from David a son who will be God's son, and that God will be his father. The son to be brought forth from David would come after David dies. "When your days are fulfilled and you lie down with your fathers, I will raise up after you your son, who will come forth from your body. I will be his father, and he shall be my son" (2 Samuel 7:12). So Solomon is asking for the fulfillment of this promise. When you read it on the surface, Solomon seems to be his son. No, Solomon is a state of consciousness. All of these characters are states of consciousness, and you reach a certain state when you believe God's revelation. Is it true that when David dies that out of David's body, a dead body, will come a son that will be God's son and God his father? If that is true, Lord, this is my prayer, "O Lord, thy promise to David my father . . ." David is my father? Yes. I'm a man; you're a man; David is humanity. So here we are, the whole vast world of mankind, that's David.

And you and I don't realize that we are dead. We have no concept that this is death. To us, when we say good-bye to a friend in the event we *call* death, and that's death, but this is life. Yet, this is the world of death as spoken of in the Bible. So here is David, he's dead—everyone walking the earth, the sleep is so profound, it is likened unto death. And now if the promise made to this state called death is true, fulfill it now, O Lord; bring forth from this state of death—for I am one—bring forth from me that which will be your son. Bring it out, just as you promised, from David. Bring it out and be the father of that son and let that which comes forth from me be the son of you. And so that was his promise.

Now, how did he do it? He does it just as you would do it to bring about a business success, just as you would do to bring about a marriage, anything in this world but anything. It's the same thing. For this is God's promise, the intentional dream can be done just as the unintentional dream he uses to reveal to us his secret.

Now, in this book, he makes this statement; the dream was doubled. Joseph interpreted the dream of Pharaoh, and he said to Pharaoh, "The doubling of your dream, Pharaoh, means this, that the thing is fixed by God, and God will soon bring it to pass" (Genesis 41:32). If the dream is doubled, then it's fixed and no one's going to change it if the dream is doubled. So he had a dream, he stood on the side of the Nile and out of the Nile came seven fat cows, fat and sleek. And then out of the same stream, the great Nile, came seven emaciated, thin, awful-looking creatures, never seen in the land of Egypt. They ate up the seven fat cows, and yet, you could not see after they devoured the seven fat cows that they in any way increased in weight. They were still emaciated, all. Then came one stalk and on that stalk came these seven ears; then came another seven, and they were horrible. The first seven were fat and lovely and the thin ones ate up the fat ones. And eating up all the fat ones, they had no increase in weight. And so he interpreted that. Then in this interpretation, which is the 41st chapter of Genesis, he makes the statement, When the dream is doubled—for he had a second dream using the same symbolism—whenever the dream is doubled then God has fixed that thing—there'll be no altering, you can't change it—and *soon* it will come to pass, if the dream is doubled.

Well now, let me share with you my doubled dream. I've told it before, and maybe everyone present heard it. Well, this is the technique by which you can induce a dream and make it something that is intentional. It was a year ago last Christmas, when I found myself in a mansion. There were three generations present but one invisible. The invisible one dominated the visible state. He was called grandfather. They were telling the story of grandfather: The grandfather would stand on a vacant lot and grandfather would say, "I remember when this was a vacant lot," and then he would paint a word picture of this area so *vividly* that people saw it as something objective before their mind's eye. He painted a word picture of his desire for that lot, and they all saw it.

I woke; the thing was so vivid, it was so startling. It was a little after three in the morning when I awoke; I went to my living room, and I wrote it out on a nice long yellow page in detail, just as it was shown to me in the vision. I went back to bed, I thought it quite early in the morning, and I re-dreamed the dream. This is now the double dream. It's fixed; you can't change it. I re-dreamed it with a slight alteration. Instead of hearing them tell the story of grandfather, I was grandfather. I had so completely absorbed the message of grandfather that then I told them, "While standing on a vacant lot, I remember when this was a vacant lot." Then I would paint a word picture of my desire for that lot, and paint it so vividly they all saw it. And that was God's secret to me. "Go tell it to the world."

In the end, the end is where we begin. You always begin in the end. So he goes to the end, God's final promise: I will now bring forth from your body, after you're dead, for "When your days are fulfilled and you lie down with your fathers, I will raise up after you a son that will come forth from your body. I will be his father and he shall be my son." Now, "O Lord God, thy promise made to David my father be now fulfilled"; that was his request. Well, if that is his request, what would he do?

For God revealed to me what I should do if I wanted a home. I have no means for buying the home. He doesn't ask me about means. I don't have the qualifications for entering that neighborhood. He doesn't ask for that. I don't have this. He doesn't ask me that. He only tells me what to do. Well, what do I do? You stand on the vacant lot, and you see it as you would see it were it true, that it fulfilled your dream of your future. But it must be *now*. And so I go into the end, and dwelling in the end, I see it as I would see it were it true. And living in that state—this is now the intentional dream—and I call it incubation dream; I incubate it. You stand on the empty lot, empty of anything, without any qualification in the world, and standing in it, you paint your word picture mentally; and you see it come into being to your own satisfaction. You did it. That's all that God told me to do, and then he repeated it.

So in this 32nd verse of the 41st chapter of Genesis, he tells you: Whenever the dream is doubled, if it is ever doubled, the thing God has fixed and will shortly bring it to pass, if it's doubled. Well, that night it was doubled. I woke a little after three, wrote it out in detail, went back to bed, and re-dreamed the dream—here's the double dream. But I so completely absorbed the message that *I* am telling it now. Everyone who will listen to me, I'm telling them. You know what you want? You really know what you want in this world, and you don't have it; therefore, it is empty, isn't it? It doesn't exist. Well, this is what I'd do were I you. So the lot is empty, the space is vacant. Stand right now. You aren't married, are you? You know you're not happily married? All right, if you were, would the world see you in that light? Yes. Well now, this is spaceless because you are not in that way. Well now, *be* in that way. Wear the ring. See the faces of your friends; that is, an expression on your friends' faces, see them all seeing you as they would see you were it true, and lose yourself in that state. That's the end. The end is where we start from. Now, then you are incubating the dream. You actually, I would say, make it alive, and make it real, for this cannot fail.

I'm telling you from an experience. My dream that night was the double-dream. ___(??) and if the dream is ever doubled, God has fixed it; it's part of the eternal law, and you can't change it. So I'm sharing with you his eternal law: it's the *end*. So I go to the end of anything in this world, I don't care what it is, and then see the fulfillment of the dream because that's the end. The end is all fulfillment. I open my eyes and I come back to a seeming empty lot, but to me it isn't empty; I saw the end. Having seen the end, I am sustained by the end, and I walk through all the things of the world sustained by the end. I saw it, I am still seeing it, I continue to see it until that which I am seeing and living in is perfectly realized in the world. So that's the story of the dream.

But we ask for the most fantastic dream. As many of you have said to me, "Neville, I would give anything in this world"—and you should, you should give everything in the world, not anything, but everything—"for the fulfillment of God's promise to man." When you die—and this is death—and you go into it, I will raise up from you, your dead body, my son. He'll come forward from your body, but he's *my* son; I'll be his father. Can you conceive of anything that the wisest man that ever lived would want more than that? Well, Solomon was called the wisest of all men. That was his outstanding request. And when he came before God and God said, "Ask of me what you will, anything" and that was his request, "O Lord God, O Jehovah Elohim, thy promise to David my father be now fulfilled"; that's what I want. It's not a man called Solomon, it's the state of consciousness that man reaches when he can really want that more than anything in the world. When he wants that more than anything in the world, he's Solomon. He's at that point, that state of awareness, where he is concerned in the depths of his soul asking, instead of asking for an extension of life in this world of death. He didn't ask for long life. He didn't ask for riches. He didn't ask for the life of his enemies. All these things were given him, but he didn't ask for them. He asked for the one consuming desire of his heart, and that was the fulfillment of God's promise to David his father.

And humanity is David; this is the Son of God. And out of this son he brings a *real* Son, the Spirit that is one with the Father. For God is Spirit and those who worship him worship in Spirit and in truth. So he brings out of this decaying, dying body that which cannot die, the immortal you. He brings it out and it's you and you're one with God. Then you see the symbol of the child, proving that he gave you himself, because he takes the whole vast world of humanity and puts it into one single Son and symbolizes the whole humanity in a single Son.

But to make this practical, if you haven't that longing of the heart—I know in this audience there are a few of you who said to me, "In your prayers remember me in this hope: I want that more than anything in this world"—and so there are in this audience tonight a few who have asked that of me, but the majority would like more of the comforts of this world. And it's perfectly all right. No matter what it is, it is the same technique. "Neville, go and tell them to go to the end." Go to the very end. What would be the end if you were *now* the man that you want to be, now the woman that you want to be? How would you see the world? That's the end. Well now, see it just as you would see it were it true.

And that is intentional dreaming. I call it, in one of my books, "thinking *from* the end instead of thinking *of* the end." When I think *from* the end, I'm in it, and the whole vast world mirrors that end. If I'm thinking *of* it, where *am* I when I think of it? For where I am is what I'm going to resurrect, what I'm realizing. So the state called Solomon puts himself in the end, where God did grant to him the promise that he made to his father David. So everyone gets into the state called Solomon, and there he brings out God's promise.

Somewhere along the line, everyone has to enter that state. You might just as well enter that state tonight because somewhere, "You see yonder hills, the sesamum was sesamum, the corn was corn, the silence and the darkness knew; so is a man's fate born." You mean my fate is born in that manner? Yes. And the silence and the darkness knew it? Yes. Well now, I'll take the silence and the darkness and manipulate them—no one knows it. And I will go like Solomon and stand in the silence and the darkness, and I will ask in the depths of my soul to have granted to me the promise he made to my father David. For maturity comes to the individual when that individual becomes his own father's father. Here is David, the whole vast world of man, and then suddenly out of him comes something that is God's son. And God's son turns because he's one with his father, and "What think ye of the Christ? Whose son is he?" They not knowing said, "Why, David, son of David." "Why then does David in spirit call him Lord?" Why did he call him "my Father"? "If he calls him my father, how can he be David's son? And no one asked him any other questions" (Matthew 22:42). He who is David's son becomes David's father. That's when maturity comes to man.

So tonight, if I could aid you in building that picture, just imagine you could tell me tomorrow that it happened to you, just imagine. Well, that's the end. You could tell me *after* the event, couldn't you? You can't tell me before the event; that's only a hope. So he's asking, Grant to me this night, now, the promise you made to my father David. Do it now. Well now, if it happened to you tonight, when we meet next Tuesday, or in the interval, or beyond ___(??), wouldn't the first thing you would tell me would be it happened to you? Wouldn't you tell me you saw him and he called you "Adonay"; he called you "my Father, my Lord, the Rock of my salvation"? You couldn't *wait* to tell me! You wouldn't wait 'til Tuesday, you'd call me tomorrow on the phone ___(??). You'd seek an audience right away. Whether I had a thousand people to see or not, you couldn't restrain yourself. Well now, what would the feeling be like were it true? Well then, do that.

That's exactly what Solomon, the state called Solomon, did. In other words, it was intentional dreaming, not unintentional. In the unintentional dream he speaks to me every night. We're all past masters at misinterpreting the dream if it is symbolical. If it is a simple direct statement, like when I was in the army and I sought my honorable discharge, that was a direct statement, no confusion. The voice spoke to me in plain, plain language that no one had to interpret for me: "That which I have done, I have done. Do nothing." And then he added to that by showing me my discharge papers, where the hand wrote "approved" when formerly, only a matter of hours before, he had written "disapproved." So here, on my application for a discharge, the colonel wrote "disapproved." That night, in a simple direct message—no need of any interpretation—the same application came before my eyes, at four in the morning, and a hand, from here down, scratched out the word *disapproved*, and it wrote in *approved*. Well then, to make it very simple and very clear, the voice spoke to me and the voice said to me, "That which I have done I have done. Do nothing." I woke; it's four; I did nothing. And the very person who had disapproved the application was the one who approved it nine days later. That's *direct* communication. That's simple.

But, when it comes now, say, to the little pig, when suddenly, I find myself in a huge big area where all the plants are being displayed and it's closing time and I see a little pig. Being merciful at the moment, I took the little pig and tried to give it some food and some protection. So I did the best I could from all the leaves and the bushes and the things around, all the flowers. I thought at least if it didn't want it as food, if it got hungry enough it would eat it. And so, I took flowers and took leaves and put the little pig on a table maybe four, five feet tall. Then the scene changed, and I am in a huge big supermarket. Here in the supermarket with everything displayed, I look down and here's the pig. He's not a little runt where I found him a moment before; he is now a tall *rangy* pig, very rangy and very tall. In other words, he had grown in the interval, but he had not been well fed. I knew he should have been better fed, and so I started getting a meal—I started fixing meal. My brother Victor said to me, "What are you doing?" I told him, "I'm going to feed my pig." And so he took some lovely thick white gravy-like and added it to my meal and I began to mix it because I thought that would give him substance, far better than plain meal and water.

Then I sent my daughter over there to get me some crackers. She said, "What would I use for money, Daddy?" I said, "This all belongs to us. You don't need money here, everything is ours, just go and take it." So there's a huge big pyramid, and she took from the base of the pyramid a package of crackers and dislodged the balance and the whole thing fell, revealing a single little candle about four or five inches tall, and the candle was lit. I said to her, "That's my candle. It must never again in eternity be covered. Never must that ever be covered again; it's now lit and it'll be lit forever." The words of Job and the words of Proverbs came rushing through my brain: "When his candle shines upon my head, by his light I walk through darkness" (Job 29:3; Proverbs 20:27). So here, it was lit. But I didn't know the symbolism. Here's the pig.

So God spoke to me that night, not directly as he did when I was in the army—that was no symbol in the army. It completely comforted me. I didn't ask anyone to do anything in the interval of nine days. I knew I was out. But this is all symbolism. And what is this little pig, for he dominated the entire picture? Here's a little pig, at the end of the closing of the day. I found him, cushioned him, and put flowers, leaves, all kinds of things around him. And then it changed from the interior and the display of plant life to a huge supermarket, and here is the pig, but now he's a tall rangy fella. Without the aid of the language of symbolism, I would have been lost, because until that moment—unless I had completely forgotten it—I never associated Christ with a pig. A lamb, yes. I've always thought of a little lamb. She is the sacrificial lamb, the Passover lamb. I had heard of other things, but never . . . the fish, yes. You can take an acrostic and spell the word Christ out and it comes to fish. And so, yes that, but never a pig. And so here in the language of symbolism, all over the world, it's a universal language, in every land in the world the little pig has always been the symbol of the Savior and the Redeemer of the world.

Well, I found him. I found him this little tiny pig, when I first discovered the creativity of my Imagination. So I imagined a certain state, lost myself in it, and in time it became a fact. It took all the things of the world and molded them to produce what I was imagining. So I found him. But in the interval between discovering that Christ was my own wonderful human Imagination and that moment in time, I had neglected to properly feed him. I had seen so many opportunities in the world to do a loving thing *mentally*, not physically. There's no need to go to the bank and write a check to take care of someone who is distressed. He isn't asking for that. He asked me to simply use my Imagination. And I had seen the need and didn't do it, so I wasn't *feeding* the pig properly.

He told me exactly what to do: Now that you have me, feed my sheep. These are all my sheep. You have found me? "Yes we know. I have found you, Lord." Well, feed my lambs. "You know I feed your lambs." "Lovest thou me, Peter? Yes, Lord. Well then, feed my sheep. You *know* I lovest thou, Lord." And three times, he comes back because he *thinks* he loves him. Because we still, conditioned as we are, we are thinking of some other external Christ. Raised as I was raised in the Christian faith, it was the most difficult thing in the world to stop thinking of an external Christ, something that came on the outside that belonged to the pages of history. I *found him* in myself as my own wonderful human Imagination, but because I was conditioned as I was conditioned, raised in the environment in which I was raised, automatically the mind jumps back to an historical Christ, not the *living* Christ that walks with us as our own wonderful human Imagination.

So in the interval of discovery of Christ and the interval thereafter, so many opportunities I missed. So he was tall and rangy. He lived all right, for Christ is the living Christ, but he wasn't fat enough; he wasn't well fed enough. I should have in that interval exercised my Imagination lovingly unnumbered times. Every time I did it, I was feeding him; and when I didn't do it, I neglected him. He was hungry, and I gave him nothing. He needed shelter, and I gave him nothing. He needed something, some comfort; I gave him nothing. And yet, every moment of time was an opportunity to feed him and make him a lovely, big wonderful fatted pig.

Now I know the very word offends people, to say that Christ is symbolized as a pig. But that is universal—all over the world the pig has always symbolized the Savior of the world. Here, we have hundreds of millions of people in this world today who will not eat the pig. That's all a symbol: they will have no part of Christ, so they will not touch the pig, they will not touch the pork. There are 400 million Mohammedans who will not touch the pig—it's the unclean animal. They will have nothing to do with the concept of Christ. And here is the Savior of the world; they will not touch it.

And yet it's not the pig. My old friend, Abdullah, he was born in Ethiopia. He was born of the black race, of the Hebrew faith. He was a strict vegetarian for other reasons because that is not part of the Hebraic faith. But he never in his life touched pork, never, not in any form. One night, God spoke to him, as he spoke to me, and he said to him, "If you will not eat the food that *they* place before you, why do you expect *them* to eat the food *you* place before them?" He was teaching. He would go to a place, and they would prepare special physical food, knowing he did not take pork. So they would go out of their way to prepare things that they thought he, a strict orthodox Jew plus a vegetarian, would eat. He had been a strict vegetarian for forty-odd years. Then, after the vision, he was invited to a banquet where he was the honored guest. And what do you think they served that night? They did it not to hurt him, not as a jest; they simply did it and thought it the most marvelous thing in the world. And he grew up a strict vegetarian and had never in his life eaten pork.

When they brought on this fabulous table and the honored guest was led into this dining room, here was a lovely little suckling pig, with a sweet potato in its mouth, beautifully roasted. He broke his diet on pork. He had not in forty-odd years eaten any kind of meat, but *never* pork. And after the vision of God begins, "If you will not eat their food, why do you expect them to eat yours?" So he was teaching this principle, as he understood it through revelation, yet he was restraining himself. You see now why a savior comes into the world and he's called a glutton; he's called a winebibber, a drunkard; he has no taboo. He eats whatever man puts before him because if he eats what man will give him and serve, they will then take his food. And so in the Book of Acts, Peter said, "I cannot eat meat from unclean things." Then comes the vision and a sheet descends from heaven; on it was *all manner* of food, and the voice out of the depths of his soul speaks, "That which I have cleansed I have cleansed . . . slay and eat." Nothing is unclean in all my holy mountain, eat it. If you eat everything—it's all mine, I made it all—well, then, you will be able to tell my story; and they will eat the food you will give them if you in turn eat the food they are capable of giving you. And so that was the story (Acts 10:14).

And so, when I met Ab, I was a strict vegetarian and had been for seven years. When I saw the dinner he first prepared and invited me to sit with him, I wouldn't sit. I wouldn't touch it. I had a little of this, a little that on the side. He started off with three or four huge big shots of Rye, and then this enormous amount of food, which he washed down with many, many bottles of Porter, a good strong—if you don't know Porter, it's strong as beer.

But many bottles would wash it down. And after all this Rye and all this Porter, he then had a huge big, enormous helping of ice cream. I said, "Ab, what are you doing to your stomach?" He said, "Oh, you couldn't eat it." I said why? "Because you have ___(??). It would poison you. Can't poison, Ab." And so, it didn't poison Ab. Last time I saw Ab, he was well over a hundred years old. I'm told he went back to his Ethiopia to lay the garment down that he picked up in Ethiopia a hundred years before. So here was his story.

So I tell you, he speaks to us through the medium of a dream, the medium of a vision. He has shown me so vividly by repeating the vision in one night that if I go to the end, and tell you to go to the end of anything and paint the end as it would be seen by the world were it true. You want to be, you name it, a successful businessman? You really want to be? A great artist? You really want to be? Would the world see you were you such a great artist? Would the world know of you if you were a great success in your chosen field? Go to the end and let the whole vast world see it, or that section of the world that would see it were it true. Don't quiver; go to the end. Dwell in the end and *see* the end. Then, as you see it, feel the thrill that is yours because it's true. Paint it as Grandfather did. When you open your eyes, you're back here seemingly, and the lot is still vacant. You forget it. You prepared the end, and the end is where we start from, "In my end is my beginning." And so I go to the end and start in the end. Then in a way that I do not know and need not consciously devise, I move across a bridge of incidents, a series of events that leads from where I am now at this moment to the fulfillment of that end that I had imagined and made real in my world. So this is the story of the dream.

So the whole thing begins with a dream. He tells us in the very second chapter of the Book of Genesis, and "he caused a profound sleep to fall upon the man, and he slept" (verse 21). There is no statement in the entire Bible, save the very end of the Bible, "He is the first fruits of those who slept" (Revelation 1:5). All through the Bible the call is, "Awake, O Lord, and rise from the dead. Why sleepest thou, O Lord? Awake" (Psalm 44:23). God is sound asleep in man dreaming all these things in the world, but the sleep is so deep it is likened unto death. And then comes the use of this same technique by which I dreamed all the unlovely things to dream the lovely things. But the wisest of all, he remembered, or he heard of, a promise that God made to David. And when he came into the presence of God, and God said, "Ask what you want of me," he didn't ask for the things that man could ask—long life, riches, the life of my enemies—"O Lord God, thy promise to David my father be now fulfilled." Can you imagine having that clarity of thought in the presence of God to ask for that? Well, that's the Spirit.

So how would the world look to you? Well, forget it, because the world to me is the same world, but I am not the same to myself. So you could not keep it to yourself, any more than I can. I've shared it with every person that I met, so you would share it too. So with whom would you share it tomorrow if it happened tonight? Well, then, tonight, in your mind's eye let that be your request. If it doesn't happen tonight, at least you have *incubated* the dream. You've accepted it. You heard it and heard it to the point where you're willing to ask for it more than anything else in the world. And so you incubate the dream. And because all visions have their own appointed hour, and they're all ripening and they'll all flower; this, the dream, it will ripen and it will flower. And when you least expect it—it always comes like a thief in the night, suddenly—and then you are born from above and David stands before you; the temple is split in two, and you're never the same. You enter into heaven.

And the greatest in this world was called John the Baptist. "No one born of woman is greater than John, but I tell you, the least in the kingdom is greater than John" (Matthew 11:11). So the first one in, and everyone in thereafter, is greater than the greatest who walks the face of the earth. There are those today—and you don't condemn them if that's their request, leave it just as it is—they will have unnumbered fortunes, but they want more. That's their security. But your security is in God and his truth. You'll know the truth and only the truth can set you free, nothing else. You aren't free because of anything you own in this world, it's only what you know of God and his truth. And so he speaks to me, speaks to you. Every dream is God's communication within the dreamer, and the dreamer is God. For the dreaming one is imagining and imagining is God in action. That's the only source; but the only source of all dreams, all visions, happens to be God, and God is your own wonderful human Imagination.

So this whole wonderful play has been laid out, and no one's going to change it, but no one. Now, don't be disturbed no matter what headlines you see tomorrow or in the future. God is still in control of the entire play. Everything is going to come out as he planned it. His only purpose is to bring out of David, after he dies, a son who is God's son; and the one he's going to bring out is you. He brings *you* out of the pit, part of the great structure of humanity. And then he summarizes the whole vast world of humanity in a single youth, and his name is David. He doesn't have to tell you, you know it; he knows it; and you both know it, and he calls you Father. Just imagine the thrill when every person that is now fighting in this world, all these racial conflicts, just imagine that *every* person in the world is destined to be the Father of David, but everyone. Because he has *one* Father, *one* Son, we're all one.

What a play! The most glorious play in the world! Everything is a play, and God is playing all the parts. The day will come every being that is now walking the face of this earth, I will know that I am not just *like* him, *I am* he. And you know the same thing. We look together—there are billions of us—and all will only see one Son, and all will know it is "my Son." The most intimate relationship in the world, my Son, and he's God's Son; therefore, I know who I am. If my Son is God's Son, I need not ask anyone in this world, "Who am I?" He asks the question, "Who do people say that I am?" They answered, "Some say you are John the Baptist come again, some say Elijah, some say Jeremiah, others say one of the prophets of old." "But who do *you* say that I am?" "Thou art the Christ, the Son of the living God." "Flesh and blood could not have told you this, but my Father who is in heaven he has revealed it unto you" (Matthew 16:13).

No man in the world can tell it. It takes the Son to tell you, for the Son calls you Father. So, "What think ye of the Christ? Whose Son is he?" "The son of David." "Then why did David call him, Father?" And so, what think ye of the Christ? Well, you ask the question, and they bring all kinds of answers. But he does not respond to these answers. "But whom say *ye* that I am?" "Thou art the Christ, the Son of the living God." And then he knows, and that Christ is the Father of David. That Christ says to all, "When you see me you see the Father. Don't ask to see the Father, for when you see me you see the Father." Father of what? Well, the only Father; there's only one Son, David. And so, that is the story of the Dreamer.

Tonight you can dream, intentionally, as I did to get out of an imprisoned state. Took me nine days. I did nothing after my intentional dream the first time. That's exactly what I did. While wearing some sweaty old army fatigues, I simply imagined that I was living in my own lovely bedroom, and it had an odor so *unlike* the barracks of the army. So I reveled in the change of odor, the change of fragrance, and then I saw what I would see, and could only see, were I there. I saw nothing that I would see were I still in the barracks; I saw everything I would see were I at home. The actual distance was over 2,000 miles apart, 1500 miles from it. And there I reveled in all these things. And then, I got into my imaginary bed in my New York apartment and slept. And then it happened. That was an *intentional* dream, a controlled waking dream. Then, nine days later, I was on the way to fulfill that state. And because in those days we were all shunted off the place to give right of way to more important traffic, it took me three days to make the trip. ___(??) three weeks, I was on my way. That's all that matters. There I was, honorably discharged, a civilian once more, by the simple technique that God taught me and I'm teaching to you.

And now, *don't* do what I did, for he reminded me of my neglect when he once more showed me the pig. That was a double dream, all in one. For in Pharaoh's dream: seven cows, seven lean cows, the lean cows ate up the seven fat cows; seven ears of corn, seven lean horrible ears, and the seven horrible ears ate up the seven fat ears. One dream repeated, in my case, a little pig. And then in the same dream, the same pig grown now, but skinny, and he should not have been. That's how God showed me what I did in the interval between the revelation of Christ and my neglect of Christ. So don't you neglect him! Every moment of time is an opportunity to feed him, and you're always feeding Christ every time you use your Imagination lovingly on behalf of another.

Now let us go and feed him.

* * *

Q: (inaudible)

A: My dear, I could not do justice to that . . .

Q: ___(??) an experience I had recently which approximates your army experience and I ask this question searchingly. Your presence in the army, was that a function of somebody else's imaginal act, whereby you became the reactor? Or was it an imaginal act that slipped into your sleep in an unguarded moment? Certainly it was not a voluntary imaginal act that you be in the army, was it?

A: No, it was not a voluntary act, I assure you. But I was of the country. I am part of America, and as an American, I'm subject to the laws of our land. And so when they sent me a notice stating, I was then not a citizen, but they gave you a little notice where as a foreigner, would you object to serving in the armed forces of the United States Army? Well, I wrote right back and immediately said no. Then, right after that, I was called within a week and right away, they said, "You are A1 classified." All right, ___(??) I was A1. I didn't want to be a 4F to get out of the army. So I was A1, and then in the immediate present with all the other foreigners, I was drafted.

Q: ___(??) was that somebody else's imaginal act that . . .

A: I was part of the system. As they said, "Tell me, do you pay taxes?" and he said, "Give me a coin. Whose superscription is this?" They said, "Caesar's." He said, "All right, then render unto Caesar the things that are Caesar's." I'm in the world of Caesar, and Caesar said we are at war and we need manpower. I was an American; therefore, as an American I must be subject to the laws of the country, whatever this administration dictates, the policy dictates. But within the framework of the dictate of policy of the country—I wouldn't violate it—I still exercised God's freedom. And so, they did not think it strange when they had a change of heart.

First of all, my request was within the laws of the land. I was over thirty-eight, so I requested my discharge based upon what the law allowed. It was *disallowed*, even though I was within the rights based upon law, because I was over thirty-eight when I made my application. Then, anyone over thirty-eight could apply. It rested with his commanding officer whether he would be allowed that application or not. Mine disallowed it. But that was his privilege and his right. But I also had a right; and within my heart, I did what God told me to do, "Go to the end." I slept in my home in New York City, 2,000 miles away, and then in nine days, he had a change of heart. And he thought he initiated that feeling toward a man called Neville Goddard. Well, I wouldn't disillusion him.

I know what I did, and I know what happened, how it worked. And it works that way. ___(??) run away from the army. This is a country; it's organized, and so if the law is all able-bodied men must serve, well then, let them serve, but within the framework of that law. But it's a natural thing if a man exercises his freedom. And then your commanding officer will say to you, "I don't think I want you here. You disturb me." And so you disturb him to the point where he wants to get you out, so he gets you out. He's only fulfilling what *you* want. Happens all the time.

My mother used to "let" my father do these lovely things for her. My wife does the same thing. I learned a wonderful lesson from her. When she wants—of course, I do all the dishes anyway, but even before I started doing them, she would say to me, "You know, I'm going to *let* you wash the dishes tonight." How can you say no if she's going to *let* you do it? "I'm going to *let* you make the bed." "I'm going to let you sweep the floor." Well, she's going to let you do it. Well, you can't say no. But if she said to you, "You will sweep the floor tonight." Well, you aren't going to sweep it. So she knew exactly how to let me do things that she didn't want to do herself. So she let me do all the things, and today it's become a habit.

Good night.

THE SIX-POINTED STAR

May 14, 1963

A man's true environment is in his Imagination. The thing to do with a man is to get the true story *that* reveals to man into man's Imagination that he may be guided by it. A man is overwhelmed by that figure in his Imagination. And I firmly believe that the Bible reveals that God became man to get into us the true picture as revealed through the prophets. For man's entire life is determined by that figure, that dominant figure, that he holds in his Imagination. He believes himself to be this, that or the other, and it's going to influence his every action in the world. He can think that he's wanted or unwanted, wise or unwise. No matter what he thinks, that dominant figure will influence everything that he does. For man's *true* environment is really in his Imagination.

Now, an event can only be made known as it is borne witness to, as it is proclaimed, as the story is told. So tonight, I hope to be able to tell you the story, and I bear witness to it because I have experienced it. The Bible begins with God and ends with God. But man has not been told the true story. The Bible begins with the words, "In the beginning God created the heavens and the earth," and it ends, in the very last part of the Book of Revelation, it ends, "Come, Lord Jesus." The very last verse is like signing off a letter, for I would say to you having written a lovely letter to you, "Blessings upon you and yours." The last verse of that twenty-second chapter reads, "And the grace of the Lord Jesus upon you." There are many translations, "upon all the same," but the best manuscripts omit the word "all the same" and other manuscripts omit the word *all*. So the best manuscript has "And the grace of the Lord Jesus upon *you*." It's addressed to you personally.

But the verse before that, it is the very last word, "Come, Lord Jesus." It begins with God, and it ends with God. But man cannot believe that God became man that man may become God. It's the most difficult thing for man to accept. And because you've been taught to believe that Christ Jesus is something outside of yourself, you rebel against it. The whole vast world, those that call themselves Christians, and there are 900 million Christians, they believe that Jesus Christ is something other than themselves. They really believe it. They make little statues, all kinds of paintings to a being that they call Christ Jesus. They cannot believe the words of Paul, "Jesus Christ is *in* you." "Do you not know that Jesus Christ is in you?—unless of course you fail to meet the test" (2 Corinthians 13:5). He invites us to put him to the test—for all things are possible to *him*—inviting them to put him to the test. They can't believe that the being in the mirror, seeing something that does not fit their concept of Jesus Christ, they cannot believe that Jesus Christ is in them. So they rebel.

Now, this is the path. You follow this closely. It begins with God; it ends with God. In between, there is a drama, a horrible tragedy, but a *frightful* tragedy, that is essential to awaken us and make us sons. Can't do it without the tragedy. So after the statement, "God," God makes a selection and he chooses Israel: "Israel is my choice." And you think of a race of people. Israel is *not* a race of people; Israel means "the pure in heart." By pure in heart, it doesn't really mean that you are namby-pamby in this world. It means that you are incapable of deceit. You would die, you'd be cut up into pieces, rather than deceive another for personal gain. That's Israel. So when he finds an Israelite, he said, "I have found a man after my own heart." It has to be the heart of God, the pure in heart, for only the pure in heart can see God. So after "God," the passages of old, he now has put his model, and the model is Israel. Nothing but Israel can be salvaged from this entire play, the pure in heart.

So he said of Nathaniel when he saw Nathaniel, "Behold, an Israelite indeed in whom there is no guile" but none whatsoever. That's the first chapter of the gospel of John, when he sees Nathaniel, a pure Israelite in whom there is no guile. So the next is Israel. Then the next is the play, the stage, the battleground, and that's called the Holy Land. The Holy Land is not in the Near East, where today modern Israel is established; no, the Holy Land is your mind—that's the Holy Land. The whole battle, the whole drama, takes place in the mind of man. That's the Holy Land of God, and on that battleground, he's going to bring out Israel. So here we first find Israel, then we find the Holy Land.

Then after that, God reveals a law. It's called the Torah. The Torah is a law to lead man in exile, where he passes through this barren land of Egypt; and yet with the use of the Torah, with the use of this *wonderful* law, man can cushion the blows. For there are blows and they are coming, and you can't stop the blows. But you can cushion them through the wise use of God's law. God's law is conditional. It is all mental, but man did not know it was mental. He thought it was an external behavior, that if I would attend school, do all the things on the outside, that this in some way would comfort God or protect me in his presence. And so man still today in 1963 observes the outer actions in his temples, believing *that* is keeping the law of God.

But the law of God was explained to us in the Sermon on the Mount, that when you do something physically, yet mentally it's in conflict with what you're doing physically, it's what you did mentally. Listen to the words, "Any man who looks on a woman lustfully has already committed the act of adultery." Now he didn't commit it. He might have restrained the impulse because he was afraid of the consequences of his act, but that does not excuse him from the act. To look upon a woman with lust is to have committed the act.

Now, in the Bible, in the Old Testament, we are told one should not commit adultery. Man thinks adultery is an act, a physical act, where a married person is known by another other than her husband, or vice versa. Then we are told that is not adultery in the true spiritual sense of the word. Adultery is to look upon another with lust and want it, even though you do not perform it because you may contemplate the consequences of your actions—how it may bring about disgrace to you and your family. But that is not good enough. The very contemplation of the act *was* the act. So the whole thing is lifted to a *mental* level.

But here we have a Torah, a law by which we live. So I may be tonight unemployed and the world tells me I can't get the job, that all these are being displaced by automation, and so I accept that. I *want* the job, but I am told by those who are supposed to know, I can't get it. I am told that creation is *mental*; it is not based upon any physical law in this world. Creation is completely mental, that all causation is in my Imagination. That's where my entire environment exists. And so I want to work. In my Imagination I'm gainfully employed, and I go to sleep in that state as though I am gainfully employed. I have never earned so much, I have never contributed so much to the world's good, and I have never been so happy in what I'm doing, all in my Imagination, regardless of the evidence of my senses to the contrary. So that's the Torah.

Now, first comes Israel. I'm going to make a heart so pure—not pure as the world calls pure, I mean pure in the true sense of the word: guileless. He could stand in the presence of nothing, and couldn't raise his finger to put something into his mouth to satisfy a hunger if that is at the expense of another for personal gain. *That* is the pure in heart, the guileless, the Israelite. Now I'm going to give him a law by which, as I send him through the most horrible furnaces of the world, I'm going to give him a law where he can cushion the blows and play the part to aid in the awakening of myself in him, and comes the Torah.

After the Torah, we get the prophet, and the prophet reveals God's promise to man. This is God's promise to man—we read it in Isaiah, all the prophets, really—"And I have called Israel in whom I will be glorified." I'm going to be glorified in Israel, only Israel, nothing but Israel. Forget a race of people and think only of the pure in heart, regardless of the pigment of the skin, regardless of the national, racial background—only the pure in heart is Israel. And I'll call Israel in whom I will be glorified. That's his command, and his command will not fail. He's going to be glorified in Israel. So read it in the 49th chapter of the Book of Isaiah.

Now, he tells us what will happen before he reaches the end, which is himself; for the end is Jesus Christ. You are Jesus Christ, but you don't know it yet. You *are* Jesus Christ; and the day is coming that God will awaken *in* you as man, and Jesus Christ is God the man. God becomes man, and man became God. So the end is Jesus Christ. The beginning is God; it ends with Jesus Christ; and in between comes Israel, the Holy Land on which the battle takes place. Then comes the law, Torah. Then comes the prophets, the promise to man and the fulfillment of that promise. The promise is that he will make you himself.

So the cry is, "O Father, glorify thou me with thine own self with the glory that I had with thee before that the world was" (John 17:5). He's asking for one thing in this world: for the glory of God. And God cannot give his glory to another. Now listen to it carefully; the glory is given to us *after* the furnaces. You listen to it; it's now the 48th chapter of Isaiah: "I have tried you in the furnaces. For my own sake, for my own sake I do it, for how should I give my name to be profaned and my glory to another?" Now he calls Israel, "And Israel, whom I have called; I am He, I am the first, and I am the last" (verse 12). If I am the first, I am God who created it all; I am the last, "Come, Lord Jesus!" The beginning and the end of the entire story: I am the first and I am the last.

So here, "I have tried you in the furnaces of affliction. For my own sake, I do it, for how should I have my name profaned?" And what is his name? His name is Father. The heart of God is the heart of a father. So the cry is, "O Father, glorify thou me with thine own self . . . for I will not give my glory unto another." He can't give it unto another; he can only give it to himself. He has to make us himself. And it takes all of the furnaces of affliction to transform us into that part, incapable of deceit, incapable of taking advantage of another because in the end there is no other; there's only God. When man thinks he got the better of another, who is fooling whom?

There is no other, there's only God. 'Hear, O Israel, the Lord our God is *one* Lord." There is no other. And so when I think something moving across the face of my world is other than myself and I can take advantage of it for personal gain, I am still asleep. I still must go through the furnaces to burn away that concept that blinds me from the oneness that is God.

So here, there are six definite states. You may call it the Mogen David if you will, the six-pointed star. It is God at the beginning. Then comes, "My choice is Israel." Then comes the Holy Land—the mind of man is the Holy Land on which the battle takes place. There is no other land. No matter where you go in the world, the only Holy Land is your mind. Then comes a law by which, in that land when the battle rages, you can cushion the blows. If you find yourself in jail, you could while in there imagine yourself elsewhere; and the doors will open, and you will go where you're imagining yourself to be. You could find yourself this night unemployed, and you could imagine yourself gainfully employed, and the doors will open from that prison state, and you would moved toward a wonderful job where you're gainfully employed.

So the Torah is a conditional state. You cannot be in one state and not suffer the consequences of not being in another state. They're only states. So he doesn't blame any being in the world. The being who played the part of a thief and the being who played the part of the judge who sentenced him are played by the same people. The supreme actor of the world is God. "God only acts and is in existing beings or men."

So tonight in this room, only one being is present, and I am a speaker teaching the law as I understand it, as I have experienced it, and you are listening. The being listening and the being speaking are one and the same being. There aren't two of us, there's only God. So the man who is shooting the so-called culprit tonight because he was picked up as a spy, the one who was actually executing the order and the one against whom it is executed, are one and the same being. To tell you that Stalin and the Pope are played by the same being, you might be shocked, but there is no other being to play the part. It's all a play, the whole vast world is a play, and one being is playing *all* the parts. In the end, we are all Jesus Christ, the God that became man that man may become God.

So in the end, no man by the wise use of law could redeem himself, no man. I can know the law so intimately, know it so well, that I could cushion every blow. Knowing that, I could imagine myself now while I'm in prison to be elsewhere and actually *move* elsewhere. When I am there, another change in pattern and once more I'm encircled, imagine myself to be elsewhere and I would *go* elsewhere. I could play it so beautifully that no one could ever long encase me in any prison. But I cannot redeem myself no matter how wisely I use the law. Redemption comes *only* by the act of God. Divine mercy steps beyond this fabulous world of horror, really, and raises me and redeems me in the body of Jesus. I am redeemed in his body. I am one with him.

Standing here tonight to tell you I am one with his body, it seems so stupid, for I respond to the name Neville. If you call me Neville, I will answer. If you called me Jesus when I walk the street, I wouldn't answer. If you said, "Jesus Christ," I might be curious, but I would not think you mean me. I wouldn't turn around. But if you say Neville, I would turn around and respond to the call called Neville, but I would not respond to that called Jesus Christ. Yet I do know from an actual experience I was absorbed into his body and became one with him, and I was the very being, by an actual experience.

So I tell you, by this experience, the event can be made known only as it's borne witness to. So I told you my experience and recorded it in book form that it may outlast this little earthly garment. I've told you the story from time to time and will continue to tell it, for that's the only way that I can proclaim it and have someone hear it. But it has been mistold through the centuries; it has not been told correctly. We're all one, the whole vast world is *one*, and God is playing *all* the parts. And this is the sequence through which it moves. God, in the beginning . . . "In the beginning, God created the heavens and the earth," then selects the mold, the model, the Israel, the pure in heart. And then he has a stage, and the stage is the Holy Land, and the Holy Land is the mind of man. There is no other Holy Land. Then comes from that, the law. He reveals the law, and the law is made conscious to us and unveiled to us in the form of a *mental* approach to life: that causation is mental; it isn't physical. When man discovers it *is* mental and it's not physical, and he abides by it, and applies it, he lives beautifully in this world.

But he can't redeem himself; he has to be redeemed by God. He's buried in the sepulcher called "the skull of man." That's the only Holy Sepulcher in the world, your own skull. And then comes a prophecy and man discovers the prophecy by reading scripture. God has promised man that he would raise up out of man something that will come forth from him as though it were his son; and yet, it will be God's son, and God will be his father, and this which came out of man will be God's son. That's the promise made in the 2nd Samuel, the 7th chapter: I promise you I will do it. And then the years go into years, and centuries into centuries, and where and when will it happen? Because the world thinks it's going to happen once and for all.

Today, all the churches teach that *once* upon a time an individual was raised from the dead, and his name was Jesus Christ and that is it. Now listen to these words, and he mentions some teachers in his letter to Timothy—this is Paul writing his second letter to Timothy, the 2nd chapter—"They have swerved from the truth by teaching that the resurrection is past." The resurrection hasn't past; it is taking place. If you think that Jesus Christ is a single being that lived and died and was resurrected 2,000 years ago, and that's it—you don't know the story and you don't know the mystery. Jesus Christ is God himself *buried* in every child born of woman, but *every* child, regardless of race, regardless of pigment, regardless of any background. In every child God is dwelling. God became man and becoming man is Jesus Christ. It's in man, buried in man.

Now it's Jesus *Christ* that has to do the resurrecting. God's mightiest act is the resurrection of Christ *in* man *as* that man. So you come out of your *own* skull, which was a tomb; and while it was a tomb, God transformed it into a womb. And out of that womb, your own skull, comes you. But you're individualized. You don't respond to the name of Jesus Christ, but you are he. For the only one that he is resurrecting is Jesus Christ, the man that is God, but it's you, John or Mary or called by any name. When you come out, listen to these words now; these are from the Book of Galatians: "There is no bond, no free, no Greek, no Jew, no male, no female, in Jesus Christ" (3:28). That which comes out is above races, above sex, and above everything known to mortal man. There is no bond, there is no free, there is no Greek, there is no Jew, there is no male, and there is no female in Jesus Christ. He's completely above the organization of this world. It's an entirely different world, a new world.

And it takes a *new* man to function consciously in the new world. All of the blows of this world were necessary to produce that man. So in the midst of tragedy, don't forget the glory. This was given to us in a very simple little way in the Book of Revelation: "And I saw a little scroll . . . and he offered me the scroll. He said to me, 'When you take it, eat it; it will be bitter in your stomach, but sweet as honey in your mouth.' And so I took it; and it was in my mouth sweet as honey, but in my stomach it was bitter" (10:9). For that's life, like a Jewish wedding, have you ever attended a Jewish wedding? They have two glasses of wine, one is sweet and one is bitter. The bitter one has very little in it, not much, and the sweet one is almost up to the brim but not quite. During the ceremony, you partake of both; you take the sweet and you take the bitter because that's life. "Joy and woe are woven fine, a garment for the soul divine." But there is more of sweet than there is of bitter. So in the midst of tragedy when the things are falling all around you, don't forget the sweet, the glory, and the promise of God, for he's giving you himself. So if today the whole world collapses all around you, don't forget the glory, don't forget there is more sweet than there is bitter in life. So in this marriage ceremony, you take both—you take the sweet and you take the bitter. There is more of the sweet than there is of the bitter, and so you go through life that way. But man in the midst of tragedy, he forgets the glory.

So Paul makes this statement in the 8th of Romans, he says, "I consider that the sufferings of this time are not worth comparing to the glory that is to be revealed to us." I don't consider even comparing them. A man may be in pain, or he may not be physically in pain, but he may be embarrassed because of some behavior of a relative or his family or his, well, inside himself in conflict. His country may be embarrassed, and he is hurt because the country's embarrassed. But I can't consider that I should even compare the sufferings of this time to the glory that is to be revealed to us. So consider the whole vast thing, you can't compare them. The little bit of wine that is sour and bitter, you can't compare it to the sweet that is ours. For when man is completely unveiled and he's God, this whole vast world then disappears; it vanishes from consciousness. He is in a world that is completely subject to his own creative power. That's God.

So here, don't forget the six-pointed star, the Mogen David. You begin with God and you end with God. Here you have, your second is God's choice, that is the mold. He uses the pure in heart, the guileless being, called Israel. Then comes the stage. He gives us a stage on which he's going to play the drama, and that stage is called the Holy Land; and the Holy Land is your own wonderful mind. That's the Holy Land. Then comes the law, a simple wonderful law, which is conditional.

All things are conditional in God's law. If I go in a certain direction, I will encounter certain events, but I am free to change my direction and that is called in the Bible repentance. Repentance means change of mind. I may at any moment in time change my mind. Repentance does not mean what the world tells you it means, such as feeling regretful or remorseful or in any way sad of heart, no—no sense of guilt. I know what I am; well, then, I change my mind. A change in attitude toward life is a change of the world in which I live, an automatic change if I remain faithful to the change. So repentance begins the law in its spiritual sense. So the whole concept is "Repent, for the kingdom is at hand." Well, that change in attitude of mine toward life is a complete change in myself in this world. That's the Torah in a spiritual sense.

Then comes the promise, the prophecy, and he prophesies to man what he's going to do to man: He's going to give you himself. It is God's purpose to give us himself and to give us himself so completely it is as though there were no others in the world, just God and you. Believe that, and the most fabulous story that I'm telling you becomes permanent and, I tell you from experience, possible. For in one short little interval of nine months in human time, three fantastic events will unfold in you, all leading up to the fulfillment of God's promise to man. You'll be born from above, out of your skull, just as a child is born from below from the womb of a woman. Just as a child is born, as you and I were born from our mother's womb, *we* will be born from our own skull, and come out in the same way of a child coming out. Only we're not little babies. It'll be symbolized as a babe, but we will be adults coming out, a fully-grown being coming out of our own skull. And the whole drama is symbolized just as told us in the Books of Matthew and Luke.

But man has completely misunderstood the story, and they say a little child was born of a woman called Mary 2,000 years ago. It isn't so at all. It never was so. The only Mary in the world is the skull of man, the *only* Mary, never was another Mary. And out of this wonderful skull of man, this divine womb of God, comes man; but his birth is symbolized in that of a little child, wrapped in swaddling clothes. The little child is discovered by men of the same age, right here. They can't see the one who came out because this being is something entirely different. He belongs to an entirely different world, not wearing these garments at all.

But they know *of* him, and they know he is born. So they speak of him, and they will say, if your name is John, "How can John have a baby?" They still are ___(??) the concepts of this world, so they think the being found is not a sign, it's a fact. That's not the fact; it's a *sign* bearing witness to a fact they cannot observe. And he who is born stands in their midst, and he looks at them, well, they're just like toys to him. He is now so powerful, so wise, so altogether omniscient and omnipotent as he stands in their presence, yet invisible to them. And harmless—he's as harmless as a dove. He wouldn't hurt one hair of their head. Because of their ignorance they can't see him. Not a thing that he can do to make himself visible to them because they haven't eyes to see the kingdom of heaven and they haven't ears to hear the sounds of heaven. So he stands in their presence, a man clothed in the garment of heaven, invisible and inaudible to all who are present. But all the signs are present bearing witness to the event that took place in his case.

And after the event comes God's promise to give himself to one that he succeeds in raising from the dead, which is to be born anew, born from above, and he gives him his Son as his own Son. He doesn't give him his Son ___(??) planning to walk the street with him; he gives him his Son as his own son. And that being, invisible to the world, is the Son, and it's David, the immortal David that is the sum total of humanity. So he gives you humanity symbolized in one youth, and it's called David. You have no doubt as to who he is when you see him.

Then, God separates the veil. There will be no need as far as you are concerned to ever go to any intermediary to reach God. For when that veil is severed you have direct access to God. You don't need any priest, any rabbi, any pope, anyone in this world to go to God. You're one with him. And so, the temple is split right down from top to bottom. When it's split from top to bottom, the prophecy is fulfilled: "As Moses lifted up the serpent in the wilderness, so must the Son of man be lifted up." And that Son of man is lifted up *as* God, for he beholds his own Creator and knows it to be himself. He is now self-begotten. There's only God. He can't beget other than himself, and the whole vast play is to bring him out. He created the whole vast world for the purpose of bringing them out.

I think Blake put his finger on it when Blake said to Max Beckman in vision one night, "Have confidence in objects, do not let yourself be intimidated by the horrors of the world. Everything is ordered and correct and must fulfill its destiny in order to attain perfection. Follow this path and you will obtain from your own ego a far deeper perception of the eternal beauty of Creation: and then you will attain greater and greater release from what to you at this moment seems to be so sad and so horrible." You will be released from the horror of it all if you follow this path. Yield completely to it; let it be.

And this is the play. This whole vast tension today in the world between races and nations, all these are part of God's play. And when it's all over, the scenery will remain, the ___(??) may remain, but you and I will be extracted, and all are one. If tonight you played all the parts of Hamlet, just suppose you played all the parts of Hamlet—you played Hamlet, you played his mother, you played the uncle, the ghost of the father, you played all the parts. At the end of playing all the parts, who are you? You're not Hamlet and you're not the mother or the murderous uncle, the wounded and dead father, or any part. You are the actor. Well, "God only acts and is in all existing beings or men." And so the supreme *actor* of the world . . . God is not a passive observer of this pageant of Israel, he is the supreme *actor* in the drama.

And so God *in* man is I AM, that's God, and he's playing *all* the parts. If I'm playing all the parts of Hamlet tonight, but every one, if the play came down and I changed my costume and came back as the mother, changed my costume and came back as the father, the ghost, changed, came back as the uncle, the murderer of the king, I'm still the same actor. Well, do you know that God is playing all the parts? There is nothing but God in this world. But he's playing it for a purpose: to individualize himself as Jesus Christ; and when the play is done, *you are* Jesus Christ. Everyone will be Jesus Christ.

Now let us go into the Silence.

*   *   *

Q: Neville, we were hoping you would give a lecture on Revelation before you close the series. Would you tell us the lecture before because I have a friend most anxious to hear that?

A: All right, my dear. Now to get back ___(??). Bear in mind, like tonight's subject, there was more of the sweet wine than the bitter in the wedding, and there is more of the sweet than the bitter in the little book that John was so eager for in Revelation. So in going to the ark, there were more of the clean animals than the unclean animals. But life would not be complete if everything was without choice on the part of man. If there were no evil in life, there could be no knowledge of good. If man had no choice, he would be an automaton; he'd be a puppet. So into the ark, and man is the ark of God—"I'm either the ark of God or I'm a phantom of the earth and the sea." But I'm not a phantom. I am the ark of God, and in that ark goes everything, the clean and unclean animals, and man has to choose. It's not an animal—these animals are but simply states. These are symbols of states of consciousness, and it's entirely up to man to choose the states into which he will go. He may fall into the unclean, officious state unwittingly, or he may wittingly go into it. But it's entirely up to man to choose the thing he will serve. And so the ark has been stocked with all animals; there are more clean than unclean. I have seen the Jewish service of the wedding; there's more of the sweet wine than the bitter.

Now if I decide to give a talk on Revelation, I promise you I'll let you know a lecture or two before. I have but two and a half weeks left . . . I close at the end of this month on a Friday night.

Q: (inaudible)

A: ___(??) individualized, the minute he knows salvation is mental and not physical, and up he goes from Egypt and the great exodus is on, leaving this whole vast world.

Until Friday.

THE CROSS

May 17, 1963

___(??) very practical and yet you'll find it very spiritual, which to me *is* the most practical. When you see a cross, do you think of suffering? And you hear someone say he was crucified, do you think, as the world undoubtedly thinks, that it is a suffering state? And if I told you that the cross is a spiritual wedding ring, would you believe it? When you see someone wearing a wedding ring, you know that there's a union, there's a marriage, and there should be love in that state, there should be. But may I tell you, when you see the cross hereafter think of a spiritual wedding ring, for it really is. For the cross is the symbol of God becoming man that man may become God, and that's the cross. The central teaching of the Bible is the cross. He actually becomes us, nails himself upon us. For we were dead, and he was alive, and he so loved the creature that he became his own creation to convert it, to transform it—like a Pygmalion and a Galatea—into himself.

Now, we are told in Genesis, a little man is given seemingly to another, but all the commands in the Bible are to God by God. For man was not alive. And he commands man to leave everything and cleave to his wife, and then they become *one* flesh. So when we read the Bible and saw the bodies male/female, you might think when you read of a woman that it means a female, no, it doesn't; when you read of a man it means a male, no it doesn't. Whether it be male or female, it is speaking of us. And woman, we are told in Paul's first letter to Timothy, "And woman will be saved by the bearing of children." If you take that phrase "the bearing of children" and go to the bottom of the page—it should be in your Bible, it is in my Bible, in all my Bibles, I have many—there's a little note at the bottom of the page which tells us that that phrase "bearing of children" literally means "by the birth of *the* child." Definitive, *the* child. So woman is saved by the birth of *the* child (2:15).

Well, I am that woman. I am a man, a male. I have sired two children. My children live in this world. I'm married. But I am the woman spoken of in that passage, the last verse of the second chapter of Paul's first letter to Timothy. I am the woman; *God is* the husband. Listen to these words carefully, Sing, O barren—it begins Isaiah 54—Sing out, you barren one . . . for you will be more fertile than those who are married (verse 1). In the same chapter, Isaiah 54:5, the statement is made, "Your Maker is your husband, the Lord of hosts is his name." My Maker is my husband; the Lord of hosts is his name. Now I am told he has to become me and cleave to me, for I am his wife. He had to leave everything and forget everything and so cleave to me we become one flesh.

Now, Paul tells us, in the very end when he completes the job, Paul makes the statement, "Henceforth, let no one trouble me, for I bear on my body the marks of Jesus" (Galatians 6:17). Not little holes through here or a crown of thorns on my head or a gash in my side or holes in my feet, but everything said of him you experience *seemingly* in your body. You go through all the experiences, and it takes place in your body. His birth, his fatherhood, everything in the world takes place in you. So you bear on your body the marks of Jesus.

Now, in the meanwhile, let us now turn to what came after this comment was made to man. It came, if you read Genesis it's only 400 years; if you read Exodus and the letters of Paul, it came 430 years *after* the promise, and this is what he calls the law. He said, "No man is justified before God by law." Yet here was the law, and God gave it to us because of transgression. It pays to the *n*th part, to the most simple iota of one's transgression, whatever it is. And here, use it, but you can't be justified by it. But learn the law, for we are told in the 1st chapter in the Book of Psalms, "Blessed is the man who delights in the law of God, for in all that he does he prospers." This is a promise. Dwell upon it. It's not the *real* promise, but this is a promise concerning the *law* of God. The *real* promise preceded it by 400 years if we read one book and 430 if you read another book. But regardless, it *precedes* this law. "But blessed is the man who delights in the law of the Lord, for in all that he does he prospers." You can't fail in the law.

But no matter how wisely you exercise your talent, which is the use of law, it doesn't in any way qualify you for the marks of the body of Jesus. That is grace, that's the gift. It will happen regardless of what you do in this world. Not one person in this world will fail. It can't fail because you, personally, are not doing it. You are the bride of God. It is God who is doing it, and God is doing it on us. He fell in love with us, as told us in the 1st chapter of Ephesians, "He chose us in himself before the foundation of the world." So I was his choice before the foundation of the world. He selected me, as a man will go out to find a woman that he wants, and he wants her with all of his heart to bear his name and bear children, if he can have children.

In this case, only one child God is going to have from you, only one. *Only* one, as told you in the 3rd chapter, the 16th verse of Galatians: there will only be one. Everyone's going to have one to prove that God loves you and became you. The one is going to be *God's* child, and it's going to be *your* child because *that* child is going to call you Father. Although I am his bride and seemingly female, in this state, a wonderful statement is made, "We shall all be *one* in Jesus Christ." And the phrase in Greek "all be one in Jesus Christ," "all will be masculine." Why they didn't use it, I will never know, but there it is. We shall all be one, and that phrase *all be one* literally translated "all be masculine." He fell in love with man, generic man, in a capitalized sense, though in this level, we're all split in two, male and female.

Now, we come back to the law. In all that you do you will prosper if you abide by the law. And the law is just as simple as this: as I stand here now I could in twelve seconds be in twelve different states of consciousness. I can think of you, think of you, think of the other one; and then all of a sudden, everything that I think of, that's a state of consciousness. I could be in as many states as there are seconds in the time that I'm thinking. But the state that I'm going to externalize and objectify and make real in my world is the state that I occupy more than I do others. That state to which I most constantly return constitutes my home, my true self.

And so, I go into a state. If tonight you want wealth, let no one in this world tell you, you shouldn't want it. If you want health, let no one tell you, you shouldn't want it. I don't care what you desire now in this world. You may after you realize it tire of it. We know that in the world. There are people who build a home, spend a fortune on the home, they're in it just a matter of moments and they tire of it. Not just the home alone but family relationships in the home change, and they don't want any part of that home because it ___(??) the relationships that occupy it. They don't want the home, they don't want the relationships, and they don't want any part of it. And yet they wanted it, seemingly, forever when they got it. That's life.

There is no static thing in this world because man at every moment in time could change a state. So when you *know* what you want, I don't care what it is that you want. You want to be happily married, perfectly all right. There are people all over this world today, many of them are in the limelight, running for the highest office in this land, who wanted a change of marital relationships more than the highest office in the land.

Because if they wanted it more than that change, they would have subjected themselves to what they considered the unlovely relationship in the hope of fooling the voters tomorrow because they wanted *it*. No, they wanted a change of this relationship more than they wanted the highest office in this land, and did it.

So I say there is no static picture in this world. Tonight, let no one and ask no one if you should want it. For let me quote one of the truly great awakened minds of all eternity, Blake, "I do not consider either the just or the wicked to be in a supreme state, but to be simply states of the sleep which the soul may fall into in its deadly dreams of good and evil" (*The Vision of the Last Judgment*). So I fall into a state. It seemed to me good, and it's good because I so hungered for it. I am in it. I may tire of it in a matter of moments or in a matter of thirty years or in a matter of some other length of time. It was neither good nor evil, simply a state.

There are infinite states in the world into which man falls. But when you come here, you shouldn't *fall* into states, you should *deliberately enter* a state. Even though you think, well now, this is a state, but don't fall into it. With your eyes wide open, "I want to be wealthy!" as you conceive wealth to be. All things being relative, what you and I consider a normal income to live graciously in our present world would be a millionaire's income in most of this world—if you think x-number of thousands you require to live well in this world we live in. But you go to ninety percent, maybe ninety-five percent of the world, if you had that sort of income, you would be a king of kings in their area. So all things are relative.

So where you are, what do you want? And you name it. Well, when you know *exactly* what you want, listen to the words, "Blessed is the man"—this is a Beatitude—"Blessed is the man who delights in the law of the Lord, for in all that he does he prospers." You can't fail if you delight in the law of the Lord. You don't feed your mind with anything other than the image desired to be externalized in your world. If today reason denies the image, you deny reason. If anything in this world, if your senses dictate that these are the facts of life, but they are in conflict with the image that you want to externalize, you deny your senses. Completely deny the senses and reason and entertain the image, for this is God's creativity.

And so I live this night in the assumption that I am the man that I want to be, even though everything, reason and senses, deny it, but I live in it—and I'm speaking from experience—then at the end of the not distant future, I begin to crystallize it and externalize it. And then I duplicate it. I tell the story to others and they begin to duplicate it, and then they tell it to others. At the end of a few years we have hundreds and hundreds of witnesses to this principle. Does it matter what the world thinks? Does it matter what anyone in this world would tell me about it if I can duplicate it and prove it by experience? Well, this is God's law.

The law is conditional. I can't be feeling sorry for myself and expect to call some practitioner who will push a button, leaving me as I am, and then produce results for me. I have it all the time. Someone will call up and say, "Will you do so and so?" The purpose of it all is to produce a change in the individual, not just a change in the circumstances round about, where it vanishes like a snow when the sun comes out. It's to produce in the individual a change that *sustains* the change when it externalizes itself in the world. But someone will say, "You know, my people aren't paying the rent. Three of them are now in arrears, they owe me three months," and they want you to in some strange way produce some little miracle where they all put their money down. And they remain just as bitter as they were prior to the loss of the three months. They remain just where they were prior to the call and think that the little pushing of the button is going to produce a change in their life. That call will come through day after day, week after week, month after month, year after year until you can produce in *them*, the caller, a change in their own heart. When you produce it in them, they need not call you ever again, for the simple reason that the change in *them* externalizes itself in their world. And it works that way.

So if there's a practitioner here, you don't ___(??) push buttons, you produce changes in them. And may I tell you, you don't need the income from any being in this world. If they pay you, all well and good, but don't depend upon any person's income in this world. You don't need to. Your own consciousness of wealth will produce wealth. You'll have everyone in this world, and it will simply flow like a river toward you. Don't depend upon anyone. No one is your source of supply. The only source is God, and his name is I AM. That's God. There is no other God.

So if they call, let them call. Try to persuade yourself that they have changed their attitude toward self, toward life. That change in them will automatically result in a change in their lives. They can't help it. But when someone makes them feel; and here, I tell you this because of a recent call, where in the city three different ones from different groups, not all in the same so-called -ism, different -ism, and they tell her, "Forever you will have to depend upon me to produce these things for you." Well, here this poor child believes it, and so she sends x-number of dollars every month to this one, this one, the other one, and then she calls the speaker. I've always warned her, "Don't you send me one penny"—which she doesn't have a dime—"Don't you send me a nickel. I want to produce in *you* the change." But she so completely believed that they could influence her that unless she calls upon them these things will recur. But they recur and recur and recur.

How to get her to really believe in God? The *only* God in the world is her own wonderful I-am-ness.

Now here is the story. He loved her; he loved her more than any man in this world could ever love her. I love my wife, and she and I together produced in this world this glorious child, and we revel in the daughter that we have. But I could not in eternity, as a man, love my wife to the degree that God loves us. God so loved her he became her, and he's one with her. And his name is not Neville; his name is I AM. That's his name. He's anchored upon her, crucified upon her. She was but a thought, that's all she was to him, and he so loved her he nailed himself upon her and completely forgot his divinity. He actually cleaved to her, and he will not let her go until they become one, not two. They were two in the beginning, God and this one that he loved; in the end, only one. And to him, he is so lost in his identity that when he rises in her, it's she, it's not another. It's just the individual that he fell in love with.

He gives his *name* to her. She had none. He gives his name, and she bears the name, and it's I AM. ___(??) and she wakes now. "Henceforth let no one bother me, don't let them trouble me, for I bear on my body the marks of Jesus." And these are the marks of Jesus. You aren't going to find them as the religious world tells you with the stigmata, bleeding hands and bleeding head and bleeding side and bleeding feet. They are *not* the marks of Jesus. I have had these, and they're marvelous. It's a thrill beyond the wildest dream when you feel yourself sucked in like a vortex, or a series of vortices, sucked into this body. I've had that. But they're not the marks of Jesus.

The marks of Jesus are all written out in dramatic form in scripture. The *first* mark of Jesus, but the very first one, is the resurrection, that's the first mark. How do you mark that? When the individual in himself awakens from a profound sleep to find he really, prior to this moment, was dead, for he awakes in a grave and no one but the dead are interred. So you inter them. And if a person is now in a sepulcher, the Holy Sepulcher, he awakens to find himself awake and alive, but he's in a grave. Then he must have resurrected. That's the first mark. The second mark is his birth. He comes out of it, and he comes out of that sepulcher just as a physical child comes out of a physical womb. And then come the other marks in discovery.

Then you look at it. "When the fullness of time had come, God sent the Spirit of his Son into my heart crying, 'Father.'" When the fullness of time had come. When the nine-month pregnancy is over. Nine months could be nine ages. But when the *fullness* of time had come, God sent the Spirit of his Son into my heart crying, "Father." So in my being when the fullness of time has come, his Son comes and calls me, "Father." If he calls me "Father," God's work on me is complete. For he used me as his bride, he cleaved to me and wouldn't let me go. But he had to produce his creative power, and he had to produce it by producing a son. He produced in me a son that calls me, "Father" after the fullness of time had come. So when the fullness of time had come—if you want it, the 4th chapter, the 4th verse of Galatians—"When the fullness of time had come, God sent his Son forth into my heart crying, 'Father.'" And then the Son calls me, "Father." His work in me is complete.

One more step to bear the marks of Jesus. But he takes it—and this is now the 10th chapter, the 20th verse of Hebrews—and he strips me down from top to bottom, and it's called "the curtain that separated man from God." There's one little membrane to be severed, and that which separated man from God is now split right down the middle; and it's called "the curtain that is his flesh." You feel it all on your body. Everything that I am talking about, you actually feel it is taking place here. But it's not on this, but you feel it here, for this is the shadow of the real body. So it actually, in some way, has all the effects that you get in the depths. The real body, the immortal body casts its shadow upon this and you feel it is taking place here. But it's not. It is in the soul, the real you.

So here, you could this night wisely apply God's law, and no being in the world can stop you from becoming what you want to be. If you stop for one moment and look over the roster of the world, take all the big so-called intelligent, wise, wonderful men in the world, all the great politicians of the world, any of them, go back, oh, just so short a time and you will see they were all just as you are now. They had no reason in the world to believe that they are what they are today, but none. Not one is endowed with any more intelligence, with any more power. Undoubtedly, ninety-nine percent of them stumbled into these states. I don't want you to stumble into it; I want you to go deliberately into these states. If you stumble into a state, when the convulsion takes place as it always does in the world and you are emptied from that state, you may not know how to get back into it because you didn't go into it deliberately.

If you go into these states deliberately, it wouldn't make any difference what convulsion took place—and they will take place, they always take place—how to go back into that state if it's a comfortable state to be in. You may go into any state in this world that you want. But if you don't know you are in a state and you think, well now, this is simply a natural thing based upon my birth. Well then, when you are emptied from that state you may never find your way back into that state. But you can. Everyone in this world could go into the state of his choice. I'm speaking from experience, when I have over 900 letters at home each testifying to a deliberate entrance into a state from people who knew nothing of this before. But they simply decided to take a state into which they would go; they entered that state, viewed the world from it as though it were true, and then in a way that they could not consciously define or devise the state appeared and became real in their world.

Everyone can do it. But don't forget, don't fall into it; go into it deliberately. Tonight if I would be, and I name it, anything in this world, then let me assume now that I *am* the man that I want to be. Remaining in it, let me view the world and see it mentally as I would see it were it true. If I do, I am delighting in the law of God; and in *all* that I do, I prosper. No one can stop it. But no matter how I do it, I cannot earn the grace because the grace cannot be earned. The grace is a gift. Because it is a gift, it is unconditional, and that's my glorious concept in this world. No one can fail. So if tonight you be a pauper of paupers, when in the fullness of time God is calling you, you'll receive the kingdom. And the greatest in this world does not compare to the least in the kingdom. So you may be at the moment when you are called unknown, poor as a church mouse with not a thing in this world to support your entrance. But you don't need it; you become heir, the heir of God, at that moment when the fullness of time has come.

But in the interval, waiting for the fullness of time, use God's law. God's law will never fail you, but it doesn't qualify you to receive his grace. If you could qualify to receive his grace, then it isn't grace. For grace means "unmerited gift," something given without merit on your part. It is love in action that isn't earned by the one to whom it is given. You couldn't earn it. On the other hand, if you have done something of which you are ashamed, may I comfort you, the 11th chapter of Romans, "God has consigned everyone to disobedience, that he may have mercy upon all" (verse 32). Were it not for divine mercy no one could be saved, but divine mercy chose us in himself before the foundation of the world. He chose me, he chose you.

When he emptied himself upon me, I do not remember. I have had moments where I have had remembrances of the thrill. It was a thrill, may I tell you. It wasn't pain to me. Whatever it was to God who nailed himself upon me, that I don't know. But to me on whom he nailed himself—for I'm the cross, this is the tree on which he hangs—and when he nailed himself upon me, the tree became alive, and it was a thrill. There was no pain whatsoever, as far as I'm concerned. It might have been a pain to him who so loved me that he hanged himself upon me, it may be. And so we're told by Blake, "The gods of the earth and the sea sought through nature to find this tree; but their search was all in vain: there grows one in the human brain" (*Songs of Experience*).

So here, on my brain, he is nailed and the extension is right on this body. But as far as I'm concerned it was no pain. It was ecstatic delight, supreme delight, when he made me alive. And then, he cleaved to me, remained faithful to his love, and then he awoke me. Today I can say with Paul, "I now bear on my body the marks of Jesus." The birth from above, the memory of it is so vivid; the resurrection from the grave is so vivid; the discovery of David is so vivid; the splitting of this body from top to bottom and the ascent up the spinal cord into my skull are so vivid. All these marks of Jesus I bear upon my body. So I know that this is the last time; he has completed his work in me.

And he had to bring forth only one child. Listen to the words, the 3rd chapter, the 16th verse of Galatians, and here he promises to bring forth one. The Greek word really means "seed," and the King James Version translates the word as seed, but to give it meaning in the modern translation, the Revised Standard Version, they translate the word seed as offspring. And so we're told in Galatians 3:16 that this offspring—and then they said, "He does not say offspring, meaning many; but offspring, meaning one, which is *your* offspring, which is Christ."

Now when you hear the word Christ, you think automatically, if you're a Christian, of Jesus Christ. The word Christ in Greek is the identical word of the word Messiah in Hebrew, identical: The word means "anointed." So I bring forth Christ, *my* offspring, and you think only in terms of Jesus Christ. Go back, "Anoint him; this is he." Go back into the 1 Samuel and who is spoken of? "That is he; rise and anoint him. He is my chosen one" (16:12). It's David. "Thou art my son, today I have begotten thee" (Psalms 2:7). He is the anointed. It is David who appears; *David* is the anointed. Well then, who is Jesus? God himself, you are he. For when God succeeds in giving you himself, who gives you himself? Therefore, you, who began in time, when he, your husband—"your Maker is your husband, the Lord of hosts is his name"—the husband must leave everything and cleave to his wife until they become one. When you become one, he who was your Maker, who so loved you, who became the husband, when you become one, *you* have an offspring. The offspring proves to you who you are. But the offspring is God's only begotten son, who is the anointed David. And then you see him. Everyone will bring forth only *one*, and that one is God's son.

People can't quite see the mystery that Jesus . . . the word Jesus means "Jehovah saves," that's what the word means. It is really Jehovah and Jehovah's name is I AM. And so when the child appears, he is the son of I AM. In the Old Testament, it's revealed to us in the most marvelous way, but man can't quite believe the word Jesse means I AM. We have all kinds of Jesses in the world. People name themselves Jesse, Jesse this, Jesse that, Jesse that, and to them it's a name. The word Jesse is I AM. Well, "Whose son are you?" "I am the son of Jesse," that's what David said. And who is Jesse? I AM. So when you come forward, *you* come forward, because he so gave you himself you are one with God. But how will I know it? Wait, just wait a little while, and then a child will be brought from you. When the child comes, you'll know him. He was always the Son of God. Now he's *your* son, therefore, you are God. So the purpose of this whole fabulous wonderful drama is to bring forth his predetermined purpose. And the purpose is to give himself to me, to you, to all of us, as though there were no others in the world, just you and God in the beginning, and finally only *you as* God. That's the great sacrifice: he completely gives himself to you; there aren't two anymore. The only heaven is your son bearing witness of your fatherhood, and the son is David.

But in the meanwhile, we apply the principle of his law. "Blessed is the man who delights in the law of the Lord, for in all that he does he prospers." And the law is conditional, no respecter of person. You could be the wisest, the loveliest, and the kindest person in the world. You begin to feel sorry for yourself and you're entering the state that will bear the fruit of that state, and you'll have every reason in the world to feel sorry for yourself. Don't envy anyone; they're only in a state. They're either in that state deliberately, knowingly, or they entered it unwittingly. I ask you to enter every state knowingly. You can be healthy, you can be wealthy, you can be famous, and you can be anything in this world. And there is no man in the world based upon the state that he occupies today [who] is worthy of your admiration, no person in the world. Someone is in a *state* where he's acclaimed as a great person. It's only a state, and people bow before the state and make of it a god. There's only one God and his name is I AM.

So someone goes by . . . I have seen it. A few years ago, in San Francisco—and may I tell you I admire General MacArthur, a marvelous, to me he's a grand, wonderful man, I admire him as a true great American and a leader of men, no question about it. He entered this country after years abroad. A friend of mine in San Francisco, a very able lawyer, he acted like a little child of about three. You've never seen such devotion, such complete hypnosis when the general drove by. The crowd was hailing him for what he'd done for our country in the last war and in the first war; but this man, he would have followed him right straight to a gallows, and put his neck in place of the general. You've never seen such worshipfulness. And I wondered, I said to myself, "What is it all about? He's been coming to my meetings for years, and he can't see a state moving by."

Recognize the state of greatness. Recognize a state, but to identify the individual as the state, he could tomorrow fall from that state and the same one will wonder what happened to his hero, not knowing it was a state. Where is Stalin? Where is Hitler? Where is Goering? Where, mention all of them, Trujillo, with all their statues and cities and towns named after them to be perpetuated forever? Suddenly the state is vacated and the little occupant is decapitated. ___(??). These are all states.

So don't worship any being in this world. Worship only God, and God is really your husband. Love the man whose name you bear, love the woman who bears your name, but in the end they are shadows of the relationship of God and man. These are only shadows. Your real husband is God, and he's more faithful than any man in this world could ever be to you. And so, they're married for fifty years and sired many. I think of one mentioned earlier. So after thirty-odd years, leaving behind his many children, he marries another one who has four children. No criticism, perfectly all right. His father outlived his mother by a couple of years, and then he married a widow that he'd known through the years. Perfectly all right, and so he married her.

God will never marry anyone other than you. But no one in this world he loves more than he loves you; and you are, individually, his only love. That's the mystery. He could never divorce you for another. And in *his* life because he is life itself, you could never die because *he* is life. He is wedded to you, and he's so wedded to you that he's determined to prove to you his love in the begetting of his son. And when he brings his son forth, it's your son, your boy. And strangely enough, in that little phrase "one person in Christ Jesus" is a phrase used in Matthew, you're his father, for God is a father and the heart of a father. Though he picks you out as his bride, when he completes the process, you are he. But he wasn't a bride; he was *father*. That's the mystery. He transforms you into himself. And he was, before he wedded you, a father, and so he transforms you, his bride. You are his emanation yet his wife 'til the sleep of death is over. When the sleep of death is over, you're transformed into him; and he was, before he wedded you, a father, and so you are a father, and there is your son.

Now let us go into the Silence.

*   *   *

Q: (inaudible)

A: The question is, I speak so often of the fullness of time—this is taken from the Book of Galatians, the 4th chapter: "When the fullness of time had come, God sent forth his Son, born of woman, born under the law, to redeem those who were born under the law" (verse 4). Everything has its own appointed hour, all pregnancies in the world.

At what moment in time after the nailing of the cross within you he impregnated you with himself to beget you in his own likeness, I do not know at what moment in time. But at that *fullness* of time no one can stop it. What is that fullness of time? No one could be animated in this world, no one in this world could live and breathe were it not because of God nailed upon him. The 2nd chapter, the 20th verse of Galatians: "I have been crucified with Christ; it is not *I* who live, but Christ who lives in me; and the life I now live in the flesh I live by the faith in the Son of God." There are two; one says "by the faith in the Son of God," and one is "in his faith." So you can take your choice—either because of *his* faith or my faith having felt him. But I am crucified, for I *have* been crucified with Christ.

So the act is finished, my crucifixion is through, yours is through, everyone's is through or we couldn't be here. But at one moment after the union—for to me a cross is a spiritual wedding—so it's done. At that moment the wedding takes place. But when, after the union, were you impregnated with himself? He animates you, I am alive, but when would I be impregnated? I rest assured when the fullness of time has come, his son will come forward and call me "Father." It has to, for the son only has so much time between impregnation and externalization. So when will he come? Well, again, Habakkuk, "It seems long, wait; for it is sure and it will not be late." "For every vision has its own appointed hour; it ripens, it *will* flower. If it seem long, wait" (Habakkuk 2:3).

So I cannot tell anyone. Was this the night that infinite love embraced me? Was it that moment in time when I stood in his presence and he embraced me and I became one with his body that he impregnated me? I must confess it was *infinite* delight; it was sheer ecstasy when he embraced me and I became one with his body. Was that the moment of impregnation? I don't know. I know he knows today I bear the marks of Jesus on my body. So he can't impregnate me with anyone but that, and brings forward David to cry, "Father." Now, whether that was that moment in time? That doesn't go back very far, you know. I go back to the age when I was about twenty, twenty-one. And so this happened in 1959, and so it wasn't too long, if *that* was the moment. But I cannot speak with authority. I know what's happened, but I cannot definitely state that *that* was the moment of impregnation.

Prior to that I lived as everyone lives in the world, and I'm an animated being as we all are animated beings. But was that the moment when I stood in his presence and answered correctly that love was the greatest thing in the world? For he can only bring forth love: he calls David. But the very word David means "my beloved." And so was it that, when he said to me, "What is the greatest thing in the world?" and I answered, "Faith, hope and love, these three, but the greatest of these is love." Then he embraced me, and we became one, but *really* one, not two. And I *was* the body of the being who asked the question, and I stood in the presence of infinite love who is God. So was that the moment of impregnation? I don't know. If that was, doesn't take long between ___(??) and fulfillment.

Good night.

OUR REAL BELIEFS ARE
WHAT WE LIVE BY

May 21, 1963

___(??). Now we can make a habit of this and not really take it in. ___(??). I would like everyone to really pay all attention. Our real beliefs are what we live by. Therefore, it is so important to get truth. For the belief, whether it be true or false, if we really believe it we live by it. And we need not, may I tell you, experience what we said we believe to really believe in it. I'll give you a very graphic example. I personally have never, and I don't think any of you have, jumped off a tall building. We haven't had the experience, but we believe that if we did it would either be fatal or crippling. And so we haven't done it, and yet we have not experienced it. So a real belief is tantamount to knowing. You can't distinguish between the two, believing and knowing, when it's a real belief.

Now a real belief may be a lie, but it's just as knowing as a true belief. So it's so important that you and I are exposed to the truth. Nothing is more important than that the testimony of Jesus be heard and responded to. Nothing is more important—I don't care what it is in this world—than that the testimony of Jesus be heard and responded to. I am not saying that your response will be affirmative; it may be negative, as told us in the last chapter of the Book of Acts. Paul spent the day from morning to evening trying to explain to them the kingdom of God and trying to convince them about Jesus. He used the argument from scripture—there's only the Old Testament, so he used the argument from the law of Moses and the prophets—and we are told that some were convinced by what he said and others disbelieved. Now that's your privilege, to believe it or disbelieve it, but you should be exposed to the testimony of Jesus. For we are told, he is the first fruit; he is the first fruit that awakened from the dead. He is the pioneer and pinnacle of our faith. So God succeeded in his purpose, and here is the first success. No greater than you when he succeeds in you, no greater, but here is the first one in whom he succeeded in producing his prophecy, his purpose. And listen to his testimony, for he tells us, "These words are not mine. They are the words of him who sent me. And all the words that I speak are the words of my Father." And so he's only echoing what was dictated to him by the one who raised him from the dead.

Now we come down to this level and take one of his statements. Here is a statement, "Whatever you ask in prayer, believe that you received it, and you will." Now, unnumbered hundreds of millions of Christians have repeated that statement. Do they really believe it? Oh, they will quote it from scripture; do they really believe it? I have taken that same statement and put it into our modern tongue in these words, "imagining creates reality." I know it from experience: I will say, "Imagining creates reality." Many of you who come here you've proved it. There are many of us who've proved it in a way, but they will repeat it and give it lip service. But I say if it gets real to the individual who has heard it because the habit of worry discloses a lack of faith in that saying. If I worry, I'm imagining, am I not? Am I not fulfilling the statement of Job, "And my fears have come upon me"? So if I worry about a problem—he can't find a job, things are going from bad to worse, I can't pay my bills and I'm worried—do I really believe that imagining creates reality? Really believe it as I believe something I haven't actually experienced, like jumping through the window? I know I'll break my neck or injure my body, I'll cripple it or kill it, I know it. And I haven't experienced it but I know it. That believing and knowing have become one. But when it comes to that, well, do I believe that I know it with the same intensity? Do I really believe that imagining creates reality? If I do, I couldn't worry, for worry is to only conjure what I fear in this world. For worry is an imaginal act. I couldn't possibly be concerned about anything if I really believe that imagining creates reality.

So I say nothing is more important to us than to hear the testimony of Jesus and respond to it. I'm not saying that everyone who hears that statement will accept it. We're told he was rejected in this world. Who was rejected? He was rejected. Now let me show you who he is. We're told that he was rejected by the majority of the people of the world, and in spite of the numbers today, nine hundred million, I would safely say almost nine hundred million reject him because they don't know him. They think they know him, but they do not know who he is.

Now, you take these words and you put them together and try to come up with your own answer. Here is one taken from the works of Paul; it's the

5th chapter of 2nd Corinthians: "From now on I will regard no one from the human point of view; even though I once regarded Christ from the human point of view, I regard him thus no longer" (verse 16). Listen to it carefully. He saw him once as a man, and now he regards him thus no longer. The same author, Paul, now in his letter to the Galatians—he only wrote one—so in his letter to the Galatians, the third chapter, in which he tells us that our offspring is Christ. If you want it, it's the 3rd chapter, the 16th verse—our offspring is Christ. Turn the page over to the 4th chapter, and he tells us, "My little children, with whom I am once again in labor until Christ be formed in you" (verse 19). Now he sees the mystery. Now he sees who Christ really is. And when I tell you everything in this world is human, everything, mountains, cities, rivers, everything in this world takes on human form when man begins to awaken. So Christ takes on human form. But the same author, Paul, defines Christ as "the power and the wisdom of God." How can power and wisdom take on form, human form? May I tell you, it does. It actually comes out of you and takes on human form, but it's your very self.

So before we come to this—this is the depth of the evening—let us go back now to the statement "imagining creates reality." I received a tape last week from the state of Maine. A friend of mine brought his machine home and played it for me. And as I listened to it, here is a lady that I met eight years ago in San Francisco. On the tape, she said, "I feel I should give you a resume of the things that have happened to us since I first heard you. I heard you in San Francisco eight years ago. I remained there for the next two years, so I heard you twice. I really believed you. From the very first day I heard you I believed you. So I went out, I rearranged my home and I sold it, bought another, fixed it up, and sold it. Then on the second year when you came, I decided I am really going to travel. All we had then was a home fixed up."

I recall vividly the night that they came by Beverly Hills. I had no idea that this lady and the other lady in the car and the two children and the dog were reduced to eight dollars. I had no idea. But in her tape recording, she tells me the story. She said, "I firmly believed you when you said 'Imagining creates reality.' And so we started off, that is, we *started* off." She and her friend who had two little girls and a dog, a huge big poodle, whose name was Doris. I can see her now. And Doris was a perfect lady. So she stopped in front of our home—we lived on El Camino—I went out to see this peculiar thing, an old car and an old trailer. They were on their way to the east, and I mean Maine. You can't get any further east ___(??) the water, and they only had eight dollars between them. She was putting into practice imagining creates reality.

That night they started off. The next stop was Palm Springs. They went into an employment agency and asked if there were any jobs available. They said, "Well, if you can paint." Well, they were painters but artistic painters, I mean, they were not house painters. But they painted lovely things. She said, "If I can paint these things, I can paint a house." So they said, "There was a shortage at the moment of house painters, and there is a home here hungry for work to be done. If you want to take the job, it's yours." So the two ___(??) and painted the house and did a wonderful job, recouped their finances, and started off to Arizona. They did something similar in Arizona.

Well, when it ended, they were in Maine. They still had very little, naturally, going all across this country, feeding four mouths and the dog, and buying gas and oil for the old, old jalopy. When they got there, they were there not more than a week when they received a letter via the bank that the house that they had sold in San Francisco on a long-term arrangement, the man came in to some money, he inherited some money in that interval, and wanted the entire thing completely cleared, and paid off all mortgages on the house. They gave him twenty years to pay and he paid the entire thing in two weeks. So they got their check. With that they bought a home, changed it, modernized it, sold it and made a profit.

Next thing they knew, they were on their way to Spain. They went all over Paris, all over France, all over Europe, came back to Spain. There they stayed five months and bought themselves two acres of land in Spain. No house on it as yet. That's for the future, they say. Then they came back to this country where they're now living, back in Maine. And she thought she should tell me and give me a resume of her experiences based upon the one simple statement "imagining creates reality." To them that became a real belief. It wasn't given lip service. The whole vast world will give it lip service, "Imagining creates reality," and the first thing you know they do everything but imagine the solution of the problem. They never imagine the end and lose themselves in the end, they only say, "Imagining creates reality."

Now we go back to the 11th chapter, the 24th verse, of the Book of Mark, "Whatever you desire"—whatever, doesn't have to be good for you—"Whatever you desire, believe you received it and you will." That's the promise. I say nothing is more important in this world than to hear the testimony of Jesus and respond to it. They'll say, "That's nuts. That's a lie. I don't believe it." All right, respond to it anyway. Or respond to it in the affirmative and say I believe it, as the girls believed it. They believed it. Today, leaving here, more than three thousand miles away, and started with eight dollars and an old car, two children, two adults, and a dog, and making it, and then going off to Europe.

And they had some peculiar happenings; they bought their ticket on a freighter and then came a strike and that line was struck. Now all these lines need to open, so they work with each other. And because the line was struck, based upon some longshoremen's strike in New York City, they called up, of all lines, the Queen Mary. They didn't do it; those who sold them the ticket did it. They said, "We have passengers here and the line is struck, can you accommodate them on the Queen Mary?" There was no accommodation in second or third class, only first class, so they went first class on the Queen Mary. I tell you this thing never fails. And you can't half believe it; you've got to believe. A real belief is that by which we live; you really live by it.

Now, listen to the testimony of Jesus, for you're told the testimony of Jesus is the spirit of prophecy. Everything that happens to him must happen to me, must happen to you, everything. I don't care what the state; it must all happen to us. For the spirit of Jesus, the very testimony of Jesus is the spirit of prophecy. And what happened to him? He was born in an unusual way, a unique manner, the Son of God, begotten of God. Listen to it carefully: God is begetting himself. When God begets himself, the self-begotten is still God. He's not begetting another; he's begetting himself. So God is begetting himself, and when he begets himself, he is still himself. But the self-begotten would have to be son and the begetter would be father. But if the Son-begotten is one with the begetter who is Father, the Son can say, "I and my Father are one." Can't be another. He is begetting himself; he is not begetting another.

So if he begets himself, the thing begotten would be Son. But because it is himself, and he the begetter is Father, the state or self-begotten is also Father, is it not? He said, "I and my Father are one. My Father is greater than I." But if the self-begotten though Son, yet Father, for he only begets himself, and, therefore, the begetter is a Father; the state begotten is Son. But he's only begetting himself; therefore, the Son-begotten is also Father. If he is Father, then he must have a Son.

And so, here is the great mystery of the appearance of David. David is set up in the beginning to prove to all that he begets that he gave you himself that is Father. And so God begets himself. And when he begets himself in you, it's you, it's not another. You come out of this tomb; and it's you, but it's God. God and the state begotten are one, for he can't beget another. And, therefore, begetting is Father, begotten is Son. Well, the Son and the Father are one. But because the Father is father and the Son is one with him, he has to be a father; therefore, "Where is my son?" Then comes David. David comes into his world and reveals him as Father. See the mystery?

So I say nothing is more important in this world than that the testimony of Jesus be heard and responded to. One should respond to it negatively or affirmatively. I hope you will respond to it affirmatively. Because if you believe it tonight with the same intensity that you now believe what you have not yet experienced, like dropping off the house—you haven't experienced that—but no one in this world could argue you out of the belief that if you dropped from the top of this house you'd break your neck or cripple your body. That you would do it to disprove these statements; you would do it. Because to you, without the experience, belief has become ___ (??). To know is tantamount to knowing and yet you haven't experienced it. So I ask you to believe this with the same intensity even though you haven't experienced it. I have experienced it and I want to speak with the conviction of having experienced it that you who have not experienced it may believe it with the same intensity that you now believe that if you dropped off this house you would either cripple or kill yourself.

So this is what I'm trying to get over tonight. We only have a few left, three more after tonight, and not to give lip service to these revelations of Christ: For he said in his words and in our words "imagining creates reality." If you worry and it's a habit, you are disclosing a lack of faith in the claim that imagining creates reality. How could you actually worry about anything in this world and still believe that whatever you imagine will come to pass? For whatever you ask in prayer, believe you received it and you will. If you actually believe that, really believe it, not just give it lip service, you could not then worry, you couldn't. For worry is simply a confession of your lack of faith in the claim that imagining creates reality.

So I'm not asking anyone here to take a secondhand car and start off for Maine. But if you only have a secondhand car and that is your objective, may I tell you, we have tangible proof that it works. Here we have in our latest book forty case histories culled from over, well, close to a thousand. I could have used them all, all based upon this simple claim that imagining creates reality. But you see, until it becomes something just as permanently fixed in our minds as an experience of falling off and yet not experienced, but believing to the point where it becomes knowledge, we can go back unnumbered times to former beliefs and not really persist in believing and applying this principle.

And so many of us, even in the book, there are forty stories told. I hope they're all still faithful to the picture. How faithful they are, I do not know. But even though their stories were used in the book, they could still go back to their former way of thinking and say within themselves, "Well, you know, maybe it would have happened anyway." That's quite possible. I only ask you to believe, believe it with that same intensity that you believe something you have not experienced. There are so many things I could tell you that you have not experienced that you so believe that you know. You wouldn't take a razor across your throat, and you haven't experienced it. You know without experience that if you did it you would be dead. You haven't experienced that, but you know it. So not everything that one actually knows is based upon experience.

So he comes, and he reveals to us the most glorious thing in the world and tells us what God has in store for us: to give himself to us, no strings attached. No intermediary. He gives himself to us ___(??) the Father. The Father actually becomes the state begotten; he begets himself. And he so begets himself he gives to the state begotten fatherhood, and David bears witness of that self-begotten as Father. For David calls him Father to fulfill the prophecy of the 89th Psalm: "I have found David and he has cried unto me 'Thou art Father, my God, and the Rock of my salvation'" (verse 26); Psalm 2, "Thou art my Son, today I have begotten thee" (verse 7). So here was this thing set up in the beginning of time to reveal God's purpose. When he begets himself in us and we come forward out of our own being as son, we have to be father. Although we are brought forward as God's Son, the Father and the Son are one, but he's one and the Father's father, the Son has to be Father; therefore, "Where is my son?" Well, the cry in the very last book of the Old Testament, the Book of Malachi, "The glory of a father is the son. If then I am a father, where is my son?" (1:6) If I'm really begotten of God and God is father and I am one with my begetter, we're one, I'm self-begotten, and my Father and I are one, then where is my son? And then comes David and David calls you Father.

So if you have not experienced it—and I take it so far you haven't—may I ask you to believe it with the same intensity that you now believe things you have not experienced. You have not had the experience of falling off the Empire State Building, but you know if you did you would die. Yet you haven't experienced it, but you *know* it. So knowing and believing are equal when faith develops in man. As faith develops they become one. So I ask you to know this story, that it's true, with the same intensity that you know things you have not yet experienced.

So this is this story tonight. To repeat it, "Our real beliefs are what we live by." It's so important then that our real beliefs are true; they could be lies. The last war is the result of the belief in lies. Every war, every violence is the belief in lies. But they will use the gun. We believe in an army. ___(??) believes in an army and came the convulsion of the world. So the one truth is "I am the truth." Listen to the words, the 14th of John, "I am the way, I am the truth, I am the light" (verse 6). You're the way to what? "I am the way to the Father; no one comes to the Father, but by me," but no one. "This is the way to the Father, and I am the truth—everything that I have said is true. They're not my words, the words of him who sent me." And so he tells the truth. Although they're not understood, he tells the truth. He said, "If you do not believe my words when I tell you of things of the earth, how could you believe me if I tell you things of heaven?" (John 3:12). How could you understand if I told you the things of heaven, if you do not understand the things I tell you concerning the earth? And he tells them the things of earth, and they do not respond affirmatively. He said, "I am the life . . . and no one comes to my Father save by me. I am the way to the Father." This is how it happens. He begets me, and begetting me he brings me forth, and he and I are one.

Now if you haven't had that experience, believe it. ___(??) believe it. I have had the experience; just as it is recorded in the scriptures I have experienced it. And that's exactly how it happens. It's going to happen to every being in this world. You know why? Because the God in you . . . if I ask you now, "Who are you?" Even if you didn't use the words or the words "I am" and you answer me, you might say, Grace, you might say, John; but before you said it, you're actually saying, "I am Grace. I am John. I am so and so." Well, I AM is the name of God. But before you can say anything of yourself, you say, "I am"—that's God. Well, God is begetting himself in you, and he's going to actually beget himself. And when he begets himself, you are actually formed. Listen to the words in the 4th chapter of Galatians, "My little children, I am once more in travail with you 'til Christ be formed in you!" (verse 19). Christ is being formed in you as you. All of you have to give birth to Christ, for Christ is the Son of God.

Now I ask, how can he be the Son of God, when Christ is the power and the wisdom of God? In eternity everything is human, but everything is human. The power, when you see it, takes on human form. When you see wisdom, it takes on human form. When you see might, almightiness is human. Everything is human. Everything comes out of you because you are man. All of the attributes of the mind of man take on human form. Many years ago, it must have been thirty-seven years ago, I sat in the Silence, and there I was lost in contemplation; and then before my vision, my inner eye, appeared a huge rock, a flint. And then before my eyes it broke and many pieces scattered all over. Then invisible hands molded it into the most beautiful figure of a meditating Buddha. And here was Buddha in meditation. I was glued to this beautiful figure. As I looked at it I became more and more excited. I am looking at myself. I was that meditative Buddha that I'm contemplating. And then it began to glow, and when it reached the limit of luminosity it exploded. It took on the luminosity of a sun and then exploded.

The day will come when out of your own being you will actually come forward and it's Christ and he's just like you, just like you. You're bringing forth your own being; God's bringing forth himself. And the self brought forth is a form: the form, the unbegotten, begetting himself . . . and it's you. Christ is your offspring. When he comes forward, as you look at him, he is yourself. Then you understand that 1st John, the 3rd chapter, "It does not yet appear what we shall be, but we know when he appears we shall be like him, and see him just as he is" (verse 19). For I saw the meditative figure, all out of stone. We are just dead as stone in the beginning. And here it broke, molding into something that was a statue. And then out of it came a glowing, living being and I am the being I am contemplating. So God is contemplating himself in you, begetting himself in you. And when he brings you forward you are Christ . . . and it's just like you, you raised to the apex of perfection. You couldn't improve upon the glory or the beauty of the being you're bringing forward out of your own self.

So here, we can start on one revelation, just like the girls chosen at the door of the coffeehouse. And try it there and you'll prove it to your own satisfaction, as they have. But before you prove this I ask you to believe it with the same degree of belief that you believe things you have not experienced. You don't have to experience many things in this world to really believe them. And so if I am going to start to believe—for my real beliefs are what I live by—I should believe only the truth. Therefore, nothing is more important in this world than that the testimony of Jesus be heard and responded to. And so respond to it. Believe it. I hope you do, because ultimately, you will anyway because God will not stop his purpose. His purpose is to beget himself in you and the mold is himself and the mold we have in the pioneer and perfecter of our faith called Christ Jesus. That's the mold. When it comes out, you the begetter and you the begotten are one. The begetter is a father; therefore, the begotten though son must be a father. Therefore, "If I be a father, where is my son?" And then David appears and David calls you Father. And then you go back and search the scripture. Then you find all the evidence for the experience. So David is supposed to call the Lord God, Father. "He has cried unto me, 'Thou art my father, my God, and the Rock of my salvation."

So whom do you speak of? Who is David? And who is Christ? And then you find all these answers coming into you. He called me Father. If he called me Father, how can I be his son? So Christ is the begotten of God. But he's one with God. If he's one with God and God is father, he has to have a son, and David calls him Father. So he asks the question, "What do you think of the Christ? Whose son is he?" And they answered, "The son of David." And so he replied, "Why then did David in the spirit call him Lord? If David called him Lord, how can he be David's son?" (Matthew 22:42). And so they said to him, "Show us the Father, and we will be satisfied." He said, "I have been so long with you, Philip, and you do not know me? He who has seen me has seen the Father; how then can you say, 'Show us the Father'? And they asked him no more questions" (John 14:8).

Do you see the mystery? When you open that Bible, you're reading God's history, you're reading a mystery. It's not like any other book in the world. And a mystery, as I've told you time and again, is not something to be kept as a secret, but it is a truth that is mysterious in character. How to unravel? Well, in my own case, it happened. The whole thing is unfolded in me. I'm sharing with you my own experience, asking you to believe it without the experience that you may aid the forming of the unbegotten within. Because you will believe anyway; man lives by his beliefs. So don't accept these lies and distort the picture, for it can't come forward until it's perfect. For we are told, "Be ye perfect as your Father in heaven is perfect." So you cannot bring to birth any imperfection; it has to be right. And so you must be holy, for the Father, the Lord your God, is holy. But I can't bring forward anything but the holiness, but the perfection. So if you believed a lie, then there's a distortion and you can't bring to birth anything but perfection.

So not a thing in this world is more important than the testimony of Jesus, and it must first be heard and then the response to that testimony. I hope that you will respond to it, as I desire with all my heart, with complete acceptance. Accept the testimony. It's true. One day will come, who knows when, maybe tonight—it is my hope, tonight, tomorrow, but in the immediate present—that you'll bring forward the perfection that is Christ. For you have to give birth to Christ and Christ is yourself. You don't meet something going out of yourself; you go out. You actually come forward and you are born. And all the witnesses as told in scripture are present and they bear witness to that invisible presence. You are more conscious of being alive than anything in the world; but no one sees you because God is Spirit. It's God that is born. God is Spirit; therefore, his Son is spirit. In God, there is life; in the Son there is life. You are the most living being imaginable at that moment when you come forth out of your being, self-begotten. For God only begets himself.

Now let us go into the Silence.

*   *   *

Q: (inaudible)

A: ___(??) Bible, the gospel of John. The first narrative begins in the first chapter; I think it's in the thirty-third verse through to the end. It begins by showing the disciples finding, seeing and believing in him, that's how it starts. First they find him, they see him and they believe him. The last narrative, if you take the 20th chapter—there are twenty-one chapters but all scholars are agreed the 21st chapter is an epilogue—so really, the end chapter of the gospel of John is the 20th chapter. And the last narrative is this: seeing and believing. But we have it moving forward to a faith which is not dependent upon physical seeing at all. The beatitude is given to the one who sees not and yet believes. For even all the witnesses brought together into believers, they still move forward with an imperfect seeing and certainly never fully realized goal. Abraham didn't. No, not one prophet, not one patriarch fully realized or obtained the goods, but they still moved forward with an imperfect seeing, an unfulfilled goal. And all these were brought together, cumulatively speaking altogether, in a massive state to show what is produced by man. Because behind this stands all of these characters, aiding us is our beliefs, they surround us. So the gospel of John begins with finding, seeing, and believing; it ends with seeing and believing. But it goes beyond that, and then the beatitude is pronounced upon the one who has not seen and yet believes.

So I ask you to trust me. I ask you to believe in me. May I this very moment—and I have no desire to go; the moment I go doesn't really matter—but if I haven't told you the truth this night as I have experienced it, may I never speak again. Just about ___(??). I haven't contrived it. I haven't for one moment tried to develop some workable philosophy of life. I have no desire to establish a church or a religion or any organization, none. I'm simply telling you what has happened to me, and what has happened to me is all written out in scripture.

So without seeing . . . for Thomas insisted on seeing, and so he appeared. The door is closed, in the midst of them all he appears; and then, Thomas, because he sees the risen Lord and believes, he says now, "Do you believe now because you see me, Thomas? Blessed are those who do not see and yet believe" (John 20:24). He didn't pronounce the blessing on Thomas; he pronounced the blessing on those who did not see, who didn't have the experience and yet believed. So I tell you, begin to believe now. It's true; everything I've told you this night is true.

And so the massive evidence accumulated in the eleventh through the twelfth chapters of Hebrews; he names them all, beginning with the first one, Abel. Comes all the way down, and then he said, "Unnumbered," after he mentions all of the great patriarchs. Then he couldn't mention any more. But they did not receive the promise, he tells them, because God had a greater picture for us, that we're all coming together. It was not really for them but for us because the time was not yet fulfilled for one to be born. And they inquired when and who ___(??).

Listen to the words we used earlier, quoting from Paul's letters, "I know who I have believed." Not what I have believed—I know who I have believed. He personified his own wonderful Imagination, for it happened to him. And so that which seemed to be an impersonal power—he is the power and the wisdom of God—and then suddenly it takes on human form and it is he. So I know who I believed. Now who are you going to believe? Well, I know what I did. I believed. (Tape ends.)

THE STORY OF SALVATION

May 24, 1963

___(??) by one of our great educators—whether you agree with his political opinions or not that's irrelevant, really—but his name is Robert Hutchins. Regardless of what you think of a man's political opinions, if the man has accomplished much in this world as he has, then listen to what he has to say. He said, "When I taught Macbeth as a professor in school"—now here are these great schools preparing our young men for great universities—he said, "My pupils looked upon it as a blood and thunder story. That's all that they saw in Macbeth. They could not understand Macbeth as Shakespeare *meant* it to be understood by us without the experience, vicarious or actual, of marriage and ambition. For that's the story of Macbeth. They thought it was simply a great Scottish western. And so these are fellows just entering our great universities. But you couldn't understand the great story unless you had either a vicarious experience of it, someone who had experienced it and told you, or that you yourself experienced it. And here is one of the truly great tragedies of all time taking as its theme marriage and ambition. What it can do to man, distort all values in this world, if ambition goes outside of the bounds of your moral and ethical code—what it does to marriage.

So here, I say the same thing is true of the greatest story ever told, and that is the story of salvation, as given to us in the scriptures in the life of Jesus Christ. You cannot fully understand it save vicariously or unless you have the experience. I hope that you will listen to one who has *had* the experience and believe it. For salvation is pinned upon hearing the true story of salvation, understanding it, and believing it. For belief is essential for it to take root in man.

Now we will turn to one of the many stories told in the gospels. This is the gospel of John, the tenth chapter. In essence, he calls himself "a door."

He says, "The sheep cannot enter save they come through this door. They will hear the voice of no one but the voice of the shepherd. The shepherd will lead them first, and they will follow the shepherd." Well, that's not the point I want to make tonight. The point in the same chapter is this, "I and my Father are one." It's the boldest claim that man ever made, the 30th verse of the 10th chapter of the gospel of John: "I and my Father are one." Then we are told, the Jews took up stones to stone him, and he answered them saying, "I have shown you many good works from my Father; for which of these do you stone me?" They answered, "For no good work do we stone you but for blasphemy; for you being a man, make yourself God." Then he answered, "Is it not written in your law"—now bear in mind he was born and raised a Jew, fully familiar with the law—"Is it not written in your law that 'I said, you are gods'? If they are called gods to whom the word of God came, (and scripture cannot be broken), then why do you feel that the one who is consecrated by the Father and sent by him into the world blasphemes when he has said, 'I am the son of God'? If you do not believe me, believe the works. Believe it just for the works sake if you cannot believe me that you may know and understand that the Father is in me and I am in the Father" (verse 34). Then we are told they tried to arrest him, and he escaped from their hands.

Now here is the boldest of all claims, "I and my Father are one." My Father can never be so far off as even to be near, for nearness implies separation. He can't be so far off as even to be near, for it implies separation: We are one. And then he turns to that wonderful scripture, the 42nd Psalm, where it's a sad, it's a lonely psalm, "As the hart panteth after the water brook, so panteth my soul after thee, O God" (verse 1). And then he paints a word picture of the sadness of life. He has a thirst that nothing can change but an *experience* of God. Then he speaks of his own tears, he said, "My tears have been my food day and night"—intensifying the ___(??)ness of the tears, intensifying these things—"while men say to me and say continually, 'Where is your God?'"

They'll do it all the time. If you dare to claim that I and my Father are one, let the smallest little thing happen to you in this world, a toothache, let there be a rip in your hand because you simply got your finger cut, let anything happen to you, and you'll find crowds liking to say, "Where is your God?" You dare to claim that I and my Father are one and you go further and say, "My Father is he whom you call God; but I know my Father and ye know not your God." Make these bold assertions and see how the whole vast world—when your food day and night happens to be your tears, and you think you can conceal them; you can't conceal them—men will say to you and say continually, "Where is your God?" But in the midst of it all you still must persist in identifying yourself with God. You're one with God, and he's molding himself on you, in you, as his very being.

Then you start from there to prove *things*. As he said, "You don't believe me, then believe the works." Believe the works, for you must begin to believe for the thing to take root in you. If it doesn't take root in you, it can't grow. Salvation *depends* upon hearing the story of salvation, hearing it, understanding it and believing it—that you don't see it as blood and thunder. For if you take the story as it really is presented by the churches of the world, it's blood and thunder, a little child, and they try to snuff out the little child and slaughter the innocents. Tens of thousands of innocents were slaughtered in the hope of reaching the one. That's how the story starts, blood and thunder.

Then, his family denied him, his brothers wouldn't believe him, no one believed him as the story began to unfold within him. No matter what he did in the world, all the signs of the world did not convince them that he was the one promised who would come into the world. For the world looked for something entirely different, some conquering hero would come out of the clouds and enslave the enemy of Israel; and then himself would set up as this conquering hero, and that would be the one they called Messiah. Messiah doesn't come that way. For Messiah makes the statement, "My kingdom is not of this world." It's not of world. Everything you see here is fading; it's vanishing, but everything is vanishing like smoke and everything is wearing out, just like a garment. There isn't a thing in this world . . . all the medals of the world will be poured out and emptied. This building, solid as it is, will make way for something greater than what it is today, or maybe just an empty parking lot, like the one next door. That was a lovely old building too just a matter of months ago; it's now a parking lot. So everything is changing in this world and nothing endures in this world. But says he in the 51st chapter of Isaiah: "Lift up your eyes and see; look at the heavens, they'll vanish like smoke, and lower your eyes to the earth, it wears out like a garment; but my salvation will be forever, and my redemption will never come to an end" (verse 6).

So listen to the story of redemption. How is it done? It's a simple story. The most impossible thing in the world but it's true. I stand here because I only have two more lectures; and if you've heard it a hundred times, hear it again. For if tonight you got a million dollars by the application of God's law and you didn't know the story of salvation, and didn't understand it so that you could believe it, the million dollars would be as nothing. That's part of the earth that wears out like a garment, that's part of the heavens that vanish into thin air, leaving nothing. But there is a plan that God has for the whole vast world, to redeem the world, and he redeems it with himself.

So his statement, "I and my Father are one" is a true statement. For when God redeems *you* it's himself because God himself became as you are that you may be as he is. That's a true statement. God actually became you, taking upon himself all the limitations of this fragile little garment and all the weaknesses of the being called Neville, but all of them, not a few of them. He actually entered into me and partakes of everything that I am in this world, to redeem me. He redeems me by a predetermined plan. It's a blueprint inwoven into the soul of man that is God's prophetic blueprint. And at a certain moment in time it begins to unfold.

When it begins to unfold, go back into scripture, and then you'll see it all foretold. Every word was in scripture, beginning back in the Book of Genesis and coming all through the thirty-nine books of the Old Testament. But no man understood it until it happened. When it happened, the one *in* whom it happened then told it. But that's not the way they thought it *should* happen, so they didn't believe it. And still today they don't believe it because the churches are not telling it. May I tell you, no church in this world can save you. No church in the world can in any way produce a Christian. A Christian can only be produced by the hearing of the story of salvation, hearing it with understanding and believing. It's the most incredible story in the world.

To understand a picture of it, let us go to the 7th chapter of 2nd Samuel. This has been completely violated throughout the century, and yet it's essential to the picture. I say now to my servant, my prophet Nathan, "Go to my servant David." David is humanity. David is not the little individual; David is symbolical of the whole vast world of humanity. Go and tell mankind not to build a house for me; *I* will build a house for him. The word house has a peculiar meaning; it means "a dwelling place" and it means "family." Mankind must not build a dwelling place for me, "for I the Lord do not dwell in buildings or houses made by hands" (Acts 7:48). I dwell with them who believe in me. That's where I dwell: right in the heart of all who believe in me. I will build a house, meaning now a family, for him. He personifies David as a single individual. Although David represents the whole vast world of humanity, in speaking to David he speaks to David as a unit, as an individual being. Let him not build for me, I will build for him. I'll build him a family. And that's the great secret of salvation.

God in the soul of man is building a family for David. He's building out of David—this is David—he's building out of David and *in* David, a father. For David could not call him, Father; he always spoke of him as The Lord, as God. But he's going to build in David, and out of David, a father, and when David sees him he can't restrain the impulse to *call* him Father. This is what he promised David: "When you sleep with your fathers"—in other words, saying, when you die, and this [world] is death—"I the Lord will raise up your son after you, who will come forth from your body. *I* will be his father, and he shall be my son" (2 Samuel 7:12, 14). So out of David—you, the speaker, every being in this world—God is actually bringing forth himself, for the words I first started tonight with, "I and my Father are one." He isn't bringing forth another, he's bringing forth himself: "I and my Father are one."

So he's bringing out of David himself. He is begetting himself on David. So begetting himself on David, the thing begotten is his son; yet it's one with himself that is God the Father. The minute he completes it, David awakens and David sees what came out of him. But David has to call that which came out, Father. He redeems humanity. He redeems the individual first, and eventually redeems the whole vast world of humanity by this wonderful process of salvation. He redeems the individual by bringing out of that individual, himself. But the thing brought out has form; it's begotten, and the being who brings it out is the unbegotten; it is God. And so the being begetting is the Father; the being begotten is the Son. The being begotten is the father of that out of which he came.

And here is a mystery. He comes out seemingly as the Son of man. Well, he is; he came out of David—he comes out of you, comes out of me. If he comes out of me, then he's the Son of man, yet the Son of man is the Son of God. For what comes out of man was begotten by God. And yet you can't deny it came out of man; therefore, it is the Son of man, and yet it is the Son of God. So the Son of God makes the statement, "I and my Father are one." You'll say to me when he calls you God, and who hears the word of God is called the Son of God. And he's quoting in that chapter, the 82nd chapter of the Book of Psalms, it begins, "And God has taken his place in the divine council; in the midst of the gods he holds judgment." Then he turns to those that he brought forth, "I say that you are gods, all of you, sons of the Most High." Well, then he told them the story, before this was accomplished, "I say, 'you will die like men and fall like any prince'" (verse 1 and 6.) And so you and I die like men and fall like any prince, although, eventually, what is brought out of us is begotten of God and, therefore, the Son of God. But it came out of man, and therefore it is the Son of Man. So the Son of man can say, "I and my Father are one, though my Father is greater than I."

Let me repeat it, my Father, if I *really* believe it, can never be so far off as even to be near, for nearness implies a separation. So in that 42nd Psalm—it's a very lonely psalm—he turns and he communes with himself, that's how he finds God. He turns to himself. And then, at one moment, it didn't come to him, that communion with God, and then what does he do? He turns to memory, he said, "I remember thee." Then he turns to memory, and that's it: there is the secret. He's revealing to us the means of escape.

So tonight if I am now troubled because someone said, "Where is your God?" Haven't you had it? One Sunday night, I am lecturing in New York City but hadn't the slightest idea I ever had a gall bladder. Had no knowledge whatsoever that I had such a thing as a gall bladder. Here I am lecturing in town hall—but a dinner party is scheduled the next night, and then that Sunday night, when I came home from my lecture, colic beyond the wildest dream, pain, excruciating pain. So my dinner party I wouldn't cancel. I left my wife to be the hostess of the evening, and I remained in my bedroom. Came eleven that night, when the pain did not subside, not a thing I could do; they rushed me to the hospital, and that was it. Then came my wonderful friends, "Where's your God, Neville?" It only fulfilled the 42nd Psalm of David. I came to fulfill. Everything is a word in the word of God, I must fulfill. If I didn't have a friend in my world, who would say to me, "Where is your God?" part of my scripture would be unfulfilled. I can see him coming through now, before he even started to know that this is Neville; he was asking the question on the outside, "Where is your God, Neville? Why did it happen to you?" In other words, I'll go back now to my own concept of God, whether it be lighting a candle or saying a little prayer on the side or giving to charity in the hope of appeasing something up in space. But someone must have sent to me here, as you know he is, because were he here, one with me, and he and I one, why should you be there in that bed? And so this happens to everyone that's in the world.

So I have come, said he, to fulfill scripture. And every word of scripture must be fulfilled, for scripture, said he, cannot be broken. When he's quoted in that 10th chapter—the words are set aside, "scripture cannot be broken," the 10th of John—and calls you gods (verse 35); and yet he tells you you'll die like men and fall as any prince? And the one that he's consecrated and he's sent into the world and you tell me he blasphemes because he said, "I am the Son of God"? Well, "Don't believe me now, believe the works." "Have you seen the many things that I have done?" said he. Well, believe the things that I have *done* if you don't believe me. Well, the things that happened to me I can't share them with you, but I can share, the eyes being open, I can share those who wanted to dispose of ___(??), and dispose of it to celebrate the thing that they used: the imaginal act. I can share with you the *unnumbered* things that happened in the world when I told of my Father's law, that imagining creates reality. If a man dares to imagine that he is the man that he wants to be and remains loyal to that imaginal state regardless of what happens in the world, if he is loyal to that state it *must* become an objective fact in his world. And it does!

Have you followed the story? said he. It all happened, didn't it? They conceded that it happened, they were miraculous. But no matter how many and how multiplied the number, neither the number nor the nature of the signs that he produced in the world evoked faith. They had no more faith because he did all these things. So he asked us to believe in the *things*, if you can't believe in me. For he couldn't take them into the depths of his soul where these things take place and really show how they took place. He could only tell them.

So to come back to the first statement, the little pupils did not believe it, and they could not understand it without the experience whether that experience is first vicarious or actual. And so a vicarious experience is all I can give you. I ask you to share with me my experience, and to you, before you experience it, it's vicarious. After you've experienced what I tell you, you will know how true it is, and then, it is something that is *real* in your life. And you will not look upon this as blood and thunder. For the story of Jesus is really blood and thunder, for that's the story of life. Every child born of woman goes through all these horrible experiences in the world.

It's the story of Job. And in the very end, he's salvaged, he's saved. How is he saved? He's saved by God who saves himself because *God* played all the parts. Only God is playing the part in this world today. No matter what the man is doing, whether he's the most horrible beast in the world, God is playing that part, because there's no other being to play it. "God only acts and is in all existing beings or men." God actually became just what I am. I've done so many things of which I am not proud, but today I know, in the very end "Though my sins be as scarlet, they shall be white as snow." In the very end, *all* is forgiven, because in the end I am one with the being who begot me. Then he lifts me up completely, beyond this level, and I'm in an entirely different world.

So the story of salvation, although difficult to grasp, I am not repeating it because I heard it. I am like Paul. It was revealed to Paul, in the sense that he experienced it; it was revealed to me in the sense that I experienced it. And although these events are separated in time, they form a single complex, and they start with resurrection. You can completely forget the crucifixion. You were crucified with God in the beginning of time. That's behind us. Forget that, you aren't facing that; that's behind you. But what is ahead of you, and the first event in the series that awakens the entire drama is resurrection. You only resurrect if you're dead. Therefore, when you are resurrected, you come out of the grave, the grave of your own wonderful skull. Coming out of that is in itself a birth.

The next event is the discovery of the relationship he promised David, "I will build for you a family." David doesn't know, but he promised him,

"I will build for you a family. Do not you build for me a dwelling place; I will build for you a family." And so he builds a family using you, his own begotten self, as the father of David. So David has a father. What is the father's name? Your name. What in the Bible is his father's name? Jesse. What does Jesse mean? I AM. So who is your father? My father's name is I AM. So he builds David—he keeps his promise, he never fails in his promise—so he builds for David a family, a relationship of father-son.

Then he takes the next step and he tears the curtain of the temple from top to bottom so there's no more intermediary between his son and himself: they are one. Then the son *as* the father—his own begetter, his own redeemer, his own creator—move up and ascend into Zion. They move up in this wonderful living liquid light state, right into Zion, into the skull. And then he remains for the few remaining years to tell his story. He tells it to as many as will hear it. Let them all be exposed to it, but they must hear it as it really took place, hear it and understand it, and believe it. So that is how salvation takes place in the world.

For no priest, no man, no church in this world can make you a Christian. Christianity is the unfolding of the promises made to Israel. The New Testament is simply the unfolding and fulfillment of the Old. It's not a new religion, one as old as the faith of Abraham, one scripture. And so you hear it with understanding. You're told that it first took place in *one* person and naturally rejected because it wasn't as they expected it. Forever it's the same, same story. They called him a drunkard, they called him a glutton, one who loved harlots, one who loved tax collectors, one who loved all kinds of things that the good people thought should not be done by one who makes such a claim. For they had their own concept of what the one should do in this world if really he was anointed by the Lord. He certainly shouldn't do the things that they would judge harshly.

And yet every time it comes, it comes in the same way. He could never be accepted by those who have their own standards, their own codes by which men should be judged who make the claim that God has consecrated him and sent him into the world to tell the story, one in whom the entire thing unfolded itself. We don't *look* the part, and so if he is a stumbling block in the world, all he can say is "It happened, anyway." But invariably he is a stumbling block to everyone in the world who's looking for an entirely different personality, a different character, something different, a mental giant, or maybe a physical giant, or maybe a combination, or maybe someone with a marvelous social background, a great wonderful background, but he isn't that at all. When he comes, he comes into a very simple environment, completely unknown.

But then the time is right in the eye of God for the seed that was hidden in the soul of man to begin to unfold, and at the appointed hour, it unfolds in the individual and all he can do is tell about it. If they believe it, all well and good. If you won't believe, he will say to them, "What do you want? I will tell you how to get it." And then he will tell them the simple story of causation: That causation is mental, as told us in the Sermon on the Mount. It's all mental, not physical. You see that woman? You like her? Would you like to know her intimately? Yes. You really would? You have already committed the act of adultery. Your very longing to know her in that intimate state is the act, therefore, causation is mental. That's what he's saying right away.

Now if causation is mental, I'll show you how to create. It's very simple, for here was the act: by a longing on your part, you committed the act. And this is what we do. Causation is the assemblage of a mental state which occurring creates that which the assemblage implies. And so I would like (and I name it). You would? Yes. Well then, what would happen *if* you had it? Well, I would do so and so, and they would say so and so to me. They would? Well, then, bring so and so into your mind's eye and let them say to you what they would say were it true. Would you? Yes. Well, then do it.

Last Tuesday night my friend at home, who drives me home from these lectures, he said, "I've been thinking over your very, very brilliant statement, 'Assume the feeling of the wish fulfilled. What would it be like were it true? How would I feel were it true?'" And then said he to me, "Here is a statement, a very common statement, but it really fits" and this is what he said, "Try it on for size." It's a very marvelous statement. Try it on for size. You want to be (and you name it), something much bigger than you've experienced before, much bigger. Well, it's too big! But try it on for size, and then we can adjust it. We can fit it. Try it on. How would the world see you were you now the man that you want to be? How would they see you? Well, I'm embarrassed, it's too big. Well, we'll cut it down, bring it down until finally it seems natural. You do it until it seems natural, when it seems to take on the tones of reality. What's real to you, what's natural? Well, try it on for size. What would the feeling be like were it true? And so, you feel that it *is* natural and it feels natural. From that moment on, things will begin to happen. It's going to come into this world as a perfectly normal, natural fact.

Now, the world will know of it, because you will tell, others will tell it, and they'll have all the evidence in the world. And they will say, "Well, he told me this law and this is what happened; and this is what he did and that's what happened." Well, let me meet him in the flesh. He doesn't look like a person who ought to be person that God consecrated. I once met him at a party and he drank much too much, and I'm quite sure he ate too much.

And so all the stories go concerning the person, the individual, the external garment that he's wearing, and they judge him by the garment; because they haven't ears to hear and eyes to see the God housed within him. They don't know that being at all, and they can only judge from appearances.

But when he comes into the world, as told us in the 11h chapter of the Book of Isaiah, he judges not by what his eye sees, nor does he decide by what his ears hear. He doesn't, he can't. He doesn't care what you look like. All he asks, "What do you want? 'What wantest thou of me?'" and you name it. Well, he knows causation, so he assembled in his mind's eye the necessary imagery that would imply if true that you are what you want to be, and he remains loyal to that assumption. He doesn't waver in his loyalty to the assembled imagery, regardless of what happens to you in the interval between your request and the fulfillment of that request.

So when it happens, you may turn back like the one percent and say "Thank you"; or you may, like the nine percent, forget it. Nine percent ___ (??), but it really is ninety percent, for there were ten and one turned back, and nine never turned back. So nine will receive the word and go their way, oblivious to the fact that one heard good news for him, and off they went unmindful of the act. He doesn't care. He only asks a very simple question to go on record for the word of God: "Were there not ten of you? Where are the other nine? For you're all cured of leprosy, so where are the other nine?"

And so, here is the entire story of salvation. Hasn't a thing to do with a church, lovely as they are, but I am warned in the 2nd Book of Samuel, the 7th chapter, not to build him one. Let no one—David is the whole vast world—Let no one in the world of humanity build me a church; I will build for you a family. The word is a play on the two meanings of the word house. Do not build for me a house; I will build you a house. And David ___ (??) do not build a dwelling place, for I do not dwell in buildings made by hands. I dwell in the heart within who believe it. But I will build *you* a house, in other words, I will build you a family. And then he builds me the family, and David doesn't know until finally the Father appears, and then he calls him Father, automatically. The two view each other as though they knew each other forever. He builds him a Father; he builds him a family, and this relationship goes on forever and forever; it never comes to an end.

So he hid him in man, and then brought him forward as man's son. You can't call it a reward because this is grace, and grace is an unmerited gift. But he brings him forward as the most glorious gift in the world, the gift of a son. Now we are told in Isaiah, the 9th chapter, "To us a child is born, yes, but to us a son is given" (verse 6). It's a gift: David. And to us a son is given and David is given to us, individually, as son. Then in the very end when the curtain comes down on this drama *everyone* will be the father of one son, and that son is David. The father can say of his own begetter, "I am the son of John," but in this case "I am one with my Father." For the being begetting is one with the self-begotten. He isn't begetting another; he's begetting himself. So God is begetting himself, but as he begets himself, the self-begotten is God. And you are God. So don't be embarrassed.

And when they start throwing stones, and a stone is not a stone we see, the stones are the literal facts of life, these are the stones. So they pick up the stones in their mental hands and show you that they know who you are, when you were born, how old you are, the limitations of your background, both intellectual, financial, social, and every other way. They name them all. These are stones they throw at you: the facts of life. So they throw all the literal facts of life to stone you. Then you will ask a simple question, "For which good works do you stone me?" and they will say, "Not for any good work but for blasphemy. Because you are a man"—I know you, I know where you were born, we have your birth certificate, all about you—"and you being a man dare to make yourself God." And if you say to them, "Is it not written in your law 'I said that you are gods'? And if he calls them gods to whom the word of God came (and scripture cannot be broken) then why is it blasphemy when the one whom God consecrates and sends into the world makes the statement, 'I am the son of God'?"

Now, you don't believe that? All right, you don't have to, believe the works. Ask nothing but the works—don't ask him how it happens—where it's a simple, simple mental causation. Do not believe in the one in whom the whole thing happened, believe the works. And then at the very end they were still denying ___(??).

Now let us go into the Silence.

*　　　*　　　*

Q: (inaudible)

A: ___(??) Cinderella? Well, they have far more of vision, real vision than all the morning papers put together. ___(??) *Alice in Wonderland*, you read it and think, well, that's a lovely story; and you forget it. It is filled with vision, filled with it. Now that's where the two little girls, I mean, where Alice comes. Tweedle Dee and Tweedle Dum and they say, "Let us go to see the king." And then, of course, the king is sleeping. Then Tweedle Dee says, "But he is sleeping, he's dreaming. I wonder what he is dreaming about." Alice replies, "No one can know that." Tweedle Dee exclaims triumphantly, "Why he's dreaming about you. And what do you think would happen to you if he stopped dreaming?" You look at and smile. ___(??) of that story is true, what would happen to us if God stopped dreaming? He isn't going to stop dreaming until he awakens us as himself, because the dreamer must be awakened. Because if he stopped dreaming this dream, we all would vanish into thin air and leave not a rack behind. Only those in whom he awoke would be one with him, the dreamer. If he stops the dream before he awoke in all, those in whom he has not awakened would vanish like smoke. And so this great author saw it, saw it clearly, and put it into picture form. So little Alice goes and the king is sound asleep, and Tweedle Dee ___(??) said, "Why it's the king and I wonder what he's dreaming about? And the poor thing, she replied, "No one can know that." He said, "Why he's dreaming about you. And what do you think would happen to you if he stopped dreaming?" We go blindly on thinking that's a . . . isn't that lovely, it means nothing. That's how sound asleep we are. And that is a child's story.

I'll see you Monday and I'll reread my Cinderella. ___(??)

JESUS ONLY

May 28, 1963

Now tonight's subject is "Jesus." Last week, a friend of mine said to me, "You know, I've heard you so often, but really over quite a period now, and I'm not quite sure that you believe in Jesus." Well, that's my friend's opinion, perfectly all right. If I said to you, "Do you believe in God?" the chances are everyone here would say yes, without batting an eye. And if you asked me, "Do you believe in God?" I would, without hesitating, I would say, "Why, certainly I believe in God, but, you know, you and I may be miles and ages away in what we believe."

Today, I said I believe in democracy. Well, so does Khrushchev, but it's not my concept of democracy. Or maybe . . . how old is the United Nations, I don't know, but the Australian Ambassador, who represents Australia at the United Nations in San Francisco, ___(??), he defined for us his country's concept of democracy, which is my concept, but it may not be yours; and certainly, it is not Khrushchev's. He said, "Democracy to us in Australia is based upon the principle of compromise, but not upon the compromise of principle." All the difference in the world! For that's my concept of democracy: this two party system, where this area of the world, our world, needs help, but it doesn't—someone in the mid-West they don't need the same kind of help, but they will cast their vote with me, representing this part of the world, that I may get the help I need for the people I represent. And so I don't need what he wants when the vote comes up and he's putting it forward, but I remember his kindness to me and so I will throw my vote with him. That's not compromising principles; it's simply the principle of compromise.

So when I was asked, "Do you believe in Jesus?" I said, "Well, I don't think anyone walking the face of this earth believes more in Jesus than I do."

But, who is Jesus? The poet said, "Truth embodied in a tale shall enter in at lowly doors." Well, the authors of the Bible, and no one to this day knows who they are, no one knows the author of the Bible, save it's inspired and dictated by God. So when we read Jeremiah, Isaiah, and all these names, no one knows the true prophet who received an inspiration, this Word of God. But they knew, as the poet I just quoted knew, that we understand best not bare truths but thoughts put into stories. Man wants to *see* the truth, and so, they presented the story in such a manner that we could *see* the truth. But over the years, man has mistakenly taken personifications for persons; they've mistaken the vehicle that *conveys* the message for the message; the gross first-sense for the ultimate-sense intended. So today, we have idols made out of the personifications of truth.

So here, let me this night try to explain to you what I mean when I use the word Jesus. You see, you and I name a child because we like a relative, or a friend or maybe the sound of the name. You will say, "Well, I like that, that sounds well," so we give a child a name based upon sound, or based upon the fact that we like our uncle or our father or our mother, or maybe some friend. But in the Bible, this great book of God, it is not done in that manner. In the Hebraic world, names are chosen for their meaning in ___(??); so all these names are chosen for their *meaning* in the great drama of God. So what is the name Jesus? It's the Anglicized form of the Hebrew word Joshua. It means "Jehovah is salvation." Jehovah is a savior. Therefore, the 43rd of the Book of Isaiah tells us, "For I am the Lord your God, the Holy One of Israel, your Savior. I, I am He, and besides me there is no savior" (verse 11). Call him Jesus, for he shall save his people from their sins. So he's called Jesus, and the only savior is Jehovah; and Jehovah's only name is I AM.

So who is Jesus? He's the savior, the only savior. He will save all people, his people, from their sins, and his name is Jesus. The word Jesus is spelled the same root as Jehovah. It begins Yod He Vau—that is the *root* of the name of the Lord, which we call the Lord. Which in Hebrew, don't even sound it, it's so sacred a name you don't sound it. But you've got to sound it; if you could, they translate the word "the Lord." But he is called "the Lord." And so, Jesus and Jehovah are one and the same. But the name of Jehovah—and man forgets it, he just can't keep the tense with him—the name is I AM.

So, when I make the claim that God so loved you that he became you, I mean that *literally*. That's not some poetical statement; I mean it literally. He so *loved* you that he became you. It is God's purpose to give you himself, as though there were no others in the world, just God and you; and *finally* only you. The gift is complete and it's only you, for his name is I AM. So when we are told he bears all the sins of the world, all the blows of the world, that's to be taken as literally true.

Many years ago, when I was in the theatre, this goes back into the twenties, the early thirties, there was quite an argument going on in our little circle in New York City as to the true author of Shakespeare. Many believed it was Bacon, others believed other people, but no one would accept the fact there was a man called Shakespeare. And so, someone presented the argument it was an acrostic and they brought me the book of *The Tempest*, written in 1611, the year that our Bible came out in English—that was the year that the King James Version was presented to the public. So Shakespeare wrote *The Tempest* in the atmosphere of that beautiful English. And no one understanding English would put anyone in Shakespeare's class when it comes to the use of English. We love Mr. Churchill—I love him as a man; I love all of these great men, men and women that walk the face of the earth over the years, over the centuries—but you have to really, well, you must be able to read the English tongue to put anyone in a close race with Shakespeare and the use of the English tongue. Whoever he was—I don't know whether he was Bacon and I question that seriously—but whoever he was, there was a master. And he had but 300 years and no one truly knows who wrote Shakespeare.

But here is the year 1611 and he brought out *The Tempest*. In the first act, second scene, the heroine of the story, Miranda, turns to her father, Prospero. He was the banished Duke of Milan and shipwrecked. And so he had the power of enchantment and so using his magical powers he created storms and lightning, and all kinds of disturbances, turbulence to rescue the usurper of his title, which he did. So Miranda turns to her father, Prospero, and it's a very simple little story. But, instead of using the acrostic in this, which they try to convince you Shakespeare did it, I thought of only what was there. It has stuck with me through the years. And this is what she said to her father: "You have often begun to tell me what I am but stopped and left me to a bootless inquisition, concluding, stay, not yet." Here she's asking, Please tell me who I am. Tell me. You've often begun to tell me what I am but stopped and left me to a bootless inquisition, concluding, stay, not yet.

Well, whoever was Shakespeare was a giant, a mystical giant to have written that little speech of Miranda. For here, *we* are Miranda, left to a bootless inquisition. I need not tell you about the word inquisition, where a man is put through the tortures of hell, bootless. Well, a boot covers the foot and the foot has always been the symbol of the generative organs of man, always, in all the languages of the world. When I wash the foot, I am cleaning the creative organ of a man. When I take the linen cloth from you and I wipe that foot, I am exposing the creative organ of the man. When I say, "Take off your shoes, for the ground on which you stand is holy ground," I am telling you to uncover the creative organ of the man. On that eighth day, the circumcision is the unveiling of the creative organ of a man.

So here, it is an unveiling of this power, where man is then subjected to the most violent rape in the world. Not only sexual rape but all kinds of rape: revolutions are rapes; wars are rapes. All the violence of the world is the bootless inquisition. And so, "You have left me to a bootless inquisition, concluding, stay, not yet." It isn't yet time for you to know *who* you are and *what* you are. I can tell you this night who you are in the hope you'll believe it, but with all of my faith and my intensity I question seriously that you will believe it. I tell you that you are Jesus, the only Jesus. There's nothing but Jesus, and Jesus and Jehovah are one. There's nothing but God in this world. And Jesus is playing this part and he was left to the bootless inquisition, where they spat upon him, where they hurt him, where they did everything in the world conceivable for man to do to man, as Browning said, "Man's inhumanity to Man." It's part of the drama.

And so, "Tell me. You've often begun to tell me what I am but stopped and left me to a bootless inquisition, concluding, stay, not yet." If you have an original portfolio, I don't mean the original, I mean a facsimile, I have one at home; and when you see it printed it does spell Bacon, no question about it. For the beginning of every line is capitalized and so the first line is indented, so that's not intended to be read. "You have often," that's indented, and it begins with "Begun." Well, "Begun" is a ___(??) "B." "Begun to tell me what I am but stopped." Then you come back to the next line, "And"—and "And" is capitalized—"And left me to a bootless inquisition." Come back to the next line, "Concluding," well, "C" is capitalized. "Concluding, stay, not yet." So you come down the first capitalized line and it spells B-A-C, but there is no other line. You go across the bottom line and it spells O-N. So that's how my friend, who tried to persuade me Bacon was the author, told me where in an acrostic the author was concealing his identity. But that's not what I got from that wonderful, wonderful speech of Miranda. *We* are Miranda, and we are left to this bootless inquisition, until that moment in time when the waiting is over and, like Job, we cry out: "You know I am guiltless. Why then do you by this agony try to win from me a concession of guilt?"

So *we* are the Jesus. We are Jesus. But it's part of the great plan to awaken us as God. And so I do believe in Jesus, but my Jesus is not the concept of the world's concept of Jesus. He's not something detached from me, something out in space to whom I pray, like an idol. No, my Jesus is *in* me as my own very being, the only being that I really am. That's Jesus. Only Jesus is resurrected. Only Jesus ascends; the Son of man. If he is not *in* me, I can't ascend. If he's not *in* me, I can't resurrect. If he's not *in* me, I can't be saved, for God saves himself. It is God *buried* in man. Who went into the sepulcher? Ask the question, "Who went into the sepulcher? They put Jesus there. Well, who was resurrected from the sepulcher? Jesus. Did anyone else go in? They went in only as ___(??), but the one who resurrected was he. Well, the sepulcher is your own wonderful skull, that's the sepulcher. In your skull Jesus is buried; out of your skull Jesus will come. And when he comes out he's not another, you don't see another; it's your very being. Listen to the words, "It does not yet appear what we shall be, but we know that when he appears we *shall be like* him" (1 John 3:2). How can I be like him and not be he? "It does not yet appear . . . but when he does appear we shall be like him." "Stay, not yet." You don't quite know who you are? It's not quite yet.

But I'll give you a cue as to how to bring it to pass. It begins, the very first words put into the mouth of Jesus in the earliest gospel, the gospel of Mark, he makes the statement, "The time is fulfilled"—it has to be filled up first, all the ___(??), like pregnancy—and "the time is fulfilled, and the kingdom of God is at hand; repent, and believe in the gospel" (1:15). Repent is a prerequisite to entry into the kingdom. And repentance hasn't a thing to do with remorse or regret; it has only to do with a radical change of attitude toward life, that's repentance.

This is what I mean by practicing my religion. If I say I believe in him, all right, then repent. Who repents? Jesus repents. Jesus? What did he do that was wrong? *You* are he. Nothing wrong, it's simply missing the mark, that's sinning. If I miss the mark in life, I must repent by changing my attitude radically toward that state, and see it as it *ought* to be seen. Who, by me? No, by the world. And believe in this changed attitude of myself toward anything in this world, and fix it, believing in it. If I live in that assumption just as though it were true, it'll become true. So I produce the signs. These are the wonders of Jesus; all these signs come to pass.

And when I least expect it—I'm still in the sepulcher—I will awaken. And may I tell you, if Jehovah and Jesus are one, when he is awakened, is he not awakened by himself? When he is born, Jehovah has no father and mother; therefore, if I am born and I am Jesus, am I not then self-begotten? Then don't I come out of my own being by myself? And I'm telling from experience exactly what happened, you are self-born, self-begotten. When God actually becomes you, he becomes you; there's no one on the outside. He actually gives himself to you, as though there were no others in the world, just *you*, and you are he. So when you come out you are born.

So to me, when I use the words Jesus Christ I speak of the way, the truth. What way? The only way—the way to what? The way to everything in the world: the way to health, the way to wealth, the way to everything, but, specifically, the way to the Father. "No man comes unto the Father save by me," but no man, and yet, "When you see me you see the Father" (John 14.6). You can't come to the Father in any way save by me, for "I am the way." And those who were in Christianity in the first, second, and third centuries were spoken of as "the people of the Way," capital W. They were not all Christians; that came later. They were called "the people of the Way." You can read it in the Book of Acts, the 9th chapter. He goes to persecute the people of the Way; and then he finds who Jesus really is: he finds him within himself, and he reveals the Way, and the Way is rejected. God has planned everything as it has come out and as it will be consummated, but everything in the world. Let no one tell you it's going to pot, that others will take advantage, no, you're still to be exposed to this bootless inquisition, like Job. And when the drama is over in the individual case, well, then he starts on the Way.

Now here is the first recorded word of the teacher in the Book of Luke. He asked for the Bible. There was only the Old Testament, so they gave him the Bible, the Old Testament, the covenants of Jehovah, and he opened it up to the 61st chapter of Isaiah. For even to this day, the first five books of the Bible are read over a period of three years, but the reader has freedom of choice as to what part of the prophets he will read. And so, they read—and it takes three years to complete the reading of the first five books, called the Torah, the law—but you're free while you have your congregation to read any part of the book. And so he opened up to Isaiah 61 and he only reads the first verse and the first-half of the second one. He doesn't complete the second when it comes to vengeance. He stops at the first half of the second verse. The verse begins: "The Spirit of the Lord God is upon me . . . he has anointed me to preach good news to the poor . . . to open up the prison doors to all that are in prison and to set free all that are bound; and to proclaim the *acceptable year* of the Lord."

Our earliest fathers in the church in the second century took this passage of Luke and they went out and preached it. It is still in print from the earliest fathers in what is today the Catholic Church. So that was the beginning of it all. And this father made the statement that this first passage read from Isaiah meant that God's work was completed in a year, proclaimed the *acceptable* year of the Lord, and he took it to mean that whatever that work was it was done in a year. And he was right. In spite of all that has happened in the interval, he was perfectly right. After this exposure to the bootless inquisition, when we are now lifted up, it only takes one year to complete that passage, from resurrection, birth, discovery of David, and the splitting of the temple and the ascension right into Zion, all within a year. And it happens in three nights, spread over a part of the year. Again, "in three days, three nights, I will rebuild it." This time it's the perfect temple that is Job. So it is that first part of that second verse of Isaiah, "to proclaim the acceptable year of the Lord." And so, he proclaims it and he tells them all, "There's only one Way to the Father."

So follow the story of Jesus. Read it carefully, all that they say about him, and then know it's *your* story. The day will come that all these things will happen in you. The Bible is not *chronologically* exact, but it's a beautiful story. But the story is simply assembled into a nice arrangement, as Luke implies. He does not claim any great chronological exactitude. He claims only that his arrangement is a better arrangement than his predecessors. You read the first four verses of Luke and you'll see he's implying his is a better arrangement of the source material. So he has the source material and then he arranges it in story form that people could *see* the truth. For man insists on *seeing* the truth. So to see the truth he personifies it. And so you personify truth, you personify the Way, you personify life, you personify everything and they take on human characteristics. And so if you insist on seeing a Jesus other than yourself you're going to see another.

What individual it was in whom the *only* Jesus awoke, who knows? Who knows what the individual's name was? It means nothing, for its only Jesus that matters. So what was the mask that he wore when he awoke? What does it matter? He could have been in any form, in any sex, because, as we're told in the last part of the 3rd chapter of Galatians, "In Christ Jesus there is no Greek, no Jew, no bond, no free, no male, no female" (verse 28). So he is beyond the organization of sex, beyond freedom and slavery in *this* world when he awakes. When he awakens he's completely above it all.

And the only thing I speak of here is Jesus. He's your own wonderful human Imagination, that's Jesus. He's your own wonderful I-am-ness, that's Jesus. Now, test him and see. For you're told, "Examine yourselves to see whether you are holding to the faith. Do you not realize that Jesus Christ is in you?—unless of course you fail to meet the test." I hope you will discover that we have not failed. Now this you will read in the 13th chapter of 2nd Corinthians. He's asking you to test it. If he is *in* you and by him all things are made, and without him there's nothing made that is made, then test him.

Test him in the most simple, simple way. If he is my Imagination, and imagining is creating reality, I could go into my inner being as it were and assume that things are as I would like them to be, and if my premise is sound, if it's true, it should prove itself in performance, shouldn't it? And so, I go to bed in the assumption that I am now the one that I would like to be, just now. And then, in the not distant future, I reshuffle the world to mirror my accomplishment; the whole thing worked; it takes on form. But if it does and I repeat it and it works again, and I repeat it and it works again, haven't I found the Creator? For by him all things are made and without him there's nothing made that is made. Well, suddenly, I make something out of nothing. I didn't ask anyone's help, I didn't turn to anyone to assist me. I simply dared to assume that I am what at the moment my reason and my senses deny, and remaining loyal to my assumption it objectified itself and became a fact. I remembered what I did. Remembering what I did, I am faithful now to him. I found him.

But now you don't go and say "I am Jesus." No one must go out and say "I am he," for you're bragging. No one can brag because *everyone* is Jesus, but they don't know it. All you can do is tell them that they are, and when you tell them who they are ninety-nine point ninety-nine percent of the world would be offended, embarrassed because you have insulted their God. They can't feel *equal* to that. They feel unclean. They do not feel they could possibly come near that state, therefore, when you tell them, that's blasphemy, and they'll tell you it's blasphemy. But I tell you it's not blasphemy. I and my Father are one. But we *are* one, and you can make the same claim.

The day will come and everything that I've told you concerning the Way will prove itself in you. I'm speaking from experience, I am not theorizing. This is not theory with me; it's all experience. Hasn't a thing to do with any orthodox training whatsoever. I've had none of it. Only the simple training of a boy raised in a Christian environment, where we had Sunday school and regular meals and the usual discussions in a Christian home where we discussed the Bible. That was my only training. So I have had no orthodox training. This was not from anything man has told me. It's all based upon what I have experienced, all by revelation. It came unsought, unexpectedly, and all within one year—the acceptable year of the Lord. When that moment comes, you move up that moment of resurrection through the birth, through all, right into Zion, the house of God, all in a year, remaining clothed in this garment of flesh that you may tell the story until you take it off for the last time. And you will take it off for the last time *after* you've gone through that acceptable year of the Lord.

And so, I've tried to tell it as clearly as I can. I have not embellished it, I haven't added to the story, just as it happened to me. I have told it in the very last chapter of my latest book *The Law and the Promise*, and I quoted with words from the scriptures. So I have presented two witnesses. When you bring two then you have conclusive evidence if they agree. For two by nature would be opposition, would be enmity, it would be difference. For when two different persons agree in testimony it is conclusive. And so, if I had the experience and then searching through the ancient scripture I found supporting text for the experience, so here is agreement in testimony and, therefore, it's conclusive. And so I gave you the story as it happened to me and gave you that text in scripture that supports that experience.

And some lady said to me tonight before I took the platform, "I wanted to give a few books away to my friends and you haven't *Awakened Imagination* at the moment, would you recommend some other title." Well, I recommend that among one of the three. I said, "My friend, pick three different titles and have them exchange the books. Well, here's my latest book. It's one I recommend." "Well, she said, "I'm quite sure that if they read the last chapter first, they'd tear it up." I hope not. For the purpose of the book is to tell all how God's law works. But what would be the law without the promise? And you could have this law so down, so perfectly under your control that you could own the earth, and yet not have the promise fulfilled. Because no one is justified by law before God, you can't be. It's only the fulfillment of the promise. And the promise is *given* to man; it's grace, after he has gone through this bootless inquisition. And I mean bootless too.

God in his infinite mercy hides it from himself in the sense he has taken from me the memory of my past. For if man could only see what he had to live through to reach the fulfillment of the promise, I doubt that God himself would venture forward. He had to go into this horror and this really ___(??). The churches speak of hell, and they're in it, and they don't know that? They think of some greater hell on the outside when they are in hell and they don't know this is hell. When some individual consumed with a passion unsatisfied, isn't that hell? That passion may be any kind of passion, an ambition beyond the wildest dreams of man and you can't satisfy it, that's hell. Look into the world, and see the horrors and see all the things that are happening morning, noon, and night. There isn't a morning's paper that you can't pick up and see a page of hell.

And so we are in it, we are in this bootless inquisition until seven times over, ___(??) heated seven times more than they were wont to be. Well, when you are brought out, just pure gold, pure gold. And we are the very being who walked through it all. For in the furnaces there were threefold men and then came the Son of God. But here we have a threefold man. Know what's a threefold man? You're a threefold man. But in the presence of it all, one untouched, not even the stench of smoke upon him, was the Son of God. Read it in the Book of Daniel. In the furnaces behold the three-fold man, but the fourth is Jesus. And Jesus is the reality of every being in the world. There is nothing but Jesus. So when they asked Blake, "What do you think of Jesus?" Without batting an eye, he replied, "Jesus is the only God," but quickly added, "But so am I and so are you." Crab Robinson to whom he said this couldn't understand it, just recorded it in his diary. Luckily we have his diary. And Blake did not elaborate, didn't go beyond it.

But I am telling you, when you go to bed this night and you feel sleepy and you say "I am," that's his name. And you believe in him, well then, believe that he is actually creating. There's nothing impossible to Jesus. Well then, at that very moment believing that Jesus is your own wonderful I-am-ness, what would you like to be? Assume that you are it and go sound asleep just as though it were true. That's how it operates: Feel as you would feel were it true. Name what you would like to be true, and then go sound asleep.

Now, don't put this in the closet until I get back in November. This is something to *live* by. Religion should be practiced and we don't practice religion by simply going to church and listening to whatever the minister has to say, ___(??) lovely as they are. And I'm all for it, perfectly fine, but that's not practicing religion. Practicing religion is living it every moment of time while we're here, and you practice it best by practicing repentance. Listen to the words, "The time is fulfilled, and the kingdom of God is at hand; repent, and believe in the good news, believe in the gospel." But repent. And repentance tests man's ability to enter into and partake of the nature of the opposite. And so I am, and I name it. But I don't like it. Well now, can I persuade myself that I am exactly what I would like to be, which is opposed by what I seemingly am? Then I persuade myself that I really am what I would like to be. That tests my ability, my Imagination, to do such a thing. But can I do it? Well, try it.

Can I, while sitting here physically, assume that I am elsewhere, if I want to be elsewhere, when there's no way to that other place? No money to take you there, no time to allow it, but nothing. Well, can I assume that I am, knowing that something will change in my world if it's a radical change to allow this journey to take place within you? And I'll make it across this world. Well, try it. I have tried it and it works. I've tried it so that now I don't allow myself to experiment if I am not serious. Because, if I do it just for exercise and I don't do it with something I really want to realize, the being I really am doesn't forget it. They'll teach me lessons and bring it to pass when I least expect it and don't want it. So, I only experiment with serious things, things I *really* want to bring to pass. And I tell you it won't fail you, but you are the operant power. It doesn't work by itself; you have to operate it.

And so, I tell you, you are Jesus. Let no one tell you that you are not. There's only Jesus in the world. Yet he's housed in every being, even those who said there is no God, in every being in the world. Those who call themselves atheists and are proud of it, he's housed in them or they couldn't even breathe. Nothing in the world could breathe and live were it not that Jesus is buried within him, in the sepulcher of his own wonderful skull; and there he remains while he goes through all the pains of the world to awaken himself as that individual. So you'll understand the words at the grand transfiguration. When they looked up, Moses was there, Elijah was there, one personifying the law and one personifying the promise. And then came the awakening on the part of the disciples and then there was *only* Jesus, Jesus only. He had fulfilled it all, fulfilled the promise, having fulfilled it, Jesus only. And so, you are destined to awaken, completely awaken, *as* God.

Now let us go into the Silence.

ON THE BOOK OF REVELATION

May 31, 1963

It was asked by someone present, would I please talk on the Book of Revelation, and I in an idle moment said yes . . . because here is the end of the play. You see, the whole vast world is a play. The word genesis means beginning; an apocalypse is the end—a complete unveiling of the purpose of the play. So I could no more explain Revelation in one hour than I could do the most impossible thing in this world. I wish I had asked you all to bring Bibles and simply ask me questions from the book, because you can't separate the last scene of a play from the play and give it any meaning. You can't possibly do it.

I can only tell you that God conceived the play. He not only conceived it and wrote all the parts, but he built all the scenery; and God and God alone is playing all the parts. His name is I AM. So you can say "I am"—that's God. He's playing that part that we call Mary or Jane or John, or by some other name. He's playing that part. We are the incarnation of the tragedy and the glory of this divine play. We must not forget the glory in the tragedy. There's more of the glory than of the tragedy, but when we are in that tragic state we tend to forget the glory. Now, to cover this would be impossible. But there are a few aspects of the great play that will stick into the mind of man and I thought I would pick these out tonight. Then when we come to the question period, then you can ask anything that I have forgotten or didn't have the time to cover.

It's a play in seven acts and each act has seven scenes. The first chapter is a prologue where it states the star of the play, and the star of the play is named Jesus Christ. You'll find it in the seventh verse. Although the book itself is titled *The Revelation of John*, the first verse tells you whose revelation it really is, the Revelation of Jesus Christ. Yet all Bibles will give you a title and call it the Revelation of John; yet the first verse tells you exactly whose revelation it is. In this prologue, the whole thing is set up what God intends to do. The last chapter, the twenty-second chapter, from the sixth through to the end, is . . . you may call it an epilogue. Where in the beginning, which is Genesis, he needed a sun; in the end, there's no need for the sun—we are light unto ourselves. In the beginning, there was an earth; in the end, there is a new earth. In the drama there is tragedy and tears, horrible things; in the end, he wipes away all tears. So Revelation is a complete wiping away of the entire picture as it started in the beginning.

Here, he speaks in Genesis of a serpent, which was the beginning of the exit from a state of bliss—and they speak of the serpent in Revelation. You might think, as I was taught to believe, it's some horrible monster that in some strange way came into God's picture, and it isn't. There's only God in this world. Did you ever run, as child, an obstacle race? Well, in little Barbados we had those. Our teachers would simply put a tarpaulin down, and it was as flat as this desk, and we had to run through this very tightly formed canvas, where it was anchored on both sides. Then, when we came out we were exhausted from getting through this very tight canvas. Then you were confronted with barrels, and you went through barrels. Then you jumped over some kind of obstruction, and then you climbed a greased pole. Then, maybe it was more difficult, you had to catch the greased pig. And that is life: an obstacle race. The opponent in this is God, and the being playing the part is God. And it's called in the drama "the serpent."

May I tell you from actual experience, one day you will see him, the opponent. The opponent is called a slimy, greasy, horrible being, a monster. And the hero of the play is also a serpent but a *winged* serpent, a radiant winged serpent, while the opponent is the crooked serpent from the 27th chapter of the Book of Isaiah. And here is that strange monstrous being, as it begins the 27th of Isaiah. But in Isaiah 27 we are told, "We are called and redeemed one by one." So redemption is not something that takes place as the world has been taught to believe, suddenly, where billions of us are suddenly brought to the end. No, the play is on and we are playing it, God is playing it, and we go through this horrible obstacle race. As Paul said in his final letter to Timothy, he said, "The time for my departure has come. I have fought the good fight, I have finished the race, I have kept the faith" (2 Timothy 4:6). That's what everyone has to do, fight the good fight, finish the race, and finish it only by the keeping of faith.

Now, there are seven letters, which begins with the second chapter. No one can read these seven letters . . . it only takes two chapters to read them, they're short letters addressed to seven churches. Now, seven in the Hebraic tongue is "spiritual perfection." So when one has been brought to the limit, to the end, it's spiritual perfection. And here, he addresses ___(??) and every one as you read it he emphasizes, he doesn't criticize them, he praises them for what they've done; but there's something lacking and the one thing lacking is repentance. Repent. I know you've done it. In the midst of the horrible world you kept the faith alive to an extent, but you have not quite fulfilled the command to repent.

Now, to repent means a radical change of mind toward what you see in the world. Here is the obstacle race. It's a horrible race that God set up to develop himself, to bring forth himself as you, as me, as every being in the world. And the only way we can go through it is to repent. To repent means a radical change of attitude toward life. It hasn't a thing to do with remorse, with regret. I see you and you do not look as I would like you to look, and you, in a conversation, you tell me things are not going well. I am supposed at that very moment not to wait, at that moment to change you in my mind's eye and to see you as you ought to be seen by yourself and by me, and remain *loyal* to that changed aspect relative to you.

But every church is told to repent. They are catholic in what they have done. In the midst of the horror of the world, they have, in a way, remained loyal but not good enough. The one thing that he told one church after the other, they must repent. Teach the principle of repentance to the whole vast world. And the principle is this: When you see anything, beginning with yourself, and things are not as you would like them to be, *assume* that they are as they ought to be, and *dare* to live in the assumption as though it were true, just as though it were true. And then you go through this strange obstacle race quicker, easier, by repentance. Because, in the end, the goal is God. When God takes himself through, he gives himself to us at the very end. It is God's purpose to give himself to you as though there were no other in the world, just God and you. And at the very end, when the gift is given, it's only you: You are he.

It's a new world, a new kingdom; everything is new. No need even for a sun—you are light unto yourself. No need for anything you have here, not even for the sea. If there's need for a sea, you'll create a sea. For the whole vast world will be subject to your imaginative power. It's *all* Imagination that's playing this wonderful, wonderful drama. Divine Imagination creates it, Divine Imagination is playing it, and when he comes out, your wonderful human Imagination is Divine Imagination, creating everything, as it desires in this world.

Now it comes, after he tells these stories to the churches. There are seven churches, seven bowls, seven lamp stands, seven seals that would seal the book, and seven all the way through. But so many people who I discuss the Bible with them, when it comes to Revelation their minds . . . as someone

came to my door about two months ago and said to me, "Don't you know
only 144,000 will be saved?" So that's in Revelation. It's not in any other
part of the Bible—there are sixty-six books—that's in Revelation. Then
came, about two weeks ago, a fine wonderful looking lad, about twenty-six,
twenty-seven years old, and he had the Bible all marked and there he was
with all these marks. He started to open the book—the same concept of
life—and he's going to prove to me something about the Bible. And he
goes to Revelation, about a beast, a beast that is six hundred and sixty-six,
that's his number. This you will read in the thirteenth chapter and here at
the end of the thirteenth chapter they speak of a beast. But you must read
it carefully. He tells you this calls for wisdom, this calls for understanding,
when you hear about this beast, for the number of the beast is a *human*
number. It's the number of a man.

   Well, I have heard all kinds of arguments about Nero was the man,
Hitler was the man, Napoleon was the man. They can make it fit any
name in this world. It hasn't a thing to do with any individual man in this
world. That Hitler represented a monstrous thing, no one denies that. That
Napoleon did, no one denies that. That Stalin did, no one denies it. But
this hasn't any reference whatsoever to any individual man in history. The
beast that opposes me happens to be myself. I am opposed by myself; for
the number is the number of a man; it's a human number.

   For man was created on the sixth day, so the number is 666, raised to
the nth degree, three sixes. And I am man. You, though you are female,
you're man, you're generic man. Everyone is man. And we are opposed *only*
by ourselves. We have to overcome our beliefs in this world, no matter what
we believe in. That I am unwanted in the world? I've got to overcome it.
Not by hitting the one who thinks that I think he opposes me, no, I must
overcome that belief in myself. That I am unwanted? I've got to feel I am
the most wanted being in the world and not crush anyone who reflects my
unwantedness. I will actually feel, in spite of that reflection, I am so wanted.
When I look at the same being, he wants me, and he reflects the whole vast
world.

   So the beast is not Nero—and you can take the name, yes, in a certain
way you could write Nero out and give numerical values to the letters,
and make it come to 666. I've seen it done with the name Hitler. I've seen
it done with the name Stalin. But that is *not* scripture. They were not
prophesying existence of a Hitler or a Stalin or any other being in the world.
The only beast is man. And the 4th chapter of the Book of Daniel reveals it
to us. Daniel is the apocalypse of the Old Testament and Revelation is the
apocalypse of the New Testament. And in Daniel, when the tree is felled,
they are told to strip off the leaves, cut off the branches; bring it down just

to a root. And then, strangely enough, a tree, which is referred as "it"—"take off its leaves, strip its branches"—suddenly it's personified as man. Then we are told, "Take from *him*"—it's a tree now, a tree of life—"take from him the mind of a man and give to him the mind of a beast, until seven times passes over him" (verses 14, 16). Here we have seven again. Heat the furnaces seven times more than they are wont to be, because only pure gold must come out. Seven times more, so let seven times pass over *him*. It's a tree. Suddenly the tree becomes humanized, and it's man.

Now, in this picture of the 666, I tell you it hasn't a thing to do with any being outside of yourself. The whole vast world is the animal that opposes you, but it's yourself. Because, "All that you behold, though it appears without, it is within, in your Imagination" and this world of mortality only reflects that which is taking place within you. But if you think you're unwanted? All right, as long as you think you're unwanted and you try to force the issue and break it down on the outside, you're fighting the most horrible tyrant in the world. You've got to assume that you are the most wanted being in the world, that your contribution to the world is so great the whole vast world rushes to praise you. And when you live in this wonderful dream as though it were true, you produce whatever is necessary to make the world see it and praise you, *regardless* of where you are today. That's how you overcome the beast.

And, may I tell you from my own experience, you will see him. He will fill this room, may I tell you. He is the most horrible, slimy, loathsome thing that you have ever seen. You don't see yourself because they're in opposition. You the being that is really the star of the drama, you are a winged serpent, a radiant winged serpent. But you don't see yourself; you see only the opposition. The opposition is the crooked serpent of the 27th chapter of Isaiah. You see him as a green . . . when I saw him he was green, a greenish yellow-green, I can't quite describe him, but a monster that would fill this room. There he came toward me and I'm trying in some way to corral him, not to kill him but to make him impotent. And I got him. One time I got just the head into a vice that was smaller seemingly than the head; he couldn't dislodge it. But you don't kill him. He's *always* there to oppose you. He takes on all these forms and he's always ready to once more dislodge that head, and once more because he's slimy he can pull it out. So you think you've got him for a while and there he is. The vision is a true vision. I have had it. I have had the vision of this monstrous leviathan as told us in scripture.

Now we go to the next chapter, the fourteenth chapter, another number. Did you not know, said this lady to me, only 144,000 will be saved? That's the fourteenth chapter—right after the beast appears. In the 144,000, you are told here they are the perfect ones redeemed from earth, redeemed from humanity. And they will sing a new song and no one in the world can sing this song but the 144,000. No one could even know it; only the 144,000 could know it. And they're going to sing a song. May I tell you the song? Because only the 144,000 can sing it, and you think that 144,000 persons; no, 144,000 is the number of man. It's Aleph is one, Daleth is four, and Mem is forty. One plus four plus four is nine. No matter how many zeros you add to it, it still remains one plus four plus four, which is the number of Adam which is nine. So the 144,000 tells you *everyone* in the world will be saved, none can be lost. I don't care what the world will tell you, no one can be lost, for God is playing all the parts. His opponent is himself. The opponent is a slimy, horrible, crooked monster; and he is the winged, radiant serpent, the cherubim. So the 144,000 represents not 144,000 persons. That would be horrible. There are three billion people living in the world today. There may be six billion in another twenty years. There may be twenty billion in another hundred years. And 144,000 literally? No. Don't believe it. This is all symbolism. *Everyone* will be saved.

So here we are told 144,000 sing the new song. And I'll tell you, because I heard it, he's going to call your name when you are called. And they will ___(??), the most heavenly chorus that you have ever heard, it's a heavenly chorus, and the song, the new song, calling you by name—no impersonal thing saying he, she or it—but your name, your eternal name. They'll call it and you'll know it. You'll feel yourself lifted up, right through your skull. And you'll feel yourself in the most glorious world where there is no sun. You are light unto yourself—there's no need of a sun. You radiate light from your own being. You are luminous. And you will come upon this most wonderful world, a world of imperfection—the blind, the lame, the halt, the withered. And as you come upon them, the choruses sing, calling you by name. Whatever your name is, if it's Jane, they will say "Jane is risen." It will be simply a repetition of the same theme "Jane is risen." They don't change it. Not even something other than that. But in the most marvelous way that one little theme is made the most glorious thing you have ever heard. "Jane is risen" is multiplied in the numberless ways of telling it, as the chorus exults, and you are the being of whom they speak.

You walk by this sea of imperfection, and as you walk by they are all transformed into beauty. Those who are blind, they are made perfect. Those who are deaf begin to hear. Those who have lost their arms, arms come out of nowhere and the arms are returned, everything is returned, and everything is made perfect. And then you will understand the words, "And those I will call forward, the lame, the halt, and those whom I have afflicted I redeem" (Micah 4:6). Read it. I'll call them all and those whom *I* have afflicted. Haven't I afflicted in my world? Haven't I fought with my shadow? Haven't I seen someone who I thought was my opponent and fought with them? And haven't I, in my own mind's eye, whittled him down to a smaller state so that I could take advantage of him? So I have whittled down everyone in my journey, from the beginning to the end. So all that I have lamed and maimed and I have hurt, I'll call them all and redeem them.

And the song of the 144,000, because no one knows the song but the 144,000. It's a new song. So forget the 144,000 persons, it means humanity. As you are lifted up you join the 144,000 and you don't expand it to 144,000 and one, it's still 144,000. And when all of us join that, we are still the 144,000. We know the new name and the new name is every person's name as it's given. For you're called by name. You are loved by God. You are not known as humanity, you are known singly, individually. "I call you by name" as told us in the 48th chapter of Isaiah, just where the name and all of these are brought together. All that I have injured, all that I have hurt, I will now bring and redeem, and in that same 48th of Isaiah, I will now call one by one. Everyone will be saved. At the very end of the chapter, "He calls us one by one." But he tells us he maimed us, he hurt us, everyone, and then in the end we're all redeemed.

So here, to take this fabulous book, I couldn't do it if I talked through night after night for several months. There are only twenty-two chapters but I could take any one verse. For he tells us: To him that overcometh, I will let him sit with me on my throne, as I myself overcame and sat down with my Father on his throne. So here is a form of overcoming. But he gives us the clue in the very beginning: we overcome by repentance and repentance is a radical change of attitude toward the world. Instead of thinking that "he" is opposing me, it's because *I* felt myself inferior he rises in my world against me. I know it. I'm speaking from experience.

When I came to this country unknown, uneducated, with no one to receive me, and I felt, being a stranger, that naturally the world stood against me, the world *was* against me. And then I began to have my visions. I began to appropriate them and put them into practice. So I can safely say and honestly say to you I have never been barred—and I have no high school certificate—I have never been barred from any club in this land where I was invited. I have been invited to the most exclusive clubs as an honored guest, from east to west, *never* any bar, because I overcame the bar in myself. I had all the limitations in the world against me, uneducated, unknown, with no social, no intellectual, no financial background, but none. And then, I overcame it within myself. When I did, I met those who were members of these clubs and they invited me as their honored guest. There was no question asked, I was simply welcomed as an honored guest.

So Revelation tells us, "To him that overcometh." I don't overcome the other by hitting the shadow and destroying the shadow, for I am ever casting the shadow. If I destroy the shadow at this moment and remain where I am, I cast a similar shadow one moment later. And so, I may kill John, who offends me, well then, Peter will rise in my midst and reflect the same distortion in me that I hold of myself. So everyone has to simply change his own concept of self. As he changes the concept of himself, he changes the world in which he lives, and goes on overcoming, overcoming and overcoming until he comes whose right it is to rule, and it's *yourself.*

For God is playing the part. God's only name is I AM. Can't you say, "I am"? If you couldn't say "I am" you wouldn't be here tonight. Before you say anything you say "I am"—that's God. And he's playing the part *against* himself. He sets up the opponent. And there are two serpents in the scripture. Now listen to this one at the end of the third chapter where the serpent appears in the Book of Genesis. At the end of the third he banishes man, he drives man out, and then he takes a cherubim with a flaming sword that moves in every direction to guard *the way* to the tree of life. To guard the *way*, and the way is "I am the way." There is no other way. So he sets him up to guard the way to the tree of life. Who was it? "I am the way. I am the truth. I am the life." There is no other way. The way to what? The way to everything in this world, but *especially* to the Father. No one in this world can come to the Father save they come through this way. And he tells you he is the way. Know who he is? *You* are he: it's all hidden in you.

And the day will come, it will begin to like a flower begins to unfold, unfold in the most wonderful series of mystical experiences. When it begins to unfold, you stand amazed at the beauty of this story. And may I tell you, you are told that the kingdom is taken by storm? It's true. When you move into it, and it's called Zion: "And I looked up and behold there was Zion and the Lamb, and around the Lamb 144,000." And it's all here, it's all in your own wonderful skull, that's where he's buried. And may I tell you, when you go into it having ascended that wonderful spine of yours, you will make the most tremendous effort *ever* to get out. You've never heard such a storm. But you cause the storm. So when we are told, "And they take it by storm today," when you get in, you make every effort in the world. You've never heard such an earthquake, never heard such frightful, I would say, vibration that *you* cause. But you don't get out. There's no other place to go; it's all within you. "So the whole vast world, though it appears without, it is within, in your Imagination, of which this world of mortality is but a shadow" (Blake, *Jerusalem*, Plate 71).

The Bible begins with the words, "In the beginning God," and it ends with the words, "Come, Lord Jesus." Jesus is God—the world does not believe it—and Jesus is playing the part. When you say, "I am," that's he; but he's individualized when you say, "I am John, I am Peter, I am Ray, I am Mary." But it's the same Jesus. There's only Jesus in this world. There's nothing but Jesus, and Jesus is God. So, "In the beginning *God* created the heavens and the earth," and the end of the book, "Come, Lord Jesus." Come, let him awake within you, for he had to die to become you. So we are told, "I am the beginning and the end, the Alpha and the Omega. I am he who is, who was and who is to come. I am he who *died* but is alive again." All this is Revelation.

I am he who died. I had to die. He had to die to become me, to make these that are dead alive, for I was dead. He created a whole vast world, God did. It existed only for him, not for itself, just like a picture exists for the artist but not for itself. And then the artist falls in love with his picture. He so falls in love with his picture that he wants to make it alive for itself, and so to do so he has to *become* his picture, his sculpture. So he actually enters this dead thing called Neville, called you, by any name, and he enters us, and he lies down in the grave of the thing created. And then he starts his dream, dreaming that he's you. Then he sets up the opposition to bring forth the dreamer and to awaken the dreamer *as you*. But the dreamer is himself—that's God. And he's dreaming he's you and brings it forth through opposition.

For without opposition not a thing could happen in this world. I couldn't leave the platform unless I was opposed, the car couldn't move unless opposed, the bird couldn't fly unless opposed, the plane couldn't take off unless opposed, the fish couldn't swim unless opposed. Everything in this world must be opposed in order to *move*, so God sets up that opposition. And then in me, the dead, he sets up the opposition and then he moves. And I'm frightened to death with all the things that scare us. But in the end, when he takes me through, he awakens and I am he. You and he are one. We are one.

Then you'll know why that wonderful question when it was asked, "What is the greatest commandment in the world?" and he answered, quoting from the Book of Deuteronomy, "Hear, O Israel: The Lord our God is one Lord" (Deuteronomy 6:4). "Hear, O Israel; The Lord"—the word translated "the lord" is Yod He Vau He, which really means I AM. The word translated "God" is Elohim, it's plural, and then goes back to I AM. So, "Hear, O Israel: I AM, our God, is one I AM." Here is a unity, a *one* made up of many. It takes all of us *awake* to be Jehovah. Everyone in this world will be awake, but it takes all of us completely awake to form one Lord. So, "Hear, O Israel: The Lord"—that is Jehovah, I AM—"our Elohim"—we are the Elohim—"is one Jehovah." So all of us completely awake will be one Jehovah—that's God. No little thing left behind, just God.

And what is the next? As the poet said, "Be patient. Be patient. Our playwright will show in some fifth act what this wild drama means." And what you and I, completely awake, forming one body, will create tomorrow will put all this fabulous world into kindergarten. What we will do in our *next* creative power when *we* are awake will make it all look as though this was really kindergarten. And yet, we pass through it as though it's the most horrible thing in the world. So take comfort, he who created all became you because he loved what he created when he created you, and he's buried in you.

Now take the message of Revelation and practice the art of repentance. You start to read the letters and the emphasis in each letter save Philadelphia—Philadelphia means "brotherly love"—they so practiced brotherly love that he did not give to them this suggestion to repent. So the Philadelphians, which came in the sixth letter (which is man), so he didn't do it to the sixth. But he starts off Ephesus and he goes through, and each one he emphasizes the art of repentance. But when he comes to one who loves, he doesn't. If you fall in love with someone without trying to change him, just simply love, he allows that because God is love. And if you don't change him in your mind's eye and make him what you would like to see him in this world, that is permitted, that's permissible. So Philadelphia did not receive the suggestion to repent, for it means brotherly love, the city of brotherly love. All the others had to repent.

Now let us go into the Silence.

*　　　*　　　*

Q: (inaudible)

A: ____(??) in Revelation the 144,000. You will read the 144,000 were chaste—they were not defiled by women. That's been a complete misunderstanding of scripture—those who become celibate, those join the monasteries, and all these things of the world—it hasn't a thing to do with sex. Because fornication in the Bible was always equated with *idolatry*. Therefore, to worship anything in this world other than God is idolatry, whether it be the emperor, whether it be our president, whether it be the government or anything in the world, that is fornicating. For we are married to God and to go apart from him is to fornicate, to commit adultery. We're told in the 54th chapter of Isaiah, "The Lord is your husband" (verse 5). Well, if the Lord is my husband, I must find out who he is, and I'm telling you who he is: he is your own wonderful human Imagination. So to believe that any power in this world is causative other than your own wonderful Imagination is to fall in love with a power you believe to be causation and therefore you are attached to it, and that is fornication. So when you read it—I didn't cover it, but I must before I leave—so this so-called "they were chaste, undefiled by women" hasn't a thing to do with sex as we understand the word; it has all to do with idolatry. And so you actually believe in some creative power other than your own wonderful human Imagination is to have another man or woman in your life.

Q: What about the child, the woman with the child out in the wilderness?

A: Well, that comes from the 12th chapter of Revelation. ___(??) there's a woman in labor giving birth to a child and then this dragon, the red dragon appears to devour the child, but as she brought forth the child it was caught up into the presence of God. But remember, the birth took place in heaven; it just simply moved into the presence of God. And so the dragon is *always* in the world ready to oppose any progress of the individual who is God. He's always present. And if I go back to my own personal experience, when the child is presented and I held him, suddenly it was all vanished, all gone. No one could take him. And it *did* take place in heaven; it certainly wasn't on earth, as we understand earth. And so, here was the discovery of the symbol of the event that took place. I held him in my hand, looked into his beautiful face and called him by an endearing term, "How's my sweetheart?" and then at that moment, the sudden vanishing of the entire scene. So we're told in the thirteenth chapter, as the red dragon came right into the presence of the woman in labor, she was bringing forth *the* child, a male child—and as she brought him forth he was caught up so the dragon could not devour him. It's all symbolism, but it's true. It actually takes place in the consciousness of man.

Q: When the beast is thrown into the lake of fire, he is enchained for a thousand years. What does that mean?

A: It's thrown into the lake of fire. He's been enchained for a thousand years. Now what does that mean? Well, I can only give you my own experience. When the dragon is cornered by you, you don't kill him. It seems that man always needs opposition for growth, and growth is forever. So these two serpents are antagonists. One is the radiant, winged being that is Jesus Christ, and may I tell you, he is that, and *you* are that. And the other is the slimy, crooked monster.

But you *need* it for opposition. So you enchain it while you revel in your accomplishment. But there must be another journey; there is no end to the unfoldment of an infinite God. If I could unfold and that was all I could ever accomplish, that would be stagnation and that would be worse than death. This is *constant expansion*. There is no limit to luminosity, to expansion; there's only a limit to opacity, to contraction. So we reach the limit of opacity, of contraction, and then we start a journey that never, but never, comes to an end. Because, it never comes to an end, I couldn't move forward without opposition. And that's the drama. What will be my opposition in the next great drama, I don't know. But he will be that serpent.

I didn't kill him. I've never succeeded; strangely enough, he's a very frightening thing. He would fill this room, may I tell you, this monstrous thing, slimy, crooked, subtle. I only encountered him a week ago. So, how many times, I don't know. I still encounter him. But I got him. It means that you expand to a certain point where you arrest him, but he's very much alive. It's all you. There is nothing but God in this world, but nothing, and God opposes himself for God's expansion. He has to set up his own opposition.

When I was a child going through these things, who created it? Man did. And they tied that tarpaulin down so tight, and we were only little tots, but so tightly stretched, how to get through it, and it was a very long one. By the time you got through you were exhausted, and you looked up, others were coming through too, like cats crawling. Then you have to go through barrels. That's the next one. Then you jump over some hurdle, and then you climb a greased pole, and then the greased pig. There is always a prize at the end, but there is opposition for the race. We are, as Paul said, "The time for my departure is come. I have fought the good fight. I have finished the race. I have kept the faith."

Well, I'll be back. (Tape ends.)

WE HAVE FOUND HIM

November 12, 1963

___(??) I wondered if I should start with what most people need ___(??), the normal sphere of how to get a house or how to get a better job or how to get a fortune. I said no, time is short as far as I am concerned, so I must tell you what I have discovered. And so, in the course of time, you will know how to get a house and a better job, and more money and all these things ___(??), but for an opening night I thought I couldn't compromise and I had to tell you about him. For I have found him. I have found him of whom Moses and the law, and the prophets wrote. Yes, I have found Jesus Christ. So when you find him, if he is all that you feel that he is, you can't keep him to yourselves, you must share him. And so I want to share him with you.

So we are told, "If anyone ever says to you, 'Look, here is the Christ!' or 'Look, there he is!' do not believe it" (Mark 13:21). And that I will endorse. If anyone, no matter who he is, says to you, "'Look, here is the Christ!' or 'Look, there he is!' do not believe it." And yet this night I'm going to share him with you. But I can't point to another and I can't point to myself, and yet I will share him with you.

The first book written in the New Testament was written by Paul. Scholars are divided whether this book was Galatians or Thessalonians, but both were written by Paul, so it doesn't really matter. But they all are agreed that Paul wrote the first book in the New Testament. In the letters of Paul there is no trace whatsoever that man can find an *historical* Christ as we today use the term, none whatsoever. Yet, if man wants to see Jesus Christ, he's always sure to see him more clearly if he looks at him through the eyes of Paul. For Paul saw him clearly. Paul saw, also, the deep mystery of its meaning.

Now, to Paul it's about a mystery. He said, "Great indeed we confess is the mystery of our religion." A mystery is not a matter to be kept secret but a truth that is mysterious in character. So I will reveal the mystery; so look at it now through the eyes of Paul. Paul made the statement that "The gospel that I have preached is not man's gospel. For I did not receive it from a man, nor was I taught it, but it came through a revelation of Jesus Christ" (Galatians 1:12). Revelation to Paul was an act of God in self-revealing. God revealed himself. So, Jesus Christ to Paul was God himself, not a man. He said, "I regard no one from a human point of view; even though I once regarded Christ from a human point of view, I regard him thus no longer" (2 Corinthians 5:16). No one from a human point of view, no, not Jesus Christ. Well, then who is he and where is he? How can I share with you my discovery of Jesus Christ, and not point to another; and not point to any being in this world, and make no image of him? Well, how can I show you who he is? Well, that's my task this night, and I hope I succeed in showing you Jesus Christ.

We turn now to what I think is the earliest book, the Book of Galatians: "Paul an apostle—not from man nor through men, but through Jesus Christ and God the Father, who raised him from the dead" (Galatians 1:1). And "When it pleased God to reveal his Son *in* me . . . then I conferred not with flesh and blood" (Galatians 1:16). There was no one to whom he could turn to explain why it never happened in eternity before. "Then he spent his days from morning to evening expounding the matter to all who would listen, trying to persuade them, to convince them of Jesus, both from the law of Moses and the prophets. Some were convinced by what he said and others disbelieved" (Acts 28:23). That's the eternal story: The man who finds him cannot convince them, for no man can see David in bodily form and show who the Son is. They can only invite you to come with them . . . and then they turn back to scripture and show you what was foretold; and tell you, hoping that you will believe what they have experienced that matches what was foretold, that you may see who he is. And some will believe it and others will disbelieve it.

Now he turns to his letter to the Galatians, he says: "O foolish Galatians! Who has bewitched you, before whose eyes Jesus Christ was publicly *portrayed* as crucified? Let me ask you only this: Did you receive the Spirit by works of the law, or by hearing with faith? Are you so foolish? Having begun with the Spirit, are you now ending with the flesh?" (Galatians 3:1) Now listen to the words carefully. He uses every word as a poet would use words, with great caution. Every word has significance. "Before whose eyes Jesus Christ was publicly portrayed as crucified." The word portrayed means "represented naturally and vividly, whether by drawing, painting, verbal description, or by action." So the entire drama, whether you saw it painted, just in drawing, or someone like Paul verbally describes it to you in his letters, or, whether you sat in an audience, and the curtain rose, and before your eyes was portrayed a man—so that the entire drama of Jesus Christ crucified was *portrayed*, as you would go to the theatre and see it on the stage.

So everything was vicarious—the suffering and the shameful death—like an actor being slain this night on the stage, he is not dead and you know it, and the one who so killed him, as it were, didn't really kill him. The curtain will go up tomorrow night and the same actors will reenact the part. One will perform the action of murdering and one will drop as though murdered. And yet, night after night, they reenact the part. So it was *portrayed* as crucified. It was not a drama that took place 2,000 years ago; it *takes* place in the soul of man.

This past month I went to the Metropolitan Museum of Art to see one grand picture, the picture by Rembrandt of Aristotle contemplating the head of Homer, valued at a million and a half. It was a perfectly marvelous painting. There were guards all around, and we, the viewers, were separated from the picture by, say, five feet. We could get no closer, all roped off. I don't blame them, because there are certain fellows in the world who would throw something on it and disfigure this masterpiece. But in the same gallery there were pictures of the crucifixion, valued in the hundreds of thousands. They were portraying a drama that I personally have experienced, and they did not portray it correctly. For here, one has the stigmata on the left side, the hands, the feet, the head and the left side. That is an incorrect portrayal of the drama. There were others that had it correctly done, hands, feet, head and right side. But even that isn't true. For they had nails driven into fleshly hands upon a wooden cross, and that is not true.

That which binds God to the real cross that is man is a vortex. And may I tell you, the expression on these faces that I saw and these priceless masterpieces by these great artists is a sad, sad face. And it's not a sad face at all. May I tell you, when you experience it this will be a recurrence, because you have already experienced it. But when it is once more brought back to memory and once more you feel it, it will be an ecstasy that you cannot describe in words. Your hands, your feet, your head and your right side, you are nailed upon this by vortices, not nails. And yet in all of these great masterpieces ___(??) if they knew it, they would have painted a vortex honing into my body as it were. But they nailed my body to a wooden cross. It's no wooden cross. I am actually nailed to a tree, but the tree, as Blake so beautifully brought out: "The gods of the earth and the sea sought through Nature to find this tree; but their search was all in vain: There grows one in the human brain" (*Songs of Experience*, page 217). It's on that tree that we are nailed, and we are nailed by vortices, not by any nails, as depicted on the canvases that I saw only this past month in the Metropolitan Museum of Art. Where within that confine you couldn't buy it for, maybe, a billion dollars or two if you took the value placed upon these canvases by men who are supposed to know what they are addressing. So here was *portrayed* the great drama of life through death, but not properly depicted. It wasn't true.

So I want to share with you what I know from experience. And I can't conjure a being and point and say, "Here is the Christ! Or there he is!" for that would be a lie. It is a *way* of salvation, just a *way* of salvation. And may I tell you, when you receive God's grace, which is God's gift of himself to you, and you are fully aware of it, you find yourself ascribing the entire process of your salvation to God's actions. You, yourself, will confess you had not a thing to do with it, nothing whatsoever. Your very faith, in your eyes, was a gift of God. You had nothing to do with it. It's all God's gift, therefore, *all* will receive it and *none* can fail. Every being in this world will be salvaged by God's grace, grace and grace alone.

By grace we mean, "saved through faith." It is not your own doing, it is the gift of God: "Not by works, lest anyone should boast. We are his workmanship." I am his workmanship. Well, how can I, the thing worked, the pot, say to the potter "Why do you make me in this form?" I have no choice in the matter. He has made me as he desired me, and then endowed me with life by giving me himself. Then, it's by grace he ascends from faith and it's not my own doing. Then salvation by faith is really salvation by the faithfulness of God.

So I know there are many in the world, especially today in this nuclear age, those who call themselves scientists and great philosophers and the wise men of the world, they will ask such—*nothing* beyond what they call the world of Nature. No explanation whatsoever unless it comes within the confines of what they say is the world of Nature. And so I can't speak to them. If you're present, my words would be simply an idle tale, wouldn't mean a thing to you, because I am not speaking of this world at all. Like Paul I did not receive it from a man, nor was I taught it, it came to me, too, by the revelation of Jesus Christ.

And what is this revelation? God unveils himself in us at his own appointed time. And, we are told, God's vision of man "has its own appointed hour; it ripens, it will flower. If it be long, then wait; for it is sure and it will not be late" (Habakkuk 2:3). So don't try to hasten it. Don't ask "When will it happen to me?" for no one knows the time or the season. As we are told, Wait for the promise of the Father. Do not ask the time, ask the season, for it's not yours to know. For the Father has fixed it by his own authority. Just wait, wait for the promise of the Father. But power will come to you when the Holy Spirit has come upon you; and then you will be my witnesses in Jerusalem, in all Judea, in Samaria, to the end of the earth (Acts 1:4-8).

Well, how will you and I be witnesses to all that is told us? For the Father is God's witness. You are told, "The testimony of Jesus is the spirit of prophecy." All that is prophesied is going to happen to you. Not a thing matters, really, outside of the fulfillment of God's word—your homes, your position in the world, socially, intellectually, financially, in the intellectual world, all will vanish and not even leave a trace of ever having been present. But God's word will remain forever, and he has to have *witnesses* to the truth of his word, "For thy word is truth."

Well, how are we going to have witnesses? When it happens to you, when it happens to me, we witness. As we are told, only by the evidence of two witnesses or three witnesses can charges be sustained. I can't bring one witness. I can know the Bible backwards and say, "Here, this is the witness." Well, that is true. But I can't defend it as one witness. I must have two witnesses at minimum, three, yes, and the more the better. But I can't have just one witness. So I will say, I'll memorize the Bible; I know it backwards. I'll present that as my witness, that God's word is true, and it's very good to know the Bible, but that's not what God will accept. "For God has taken his place in the divine council, in the midst of the gods he holds judgment" (Psalm 82:1, 6). So when God enters into that divine council, he has to have two witnesses. And the external witness we all have—that's the Bible. We must have an *internal* witness, where our internal list of experiences parallels the Bible.

And so you step into his presence and you don't have to say one word. For God does not judge you by your social position in this world, by your intellectual position in this world, for the wisdom of man is foolish in the eyes of God. So when you're brought into the divine council, he sees only the heart. He does not see outward appearances; what you did in this world, what you made, what you accomplished, that is as nothing. He's only looking for the witness, the witness that parallels his prophecy of what will unfold within the mind of man. So you stand before him and he sees the Father. And then it parallels this way of salvation. And the way of salvation is this. It will happen to everyone born of woman. I don't care if you are dead now and it didn't happen to you before; you haven't really died. That's also a grand mystery. Your body was consumed by the fire and scattered in the four corners of the earth, but you really haven't ceased to be. Man does not terminate at that point where my senses cease to register him. He still is a living reality, whether he has experienced it or not. But he *will* experience it, because to himself he is just as solidly real as he was here to us who touched him and felt his bodily presence.

But he has to come one day into the divine council where God sees the witness that no man can see. And when they are parallel so that the birth spoken of Christ Jesus, he has experienced; and when David, the eternal David, calls him, Lord, he has experienced; and when his departure from Egypt, which is always symbolized by the turning of a rod ___(??) into a serpent, when he has experienced that; it simply signifies his departure from Egypt, meaning this age. He doesn't have to say he's done it it's so obvious to the one who sits in judgment. So when these experiences are paralleled by the external witness of scripture, he enters the divine council.

Now we are told the day is coming that the Lord will reign as king over the whole land; on that day the Lord will be one and his name one. That name is Christ Jesus—only one, Christ Jesus. It's Christ Jesus that David calls Adonay. He calls him "my Father" in fulfillment of the 89th Psalm, "I have found David . . . he has cried unto me, 'Thou art my Father, my God, and the Rock of my salvation'" (verses 20, 26). When you find him and he calls you the same thing, then you know who Christ Jesus is: Jesus Christ is God the Father. And everyone one day will be called by David, "Adonay," and when he calls you "Adonay," he knows who he is. Well, "What think ye of the Christ? Whose son is he? And they answered, 'Why, the son of David.' He said, 'Why then did David in the *Spirit* call him Lord? If David thus calls him Lord, how can he be David's son?'" (Matthew 22:42). Well, you're going to have these experiences, and then because he only calls in scripture, he calls Christ Jesus "Father," when he calls you that you know who you are. For on that day the Lord will be one and his name one. So in the end, when all awaken, there's only one; and that one is God the Father.

So Paul recognized no intermediary between man and God. He completely repudiated all institutions, all authorities, all customs, all laws that interfered with the direct access of the individual to his God. So man is sure that between himself and God is Jesus Christ. Don't believe it! No intermediary between the self and God. But God is *personified* in scripture as Jesus Christ, and throughout the centuries man has mistakenly taken personifications for persons; and the acted parable for history; and the gross first sense for the ultimate sense intended; and the vehicle that conveyed the instruction for the instruction itself.

So here, Jesus Christ is not *someone* that lived 2,000 years ago. Jesus Christ is God himself, who became you that you may become God. He is actually the life of your being, as told in Paul's letters to the Corinthians. And he acted as though he's shocked that they didn't know, "Do you not know that you are the temple of the living God and that God's spirit dwells in you?" (2 Corinthians 6:16; 1 Corinthians 3:16) Well, if God's spirit dwells in me, I should know it. If not now, eventually I should discover him, for God could not emerge from a man in whom he did not exist. He exists *in* you, and one day he will emerge by a series of revelations so that I will know him. And when he unveils it by the series of revelations, I will know him, and when I find him I find myself. It's the unveiling of myself that *is* Jesus Christ.

So, Jesus Christ is the *way* of salvation, personified for us as a man. And so in this year 1963 we are still bowing to a being who lived 2,000 years ago. We have made an idol of something that we were told, "Make no graven image unto me," but none. ___(??) the second commandment, "Make no graven image unto me . . . and if anyone should ever say to you, 'Look, here is the Christ!' or 'Look, there he is!' believe it not." But *in spite* of that we still make these images. And there are unnumbered images that man will conjure in his mind's eye when he hears the word Christ Jesus and see it as something objective to himself. You will not in eternity find him until he unveils himself in you *as* you . . . when he unveils it in the most marvelous way by that which was God's mystery, the Bible.

So the whole thing begins to unveil in you—you have the experience. You go back and read the scripture, the Old Testament, and there you see exactly what was foretold. But you could not foresee it. Yet there it was; it was foretold. Then suddenly . . . whoever would think, in this modern day, that he or she is father of the David of biblical fame until it happens? I share with you—I can't say I will persuade you to believe it, any more than Paul succeeded in persuading those who listened from morning to night, as told us in the 28th chapter of the Book of Acts. And so, he spent his day from morning to evening, telling them about the kingdom of God and trying to convince them about Jesus, both from the law of Moses and the prophets. And some of them believed on what he said, while others disbelieved (verse 23).

So what percentage this night will accept it, I do not know. I have not the slightest idea how many will believe it without having the experience. Many find him not because they sought for him, but those who found him brought them to him. And so, I found him and so this night I will share him with you, but I can't *persuade* you that it is true. But the day will come you will have the experience and having it, you will be automatically taken right into the divine council where God, in the 82nd Psalm we are told, has taken his place in the divine council; in the midst of the gods he holds judgment. Not to condemn; no one is condemned. He's not a God of retribution. He's waiting for the second witness, for you can't come into his court bearing only one witness. You could be the greatest scholar in the world, memorize the entire book so you could repeat it word after word as it was in the original tongue. That's not what he wants. Have you experienced the ___ (??), those who bring the second witness? You have the external witness of scripture; you must bring the internal witness of the Spirit. Standing in his presence he sees, because he doesn't have to ask questions, and seeing it, you become one with the body of Christ Jesus. You *are* then Christ Jesus. And so when Blake was asked, "What do you think of Christ Jesus?" without batting an eye he replied, "He's the only God" and then quickly added, "But so am I and so are you." Well, he who asked the question did not know it. Blake did, for he had the experience.

And so, I know I have found him. Having found him it's my duty until the end of days when I take it off for the last time to share that discovery with everyone who will listen. For like Paul when he said, "The time for my departure has come," he didn't mean a little physical death that all go through, he meant the end of an age. "The time of my departure has come. I have fought the good fight, I have finished the race, I have kept the faith. And now, henceforth, is laid up for me a crown of righteousness" (2 Timothy 4:7). So he meant the end of *this* age for him. It was not what the world would call death but a coronation. That crown of righteousness was his and he would be that king. And only one king, not a bunch of kings; for "The Lord will become king over all the earth, and on that day, the Lord will be one and his name one." So, there aren't to be numberless little Christ Jesuses running around, but one. You will not lose your identity, any more than I will lose my identity, but you will have a greater self. For we are heirs not only to his promise but to a person. We actually *inherit* God, and without loss of identity. All will know each other and yet all Christ Jesus.

Now, you try it. When you go home, you dwell upon it. You dwell upon these two witnesses. Try to read it in the scripture. If you do not now do it, make a habit of it, just read it. Much of it will mean nothing to you, but read it anyway. Just read it and dwell upon it. When you hear the story of Job and Job ___(??) and cries out, "Oh, that I could find him." He heard about him, but he hasn't seen him: "Oh, that I could find him." Tonight the whole vast world is trying to find him outside of self. Until the very end of Job, in that last chapter, "I have heard of thee with the hearing of the ear, but now my eye sees thee" (Job 42:5). I *see* what you meant in the beginning of time, but I was looking elsewhere. I was looking for some external savior I thought would come in some miraculous way and conquer my enemies and then set me up in some wonderful way. So I was looking for an external savior. And then it happened in me. It wasn't an external savior; it was God's *way* of salvation.

And so, Paul taught Christ crucified that all might see not God's weeping but God's love. All the difference in the world. The whole vast world sees on the crucifix, they see God weeping, the crying, weeping God. That was not what Paul did at all. He ___(??), in every letter he did, that we might see God, not his weeping but his love. That's what he did. He portrayed the dying and the rising Christ in every letter, the mystery of life through death. "Unless I die thou canst not live; but if I die I will arise again and thou with me." [*Jerusalem,* Plate 96] And so God dies by actually becoming one with this tree called man, and then putting himself through the furnaces of affliction. In the end, known only to God he unfolds and ___(??) himself by unveiling himself in man as man. Then man sees who he is . . . and he *is* Christ Jesus.

So let no one tell you that they know a man and then take you to meet a man, a holy man. Run in the opposite direction. Let no one fool you that they have found him in the form of some man that they have met. I meet them everywhere I go, these so-called holy men. And so, having gone through the furnaces myself, I invariably turn in the opposite direction. I have found him, so I am not looking for him. But until that day when this garment is taken off for the last time . . . for the one single thing in scripture that is given to us that signifies our departure from this world is the turning of a rod ___(??) into a serpent. It has happened to me. And so having happened to me in the core of my being, I know this is my exit from this age into an entirely different age, where all things are then subject to my imaginative power. While I'm here I must, in the world of Caesar, obey the laws of Caesar and use God's law to the best of my ability within the framework of his purpose. But at the end, there too waits for me the crown of righteousness, where I am one with the *only* being that reigns over all the earth.

Until then, play the part well, play it lovingly and tell everyone in the world who will listen to you that you found him. And try to the best of your ability by verbal description to describe who Christ Jesus really is. I love engraving . . . I can't do it by engraving, I can't paint, I can't draw, and I'm not a playwright to write the play, but I can to the best of my ability by verbal description share with others my discoveries of Christ Jesus. And so I hope this night that you will exercise your own powers of perception to come with me and actually try to test what I've tried to tell you.

Only a few of the Galatians are well-favored to use their own power of perception. They couldn't seem to put two and two together as he was talking to them, and so he accused them of being foolish: "O foolish Galatians! Who has bewitched you?" You started with the Spirit, didn't you, and now ending with the flesh? And so, anyone who has some visible

objective picture of Christ Jesus is ending with the flesh. You started with
the Spirit and now are you ending with the flesh? Who bewitched you
that you would turn back to the flesh having heard it with faith? "Did you
receive the Spirit by works of the law, or by hearing with faith? Now are
you so foolish having begun with the Spirit, are you now ending with the
flesh?"

So tonight, make no mental image of any being external to yourself as
Christ Jesus, for you're only having an idol. An idol has no power, none
whatsoever. But wait patiently for the promise of the Father. Do not ask
when he's going to give it, for a time and a season are not yours to know; but
the Father has fixed them by his own authority. We simply wait patiently for
the grace that is coming to be given. When it comes, it will come in the
form of a power. And power is given to you when the Holy Spirit has come
upon you. At that moment the veil is lifted, and then a series of mystical
experiences you will go through, all parallel to scripture. Then you will
become one of the witnesses. There will be crowds and crowds of witnesses
to the truth of God's word. Everyone one day will witness to the truth of
scripture, which is God's word. And God's word is truth.

So the testimony of Jesus is the spirit of prophecy. So wait, it will come
and it will not be late, that I assure you. It came on me like a thief in the
night; when I least expected it, it happened. I had not the slightest idea
that this thing could happen. For as a boy I never heard it from a man. I
certainly was not taught it by a man. No one ever shared it with me before.
It came suddenly out of the blue that he shared his experiences with others,
but I did not have the perception to see what he had left behind him in the
form of letters. And so, no one ___(??) to see it or they would have shared
it with me, but they did not. So, like him, I did not receive it from a man
nor was I taught it, it came by a revelation of Jesus Christ when he *unveiled
himself* in me as my own being. For the one who calls him Father called me
Father.

And so you say you're looking for the Father? "Have I been so long with
you, Philip, and you have not seen the Father? He who has seen *me* has
seen the Father; why then do you say, 'Show us the Father'? And they asked
him no more questions" (John 14:8). They should have asked him, "Then
where is your Son?" Well, you can't be a father unless there's a son. But no
one asked him, "Where is your son if you're a father?" So he brings up the
matter and answered it for them, "What think ye of the Christ? Whose son
is he? And when they answered, "The son of David," he then in turn said,
"Why then did David in the Spirit call him Father? If David thus calls him
Father, how can he be David's son?" (Matthew 22:42) So he answered it.
He tells them who he is and there must be a son. You go back and you read

scripture. Well, in the 2nd Psalm, "Thou art my son, *today* I have begotten you." To whom is it spoken? To David . . . by the Lord . . . and David calls Christ Jesus the Lord, or my Father.

Now let us go into the Silence.

*   *   *

N: So, Ina, the time has come for your departure.

I: Thank you very much.

Q: (inaudible)

A: ___(??) I understand correctly as I told you that the individual's faith is also the gift of God. ___(??) I once confessed that having received the grace of God I not only found myself ascribing the process of my salvation to God's actions, I also found myself thoroughly convinced that my own faith was the gift of God.

Any other questions, please?

Q: (inaudible)

A: ___(??) is a quote from Blake, and I endorse it one hundred percent: "Man is all Imagination and God is man, and exists in us and we in him. The eternal body of man is the Imagination, and that is God himself." [*Annotations to Berkeley*; "Laocoon"]

Good night.

HE IS MEDITATING ME:
THE ROCK

November 14, 1963

Tonight's subject is "He Is Meditating Me." The principal source of religious insight is revelation. Revelation makes us sure; without it all seems obscure. You can sit down and rationalize from now until the end of time on this greatest of all books, the Bible. Unless it's revealed to you, I do not see how you can really grasp it. It is God's word, and, may I tell you, it is true; every *word* of it is true. All the symbolism is true, all the imagery is true, and it gradually unfolds within the individual. Everyone will experience it.

So tonight, in this strange subject "He Is Meditating Me", well, who is meditating? When I say, "I and my Father are one," am I the being really meditating myself, projecting on the screen of space this thing called Neville, having experience within the limitations of these dimensions? Well, listen to the words of Peter. It's the first epistle of Peter, the second chapter: "O come to him, to that living stone, rejected by men, but in God's sight chosen and precious. Become living stones, built into a spiritual house . . . that you may declare the oneness and the wonderful deeds of him who called you out of darkness into his light" (verses 4, 5, 9). Read it in the second chapter of Peter's first epistle: He calls us out of darkness into light.

Well, many years ago, 1934 to be exact, I was sitting in the Silence, not thinking of anything in particular, just simply contemplating this interior structure of the brain as it were. If you turn your eyes, mentally turn them inward and just let them rest upon the interior of your skull, in a little while all these dark convolutions of the brain grow luminous and they fascinate you. The whole thing becomes liquid and golden liquid light. So while watching this wonderful golden liquid light, suddenly out of the nowhere came a stone, a rock. There's nothing more sterile, nothing more opaque, nothing more contracted as far as imagery is concerned than a rock. So here was a rock, this quartz. As I looked at it, just simply looking at it, not wondering why it's before me, but there it is before me, and suddenly it became fragmented, broken into unnumbered pieces. Then all these little pieces were gathered together, but not re-formed into the rock (the original form) but into a human shape. And here it takes human form. Here, I am seeing a man seated in the lotus posture. I became intrigued. As I looked closer, I'm looking at myself. I am the being that I'm contemplating. Here he is seated in the lotus posture and just the very image of the being I knew myself to be. As I looked at him, he began to glow and he increased in luminosity until he reached the limit of intensity, and then he exploded. Then I returned to this level with only the memory of what I had experienced.

We are told, "The Rock, his work is perfect," the thirty-second chapter of Deuteronomy. The rock, which is now inanimate, "his" work, it becomes personal now. What was a rock takes on the form of a person . . . "his" work is perfect. "And of the Rock that begot you, you are unmindful and you have forgotten the *God* who gave you birth" (verse 18). Here, a Rock begot me and God gave me birth, so God is the Rock. That's Deuteronomy 32. Here's a Rock, it begot me, and I forgot the God who gave me birth. If I was begotten by a Rock and born of God, then God and the Rock are one. So here, the invitation: "O come to him, to that living stone, rejected by men, and yet in God's eyes chosen and precious." It tells you: *you* will become living stones and be built into this spiritual structure. Then you are told that you may declare the wonderful deeds of him who really begot you, these wonderful deeds of him who brought you and called you out of darkness into his marvelous light, from darkness into light. Now, when I had the experience I didn't understand it. I simply recorded it. Understanding comes over the years. You record the experience. You can't deny it, you had it. It's not theory, you didn't seek it, it just happened. And then suddenly, as years move on, awakening comes and you begin to understand what has happened to you.

Now, last year a book was given to me. I read the review and my daughter and my wife said, "What do you want for Father's Day?" Well, we don't share presents for Father's Day and Mother's Day and all these things. But they said it to me in a kidding manner and I answered in the same manner, I said, I have just read a review of a book. It's Carl Jung's latest work and so I would like to have it. So I gave them the title *Memories, Dreams and Reflections*. He died in 1961 and the book came out in 1961. So it's not only his latest, it's his last work. It is really an autobiography; although it is not claimed to be one, it is written in the first person. Well, in this, Jung made this observation. Mine happened in 1934, what I've just told you. His happened in 1944—not the full vision, only the middle section of the vision. He found himself in 1944 in a dream, but in a dream awake. And true vision is when you are in a dream awake. This, you may not know it, this is a vision. But because you are completely awake, you don't call this a dream because you are in it and you are awake. For when you are really in a dream and you awake in it, it's just like this. So a vision is in a dream awake; what Blake called "fourfold vision." So this is the four-fold vision of Blake. But we are now completely awake in it and it has continuity, so we don't even realize it is still a dream.

But this is the vision of which I speak. So, he found himself in a dream, walking along a little country road, and he came upon this wayside chapel. The door was ajar so he stepped in. As he walked into this little chapel, he walked toward the altar. And to his amazement there was no image of the Virgin and there was not anything that would remind him of a Christian chapel, yet it was. There was no crucifix and no image of the Virgin, but in place of these two images, this wonderful display of flowers. And then, looking down below the altar he noticed a Yogi seated in the lotus posture; and looking closer, this figure had his face. It startled him; and he awoke frightened, and said he to himself: "So it is he who is meditating me. He has a dream and I am it." Then said he to himself, "And I knew that when he awakened I would no longer be." Then said he—being the great analyst that he was—"This is a parable and what is its message to me? For here I am being confronted with something from the very depths of my soul, what is it trying to tell me?" And said he to himself, "The central jet of truth that this thing is trying to convey to me is this: on this level of my being I think *this* is causation and *that* is effect; and here now it's revealed to me, *that* is causation and *this* is effect. That myself retired in meditation, and meditated this human form to have the experience in three dimensions of space and time; and then by this experience, I would increase my awareness, and this increased awareness would further my realization. So the whole story is to reverse *in me* my thinking about causation: causation isn't here; it is there. And I saw the being who is meditating me." He didn't see the rock and he didn't see the light.

The *limit* of contraction is the rock, the most sterile, the most opaque that you could think of in this world. If you thought of an image to convey these qualities, think of a rock, a quartz. And then it becomes fragmented. And then when re-gathered, it doesn't take the original form, it takes the form of man. Then the man glows, becomes a breathing, living being, and then it glows and glows and glows, and reaching the limit of brightness it vanishes. The job is completed and it vanishes. And we are told, "I have brought you out of darkness into light." For God is light: "I am the light of the world" (John 8:12). And yet I do not lose my identity, I do not lose the being that I am; only I inherit the greater being, the light of the world. So here, in this vision revealed to me, I will now share it with you. What is the stone then that men will reject? "Come unto him, to that living stone men rejected." What is the stone? For the stone I saw was only a symbol. I certainly was not the stone. What is the stone, that opaque contracted state that men rejected as causation?—your own wonderful human Imagination.

The Bible recognizes only one source of dream, only one: all dreams and visions proceed from God. Well, I don't have to be a giant in mind to discover who he is. I stand here and I think of my home that I left an hour ago. Well, that's a dream, a daydream, but a dream. It doesn't differ from the dream of the night save in one respect: when I fall asleep tonight and I have a dream, in that dream I am the victim of my attention, not the master of my attention. Here, in a daydream I am in control of the direction of my attention. So I can simply direct it and if it doesn't please me, I can change it. But in sleep this night, if I dream, I may not be awake as I am now and become the victim of the direction of my attention rather than its master.

So, if all dreams proceed from God, but *all* dreams, I don't have to go very far to discover who God is. For here, in this moment I was sitting in the Silence and suddenly before me comes a rock. Only a symbol, a symbol of what was recorded in scripture in Deuteronomy 32 and all through scripture, really: Isaiah 28, "I am laying in Zion a stone." Zion is called the eternal home of God. "I am laying in Zion a stone." And here, in this Book of Peter . . . and Peter, the word Peter means rock. The very word Peter is a rock, is a stone. So what is this stone *symbolizing* in my world? It's symbolizing my own wonderful human Imagination that I, through the years, rejected. In my search for God I thought he was another and found him because others thought he was out there. They showed me pictures of him and showed me all kinds of things of a God, and in my innocence I believed them. And so, I kept on rejecting the stone, the *living* stone. I hadn't touched it. And one day, I touched it and then *I* became a living stone. The stone became alive. You read it carefully—it begins on the fourth verse—how by finding it, you that you rejected, accepting it you are accepted. By association you touch it, and you that you rejected become a living stone. And then you can declare all these wonderful deeds of he who called you out of darkness into light.

So here, we call that the projection on the screen of space of things I would approach. And then I knew, in the depths of my soul, I knew I would one day accept the one I had rejected. For I could not believe, trained as I was trained, that I, and I myself, was the cause of the phenomena of my life. I didn't believe it, that I was the cause of all the strange things happening to me, all the misfortunes, all the strange things in the world. I couldn't believe it, so I rejected that. I rejected the stone that begot me, and the God who gave me birth.

One day I found him, I accepted him, and then came the unfolding of all this wonderful symbolism as recorded in scripture, all the imagery, and it's all imagery. Who would have thought on reading that that you were in conflict in the depths of your own soul and really encounter the symbol of the stone? But who saw it? I saw it. Well, where did it come from? It came out of my Imagination. For if all dreams proceed from God, and I know exactly what happened to me . . . I sat in the Silence thinking of nothing in particular, turning my attention inward into my brain and contemplating these dark convolutions of the brain, and as always happens they grew luminous. As they grew luminous, I am simply looking at this luminous cloud forming in my head, and suddenly out of nowhere, comes this quartz, this enormous stone. I didn't do a thing, just simply looked at it. And it fragmented, the whole thing broke into unnumbered pieces. Not a piece was lost but re-gathered by some invisible hand. As it was re-gathered, it was not the original form, now it takes the form of man.

So Jung makes the statement that "I myself retired in meditation, and meditated me in human form." But he does not mention the fact that his dream encompassed the stone and the light. That out of this dark opaque state suddenly came light, light beyond the wildest dream of man. But I tell you, you have meditated yourself and brought yourself right into being right here in this world, that you may increase in experience and by this increase of awareness further your own wonderful self-realization. And that is forever. There is no limit to translucency. There is only a limit to contraction, to opacity, and the stone is the symbol of the limit of sterility, the limit of opacity, the limit of contraction. But there is no limit to man's expansion, man's translucency. So when I saw this thing reaching seemingly a limit, it exploded, proving to me that there could never be a limit to the expansion, to the translucency of my own being. So, everyone is simply on the way, expanding, *after* he sees this wonderful thing taking place within him.

Until you see it, may I tell you, share with me what I have experienced. You don't have to wait to see it to test it in this world. For if all things come from him and without him there's not a thing made that was made, I don't have to wait to prove it. I just have to test it this night. And actually, if I *know* that my own Imagination *is* God, the rock that I rejected, the God I rejected . . . I went in search of a strange God, some God that didn't really exist, that someone painted on the wall, or carved in wood, and some peculiar thing outside of myself. But then, if this really is what all along I rejected and now I will accept, then comes testing me ___(??). So we are told: "Come test yourselves and see. Do you not realize that Jesus Christ is in thee?—unless of course you fail to meet the test!" If you want to search it, it's the 13th chapter of 2nd Corinthians: "Come *test* yourselves and see. Do you not realize that Jesus Christ is *in* thee?—unless of course you fail to meet the test" (verse 5). Well, if he is in me and by him all things were made, and without him was nothing made that was made, I certainly should be able to test him. Well, how did he work in this world? Read this now, "He called a thing that is not seen as though it were seen, and the unseen becomes seen." That is the fourth chapter, the seventeenth verse of Paul's letter to the Romans: "He calls a thing that is *not* seen as though it were seen, and the unseen becomes seen."

I've just returned from New York City, and last month on a Wednesday evening this lady came in from Baltimore. That's quite a long journey, and she came to bring me good news." She said, "A friend of mine, working in my office, last July" . . . now last month October . . . "last July, her purse disappeared, her pocketbook. She reported it to the office, they made a thorough search, and no trace of it." She said, 'All I had in it as far as money was concerned was $1.35, just lunch money. But I did have a lovely bracelet that I valued—not only to me, it was of great value sentimentally—but I also thought it had great value in a monetary sense, so I placed a double value on it. But I wanted the bracelet, not the $1.35 that was in my change purse. And not one little thing happened to retrieve this purse.'" This lady who came to my meetings told her of my work and told her what to do, and then she gave her a complete set of my books. And this is what the lady did. She imagined that she was wearing the bracelet, that's all that she did. She imagined she was wearing the bracelet. If she wore the bracelet, well then, it wasn't lost. And day after day she wore that bracelet.

This lady who came from Baltimore on Wednesday night to tell me the story could tell me the previous day, on Tuesday in October, the purse was found in this strange manner. The firemen were called in to give some estimate on structural changes because they suggested certain changes for safety. And then they brought the firemen in to make these so-called suggestions. One fireman simply took a certain ___(??) should come out, and as he did so, behind this thing that he pulled was the purse. The only thing missing was the little change purse of a dollar and thirty-five cents, and there was the bracelet.

If "By him all things are made and without him there is nothing made that is made," well then, I can test it. If I test it and he proves himself in performance, I've found him. But, if *all* things are made by him and without

him there's nothing made that is made, doesn't she know this night who
Christ Jesus is? Who God is? She found the one who made it. But she may,
in spite of this, tomorrow still reject it. That's life. I can find him this night
and then tomorrow, by the confusion of the world, reject him as not really
the God who creates everything in my world. At least she's proven in one
instance from her own satisfaction she has found a causative power within
her. She may not want to feel it is Christ Jesus, although scripture tells you
it is, the Bible tells you it is, but churches tell you that it isn't.

The churches want to lead us on the outside and point to some being
hanging on a wall or to something in time and space 2,000 years removed
from now, and call that Christ Jesus. And they have organized around
a certain idea and mislead man. I don't say they do it consciously and
deliberately; they do it unwittingly. They don't know Christ Jesus. They can
dress themselves up in all the flowing garbs of the world and that does not
mean that they've experienced Christ Jesus. For when they experience him
then it's so simple, it's so easy, it is so wonderful.

And one day, you have all these marvelous experiences spoken of in
scripture. I can't tell anyone the thrill that is in store for you when you
move up from *this* age into *that* age. A body already prepared for you, not of
your own choosing, and certainly you did not earn it. The body prepared,
completely prepared, but waiting for you to fill it. And you become
molten light. As molten light you move up and fill this infinite garment,
an immortal garment, already prepared for you. And you fill it in one
marvelous circular motion.

This temple of yours will be struck like lightning, as told you in
scripture: "Tell me, Master, what is the sign of your coming?" and he
answered, "As lightning comes out of the east and shines as far as the west,
so will be the coming of the Son of man!" (Matthew 24:3, 27) And it's just
like that. It's a bolt of lightning right out of your own skull, and it splits
you in two from top to bottom—the bottom being the base of your spine.
It's just the torso that is completely torn in two, and you see it separated
by several inches. And at the base of what *was* your spine is molten golden
liquid light. As you look at it, you can say with Blake, "I know it is my Self,
O my Divine Creator and Redeemer" (*Jerusalem*, Plate 96) I am one with
the very thing that I contemplate, and then *as* it, in serpentine motion up
you go into Zion. And you fill a garment prepared for you. That garment
is unseen by mortal eye, because no mortal eye could behold the beauty of
that garment. It is beyond the wildest dream of anything known to man. It's
not man as you understand man. Yes, a human face, human hands, human
feet. But how could you describe the body that is yours now when you move
up and take possession of it? And then you are in Zion.

So I say to everyone, it's going to happen to you, to every being in this world. For you don't earn it, it's a *gift*; it's given to us. And as he gives us the gift of himself, he gives us the garment already prepared for us. All will get it. And no two . . . he doesn't tell the other what garment he is preparing for the other . . . but all will be molded as living stones into his living wonderful temple. It's a living thing, not made of dead stones. The stone was converted into something alive, and suddenly the whole temple becomes alive, and you and I form the stones of that temple. You can't describe the beauty of the body that forms.

So here, who is meditating me? I am meditating myself. God became me that I may become God, and in becoming me he passes me through all these furnaces of affliction. At the very end, then he draws me out, singly. He doesn't draw me in a pair. I'm unique in the temple. I cannot be replaced in the temple. You cannot be replaced in the temple. So he draws us, as told us in the Book of Isaiah, the 27th chapter: "I will gather you one by one, O people of Israel" (verse 12). One by one . . . I don't bring two. It's unique; this temple is unique, only one can come at a time. The door is narrow and only one can get through. And God draws us "one by one, O people of Israel" into this temple that he's building. It's a heavenly structure, something altogether, well, you can't describe it. Not a thing on earth could even be a shadow of it. That's how unique you are, how perfect you are in his eyes.

So you don't reject this night the stone that begot you. The stone that begot you is your own wonderful human Imagination. That is God. "Man is all Imagination and God is man, and exists in us and we in him. The eternal body of man is the Imagination, and *that* is God himself." (Blake) And if God makes all things, well, then test it. I will this night imagine that I am the man I would like to be, and although reason denies it, my senses deny it, and everything denies it, I will walk in that state just as though it were true. Like the lady wearing the bracelet. It was gone between July and October. She believed her friend who came to my meetings, who gave her the books. She read the books, she never met me in person, never saw me, only from the books. And she began to make a game of it and she wore her bracelet day after day. And then, seemingly out of the nowhere, there must be structural changes in the building. And the firemen come in and they say what they will allow and what they would disallow, and "this must go." One fireman—why did he do it?—he takes some little thing and pulls it from the wall and says, "This must go. This is a fire trap." As he does so, behind it here is a pocketbook, and in the pocketbook the one thing she wanted. And the only thing lost was the change, the $1.35. But the *bracelet* was there! Well, didn't she find God?

Now many don't believe that is God. Maybe you can't quite feel that Imagination could be personified. May I tell you, I stood in the presence of God. He is just as described in the Book of Daniel, just as he's described. And standing in the presence of the Ancient of Days, I answered in scripture, that's all that I answered. He asked me the simplest thing in the world, which you may not know if you were asked that suddenly. But you don't have to know, as told you in the Book of Luke: Don't be concerned when you are brought into the Divine Council, brought in before the authors, or rather, the rulers of the synagogue (Luke 12:11, 12). For a synagogue is simply a place of assembly; it's the assembly itself or those assembled. But they only read in synagogue, that's all that they do. They don't give sermons, it's simply the reading of scripture that all may hear it, as told in Nehemiah, hear it with understanding. Read it so they understand you when you read it, the 8th chapter, the 8th verse. Read it so those who hear you understand what you say. And so, read it, that's all that is read in synagogue, it's simply the reading of scripture.

So when you're told, "Bring your ___(??) into the synagogue before the rulers and the authorities of the day, do not be anxious how you will *answer*." Well, if I'm to answer, something was asked me. I can't answer unless something was asked of me. So, "Do not be anxious how you will answer or what you will say; because the Holy Spirit will teach you in that very hour what you *ought* to say" (Luke 12:12). So you are supremely and divinely prompted what you ought to say. That gives man freedom to disobey. That is the only place in the Bible I can find where a man could really disobey to the point of sinning against the Holy Spirit. Having been prompted what to say then not to say would be a sin against the Holy Spirit. Well, I can't conceive of any being in the world being divinely prompted what he ought to say failing to confess his faith.

And so I was asked, "What is the greatest thing in the world?" and my automatic reply was, "Love." I said, "Faith, hope and love, these three abide, but the greatest of these is love." With that the Ancient of Days embraced me and I became incorporated into his body, one with his body. I *was* the very being who embraced me. I have had no sensation from that day on of any separation or divorce from that union. It was a union that has been abiding since. And slowly he who embraced me is rising within me, instructing me as to all my visions that I had and recorded without understanding. Then understanding comes slowly as he rises within me. When he completes his rising fully within me, I am he. Then all the things foretold will be mine. And so they come week after week and month after month.

Well, just imagine going to bed, fully convinced of the reality of God having experienced it, and asking him as you would a person, "Why did you make this? What is the purpose of it all? Why?" Not doubting for one moment that he created it, I'm not asking him to define his act. *How* was it made, that isn't my concern, but *why*? What is its purpose? And then from the depths of your soul one word comes in response to your inquiry, and that one word is "hatching," just "hatching." For hatching the whole thing was made. Then your mind goes back and you remember the words of Blake in his *Gates of Paradise*. Here he has an egg, and he breaks the egg in a drawing, and out of the egg comes a cherub, this thing you couldn't see to be a cherub with the shell unbroken; you wouldn't know what it contained. But within the egg it contained a cherub, a winged immortal creature. And then Blake drew an egg, broke the egg, and out of it comes a winged cherub. And the caption of that winged cherub is this: "At length for *hatching* ripe he breaks the shell." So, why did you make it? "For hatching" came back the answer. The only purpose of the whole vast universe is for hatching out sons of God.

But being a son in the process of becoming, we are invited to imitate him as dear children, and hatch out our dreams as he is hatching out his dream. His dream is to beget sons more numerous than the sands of the sea. All the sons, these are the Elohim that go to make the one God, the *only* God. So, "Hear, O Israel: The Lord"—that is one—"our Elohim"—that's a plural word—"is one Lord" (Deuteronomy 6:4). It takes *all* of these completely awake to make Jehovah. All one. So here, the word came back, why did you make this? And the answer came "For hatching." The only reason for the whole vast universe was for hatching out sons of God. As told us in the 8th chapter of the Book of Romans: "The whole creation groans waiting for the unveiling of the sons of God" (verse 19). Everything is waiting for that moment in time when the whole curtain is lifted and all the sons are born. And all are he, and altogether form God. So I tell you, I share with you that revelation: it's only for hatching.

So tonight you can hatch out a dream. You want a home? Dwell in it, just as though you were in it. You want to dispose of one? Keep out of it mentally as though you had sold it. You want to get married, be happily married? Wear the ring as this lady wore the bracelet, and be as persistent in the wearing of it as she was in the wearing of the bracelet. Whatever you want, hatch it out! For the whole world is only for hatching. Everything in the world is hatched out by God. But don't reject the God *in you* that is one with the God that brought the whole thing into being. Your human Imagination keyed low is still one with the God that brought the whole vast universe into being. And if he brought the whole vast universe into being for the hatching of his sons, keyed low as we are, we can hatch out ours, jobs, income, anything we want in this world. For it's only for hatching.

This is not something manufactured; this is revelation. For when you hear a word, one word, from the depths of your soul, and it comes in response to your inquiry; don't neglect it. Share it with everyone who will accept it, and it is only for hatching. So you can hatch out anything in this world, I don't care what it is. Someone wants to be a president; he hatches it out. It doesn't mean anything in the eyes of God. For in the end, when we awake as God, we inherit God. Then all the little things of earth will wear out like a garment and dissolve like smoke. So your human history will be as nothing.

It's only your divine history that is already written for you in scripture; and all that is written in scripture you are going to experience in the depths of your soul. And if you can't understand it the very day you experience it, wait, it will happen. I had mine in 1934. I didn't understand it. I have had visions all through my life. I didn't understand them but I recorded them. So these things are indelibly impressed upon the mind. It's exactly what has happened, but then you didn't understand it. And so, you go through life waiting, and finally the *real* series begins to unfold within you, and then understanding comes. And all the things that previously happened to you without understanding suddenly begin to unfold like a flower and you have the full meaning of it. You go back to your scripture and there it was. "Come to him"—to him? And then the very next line tells me that this one spoken of as a person is now a living stone? And you couldn't understand it. And to see a stone, this inanimate sterile thing, broken, reshaped into a human form and that human form becomes living. Then you understand it. A living stone and the living stone is human. Then he calls you out of darkness into the marvelous light that is he. He brings you into his own light and you are one with him.

So here, tonight you test it. Take your dream this night that you want to realize in the not distant future. For man's span is short in this little world of ours, three score and ten. You haven't too many months or years to wait for the fulfillment of the dream. And this revelation is true: "Why did you make it, O God?" "For hatching." Well now, be imitators of God as dear children. As we're told in Paul's letter to the Ephesians, in his fifth chapter, "Be imitators of God as dear children." Well, if he brings it this way, by calling a thing that is not seen as though it were, and I must imitate him, well, then I will imitate him. I will dare to assume that which is not now seen, and then I will be faithful to my assumption as though it were true and bring it into being. For the world is for hatching. This is God's wonderful nest that he made. It's the nest and he's hatching out.

So then, that wonderful picture of Blake's; when you see it the next time, you will see it based on understanding. "At length for hatching ripe he breaks the shell" and out comes this winged creature, the immortal you, out of the shell that you could not have seen the contents until the shell was broken. Who looking at a caterpillar could predict his future as a painted butterfly if you've never seen a butterfly and didn't know the source of the butterfly? How could you look at it and see a painted butterfly? How can you look at man—as it was shown me so vividly and explained to me so clearly that man to the higher world is simply this carnivorous bowel, giving off the most offensive odor? And how could you now look at man seen from a higher level—as we would now look on the lower level and see a caterpillar, for that is all we are to the higher level—and see this cherub, see this God coming out of this carnivorous bowel? For that's all that we are.

The night that it [the dove] descended upon me and smothered me in affection with kisses, and then this woman to my left explained to me what we were to the higher world. But she explained to me that he who came in the form of a dove came because he so loved me; and he demonstrated his love to me, and all over my face this dove smothered me in kisses. And she told me how we offend the higher world, for to them we are only a carnivorous bowel. But out of this carnivorous bowel, as told us in the Book of Daniel, how we were given the garment and the heart and mind of an animal, and then seven times must pass over us until the people know that the Most High rules (Daniel 5:21). Then something comes out. It's a hatching out process. So we are just like the bowel, that ___(??) picture of the bowel than the caterpillar? And yet out of it comes the painted butterfly. So if we are to the higher world a carnivorous bowel, out of it comes God. He buried himself in us and then brings himself out completely awake, and we are he.

Now let us go into the Silence.

*   *   *

Q: If what I want to hatch appears as if it would cause unhappiness to someone else, do I have to worry about that?

A: Did you hear the question? If what I want in this world appears that it might cause unhappiness to another. Well, let me give you a personal experience, very personal. When I fell in love with the girl who now bears my name and is the mother of my daughter, I was terribly involved. I was married at the age of nineteen, separated at twenty but not divorced. In the meanwhile, I became a dancer and everyone who knew us as a dance team thought that if I ever got a divorce, or my wife got a divorce, surely my dancing partner and myself would get married. That was taken for granted by everyone who knew us. But here, I was now not only not divorced, I was already committed to someone else. Then I found the girl I wanted, who was not my first wife or my dancing partner. Well, if I married her, on the surface of things I would hurt my dancing partner, wouldn't I? I didn't want to hurt her. I'd rather *die* than hurt her. I just couldn't hurt her. So I kept on postponing what I knew I should have done. I should have assumed that I hurt no one.

And so, one day I said to myself, I'm not applying this principle that I know so well. I'm trying to unravel it on this level and you can't unravel it on this level. So I began to fall asleep in the assumption that there was a bed over there occupied by my *second* wife, not occupied by anyone else. She slept there. I slept in that assumption for one solid week. At the end of a week, my dancing partner said, "I've got to talk to you about something. It's very important." I said, What is it? She said, "You know it's always been assumed that you and I would get married, but, really, you are like my brother, I couldn't marry you. I am in love with Dr. so-and-so and we have been for quite a few years, but I didn't have the courage to tell you. But now I can't let it drift any longer, and so I must tell you that I could never marry you. You're just like a brother of mine." So I had been carrying that burden for the longest while and she had been carrying the burden; we didn't tell each other, and she didn't have the courage to tell me until I assumed that I was happily married to the girl who now bears my name.

So, you don't hurt anyone if you really go beyond appearances to a higher level. I could not honestly or consciously hurt my dancing partner. I would rather have died than to have her hurt by marrying someone else. But I assumed she was not hurt. When I went to bed, I made it quite clear to myself that I am sleeping in the assumption that I am happily married, which I could not be at the expense of another. So, if I am happily married, she is not hurt. Then suddenly at the end of the week she comes forward and tells me that I am her brother and she doesn't believe in incest. So that's the picture.

So I hope I've answered you. You don't hurt anyone if you go above this level into the real level of your wonderful Imagination and see things as they ought to be through the eyes of love. So every time that you exercise your Imagination lovingly, you're doing the right thing. No matter what you do, you're doing the right thing. But on this level we wrestle with ourselves trying to unravel and you can't unravel it here. This is a shadow world. As he said earlier when he saw this figure of himself meditating him, he knew the central jet of truth was: It was trying to tell him to reverse his belief of causation: causation isn't here, causation is there. So, revise the level of causation and he has causation

___(??) a shadow in this world that the world calls reality. Is that clear? Thank you, Bill.

Q: What is the correct definition of Selah.

A: Selah, in all the Psalms? It's just simply a pause and a conjunction. When you read a psalm at the end of it is Selah. Then it means that that reader of the psalm he broke it to be joined to the next. In other words, in the original manuscript there is no punctuation mark between even words or paragraphs. There are no verses, no chapters, simply a string of consonants, not even in the original manuscripts, vowels. And so man had to simply break them down in to what he would consider a word, a verse, a sentence and so on. And so, we broke them into chapters. But Selah means simply "joined to the next to give meaning to the two." It's not really an ending, it's simply move forward and read the next psalm with it, because this is an arbitrary break of the original manuscript. And this break didn't take place until the fifteenth century. So the scholars in the fifteenth century worked upon the scripts and tried to give it some kind of meaning for us.

Even to this day, you take this one statement when he said, "Behold, I say unto you today, thou shalt be with me in Paradise." Suppose I changed the comma, "Behold I say unto you, *today* thou shalt be with me in Paradise." All the difference in the world. But the comma was placed after "today." And yet, in the script he was made to say, "Do not touch me, I am not yet ascended in Paradise." And yet, the world today puts the comma after "today": "Behold, I say unto you *today*, thou shalt be with me in Paradise." "Behold, I say unto you, today thou shalt be with me in Paradise." All the difference in the world.

So that's punctuation, and these are all, well, scholars did a marvelous job. You can't condemn them. We are heirs to their great work and they did a fantastic job on these scripts. I have many scripts at home and no two really agree. But they always give me something, every one. I like Moffatt's, not for the entire book but for the poetry that the regular translation has lost. Moffatt's tries to catch the poetry of it, and to me I just love the poetry. They are closer to the divine inspiration.

Q: (inaudible)

A: Did you hear the question? Well, first of all, I find that the lighter one treats it the best. First of all, if I assume that it's done and make no effort to make it so, I am living by faith. By faith all things were made, as we're told in Hebrews 11, it is by faith. So if I *really* believe the thing is done because I've imagined it done, believe in the reality of my imaginal act, well then, the lighter I treat it the better. If I make a problem of it, it's the *lack* of faith. I'm almost confessing the absence of faith. But to treat it lightly, in confidence, then it will. But if I make it a problem, well then, I make it a difficult thing.

Q: (inaudible)

A: Yes, it's all hatching, everything is for hatching, everything in the world. To me I think it's a profound revelation. One word comes back, not a long sentence, "hatching." And then my mind rushes to the quote of Blake, and here is this angelic being coming through an egg, and he uses the caption, "At length for hatching ripe he breaks the shell." Now Blake saw it clearly, but having this artistry that was Blake he could draw it and present it. And having this wonderful spiritual ___(??), he also captured it. But when you only hear it ___(??) only describe it verbally. But he could describe it in drawing, in painting, in poetry, in everything. But here is that one little thing . . . and the egg is broken ___(??) the cherub, and he uses the word "hatching" And out of the depths of the soul comes the one word "hatching." That's why he made the whole vast world: only for hatching.

And tonight, you have an idea; that is to you like an egg. And so, warm it by simply accepting it and let it hatch. Because it contains within itself all the necessary power to express itself. It takes your acceptance of the fact that it does and it hatches.

Until Tuesday. Thank you.

COUNTING THE COST

November 19, 1963

Tonight's subject is "Counting the Cost." In the gospel of Luke, the fourteenth chapter, he asks a certain question, "Which of you desiring to build a tower does not first sit down and count the cost, whether you have enough to complete it?" (verse 28). So you and I are called upon to count the cost. It's not in dollars and cents. That's not the coin that you use. God counted the cost when he decided to transform us into himself. It's a frightening cost! Because, God actually became us; he didn't pretend to become a slave, he became one. As we are told in Philippians: "Jesus Christ, who, though in the form of God, emptied himself, taking upon himself the form of a slave, being born in the likeness of men" (2:5).

He actually took upon himself the form of a slave and this mightier self that is our self who is Jesus Christ, is your own wonderful human Imagination. Completely emptied himself and assumed the form of a slave, and now he serves us in the capacity of a slave. A slave does not question the order given by his master, he only obeys. For today he serves us as indifferently and as quickly when our will is evil as when it is good. I can conjure in a second, a split second, the most horrible picture or the most wonderful loving picture, and he does it. He is my own wonderful human Imagination, who gave up his primal form, his prenatal wholeness, and took upon himself the form of a slave, which is my own wonderful human Imagination that serves me in this capacity.

Now tonight, I want to take it on this level, this level of Caesar, and show you how on this level we do the same thing. Just as he gave up everything to become me to transform me into himself, so that I may wear the form of God and wear that primal form that is eternal, so today I give up, too, certain things. But I must count the cost. Well, how would

I go about counting the cost if I wanted to be other than what reason tells me that I am? Well, this is how I do it. First, I must know what I want to be, and then I conjure in my mind's eye a certain imagery which imagery implies the fulfillment of my dream. And then, this is where I now count the cost. Do I have the necessary persistency, the necessary faithfulness, the necessary power that in spite of all things to the contrary I will persist? Do I have these virtues? Am I willing to start with what I have in the hope that it really is enough to build the tower? For the word translated tower means "a simple watch-tower." As we are told in Habakkuk: "And now I will stand, and watch, and take my station upon the tower; and I will look forth to see what he will say unto me, and what I will answer concerning my complaint. The Lord answered me and said, 'Write the vision; make it plain upon tablets that he may run who reads it.'" And then comes the promise, "For the vision has its own appointed hour; it ripens; it will flower. If it be long, then wait; for it is sure, and it will not be late." Here you find these three verses of 2nd Habakkuk (:2, 3). This is the tower spoken of in this Book of Luke, "I will stand upon my tower."

So I bring before my mind's eye a certain imagery. I bring you, my friend, and hear you discussing each other and your discussion is all about my good fortune. I listen as though I actually heard you say what I want everyone to say. I listen and persuade myself I'm actually hearing it. And then have I now the courage, in spite of tomorrow when everything denies it? Have I the persistency? Have I the faithfulness? By faithfulness I mean loyalty to this unseen reality. So here, it is unseen, but to me it's *real*. I'm seeing it vividly in my mind's eye, but it hasn't yet objectified itself upon the screen of three-dimensional space so that you may share it with me. Well, can I remain faithful? Can I remain loyal to this unseen reality until it becomes something I can share with the world? Have I that coin?

So the coin I use is not the coin of Caesar, it's the coin of God. He knew exactly the price he had to pay when he decided to transform me into himself, for he had to grant me all the freedom in the world to make mistakes. He had to become my *slave* and wait upon me just as swiftly when my will was evil as when my will is good. He couldn't discriminate and say you shouldn't do it. He has to wait upon me and let me make all the mistakes in the world as he slowly transforms me into his form, that I, too, may bear the form of God. So just as Jesus Christ, who, though he was in the form of God, emptied himself and then took upon himself the form of a slave, and was born in the likeness of a man. Not *a* man 2,000 years ago, *you* are the man in which Jesus Christ is born. Every child born of woman is Jesus Christ, born in the likeness of man. And now in the depth of that soul is one's own wonderful human Imagination, which is Jesus Christ, a slave of that man.

And he takes the part of the slave in the true sense of the word: he only obeys. He doesn't suggest anything in this world, only obeys your wonderful vision and he will in the twinkle of an eye conjure up the most horrible animalisms in the world and lust at the call of your desire. And the same one does it that will conjure to me, if I so desire, the most loving thing in the world, the same being, not another being. There's only one God and that God is Jesus Christ. Forming us from what we are into what he was when he gave himself up to become us—and that is God himself.

So here is a story. Last month in New York City this lady came to me, she brought her husband—nice looking chap, tall, fine, handsome looking fellow. She said, "Do you recall my story of last year? I was at my wit's end, and I told you my husband, who I consider a very fine lawyer, he graduated from one of our greatest universities, and here at his age, he was then only forty, he was only earning eighty-seven dollars a week in a very large law firm. I asked you if I could apply this technique for him, without his consent, without his knowledge, because, trained as he is in the legal world, he could not conceive of the rational side of this picture at all. It made no sense whatsoever to him. So could I, without his knowledge, without his consent, use this technique to increase his income? And I asked you if I could take it and double it. You said to me, 'Double it? Treble it! Make it three times or make it more than that. A man trained as he is trained—years at a great university, at the age of forty, only making eighty-seven dollars a week? Why that's insane. Treble it!'" Well, she said, "Now I want you to meet my husband." So I met her husband. She said, "He's now making $300.00 a week. Now, this is what I want, Neville, I want him to be a judge." I said all right, does he want to be a judge? So I said to him, "Would you like to be a judge?" He said, "Yes. I think I would be a very good judge. I have all the qualifications and I think I'd be a good judge."

I said now to her, I said, "Now you did it, he didn't do it. He didn't have a thing to do with this $300.00 a week. It simply came over the year to him and now he is earning $300.00 a week. But *you* paid the price. You were very vigilant, you were persistent, you were faithful to the vision concerning your husband. Now, I'm telling not to him, I'm telling to you. Now that you are making $300 a week, don't you have someone who helps you out with cooking the meals, or maybe serving the dinner in your apartment, or cleaning the house?" She said yes. I said, "All right, from now on, you only think of your husband as a judge. And so now you say to your servant, take a certain product to your husband, say, a glass of water, a cup of tea, or whatever it is, you refer to him as *the judge*. Take this to *the judge* or 'Would you please take to *the judge* an ashtray.' Whatever it is you want to send to your husband, he is *the judge*. He is not just your husband, Mr. So and so, ___(??), he's earned the right to be called Judge and you refer to him as Judge. When I come back here in May next year I want him on the bench as judge." And do you know he's going to be judge if *she* will pay the price. If she is persistent, if she is faithful to that vision, referring always in her mind's eye, that even in her dream, she refers to him as "the judge."

I have a brother who is a doctor and from the day he was married—and I give his wife one hundred percent credit for this—she always referred to him as "the doctor." She never once spoke to anyone in her household—she has a full complement of servants; there are five in the house and three in the yard—but anyone who had to take anything to my brother Lawrence, when his wife suggested it, "You take this to 'the doctor' or 'the doctor' wants this done or 'the doctor' wants that done." Then she has two sons who are doctors, and she discriminates between her husband "*the* doctor" and her two sons that she calls them by name, Dr. Michael and Dr. Robert. But they are not "*the* doctor." In her mind's eye her husband, my brother Lawrence, is "*the* doctor." Today in Barbados he is the most prominent doctor, he has the biggest practice, many doctors working for him, and a clinic with thirty beds. And so, he's the most busy doctor in the island of Barbados.

I go back to my sister-in-law Doris' concept, which people laughed at when she started. For when he came out of McGill as a young doctor, in her mind's eye he was "*the* doctor" and always referred to him as "the doctor." And Lawrence grew and grew and grew in the world of medicine. So I said to her, from now on he has to be "the judge." "You take this to 'the judge'." There's only one judge in your mind's eye in your household and that is your husband. You take it. Not only is he earning $300.00 a week, but the dignity that would go with his new position and increased funds and responsibility.

Another one came from Baltimore and he said, "Do you not remember my problem, Neville? My problem was money. Well, I want to tell you I am making four times what I made a few years ago when you and I discussed my problem. I think I can say from the actual evidence I was vigilant, I was faithful. Today I am making this four times more and making it more effortlessly than I did when I made my bit of money when it was really my problem."

Now, this is the price you and I pay. Causation is mental; it is not physical. Causation is the assemblage of mental states which occurring creates that which the assemblage implies. You can put it down. That's exactly what causation is: it's the assemblage of mental states which occurring creates that which the assemblage implies. So I create a scene . . . and so I have a servant in my house and I'm saying to the servant, "Take this to 'the judge'." Here is one image, a servant; another image, something

I'm giving to her; and then another image, a man. I refer to him as "the judge." So here is the assemblage of mental states which occurring creates that which the assemblage implies.

What does this imply? He's not a judge at that present moment in time, but what is that conversation *implying*? It implies he *is* a judge. I'm asking to take this to 'the judge', and so, she takes it to the judge. Then I must be persistent, I must be vigilant, I must be faithful, I must be courageous. Regardless of tomorrow's denial, I must be courageous and still live in this state. And when the day comes, I cannot predict it, I cannot tell you how it's going to happen, but they will see in him the man *they* want to be judge. Some party, a ___(??) party, either the Democratic party or the Republican party or someone, they're going to see in him the man they want to be a judge, and he will have no choice in the matter. Because one woman unknown to the party sat in a certain mood and she was faithful to that mood, and then they had to see him as she always saw him, she saw him as the judge.

Well, this is how this fabulous law works. My brothers came to New York City last month and stayed two weeks with us. We got a suite of rooms on our floor at the hotel, so we were in constant contact. I bought a dozen shows for them, that is, seats to go to a dozen shows, all in two weeks. But there was one thing my brother Lawrence wanted; above all things he wanted to see *Aida*, the opera. He loves music, he appreciates music, he understands music. My brother Victor had never seen an opera, so anything would be exciting to him. But Lawrence wanted to actually see and hear *Aida*. This year they've changed the format of *Aida*, the same music but new costumes, new scenery, and new format. And it's a sellout. You can't get near *Aida* in New York City now. In fact, in New York City all the operas are sold out, anyway. But when it comes to this present presentation of *Aida*, well, it's just like asking for a ___(??). Just can't get near the place.

Well, he wanted to see *Aida*. So, I said, All right, you're going to *Aida*. Went down to the Metropolitan Opera, the four of us, my wife, my two brothers and myself. We got there around 11:30 in the morning and there were two long lines, two windows serving this entire crowd. They always sell ten seats in advance at the Met, that is, ten operas. Not the same opera, but the next ten performances are always sold in advance. So I got into one line—it's a very long line—and then the other line was maybe five or six shorter. But my line wasn't moving. It was simply a static line because the one up front was asking a thousand questions: "Can I see from this one, can I hear correctly, and are these good seats for the money I'm paying?" Well, the man was very kind and very considerate and he answered her very gently, but it wasn't moving. I saw this line began to move, so I broke line and just went over to this, and got at the very end of it. It moved rapidly down toward the teller.

When I got to the teller I was the second now in line. The man in front of me bought two seats for some opera, which opera I don't know, but the two seats were two little pink seats and they were stuffed in an envelope and just about to be pushed to him. At this very moment, just as the man is pushing the seats to him, a tall man about six foot five or six foot six stuck his hand over my head from my side, and he registered this man's attention and called his attention to the side. So the teller looked up this way and began to answer the man's question. At this moment, this man took the two seats and pushed some bills under the window, and started toward the door. The man thanked him after the questions were answered, and then the teller looked back and he sees four one-dollar bills. So he said, "What is all this?" And the man is now almost to the street. So he looks through the window, and he calls out, "Mister!" and the man doesn't respond. "Mister!" he calls a second and third time. He doesn't respond. So I turned around and said, "Sir!" At that he stopped. I said, "You! You come right back here." So he did that. So he came right back, came in front of me and the man said, "What have you done here? These are four one-dollar bills." He said, "I gave you twenty." He said, "Oh, no you didn't." He said, "I gave you twenty." I said, "Oh, no you didn't. You only gave him exactly what is there, because I was standing here and saw exactly what you did. Whatever that is that's all you gave him, you gave him no more, because I was standing here." He looked at me this way but did nothing. He just simply looked. And then he opened up his wallet. I could see a bunch of ones in the side of the wallet and a twenty-dollar bill tucked in the side.

So then he said to the man, "I gave you twenty dollars." The man said, "You didn't." Closed the other window, he came around, "You heard the man. He said that he was standing next to you and he saw exactly what you did, so that's what you did." So the man now takes his four dollars back, puts the twenty dollars into the window, and then says, "When will you discover your mistake?" The teller said, "I didn't make a mistake." He said, "When will you discover you have more in your cash box than you should have? Tonight?" and the teller said, "No, not tonight." He said, "When?" He said, "The end of the season." Could he argue with him? And they all loved that. This whole thing is unfolding just as I'm telling you, all by one's wonderful human Imagination. So when I stepped forward, after the man takes his seats and leaves, and then I said, "What is that horseshoe ___(??) right over the orchestra? I want it right over the orchestra and I want two seats in the center for *Aida* next Tuesday night." He said, "Well, that horseshoe ___(??) is called the Grand Tier." I said, All right, then I will take two in the center of the Grand Tier for Tuesday. He didn't hesitate a second. He pulled the two seats out, and I got my two seats.

This is how the law works. I could not have plotted that. In that line was one in the *state* of a thief. No one's a thief, no one is honest, no one is this—they're only states. And so, here in a line, and the line is broken. There's no one in *that* line that's in the state of a thief, but in this line there's one that will play the thief. I am determined I'm going to get two seats for my brothers. And so, this line is frozen, this begins to move, and the depths of my soul moved me from this line, right here, next to the thief, the one who's in the state of the thief. For he and the tall fellow were working together, the tall one waiting at the door for him. And so, when this one paid the twenty dollars, took his four dollars back and his tickets, at the end the two began to talk, the very one who diverted the teller's attention. It was all a set up job. These were states. He wanted to defraud the man of sixteen dollars. I was not in the state of the thief, and walking down, my Deep Being put me right behind him, so that I could say, "You didn't do it at all" and protest this attempt to steal sixteen dollars.

The teller now seeing that I protected him and saved him sixteen dollars gave me two house seats. These are reserved always for the VIPs, people who come at the last moment, like a president, or a governor, or some so-called great, important person. They are always kept back to the last moment to be sold only to VIPs. But having served him faithfully and saving him sixteen dollars, he didn't wait for one second to pull the two out, and I got my two for *Aida*. And it's a sellout; the sign is up "Sold Out." You can't get it. I never saw the sign. I just got right behind, in this wonderful drama, a thief and protested. And so, the wonderful words of Lincoln, "To remain silent when we should protest makes cowards of us all." And I have never once felt like being a coward. I'd rather die in the attempt to be what I would call the decent person than to be a coward by being silent when it's so obvious the man is trying to steal sixteen dollars.

And so, this is how this wonderful law works. You don't have to worry about *how* it's going to work. You must count the cost, are you willing to pay the price? And the price is simply your own vigilance, your own faithfulness, your own persistency, your own courage. Are you going to pay the price using this coin? Then your dreams will come true. I don't care what the dream is. So you want something that can't be obtained? It doesn't matter what the world says: "Sold Out" means nothing. Hasn't a thing to do with it. You just get into the line, and the line isn't moving? All right, the depth of your soul will move you out of this line to this line. But not just this line, he put me behind the very one who is plotting and planning his little scheme to get sixteen dollars. And you are going to protest, because you haven't ___(??) him. Puts you right behind him, and so right as he said, "I gave you twenty dollars," you automatically say, "You didn't. I was standing right there, didn't do it at all." And so he's taken by surprise, he looks at me, but can't raise a finger to slap you, can't hurt you. You know exactly what you saw and you do it.

So this is how this law works. Are you willing to count the cost? "For which of you desiring to build a tower does not first discuss and count the cost, whether he has enough to complete it?" Will you tonight count the cost and say I will complete it? Tomorrow will deny it, reason denies it, my senses deny it, but I will complete it. I will persist in feeling that which if true implies the fulfillment of my dream. And if you do it, no power in this world can stop you from realizing your dream, but no power. Because causation is mental, it is not physical. And so I know, just as this lady, without the consent of her husband, raised his salary from his eighty-seven dollars a week to over $300.00 a week, she will raise him from his present position in his present office to judgeship in the city of New York.

And the other chap, who is a Kennedy, he's now earning many times what formerly he earned. He can go beyond it. As I said, "You have a daughter just about ready for college and I know if you want to send her to a private college you're going to have to think in terms of not less than $5,000 a year. And so, you think in terms of an extra five or ten thousand dollars a year." You say that is selfish? Forget it! It's all part of your own wonderful Imagination. If you can imagine yourself earning x-number of dollars, and you are persistent, and you believe it, and sleep as though it were true, in a way you do not know, and no one could devise the means by which it will become a fact, it will become a fact. *If* you are persistent. *If* you are courageous. *If* you view yourself as such a person. This is how it works.

And so, he actually—from the depths of my soul he waits upon me just as indifferently and as swiftly when I am evil as when I am good. Let no one tell you that he only sells the good. No, ___(??) both for good and evil. "I kill, I make alive; I wound, I heal; I create the good, I create the evil" (Deuteronomy 32:39). But you are invited to choose the good, to choose the blessing, but we aren't *compelled*; and he who serves as our slave will serve us just as swiftly when the will is evil as when it is good. So let no one tell you he is not your slave. "Jesus Christ, who, though in the *form* of God . . . emptied himself, taking upon himself the form of a slave, and was born in the likeness of men" (Philippians 2:7). And so, as you're seated here now, the slave, your slave that will make everything for you is your own wonderful human Imagination. That's Jesus Christ. He's actually buried in you and will form anything in this world, if you will pay the price. Sit down and count the cost, are you willing to be that persistent? Are you willing to stand upon your tower and actually watch faithfully? For you're building a tower and the tower is only a watchtower; and I will watch and watch faithfully until what I am seeing comes to pass.

So we are told the vision—what vision? your vision, my vision—it has its own appointed hour; it ripens, it will flower. If it be long, then wait; for it is sure and it will not be late. So, you know exactly what you want in this world, either for yourself or for another. This lady did not consult her husband. She said he's too rational, he's trained in the legal world and the mind is trained rationally. And so you couldn't possibly explain to him that this could work. So don't explain it to him. You bear his name and you want him to succeed because his success is your success, well, then do it. And so, I go back one year later, and then he is brought, not reluctantly this time, he's brought, introduced to me, and he did not blush when I said to him, in her presence, "Do you really want to be a judge?" And he didn't say timidly, he said yes, quite openly. "Yes, I would like to be a judge. I think I'd make a good judge." Then I ___(??) and I addressed him as judge. Then I told her exactly what to do, and when she does it, he will be a judge.

So do you know what you want to do? Maybe you will not bear a title like professor or doctor, where someone could refer to you as that. Doesn't matter. You conjure in your mind's eye a certain scene which if true would imply a certain fulfillment in your life. Well then, see the scene and enter into that scene just as though it's taking place now, and persist in it, and that scene will come to pass and give birth to what the scene is implying.

So, causation is the assemblage of mental states which occurring creates that which the assemblage implies. You can put it down and dwell upon it. That's how this law works. Because I tell you these stories, you could not for all the money in the world have bought the two seats. I paid no more than the twenty dollars for the two seats. That's exactly what they were selling for, twenty dollars. I didn't go to some scalper. I didn't go to some agent. I went straight to the box office. And here in the depth of my soul, because I knew exactly what I wanted, I wanted my brothers Lawrence and Victor to see *Aida*—and so I went straight to the box office, and he puts me right behind one who is in a state of a thief and causes him to act. And then causes me to act in such a way that the teller is grateful for my defense of his honesty, and gives me the seats.

Now, the man wasn't a thief. He may play the part of a thief for the rest of his days, but no one is a thief. He's in the *state*. When you are in the state of a thief, you can't do anything else but steal. You can't do it. They're only states, infinite states. So Blake said, "I do not consider the just or the wicked to be in a supreme state, but to be every one of them states of the sleep which the soul may fall into in its deadly dreams of good and evil."

(*A Vision of the Last Judgment,* pages 91 and 92) And so, he fell into a state, and that state was to get the better of other people all through his life. He will continue to do it until he gets out of that state. Either he gets out by his own efforts or someone who will love him enough to get him out of that state. If he has a wife or a mother or a friend who knows the kind of a state that he dwells in and would like to see him out of that state, making just as much money but this time honestly, they can get him out of that state. He is only in a state.

All things are states. That's why in the end you can say, "Father, forgive them; they know not what they do." So if I'm only expressing a state, then don't condemn me. It's a state, and the states are permanent and men move through these states. Not knowing they are only states, they express the state that they are in. And so, if I return constantly to one state, you can call me by the name of that state. If I'm always stealing, I'm expressing the state of stealing. But if I live in it constantly, it's perfectly all right to call me a thief because I'm so identified with that state. So the state to which I most often return constitutes my truest self. But no matter how often I've been in the state of stealing I could get out of it, get out of it permanently, and never fall into it again.

So everyone is at every time in his life just in a state. Now get out of the state that is not productive. If you aren't pulling your own weight in this world, that's embarrassing. Now construct a scene where you are not only pulling your own weight, more than yours. Actually feel it and see a scene implying that you're doing it. Let's have a scene ___(??) when—that was one of my visions—"I remember when." That vision came to me so vividly a few years ago where I found myself in a scene and the scene is giving me the most fantastic story to tell the world. The story is this. I found myself in an enormous mansion and there were three generations present, grandfather, and then the other two generations. The two were now enjoying this great, fantastic estate brought in because of grandfather's vision. They would say—and I was taken in Spirit into this mansion—and they would say, "Grandfather would stand upon a lot and while standing upon an empty lot he would say, 'I remember when this was an empty lot.' And then he would paint a word picture of his desire for that lot and paint it so vividly you saw it existing as an objective fact."

Then I woke and wrote the vision down. It was early in the morning, about three or three thirty, so I went back to bed and I re-dreamed the dream. Re-dreaming the dream I had a slight change in the dream. Instead of saying that grandfather said it, I had so absorbed the faith of grandfather, I became grandfather, and *I* said "*I* remember when this was an empty lot." Then I would paint the picture of my desire for this empty lot and paint it so vividly everyone who heard me saw it as something objective to them. And then, going back, as we are told in scripture, if an event in your life is foreshadowed by a word of scripture it's predestined, it's fixed. So I went back and reread scripture, and here in the 41st chapter of the Book of Genesis, the doubling of a dream means that the thing is *fixed* by God and it will shortly come to pass (verse 32).

So my dream was doubled that night. I was taken in Spirit into this fantastic mansion and heard a certain secret of creativity. I woke, recorded it, fell asleep again, and re-dreamed the dream. So it was the doubling of the dream, and the doubling of a dream means that God has fixed the thing and it will shortly come to pass. So when we double the dream, well, we need not fall asleep in it, you can double it in a waking dream. You can take it this night and see yourself as you would be seen by the world were you the man, the woman that you want to be. All right, that's a dream. That's a waking dream but it's a dream. The same power that created the dream of the night is creating this. It's Christ Jesus in you, your slave. Now tomorrow do the same thing—that's a doubling of a dream. And you can treble the dream, and that's persistency, that's vigilance, and that's faithfulness. And it will come to pass.

So you take your wonderful noble dream for yourself and for your friends, and for others. Regardless of the circumstances of the moment, if they're not in tune with your desire for what you want, well then, ignore it and remain faithful to the dream. And then double dream. For that was shown me so clearly for I was lifted in Spirit into the mansion. I heard the conversation: Grandfather used to stand upon an empty lot and as he stood upon it he would say "I remember when this was an empty lot" and then paint his word picture of his desire for it. Well, I can say of a friend, "I remember when he was unemployed." Well, if I say I remember *when* he *was* unemployed, I'm implying he's not now unemployed. "I remember when he only earned" and I name an amount. "I remember when he only earned x-number of dollars a year." Well, if I remember when he *only* earned that, I'm implying he isn't earning that now, he's a way beyond. "I remember when she was not well." Look at her now. She must be radiantly happy and healthy if I remember *when*.

And so you take this technique and apply it to everything in your world. That conjures a picture. You bring someone before your mind's eye, "I remember when he was simply unknown." Then what am I saying? He must be known. Of course, you can do this in a negative, too. You can use it and just as swiftly Jesus Christ in you, your own wonderful human Imagination, will answer the call. You can say, "I remember when he was known, when he was someone, when he had money" if you want to use it negatively. So I tell you, I acquaint you with God's law and leave you to your choice and its risk. For he in you will serve you as indifferently and as swiftly when the will in you is evil as when it is good. So I can't deny that he will serve you even when you are evil. So I leave you to your choice and its risk. It's like electricity. Because it *could* kill I shouldn't deny man's use of it. Because it has done so many wonderful things in the world, but it could destroy. So because it *could* destroy, why not use it constructively where it doesn't destroy and helps man ___(??).

So I tell you God's law. As we are told, "Blessed is the man . . . who delights in the *law* of the Lord . . . for in all that he does he prospers." That's the 1st Psalm. "Blessed is the man . . . who delights in the law of the Lord . . . for in all that he does he prospers." So if you know the law and you delight in it, you will prosper. I only hope you will not use it negatively. But, may I tell you, I have no power to stop you from using it negatively. I still must acquaint you with it and hope that you will use it constructively. But you could use it negatively, and he will wait upon you and respond to your call just as swiftly as though you used it in the most glorious manner in this world.

But in the end he is faithful to his picture for you and brings you out just like himself. I only hope you will not use it negatively, because I don't believe, in his case, that the hatching out is going to be delayed. But if you use it destructively, it may be a more painful process of coming to the end. But I can't conceive of delay in his vision for man, and as a vision for man, individually, he calls us one by one. And so, he's seen you in his mind's eye and he so loved you he emptied himself of his primal form and took upon himself the form of a slave and became born in the likeness of you. And *as* you he goes through all the furnaces of affliction, obeying your will, even ___(??). But he has a fixed date for the bringing of you out into his own wonderful primal form. So I do believe, and yet I cannot say that it's true, I believe if you use it negatively you may find the birth more painful.

Now let us go into the Silence.

*   *   *

Q: (inaudible)
A: No, my dear, I never consider the cost of what I want. I didn't want to see *Aida*. I go to the opera occasionally when I'm in New York City, ___(??). When ___(??) willing to pay the price as God was willing to pay the price when he became me, when he became you. He did not impose upon us limitations of the use of him; he's our slave, and we could use him lovingly or unlovingly. But he knew the price he had to

pay, and he is suffering. People don't believe it. If anyone wants to know the price that God paid to become you to make you God, read the 53rd chapter of Isaiah. Read it over and over and over. That's the price to be paid. All the sicknesses of the world, God bears them. All the iniquities, he bears them. But there is one verse in it: he saw the fruit of his soul in travail and was satisfied. ___(??) the result of his suffering when he decided to become me to transform me into the form of God. Does that answer, David?

Q: (inaudible)

A: All right, if I want, say, x-number of dollars more than I earn, I must always be willing to assume the responsibility that goes with increased earnings. There are responsibilities. Some people do not accept it but there is. If they don't accept it they suffer. I must be willing to assume the full responsibilities of increased responsibility. It carries with it a certain burden. But, it will not be a burden when you assume it. I can't foresee now what will be asked of me if I should transcend my present position. But something will be asked of me that I do not now foresee. But if I want to transcend it, let that be the vision and then others will come, and I will have the ability to really play the part well, I will.

Q: Would you care to comment on the phenomena of meeting people in dreams who have passed on years prior and have received instructions on certain ___(??) phenomena?

A: You're told in the Book of Numbers, the 11th chapter and 12th chapter: "Would that there were a prophet among you, for I the Lord God will make myself known unto him in a vision and I will speak with him in a dream." So we have in the scripture only one source of dream, and that one source is God. All dreams proceed from God. So every dream has a great significance. I am not saying that we are masters in interpreting the meaning of dreams; many of us misinterpret them, but it does have a certain message for us if we can only interpret.

For instance, there is a lady in the audience here tonight. May I tell you the lady is Nordic. She is blue eyed. She's a lady my age. She has been here tonight. And God was speaking to her. She saw a couple who are now dead. They knew her well when they were alive. They were Nordic. He was an engineer. She looked at him and remembered, remembered him well. Then she looked at the wife and it's not the wife she knew here, much younger, but the wife was Nordic. And then looking back the wife is not the wife; she is Negress. But it seemed so natural. But she was startled by the Negress, and she is still Nordic. Then she looked back at him, he is Negro. Looked back at the girl and she is Nordic.

In the same dream, she goes to bed (the lady in the dream), and she finds herself sleeping in a reverse position in the bed. Her head is where formerly her feet would be. The whole dream is trying to show her something in the depths of her soul of a reversal. There's a great reversal taking place in man where man is being transformed into God; that he's not reptilizing here forever on this level, he's being transformed. And all these are reversals—that God is not a white man or a black man or a red man. The form that was the primal form of Jesus Christ—before he emptied himself, and *then* took upon himself the form of a slave and was born in the likeness of men—it's *that* form that man eventually will be raised to wear. And it's not *this* form.

So she was shown, and this lady, as I say, she is the essence of the Nordic, blue eyes, and undoubtedly when she was young I think her hair must be very blond, I don't know. I only know her in the years that I have known her here, in the last eight years or so. But she is very, very fair-skinned. And yet, in this it didn't seem strange to her. She knew the people and the man, who was an engineer, when she saw him, she knew he was the same man, but suddenly he's not the Nordic, he's Negro. The girl was not the wife that she knew. She was married, the same girl, and she's Negro.

So what was this fabulous dream trying to tell her? It's trying to tell her a marvelous story. Don't be concerned with all the conflicts of the world, that's not the plot at all. That isn't God. Just remain faithful to his promise to you . . . and he's promised you to give you himself. And he's not this [body]. The form that he gave up to take on this is the form one day you will wear, and you will be God. And there is only Jesus Christ in the world. He gave it up, his primal form, and took the limitations of this state, your own wonderful human Imagination, and then was born in your likeness. And tomorrow, he will not be anything you see here. He'll return to his primal form and the form is God, and you will be like him.

So the dream of the night . . . I could not honestly . . . I am not an analyst in the sense of trying to analyze dreams. I would like to ask every person who comes to me with a dream, what does the symbolism mean to you? What does this person in your life represent when you knew him here? And so if I could get an honest response from this individual as to what he meant, then I might be able to throw some light on the experience that he had with that person. Because, I don't know. If it comes to me symbolically, well then, I would try to find help by going to, say, my works, *The Lost Language of Symbolism*. And try to open up ___(??) and read with an open mind why did I encounter the rock, why did I encounter the pig, why did I encounter the dove? What is the sense of the meaning of it, for these are simply a universal language. But the other, when I meet individuals that I know well, they may be here or on the other side of the veil; what did they do to me when I knew them as friends or enemies? ___(??) what's the significance . . . (tape ends).

ADVENT: THE FOUR TEARS

November 26. 1963

Tonight's subject is Advent. And I'm not referring to that tremendous tragedy and great advent that all of us have experienced in this past weekend, for that really was an advent [JFK], but I'm speaking of God's Advent. Advent is the term used to designate the coming or the second coming of the Christ at the end of the age. The purpose of his coming is to redeem man from the wheel of fate, the wheel of recurrence. There's a definite pattern by which it is done.

Advent will begin next Sunday in the churches. Now this does not mean it *actually* begins next Sunday, but that's part of the ritual. It always starts on the Sunday nearest to the day of Andrew. Andrew's day is always the thirtieth day of November, and the nearest Sunday to that day begins the season of Advent. And it runs four Sundays and culminates on the day of Christmas, the birth of Christ—because, Andrew was the first, in the most mystical of the gospels, to behold Jesus. Andrew first found him and told his brother Peter. And so, on the day marked as Andrew's day, here comes the great watch: It is the longing for the coming of the Savior of the world.

Now, man has been taught to believe that he comes from without; and the way he comes the world finds it difficult to believe that he did come. So Andrew who found him could not have found him on the outside. He never comes from without. The only way that you will know that he came is to compare what is happening *in* you to what was foretold in the ancient scriptures. You go back and you read the ancient scriptures, meaning the Old Testament, and there it was all foretold . . . but *not* through any one prophet. And suddenly it happens in the individual, and he finds in the ancient scriptures confirmation of what is taking place in him. And he tells of the coming of this great event.

So Advent is the coming of the great event. It's really a *series* of events where the structure is unveiled. It's the unveiling of Christ in man, and this unveiling takes a certain series of events. It's told symbolically. And they looked at him, and then they tore his garments into four parts and each took a part. But they said, "Let us not tear the tunic, for it's woven without seams from top to bottom; let us cast lots to see who will get it" (John 19:23, 24). And there were four who cast lots to see who would get it. There are always four, because the fourth one falls heir to the next unveiling of the temple. For, "He who began a good work in you will bring it to completion at the day of Jesus Christ" (Philippians 1:6). That day is not at the end of history; it is within history. It happens tonight—I hope it does to many of you—but it comes at the moment that you least expect it, when the scaffolding comes down, and the scaffolding is torn apart, in four parts, and then the building is revealed. It's the immortal body you will wear. The same identity, now no change in identity. But with all the changes of identity there's a radical discontinuity of form. You don't wear *this* form. *This* is the scaffolding and it is *this* that is torn.

May I tell you, I speak from experience. I have no scars to bear witness to the tearing, but I felt and experienced and observed the tearing of this scaffold. It starts in the head, and here the very first blow is in the head, an enormous blow. You think this is it, meaning, well, oblivion. But it's not oblivion. Suddenly you awake and you had no idea that you were asleep. Suddenly you begin to awake for the first time in eternity. Although that is measured in time, you feel you've never before been awake. Blake calls it a period of 6,000 years: "I behold the visions of my deadly sleep of six thousand years dazzling around my skirts like a serpent of precious stones and gold. I know it is myself, O my divine creator and redeemer" (*Jerusalem*, Plate 96). He beholds himself after six thousand years of the most horrible dream in the world. So said he, "Do not let yourself be intimidated by the horror of the world. It is all ordered and correct and must fulfill its destiny in order to attain perfection. Follow this path and you will receive from your own soul an even deeper perception of the eternal beauties of life. You will also receive from your own soul an ever increasing release from what now seems to you so sad and terrible" (Blake to Max Beckman, *Looking at Modern Painting*).

So you see the drama taking place here is all the scaffolding. Someone is blown apart, gone from the world, and someone played the part of blowing him apart . . . and then he is blown apart. All this confusion in the world, that's all the outer picture. For, "He who began a good work *in* you"—not on the outside, *in* you—"is bringing it to completion at the day of Jesus Christ." And he unveils *in* you Jesus Christ. There's only one being in this

world that is ever resurrected and that being is Jesus Christ. As told us in
the 1st epistle of Peter, the 1st chapter, the 3rd verse: rebirth is through the
resurrection of Jesus Christ from the dead. There is no other rebirth in the
world and yet everyone *must* be reborn. You must be born from above: "For
unless you are born from above, you cannot in any wise enter the kingdom
of God" (John 3:3). And rebirth comes in only one respect, only in one way,
and that way is through the resurrection of Jesus Christ from the dead.

Well then, who is Jesus Christ from the dead? It never occurred to me,
raised as I was in the Christian faith, that when it happened to me it was
the resurrection of Jesus Christ, for the simple fact *I* was resurrected. I was
awakened in a tomb and the tomb was my skull. Well, if I find myself in
a tomb I must have been dead or someone thought me dead and placed
me there. And was I placed there six thousand years ago? Is this some
strange peculiar recurrence? Is this a mystery where a man at the end of a
few score years here, and the body decays, and yet he doesn't? Is he placed
in a peculiar wheel where he experiences death and restoration, and death
and restoration, and finally redemption from the wheel of fate, completely
removing that individual from the wheel of recurrence? And that's what it is.
So we are all on the wheel of recurrence, actually imitating the great mystery
of death and restoration.

Then comes that moment in time when God, as we are told, he
resurrects us by his glory. And he looks upon us, and looking upon us we
receive his glory. As told us in the Book of John: "Glorify thou me with
thine own self" (17:5). If God would only glorify me I would awaken. For
he will not give himself to anyone but himself, as told us in the Book of
Isaiah: "I have put you through the furnaces of affliction. For my own sake,
for my own sake I do it, for how should my name be profaned? I will not
give my glory unto another" (48:10). So when the cry is "Glorify thou me
with thine own self," I'm asking God to give me himself. He shines upon
me and by his shining upon me he awakens me.

Well then, why was I ever placed in that tomb? Listen to the words
carefully from the 8th chapter of the Book of Romans: "And the creature was
subjected unto futility . . . not of his own will but by the will of him who
subjected him in hope; for the creature will be set free from his bondage to
decay and obtain the glorious liberty of the children of God" (verse 20).
It's the grand mystery of life through death, and I, *not willingly* but by the
will of him who subjected me, I was placed in a tomb and the tomb was
my skull. Then in that tomb I appeared dead; but it was a profound *sleep*,
and then I dreamt the dream of this world, the most horrible dream in
the world. So I dreamt all the horrors of the world I was subjected to as
I dreamed it. I dreamt that I was shot while I was a president. I dreamt I

had the most wonderful fantastic funeral, where the whole world mourned because of my exit from this world. And then I dreamt I was a poor man and couldn't buy a loaf of bread. And I dreamt I was mutilated. I dreamt I was honored, I was dishonored. And all these were my dreams in this world.

At the ending, God stepped beyond and by his wonderful mercy he looked upon me. And I always become what beholds me, as I become what I behold. So God beheld me and he, beholding me, resurrected me. And the first act in the great Advent is to awaken. I awoke one night four years ago; I awoke in a sepulcher to discover the sepulcher was my own wonderful skull. It never occurred to me that I was *really* dead prior to that moment, that I had slept prior to that moment, save the nocturnal event night after night. But to find that I had been asleep for 6,000 years and then I awoke, and here I am completely awake in a tomb and the tomb is my skull! That's the beginning of Advent.

Now there are four Sundays to it. They take my robe and they tear it into four parts. They dare not touch my tunic for it is woven from head to foot, and it is woven so beautifully it's without seam. They must cast lots for it, for scripture must be fulfilled. The 22nd Psalm tells me, you cannot fail. Tear my robe apart. For a new way is now opened to man; it's through the curtain of the flesh . . . and it is the flesh. I bear no scars to prove what I tell you, but I felt everything in my flesh. As told us in the 10th chapter, the 20th verse of the Book of Hebrews, this is the new way that is opened.

Now, no ritual in this world do I need. I need no individual to lead me to God. From then on, having torn the scaffolding away, I have direct access to my Father because he and I are one. He built that garment that he wanted me to wear and this is the garment that he built. How can I describe it? You have to experience it. He took a garment into which I was encased, an animal garment and transformed it into "the human form divine." My face remains, what you see now, only raised to the nth degree of majesty. Hands remain but raised to the nth degree of beauty and expression. Feet remain, the body not. He transformed me into the human form divine.

Now listen to the words of one who not only saw it, as I have seen it, but he had the ability to tell it as I have not arrived so far to tell it. He was the grand poet, Blake.

> Mercy, Pity, Peace, and Love
> Is God, our father dear.
> And Mercy, Pity, Peace, and Love
> Is Man, his child and care.

For Mercy has a human heart,
Pity the human face.
And Love, the human form divine,
And Peace, the human dress.

Well, how could I describe to anyone "the human form divine"? And yet I stood in the presence of "the human form divine" and it was infinite love. Infinite love embraced me and incorporated me into the form of infinite love. But I can't describe what the body is, not to the satisfaction of anyone in the world before he experiences it. But the face, yes, the sameness of identity but a radical change as to form.

And so, Advent is the unveiling of Christ in man. That's what it really is. You take the curtain apart and you unveil Christ in man. And you do it in four great tears in the flesh. The first is in the skull. And you can take it in this way: when you awake in your skull and then you come out of your skull, which is called the birth from above, it's really one. It takes place in one night.

The second one is an explosion, a fantastic explosion, and then it comes where you know who you are. That second event reveals who you really are. And it takes the Son to reveal the Father, and the Son appears and calls you Father. Then and only then do you realize who you are. That God fulfilled his promise to give you himself as though there were no others in the world, just God and you; and now, because he gave you himself, just you because you are he. Prior to that moment you did not know what you would be like, but you knew that when he appeared you would be like him. And so, when his Son appeared you were the Father. You didn't know what you would be like, as told us in the 1st epistle of John, the 3rd chapter: "It does not yet appear what we shall be like, but we know that when he appears we shall be like him" (verse 2). And no one can reveal him save the Son. So the Son appears in your world and he calls you Father, and you know that then you are *like* him. You are the Father because the Son calls you lord, he calls you Father. You have no uncertainty in your heart as to the reality of what is taking place in your world. That was the second tear of the garment.

Then comes the third tear. He tells you, I will come in this manner "The earth will shake and every stone will be split right through" (Matthew 27:51). That's when I come; that's the third tear. And every stone is really split, every segment of your spinal column is completely severed in two, and you see them separated by inches, fulfilling the 27th of Matthew. He will come and every stone will be split, and there is an earthquake. You have never felt anything comparable to it. That's the third tearing.

The fourth one is when you take off the garment for the last time. Because then when it actually comes off, the tunic that is made without seam, woven from the top to the bottom, is your immortal garment. It's the garment of love, for then you wear the "human form divine" and the "human form divine" is all love. There's nothing but love.

So, when you experienced as we all ____(??) day, experienced this past weekend, this horror, may I tell you, the one who played both parts was God. God played both parts. He also played the third part of horror, for there's *nothing* but God in this world. And in the very end when the curtain comes down, "God who only acts and is in all existing beings or men" will call us all together—for we're incorporated into the body of love—and reveal the meaning of the play. And the four acts will be over. The four tears will be over. Then in some wonderful fifth act he will display the purpose of these four acts. For then you and I will be although identified as to face, no loss of identity, but with this radical change of this immortal form, we will play the fifth act. And, oh, what an act! But then we are qualified to play it. We have the garment with which we can play it. We couldn't play it with these. It takes these, the outer structure, to play this so-called horror of the world.

Now, I am not speculating. I am giving you and sharing with you my vision. I've experienced it. But I cannot in any way describe it save in words. I cannot, on this level, do any more than I am doing now—using words to tell you what I have experienced. For if this seems to be a horrible play, then I ask you to believe God played all the parts. The so-called insane part that blew one that we all admired so much into seeming eternity. It's not eternity. It could be that very moment in time that impact was the tearing of one section of the garment, who knows? For he's on the wheel of recurrence. Haven't you seen where—we go back to 1840—and he elected every twenty years made his exit while in office? Now, we've gone beyond the hundred years. Can't you see the wheel of recurrence? This is now beyond a hundred years. We started back in 1840 with a change in pattern. Not really a change, but to those who had memories it seemed to be a change because memory is so short.

If you could go back as Blake went back and he said: "I behold the visions of my deadly sleep of six thousand years." Six thousand years. Well, what man can go back 6,000 years? If you could, you would see everything, as it is about to appear. And what is more horrible in this world than to sit in a play in the presence of one who saw it, and who is talking, who tells exactly what's going to happen? You go to a picture, and all of a sudden someone who wants you to know they saw it before, "The one going through that door, he's going to shoot that one." And you don't know that, you don't anticipate it, but it comes to pass, and you get annoyed with him. But he keeps on talking about it and he tells the entire play as it unfolds. Wouldn't you want to hit him over the head? Well, that's the play, this fantastic play.

But don't feel yourself a slave; within the framework of God's play as actors you and I can modify the part, we can change the part, but we are playing a part. And an actor to play a part well must to some extent feel the part that he's playing, and to the best of his ability he must imagine himself as the character that he is depicting. And so, I am playing a part. I was cast in this role. I stood in the drama in the depths of my soul and cast lots for his robe, and got the fourth part. So I came into the world playing the part of the fourth and had to play what I am playing.

This all goes back and anchors on the one called David. The earliest manuscripts, but the very earliest manuscripts, know only one ancestor of David and that is his father Jesse. He had no mother. And for this you may go back and search the *Encyclopedia Biblica*, the most scholarly work on the Bible to date. They say, as far back as we can go we can find no ancestor of David, other than his father whose name was Jesse. Furthermore, they say, in the earliest manuscripts there are only four brothers and he was the youngest of four. Others are mentioned as brothers but not named. And in scripture unless a thing is named it doesn't exist. And so, there could be seven brothers, as they're told, and eight brothers, as they're told, but they *must* be named. Only four are named and the youngest of the four named is David.

"So tell me, whose son are you, young man?" And he answered, "I am the son of thy servant Jesse the Bethlehemite" (1 Samuel 17:58). And Christ is made to say, I came not to serve, or to be served, "I came to serve, I came as a servant" (Mark 10:45). "I am the son of thy *servant* Jesse the Bethlehemite." And the word Jesse is I AM. The word Jesse means Jehovah. Jehovah comes not to *be* served but to serve. Well, who serves but the actor who is playing the part, playing all the parts. And, the one who discovered this father . . . as we are told, and David brought down the giant. Having brought down the giant, the promise now must be fulfilled. And the promise is: "That he who brings down the giant, the enemy of Israel, I will set his father free in Israel" (1 Samuel 17:25). Well, who is the father? The father is Jesse. The father is Jesus Christ—that's Jesse. And so, suddenly he looks and he calls you Father. There is *only* Jesus Christ. So we go back, your rebirth, the unveiling of the works of God in you, is through the resurrection of Jesus Christ from the dead. The only one who is resurrected is Jesus Christ. So when *you* are resurrected, *you* are he. There is only Jesus Christ.

You too will say in the end, as you will say this night when you read all the papers, as you saw the TV, "Father forgive them, for they know not what they do." He knew no more what he did driving in the open car than he who fired the fatal bullet, and the other one who fired that bullet; and you and I, on this level, will speculate and do all kinds of things, and it was all a play. You go tonight and you see *Macbeth*. And sitting in the audience stirred by the emotion of the play when she wants that spot rubbed out, and you in the play crying because of what she has done and what she prompted her husband to do, you hope it will never in eternity be wiped out. You hope that spot remains on that hand as a reminder of her violence, the horrible ambition that resulted in this innocent murder. But the curtain comes down, and you really don't want that spot to remain if you know she's a grand actress. You only want it to remain on the part she played, but not on the actress who played it. But while you're carried with emotion you *want* it to remain. Well, in this wonderful play of ours you want this one snuffed off and that one snuffed off, and all these things, just because we don't know it's a play.

But I'm telling you from my own experience this is a play, the most glorious play that God could conceive. And the purpose of it was to create in us an immortal structure, the human form divine. And the human form divine is all love, there's nothing but love. One day, I prophesy, everyone in this world—the insane today, the imbeciles today—all will play all these parts. But one day, not be playing these parts, and be brought into the presence of infinite love. He will embrace them, incorporate them into his body. And in the end, when the curtain comes down and the play is over, *everyone* is wearing the human form divine. And everyone will have the heart of mercy, everyone will have the face of pity, and everyone will be wearing the dress of peace. But the form itself will be the human form divine, and that form is infinite love.

So I ask you not to despair. I know tonight the whole country is disturbed—maybe not tonight but certainly last night—and wondering. And so to repeat Blake: "Do not let yourself be intimidated by the horror of the world. Everything is ordered and correct and must fulfill its destiny in order to attain perfection. Follow this path and you will receive from your own wonderful soul an even deeper perception of the eternal beauties of life. You'll also receive an ever increasing relief from that which now seems to be so sad and so terrible." You will. You'll suddenly awake from it all and you will see the reason behind the play, and you will allow it. Although the face will be yours forever and forever, the form by this horrible play is transformed into the human form divine. And that form is infinite love.

But in the meanwhile, use God's law. Use it to create and modify all the things in this world. Create things you want and cushion the blows of the play. Because, like actors you can play it differently—the same play, same part, but you would play it differently—without the blow that would be the inevitable blow if you did not use God's law wisely. The play, the part I'm playing using this law and play it wisely, everyone can do it. And you play the part wisely when you use your Imagination lovingly on behalf of yourself and others. That when you hear the most horrible story, you revise it. When you hear anything, you revise it. All that is allowed within the play; it does not change the outcome of the play. God planned everything as it has come out and as it will be consummated. As we are told in the 14th of Isaiah, "I have planned . . . that which I have planned shall stand, and my purpose is forever" (verse 24). I have planned it just as it is and my purpose is forever. No one will change it. You read it carefully and you will understand ___(??).

But in the end, when the scaffold comes down and the building is revealed, I just can't tell you the glory of that building, for it's the glory of God. I can't tell you what it is to wear the garment of love, and yet, this remains until the *final* tearing. There are four tears and no one gets the fourth tear until he makes his exit from this world, then comes the fourth one. All these other things appear, like the dove, and all these things that are part of the eternal story, they all appear to show you how true the story is. But the fourth tear, when the garment is torn into four parts, and then others will cast lots for the untorn garment to play that part. For the fourth one is the one who comes through the door. And maybe tonight you may be that fourth one. I cannot in any way determine who will win the garment, but God knows exactly how he is unfolding this fantastic drama ___(??).

So you read it carefully. Only one relative and the relative was father, born without a mother, begotten of God, begotten of the spirit and not of flesh and blood. And the being begotten is beloved, David. David is the one, the second tearing of the garment. And when the garment is torn a second time, it exposes David as the Son. David looks and he calls you Father, and then you know. That's the second tear.

And then comes the third tear and your departure from Egypt, where in the most fantastic way you can take the imprint of God. Because only if you are in the state of molten gold can you take the impress of God. And so, we are taking the seal of God. But you can't take the seal that comes sealed upon wax or upon clay. But then wax or clay must be in a molten state to take the impress; and so you see the gold, and you are it. Then, suddenly the gold becomes serpentine, and up it moves, up the shaft of what was formerly split. You move up the shaft of your own spinal cord and here you take the impress upon the face of God. But God dwells in Zion and Zion is your skull, and it's in there that you go. You make the most tremendous effort to get out. But you don't get out. You just press into that skull and take the impress of the face of God . . . yet no loss of identity. But you'll wear forever the form of God, without loss of identity.

As you are told, "From John the Baptist till now, the kingdom of God has been preached and everyone who enters the kingdom does so with violence" (Matthew 11:12). And may I tell you, you've never known such violence in your life as at that moment in time when you move up with a power that you've never felt before. But that power pushes into that seal and you take the face of God. But it will not be unveiled to you until the last tear, which is the taking off of the garment. So what you have inherited, your heavenly state cannot become actual or is, at least, not fully realized by you so long as you still wear this, waiting for the last tear. And then the garment is torn, as you are told, into four parts, and you're clothed in that seamless robe, wearing, without loss of identity, the human form divine.

Now, let us go into the Silence.

WHERE ARE YOU FROM?

December 3, 1963

Tonight's subject is "Where Are You From?" This you will find in the 19th chapter of the Book of John. And the rabbi said to Pilate: "We have a law, and according to that law he ought to die, for he claims he's the Son of God" (verse 7). And their law would not allow that. For we know where this man is from, know all about him; and when Messiah appears, no one will know where *he's* from, so his claim is false. So when Messiah appears, it will be mysteriously done. And yet we know exactly where this man is from. Even his own brothers do not believe in him. And he said to his brothers, "My time has not yet come, but *your* time is always here." And then he repeated it but qualified it: "My time has not yet *fully* come" (John 7:6). He knew his time. He is speaking of two entirely different times, two entirely different worlds, two different ages. So, "My time has not yet fully come, but *your* time is *always* here." It's not a ___(??) for it, it is always here, but my time has not yet fully come.

So, Pilate said to him, "Where are you from?" and Jesus gave no answer. And Pilate said to him, "You will not speak to me? Do you not know I have power to set you free and power to crucify you?" And Jesus answered him, "You have no power over me unless it has been given to you from above; therefore he who delivered me to you has the greater sin" (John 19:11). He does not answer Pilate's first question, but he corrects Pilate's misunderstanding of power. He does not answer "Where are you from?" He doesn't tell him, because Pilate would never understand; but he corrects Pilate's misunderstanding that is the world's misunderstanding of power. Pilate thought he had the power to set him free or to crucify him. He was simply telling him he had no power whatsoever unless it had been given to him from above.

462

For one day you'll have this experience and you will taste of the power of the new age. And you will see a scene just like this. As you taste of this power of the new age you will know it is all animated, and *you* are the power animating it. You will arrest within yourself an activity that you sense. At that moment of arrestment, everything stands still and it's dead. It's made as though it were made of clay. Not just the outer aspect but your brain that is so fluid and so alive and so pulsing, that too if you opened up the skull would be like clay. The heart that pumps and pumps, that too would be like clay. The whole thing including all the inner works would be frozen. Then you would release within yourself the activity which you had arrested and everything would once more become animated and would continue in its course, and would perform its intention. Then you would know what he means by "this time" which is forever as against "his time" and when he said to his brothers, "My time has not yet fully come, but your time is always here."

Now, man's view of time, man's conventional view of time, including our great scientists, is that the future develops continuously out of the past. But that's not the biblical view of time. The biblical view of time is what appears to be so new in our world is only the appearance of the return of phenomena already old. The whole vast world is moving on a circle and all of this is already so, so that the entire space-time history of the world is laid out, and we only become aware of increasing portions of it, successively. But it's on a curve, and therefore what seemingly was past isn't, really, from the biblical view, it's your tomorrow. It hasn't really receded into a past, it's advancing into a future. And it is forever.

Now listen to the words from Ecclesiastes . . . and our scientists ___(??) can't understand it, therefore they say the book was uninspired, not really an inspiring work. But it's one of the cannons of history of scripture. Listen to these words: "What has been is what *will* be and what has been done is what *will* be done; and there is nothing new under the sun. Is there a thing of which it is said, 'See, this is new'? It has been already in ages past. There is no remembrance of former things, nor will there be any remembrance of later things to happen among those who will come after"(Ecclesiastes 1:9-11).

Well, who will accept that? The conventional view completely denies it; it couldn't possibly be true. He is telling me that I have a memory of my youth. I can't quite remember the moment of my physical birth. I vividly remember the moment of my spiritual birth, but I can't remember the moment of my physical birth. But he's telling me it has been, that I do know. And everyone here without memory of that physical birth, they can't deny by observation of other people being born that they, too, must have been born in a similar manner. So, they say it has been. Now he tells me,

"That which has been done"—which is my birth—"is that which will be done." That I am moving toward that thing on a wheel of recurrence, that same thing in this world of Caesar, and only divine mercy can redeem me from the wheel. That, "What seems to be, is, to those to whom it seems to be, and is productive of the most dreadful consequences to those to whom it seems to be, even of torment, despair, and eternal death; but Divine Mercy steps beyond and redeems man in the body of Jesus." (Blake, *Jerusalem*, Plate 36) So here the wheel is turning.

Now, let me share with you a story told me last Tuesday night, a week ago tonight. The lady is present. She gave me a letter just before I started. I had no time to read it before my meeting and had no time until just before I retired that night. So about midnight I read the letter, and this is the letter. It was dated November 23, which as you know was a week ago last Saturday, the day after the great event in this world that took place on the 22. She states in the letter: This is my experience of ten days prior to November 22, that is, November 12. I go from my office, home and back, always in a certain manner, a certain road. It is my habit that when I get to a certain intersection that I turn and read the headlines at the newsstand. For quite often, in fact usually, a red light is with me, and so I have a moment to turn and read the headlines. This time when I went home it was dusk, the sun was setting, a few cars coming from the opposite direction. I am moving west into the setting sun and a few cars moving in the opposite direction had their headlights on because it was dusk. I was in the right-hand lane, but the traffic was moving; it was a green light. But habit in some strange way possessed me. Although the car was moving, I turned to read the headlines, the words to the left. And so I turned, I saw four papers on the rack—three the usual black and white, and one was a green sheet, and this enormous black type as a head mast read "Kennedy Shot." This is November 12. I almost put my foot on the brake to turn, but I was in the intersection. But reason prevailed, I said, No, it's the headlights, it's the dusk, it's the sun that is setting, and surely above all things in my office where I work the radio goes all day long, and such horrendous news would be on the radio. So that capped it. Reason prevailed, and I knew that I had not seen correctly. But I saw on this green paper "Kennedy Shot." Well, I kept going across the intersection. How long does it take, she said in her letter, two, three minutes, three seconds, two or three seconds? And so, at the end of three seconds I crossed the intersection and kept moving. It wasn't one block before I completely forgot the incident . . . completely forgot it.

And in my office, ten days later, on Friday the twenty-second, I came to the office late. Two radios were blasting, a TV is going, and nothing but this news on the air. Some are crying, many are talking, others are cursing. And

I wanted some quietness to do my work. I'm at the typewriter. Three-thirty in the afternoon I'm still trying to remember a dream, a dream that is related to what I'm hearing. But I couldn't call back the dream. I'm trying to remember the dream. I know that something I dreamt is related to what I am hearing on the radio, what's coming across TV too, but I couldn't bring back the dream. A co-worker leaves the office. He is gone not more than a few minutes when he returns bringing in a paper, a folded paper. He comes in my direction and he calls me by name, he comes over to my desk and he slaps it down on the table, and said to me, "Isn't it amazing how fast these papers can move!" And he intended that I should have the paper. So I took the paper and opened it and here is a green sheet, the outer covering is green, and only two words as the masthead "Kennedy Shot!" Then suddenly, what happened to me ten days before springs into my mind, and here I am seeing the entire scene as I drove home, going west, and watched this headline on this newsstand.

I took that letter, so it meant a tremendous thing to me, and read it over and over to my wife. She and I reacted as I would expect her to react. I knew how *I* would react. But last weekend, a friend of mine who sponsors my meetings in San Francisco came home, and so I invited four mutual friends that knew her well to dinner. So we were . . . there were the seven of us at home. And I ___(??) the letter and read it, and gave each to see the letter and hold it in their own hands ___(??). There was only a moment of surprise of a strange coincidence, no more. Within a matter of seconds, just as the lady said, in three seconds she had completely forgotten the incident and tried so hard to bring it back to memory, like a dream; for the event is now turning something in the depths of her soul that she experienced this. But she couldn't bring it back until the fact was presented when the paper was put before her in a physical manner, and then she saw it. Through the evening they discussed all kinds of things relative to the great drama, but they thought that the FBI, the Secret Service, the local police, all these people should have done what they did not do. And here, it is stated so clearly in the first chapter of the Book of Ecclesiastes.

So in her letter to me she said at the very end of the letter: "When the man looked at me, having given me the paper, and I saw it, black type on green, I must have turned green myself because he said to me 'What's the matter?' And I couldn't answer him, because how could I tell him that Creation is finished? How could I tell him that this is a drama and it's finished? That because it's animated, blood flows instead of tomato juice as it does on the stage?" But having had the experience of arresting in me an activity which animated the scene I saw, I know that it's no more than that on the stage. But it's for a divine purpose, and the purpose is that God is individualizing himself. He individualizes himself through this play. And when he comes out individualized, that's Jesus Christ, the only name that the individualized God bears. So in each, as he comes out individualized he is incorporated into the one body. For the Lord on that day, "the Lord will be one and his name one . . . and the Lord will reign as king over all the earth." But on that day the Lord will be one and his name one (Zechariah 14:9).

Then she said at the end of her letter, "Could my reason—that is, my refusal to recognize as true what I actually saw—be the lines spoken of in the 30th chapter of the Book of Isaiah?" Then she quotes the ninth, tenth, and eleventh verses: "These sons, these lying sons who will not hear the instruction of the Lord; who say to the seers, 'See not'; and to the prophets, 'Prophesy not to us what is right; speak to us smooth things, prophesy illusions, leave off the way, leave the way, turn away from the path, let us hear no more of the Holy One of Israel.'" Yes I can answer her; they are (these lying sons) your reason. They took everything that night—the setting sun, the dusk, the absence of the news from the radio, everything, the headlights—to persuade you that you had not seen what you actually saw. And it went so deep into your being that even when the news began to blare at the office, you thought it was related to a dream. This was a waking dream, just like another dream, and you tried to bring back memory and you couldn't recall what you actually had experienced.

But, it also struck me in a very forceful manner because in the same 30th chapter of Isaiah I took the verse I wanted for the title page of my latest book, *The Law and the Promise*. I took the eighth verse. She took the ninth, tenth, and eleventh verses, and I took the eighth: "Go now and write it before them on a tablet, inscribe it in a book that it may be for the *time to come* as a witness forever." And so I took that verse for my title page that I would inscribe it in a book, whether one believed it or not, for I *know* it's more true than anything being discussed this day concerning what happened in Dallas. For they all think it should not have happened. They don't know *this* time as against *that* time.

So he said to his brothers, who did not believe in him: "My time has not yet fully come, but your time is always here." These garments are part of the eternal structure of the universe. This thing here, I will one day vacate it; but it remains as part of the eternal structure of the universe, like *Hamlet* remaining after Lawrence Olivier makes his exit from this world. And so, he remains as part of the eternal structure of the play called *Hamlet*. So, tomorrow another one, unborn today, will put on the costume of a Hamlet and play Hamlet as conceived by Shakespeare, as you will put on this thing called Neville, as conceived by God, because I will have vacated it for the last time. But, it's here to be worn, and all these are to be worn, and worn forever and forever until he completely individualizes himself. And more than the sands of the sea, we are told. He is the grand Abraham of scripture, the father of the multitudes, individualizing himself. And there's a series of events by which he breaks this invidious bar; and then causes the individual whose shell he breaks to separate and escape from this strange wonderful wheel of recurrence. And so, at what moment in time this series of events begins to appear within you, that's his secret.

But, everything is here. And that bullet in the brain of Kennedy is part of the eternal structure of God's world and God conceived it. So the one who pulled it God conceived it, and that's a part to be played and played over and over and over. And men can't quite see the drama, because it doesn't make sense. Because he thinks it's here. It isn't here. This is forever as the play. But he's speaking of another time: *My* time has not yet fully come. My time belongs to a world where I am really free, where I am now in a world where everything is subject to my imaginative power, but everything. And I too will be part of that world animating this, and seeing it differently, so that the bullet and the one who pulled it and those who weep will not really disturb me from *that* level.

So Blake made the statement: "Hear the voice of the Bard! Who present, past and future sees; whose ears have heard the Holy Word that walked among the ancient trees." He is telling you he experienced the 3rd chapter of Genesis: "And the voice was heard of the Lord God, as he walked in the garden in the cool of the day." Then, in the 4th chapter of Daniel: "And this Holy One that walked in that garden gave the command, 'Hew down the tree.'" *We* were the tree in that holy garden, but innocent trees, and we had to fall into experience to awaken into the world of Imagination, where *everything* is subject to our imaginative power, awakened as God. So here, "Hew down the tree, cut off its branches, strip off its leaves, scatter its fruit. But leave the stump of its roots. And then let him be watered with the dew of heaven" (verses 14, 15). Take from *him* now—it's a tree and suddenly it becomes a person—"Take from *him*," even though that was a tree. ___(??). "Take from him the heart of a man and give him the heart of a beast and let him dwell, and his dwelling place be among the beasts. And let seven times pass over him until he knows that the Most High rules the kingdom of men, and *gives* it to whom he will, yes, even to the lowliest of men."

So here, the tree is felled. And again with Blake: "The gods of the earth and sea sought thro' nature to find this tree; but their search was all in vain; there grows one in the human brain" (*The Human Abstract*). So it's turned down into generation and suddenly it becomes an animal. This is an animal, this is an animal form. Everything we call human that's animal is related to the animal world; it has an animal heart, the animal mind. And seven times pass over. What is a "time" in the language of scripture? Blake implies approximately nine hundred years. So seven times must pass over him. Blake leaves off the little additional three hundred and speaks of a solid number of six thousand. And he said: "I behold the visions of my deadly sleep of six thousand years circling around thy skirts like a serpent of precious stones and gold. I *know* it is my Self, O my Divine Creator and Redeemer." (*Jerusalem*, Plate 96)

So here, he saw the whole thing clearly. The Holy One he heard, the Holy One walking in the cool of the day, in this world called the Garden of Eden. And he tells us by implication that he actually heard the command "Hew down the tree," so said he in this very opening to what he started in a series but only gave us one. He calls it *The First Book of Urizen*, but he deleted the word "First" afterwards because he only brought out the one. But in this, he addresses the Holy One, the Immortal and calls them "Eternals." "Eternals! I hear thy call gladly. Dictate swift winged words and fear not to unfold your dark visions of torment." This I am quite willing—when I see the result of passing through this horror—I am quite willing that I seek in my mind's eye the vision which is your vision for me when you complete your dream and you individualize yourself.

So Los beheld the vision and he was faithful to the vision in time of trouble. So I ask *you* to be faithful to the vision in time of trouble. So when you go through it, know it has happened and happened and happened, but you have no memory. In some strange way this lady, in ten days, within one block, it so passed from memory that even when the radios began to blare and the TV, and people are weeping and cursing, and talking, she is prodding herself to remember a dream. And only when the facts of a paper were placed before her and she saw the green page and then the headline "Kennedy Shot!" the whole thing ran into her mind like some photographic plate. She remembered the intersection where she saw these four papers on a rack—three the normal black and white and one the green with this headline—and the struggle with herself as she crossed the intersection which only takes two or three seconds. Then, all of a sudden, it rushed into the mind.

Our theologians for centuries have been trying to delete from our book the Book of Ecclesiastes because it doesn't make sense. Because the normal view of time is that the future develops continuously out of the past. I was born as a babe and so I will, as any person in this world, grow to manhood, and then having waxed, I will then wane and vanish. That's the normal progression on this linear motion of time. And that's not the biblical view of time at all. It's something entirely different. And he separates the two times, he speaks of "your time" that is always and "my time" that has not yet fully come.

So, I picked up that one on Time when I chose the verse I wanted for the title page of my book: "Inscribe it in a book that It may be for the time to come." For that's what it is. I'm not speaking of this. The law, yes, I still say within the framework of God's grand dream there's another dream, my dream, your dream, and we can have unnumbered experiences. We aren't going to change *his* dream for us. But we can modify and change within the framework of *his* dream the things that we will encounter. And if I use the law wisely, I will avoid repetition tomorrow when the wheel turns again. I won't break the foot the next time. I won't have the distorted arm the next time. I won't have anything the next time if *now* I revise it. So I say, if there is one thing I have been brought into this world to tell you, it's the secret of revision—that something today is unpleasant, you don't like it, don't let it slip by. The Bible speaks of redeeming the time. Every moment if it's unpleasant it should be redeemed because you're going to meet it tomorrow as the wheel turns. So don't let the night descend and catch you with the unredeemed day. Take the day and redeem it. You may produce the results now, in the immediate present. But if you redeem it, when the wheel turns, because you haven't yet, you've not hatched out . . . for as Blake . . . "For hatching ripe he breaks the shell." But if the shell isn't yet broken by the series of events which detaches you from this wheel of recurrence, then revise the day, so that the next time when the wheel comes around, you are not going to relive the unpleasant thing of this moment in time.

But I tell you, "Your time is always here; my time has not yet fully come." It takes one more link to break it, for it's all, it's only hanging by a link. To be part of the world where having once tasted of the power of the age to come, then to return to the world where you're part of "this" age and be animated. As he confessed, "You would have no power over me had it not been given to you from above." Here is one who is confessing he's only at the very brink of leaving it; but while he's in the world of Caesar, having tasted of the world to come and the power that belongs to that world, while in the world of Caesar wearing an animal garment, then no one has the power over him unless it was given to him from above. So the one who gave it to you, he has the greater sin if now he sends me to the gallows. The God who sends me to perform an act that is condemned by society, you have the greater sin, for it is part of the great play.

And this dual time is so difficult for man to grasp, but I am only quoting from scripture. He speaks so often of time, and he separates the two times: this time which belongs here forever and that time, this world and that world. So he speaks of two ages, *this* age, where there is rebirth but it doesn't mean reincarnation. For, that which has been done is that which will be done. Were you once born of your present mother? You will be. It's happening all over again, at the moment in time when the wheel turns, and we will get the same surprise that is conceived as reincarnation, being born of another mother. But they can't conceive of returning, being born in the same manner of the same mother. Because they can't see these garments . . . and they think these are themselves. And these are *garments* that God wears.

And so, the whole vast world will say, "Oh, yes, I believe in reincarnation. It justifies the inequalities of life." Nothing justifies the inequalities of life, as you are told of the blind man, the 9th chapter of the Book of John: "And they said to him, 'Rabbi, who sinned, this man or his parents, that he was born blind at birth?' He said neither this man nor his parents: but the works of God be made manifest" (verses 2 and 3). All these are the experiences through which God goes—the blind, the lame, the withered, the halt, everything. And it's not any justification, because the God of whom I speak is not a God of retribution. In spite of the horror of the play, he's a God of love, because in the end he individualizes himself, and you are he. If it took six thousand years of horror, the end result justifies the means conceived as a play to bring it out.

But I ask you, don't forget the lady's letter. Don't do what my friends of last Saturday night did. So when they departed and I started washing dishes in the wee hours of the morning, I said to my wife, What a strange reaction! Now this lady sponsored me. She has sponsored me for the last seven years, and prior to that she came to my meetings when she was not my sponsor. She sells all of my books. And all of my other friends have known me here on the West Coast for the last fifteen years. And so, it was like reading a nice little mystery and then throwing it into the ashcan—that's it—and then we go back to discuss the facts of life. "Why were not the FBI on the job and not these people on the job?" and they just got through reading that ten days before he was actually shot. By the human standard he was already dead.

But time, with a larger focus you see a larger focus; you take a larger section of time. And she, in some wonderful way, the green light is with her, she hadn't time to really focus, so she is moving forward with the green light, an intersection, she is almost on it. But habit possessed her, she turned to see, she's in the right hand lane, and here, on a green paper, the headline "Kennedy Shot!" But then it fades. But are we not told in that ninth verse of the first chapter of Ecclesiastes: "There is no remembrance of former things, no remembrance of later things to happen among those who come after." And so, she is trying when it *does* happen, that we on this level will appreciate it. She is trying to remember what she called a forgotten dream. She thinks it's a dream and she's remembering when I dreamed it, I dreamt it. And she can't bring back to memory, can't recall it, until the paper is brought in and the boy's voice said, "Isn't it amazing how fast these papers can move!" Even then she didn't. She opened up and saw the same headline on a green page. Then the whole thing rushed into the brain like photographic plates being pushed through the brain. And knowing her Bible, being a student of the Bible, she searched the Bible for something that caused her to lie to herself; and she found the three verses of the 30th chapter of the Book of Isaiah: "Lying sons, sons who will not hear the instruction of the Lord." They will not listen to him and they say to seers, those who see like a Blake: Tell us not; do not look; don't tell us anymore. Tell us ___(??). Give us illusion; tell us smooth things, pleasing things. Don't tell us things of old. Tell us smooth and pleasing things (verse 10). And so, that's the world.

But I am not sent to tell you the smooth things or the pleasing things. But I can tell you through the one thing I have brought to tell you which is revision, it isn't hopeless. You can if the day is unpleasant revise it. And if tomorrow the results are not before you and the next week or the next month they are not before you, I know you will change by the revision the events when you must once again encounter that moment in time. And so, you will change the pattern, for the wheel is turning and you can't stop it. For I saw it, and one moment in time I was part of it. I stopped it within me: and they all stopped. Not one could move, not even the bird in flight. The bird couldn't fall; there was no gravity. Gravity was in me.

And I thought, as I was taught in my little school, that Sir Isaac Newton discovered it. I almost thought he made it, because the whole thing was Sir Isaac Newton. I heard, and so no one was greater in my mind's eye than Sir Isaac Newton. As a child, I really believed that he determined how things should fall and how they should go up. And then one day I came into a taste of the power into which tomorrow I would inherit: For I will inherit the kingdom of God, with all the power that goes with it. But I tasted of that power before the last link was broken. And so, the bird couldn't fly and it didn't fall, and the grass that was moving in the wind couldn't move, and the leaves falling couldn't fall, and the people walking couldn't walk, and the diners dining couldn't dine, and everything was frozen. I looked at them. I was moving; I was not frozen. I froze *in me* an activity which froze them. I went over and looked at them and they were dead things, part of the eternal structure of the universe. Forever these are garments to be worn by God. And then *I* released it and they all moved. And the birds continued in flight, the leaves continued to fall, and the grass began to wave, and the diners dined, and the waitress walked, and everything continued to fulfill its purpose. Then I knew of a different time, of a different age, of a different use of power, and that *here* we are only an animated world.

So to repeat: "You have no power over me, unless it has been given to you from above." The word is Anothin, the same word used in the 3ʳᵈ chapter of John when he said: "Except you be born from above (anothin) you cannot inherit the kingdom of God." You are still part of the wheel of recurrence, still part of this time which is forever. But God in his infinite mercy having put seven times over you will move beyond and redeems you in the body of Jesus. Because there is only one body, he redeems you in the body of Jesus, there's only Jesus. Jesus, believe it or not, is God. People won't believe it. They smile at you and they laugh. But Jesus Christ is the *only* *God* . . . but so are you when you enter his body and become incorporated into it. Because there's only one name, only one Lord, and that one name is Jesus Christ. And *all* will be redeemed in the body of Jesus, and all will have the same power, the same being. Everyone will be Jesus.

Now, it doesn't make sense. But what I told you earlier doesn't make sense. The lady is here, and I must tell her one of my friends who read the letter knows her quite well, and she said, "You know, having seen the name of the one who signed it, I believe every word of it. Were it not that *she* wrote it, I would question it." So the questioning mind already was there, but she read the one who ____(??) it sent and trusting her implicitly, she said, "I believe every word in this letter." But still, they only allowed three or four seconds, right away she's discussing the possibilities of changing God's play and changing it radically so that he would still be here as our President. And they can't see these wheels within wheels within wheels that Ezekiel spoke of.

So I tell you, it is not reincarnation as the world teaches to justify the inequalities of life. You can't justify them. For man didn't sin and he's born blind? He didn't gouge his eyes out, he was born blind, and his parents didn't sin? And this only so that the works of God be made manifest? What a horrible God! And that's the Word of God speaking. He didn't sin and his parents didn't sin, it's *only* that the works of God be made manifest.

Therefore, revision, which in scripture is called . . . but the word is tarnished. It was taught . . . the very first word used in the earliest gospel, which is the Book of Mark, that first word spoken by the embodiment of God is "repentance." "The time is fulfilled," he speaks of time, "The time is fulfilled; the kingdom of God is at hand: repent, and believe the gospel" (Mark 1:15). Well, "repentance" really is the ancient word for the word I use today, "revision." For repentance is "a radical change of attitude, a *radical* change of attitude toward life." And if in the revolutions of this world there is *really* a revolution, it's not what took place in Cuba or in Russia or this country or in any part of the world. The real revolution is when man discovers that by a radical change of his own mental attitude toward life he can change the outer aspects of life. When man makes that discovery there is a *real* revolution in the world. A man discovers that by his own change of mental attitude he changes the outer aspects of his life. For I can't conceive of any greater revolution in the world, and that's repentance. But the churches have put barnacles on it and they teach it's to be remorseful, to be regretful. And to this very day you turn on the radio or turn on the TV, they're still talking of the event that should not have happened. They all sit in judgment of God. And here is the whole grand wonderful play unfolding.

When one really sees it in the end and when one completely awakes, he, too, will be able to say to all the characters that played the part, "Father, forgive them; they know not what they do" (Luke 23:34). No matter what they do, "Father, forgive them; they know not what they do." How could you tonight if you really believed the vision that was written to me ten days ago, how could you today condemn anyone who had a part? Whether his part was to play a lax part in not properly arranging protection, or the one who has gone berserk and bought his gun, and then hate as he did, if he did it; and then the one who came and did all these things to hush the very voice that might be able to throw light on it. All these things in the wonderful drama! And then this fantastic pageantry that we had in our country, where the whole vast world with the aid of this Telstar now saw it, all at the same time, Russia saw it, all of Europe. If there are TV sets in China, they could see it too, because by this new beam the whole vast world could see it. And what drama! A tremendous pageant that she actually saw ten days before this level could receive it.

So, where are you from? Well, "I came out from the Father," said he, "and I have come into the world; again, I am leaving the world and I am going to the Father" (John 16:28). In four short phrases he states his prenatal existence, his incarnation, his breaking of the wheel—he's going to die, leaving this wheel—and return to the Father. But he said to the others: "Where I go you cannot now come, but you will." Where I now go you cannot now come, not now. He tells you he is breaking the wheel, and therefore he departs for the last time. But he did incarnate; he took human form. He tells us by the words, the little phrase, "I came from the Father." That is a confession of a prenatal existence. "I came into the world ___(??); I'm leaving the world; I'm going to the Father." But, "When you see me you see him who sent me." And who sent you? The Father. "When you see me you see him who sent me."

Well, how could that be? But if God individualizes himself and God is Father, when he is individualized that individualized presence must all be Father. That's why he's ___(??) these are the ways to the Father. You will never know that you are Father unless God's only begotten Son appears and calls you Father. Without uncertainty in your soul, David calls you Father. No uncertainty when you look into his eyes and he into your eyes and he calls you Father. And so, God is Father. When he begets you as himself, you can't be less than God; and therefore you'll be father of the same child, not another child.

And so, this is the way by which this invidious bar is broken . . . this envious bar. For someone who has wealth, they may envy someone who has more. The one who is poor envies the one who has some. The one who is known is not envious of the unknown but they're envious of the known. And all this enmity, this strange peculiar enmity in the world that is part of God's play, these unequal discriminations in the world. And the world thinks it's going to change it in some strange way. You will change it only in *one* way: if you know the art of revision. But you will change it only to the extent when you reach that point in time, which is forever, you do not encounter what to you was unpleasant when you encounter *that* moment in time in the completed circle.

Now let us go into the Silence.

*   *   *

Q: (inaudible]

A: ___(??) someone two months ago tried to get in touch with the President to persuade him not to go. But, first of all, no one could have persuaded the President not to go. He would not have listened for one second. Today, he is now woven closely in the tapestry of martyrs because he died in office a violent death. Already they are building up the idea of a Lincoln concept. And so, given the choice of living another few years with a painful back or going this way without pain, for he didn't know it; and then to go down in history believing undoubtedly as he does in the linear concept of time, he would have chosen exactly what happened to him. But, may I tell you, that was only the part. *God* played the part. God through this is individualizing himself. But don't get off now to a man called John Fitzgerald Kennedy or one who called himself Oswald. It is the all-together pre___(??) of the whole vast fragmented state that produces the individualized God. This is the re-worn, as it has been worn by many people, many actors, but the actors all are God. It's a great mystery. And when I leave the stage, the costume worn by me, called Neville, is not going to leave the stage. It's just dusted off and hung up for the next occupant, and the occupant will always be God.

You could not have changed his values. First of all, he prided himself in being a very intelligent gentleman, and he was very learned, and he would have looked upon Dixon's suggestion as superstitious. That would have annoyed him to think that anyone could have persuaded him to cancel a political visit, thinking in terms of next year, by some superstitious concept. He would have thought the Republicans have pulled that on me. He would have found it in the one who wrote the letter, a nice Republican, because if she succeeds in persuading me not to go, well, then I have missed an opportunity to challenge the state of Texas. He would have justified it, just as the lady justified it with the oncoming lights and the setting sun and the absence of the news on the radio. Reason steps in and reason is the lying son who refused to hear the instruction of the Lord, who said to the seer—for she was a seer, she saw it—who said to the seers "see not," and to the prophets "prophesy not to us what is right, speak to us *smooth* things." Speak to us and tell us of the prophecies of illusion.

So ___(??), he doesn't want to hear the unlovely things. Everyone in high office surrounds himself invariably with yes-men. So they will find no seers among those who surround many a prominent person. If you said anything that displeased Hitler, you had your head removed. If you told the truth, that they were going to lose the war, and that millions would have suffered as a result of his attempt to conquer the world, and that he himself would have the ignoble end, he'd have you removed to death, because he didn't want anyone to speak to him of anything other than smooth things. It is said of Stalin.

But they fulfill scripture. Scripture is the *eternal* drama and man is trying to rewrite it. He's always trying to rewrite it. They'll say, "He doesn't really mean this" and you ask, "Who didn't mean it?" "Well, the one who wrote it." "Don't you believe God wrote it? Don't you believe that God dictated it to the prophets, men organized by divine providence for that communion?" They will seriously confess, "Well, maybe." "Well then, if God dictated it, you're going to change his Word? Aren't you warned not to tamper with the Word of God?" But they're always tampering with it. I read from a new Bible today, and they tried their best to give meaning to that which I quoted tonight, and it's so far removed. It's the *Modern English Bible*, only the New Testament is out so far. And what they did to the wonderful 19th of John in trying to give meaning, because he can't possibly mean what the Word says he said. But he said exactly that.

To the first question he does not answer: Where are you from? And Jesus gave no answer; he would not speak to him. "Do you not know

I have the power to set you free and the power to crucify you?" "You would have no power over me had it not been given to you from above." Well, that is stupid to Pilate who represents Caesar. Caesar is the power of the world in today's business and he represents Caesar. And, You dare to say to me, you whose background, whose origin is well known to the world ___(??)? He had a large family, four brothers are named and sisters; and he comes from a simple little family. And you dare to say to me, Caesar's right arm, that I have no power over you except that it be given me from above? Is there something above Caesar? And he's saying "from above" meaning "Anothin"—from God. Therefore, he, meaning God, therefore God determined who delivered me into your hands. He has the greater sin, if it's sin.

Good night.

WHAT IS TRUTH?

December 8, 1963

___(??) the 18th chapter of John, "It is for this I was born, and for this I have come into the world, to bear witness to the truth" (verse 37). And Pilate said to him, "What is truth?" Well, he did not answer. Then Pilate went out and he said to the crowd, "I find no crime in him. But you have a custom that I should release a man for you at the Passover; will you have me release the King of the Jews?" And they cried out, "Not this man, but Barabbas." Now Barabbas was a robber. That's what they said, "Now Barabbas was a robber." Well, what are they trying to tell us? For the story is eternal, it's forever. Here is one who bears witness to the truth. But truth is an ever-increasing illumination, so how could it answer one level to the satisfaction of a true definition of truth? On the level of Pilate, which is reason, it could not really answer "What is truth?" For he said, "I am the truth." You are asking me, Who are you? Define yourself. Tell me, what is the truth that you bear witness to in the world? And he said not a word.

Well, on this level, a true judgment must conform to the external reality to which it relates. I ___(??) the facts. And then if you discover that it is a ___(??), you say, My judgment is true. Then I say "I am" and then I define it—"I am rich, I am known, I am this." Then you investigate the facts of life concerning me and you discover that I am not rich, I am not known, I am not the things I claim, so my judgment is false. That's what on this level one would say. But here comes one who bears witness to the truth, and it isn't confined to this level, where a true judgment must conform to the external reality to which it relates.

For we are told, every word of God proves true. Well, what word now in scripture, which is the word of God, will allow me to claim that I am which at the moment my reason denies, my senses deny, and those who

477

would investigate my claim will prove false? I turn to the Book of Mark, and here we find the word, "Whatever you desire"—no restraint to your desire—"Whatever you desire, when you pray, believe you have received, and you will" (11:24). That's an entirely different level of truth. Is it true? Well, I'm called upon to test it, just test it. Dare to assume that you are what you want to be, and then try to remain to the best of your ability faithful to that assumption, and see if it doesn't prove itself in performance. If it proves itself in performance, you have risen beyond this level of Caesar, where things must be confirmed by external facts to prove that judgment.

Now, tonight, just before I took the platform, a lady saw me and told me of a vision of hers. She's never had one before. And it happened within a matter of, well, twenty-four hours or so. She heard a voice speaking to her in the ___(??) and the voice said to her, "Most people can't part with what they don't want long enough to get what they do want." She got up in the middle of the night and wrote it down. It was most startling . . . a voice is speaking to her, "Most people can't part with what they don't want long enough to get what they do want." So she wrote it down. The next morning when she got up she knew that she had written in the night and she had written down something. Before she looked to see what she'd written down, she tried to recall it and couldn't. She tried to remember what she had written down and couldn't bring one word back, but she knew she had done it. Luckily, on the paper is what she had written down.

Let me repeat it. It's something just revealed. It's been told forever, but this is something modern, in our language, not in a biblical tongue. "Most people"—that qualifies it, not all people, most, ___(??). We need not be among the majority; we can be in the minority. We can be the remnant. "Most people cannot part with what they don't want long enough to get what they do want." Well now, you here, who are coming here as you do as often as you do, you are not in the "most." You're not in the majority or you would not be here. Were you numbered among the many, you would not be here. You would be satisfied to go on Sunday morning early, so you could get off to the beach during the day, and just say your prayers, and do what you think you should be doing in order to pacify your conscience that you pleased God. But you don't . . . you come here at your own expense and time and money, and this, to me, is not included in the "most" people; this being that remnant that is not mentioned. That we *can*, coming here, get away from what we don't want long enough to get what we do want.

So here, on this level of truth, whatever you desire, when you pray, believe you have received it, and you will. If I really believe this night that I am the man that I want to be, I would see, as I fall asleep, the world as I would see it were my assumption true. I would actually see it just as though

I would see it were it true. And I would remain in that state not only tonight but when I sleep tomorrow night and the next night and the next night. I would have the persistency to remove myself from what I don't want long enough to get what I do want. That is another level of truth that is not the Jesus level; so he could not respond to Caesar.

Now, who is Barabbas in this world? The crowd wants Barabbas. They don't want Jesus, crucify him, give us Barabbas. You could take this on many levels and treat it wisely, toward the fulfillment of a desired end. But they want Barabbas and Barabbas was a robber. What robs me now of the man that I want to be?—the facts of life. My bank balance as it comes from the bank tells me I am not really the man that I'm saying I am financially. All right, so that's a robber. Then, my world as I know it, as my friends view me, everything in my world bears witness to the man that I am at this moment in time. But I don't want this. If I accept the evidence of my senses, yet I don't want to be the man that they tell me that I am, I am being robbed of the man that I could be—if I really know the one who bears witness to the truth. For he tells me all things are possible to God and if I read the story carefully I find out that he and I are one. For he comes to bear witness to the truth. Now we go on. He said, "My word is truth. I am the way, I am the truth, the life. No one comes unto the Father save by me. If you knew me, you would know the Father. Now you know the Father and you have seen the Father." We have seen the Father? said Philip. "Oh, show us the Father." "I have been with you so long, and yet you do not know me, Philip? He who has seen me has seen the Father; how can you say, 'Show us the Father'?" (John 14:6-9).

Now, a scribe said to him, "What is the greatest commandment?" And he answered, "This is the greatest commandment, 'Hear, O Israel: The Lord our God is one Lord, and you shall love the Lord your God with all your heart, with all your soul, with all your mind.' This is the second commandment"—and it's equal to the first—"Love thy neighbor as thyself. There is no other commandment greater than these" (Mark 12:29). Now, he's speaking now of a commandment, the question about a commandment. But where do we find it? He's witnessing the truth. The whole book, he tells us, is the truth and that every word will prove itself. "Every word of God proves true. Do not change his words lest you be reproved by him and found a liar" (Proverbs 30:5). So don't change his words, leave them alone.

So here are the words. The first commandment, and the greatest commandment is to "Hear, O Israel: The Lord our God is one Lord, and love him with all our heart, all of our soul, all of our mind." And then the second is equal to the first, "Love thy neighbor as thyself." Here we find the compound unity: the Lord is I AM. The word translated "our God" is plural, Elohim, the immortal, the eternal, the God—the first word translated God in the Bible. "In the beginning God created the heavens and the earth," that's Elohim, that is "our God." And then the last one, "the Lord," is back to I AM. So, "Hear, O Israel: I AM, our I AMs, is one I AM."

Well, how can you prove that? Must I love my neighbor as I love myself? Well, yes. But does he mean that? Is he witnessing that truth or is it something deeper? It's something far, far deeper. I must love him as myself because we are one. And I will show you how we are one, he tells you. Don't just love him as you love yourself, love him because you are the very being that you think to be other than yourself. On this level, God is fragmented, and every being is saying "I am," yet there's only one I AM. So the one I AM is fragmented, and all are saying "I am." I say, I am Neville, I am Jane, I am Peter, I am that—but only one. Well, how would I know it's only one?

Well, you wait. I will witness now and tell you how you will know that we are one, that "Hear, O Israel: The Lord our God is one Lord." Well, how will I know it? Well now, "our Lord" is Father. Now we go back to that 12th chapter of Mark that I quoted earlier when they asked the question, "What is the greatest commandment?" So he answers, he brings it all out, as I quoted earlier, and then the one who asked the question ___(??) said to him, Teacher, you're right; the Lord is one and there is no other Lord, just one. And all the sacrifices that man could make are not comparable to that command to love thy neighbor as thyself. He turned to him and said, You are not far from the kingdom of heaven. And then no one dared ask him another question.

So the question was asked, and now he brings in a mystery. He's going to show them how they will know that the Lord our God is one Lord. And you listen to it carefully. Nobody asked the question, but he makes the statement, How do scribes say that Christ is the son of David . . . when David in the Spirit calls him Father? If David thus calls him Father, how can he be David's son? (Matthew 22:42). And no one asks the question. Here is a mystery. He's leaving it, for he is now bearing witness to the truth. For he said to Pilate—on this level the embodiment of reason—"For this I was born and for this I came into the world, to bear witness to the truth." And now he makes the most fantastic statement in the world, because, if you take it as of 2,000 years ago and he's speaking of a being, if you take it chronologically, who lived 3,000 years ago. So no one saw David, for David was not born on the earth. David in Spirit calls him Father. If David in Spirit calls him Father, how can he be David's son? David calls him, Lord, and the Lord is one. He's telling everyone who hears him, wait, I have come to bear witness to the truth.

The day is coming that the same David will call you Father. Then you will know why I tell you, "Love thy neighbor as thyself," for there is no "other." You're living on this level in a fragmented world and everyone is saying "I am." But, really, we aren't billions of I am's; in the end, all are the Father. And you will know that greatest of all commandments, "Hear, O Israel: The Lord our God is one Lord." I AM, our I AMs, is one I AM. So he comes bearing witness to the truth. But while we are fragmented in this world, keep this in mind—and yet play it fully and wisely on this level—his invitation to ignore the facts of life and dare to assume that you are the man, the woman, that you want to be. For his words are true. He said, "Every word of God proves true. Do not change these words, lest you be rebuked by him, and found a liar."

Now we are told, "The words of the wise are like goads, and like nails firmly fixed are the sayings, the collected sayings, which are given by one Shepherd. My son, beware of anything besides these." Then he insists, "This is the end of the matter." It's all over, no other words, this is the end of the matter. Now, "Fear God, and keep his commandments; and this is the whole duty of all men. Now these are his commandments: fear God; keep his commandments; this is the duty of all men" (Ecclesiastes 12:11). And so, I seek out his commandments and I start reading, what did he command? Every word is a commandment, on different levels. So I ___(??) my world, the world of Caesar. But it doesn't really matter where I start in the world of Caesar, how many stripes against me. If I have no financial, intellectual, social or other background, it doesn't really matter if I know God's word.

It doesn't matter where you are this night if you know God's word, and you will accept that word. For his word is, "Whatever you desire, believe you have received it, and you will." And don't be among the majority, as the lady brought out this night, "Most people can't part from what they don't want long enough to get what they do want." They can't divorce themselves long enough from the evidence of their senses to actually put into practice God's word, which is that 11th chapter, that 24th verse of the Book of Mark. Whatever you desire. It doesn't say let the priesthoods of the world tell you that it's good for you. It doesn't say society tells you that you should want to transcend or you should not want to transcend your present level. Hasn't a thing to do with that. It's something entirely different. From that moment when John was arrested all things changed, that's what we're told. And here is John who is telling us to be satisfied. He tells a soldier to be satisfied with his wages; those who have two coats give one to one who has none; if you have more than you need to eat for food, give it those who have none. But then John was arrested. When John was arrested, here comes Jesus into the world. Hasn't a thing to do with doing things on this level in order to get things. Not a thing to do with it.

This past month in New York City, I had one of these marathon radio . . . it ran five hours through the night. I had two of them, really. But this night, my opponent was Rabbi Silver and Kylie ___(??), the actor, and then, ___(??) Oursler, the son of Fulton Oursler who wrote *The Greatest Story Ever Told*. He's quite a successful writer in his own name. They were my opponents and the moderator was ___(??) John. Well, the Rabbi said to me, "Don't you tell your people to give to certain charities, to give to this, to give to that, to give to the other?" I said no I don't. "Then what sort of a teacher are you? Don't you tell them that you must do this and do that?" I said, I am not in the school of John the Baptist; I am in the school of Jesus Christ. If you want to tell your congregations to give all kinds of money to your synagogue, all well and good, do it. You think you can enter the kingdom of heaven by merit. You'll wait forever. You'll rust on this level until you accept the teaching of Jesus Christ. Jesus Christ transcends John the Baptist, who said give one coat if you have two; you have more money than your needs, give it away to those who haven't; you have more food than you need, give it away.

So you go out to your congregation and you tell them all the time what you must do to earn the kingdom of heaven. You can't earn the kingdom of heaven. It's a gift. But I'll tell you on this level what I am telling you now, you will transform your world if you tell your congregation how to transform this ___(??) on this level. It isn't going to earn you the kingdom. In God's own wonderful way he'll single them out, one by one, and bring them into the kingdom. It's a gift. You don't earn it and you think you can earn it. Well, go on thinking you can earn it and remain in the world of John the Baptist. Although you do not recognize John the Baptist because you stop at Malachi, and I tell you John the Baptist is but a continuation of Malachi. They're trying to earn the kingdom of heaven by good deeds.

I'm not saying that you shouldn't be good. I find it easier to be good—I have to live with myself—to be kind, to be considerate. If someone asks help of me and I have what it takes, I will part and I will share. But I don't go out saying I've got to share in order to earn the kingdom, because you can't do it that way. So someone asks me for some money and if I have it and it doesn't distress my immediate family, they can have it. I've done it and still do it, and will undoubtedly continue to do it. But that's not the way that one goes into any kingdom. So I tell you how this thing works in this world. Well, he was against me, so was Oursler, the whole bunch, because they live on a level that is, as the lady said, "Most people can't part with what they don't want long enough to get what they do want." People go to bed thinking, only if Mr. Brown, Mr. Jones, Mr. so-and-so gave what they should give, with all that they have, to the charity he's trying to raise. It doesn't work that way.

Well, you should have heard the response—the phones ringing, the mail coming in, the wires coming in, and all kinds of things plus the letters that followed. In the next two, almost three weeks, they were still writing that program and yet the program goes on six days a week. But it was so much of an impact on those who heard it. It covered twenty-six states and most of Canada. And so, this is something altogether different. They talked about a man who claimed he was Christ Jesus. What if I say to them, "I am and so are you"? That would shock them all the more. They are all Christ Jesus. There's nothing but God in this world. God is playing all the parts. There's nothing but God, and God individualized is Jesus Christ. But God individualized as Jesus Christ is still God. And everyone who actually goes through that series of events awakens as Christ Jesus, without loss of identity. There's no loss of identity, yet Jesus Christ. There's only one body. So the Lord is one and his name is one, only one body.

Everybody will one day awaken to a series of events and awaken as Christ Jesus. And then you will know the meaning of these words: For this I was born and for this I came into the world to bear witness to the truth; and everything said of me will now unfold within you, but I can't share it with you, he said. You must believe it and trust me that I am bearing witness to the truth and everything said. For I dictated the words to my prophets of old, that's what he's saying. Everything in that book I dictated to those I organized by my own providence for spiritual communion with me, and they took it down beautifully, just as the lady did. She forgot it within a matter of hours. Didn't know what she had written, but she knew she had it. Luckily she wrote it down as the prophets did. And then she woke in the morning to find that there it was recorded on paper, that regardless of different memory that she had, she still could bring it back to the surface mind because she'd written it down. That's vision. That's revelation. So the book is written that way, and the whole thing is dictated by Christ Jesus, by God, the only God.

So he comes into the world in which the whole thing unfolds within him, and everyone will one day have the identical thing unfold within him. And he will know why the greatest commandment is that "the Lord our God is one Lord." And that if God is father before being individualized, then that in which he is now individualized must also be a father. And if you are the father of only one son prior to the individualization, then that same son must be the son of the one who is now individualized. So he appears and he asks the one simple question, "How can the scribes say that the Christ is the son of David . . . when David in the Spirit calls him Lord? If David thus calls him Lord, how can he be David's son?" (Mark 12:35) No one asked any further questions. It's a little mystery inserted into a conversation between a very wise scribe and Jesus Christ.

So he asks the question, Teacher, what is the greatest commandment? What is the first commandment? Well, you and I know from your commandments, that's not the first. It's recorded in the 6th chapter of the Book of Deuteronomy, "Hear, O Israel: The Lord our God is one Lord." But as you read the commandments it is, "Love the Lord thy God." It's something entirely different. And as far as "Love thy neighbor as thyself" as a commandment, you read that in the 19th chapter of Leviticus. It's not in the commandments. All we have are the ten. It's something set aside, but it is the second commandment and equal to the first. And then he ties it together. So "Love thy neighbor as thyself," for the simple reason this is a fragmented God, and the "other" is not really another, it's yourself.

If I could only share with you what it feels like when you reach the apex and the whole, and it's all you. For I saw the fragmented stone, the stone the builders rejected it is called by Peter, and "The stone that begot thee, thou art unmindful." The stone . . . it broke into unnumbered fragments. When it was all put together, it formed that of a man, and as you looked at it, it's all yourself. So when it's all put together and you see it, you will see yourself. And it's man. The one grand stone fragmented, then regrouped into a form, not a stone but a man. And looking at it, you look right into your own face, beautified beyond the wildest dream of this level, with a dignity of features, with a majesty of face, with a courage that you could not conceive that you could ever have from this level. And there you're looking right into your own face, when all are put together. And who are they all?—everyone here, the whole vast world is part of the being that I am.

I saw it one night, saw one being, and here is myself. But I came closer and I saw infinite people, all the races, all the nations of the world, all incorporated into one being, and I am he, the heart glowing like a living ruby. And here is a whole being. I'm looking at it and I'm looking at myself. I come closer. When the vision is contracted, you see nations, you see races, you see people, unnumbered people, and altogether form the one being that I am. And it's you. So, you'll look upon your own being, and this that is now speaking to you will be incorporated into that being. And that's the mystery. And all of us incorporated into one being—as you look at it, it's yourself—you're the only being.

So, "Hear, O Israel: The Lord our God is one Lord"—not two, only one—the greatest of all the commands; and the second equal to the first, "Love thy neighbor as thyself," for the very simple reason he is not another.

On this level, for the great mystery of ___(??) individualizing God as you, we are scattered and we are enemies on this level. But while on this level, I come to bear witness to the truth. And I know that this, if I say that this is a lectern and this is a microphone, this is a table, and you come forward and you feel it, examine it, and you will say, "Well, Neville is telling the truth. That's right. These are what he claims that they are." And all of a sudden I say, "Well, isn't it lovely." And you think, "You mean the table?" And I say, "No, the flowers. Aren't they beautiful! Can't you smell them?" You say, "Now he's gone off his nut. There aren't any flowers." There is no external fact relating to my judgment. So at that moment you think, "Now he's really gone." But I insist that there are lovely flowers here. And so I will assume that they are and I will smell flowers and feel flowers, and live as though they were, convinced that there will be flowers. And you will have, one night, the impulse—or maybe when I'm not even here, I don't have to be here to see them—there will be flowers. I have done it. I have taught others how to do it. And so, whatever I desire when I pray, believe I have received it. Whether that be for things or for a transformation of myself from being what I am at this very level to another level. So if I desire this night to be elsewhere, I shouldn't sleep in my apartment in the assumption that that is the apartment in which I slept last night. I must sleep where I would sleep were my desires this night fulfilled.

And when someone looks at someone in this world and they see them as their senses dictate and they think now that's the truth, that isn't true if that individual could be improved. It's not the truth. But what does the word say in scripture concerning such a thing? Well, "Go down to the potter's house, and there I will let you see and hear my words. So I went down to the potter's house, and there he was working at his wheel. And the vessel in his hand was spoiled, but he reworked it into another vessel, as it seemed good to the potter to do" (Jeremiah 18:2). He didn't discard that material at all, didn't discard it as you and I would discard people who are not coming up to our ideals. He simply took the same vessel and reworked it into another vessel, as it seemed good to him to do. So someone in your world is not as you think they ought to be, don't argue with them, don't discard them from your life, because it's yourself. Don't cut off a finger. We're all one. Leave him just as he is, and then reshape him in your own mind's eye, and try to remain faithful to that concept of him that at the moment his behavior denies, and live in that state just as though it were true. And see how true God's words are.

But come back to what the lady said earlier, "Most people"—and don't be among the most people—"they just can't part from what they don't want long enough to get what they do want." So don't be among the most people who cannot part with it long enough. Someone comes into your world and he's no good. He's always asking for help and you're always pouring it out, because you don't know how to say no. Well now, don't just pour it out and then do nothing. In your mind's eye do something about it because he's yourself. "Love thy neighbor as thyself," for he's an actual self in a state of fragmentation. And one day we'll all be gathered together and not one piece can be missing. "Not one is lost in all my holy mountain." So all gathered together, they form the man. When you look at that one man, you are he.

So he comes to bear witness to the truth, and the truth is an infinite, an ever-increasing illumination. So the question asked cannot be answered on any one level to the satisfaction of the whole definition of truth. But something infinitely greater than truth is love. For it is true that if a murderer came through the window right now and asked me where a certain man has gone, I would tell him, knowing exactly where the man is, I would say I don't know. I would lie. I would lie to the murderer and I wouldn't tell the truth. I know exactly where the man is hiding, but I would lie because love is greater than truth. I would lie and save myself, because the man that I am saving from this murderer is myself. And I would save myself from the violence that he intended. And so, love is greater than truth.

So when I stood in the presence of infinite love, who is Christ Jesus—I can see him now more clearly than I can see my own face—and when I answered, "The greatest thing in the world is love," then he embraced me and incorporated me into his body. We became one being. And I am that body, yet no loss of identity; yet containing a greater self, a greater presence, which is the one being gathering all together into that one body. And so, love is just infinitely greater than anything in this world.

But don't discount truth, for truth is forever going to higher and higher and higher levels of illumination. What holds good here will not be denied on a higher level but will be incorporated. Whether it is perfectly true here on this level, it doesn't exist on a higher level. I could stand suspended in the air and have no power on the outside holding me, just hold myself, because all things are subject to my own imaginative power, allow anything in motion in my world, rearrange it, without any concept of gravity, and hold it there forever if I so desired. Not one would cease to be waiting for me when I arrived at a certain point, still my ___(??), my own self. That is the world in which we all move as we rise from this level to that level.

So, "What is truth?" and he doesn't answer. And then he goes out and the crowds are screaming and he says, "I find no crime in him. But you have a custom, that I release a man for you at the Passover. Would you have me release the King of the Jews?" And they scream, "Not this man, but

Barabbas." Then it added, "And Barabbas was a robber" (John 18:40). They chose the law—the robber being the evidence of the senses. Don't release truth on higher levels, give us the robber on this level; I want to feel secure. And a friend of mine, who is a practicing psychiatrist in this city of ours, I knew him back East, and when I wrote him how I got out of the army by believing in scripture, by sleeping physically in the army as though I slept physically in my home 2,000 miles away, and in nine days I was transported physically to my home 2,000 miles away, honorably discharged; he being a Freudian and a practicing psychiatrist doesn't even answer my letter.

I met him when the war was over. He was still in it when the war was over, and I got out in March of 1943. He came out when the war was over, the end of '45, my age, dying to get out. But he was too much . . . so he chose Barabbas, because he was trained to believe in the reality of his senses. He once said to me, "I love listening to you, Neville. You know what I do when I hear you? I put my feet into the carpet"—that was in New York City where we had carpets—"I put my feet into the carpet and I would hold the chair with my fingers to keep my sense of the reality and the profundity of things." So I took him away from reality and the profundity of things. So while he was in the army, he had only a little cot to keep his sense of reality and profundity of things. I let go of the cot and slept in my lovely bed, which I still use here, I brought it with me. So that same bed, I knew it so well, I slept in it, and saw as I would see were it true that I was honorably discharged. One thing I made very sure to myself I'm not here on furlough. I'm not on furlough; I am here honorably discharged. ___(??) no AWOL, I am honorably discharged, and this is no furlough.

And so, when I got that whole mood and bathed myself in it, I slept, and I proved the word of God. And so we are told in the Book of Proverbs, I think it's the 23rd chapter and the 23rd verse, "Every word of God proves true. Don't change his word, don't add to it, don't alter them, lest you be rebuked, and be proved a liar" (Proverbs 30:5). So just take his word. His word told me to do exactly what I did. You really know what you want?—I knew exactly what I wanted—well then, believe that you've got it. But if I had it, where would I sleep if I had it? I'd sleep in my own home in New York City . . . well, that's where I slept, all in my Imagination. So when I tell you that Blake is right, "Man is all Imagination. God is Man and exists in us and we in him" (*Annotations to Berkeley*, page 775). "The eternal body of Man is the Imagination, and that is, God himself" (*Laocoon*, page 776).

Now let us go into the Silence.

*   *   *

Q: (inaudible)

A: ___(??) tell no man. Well, that's not actual, because on other occasions, "I will tell you, before it takes place." In the 13th chapter of the Book of John, "I will tell, before it takes place, so that when it does take place you may believe" (verse 19). But for those who have not the courage to face the heat when—friends will always say and point their finger at you because you confided in them and told them of your hopes and your dreams and your wishes, and so you told them—but you didn't have the strength, the faith, to persist in the assumption that you are what you told them that you are. And then when you don't actually hatch it out, they invariably point the finger of accusation at you. So, to avoid that, he said, "Be silent, tell no one." But he himself having proven the law beyond all doubt, he said, "I will now tell you before it takes place that when it does come to pass, you may believe."

And so, I tell you now having experienced the birth from above before you have it, because I know I've had it. I've experienced these things, so I don't care what the world will say. I'm telling you before it takes place in your life and when it does take place, you'll believe it. So he didn't qualify it at all. But on other things on the world of Caesar where man is more rooted to the evidence of his senses, to cushion the blow, if they haven't the faith to sustain the assumption, tell no man. When it hatches out, rejoice in the law. If on hindsight you tell them this is what you did, they may or may not believe you.

My brother Victor, who has made a fortune in this world, a real fortune, he only confided with my mother, only told mother, wouldn't tell my father, never told us. And for two years he remained faithful to a certain vision, where he saw the biggest building on the main street of little Barbados reading J. N. Goddard & Sons. He . . . (Tape ends.)

REPENT AND BELIEVE IN
THE GOSPEL

December 10, 1963

Tonight's subject is "Repent and Believe in the Gospel." When you read the words, you wonder, what is it all about? These are the first words put into the mouth of the central figure of the entire Bible, Jesus Christ. This is the earliest gospel, the gospel of Mark. You read it in the very first chapter, the 15th verse, "Repent." Then he tells us, "The time is fulfilled; repent, and believe in the gospel."

What is this time being fulfilled? "The time is fulfilled" simply means the time foreseen by the prophets, the time fixed in God's own foreknowledge. For he said, "The vision has its own appointed hour; it ripens, it will flower. If it be long, then wait; for it is sure and it will not be late." So the time is fulfilled: the time for the hatching has come. It does not say that if you and I repent that we would in any way aid this passage. But as man repents he does not in any way cooperate with God in bringing him in. Then you are God. Then you are ___(??) whether we repent or not. And so the door is open for everyone to enter; not because of their repentance. The door is open and when the time is fulfilled for the individual, then he enters, whether in the interval he repented or not.

Yet we are invited to repent. Why? Because divine history is culminated; human history is cyclic. And so, you may wait without repentance for the entire cycle, then move and move and move, and suffer beyond the wildest dream of man. At the end, when it's all culminated, then you enter. But why suffer that much? And so, he calls upon us to repent. To repent means "to turn from and to turn to." It's like praying. It's an art. I turn from what I *don't* want in this world and turn to what I *want* in this world. Turning to,

I am repenting. To repent means "a radical change of attitude toward life." But not only to turn *from* it, but to turn *to* what I want in place of what I am presenting in this world.

So here we find these four statements. The time is fulfilled; it's already happened, and the first ___(??) is broken, and all are moving through the open door, leading to a new order called the kingdom of God. So, "The time is fulfilled and the kingdom of God is at hand; repent, and believe in the gospel." Believe in the gospel—believe in the good news of salvation—that's what it really means. Hear the story of salvation and believe in it, for *every word* of it is true.

Tonight, we're going to stress repentance, but I cannot leave the platform without telling you that it *has* come and every word is true. We are told, "There are some standing here who will not taste of death before they see the kingdom of God." And many scholars have scoffed at that word. There is no record that they saw the kingdom of God, and yet they were told they would not taste of death before they saw the kingdom of God. I stand here as a witness to the truth of that statement. We are told in the 14th chapter of the Book of Luke that, here, he is giving a banquet, it's a messianic banquet: Go out into the highways, the byways, and bring in first the poor, the maimed, the lame, the blind. When he made that statement the servant said, what you have commanded is already done, and still there is room. Go out into the ways now and command all to come in. But only these four followed him, the blind, the poor, the maimed, and the lame. Bring them in. And they are all seated waiting for the coming of host, who was Messiah. Suddenly he appeared and restored to wholeness. That's the banquet. They don't gorge themselves, as we would on this level; they're completely restored. The blind began to see.

Well, if you think you haven't played these parts, may I tell you, you are not *going* to play them, you are playing them. Until the time is fulfilled in your individual cases you will continue to play them. Well then, what are these parts? I may this night be a billionaire and I cannot buy health, am I not poor? I may buy yes-men, but I can't buy real respect. I can't buy anything with my billions. Look into the world. There are people who are multi-millionaires and they cannot buy health. They can buy all the services of the medical world, but they can't buy health. They can buy all the pills in the world, but they can't buy health. Are they not poor? They do not see God's purpose, God's plan, for as we are told, "He put eternity into the mind of man, yet so that man could not find out what he has done from the beginning to the end" (Ecclesiastes 3:11). Are they not blind? Sure they're blind. They can't see what God has done from the beginning to the end. Are they not maimed? They may not be physically handicapped, but there are men living in this world who, unless they can express themselves physically, feel themselves impotent, when time takes its toll and outlaws that so-called urge in man, and they can't buy it. All the transforming of monkey glands in the world cannot produce in them what time, called Nature, has outlawed. So they're maimed, they're lame.

Now let me share with you my experience. It happened in 1946, when suddenly I found myself lifted up, and a heavenly chorus is singing that I am risen. They called me by name and proclaimed my identity, saying that I'm risen. And here I found myself like a being of fire, clothed in a garment of air. There was no sun, no moon, no stars, no need of light; I was the light. I radiated light. Not like a noonday sun, just a twilight, a soft lovely light. And here as far as my eye could see were seated the poor, the blind, the maimed, the lame. And then I came by. And as I came by, gliding—I didn't walk, I simply glided by—everyone was restored to wholeness. Not one was left untouched as I walked by, glided by. And when the very last was restored to complete perfection, complete wholeness, then the chorus exulted, "It is finished." Then I left that banquet and found myself crystallizing once more into this garment of flesh, for unfinished business here. So I have experienced the 14th chapter of Luke.

So when he said, Let them call everyone in the world, they all made excuses. He said, I did not come to save the righteous but the sinners. For there's a greater rejoicing in heaven when one sinner repents than ninety and nine righteous who have no need of repentance. So you invite this one and he doesn't think he needs anything in this world. He knows that he sees perfectly, and he's as blind as a bat. He doesn't know God's purpose, but he thinks he sees perfectly. Then you invite this one, he doesn't feel any limitations in his world, so he's not maimed, he's not lame. So he makes an excuse. Then comes another and he makes excuses. He isn't poor. He can buy a home, buy three if he wants it. He has no sense of poverty, and he doesn't know how poor he is. He said to the servant, Go out into the highways and the hedges, and you bring in all the blind, and all the maimed, and all the lame, and all the poor; and the servant said, it's already done, what you've commanded.

Just exactly like that, for it was already done when I rose within myself, rose as David rose into Zion. For we are told that no one could take Zion; the lame, the blind, the halt, would ward them off. That's all that you needed in Zion, the lame and the blind, they could ward them off. And David began to build in a circle. And he built not only a circle but he built inward at the same time, performing the most fantastic architectural feat, which is to build in a circle and inward at the same time, is to build in a spiral. That's exactly what takes place in you, when you're lifted up to give

492 NEVILLE

the grand banquet. You find yourself moving up in a spiral. You're pulled out of yourself just as though you're a whirlwind, in a spiral. And suddenly you're clothed in your prenatal wholeness, in your primal form, clothed in this being of fire, as you are fire, and clothed in air. And then you walk by and they're all seated on the ground as far as the eye can see, an infinite sea of human imperfection. And this is your banquet, the banquet of Messiah. Messiah is giving this banquet: "Feed upon me." And so they behold the one passing by, yes, even those without organs in their skulls. And as you walk by they become what they behold. And so because you felt yourself one with perfection, everyone beholding you as you walk by *feeds* upon you, and man invariably becomes what he beholds. And so, here, that story is true, every word of it is true.

And so, the time is fulfilled. Not because of anything I did as a man as to repentance. Whether I repent or not the time is fulfilled. God's period for hatching out has come and they're all being hatched out. It is my hope, but I can't prophesy, that everyone here will be hatched out this night. For the joy of being hatched out, where the circle is over. For human history is cyclic; divine history is culminated. And so, you go over and over on this wheel and finally comes that moment in time when up you go, like David taking Zion, in that spiral motion. And here, you give a banquet. And you only give it, read it carefully, everyone refuses the invitation but the blind, the maimed, the lame, and the poor.

And so, I've played every part in this world. Yes, physical poverty, physical blindness, physical maimedness, physical lameness, I've played those parts. But no matter what part I've ever played, I still incorporated in the part all of these qualities. I have a memory of being fabulously wealthy. And yet, I was, in that state, poor. I could not buy help. I could not buy the respect of people. I could buy yes-people, but I couldn't buy the real respect of people. So I have the memory of that state. Never once did I lose the sense of I-ness. You are individualized and you will continue to be more and more individualized forever and forever. You will never lose the sense of I-ness that you have now, never, not in eternity. You're individualized. And so all these characters you have played, and you are playing, and will continue to play until that moment in time when you break the surface. You break it by an act of God. It is he who breaks it, and out you come, just like . . .

Well, tonight's story is repentance. Because you're on the wheel anyway, and you can't get off the wheel; and you must continue on that wheel until that moment of hatching. "At length for hatching ripe he breaks the shell." So why repentance? Well, to ease the blow, to cushion it. For it is a play, a horrible play, may I tell you, it's a horrible play, something that is sheer fantasy if you saw it in its inception, sheer fantasy. But while it's being played, now comes an awakening. Man can, while he is playing it, repent. And repentance hasn't a thing to do with remorse, not a thing to do with regret, all to do with a radical change of attitude toward life. A radical change of inner attitude toward life results in an external change corresponding to the inner change.

It's all an inner thing, told us in the Sermon on the Mount. He said, "Do you think I have come to abolish the law and the prophets? I have not come to abolish them; I have come to *fulfill* them. For I tell you, should heaven and earth pass away, not an iota, not a dot, shall pass from the law; it will all be fulfilled" (Matthew 5:17). And then he explains the law, "You have heard it said, 'You shall not commit adultery.' But I tell you anyone who looks lustfully on a woman has already committed the act of adultery with her in his heart" (Matthew 5:27). That to restrain the impulse is not good enough. Man thought if the act was not performed he didn't perform it. And here I am told that was not it at all: the *impulse* was in itself the act. Well, that means an imaginal act is fact. For I am ___(??) mentally and performed the act, and that *was* the act, even though, physically, for one reason or another, I didn't do it. I might have contemplated the act along with its consequences to myself or my family or society and then I was afraid. But my fear, which restrained me from performing it physically, wasn't good enough. I am told, to contemplate it is the act.

Now, if causation is mental to that extent, now repent. I need not be a slave of the things as they pass before me. I can interfere with the otherwise mechanical structure of the brain. I don't have to simply watch the screen as it passes before me and observe a panorama; I can dislike it and interfere with it. So something is happening in my world, something appears on my body and I don't like it. It's something that disfigures my face or my form, and I don't like it. So why must I tolerate it? I can repent. I can revise it. If I actually see myself as I would like to be seen by the world and remain faithful to that feeling, just as though it were true, I will change it in my world. It doesn't mean I am ripening any better and any faster because of that, but until that moment of fulfillment of time, as far as I the individual goes, do it anyway. And cushion the blows as I move from where I start to where I must go for this ripeness to complete itself that I may burst the shell and come out as God.

For everyone is coming out as God. There's only God begetting himself, that's all there is in this world. There's nothing but God. And whether you believe it or want to believe it or not, the most horrible beast in the world is God being hatched out. And in the end, it is just as though he never did anything that the cyclic motion tells us that he did. Yes, a Hitler, a Stalin, or others that are not yet recorded in the world—all will be hatched out. And they were never Stalin, they were never Hitler, these are only garments that they wore in the cyclic motion of human history. So when we come out we are never these garments that we wore. As Blake said, "Oh, Satan, thou art but a dunce. Thou canst not tell the garment from the man." We see the garment and we think it's the man.

May I tell you, if I could but share with you an experience when you get to the apex and he's almost enticing you to discover himself. He's bringing you up to the very point where he's enticing you and encouraging you to discover, who?—himself. And he's you. And you see you were never this thing at all. These things that you judge so harshly, the same being is playing all the parts, but every part in the world. So while we are playing it, repent, for the time is fulfilled and the kingdom of God is at hand; repent, and believe in the gospel, believe in the good news of salvation. And the good news of salvation: at that very moment when the shell breaks you pass through a series of events that leaves no trace within you of any ___(??), and you know who you are.

So, Christianity is based upon the affirmation that a series of events happened, in which God revealed himself in action for the salvation of man. And I tell you from experience they have happened and they will happen in the life of every being in this world. Not one will fail, because you can't fail. Because you aren't doing it, the being in the depth of yourself who is God, the only God, he's doing it. We all will come out in spite of what we have done as you play the part here.

So when it comes to repentance, put it in this light. It's simple. Start with a simple process. Imagining is spiritual sensation. And take a simple little thing now that isn't here ___(??). It is not present that you and I can see it. I love to use a flower, any flower, but I like a rose. So I will imagine a rose. Well, I can't physically see it, but I can see it in my mind's eye, it's very vivid. And I can smell it. And I can feel it. So Imagination is spiritual sensation. So I can see the reality of what is not physical to the world. To me it's real. The same sensation I apply now toward repentance, no matter how I repent.

If tonight there is a lady present or a man present, who is single and who would like a companion in this world, in the right sense of the word, where they feel wanted. When they come home and he or she is not present, you will say, "Where is everybody?" If there are a dozen people present and the mate isn't present, you say, "Where is everybody?" The house is empty. No matter how many people are present, it's empty if she or he, the loved one, isn't present. That's a perfect relationship, a perfect mate, in this world. So, if this night you retired and she or he, the mate, naturally would be in the house, could you feel their presence as you felt the rose? Could you detect their presence? All right, you could feel it. You can sense it. Extend your imaginary hand and touch the individual. If you would, if it is your habit to kiss people goodnight, all right, kiss him or kiss her goodnight. And *live* in that state just as though it were true. That's repentance. To repent is simply a *radical* change, not a little change, a radical change of attitude toward life. So life is barren? Repent.

If you don't repent, you're on the wheel and you're going to play it over and over. But it does not mean you will not, when it's right, come out as God. No, it doesn't mean that you will not. So if a man does *not* repent he still is born of God. If he repents, he does not in any way cooperate with God in bringing about the new order. So repentance is given to man that while he's in this world that is a horrible play he can cushion the blows and simply make it *easier* for him in this world. But no matter how great you are in this world you're still poor, you're still lame, you're still maimed, and you're still blind.

So if you don't know what God hid in your mind from the beginning of time to the very end, and so hid it that you do not know what he's done from the beginning to the end, then you must be blind as to his purpose. That's told us so clearly in the 3rd chapter of Ecclesiastes, the 15th verse, "he hid it." I'll tell you one night before we close what he hid, for I have found it. I found exactly what he hid in the minds of man, and hid it from the beginning to the end, and so hid it that man couldn't find out what he did from the beginning to the end.

But the end has come, as far as I'm concerned, and so it was revealed to me what he hid. He hid the secret of his fatherhood: that no power in the world could show me that I'm a father but my son. So the very last book of the Old Testament, the Book of Malachi, "A son honors his father:"—the very first chapter—"if then I am a father, where is my honor?" In other words, where is my son? And that's what he hid. In the beginning he hid it until the very end of the days. He brings him out by an explosion. He stands before you and calls you Father. That's what he hid. Calling you Father and knowing who he is—he's God's only begotten son—then you know who *you* are. So it's God coming out, and only God exploding and revealing himself, and it takes his Son to show you who you really are.

As to repentance, learn the art of repentance. It's the greatest secret in the world as to cushioning the blows and making life easier in this world. Therefore, no one in this world really need despair, they can always repent. I don't care where you were inserted into the wheel, how you start life, you can always repent. And so, learn the art of repentance. As you learn it, then no matter where you start you can go where you want to in this world. You can start unknown, unwanted, unloved, and then if you desire to be wanted, desire to be loved, then completely ignore the evidence of the senses and rearrange your mind so that you are really wanted, really loved. Fall asleep night after night in the assumption that it is true, I am wanted, I am loved, and the world will reflect it, you'll be wanted and you'll be loved.

In *The Marriage of Heaven and Hell*, Blake said he dined with Ezekiel and Isaiah, and he said to Isaiah, "Does a firm persuasion that a thing is so make it so?" And Isaiah replied, "All poets believe that it does, and in ages of Imagination a firm persuasion removed mountains. But many are not capable of a firm persuasion of anything today." That I can persuade myself that I am the man that at the moment reason denies, my senses deny?—yes. It's a simple, simple technique and this is how I work it. There are many here this night who have done it and you will go along with me. This is how *I* do it and I know that some of you do it. You simply, wherever you are you imagine that you are where you would like to be or you imagine that you are what you want to be.

Well, that's a mental motion, isn't it? It's not a physical motion. If I want to be in, say, San Francisco and I'm here in Los Angeles, and I assume I am in San Francisco, well then, that's a mental motion, for physically I am here. Well, how will I know that I have made the journey? Well, motion can be detected only by a change of position relative to another object. There is no other way of knowing that something moved unless there is some frame of reference against which the object moved. So, I will assume I am in San Francisco. If I *really* am in San Francisco I should know it only by observing my world. I am looking at my world, so I will think now of Los Angeles. I should see it five hundred miles to the south of me, a way to the south of me, five hundred miles. I would think of other areas and they must be related to my assumption. If I see them as I *would* see them were this now a physical fact, I made the journey, I moved. I made my mental adjustment. I have repented.

Now, fall asleep. Though physically here, I put on the mental state and fall asleep in *it*. For man being all Imagination, man must be wherever he is in Imagination. And so, in Imagination I am in San Francisco. Time will not allow the journey, then my finances will not allow the journey, maybe all kinds of things will not allow the journey, my commitments here, but I am going to journey. Do you know that all of my commitments will reshuffle themselves, and my finances will reshuffle itself, and my time commitments all will reshuffle themselves to permit that journey? And I will be compelled to make it, whether I afterwards desire it or not. So I've gone and made the journey. Having done it *inwardly* then everything moves to compel that physical journey.

You do the same thing with finances. Say, you have no money. All right, if you had it how would you see your present circle of friends? Instead of talking negatively to them and asking them what you should do or maybe they could help you, all of a sudden they *know* of your good fortune. They knew of it. And so let the same frame of reference reflect the change in you. If your present friends know of the good fortune in your life, they'll know it. You will see it on their faces, you'll hear it in their voices, and you will simply be aware of it. Well now, make the mental journey from not having to having, and use this frame of reference to prove that you've made a motion. The whole thing is a motion in mind.

I am telling you when this whole dream is over you have never left home. You've never journeyed. You've never really made any trip whatsoever, in spite of all these trips in the world. You've been sound asleep in heaven, but sound asleep, and compelled to dream the dream of this life. And here, we have the experience of motion, all these experiences, but we never left heaven. Not in eternity have we ever left. So the expulsion was seeming, in a dream, and the whole thing is an adjustment in mind. Every adjustment in mind, if you desire the adjustment, is real repentance. So repent and believe in the gospel.

The gospel, I tell you, is *literally* true, word for word. I had no idea until 1959, in the month of July, that it was literally true. I taught it as law and got wonderful results from coast to coast in all the major cities. But I didn't know the story, that I must believe in the gospels and believing in it that it was literally true, but *no* idea. That everyone in this world would experience, when that fullness of time had come relative to him, everything said of Jesus Christ. *He* gives the banquet. *He* is Messiah. And unnumbered thousands wait for him to come by to feed them, not with bread and wine, but to feed them by beholding him, and he being whole they become what they behold. And all are transformed into the wholeness that they had lost as they play these parts in this world. The blind that's restored to perfect sight, the maimed, the lame, the poor, all restored to fullness, to the wholeness that was there.

And so, man clothed in his pre-natal wholeness, in his primal form, walks by and sees unnumbered thousands waiting for him. But no righteous is present, no complacent; only these four qualities are present, multiplied to the nth degree. I can't tell you how vast that sea of human imperfection was as you walk by it. And without effort it is all done, and that heavenly chorus, as told us in Revelation, the 144,000 formed the chorus, the redeemed singing your praise as you walk by, and then *exult* at the very end, and say it is all finished. The very last words on the cross, "It's finished" and every one made whole. Then you return here to practice and to teach repentance. Because you can't change that interval of time: For a "vision has its own appointed hour; it ripens, it will flower. If it be long, then wait, for it is sure and it will not be late." It's like pregnancy, wait, it's coming . . . and then the joy of the breaking of the shell when you come out *as he* who begot you. There's only God.

So in this 1st chapter, the 15th verse of the Book of Mark, the earliest of the gospels, where man is called upon to listen and the time is fulfilled, all that they foresaw is now upon us. The kingdom of God is *really* at hand. Now repent and believe the good news of salvation. And so, whether you believe it or not, you will be saved. But if you believe it and practice it, it doesn't in any way hasten the moment of breaking the shell, but you do make life for yourself on this *horrible* wheel of recurrence, you make it easier. And that's why I can say to everyone live so that your mind can store a past worthy of recall, because you are on the wheel of recurrence. If you don't change it now, it will confront you tomorrow.

The main events in human life, like the thing that happened two weeks ago, they seem beyond human control, completely beyond, seemingly. The lady who saw it before it happened, and saw it so clearly ten days before, she forgot. Within a matter of seconds she completely forgot that she'd seen it, saw the headlines, complete headlines, "Kennedy Shot." And in three seconds it all vanished, only to be recalled ten days later when the paper, un___(??) page, on the green sheet, was placed before her. But she didn't see it, didn't remember it. So memory failed. As you are told, "There's no memory of former things." She saw it perfectly. That was a crisis in the history, which is a type of history, secular history of the world. And so she was made to forget. Another lady who saw it and even warned the authorities, they wouldn't even listen to her warning, because they couldn't. But in the minor things of life, like getting more money, getting health, getting companionship, these are *minor*, you get all these things in the world.

This present week, telephone calls and a letter, a lovely letter from this friend of mine, who is now living down the coast, a complete change in a job and everything he did prior to the second job fitted him for the job. He is thrilled beyond measure for what he has today. He couldn't dream that he could ever get it. And everything added up to what he has by the application of this principle by his own confession in the letter. A telephone call today—a similar job from this friend about the same age, and he despaired of this other job. Now this is far bigger, more responsibilities, more money, more everything, right where he wanted, in this city—by repentance.

You don't call it repentance, because I have changed the word in my book, and I call it "revision." Because repentance has become almost outdated in the misuse of the word, for we think it means to feel regretful, to feel remorseful. Hasn't a thing to do with that. It's simply a radical change of attitude toward the effects of life. Instead of reacting and recording them and reflecting them, *affect* them. To repent is to affect life rather than to *reflect* life, and unless you repent you're only reflecting life. The whole thing is before you and you simply come upon scene after scene after scene and reflect it. So outside of these *major* crises in the world, the turning points in history, secular history, man must interfere with every little thing in this world. And we're invited to try it, to interfere.

So, the story is, you will be saved whether you repent or not. And you're not going to delay the time of your birth by *not* repenting and you're not going to hasten your birth by repenting, for the vision has its own appointed hour. But, he who first broke the shell, the first to be raised from the dead, told us to repent and invites us all to bring about a complete change of attitude toward life, even though God's fixed vision for us remains fixed and he will not change it whether we change our views or not. And in the end we come out, we all come out as God. No loss of identity, none whatsoever, only a greater being: We encompass God. You and I are the immortal parts of the immortal God, who is one, but one in a strange way, one made up of others. And we are the others . . . the immortal parts that make the one being that is God. So you could not in eternity cease to be. You can't vanish from the scene. And one day, at the appointed hour, you awaken. You aren't any better than the other, because God is one, and his name is one . . . completely perfected and made whole. So, all of the stories of perfection as told in scripture are true.

And so, as I stand before you I can confess I have given the banquet. I call all that I have played in this world, all the blind, all the lame, the poor, and the maimed, and they're all waiting for me, seated on the ground waiting for me to come. Then came that wonderful final motion, as David took Zion, and so, I found myself clothed in my primal form, a being of fire in a body of air, and walked by and fed them by letting them behold me. As they beheld me they were completely restored to their wholeness and everyone was restored. At the very end when the last was completely restored, the exultation of this choral group! And then, back here to tell you about it.

Now let us go into the Silence.

THE HOLY ONE

December 12, 1963

Tonight's subject is "The Holy One." We are told in the Book of Isaiah, the 43rd chapter: "I am the Lord thy God, the Holy One of Israel, thy Savior. I, I am the Lord; and beside me there is no savior." Read it carefully, only *one* savior: I am the Lord. I am the Lord, and there is no other savior. One has to dwell upon it, and really dwell upon it to extract from it its message. One cannot discover the true character of God by investigating or discussing him. One must let him save; then one knows. He's a savior in every sense of the word, so one must let him save. And only then does one really know the character of God. You can discuss him, investigate him, from now 'til the ends of time, but you will never *really* know God.

So tonight we're discussing this Holy One, and this Holy One is I AM. God has clothed himself with humanity, completely clothed himself with man. He's put man on as you would an outer garment, and so with the garment on say, "I am." That's God, the only God, there is no other God. Is he *really* God? Well, he tells that he is a savior: "I am the Lord thy God, the Holy One of Israel, thy Savior. I, I am the Lord: and beside me there is no savior." Is this really true? Well then, I should really test it. If when I stand here and I say "I am" before I say I am this, that and the other, is that really God? Is he really a savior? Well then, test him. See if he really can save me from my present restriction in this world. Just test him. Well, I've done it unnumbered times. I've been trying since I discovered it to share it with these aspects of my own being, for they're only my being pushed out. There's nothing but God in the world.

We think the Bible is something that records the past. It's contemporary. We think that the Israelites were saved from Egypt by some miraculous act of God unnumbered years ago, thousands of years ago, and we don't know

500

it's taking place *now*. We think the pharaohs died thousands of years ago and we don't know that they are in our present; that any tyrant in this world who can enslave you, who can restrict you, he is a pharaoh, and he will not let my people go.

So without my consent, without any desire on my part, I was picked up, like millions of others when the world thought it needed manpower, and put into the army. Then at that very moment instead of making, say, $10,000-12,000 a year, I was told from now on until they would let me go I'll make $50 a month, not a week. They'll give me my clothes. I had clothes. They'll give me my food. Well, I had food, much better food. They'll give me shelter. Well, I had shelter. I had a home. I had everything I wanted. No, they didn't listen to that, so they put me into a compound, they called it camp, and here, in this area, reduced from $12,000 a year income to $50 a month, without my consent. And I had a lease that ran for quite a while, with a wife and child to support, and all these things. They didn't consider that. Who is pharaoh in this world?

But then I believed in scripture. I believed that with God *all* things are possible, and I firmly believed that God is I AM. There is no other God. I will not in eternity know another God. But the God that I know is a present-tense, first-person experience: "I am the Lord thy God"—first person, present—and so I firmly believed him and I trusted him. So he clothed himself in me and made me alive, that's how I became alive. And now I will trust him implicitly. His name is I AM, he has no other name. There are other names but the *real* name is I AM. And so I will now trust him and test him.

And so, while in Egypt—Egypt means Camp Polk, Louisiana. So that's Egypt—I am in a compound, can't get out of it—a pass to get me out of the gate and then to get back, show the pass again, and there you are, completely restricted. My pharaoh whose heart was hardened . . . when I applied for an exit from this land called Egypt, it was denied. Same story as told us in the Old Testament. So pharaoh said "no" to the children of Israel, "You cannot go. I will not let you depart from Egypt." And so, all the pleas in the world would not soften his heart. He said no to my application. So while this night, believing in the scripture, that the only name of God is I AM, I *assumed* that I am the man that I wanted to be. I assumed that I am where I would be were my assumption realized, and there I slept.

In the wee hours of the morning, four in the morning, before my face came a sheet that resembled the sheet that I had signed and applied for my honorable discharge. And here it came back "disapproved" and signed by a colonel. Didn't sign it pharaoh, but that was pharaoh. He had the power to hold me there forever. That was the power invested in him by the laws of the land. That was pharaoh. But in spite of pharaoh, denial of my application for escape from Egypt, I believed in God. And God's name is I AM. I simply assumed that I am the man that I want to be, a man that is now a civilian, a man that is honorably discharged, a man living in the outer world, not in this compound that is Egypt.

And that night this paper came before my eyes and a hand up to the elbow. The Bible uses the Spirit of God and symbolized it as a finger, as told us in the Book of Judges, that is the finger of the Lord. It tells us in the Book of Daniel the hand appeared and wrote. It tells in Isaiah of the arm of God. So the finger, the hand, and the arm, they are symbols of the activity of God, when one believes in his name, which is I AM. So that night before my face came this sheet and then the arm came out, right to the elbow, it held a pen, and it scratched out "Disapproved" and it *boldly* wrote in above it "Approved." Then I heard the voice of God. It's my own voice in the depth of my soul and the voice said, "That which I have done I have done. Do nothing." So who can stay the *hand* of God? And so, nine days later the same pharaoh who disapproved my application for my exit from Egypt wrote in the word "Approved" and I was honorably discharged.

So we think this means a history that took place 3,000 years ago? It's *taking* place, if you believe in the name of God. There is only God. He actually clothed himself in humanity, *clothed* himself, and we the outward garment, this is the outward garment that he wears. So I ask you a question, you say I am before you say, "I am . . ." That's God. You may not believe it. You're called upon to believe it. The children of Israel found it very difficult to believe in the present tense. They addressed him as "Thou art." That's not his name at all. They speak of God, "he is." That's not his name. His name is I AM. But man can't believe that's the name of God. It's the only name of God that *works* in this world. You can pray forever to some external god and another being, it isn't going to work. Go and tell them when they ask you my name, I am has sent you. Tell to them I AM who I am, I am what I am, I am that which I am. Just say I AM (Exodus 3:14).

But what man will believe that this works? Well, I am speaking from experience. And the only God in this world that never, I would say, I would ever outgrow . . . I could never outgrow this God, not in eternity. But I could never lose the God that I know through a present-tense experience. How could I ever outgrow that God that produced my escape from Egypt? I know exactly how it works. I know exactly what I did. I fell asleep, who fell asleep?—I did. That's his name. It's one, the Holy One. So I really fell asleep. In what manner did you fall asleep? I fell asleep as though I were a free being out of Egypt, living in New York City as a civilian and honorably discharged, so that no one could ever question my exit from that area. My papers were in order. And the one who opposed it nine days later had to sanction my departure from Egypt. And we think Egypt is the northeast shoulder of Africa? Egypt is here. Egypt is wherever you are where you are confined and you can't escape. And the only exit from it is the name of God. If you don't know the name of God and do not wisely *apply* the name of God, you'll never get out of Egypt. And so Egypt is the world of restriction. And the Holy One's *only* name is I AM.

Now here is a true story. You might have read it. It came out in one magazine, oh, maybe a year ago. A man is shaving and his little girl, six years old, comes in and watches the father shave. Suddenly, out of the blue, she said to him, "Daddy, where does God *really* live?" and he, shaving, said, "In the well." In the well. And she said to him, "Oh, Daddy!" with this disgust in her voice, because the reply, the response was so silly, so stupid. So at breakfast that morning his wife said to him, "Say, what have you been telling Debbie about God living in a well?" And he said, "___(??), did I say that to Debbie, that God lives in a well?" It came so absent-mindedly he didn't know he said that. Suddenly in his mind rushed a picture that took place in his boyhood, when he was five years old, thirty-odd years ago in Poland where he was born. Then the story came . . . five years old, and here a troupe of traveling Gypsies and they always travel, they have no place where they can remain forever, and they stopped in his father's courtyard for a drink of water. This giant of a Gypsy, fantastically, marvelous man, with a short-cropped beard that was brilliant and fiery, fiery red, and he drew from that well a bucket of water. With his feet wide apart he took it as easily as you would take a cup of tea, and held it to his mouth and drank from that wonderful pail of cold water, and it dribbled down his red beard. And this little boy, five years old, was intrigued.

When he was finished with his water and placed the pail down, he bent over that well and held the side of the well, and peered into the very depths of it. The little boy was so curious he tried to climb up the side of the well to see what this giant of a Gypsy was looking at. Then the Gypsy saw the little boy and with a big smile on his face he scooped him up in his arms and asked him, "Do you know who lives in there?" The little boy nodded his head "no he didn't." He said, "God lives there." Then he picked him up in his arms, and pushed him over that well and said, "Look!" The little boy said, "Why, it's *me!*" Then the Gypsy said, "Ah! Now you know where God lives."

That's God. There *is* no other God. "It does not yet appear what we shall be, but we know when he appears we shall be like him" (1 John 3:2). There is no other God. God has clothed himself in humanity, actually clothed himself with all of us and he's wearing these garments. He is in the depth of our souls; the *only* God and his *only* name by which he responds is

I AM. You can call him Lord, you can call him God, you can call him Jesus, you can call him anything in the world—but when you call these names it's another. When I say Jesus, and the whole vast world of Christendom crosses themselves, and bends their knees, and they bow; they think of another. So I speak of the Lord, I speak of God, I speak of Jehovah, I speak of any name, but when I say, "I am", it's first person, singular. "Go and tell them my name is I AM. Well, if I say to them I met the God of Abraham, and the God of Isaac, and the God of Jacob, and they say unto me, 'What is his name?' what then shall I say?" "Just say, I AM"—the only name in the world that really works.

And I am speaking from experience. My pharaoh said no, he will not get out from this compound, he will not leave Egypt. And so that was pharaoh's decision. Then I remembered the name of God by which all things are possible, and I assumed that I am what I wanted to be, and that was 2,000 miles away. I assumed that I was not only 2,000 miles away, but I was there so I wouldn't have to run any more; I am there honorably discharged. And so, nine days later that pharaoh's heart melted and then he wrote "Approved" when before he wrote, "Disapproved." But the hand of God appeared before my face. We think this is all symbolism and it is, but, oh, what beautiful imagery! The finger of the Lord appeared, as told us in Judges 6, and then the hand of God appeared in Daniel, and this hand appeared in Isaiah. When the hand appears, it's God in action. It is God.

So the Spirit of the Lord, when it possesses man, you can dramatize that possession in the most marvelous way by seeing God actually clothing himself in that person, and actually wearing that man as though he were an outer garment. For I wore that home of mine like an outer garment. We're told, "Be ye imitators of God as dear children." If I would imitate God and God's name is I AM and he made me alive by wearing me, I'll make anything in this world alive by *wearing* it. And so, I will wear it. I wore that home that normally would not have been seen by me physically until the end of the war, at the end of 1945. Maybe they'd even send me back in 1946, as they did many. But I didn't wait for any end of the war. I didn't wait for the voice of pharaoh. There are always pharaohs in this world. And the man who played the part of a pharaoh, may I tell you, was an awfully nice chap. He didn't know he was playing pharaoh, but he played it for me to make the effort to believe in the name of God. And so, if I did not accept the name of God as reality, I would have played the part and gone through the entire five years, or whatever it was, four years.

But I remembered God's word as revealed and God's word is *contemporary*. People think it happened thousands of years ago, and that this is an entirely different age, it's a different age altogether. This is the *same* age, and all the same people that thousands of years ago believed in the historicity of the story on this level, are reenacting the entire scene. Now they're plotting and planning a trip to a holy land and they believe the holy land is on north shore of Africa. They're going to see where he was born and where he was buried in a tomb, and they don't know where he was born or where he's buried. He is entombed in the skull of man. It's out of that same tomb that he's born, whether you be here in America or in South America or in Africa or in any part of the world, or in Europe, no matter where you are. He is not born in the physical little area called Egypt. Egypt is the world, this whole vast world, and there is *always* that Egypt from which the children of Israel must escape.

So I tell you I'm not speaking from theory, I am speaking from experience. I have experienced scripture, and I know the whole thing is true; every word is true. What a man knows from experience he knows more thoroughly than he knows anything else in this world, or than he can know that same truth in any other way. Tonight, I told you what I did to escape from Egypt in spite of pharaoh's denial of my journey. And you know what *I* have done, or you believe I did it, but you will know it more thoroughly when you apply it and do it. So if tonight you are unemployed, or some loved one is unemployed, and you would only think of it, put him on, and see this radiantly happy world in which you would live after the event, and remain faithful to it. It will be hatched out just as normally as God hatched you out as a living reality in this world. But everything has its own appointed hour. And you can't, because you want it tonight, say it must happen this night. It has its own appointed hour, and it will ripen and it will flower. If to you it seems long, well then, be patient, wait, for it is sure and it will not be late.

So here is this fantastic world in which we live and the story of scripture is true, every word of it is true. You could clothe yourself this night in anything in the world, and it's the same thing that God did to make you alive. He clothed himself with you. He is wearing you as an outer garment. What is the core of that outer garment?—I AM. If I tell you, "Tell me, who are you?" before you answer, whether you use the words I AM or not, you say, "I am so and so and so." That's the core, the heart of you, that's God. But you may not believe that is God, because you identify yourself with the outer garment. But God is working in the depth of our soul and he is breaking down the wall of division between these two and making of the two one, as told us in Ephesians. He breaks it down and makes of the two one new man in place of the two, so we have peace (Ephesians 2:14).

He makes peace that way, because two is division, two simply is conflict. And so he breaks it down within himself, so the two become one to fulfill scripture. And so, he leaves everything in this world and cleaves to his wife until they become one flesh. I am his emanation, you are his emanation. Then he enters his emanation and then he leaves everything until the two become one. So he breaks down that wall of division. So I speak *of God*—that's two—I speak of the Lord, I speak of this, I speak of Jesus, I speak of Christ; but I can't speak *of* I AM, when there's only I AM. That's the Holy One—*one*, not two.

Now listen to the words carefully. It's from the 43rd chapter of the Book of Isaiah: "I am the Lord thy God, the Holy One of Israel, your savior. I, I am the Lord; and besides me there is no savior." Now the word translated, and listen to it carefully, go back, "I am the Lord"—the word translated Lord is the same "I am"—"I am *the* I am." Now the next word is "your God," that is, "*your* I am." I am the I am that is *your* I am—that's what literally it means. "Your savior"—you have no other savior but your own wonderful I am—"and beside me there is no savior."

So I could have written to the President and said, "I'm a good Democrat, and I will vote for you, and I've got the whole community behind me. I want to get out and I'm thirty-eight years old plus." Maybe he would have believed me or investigated my claim and maybe acted upon it. But I didn't write the President; I went straight to the I AM. And so, I granted my colonel his right to say no, "Disapproved." That's his right. He is pharaoh. So am I not the child of Israel asking to let me go? And so I'm pleading, "Please let me go from Egypt" and pharaoh said, "No, disapproved." And so, I slept on my little cot and I assumed that *I am*, and I named it. I clothed myself in that which I desired and I remained nine days hatching it out. So nine days later he, pharaoh, whose heart formerly was like flint, now melts, and he signs the petition without any further appeal on my part. He called me in; I didn't go see him. Nine days later he called me and said, "You still want to get out?" I said yes, sir. So he signed the petition, and then nine days later I was out of Egypt into a land of freedom.

And so I am trying to share with everyone in this world what I know God's name will do. So you think yourself poor? All right, maybe you are poor and therefore you're restricted in the land of Egypt, praying the name of God will get you out. Well, where is it? It isn't God, and it isn't Lord, and it isn't Jesus Christ, none of these, it's I AM. That's the name of God. And so when you go to bed, "I am . . . you name it" and you clothe yourself in it, just as God clothed himself—and his name is I AM—with you. He clothed himself with a man and put it on as you would an outer garment. And then he believed himself the garment; until finally he knows he's *not* the garment, he's the *wearer* of the garment. And the wearer of the garment is I AM. So you try it. And may I tell you no power on earth can stop you from realizing your every desire in this world. And then will come the most fantastic predetermined series of events, that God in the beginning to prove he could come into death, actual death, and escape from it, expanding himself beyond the wildest dream. It is God's doing . . . and God will do it.

So this is the story of the Holy One. The Holy One, the Infinite One, is seated right here in everyone. When you say, "I am" that's he. But if you identify yourself with the garment that you wear and think "I am limited," and look at the world just as you see it, then you will remain in Egypt. The purpose is to get completely out of Egypt, until that moment in time comes when you *really* get out by a series of the most fantastic mystical experiences that could ever be conceived. Normally, one could not conceive the visions. But they're all prophesied in scripture, that series will take place when that moment in time comes for you to *completely* depart for the last time from this world.

But until that moment comes, he who has had the experiences must share it with everyone who is left behind. And so they told him not to talk about it. These are his words in the 20th chapter of the Book of Jeremiah: "If I say I will not mention him or speak any more in his name, then there is in my heart as it were a burning fire, all shut up in my bones, and I am weary with holding it in, and I cannot" (verse 9). I could no more restrain the impulse to tell you what has happened to me and what I have experienced than I could stop breathing now and expect without breath to be five minutes later still in this world in what you call a life, I couldn't. I can't restrain the impulse to talk about it. If I say I will not mention him or speak any more in his name, then there is in my heart as it were a burning fire, all shut up in my bones, and I cannot take it, just cannot.

For, I cannot restrain that impulse to tell you of the true God in this world. And the only true God is housed in you as your own wonderful human Imagination. So that, "All that you behold, though it appears without, it is within, in your wonderful human Imagination, and this fabulous world of mortality is but its shadow." (Blake, *Jerusalem*, Plate 71) You have never really been included in the world that you describe. The world that is described from observation is always, as it is described, relative to the describing observer. He can't put himself into the thing he describes, not in eternity. It is always less than himself, the observer, I don't care who you are. When I describe a world it is always relative to myself who describes it, and I can't include myself, the describer, in the world as I am describing it. I am always greater than the world I describe, and that's God. And so, you simply describe a world. And then, although it is less than you, to have the experience of it, then put it on as a garment. It's less than you, but put it on as a garment. So God put this thing on as a garment, he put all these on as garments; he put the world on as a garment. But he who wears it is infinitely greater, and always will be greater than that which he wears and that which he describes. He can't include himself into his description of the universe.

So you try it. You try it this night. And if it doesn't work tomorrow morning . . . mine didn't work the next day, although I saw the picture. The very first night I did it the hand came, the hand of God, and I knew it was done. But I waited nine days, and nine days later it was done. I didn't go berserk in the interval waiting; I waited patiently; I knew it was done. And I knew, in spite of that wonderful man, who was my colonel, he had no choice in the matter. No, not even if at that very moment he had to drop dead in the world and his successor would sign the thing, it would make no difference to me, none whatsoever. I wouldn't have killed him. I wouldn't have shot him. But no matter what happened, either he, himself, as the bearer would sign it or he would be displaced and someone would sign it, that's the law.

For when the hand of God appeared . . . and "who can stay his hand, or say unto him, 'What doest thou?'" So when you see the hand, the hand is like the Spirit of the Lord. In fact, in the Book of Matthew they use the word Spirit in the 12th chapter and Luke in the 11th chapter uses the word finger: "If I by the Spirit of the Lord cast out demons," and then in Luke, "If I by the finger of the Lord cast out demons." So they accused him of casting out these things in a strange way. So the Spirit of the Lord in one book is called the finger of the Lord in the other. When you see it, all the imagery of scripture is true. They didn't make it up. The evangelists did not sit down and try to figure out some workable philosophy of life. They simply had the vision and put it down. In the Old Testament they weren't working out some philosophy of life. They had the vision and they put it down. So when one called it the finger of the Lord, and one called it the hand of the Lord, and one called it the arm of the Lord, it's the same thing as the Spirit of the Lord.

So when the Spirit of the Lord descends upon man in bodily form as a dove it never departs thereafter. But until it descends upon man in bodily form as a dove, you can have it descend upon you temporally by remembering his name and invoking it. But when it descends upon you in bodily form as a dove it never departs from that moment on. But until then, it will come in temporal form, and you can do as I did when pharaoh said no to my request. And in spite of his no, you get out anyway.

So this is the story that I have this night on the Holy One. It is One with a capital O-n-e, and "This is my name forever, for all generations" you're told—the 3rd chapter, the 14th-16th verses on in the Book of Exodus—"Go and tell them, it's my name forever; I have no other name."

The 3rd chapter of Exodus, beginning at the 14th verse, when this fantastic revelation is made to man. And so here, when you say "I am" that's he, and there is no other God. He isn't today in some high office, other than where he is where you are now. So don't go to ___(??) yourself. You'll never find him, where he was born or where he was buried. He is buried in your own wonderful human skull, that's where he's buried. And he's dreaming the most fantastic dream. I'm showing you how to change the dream by the use of his name, until that day when he awakens from the dream to find himself entombed, and then he comes out. When he comes out, the whole world changes to him. Never again will he enter that tomb. He's left it. He enters an entirely different world, a world that is prepared, waiting for the out coming of the Dreamer, who is God.

Now let us go into the Silence.

*   *   *

Q: (inaudible)

A: ___(?) since this night? No, no. ___(??) it was so vivid. In fact I should have told it, but a friend of mine who came to me in correction of the manuscript of my book when I told that story, I told the entire story to him, and he said, "Were I you, I would delete the mystical aspect of the story, because people reading the book will think they must have that vision in order to get the similar results." And so, I abided by his decision and did not tell it as it actually happened. I told the story, but deleted the mystical aspect of it, which I should not have done. But he prevailed and told me that it would be better for posterity if it did not have it attached to some mystical aspect. Because, whether you actually saw the hand or not, if you believe in the name of God and trusted him implicitly, falling asleep clothed in your wish fulfilled, it would work without the name of the hand, or the finger, or the arm. But I did not incorporate into that story the actual experience that I had for the simple reason I thought he might be wise in his recommendation. Some, never having had a vision, would think, well now, I must have the vision in order to make it work. So I believed him and so I didn't tell the story in its completeness.

Q: (inaudible)

A: The first coming? The kingdom of the Lord? I stood in his presence and I knew exactly, he incorporates his body and makes us all equal, one by one. But I would not be the first who told it. It's told in the Bible, in the Book of Daniel, the Book of Revelation. (Tape ends.)

ASK WHAT I SHALL GIVE YOU

December 17, 1963

Tonight's subject is, "What shall you ask of me?" This story we find in the Book of Genesis, we find it in the Book of Samuel, and repeated again in the New Testament. It really begins with ___(??) "What wilt thou give me?" and that is in the 15th of Genesis. Then he said, "I am childless, I have no heir . . . and a slave boy in my home will be my heir" and he was told, "The slave will not be your heir; your own son will be your heir." Then we are told, "As the sun went down, a deep sleep fell upon Abram; and a dread and great darkness fell upon him. Then the Lord God said to him, "For a surety your descendants will be sojourners in a land that is not theirs, and they will be as slaves in that land; they will be oppressed for four hundred years . . . and afterwards they will come out with great possessions" (verses 12-14). Now, there's not a word said that Abram was in any way awakened from this sleep, not a word. He fell into a deep sleep and all this was told him in a deep sleep, and there was a dread and great darkness that fell upon him.

Now this is our subject this night. He asked for a son; he was promised a son. Then we are told in the story, as he dreamed and the son was mentioned, he made this statement, he fell on his face and laughed when he was told he would have a son. And said he, "Shall a man who is a hundred years old have a son? Shall Sarah, who is ninety years old, bear a child? And said that he laughed—is this the laughter of derision, laughter of incredulity, or the laughter of rejoicing? We're told in the scripture of John that "Abraham rejoiced that he was to see my day; he saw it, and was glad" (John 8:56). You can take it in any form you want. Either you can say, well, he laughed because of disbelief, or he laughed, he rejoiced he was to see my day; he saw it and was glad.

Now when we read scripture, we're not reading secular history, we're reading divine history. Man is not aware of that. The Bible is a vision. It is a mystery to be known only by revelation. And those who think they know it by trying to analyze it they're far removed from the truth. It comes by revelation and only by revelation. If you haven't had the experience, listen to one who has had it, and either believe him or disbelieve him. Don't try to rationalize it. So I will tell you and I have told you what I have seen, and you will not accept my testimony. Seeing and knowing in the Greek are one. Seeing is experiencing. He is telling you, I have experienced it and you will not believe it, because I can't share it with you on the level where you now live.

And so here, what is he trying to tell us in this story of falling asleep and being told what must happen to man? Well, first of all, we're reading in the Hebrew. Every letter in the Hebrew world, as it were, has a numerical value and a symbolical value. He was a hundred years old. The nineteenth letter of the Hebrew alphabet is Qoph. If you want to sound it, Q-o-p-h, Qoph. We put a q in the q. The symbol of it is "the back of the head." The number, its numerical value is a hundred. A man is not a hundred years old. This is a mystery. Here is a hundred., a hundred what? The number of the back of the head. He is being told you will bear a son; it will come from the back of your skull. And so you will say, he fell on his face and laughed. That's ridiculous on this level. It comes from the womb of a woman. But he is told, he's a hundred years old, and you will bear a son, and it will come from the back of your skull. Well, you can take the laughter in any way you want, either the laughter of disbelief, or, as we're told in the Book of John, the 8th chapter, rejoicing. "He rejoiced that he was to see my day; he saw it, and was glad"(verse 56).

Now we are told in this story, your descendants will be sojourners in a land that is not theirs. It's this world. We don't belong here. These garments belong here. Every garment in this world is part of the eternal structure of this world. No matter what you do, it's part of the eternal structure of this world. When Kennedy was shot, that is taking place forever and forever as part of the structure of this world, and the one who pulled the trigger is pulling it forever as part of the structure of this world. God gets into this world as a sojourner and in this is the land that is not his as it were. In this he is as a slave: "took upon himself the form of man and became obedient unto death, even death upon the cross" (Philippians 2:6-8). Death upon the cross—we think it took place on the north shore of Africa two thousand years ago.

Now listen to the next line in this statement, "And they will be oppressed for four hundred years . . . afterward they will come out and have great possessions." Four hundred years. The last letter of the Hebrew alphabet, the twenty-second letter, Tau, has a numerical value of four hundred and the symbolical value of a cross. The symbol of Tau is a cross and it is numerically four hundred. So here, for four hundred years—not four hundred years as we measure time. No, this is the journey: we are sojourners in a land that is not ours. And while we journey we are enslaved, and while we are enslaved we are oppressed for the length of time that it takes for us to come out with great possessions. And the possession is not only the kingdom of God; we will possess not only the kingdom, we possess the King (Ezekiel 44:28). We possess a presence; the presence is God. So we go through the horror of the world and come out as God. God becomes as we are that we may be as he is.

So that's the story of this journey that is a horrible journey, frightful horror. But in the end, we possess a great man, and great possessions, and possess a presence, and the presence is God. All ends run true to origins: if the origin is God, the end is God. "You see yonder fields! The sesame was sesame; the corn was corn. The Silence and the Darkness knew! And so was a man's fate born" *(Light of Asia)*. So the origin is God and the end is God. There is nothing but God.

So in this story he makes the statement, "Before Abraham was, I am. Your father Abraham rejoiced that he was to see my day; he saw it, and he was glad." They said to him, "Why, you are not yet fifty years old, and you have seen Abraham?" He said, "Before Abraham was, I am." So I stand before you now, I am approaching fifty-nine, and yet I know there's a David, for David is my son. Is a father not older than his son? Did he not call me Father? Did David not call me Lord? "What think ye of the Christ? Whose son is he?" "The son of David." The son of David? "Why then did David in the spirit call him Lord? If David doth call him Lord, how can he be David's son?" (Matthew 22:42). But you're not yet fifty. It doesn't matter. You say he is 3,000 years from this moment in time? Well, he called me Father. If he calls me Father, am I not older than he is? Well, he called me Father. So he called me Father, am I not older than Abraham? Then who are you talking about? I am talking only, at every moment of time, about God. There's nothing but God.

So, what shall I give you? What was the answer to that statement? "O Lord God, let thy promise to David my father be now fulfilled" (2 Chronicles 1:9). Well, what was that promise? That "When your days are fulfilled and you lie down with your fathers, I will raise up your son after you, who shall come forth from your body. I will be his father and he shall be my son" (2 Samuel 7:12). Let that promise now be fulfilled. So he brings forth from humanity, from you, from the back of your skull; that's the being I will bring out of you. You're a hundred years old? That's Qoph, the back of the skull. I will bring forth from you a son. And so he laughed. The whole thing was crazy, ridiculous. It's so unnatural. It's not something that could ever happen in eternity. This is not a natural birth; it's a spiritual birth—born from above, not from below. And so he comes out. Let it happen now, said he.

But before it happens, can I ask for anything else? Certainly. Listen to these words, "If you ask anything in my name, I will do it." You want to check it? The 14th chapter, the 14th verse of the gospel of John, "If you ask anything in my name, I will do it." Well, who is speaking? They never once addressed him as Jesus. They spoke of him, but never addressed him as Jesus. Jesus and Jehovah are one and the same. When we translate the word Jehovah, Yod He Vau He, which is really I AM, we always speak of it as the Lord. Only on rare occasions do we say I AM, as in Exodus, "Go and say unto them, 'I AM sent you. I AM that I AM. I am what I am. I am who I am.'" But beyond this and a few statements, it's always translated as the Lord. So they speak of him as the Lord in the New Testament, not Jesus. No one addresses him as Jesus and then, "Jesus, tell us so and so," but "Lord, show us the way." "I AM the way." "Lord, show us the Father." "I AM the Father." So, always, the Lord is the name given to him. So when he's called the Lord, he's called the Father.

So here, "If you ask anything in my name, I will do it." So the name is not Jesus, the name is not Jehovah, the name is not the Lord, the name is I AM. That's the name. Well, how would I ask for health or wealth or fame in his name? By daring to assume that I am healthy, when the doctors give me no hope. By daring to assume that I am wealthy, when all my creditors are on my neck. By daring to assume that I am known, when I am, by reason of my senses, unknown. And so daring to assume that I am that which I want to be, when at the moment of my assumption reason and my senses deny it, is asking in his name. There is no other name. "If you ask anything in my name, I will do it."

Well then, test him. You're invited to test him. Come prove him and see. "Do you not know that Jesus Christ is in thee?—unless, of course, you fail to meet the test!" (2 Corinthians 13:5). So we're invited to test him in his name, and his name is I AM. Let everyone dare to assume that I am . . . and then name it. Then see the world as you would see it were it true. What evidence have I that I really am this before it becomes objective to the world? Well, the only evidence that I have now is to see on the faces of my friends an expression implying recognition of that which I am. Let me look at my friends mentally and see them seeing me as they would see me were it true. Let me now see my world as I would see it were it true. And then, if in the not distant future I crystallize that which I am assuming into this world, by a way that consciously I could never devise, the thing happens, then haven't I found him and I know who he is?

Well, I tell you this story is true from beginning to end, but not as the world sees it. They're trying to see it as secular history, and it's not; it's divine history. The whole drama unfolds in man. And the story of Abraham is true. In the depths of the soul God slept. It is God who fell asleep. It is God who fell to make sons, to bring us into the world as sons. And because the father and the son are one, if the father and the son are one, then the son must be father. If he's a father, then there must be a son. And who is that son? If I and my father are one, and my father is Father, then who is the son?—David. David is the Son of God. Jesus Christ is God the Father. It's Jesus Christ in us that is buried that must awaken. And as he awakens and is the father, then how do I know I am a father? Where is the son? And then comes David.

Now, the nineteenth letter, Qoph, is "the back of the head." Out of that will come the child. You'll be born, right out of the back of that skull of yours. I'm speaking from experience; I am not theorizing. Having come out of the back of the head, then there must be a son bearing witness of the being that you are. The next letter is Resh, and its value is 200. Its symbol is the head but the crown of the head, the whole head, but, above all, the crown of the head. All right, so out of the crown of the head will come this explosion and right before you one day will stand this immortal son, David. You look into his face and you see David and he will call you Father.

Now, you are only fifty years old. "And you not yet fifty years old and you know David?" Yes. Before David was, I am. Well, I AM is the name of his father. His father was called Jesse, and Jesse is any form of the verb "to be": it is I AM. And so he calls you Father. And so you look right into the eyes of David, and yet in this world of mortality you're only fifty. And you can say, "Yes, before David was, I am." Because the father precedes the son, and the son calls you Father. And so you will know in the eyes of those who are still blind you are only fifty. And they know your background. They know exactly where you began in this linear world, as one ___(??) blind as it were. So you know, in spite of what they think you are, you have experienced the fatherhood of David. And David is God's only begotten son: "Thou art my son, today I have begotten thee," the 2nd Psalm, 7th verse. It's addressed to David, in spite of the priesthoods of the world. No matter how they try to justify it and call that Jesus Christ, they are in error. They're not speaking from experience; they're theorizing. And the whole vast world takes the Word of God, and theorizes it, and comes up with false conclusions because their premises are wrong. Their beginnings are wrong.

It is David. And when you see him you know without any uncertainty that he is your son, and he knows without any uncertainty you are his father.

It is David that God buried in the mind of man. As told us in the 3rd chapter, the 11th verse of the Book of Ecclesiastes: "And God has placed eternity into the mind of man, yet so that man cannot find out what God has done from the beginning to the end." But at the end he will. When man comes to the last days of his journey, when the pilgrimage is over, and the oppression is over, and he comes into his inheritance, then David explodes out of his brain. From the top of his head this time, not from the base of his skull. He came out of the base of his skull, but the Son of God, buried in his head, comes out of the top of his skull, the king, and he is the father of that only begotten son. The son calls him Father, and he sees him, and they both meet in an understanding that no one on this level could really grasp.

So I say believe it. Believe it, because the beatitude is pronounced upon those who did not see and yet believed. By seeing they didn't experience it, and yet they believed the one who tells them he has experienced it. That beatitude is given to us at the end of the 20th chapter of the gospel of John. So they may not see, yet they believed. But many who did not see still would not believe, because they insisted on taking it on this level. I tell you, "Abraham rejoiced that he was to see this day, my day. He saw it—experienced it—and was glad."

So this is the story: What shall I give you? You can ask this night for help. You can ask for anything in this world. But the day will come that you'll have a hunger that only an experience of God can satisfy. "I will send a famine upon the land; not a famine of bread, nor a thirst for water, but of hearing the words of God"—a hunger that only an experience of God can satisfy (Amos 8:11). And so, until that hunger comes upon you, believe the one who had such a hunger. Whose hunger has been satisfied by having experienced David as his son; and can with scripture, "What think ye of the Christ, whose son is he?" And when they answer, "Why the son of David," then he replied, "Why then did David in the spirit call him Father?" He called him Adonay, my Lord, which is the name used by every son of his father. Every son referred to his father as Adonay, my Lord. So David calls him "my Lord," how then can he be David's son?

So tonight you can ask for anything in his name, if you know his name. Get down on your knees and say, "In the name of Jesus," not a thing is going to work. "In the name of God, in the name of Jehovah, name of this?"—no answer, no response. Ask in his name and his name is I AM. So without any help from anyone in this world, dare to assume "I am . . ." and then name it. "I am employed, gainfully employed." Don't ask others if you can make it. "I'm gainfully employed, making more than I have ever made in my life." Let them say what they will. Things will reshuffle themselves in this world. And you, by being faithful to his name, will externalize what you are claiming by your assumption, and it becomes fact. Then you can share it with the whole vast world.

So, "If you ask anything in my name, I will do it." Who will do it? Jesus on the outside? No, Jesus is in you. God became man that man may become God. Listen to the words, "Do you not realize that Jesus Christ is in thee?—unless of course you fail to meet the test!" I am quoting from Paul's letters to the Corinthians. It's the thirteenth chapter, the last chapter, of 2 Corinthians, "Do you not realize that Jesus Christ is in thee?" (verse 5). Well, if he is in me, and making these statements "Ask in my name," well then, I know his name. He said, "I am the truth." You mean of anything that I claim? Yes, because all things are possible to God, and his name is I AM. And I am the truth? The truth of what? The truth that is confined to the evidence of my senses?—certainly not! Truth is determined by the intensity of my Imagination, not upon the evidence of my senses. So I dare to assume that I am what I want to be, and assuming it, remaining faithful to it, I externalize it. It becomes a fact in my world.

So here, "Ask what I shall give you." The day will come you will ask, as Solomon asked, "Let thy promise to David my father be now fulfilled." And that promise: let the son be born. For he promised him that when his days are fulfilled and he lies down with his fathers, he will raise up after him his son, who will come out of his body; and that you will be the father and he will be your son. Let that now be done. Let him come out. Let him bring forth David out of me. For David, the origin is David, the end is David. Bring him out, out of me. If you bring him out of me and your name is I AM, or Jesse, and I see David, then I am Jesse. I AM the I AM of whom I spoke and others discussed, but I didn't know it.

Suddenly he comes out, and the only way in this world I would ever know that I am he is by the son. "For no one knows who the Father is except the Son, and no one knows who the Son is except the Father" (Matthew 11:27). So if I could only know it by reason of the Son, then let that Son come. Bring him out. So what comes out of David but David. He brings David out. Well then, if he brings him out of me, this garment must have been David. Humanity then is David; the whole vast world of mankind is David. But, bring something out that I know when I see him; it's altogether different. And you do. Well, then who brought him out? It came out of me. He actually came out of me and I saw him, and he called me Father.

You dwell upon it. It's something entirely different, but you dwell upon it. It's far more than if this night I put into the hands of everyone here a fabulous earthly fortune, for the earthly fortune disappears. It all withers, it all vanishes like smoke, but this of which I speak never passes away. This is the immortal faith. And so, you can have anything in this world that you want, but anything, if you ask in his name, and his name is I AM. But the day will come, you will have a hunger, a hunger that not a thing in this world—you can go from lecture to lecture, from place to place—and nothing can satisfy you but an experience of God, to know that God really exists.

And God is a person. You're a person. Well, God is a person *in* your own very being. He becomes you and raises you up through this horrible experience that ___(??). Listen to the words, "Your descendants will be sojourners in a land that is not theirs." Can't take one piece with you. If Rockefeller dies tonight, he can't take one shilling with him. Has to leave it just where it is, as his father did and his grandfather did. His grandfather left a billion dollars; couldn't take a penny with him. And then, the father left hundreds of millions and he couldn't take one-half penny with him. All the others will leave it all behind and they can't take a penny with them. Leave it just where it is.

So they will be in a land that is not theirs, and while in that land they will be as slaves. Who is not a slave? Can Rockefeller buy health with billions of dollars? Oh yes, he can have all the doctors in the world, all the services of doctors, but can't buy health. I know people sell you health out of bottles and out of health stores and all kinds of things, and those who run the little businesses from their health stores die just as young and just as painfully as the others. So they all have the same exit, with all their little things, selling you all kinds of things: "You will live forever." At forty you read his obituary.

And so, they play all these little parts. They're all slaves in this world. And they will be, as we are told, oppressed for 400 years—as long as they wear the cross of the flesh. This is the cross on which Jesus Christ is crucified, not any wooden cross. This cross, this is the 400 years, the Tau, the twenty-second letter of the Hebrew alphabet. It is on this—not 400 years by measure of time but as long as it takes to bring me out. There is one disconcerting note in the 28th chaper of the Book of Deuteronomy, which I would not fret, but the whole chapter implies that the time is not really measured as we understand time; that if at the very end of what we should think would be the whole journey we start it all over again. Start it all over again. It is not explained why, because God is playing the parts, and I can't understand how God could fail in what he has predetermined, I can't. But, nevertheless, there is the word of God in the 28th of Deuteronomy. But I will say to everyone, don't be disturbed by it. The end is determined. God will not fail.

He will not fail; he brings everyone out. And when he brings us out we're all equal. We're all God the Father, and all have the same Son. What symbol in this world would make you and I one more than to be the father of the same son? If you look into the eyes of my son and you know he's your son, and I look into the eyes of that same son and know he is my son, are we not one, one Father? "For in that day the Lord will be one and his name one." We'll be one, although seemingly many. So it is a oneness made up of many. So "Hear, O Israel: The Lord our God is one Lord." "Hear, O Israel, the Lord"—and the word Lord is the I AM—"our God"—our I ams—"is one I AM." So the whole vast world of . . . everyone can say, "I am" . . . and that forms our God. And together it is the I AM. The one Father of the one Son, and we're all the Father of that one Son, so we're all one. And that's how it unfolds in this world.

Now what I'm telling you this night I'm telling you from experience, I am not theorizing. I've gone on panels with priests, with rabbis, with Protestant ministers, with great educators, and they stand aghast, because it's not what they ever conceived. I can't blame them. It has not been revealed to them. They're speculating and I am not speculating. I'm not trying to set up some workable philosophy of life. I'm telling you what happened to me. It happened to me as naturally as a natural physical birth happens to another. So I think it, at the moment, disturbing, and then you go back into scripture and you read it to find it was all foretold.

Now listen to this lovely poem by Edward Thomas, "Now first as I shut the door I was alone in the new house, and the wind began to moan. Old at once was the house, and I was old. My ears were teased by the dread of what was foretold. Nights of storm, days of mist without end, sad days, when the sun shown in vain. Old griefs and griefs not yet begun. All was foretold me, naught could I foresee, but I learned how the wind would sound after these things should be." You dwell upon it. The new house—God enters this world of death. For we're all dead, we're part of the eternal structure of the universe, every garment in the world. It's new. He buries himself and shuts the door, and he's alone in the new house. Then the wind began to moan. In scripture, the wind and the Spirit are one and the same word. And then, the whole thing is foretold him, but naught could he foresee—the horrible oppression in the land of Egypt, this world. And only at the very end do you really realize how the wind really sounds. "All was foretold me, naught could I foresee, but I learned how the wind would sound after these things should be."

May I tell you, when this thing happens that was foretold in the beginning: I'll give you a son, when you're a hundred years old, and ___(??) to the back of your head, that's where you'll come from, and I fall on my face and laugh, it's ridiculous. It's the most unnatural thing in the world. Or, maybe I rejoice because I saw it and was glad. But then the journey starts and, oh, what horrible nights and misty days when the sun shone in vain. But I didn't quite understand until the very end. The story is "But I learned how the wind would sound after these things should be." And when it happens, now you know how the wind really sounds. The whole house vibrates like a cyclone and you don't know what is causing it, and you wonder where it is coming from. You feel it in you, and yet you feel it coming from the far corner of the room.

And then come the wise men to discover what has happened. Now listen to the words, "And Abraham sat in the door of his tent in the heat of the day and looked up and beheld three men standing before him." They were not seen approaching, suddenly they are standing before him, three men, exactly as described in the 18th chapter of Genesis. Suddenly, three men stand before him . . . and the wind begins to moan. They, too, are disturbed. And may I tell you, of the three, two also laugh. They laugh because it seems to them incredible what one is announcing, that the child is born. One announces it; and two are completely hysterical with laughter because what has happened shouldn't happen; it's incredible. But he presents the evidence of what he's declared. And then and only then do you know. So I learned then how the wind would sound after these things should be.

So believe it, and let that beatitude be pronounced upon you who have not seen and yet believed. You haven't had the experience, but believe one who has had the experience. I am not theorizing; I am speaking from experience. And a truth which man knows from experience he knows more thoroughly than he knows anything else in this world, or than he can know that same truth in any other way. You know it tonight because you believe me; I hope you do, but you don't know it to the extent you will know it after these things should be in you when you experience it. So I tell you, no matter what you hear from others, if they experience it they will duplicate what you've heard from this platform tonight. If they have not had the experience, they'll speculate from now 'til the ends of time, and might be persuaded and try to convince you of the reality of their speculations. So, it's entirely up to you. I am not theorizing.

So, what shall I give you? The last question, or the last one is, "Let it now be fulfilled." What fulfilled? The promise you made to David my father. And that is that you'd bring out of him a son, and the son will be your son, and you will be that son's father. Let it now be fulfilled. That comes from the very top of the skull, Resh. Before that is fulfilled, you have to come out of the back of the skull, Qoph. And so you are the Abraham when it happens and you are a hundred years old, though in the body you're but fifty. The hundred is Qoph and the symbol is the back of the skull. Out you come and you are born, and you see the symbol of your birth. The next one is the explosion from Resh, the top of the skull, and that which comes out is David, and he's your son.

So here, we are in the spirit of Christmas, a week from tomorrow. The whole vast Christian world will celebrate the birth of Christ, and I wonder what proportion of an nth part of one percent will really know the story. They've been taught it, but, may I tell you, they've been taught it erroneously. They're now making some great caravan to go off to Jerusalem to find the birthplace. He wasn't born there at all. To find where they put him in some sepulcher, and he wasn't buried there at all. It is God who became man that man may become God, and he's buried in man's wonderful human skull. That's where he's buried and it's from there that he will be resurrected. There's no other place in the world from which he'll be resurrected. He's resurrected right out of your own wonderful skull, and the whole drama takes place there. And so, every word of scripture is literally true in the depths of the soul, but not on the level where now man finds himself in the world of Caesar.

Now let us go into the Silence. And if tonight you really want a home, more than you really want Solomon's request—which you read in the 1st chapter of 2nd Corinthians—if you want a home or you want a job or you want money or you want these things more, don't for one second let anyone divert you. You can get them. "If you ask anything in my name, I'll do it." You don't have to ask for Solomon's request, you can ask for dresses, for suits, for homes, for fame, for anything, but ask it in my name.

*   *   *

Q: (inaudible)
A: It will happen to man while wearing a female garment. As you know, God, when we speak of man, man is neither male nor female. Male and female are garments that man wears. God being man, God became man, so he wears garments, but he's not male and not female. We're told in Paul's letters to Timothy that woman will be saved, that is a female, will be saved by the bearing of *the* child. It is wrongly translated "by the bearing of children." But there's a footnote to that word and in the footnote you will read that the actual Greek is "the bearing of the child," not "the bearing of children." So the only salvation for man is the experience of being born from above. "For except ye be born from above, you cannot in any wise enter the kingdom of heaven" (John 3:3). And the birth from above is symbolized in the sign of the child.

So whether I wear a female garment or a male garment, that birth can take place, because wearing a female garment is same as wearing a male garment. Because I am not a male and I am not a female, I am man. And man is above—in the resurrection he's above the organization of sex. "For in the resurrection they neither marry nor are they given in marriage" (Luke 20:34). That relationship belongs only here. So, because this is a divided image, male, female, it doesn't really matter which garment I wear when it happens. Of that I am convinced. I can't conceive of waiting for wearing a male garment when I'm not a male. It's from the back of the skull, and Qoph is the back of the skull, whether you're female or male. It's from there that this child is born. That's when you come out, for that's where you are.

Q: (inaudible)

A: Depending upon the request for the evening. I've had about five or six interviews before coming on the platform tonight, and I made a composite picture, and just simply assume that they all are telling me the things they would like to tell me.

Q: (inaudible)

A: My dear, as far as the great mystery of the Bible goes, I feel that comes in its own good time, I really do. I firmly believe, as you're told in Habakkuk: "The vision has its own appointed hour; it ripens, it will flower. If it be long, then wait; for it is sure and it will not be late." So God's vision for us has its own appointed hour and it will not be late. It may seem late to us. Because others will say of me, I am from a very, well, business-like family. We have no ministers in our background, we have no artists in the background, no intellectuals in my background; we're sheer down-to-earth businessmen, and they've all been hugely successful in the world of business.

A man said to me in Barbados two years ago, "But, Neville, how could this have happened to you? You are a Goddard." I said, "What does that have to do with it?" Well, he said, they're all business people. I said, Don't judge ___(??). Where do you think he went? He went with the harlots, and the tax collectors, and all the sinners of the world. He was not seen among the Sanhedrin; they wouldn't give him shelter. And the so-called prominent people in society would not entertain him. And those who were fabulously rich, they would not entertain him. Although he was kept, as told us in the 8th chapter of Luke, by wealthy women, and they mentioned three women and said, "And others also gave him of their means." But he was not seen among the prominent noble people of the world.

And so I said to him, as far as I am concerned, yes, I'm from a very successful business family, but there's no reason why God should not in his own great secret select me for the gift. It's all grace, anyway; you don't earn it. If you earned it, maybe I should come from a very pious family. But piety hasn't a thing to do with God's grace. And the secret of his selective love is his secret and not known by any person in the world. The whole vast world is taught to believe they can earn God's grace. Then it ceases to be grace. You can't earn grace. Grace is an unmerited gift.

But who knows the background of the individual soul? You are oppressed for four hundred years, and four hundred years is not four hundred years. It could be unnumbered thousands of years that you have been in Egypt, this world, on the wheel of recurrence, as told us in Ecclesiastes. And at a moment in time, God, in his infinite mercy, steps beyond and redeems you in the body of Jesus. You are incorporated into the body of Jesus; therefore you are Jesus because you are part of the body of Jesus. Therefore it's your body he wears and your body and his body that you wear. And so it's all God's love; his infinite mercy does it. So when you think you ought to earn it by joining the priesthoods of the world, or moving away to the Himalayas and sitting in the silence and being very, very holy, and then not eating this or not eating that, and not wearing certain things, not wearing other things, that is all trying to acquire merit. And you can't by merit receive the grace of God. It would cease to be grace. And it's all grace. So I can't tell anyone the moment in time when that grace will shine upon you.

Q: ___(??) wanting to move off into the Himalayas, or whatever, is that an indication of this hunger that you spoke of earlier is there?

A: That I don't know, sir. I personally never had that hunger to get away. I came into the fields of America from little tiny Barbados, and my desire was to come right down into the market place, which is America. He said, Let us build a tabernacle forever, one for you, one for Moses, one for Elijah. He said, no, you go down into the valley, you can't remain here. You must go down among the people of the world. It's there that the corners are rubbed off, as it were. How would I ever know that I could take God's law and by applying it wisely and lovingly produce the effects that I desire in any place other than the market place? And so, when I had nothing in this world, but nothing, and I was hungry, I had no desire to steal. I had no desire to take from another what I felt was theirs; I had none. And I went without food; I went without things. I had no desire to run away from it. I could have gone back to Barbados where I could have had my three wonderful meals a day and a shelter in my father's home. It was always open. I could have sent a wire, even on borrowed money, and received notice to take a certain boat at his expense. But I didn't. I had no desire to run away from it. I remained in the market place, and it was there that these things were rubbed off. I was placed in all kinds of temptations to get an easy dollar. It never occurred to me to take it.

And so, at that moment in time, then God, and only God, made the decision to simply step beyond and redeem me in his body. And so, I can tell you the story of redemption from experience. I said earlier, and I'll say it again, anyone who has been redeemed ascribes the entire process of his salvation to God's actions. He, himself, has had not a thing to do with it, but nothing. Even his faith seems as a gift of God. So you can't earn it.

I cannot honestly look myself in the face and say that I did anything to earn it. But in his infinite mercy he has hid from me the past through which he placed me, for he certainly put me through the paces. But it's not yet been revealed the furnaces through which . . . but "Whom God has afflicted for secret ends, then he comforts and heals and calls him friend." So we are told in the 48th of Isaiah, I have put you through the furnaces of affliction. For my own sake, I do it, for my own sake, for how should my glory be given to another? (verse 10) He couldn't give it to another. He has to so make you a man after his own heart that it is his heart. He can't give it to another.

And so I say, play your part fully, play it well, always tinged with love. If you are tempted to do something that isn't a loving thing, would I like it done unto me? Well, then if you wouldn't, then don't do it. Try not to do it. But in the end, when you least expect it. (Tape ends.)

CHRISTMAS: THE REDEEMING MESSAGE

12/19/1963

Tonight's subject is "Christmas, The Redeeming Message." If you owned the world, but really literally owned the world and all within it, and a billion dollars your servant, and at the end of your short journey here that was all, wouldn't that be sheer nonsense? Well, Christmas, the redeeming message, is that man lives forever.

This is the story. There is a West Indian carol called "Mary's Boy-child": "Jesus Christ was born on Christmas Day and because of this birth man lives forever more." That's a recent thing from the West Indies. But centuries ago this story broke upon the world. Men wanted it, they speculated, but they couldn't quite discover the secret hidden in the Old Testament. And they thought, and thought that by searching the scriptures, but they could not find the Christ of whom they spoke and of whose coming they foretold. They just couldn't find it, because it wasn't in the way they expected it.

Paul makes the statement in the second letter to the Corinthians, the 4th chapter, the 2nd verse, and he speaks of a treasure: "We have this treasure in earthen vessels." When you read it, you wonder what is he talking about, we have this treasure in earthen vessels. It means "conditioned by human limitation: the limitation of human understanding, human language, the meaning of words, and especially that limit set to one person's unveiling of his own inner consciousness to another." How could one who is the first really tell it, for everyone knew him in the world as a normal person? And this has been going on for unnumbered ages and suddenly "at length for hatching ripe he breaks the shell." And he tells it, and he tells it with all the limitations of the earthen vessel, called man. Well, how could he tell it to persuade anyone that this is what was foretold?

Now tonight I will tell it just as it happened. And I hope that someone in the audience—I know that there are many from time to time who may add to it memory images of what I've said. Others have taken it down on tape; others have taken it down in shorthand, but they've taken it down. The story that you're told in the Book of Luke . . . Luke, if you listen carefully, in the very first four verses: "Inasmuch as many have undertaken to compile a narrative of the things which happened among us, just as they were declared by those who from the beginning were eyewitnesses and ministers of the word, so it seemed good to me also, having followed all things closely for some time past, to write an orderly account for you, most excellent Theophilus, that you may know the truth concerning the things of which you have been informed." He does not claim he was an eyewitness, but he followed closely those who were eyewitnesses.

In scripture, an eyewitness is one who has experienced it. The one essential to be an Apostle was to see the risen Christ, as told us in the first chapter of the Book of Acts. No one can be sent—for an Apostle means one sent—unless he himself experienced the risen Christ. It's called "seeing the risen Christ." You don't see it as another; you experience your own resurrection; that is "seeing" Christ. "For Christ in you is the hope of glory." "I tell you a mystery," he said, "a mystery hidden from all ages, all generations, and now made manifest to his saints . . . this mystery, which is Christ in you, the hope of glory" (Colossians 1:26, 27). And so, the one condition imposed upon one who would be sent is that he saw, that is, he experienced the risen Christ.

Luke does not claim that he saw it; therefore, he doesn't claim he experienced it. But he claims, listen to it carefully, "Inasmuch as many"—and there were many prior to Luke—"who attempted to compile a narrative of the things which have been accomplished among us . . . a narrative compiled from the things told by those who were eyewitnesses from the beginning and ministers of this word, now it seemed good to me also to write an orderly account for you, most excellent Theophilus, that you may know the truth concerning the things of which you have been informed." Now he does not claim that his record is a greater chronological exactitude than those who preceded him. What he is really claiming, that his narrative is really a better arrangement of the source material: he heard it, these things from those who really experienced it. He heard it and compiled it into a story, into a narrative.

I want to tell you tonight the story as it actually takes place. For after unnumbered years the story has been overlaid with all kinds of extraneous things, and it isn't so at all. Next Wednesday, the whole vast world of Christendom, one billion of us, will tell the story and enact it in churches and homes all over the world. Yes, even in China, in Russia, there are those who believe it and who will tell the story, that a man and a woman had a child that was different, and that he was the savior of the world. And that is not true. The only savior of the world is God, called in the scripture Jehovah. "I am the Lord your God, the Holy One of Israel, your Savior . . . and besides me there is no savior" (Isaiah 43:3, 11). The name is, we call it, Yod He Vau He. In our language it's I AM. But, if you understand the scriptures, the word Jesus, which is the anglicized form of the Hebrew word Joshua, means the same thing. So whatever you read of Joshua or you read of Jehovah, you can read of Jesus the same. It's not a man. The gospels are not biographies of Jesus. They are really telling the story of salvation.

Christianity is based upon the affirmation that a certain series of events happened in which God revealed himself in action for the salvation of man. So you ask the question, "Did they really happen? Did they happen?" So as I stand before you, I can tell you they did happen. That I am not unique, I'm just as you are, with all the weaknesses, all the limitations of flesh, but all of them. And I had no idea the story was literally true in the depths of the soul of man. For like you I too was taught that this story took place on the surface of man, that the history of it was secular; that it actually took place in the Near East. But I know today that it didn't take place in any Near East; it takes place in the soul of every child born of woman. And when that moment arrives no one knows; only God knows. No man can predict it. No man is wise enough to see that moment in time when at length for hatching ripe you will break the shell, and then the series of events unfolds in your soul and you are Christ Jesus. Christ Jesus in man, which is God in man, is Jehovah in man. God actually became man that man may become God.

This is the story, and may someone present this night have the ability to tell it. I did my best in the last chapter of my latest book *The Law and The Promise*. Without adding to it or taking from it, I told it just as it happened. But maybe you can do a far better story. And leave out the being called Neville completely. It hasn't a thing to do with a man that stands before you now—it's the story of every being in this world—and that being will take off this garment as something that vanishes, it makes no difference. But the being that experienced it you don't see; you see the mask that he wears. I don't see the real you; I see the mask that it wears.

This is exactly how the story unfolds in the soul of man. There will come a moment in your life, and you will not suspect it, you won't have the slightest concept that it's going to happen to you. Then out of the blue, you will find yourself awakening, really awakening; and you awake to find yourself in a sepulcher, and the sepulcher is your skull. You had no idea up to that moment that you were entombed. But at that moment as you begin to awake you awake to find yourself completely awake, as you've never been awake before. And where are you? In your skull, and it's a tomb and you know it's a tomb. At that moment, you make an effort to come out and you do come out. You come out in the same manner that you came out of your mother's womb, head first, inch by inch. And you come out . . . just as you came out physically from your mother's womb you come out spiritually from the skull, your own skull. As you come out and find yourself completely out, you're bewildered. It never occurred to you before that you were dead.

We're told in the Book of Genesis: "And the Lord God placed a profound sleep upon man and he slept" (2:21). There is no thought that the man awakened until this moment in eternity. There isn't one word in scripture. The appeal is there, but there's not a word that he awoke. In the 44th Psalm, the appeal is made to God. It's God who fell asleep in man. "Arouse thyself! Why sleepest thou, O Lord? Awake! Do not cast us off forever!" (verse 23). So the command is by God to God who sleeps in man. He is individualizing himself in man. So, "Rouse thyself! Why sleepest thou, O Lord? Awake! Do not cast us off forever!" So, God awakes in man as that man. And he didn't realize until that moment in eternity that he really was asleep. He thought he was awake.

This dream has been imposed upon man, which really is God, and he must dream the dream of this world. At the end of the dreaming of the dream, God awakes. And because it was dream, no matter how horrible he was in this world, it's all forgiven. If tomorrow morning my wife said to me, "I had the most horrible dream. I murdered you and murdered our daughter and murdered all of our friends," because I love her I would embrace her and try to comfort her because of the horror of her dream. I couldn't condemn her; it was a dream. So at the end of this drama this whole thing is a dream, and the dreamer awakes, and awakening he is God. But he is subjected to the dream of this world, and the most horrible dreams we dream while we are subjected to it. And then we awaken from the dream to find we are the dreamer and the dreamer is God.

So I awoke—and you can take it down and this is true—I awoke to find myself in the sepulcher of my skull. I did not know until that moment that I had been, throughout the centuries, dead—for you wouldn't put anyone in a sepulcher unless he's dead. And so, I have been buried, buried in my skull, but I didn't know it until that moment in time. Then the most fantastic power stirred me: I was resurrected from the dead. Resurrection is God's most wonderful creative act. He awakens himself from this profound sleep that is so deep it is just like death. So I awoke from the grave, and then I came out. Now we're told in Revelation, he is the first of those who woke from the dead, the first to be born from the dead. Everyone will be born from the dead in the same way. The story of Christ is the story of man. Every man will have the identical experience when he comes out from the grave, and the grave is his own skull.

Now, we are told in the Book of Luke that three came to witness this event. For the angel of the Lord appeared and said to them that "Unto you this day is born in the city of David a Savior, who is Christ the Lord. And this shall be a sign unto you: you shall find a babe wrapped in swaddling clothes and lying in a manger" (2:9-12). And they went and discovered the thing was true. They found the sign. Listen to it carefully: "This shall be a sign unto you: you shall find a babe wrapped in swaddling clothes and lying in a manger." The child is not the event. The child is no more the event than the flag flying over the White House is the President. It signifies his presence; it is not the President. Is he in residence? Well, I don't know. Well then, look, see if his insignia is flying. And so, I will look, if the President's flag is flying, he is in residence. When he's not in residence, it's lowered. So, "This shall be a sign unto you, you shall find a babe wrapped in swaddling clothes and lying in a manger."

But that is not the event that took place in heaven. What took place in heaven: you who have been asleep throughout the ages, you awoke by God's most wonderful creative act. He woke you that is himself, for you and he are one. He simply disturbed the sleeper and woke him from his frightful dream. And then he came out of his skull in the form of being born. The sign of birth from above is always that of a child, so the child signifies your birth. But the child is not what you gave birth to: it's you. The child is simply a sign and a portent of your birth.

And three men are present. They come just as you're told in the 18th chapter of the Book of Genesis. Suddenly, he to whom the promise was made, called Abraham, for Abraham sat in the tent, in the door of the tent is in the tent, and suddenly he looked up and behold, three men stood before him. They were not seen approaching. They suddenly appeared; they were before him. And these three men are not seen approaching, they suddenly appear and they are before him. You see them and you know them. They know you but they don't see you, for you are not here anymore. This event takes place in heaven. Although they will be invisible to anyone in this world, you are invisible to them, because this is something entirely different, an entirely new age where you are born. You have broken this life's invidious bar as it were. You aren't here anymore. And you've been born after being a dreamer for unnumbered centuries, dreaming the horror of this world. Then you awake and three men witness it.

Now you're told, in the story one announces the fact and two question the fact. He does not argue the point. He presents the evidence—the evidence, not you, for he can't see you—he presents the child. The child can be seen. That's the flag, that's the insignia, that's the portent. So he who finds the child on the floor—which is a manger, the lowest point in that inn, for you're in an inn—and he picks it up, presents the evidence. You take this heavenly child in your hands and you look into his face, and you ask—if you ask the same words that I asked—"How is my sweetheart?" And he looks into your face and smiles. Just as you're told, his name is Isaac and Isaac means "he laughs." He does, he laughs. Then the whole thing dissolves and you are back on this level to ponder this fantastic experience that you've had.

And then you know who Mary is. Prior to that if you were raised in a Christian faith, you thought Mary was a woman who lived two thousand years ago. And now you know who Mary is, and yet you are male, wearing a male garment. You may be the father of children as I am; I have a son and a daughter. And yet I gave birth to myself, and it was symbolized as that of an actual infant wrapped in swaddling clothes. So then I knew: "I am Mary and birth to God must give if I in blessedness for now and evermore would live."

And so, I brought forth myself. God can only bring forth himself; he can't bring forth another. Corn brings forth corn. Everything brings forth after its kind. This was stated in the beginning that this is the law forever and forever, the law of identical harvest (Genesis 1:11). So if God is bringing forth something, he brings forth himself. So God is begetting himself and bringing forth himself. But if he brings forth himself and begets himself, it has to be symbolized. What is the greatest symbol of birth but a child? So the child is the insignia that he did succeed in bringing himself forward and he's born from above.

Now, Luke is not claiming that he actually had the experience, but he heard from those who had it. They were called eyewitnesses—and an eyewitness is one who experienced this birth—and then he wrote the narrative. Writing it as beautifully as he did men took it literally on this level. And so, you are going to find on Wednesday morning, you're going to find a woman and a little baby, and a man, and then animals around, and all these things, and that is not it at all. So if someone here this night could be like a Luke and who would actually be present to hear how it happened, they could tell the story as it really happened. For it's going to happen to everyone born of woman in this world. But that moment in eternity when it happens, no one knows; it comes like a thief in the night.

And how do I know this is what was foretold? Well, I go back into scripture and I read. I find it foreshadowed, I find it foretold in scripture. So I tried to explain to the world what happened to me. But again I come back to Paul, "This treasure is hid in earthen vessels." So I try to tell it. Because of my limitations of language and your limitation of what I'm trying to say, we talk from different premises. You've been conditioned to believe that when he comes into the world, he'll come as we came, through the womb of woman; and he doesn't come through the womb of woman. And so, you believe if he does come he has to come that way, and that's not the way that Christ comes into the world. Christ is simply God awake. And it's God in man that must awake, and when he awakes he comes out of the skull of man. It's called in the Bible Golgotha which means skull. That's where God was placed. He was buried on Golgotha. "Unless I die thou canst not live, but if I die I will arise again and thou with me" (Blake, *Jerusalem*, Plate 96). So God is actually buried in the skull of every being in the world.

Now, for those who may say, "Well, if it doesn't happen to me before I die here, will it happen?" Yes. It's a peculiar mystery: you don't really die. How can I persuade people in this world who actually die and I see the body actually incinerated, and tell them they didn't really die? It's a strange thing. You don't vanish. The world does not cease to be at the point where my senses cease to register it, it doesn't. My father at eighty-five died, as the world would see it. He's buried in Barbados. My mother died at sixty-three. And so many of my friends by the dozens have died, but they haven't died! It's a wheel of recurrence, and they are playing it as though the play will play tonight when the curtain comes down and it goes up tomorrow night. You replay the play until a moment in the play you awake. You are the author of the play, the dreamer of the dream, and you leave the play.

Now, the next stage in this . . . if I would rewrite Luke, but I don't have the qualifications to rewrite Luke, but I do know he didn't make the claim that he was writing a chronological order, an exact order, because it did not happen that way. It happened differently. The drama begins with resurrection, and it ends in the drama in Luke with resurrection. The end of all the drama in the four gospels is resurrection, and that's not so at all. It begins with resurrection. You resurrect and you didn't know you were even dead. You didn't know that you were asleep, because you seem so alive here. I am so awake! So the greatest act of God is to resurrect himself in man from the dream, this horrible dream. And it is horrible, where man seemingly dies, and he has disease, and he has pain, and he has all the frightful things in the world in this dream. And yet, at the end it is only a dream; therefore, he didn't really go through it at all. Therefore, in the end you say, "Father, forgive them for they know not what they do." They were dreaming the most horrible dream in the world. So the next stage will prove it is God, and not some little tiny thing that you thought you were in the dream, but it was God who did the dreaming, and it is still God who you are now. He has individualized himself as you. He has completed the act, his purpose, to individualize himself as you.

Well, how will I know that God succeeded in his purpose to give himself to me? Well, God is a father. If God is a father and he succeeded in his purpose, which was to give himself to me, then I'm a father. If I'm a father, then show me my son. I can't be a father unless there is a child. And so he does, he shows me my son. Then comes another explosion in your brain—it's all taking place in your skull—and this fantastic explosion. After the dust settles, you look and you understand the words of scripture: "I will open the door and no one can shut it." In Revelation, "I will open the door and no one can shut it." And then you look and here is your son, he is David, the David of biblical fame. He's leaning against the side of an open door. He turns around and looks you right in the eye and he calls you Father. You know you're his father and he knows he's your son, and then you know who you are. For David is God's only begotten son, so if God's only begotten son calls you Father, then you know who you are. There aren't two Gods in this world; there's only one God. So he calls you Father. He will call every being in this world Father; and then you will know that we are really one, that we aren't billions as we appear to be in this world. We are completely individualized, granted, and yet one.

So David calls you Father and you call him Son to fulfill the 89th Psalm. For I only must fulfill scripture. I didn't come here to make a pile of money. It's nice to have money to cushion against the horrible dream that we dream. It's nice to have the lovely things of this world, certainly, but that's not the purpose of life. The purpose of life is to fulfill scripture. Well, the 89th Psalm is: "I have found David. He has cried unto me, 'Thou art my Father, my God, and the Rock of my Salvation'" (verse 26). So I must find him. And you don't find him by going searching for him. He explodes out of your own brain and stands before you. And he's just as he's described in the Book of Samuel, just as he's described! You have never seen such beauty in your life as when you look into the eye of David. And that face of David, a youth, eternal youth, about twelve or thirteen and here, he's being personified before you, eternity. For eternity is youth, not age. It's David.

It is David who stood beside him, as told in the 8th chapter of the Book of Proverbs: "I am the first of his works of old," the first (verse 22). He created me before anything else in the world, and I stood beside him as a child. "Before he brought forth the seas, the heavens, I stood beside him as a child." It's David. And so, when God succeeds in giving himself to you, he has to give you his Son. "For God so loved the world that he gave his only begotten Son" (John 3:16). And his Son is not Jesus Christ; his Son is David. Jesus Christ is simply God Awake. Jesus Christ is God the Father. So David calls you Father. And that's how the mystery unfolds. He asks the question "What think ye of the Christ? Whose son is he?" They answered, "The son of David." He said, "Why then did David in the Spirit call him Father? If David does call him Father, how can he be David's son?" (Matthew 22:42). So, David calls him Adonay, a word used by every son of his father, when he calls him Father. So he called me Father.

And then comes another scene. And this is the chronological order as I have experienced it. This is not as Luke told it, or Matthew told it, or Mark, or John. But they were not trying to be chronologically exact. They were simply compiling these oral traditions, and putting them into a narrative. It made sense the way they put it, because, on this level, birth would come first and death last. And if you survived death, then resurrection should follow it. But that's not the order in God's mystery. Resurrection comes first. You begin with resurrection. You awaken to find yourself entombed; and then you come out, and that's birth. And the signal of the birth, or the thing that signifies it, is a babe. And "this shall be a sign unto you that something was born this day in the city of David that is Christ the Lord" (Luke 2:11). Well, what is the sign? Go and "you will find a babe wrapped in swaddling clothes and lying on the floor." That's where you find it. That was telling you that something was born this day in the city of David. Well, the city of David is Zion. Zion is not in the Near East; Zion is your own wonderful skull. That's where it was born. You come out of your own wonderful skull, and the birth is symbolized as that of a babe.

You can take this, and you, too, can compile a narrative. I think the time has come to tell it—to tell it because after 2,000 years of misrepresentation people completely lost the entire picture of this great mystery. And they're looking for a coming of another being called Jesus Christ in the flesh, and he can't come at all. He comes in us. And he keeps on coming in every individual in this world until all have hatched out. When all have hatched out all will be the father of one son; therefore, all are one. Then you will know the mystery: that "The Lord will be king over all the earth; on that day his name will be one and the Lord one" (Zechariah 14:9). Therefore, the name is Jesus Christ, and everyone will be Jesus Christ, without loss of identity.

No one will lose identity. I'll know you in eternity. But I will see you beautified beyond the wildest dream of man. I will see you with a character that is God. I will see you with the majesty that is God, with everything that is God, because you are God. All will be hatched out and all will be one. You'll not be male or female; you'll be man. Man will then, in that moment, be above the organization of sex as we understand it in this world. We don't need the divided image of male-female to create. We create because everything is then subject to our own wonderful imaginative power. But we're God completely awake.

And everyone, not one will be addled. It's his purpose to save all. Save all, he saves himself; there's no one else to save. All the commands in the world, as we read in the Bible, are given by God to God. Man can do nothing on this level. He simply is giving himself to individualize himself, and bring himself up as God. Because, there is no limit to the expansion of God; there was only a limit to the contraction of God. The contraction was Adam, humanity, the limit to opacity, yes. But no limit to translucency, none whatsoever, so that God will forever and forever be expanding. And when all are awake, and the play is over and his purpose realized, he still can expand. He can still be this composite God made up of others—one God made of all of us. We are the Elohim, and all the Elohim form Jehovah, the one Lord. Then tomorrow another act he will write, and then in that other act, a still further expansion of this infinite being that we are.

So, the story of Christmas is the story of salvation. It is God redeeming himself. Because he placed himself in a restricted area, and it was so restricted! What is more restricted than death? And the dreamers did not know that they were actually dead. They didn't know they were dreaming, for their dreams were so real they were lost in the dream. When you fall asleep tonight, unless you awake from that sleep, isn't the dream real? And don't you bleed, and don't you feel pain, and aren't you afraid, and don't you control, and don't you run from others in your dream? Then you awake from it and say, "It was only a dream." And while that dream lasted, it was just as real as this. For when you come back here, you don't think this is a dream. Oh, no, this isn't a dream, that was a dream. It's a dream within a dream until man awakes from it all.

So Shelley was perfectly right. But he wasn't speaking of some friend of his who died, as we see a friend die. He was speaking of one who awoke. For Shelley had the visions—he made his exit at thirty-six, but like all these brilliant intuitive minds they saw it so clearly. So they said he was full of incest, they said Shelley and his mother, Shelley and someone else. But, may I tell you, if I am the father of your son, my wife will one day have the experience of being the father of my son, and my son is David, yet she has borne me a child, well, isn't that incest? Why, she's myself. In the end, if we're all the father of one son, then no matter what, you can call it by any other name, it's incest. Well, they said of Shelley that he was incestuous. But this is what he said: "He has awakened from the dream of life. 'Tis we who lost in stormy visions keep with phantoms an unprofitable strife."

So we think this is altogether real; and we strive for the highest office in this country; and we aspire for the highest office in a religious sense, and we strive for a higher office in some other sense, and it's all but the dream. When we awaken from it, we are Jehovah. Jehovah's only name to be known forever and forever throughout all generations is I AM. So who had the dream last night? Wouldn't you say, "I did"? And if someone said to you, "What are you doing?" You would say, "I am dreaming." And when you awoke from it you would say, "Well, I am awake." You always precede whatever you say with "I am"; that's Jehovah's name.

So in the end, this series of events will unfold in the soul of every person in the world. But as Paul said in his second letter to the Corinthians, the 4th chaper, the 7th verse: "We have this treasure in earthen vessels." That is conditioned by the limitation of human understanding, human language, the limitation of our understanding of words, and especially that limitation of an individual who had the experience of trying to unveil it, which is something you can't share save in words to another. So tonight I have tried to unveil my inner consciousness that sailed and had that experience with you who, at the moment, have not had it. But you will have it!

And so that is Christmas. It hasn't a thing to do with some physical event that took place 2,000 years ago. There was no Mary, who didn't know a man physically, who bore a child physically from her physical womb, none whatsoever. The Mary, if Mary, is the one called Sarah, if Sarah, which is the back of your own wonderful skull. She was ninety years old and the numerical value of the word "she was ninety"; the symbolical value of that number is a fishhook. The first use of the word Jesus in the Bible is Joshua. Moses could not enter the Promised Land, that which was promised, it took Joshua to do it. Joshua is called Joshua Ben Nun, Joshua the son of Nun. Nun is a fish. He comes into the world to transform us into fishers of men, called fishermen, and he was called "the great fish." And Sarah was ninety years old and ninety has the symbolical value of a fishhook, it's Tzaddi. Look it up, the fishhook. What is he fishing for? What is he bringing out of himself? For everything comes out of man: "All that you behold, tho' it appears without, it is within, in your own wonderful human Imagination, of which this world of mortality is but a shadow" (Blake, *Jerusalem*, 71). So he brings it out and that is the Sarah or that is the Mary.

But forget the Sarah, the Mary, it's your own wonderful being and it's coming out of your own skull. You are coming out of your own skull, for that's where you're buried. And the whole drama of salvation begins with God's mightiest act, which is resurrection. He resurrects you. And you didn't even know that you were dead until that moment when you're resurrected. When you're resurrected, you find yourself entombed. What would you put into a sepulcher but the dead? And you are in a sepulcher, and the sepulcher is your skull. That's exactly what the Bible tells you: he was buried in Golgotha and Golgotha means skull. That's exactly where Jesus Christ was buried. Then Jesus Christ in you awakes to find himself entombed, and he comes out. As he comes out of the tomb, he's born from above. And then comes the series of events as described in scripture. Then, Luke says: "I heard it from those who were eyewitnesses; and it seemed good to me now to write an orderly account for you, most excellent Theophilus." Well, Theophilus means one who loves God; so if you say, I want to find the secret, God's purpose, God's plan, you are a lover of God, you are Theophilus. 'That you may know the truth concerning the things of which you have been informed" (Luke 1:03). So now you have been informed.

And to those who have been coming here over the years, and have taken it down in shorthand, tape, longhand, maybe they can compile a narrative and tell the story as it actually happened. But leave the speaker out completely, for this is only a garment that he wears. You have never seen me anymore than I have seen you, for we are veiled. This garment of flesh is a veil it comes through. I'll recognize you, you'll recognize me, but we're lifted up to the nth degree of beauty compared to what you see now. So, leave out the first narrative . . . that was born from a woman's womb . . . and tell the story of salvation. How the individual walking this earth as though he were alive, thinking he's alive and thinking he's awake, suddenly one day God hits him over the head as it were and he wakes. He didn't realize until then that he had been asleep. And when he awakes, he doesn't awake in a crib, he awakes in his skull, and finds himself completely sealed in his skull. He breaks the seal and comes out. It is now "at length for hatching ripe" and out he comes, comes out of a sealed tomb and the tomb of his skull.

Then he understands what the prophets could not see. Because they sought and they inquired what person, what time was indicated by the spirit of prophecy within them, when it was prophesied and predicted the sufferings of Christ and the subsequent glory. But they couldn't. They sought throughout all the scriptures and yet they could not find by all their searching that Christ of whom they spoke, and whose coming they foretold. They couldn't find him. It wasn't there until you have the experience. So I'm telling you the experience before you have it, that when you have it you will know that it is true.

Until it happens, continue, and knowing it to be a dream, dream nobly. You can change the dream. The Bible recognizes only one source of dream: all dreams, all visions proceed from God. So if I can think of my home right

now, that's the waking dream. Well, now who's doing it? Who's doing it?—I
am. That's God. So I think of something else, well, who is doing it?—I
am. That's God. There's only one source of dreams in scripture; and all
dreams proceed from God, and God is I AM. So if I know I am dreaming,
I can control the direction of my dream. If I don't know I'm dreaming,
then I am the servant, the slave of my attention, not its master. If I know
I'm dreaming, I can direct my attention. Directing it, I can control the
dream. Try it and see how it works. If today you're poor—that's a relative
term—but if you think you are, assume that you are wealthy, which also is
relative. But assume that you are, and remain faithful to your assumption,
knowing that God is the dreamer and all things are possible to God, and
you will actually crystallize it in your world of dreams. You can change the
dream and make it come out just as you want to, any dream in this world,
until that moment in time when you awaken from dream to find yourself
Christ Jesus, God Awake.

So while you're dreaming, dream the most noble dreams in the world. If
you don't know you're dreaming, well then, you can't change it. You are lost
in your own creation. But if you know you are dreaming, you can control
the direction of your attention and therefore control the dream. All dreams
in the world proceed from God. So tonight, just assume. When you assume
something, isn't that a daydream? You're told in possibly the greatest book
next to the Bible, the works of Shakespeare: "Assume a virtue if you have it
not. Refrain tonight, one night. It will seem easier tomorrow, and then the
next night still easier." At the very end, if you dare to assume it and restrain
the impulse to go back to habit, then your assumption will harden into fact.
You are still dreaming and will continue the dream until that moment in
time when God awakes in you as you, and he's individualized as you. So
you try it.

Now we go into the Silence, for this is our closing night until January 7.

*   *   *

Q: ___(??) the story of how would you react to things that appear
    outwardly as tragedy? Then, would this move you in any way?
A: Sir, may I tell you, returning here still clothed as I am in a garment of
    flesh and blood, I cannot fully realize my divine inheritance. It cannot
    become actual, or not fully realized by me while I'm still wearing this.
    And while I'm wearing this, it has relationships like wife, children,
    brothers, sisters and so on, and reactions may not be as intense, but
    they're still reactions on this level. Were I completely indifferent, it
    would be taken off tonight. But while I wear it, this garment that I wear

is related to certain patterns in God's eternal structure and reacts on that level. And so, I am identified today with America, and so react as an American. So any hurt or, I would say, a threat to what I consider a way of life that I like, I find myself still on this level reacting.

But my experiences I've told you and tried to record without embellishment are just as I experienced them, and they're all stories of Jesus Christ. I say it without batting an eye, without bending a knee, without in any way apologizing for it: everyone eventually will be Jesus Christ. Well, Jesus Christ is God awake. This is God's imposed sleep; to awake, and his awakening, which is an expansion beyond what he was before, is Jesus Christ. And everyone is God, and he will be Jesus Christ. In that day his name will be one, and the Lord is one. Not unnumbered little Jesus Christs running around. Just one being, and one being seemingly made up of unnumbered.

It's a strange mystery. How could I say to anyone . . . as we're told in scripture, "Before Abraham was, I am"? Well, you before Abraham and Abraham lived a thousand years before? Before Abraham was, I am. Well, I can say right as I stand here, I know it more surely than I know anything else: Before David was, I am. For the father comes before the son and he called me Father, and I knew when he called me Father I was. He never called me Father for any conviction on my part . . . I knew it. Therefore, was this not "before David was, I am"? David's father in scripture is Jesse and Jesse is I AM. The word Jesse is any form of the verb "to be": I am. He calls me Father, and in scripture Jesse is the father of David. And so here, at the age of fifty-nine, I am older than David, who predated our Christian era by a thousand years. So, before David was, I am. And if God is the only reality and all the things came after, and he succeeded in his purpose of awakening me as himself, then I can say, "Before the world was, I am." So Proverbs 8: "I am the first of his acts of old. Before he created anything, I was with him as a little child." And then he awakens me, awakens you, as himself. This is all God's doing and there's nothing but God.

Q: (inaudible)

A: ___(??) I can't take too much time. But, I don't drive a car. I have a car but it's only for my daughter, but I don't drive it. I just have never driven a car. But here I am driving a car, and seated in the back of the car to the extreme right is one whose name is Lee, and it's a woman. And the party that has the dream turns to me, the driver of the car, and she said, "What is Lee waiting for?" And I answered, "She is waiting for Mort." Well, Mort is the Latin for death. I said to her, "Only one more block and Oswald"; you can see the symbolism. No one thought of any attempt before.

Then, she said, suddenly before her came this enormous bell, the Liberty Bell, and the Liberty Bell began to toll. Well, there's no symbol in our country recognized that really is more representative of the head of our country than the Liberty Bell. What is more representative of our president than the Liberty Bell? He's supposed to keep alive the liberty that is ours and not to enslave us, that's what he is supposed to do. And we elected him to office to keep our freedoms going. Then she said, unnumbered bells tolling from churches, all over the country all the bells are tolling. The car splits in two and as the car splits in two, suddenly—as it happens in dream—it's put back together again. But the front part where I am, I'm driving, is completely protected, and the rear is completely unprotected. On the extreme right of that rear of the car sits Lee, and Lee is waiting for Mort.

Good night.

GLOSSARY

Awakening - The soul of man awakens from a profound sleep of "6,000" years to his true identity; return of long memory. Man experiences a series of six visions: resurrection/birth from above; David and the fatherhood of God; splitting of the temple of the body/ascension into Zion; the descent of the dove—over a period of three and a half years—all signs of your transformation into God by your own I AM.

Bible - All parable; not secular history but salvation history; man's spiritual autobiography. Old Testament adumbration and prophesy, while New Testament is fulfillment of the prophesies in the events depicted in the story of Jesus. (See Awakening above and Parable below).

Characters of Bible - Personifications of eternal states of consciousness (not historical persons). Two lines of personifications run through scripture, the Inner and outer; e.g. Eve (inner) culminating in Jesus; Adam (outer) culminating in John the Baptist.

David - The symbol of humanity, all of its generations, experiences, and the concentrated time in which they spring, fused in to a grand whole, and personified as a glorious youth who in vision calls you Father. God's only son (Psalm 2:7); the anointed; the Christ; eternity—a lad, a stripling. Personification of the resultant state. Symbol of your creative power.

Egypt - This age as opposed to that age; state of ignorance that I AM is God.

539

Enemy of Israel - All false gods and beliefs in causation other than the only
    God, I AM (your I AM).

Glory - God's gift of himself to each individual, achieved by an internal
    transformation of man into God by God (2 Corinthians 3:18);
    state of awareness each individual enjoyed prior to decent into man
    (John 17:5); man's true identity returned, individualized, greatly
    expanded having experienced/overcome death.

Imagination - Man's awareness of being; the inner five senses; God's/man's
    creative power; the I AM (called God, Lord, Jehovah, Jesse, Jesus);
    the Inner or Deeper Self (as opposed to outer and surface self); the
    Dreamer and the Father (as opposed to the dream in this world, the
    son, or man's creative power keyed low).

Imagining - Picturing a scene that implies the wish fulfilled, then feeling the
    present reality of it, drenching self with that feeling; then believing
    it is done, and remaining faithful to the imaginal act.

Israel - "He who shall rule as God" (all of humanity at the end of their
    journey as man); a man in whom there is no guile.

Jesse - Any form of the verb "to be" (hence I AM; God the father of David).

Jesus - The Father, the I AM (Exodus 3:14), called Jehovah, Lord, Jesse.
    "Jehovah is salvation"; Anglicized Hebrew word Joshua; God,
    individualized when you say I am.

Christ - The Son (Psalm 2:7); personification of creative power (keyed low
    in man); David; the anointed (Psalm 89:20); personification of
    the way of redemption/salvation; way to the Father (reveals you as
    Father).

Jesus Christ - Personification of awakened Imagination and man's creative
    power; God awake in man (two transformed into one); man's own
    human Imagination; the pattern, the Way of salvation.

Man - God, Imagination, is man. The son. The creative power keyed low;
    destined to awaken as God; power greatly expanded by overcoming
    this extreme limitation, opacity, and contraction.

Name - Conveys the nature and character of the state of consciousness. Name change, (e.g., Abram to Abraham) means a growth in character and expansion of the state.

Parable - A story told as if it were true, leaving the hearer to discover its fictitious character and learn its hidden meaning. (See Matthew 13:3 and 18 for an instruction on how to solve the riddles.)

Paul - To find the I AM; to desist in seeking; (as opposed to Saul, one who seeks, or humanity still suffering from amnesia). Paul is the symbol of one who awakens.

Potter - The Imagination personified. Jeremiah 18:1 also teaches revision of facts to get new results.

Pray/Prayer - To imagine: motion toward, accession to, in the vicinity of, nearness at. A mental/emotional movement into a new state of consciousness by assuming the feeling of the wish already fulfilled, and gratitude therefore. (Not supplication).

Primal Form - A being of fire in a body of air. (Not flesh and blood.)

Repentance - a radical change of attitude toward life; also called revision by Neville. Higher law than identical harvest.

Resurrection - God's mightiest act: to finish the transformation of man in to himself; you awaken in the tomb of your skull.

Time - Eternity or "big" time. Sidereal time or man's view of a past, present and future. Both exist simultaneously. Sidereal is temporary and part of the dream or illusion.

Vision - Revelation. Contains three elements: supernatural, parallels stories of scripture, and quite vivid. Issues (as does dream) from only source, God (Numbers 12:6; Job 33:14). God (your I AM) revealing self to you.

World - A dream (in concert); for purpose of sentient experience and expanding power. Animated by Imagination, otherwise dead. Also individual man.

Visions of the End (Six) - Signs to man that the internal transformation into
    God (by God, your I AM)) has been completed and the promises
    fulfilled. Every individual's destiny, eventually. (See Awakening
    above.)

A few sources of quotes used by Neville: James Strong's Exhaustive
Concordance of the Bible (with Hebrew and Greek dictionaries, for original
meanings of words); Bayley's Lost Language of Symbolism ; The Complete
Writings of William Blake; Revised Standard Version of the Bible (and 41
others).